Early Church Records of Salem County New Jersey

Charlotte D. Meldrum

HERITAGE BOOKS
2007

HERITAGE BOOKS
AN IMPRINT OF HERITAGE BOOKS, INC.

Books, CDs, and more—Worldwide

For our listing of thousands of titles see our website
at
www.HeritageBooks.com

Published 2007 by
HERITAGE BOOKS, INC.
Publishing Division
65 East Main Street
Westminster, Maryland 21157-5026

Copyright © 1996 Charlotte D. Meldrum

All rights reserved. No part of this book may be reproduced or transmitted in any form or by any means, electronic or mechanical, including photocopying, recording or by any information storage and retrieval system without written permission from the author, except for the inclusion of brief quotations in a review.

International Standard Book Number: 978-1-58549-325-8

CONTENTS

Salem Monthly Meeting

Births and deaths 1
Marriages 71
Minutes 73

Pilesgrove Monthly Meeting

Births and deaths 144
Marriages 167

Greenwich Monthly Meeting

Births and burials 174

Friesburg Emanuel Lutheran

Baptisms 177
Burials 228

Presbyterian Congregation at Pilesgrove

Membership 234
Communion 234
Baptisms 235

New Jersey Marriage Licenses 250
Index 253

INTRODUCTION

QUAKERS
The Salem meeting for worship was established in 1676 coincident with the establishment of the Salem Monthly Meeting. It was in 1681 that the Salem Quakers acquired a 16-acre tract from Samuel Nicholson and his wife, Ann. About four years later a meeting house was built on the property. A larger building was constructed in 1700. In 1772 the third meeting house was built.

A meeting for worship at Pilesgrove was organized ca. 1720. In 1720 it became an indulged meeting of Salem Monthly Meeting. Pilesgrove Monthly Meeting was established in 1794 by Salem Quarterly Meeting out of Salem Monthly Meeting. Eventually the name of Woodstown Monthly Meeting was adopted.

LUTHERAN AND GERMAN REFORMED CONGREGATIONS
From about 1745 the Lutheran congregation near Cohenzy Creek was served by Philadelphia pastors and young men in training for the ministry, once or twice a year. Most of the time the Lutheran congregation was served by a schoolmaster. As early as 1765 a Reformed pastor from Philadelphia began occasional visits to the Reformed congregation in the area. The Lutheran congregation exists today as Emanuel's Church, Friesburg, near Bridgeton. The Reformed congregation no longer exists.

PRESBYTERIANS
The Pilesgrove Presbyterian congregation formed at Pilesgrove in 1741.

SALEM MONTHLY MEETING

BIRTHS AND DEATHS FROM SALEM MONTHLY MEETING
1686-1800

"A recorde of the Arrivals of the families of Friends who came from England or elsewhere to inhabite within the County of New Salem or at least belonging to the Salem Monthly Meeting in the province of west New Jersey beginning in the year according to the English account 1675.
As also the time of the birth of their children and the place where they were borne, whereunto is annexed the children of Friends borne in every family here in this county if brought in to be recorded until the year 1688."

1674. John Pledger of Portsmouth in Hampshire intending to transport himself and his family to the province of west New Jersey shipped himself aboard the shipp called the Joseph and Benjamin. The Master's name was Mathew Paine bound to Maryland. The said John Pledger arrived at west New Jersey the 13th da, of the first month in the year 1674/5.
Elizabeth Pledger, the wife, of the aforesaid John Pledger and Joseph Pledger, their son who was born the fourth day of the sixth month 1672 were shipped aboard the ship called the Griffin. Robert Griffin being Master bound for Delaware river who arrived in the said river the 23rd day of the 9th mo, at or near New Salem in the year 1675.
John Pledger, son of John Pledger by Elizabeth, his wife, was born in west New Jersey and in the county of New Salem the 27th da, 9th mo, 1680.
1675. John Smith, son of John Smith was born in the County of Northfock in the town of Disson on the 20th day of the seventh month, 1623 who in the process of time tooke to wife, Martha Craftos, dau. of Christopher Craftos of Wooksay in Nottinghamshire, who afterwards transported themselves with four children to west New Jersey in America on board the ship called the Griffin of London. Robert Griffin being Master who all arrived in Delaware River the 23rd da, 9th month, 1675 and so to New Salem in the province of west New Jersey whey they did inhabit.
Daniel Smith, son of John Smith and Martha, his wife, was born in Wooksay in Nottinghamshire on the 10th da, of the 12th mo, 1660.
Samuel Smith born at the same place on the 10th day of the 3rd mo, 1664.
David Smith was born at the same place on the 19th da, 12th mo, 1666.
Sarah Smith was born in the parish of Pauls Shadwell in London the 4th day of the 12th mo, 1671.
Jonathan Smith was born in New Salem in west New Jersey the 27th da, 10th mo, 1675.
Jeremiah Smith, son of the said John Smith and Martha, his wife, was born at Salem the 14th da, 9th mo, 167-.
Isaac Smart, son of Roger Smart born in Greatleton in Wiltshire in or about the year 1658, who about the 18th year of his age

transported himself from England to west New Jersey in the ship called Griffin. Robert Griffin being Master who all arrived in Delaware River the 23rd da, 9th month, 1675 and so to New Salem in the province of west New Jersey. After this the said Isaac Smart took to wife, Elizabeth Thompson, dau. of Andrew Thompson and Issabell, his wife, the 26th da, of the 2nd mo, 1683.

Isaac Smart, son of Isaac Smart and Elizabeth, his wife, was born at Middleneck near New Salem the 21st or 22nd day of the 7th mo, 1684.

From the parish of Buttolph Aldgate in London came Edward Wade and Prudence, his wife, in the ship called the Griffin. Robert Griffin being the Master and brought with them these servants as followeth: Nathaniell Champney, Sr., Nathaniel Champneys, Jr., Joseph Ware, John Burton, Frances Smithey, who all arrived in Delaware River and so to New Salem where they inhabited the 23rd da, 9th mo, 1675.

Samuel Wade, son of John Wade born in Northhampton in the year 1645 who afterward transported himself from London to west New Jersey in the ship called the Griffin. Robert Griffin being Master who arrived in Delaware River the 23rd da, 9th mo, 1675 and so to Salem to inhabite.

Jane, wife of Samuel Wade and dau. of Thomas Smith born in West Chester in the year 1645 or 1646 transported herself in the ship called Henry and Anne.

Samuel Wade, son of Samuell Wade and Jane, his wife, was born the 1st da, 6th mo, 1685.

Children of Isaac Smart and Elizabeth, his wife,: Mary Smart, b. 21st da, 10th mo, 1685; Sarah Smart, b. 17th da, 1st mo, 1687; Nathan Smart, b. 20th da, 6th mo, 1690; Hannah Smart, b. 8th da, 5th mo, 1692; Rebecka Smart, b. 23rd da, 12th mo, 1695/6.

1675. Samuel Nicholson living at Dinston in the county of Nottingham in Old England, and from thence removed or transported himself with his wife, and children, who names and ages are as followeth: Rachel Nicholson dau. of Samuell Nicholson and Ann, his wife, b. the 7th da, 2nd mo, 1659; Elizabeth Nicholson, b. 22nd da, 3rd mo, 1665; Samuel Nicholson, b. 30th da, 2nd mo or 3rd mo, 1666; Joseph Nicholson, b. 30th da, 2nd mo, 1669; Abell Nicholson, b. 2nd da, 5th mo, 1672. The said Samuel Nicholson with his wife, and five children did afterward transport themselves to America in the ship called Griffin. Robert Griffin being Master who all arrived in Delaware River the 23rd da, 9th month, 1675 and so to New Salem in the province of West New Jersey.

Christopher White, son of Thomas White was born at Comrew in Cumberland in old England about the year 1642 from whence he removed to London in the year 1666 where about two years after he took to wife, Esther Beetle [Hester Biddle per London Friends Records of Marriages 1617-1668], widow who was born at Poplar in Shepney Parish nigh London. Her father's name was John Wiatt from Brooke Street in Rathlife nigh London. In the second month 1677 came the aforesaid Christopher aboard the ship called the Kent. Gregory Marley being the Master bringing with him the aforesaid Ester and her son, John Beetle as their apprentice or servant who was born at Poplar in Stepney Parish

nigh London on the 18th da of the 9th mo, 1663.
Children of Christopher White and his wife, Esther: Esther White
born at Shadwell near London about the year 1669; Josias White,
born in Brooke Street, Rathliefe night London about the year
1675. And the same Christopher White brought with him two
servants that is to say a man and a maid. The man servant
called Thomas Britton and the maid servant called Jane Ash who
all arrived at Salem in West New Jersey in America where they
all came to inhabite the 23rd da, 6th mo, 1677. Joseph White,
son of Christopher White and Ester, his wife, was borne at
Salem in west New Jersey the 5th da, 11th mo, 1678.
1677. Henry Jennings, son of William Jennings and Mary, his wife,
was born in the parish of Clemond Deane, 21st da, 7th mo, 1642
within the kingdom of England and County of Surry. After this
the said Henry Jennings on the 18th da of the 1st mo, 1666 in
London did take Margret Busse to wife, the dau.of Paull Busse
of York City in old England, our last abode was in the Thames
Ditton near Kingston on Thames, from whence on the 5th da of
the 2nd mo, 1677 we transported ourselves with one servant maid
named Martha Berket, dau. of John Berket in Esher near Kingston
upon Thames for West New Jersey in America in the ship called
Kent. Gregory Marley being Master and on the 23rd da, 6th mo,
following we arrived at Salem.
Mary Willcox, dau. of Robert Willcox in White Chappel, my maid
servant came from England in the ship called the Dorethy.
Robert Bridgman, Master in the year 1685 arrived at
Philadelphia on the 14th da, 8th mo, 1685.
Edward Bradway living in the parish of Paull Shadwell in London
transported himself with his wife, Mary Bradway and two daus.,
namely Mary and Susanna Bradway and three servants that is to
say William Groome, Frances Burkell and John Allin in the 3rd
month in the year according to the English account 1677 into
America who all arrived in the province of west New Jersey the
7th mo following and so to the place called New Salem where
they did inhabite.
Children of Edward Bradway and wife, Mary: Sarah Bradway, born
27th da, 7th mo, 1677; Hannah Bradway, b. 17th da, 7th mo, 1681
or 1682.
1677. George Deacon, son of George Deacon born in Church Waltham
in the Count of Essex, felt maker and citizen of London who
transported himself in the 36th year of his age and with his
wife, Francess Deacon who was born at Didford in the County of
Kent, with his father, George Deacon of the said Church Waltham
as aforesaid and one Thomas Edwards, his man servant to West
New Jersey in America on the ship called the Willing Mind who
all arrived safe in west New Jersey praised be God for it upon
the 3rd da, 10th or 11th mo in the year according to the
English account 1677 and so seated in New Salem and afterwards
from then to Alloway Creek in the County of Salem.
John Thompson, son of Thomas Thompson born in Kirkfenton,
Yorkshire in the year 1635 and in the 3rd mo, of that year
commonly called May. In the year 1658 the said Thomas Thompson
and his wife, Elizabeth with their two sons, John Thompson the
elder and Andrew Thompson the younger removed or transported

themselves from the aforesaid Kirkfenton in England unto Ireland.
In the year 1665 in the beginning of the year the said John Thompson took to wife, Jane Humbles, dau. of Thomas Humbles late of the county of Durham in England but now dwelling in Ireland. Thomas Thompson, son of John Thompson by Jane, his wife, born in the county of Wickloe and parish of Donard in Ireland about the beginning of the 7th mo in the year 1666; James Thompson, born in Ireland in the county and parish aforesaid about the middle of the 8th mo, 1668; Jane Thompson, born in Ireland in the aforesaid county and parish about the beginning of the 9th mo, 1672; Mary Thompson, born in Ireland in the county and parish aforesaid the 25th da, 10th mo, 1675.
In the year 1677 the said John Thompson transported himself, his wife, and his aforesaid four children and one man servant, named William Hall, from Ireland to the province of west New Jersey in America. They set sail on the 16th day of the 9th mo, in the ship called the Mary of Dublin. John Wall being Master and landed at Elsinburgh in the province of west New Jersey in America the 22nd da, 12th mo, following.
Andrew Thompson, son of Thomas Thompson born in Kirkfeenton in Yorkshire in the year 1637 and on the 29th da, 9th mo, 1658, the said Thomas Thompson and Elizabeth, his wife, with their two sons, John Thompson and Andrew Thompson removed or transported themselves from the aforesaid Kirkfenton in Old England into Ireland.
In the year 1664, on the 11th da, 7th mo, said Andrew Thompson took to wife, Issabell Marshall, dau. of Humphrey Marshall born in Silby in Lestershire. Elizabeth Thompson, dau. of Andrew Thompson and Isabella, his wife, born in Ireland in the county of Wiskloe and parish of Donard 15th da, 8th mo, 1666; William Thompson, born in Ireland in the aforesaid county and parish 9th da, 8th mo, 1669; Andrew Thompson born in Ireland in the aforesaid county and parish 13th da, 11th mo, 1676.
In the year 1677 the said Andrew Thompson transported or removed himself with his wife, and his aforesaid three children from Ireland to the province of west new Jersey in America. They set sail on the 16th da, 9th mo, in the ship called the Mary of Dublin. John Wall being Master and landed at Elsinburgh in the province of west New Jersey in America on the 22nd da, 12th mo, following. John Thompson, was born at Elsinburg the 23rd da, 4th mo, 1684.
Robert Fairbanks born in Lestershire in or about the year 1632. In or about the year 1653 the said Robert Fairbanks transported himself from England to Ireland. In the year 1676 the said Robert Fairbanks took to wife, Sarah Leonard, dau. of Thomas Leonard born in Spenceford in Summersetshire. In the year 1677 the said Robert Fairbanks transported himself with Sarah, his wife, and one dau. named Elizabeth Stribings, the child of said Robert by a former wife, and her husband, Henry Stribings from Ireland to the province of west New Jersey. They set sail on the 16th da, 9th mo, in the ship called the Mary of Dublin. John Wall being Master and landed at Elsinburg in the province of west New Jersey 22nd da, 12th mo following.

Thomas Woodroofe, son of John Woodroofe, yeoman was born in the parish of Cowley upon Costwould Hills in the county of Gloscester in old England. Thomas Woodroofe took to wife, Edeth Pitt, dau. of Joseph Pitt of Weymuth in Dorsethshire, gentleman. After the said Thomas Woodroofe with Edeth, his wife, removed to London where they had several children born to them: Thomas Woodroofe, Edeth Woodroofe, John Woodroofe and Isaac Woodroofe. In the year 1678 the said Thomas Woodroofe with Edeth, his wife, and their four aforenamed children and one maid servant named Allice Harvey, dau. of Leonard Harvey of Weymount as aforesaid transported themselves from London to the province of west New Jersey in America. They set sail from London the 24th da of the 6th mo, and had one dau. named Mary Woodroofe born at sea in the ship called the Suckcess. The Master was Stephen Nichols and arrived in Salem in the aforesaid province in the month called April, 1679.

1678. John Maddocks, son of Ralfe Maddocks, born in Chesshire in or about the year 1638. In the year 1668 the said John Maddocks removed to London. In the year 1669 the said John Maddocks took to wife, Elizabeth Burnham, late widow of Ralph Burnham. In the year 1671, Elizabeth Maddocks, dau. of John Maddocks and Elizabeth was born in St. Pulchers in London. In the year 1678 the said John Maddocks with Elizabeth, his wife, and dau. Elizabeth, and his son-in-law Richard Burnham with two men servants namely Thomas Oads and Thomas Hooton and one maid servant named Sarah Wagstafe transported themselves to the province of west New Jersey in America. They set sail from London on the 24th of the 6th mo, in the ship called the Suckcess. The Master's name was Stephen Nichols and landed in Virginia the 12th mo, following and so to New Salem the province of West New Jersey.

After this the said Elizabeth Maddocks, dau. of John Maddocks married with James Denn and had by him two children: Margaret Denn born 29th da, 4th mo, 1689; John Maddock Denn born 11th da, 6th mo, 1693.

Joseph White, son of Samuel and Reines White born the 20th da, 1st mo, 1651/2 in a town called Sulgrave in North Hampstenshire in England. The said Joseph White went from England to Ireland taking ship the 25th da, of the 7th mo, 1672 and afterward took to wife, Elizabeth, dau. of Arthur and Elizabeth Church who came from Dolbay of the Woulds in Lesterhsire in England to Ireland. The aforesaid Joseph White and Elizabeth, his wife, belonging to New Garden Monthly Meeting came from Cartharlow, Ireland. They took ship in Dublin in Ireland for west New Jersey. After eight weeks, two days arrived to Elsinburg in the aforesaid west new Jersey the 17th da, 9th mo, 1681 together with the servants mentioned as follows: Hugh Middleton whose father was of Lestershire and his mother of Glocesthershire; Mathias Belloes, his father and mother were English people; Hannah Asbuy, her father an English man and her mother born in Ireland.

After the arrival of the aforesaid Joseph White and Elizabeth, his wife, to Elsinburg a dau. was born, Reines White, 17th da, 9th mo, 1681.

EARLY CHURCH RECORDS OF SALEM COUNTY

Roger Caray, son of Christopher Caray and Margret both of the County of Devon in the kingdom of England was born in Ratcliffe Street in the City of Bristol in the county of Summerset in the kingdom aforesaid on the 3rd da, 3rd mo, 1652. About the age of one and twenty the said Roger Caray transported for Dublin in Ireland where he lived for about 5 years. Roger Caray took to wife, Elizabeth Stevenson, dau. of John and Mary Stevenson both of the Kingdom of England who transported themselves and their children to Dublin in Ireland when the aforesaid Elizabeth Stevenson was about 3 years of age near Dublin. The aforesaid Roger Caray and Elizabeth were married at the meeting in the brides ally in Dublin. Rachel Caray, dau. of Roger Caray and Elizabeth, his wife, was born in Dublin in the year 1680; and upon the 22nd da, of 9th mo, 1681, the said Roger and Elizabeth did transport themselves and their family unto America on the ship called the Adventure of London. John Dagger being Master who where landed at Elsinburg near Salem the 19th da, of the 9th mo, 1681. The said Roger and Elizabeth Caray had a dau., Mary Caray born 22nd da, 12th mo, 1685.

Rudra Morris, son of Lewis Morris born in Pembrockshire within the principality of Wales and kingdom of England in or about the year of 1658. In the year 1683 the said Rudra Morris with several others transported themselves to the province of Pennsylvania who safely arrived into Delaware River and landed at Philadelphia the 1st da, of the 9th mo, 1683 whereafter the said Rudra Morris came to Salem to dwell and from thence to Elsinburgh.

After which time the said Rudra Morris took to wife, Jaell Batty, dau. of Richard Batty born in Yorkshire at a place called Humford in or about the year 1658. After which time the said Jaell Batty transported herself with Robert Ashton for Pennsylvania in the ship called the Shield of Stockton. John Howell being Master ship setting sail from hull on the 8th da, 3rd mo, 1686 and landed at New Castle in the territories of Pennsylvania in the 5th month following.

Children of Rudra Morris and Jael, his wife: Jonathan Morris, born at Elsinburgh the 16th da, 12th mo, 1690; Joseph Morris, born 6th da, 6th mo, 1692; Sarah Morris, born 16th da, 12th mo, 1693; Lewis Morris, born at Elsinburgh 23rd da, 11th mo, 1695/6.

1685. John Smith, son of William Smith was born in Krindaill parish in the County of Kent in the year 1645. In the year 1683 the said John Smith took to wife, Susannah Mary, dau. of Edward Mary. In the year 1685 said John Smith transported himself with his wife, and two children and one man servant named Joseph Hogbin setting sail from Daile, in the county of Kent to the province of west New Jersey in the ship called the Charles. Edmond Paine being Master. In the 4th mo, in the year 1685 said ship landed at New Castle on Delaware River. In the 6th month following which after some short time were having settled in New Salem in west New Jersey the aforesaid two children died and were buried at New Salem.

After this Susannah Smith, dau. of John Smith by Susannah, his wife, was born the 8th da, 8th mo, 1687; John Smith, born at

Krindail Hill in the year 1689. [Which said John Smith, the younger afterward settled in Mannenton and married. (Added to record at a later time.)]
1681. John Handcock came from London into America by the way of Maryland in the ship called the Willingemind about the 25th of the 10th mo in the year 1679. Mary Champney, dau. of Nathaniel Champney, Sr. with her mother, Elizabeth Champney came from London in the ship called Henry and Ann, landing in the Delaware River the later end of the 7th month in the year 1681. John Handcock took Mary Champney as wife, and inhabited at Alloways Creek in the County of New Salem within the province of west New Jersey.
Children of John Handcock and Mary, his wife: John Handcock, born at Alloways Creek 10th da, 8th mo, 1690; William Handcock, born at Alloways Creek 1st da, 11th mo, 1693; Elizabeth Handcock, born 12th da, 6th mo, 1695.
John Goodwin, son of John Goodwin by Katharine, his wife, of the parish of St. Buttolph Algate in Houndsditch, London was born the 25th da, 10th mo, 1680, transported himself to Pennsylvania in the year 1701 and from thence in the year following came down to Salem and in the year 1705 was married the 4th da, 10th month to Susannah, the dau. of John Smith of Hedgfield formerly of Krindall parish in Kent.

SALEM MONTHLY MEETING'S BIRTHS OF FRIENDS' CHILDREN

Sarah Ware, dau. of Joseph Ware and Martha, his wife, b. 5th da, 7th mo, 1686.
Joseph Darkin, son of Richard Darkin and Ann, his wife, b. at Windham near New Salem the 8th da, 1st mo, 1688.
Mary Cooper, dau. of William Cooper and Mary, his wife, b. 27th da, 12th mo, 1688.
Sarah Bradway, dau. of William Bradway and Elizabeth, his wife, b. 29th da, 1st mo, 1690.
Hannah Darkin, dau. of Richard Darkin and Ann, his wife, borne 30th da, 9th mo, 1691.
Sarah Cooper, dau. of William Cooper and Mary, his wife, b. 15th da, 7th mo, 1691.
Hannah Cooper, dau. of William Cooper and Mary, his wife, b. 7th da, 8th mo, 1686.
Sarah Thompson, dau. of Thomas Thompson and Rebecah, his wife, b. 29th da, 7th mo, 1692.
Edward Bradway, son of William Bradway and Elizabeth, his wife, b. 28th da, 8th mo, 1692.
Joseph Thompson, son of William Thompson and Sarah, his wife, b. 22nd da, 1st mo, 1692/3.
Joseph Renton, son of William Renton and Mary, his wife, b. 27th da, 8th mo, 1693.
Joseph White, son of Joseph White and Elizabeth, his wife, b. 29th da, 11th mo, 1692.
John Darkin, son of Richard Darkin and Ann, his wife, b. 9th da, 5th mo, 1694.
Sarah Smith dau. of David Smith and Mary, his wife, b. 5th da,

Sarah Nicholson, dau. of Abel Nicholson and Mary, his wife, b. 9th mo, 1694. 19th da, 11th mo, 1694/5.
Rebecah Thompson, dau. of Thomas Thompson and Rebecah, his wife, b. 24th da, 12th mo, 1694/5.
William Thompson, son of William Thompson and Jane, his wife, b. 16th da, 3rd mo, 1695.
Phebe Knapton, dau. of Benjamin Knapton and Ann, his wife, b. 8th da, 3rd mo, 1694.
William Bradway, son of William Bradway and Elizabeth, his wife, b. 27th da, 11th mo, 1695.
Edith Scholes, dau. of John Scholes and Rebeckah, his wife, b. 28th da, 11th mo, 1695/6.
Mary Powel, dau. of Jeremiah Powel and Elizabeth, his wife, b. 12th da, 2nd mo, 1696.
Sarah Harrison, son of Israel Harrison and Hester, his wife, b. 14th da, 12th mo, 1696.
Mary Tyler, dau. of William Tyler and Johanna, his wife, b. in old England the 11th mo, 1677.
William Tyler, son of William Tyler and Johanna, his wife, b. in old England the 5th da, 7th mo, 1680.
John Tyler, son of William Tyler and Johanna, his wife, b. in old England the 2nd da, 5th mo, 1682.
Johanna Tyler, dau. of William Tyler and Johanna, his wife, b. in old England the 2nd da, 2nd mo, 1684.
Katrine Tyler, dau. of William Tyler and Elizabeth, his wife, b. in Salem County 13th da, 6th mo, 1690.
Philip Tyler, son of William Tyler and Elizabeth, his wife, b. 17th da, 3rd mo, 1692.
Elizabeth Tyler, dau. of William Tyler and Elizabeth, his wife, b. 24th da, 7th mo, 1695.
Sarah Hearly, dau. of Henry Hearly and Mary, his wife, b. 21st da, 7th mo, 1693/4.
James Chamness, son of Nathaniel Chamness and Elenor, his wife, b. 21st da, 1st mo, 1689.
Mary Chamness, dau. of Nathaniel Chamness and Elenor, his wife, b. 12th da, 11th mo, 1692.
Elizabeth Powell, dau. of Jeremiah Powell and Elizabeth, his wife, b. 21st da, 6th mo, 1698.
Bartholemew Wiat, son of Batholemew Wiat and Sarah, his wife, b. 4th da, 1st mo, 1696/7.
Rachel Thompson, dau. of Thomas Thompson and Jane, his wife, b. 17th da, 5th mo, 1697.
Sarah Thompsn, dau. of Thomas Thompson and Jane, his wife, b. 17th da, 5th mo, 1697.
Ann Smart, his wife, b. Isaac Smart and Elizabeth, his wife, b. 20th da, 6th mo, 1697.
John Mason, son of John Mason and Sarah, his wife, b. 19th da, 7th mo, 1697.
Jonathan Thompson, son of Andrew Thompson and Rebeckah, his wife, b. 16th da, 9th mo, 1697.
David Morris, son of Rothrak Morris and Jael, his wife, b. 8th da, 12th mo, 1697/8.
Rebeckah Tyler, dau. of William Tyler and Elizabeth, his wife, b.

19th da, 2nd mo, 1698.
Elizabeth Oakford, dau. of Charles Oakford and Mary, his wife, b. 17th da, 3rd mo, 1698.
John Thompson, son of Thomas Thompson and Dorithy, his wife, b. 7th da, 4th mo, 1698.
Mary Hancock, dau. of John Hancock and Mary, his wife, b. 15th da, 4th mo, 1698.
Rachel Nicholson, dau. of Abel Nicholson and Mary, his wife, b. 7th da, 7th mo, 1698.
Hannah Thompson, dau. of Andrew Thompson and Rebeckah, his wife, b. 12th da, 1st mo, 1698/9.
Jonathan Bradway, son of William Bradway and Elizabeth, his wife, his wife, b. 22nd da, 1st mo, 1698/9.
Christopher White, son of Josiah White and Hannah, his wife, his wife, b. 23rd da, 6th mo, 1699.
Moses Burwell, son of Moses Burwell and Dorcas, his wife, b. in New England at the town of Linn 20th da, 6th mo, 1695 as his mother reported to the Monthly Meeting at Salem in the year 1699.
Isabell Smart, dau. of Isaac Smart and Elizabeth, his wife, b. 16th da, 9th mo, 1699.
Benjamin Abbott, son of George Abbott and Mary, his wife, b. 2nd da, 1st mo, 1699/1700.
Ann Darkin, dau. of Richard Darkin and Ann, his wife, b. 31st da, 1st mo, 1700.
Joshua Morris, son of Rothrak Morris and Jael, his wife, b. 14th da, 5th mo, 1700.
Jane Thompson, dau. of William Thompson and Hannah, his wife, b. 29th da, 7th mo, 1700.
Elizabeth Chamness, dau. of Nathaniel Chamness and Rebeckah, his wife, b. 30th da, 9th mo, 1700.
Isabel Thompson, dau. of Andrew Thompson and Rebeckah, his wife, b. 22nd da, 10th mo, 1700.
Nathaniel Wamsley, son of Henry Wamsley and Dynah, his wife, b. 10th da, 11th mo, 1700.
Richard Woodnut, son of Richard Woodnut and Mary, his wife, b. 22nd da, 12th mo, 1700.
Abel Nicholson, son of Abel Nicholson and Mary, his wife, b. 13th da, 1st mo, 1700/1.
Elizabeth Bradway, dau. of William Bradway and Elizabeth, his wife, b. 16th da, 1st mo, 1700/1.
Jeremiah Powel, son of Jeremiah Powel and Elizabeth, his wife, b. 18th da, 3rd mo, 1701.
Sarah Hall, dau. of William Hall and Elizabeth, his wife, b. 18th da, 2nd mo, 1689.
Hannah Hall, dau. of William Hall and Elizabeth, his wife, b. 20th da, 1st mo, 1692.
Elizabeth Hall, dau. of William Hall and Elizabeth, his wife, b. 31st da, 10th mo, 1694.
Ann Hall, dau. of William Hall and Elizabeth, his wife, b. 19th da, 9th mo, 1699.
William Hall, son of William Hall and Sarah, his wife, b. 22nd da, 8th mo, 1701.
Mary Mason, dau. of Thomas Mason and Elizabeth, his wife, b. 2nd

da, 7th mo, 1701.
Charles and Mary Oakford, son and dau. of Charles Oakford and Mary, his wife, b. 20th da, 10th mo, 1701.
Jane Daniel, dau. of James Daniel and Jane, his wife, b. 2nd da, 10th mo, 1701.
Martha Smith, dau. of Daniel Smith and Dorcas, his wife, b. 17th da, 11th? mo, 1701.
William Mason, son of John Mason and Sarah wife, b. 23rd da, 11th mo, 1701.
Jane Morris, dau. of Rudra Morris and Jael, his wife, b. 4th da, 4th mo, 1702.
Joseph Nicholson, son of Abel Nicholson and Mary, his wife, b. 4th da, 12th mo, 1701.
Sarah Hancock, dau. of John Hancock and Mary, his wife, b. 15th da, 11th mo, 1701.
Bradway Stretch, son of Joseph Stretch and Hannah, his wife, b. 11th da, 3rd mo, 1701.
Lidia Thompson, dau. of Thomas Thompson and Doritha, his wife, b. 13th da, 4th mo, 1702.
Thomas Anderson, son of Simon Anderson and Hester, his wife, b. 25th da, 5th mo, 1702.
Hannah Chamness, dau. of Nathaniel Chamness and Rebeckah, his wife, b. 16th da, 9th mo, 1702.
Hannah Abbott, dau. of George Abbott and Mary, his wife, b. 30th da, 9th mo, 1702.
Ann Mason, dau. of John Mason and Sarah, his wife, b. 24th da, 11th mo, 1699.
Elizabeth Acton, dau. of Benjamin Acton and Christianna, his wife, b. 26th da, 2nd mo, 1690.
Mary Acton, dau. of Benjamin Acton and Christianna, his wife, b. 17th da, 10th mo, 1692.
Benjaman Acton, son of Benjamin Acton and Christianna, his wife, b. 19th da, 8th mo, 1695.
Lidia Acton, dau. of Benjamin Acton and Christianna, his wife, b. 24th da, 11th mo, 1697.
Josuha Acton, son of Benjamin Acton and Christianna, his wife, b. 9th da, 7th mo, 1700.
Thomas Daniel, son of James Daniel and Jane, his wife, b. 2nd da, 1st mo, 1703.
Nathaniel and Edward Hancock the two sons of John Hancock and Mary, his wife, b. 20th da, 1st mo, 1703.
Elizabeth Smith, dau. of John Smith and Susannah, his wife, b. 3rd da, 3rd mo, 1703.
Jane Thompson, dau. of James Thompson and Ann, his wife, b. 28th da, 9th mo, 1702.
Aaron Mason, son of Thomas Mason and Elizabeth, his wife, b. 2nd da, 7th mo, 1702.
Grace Woodnut, dau. of Richard Woodnut and Mary, his wife, b. 8th da, 5th mo, 1703.
Dorcas Smith, dau. of Daniel Smith and Dorcas, his wife, b. 27th da, 7th mo, 1703.
William Nicholson, son of Abel Nicholson and Mary, his wife, b. 15th da, 9th mo, 1703.
Mary Kasbey, dau. of Edward Kasbey and Elizabeth, his wife, b.

3rd da, 10th mo, 1703.
Mary Thompson, dau. of Thomas Thompson and Doritha, his wife, b. 10th da, 9th mo, 1703.
Joseph Wade, son of Samuel Wade and Mary, his wife, b. 28th da, 7th mo, 1703.
Jane Jeffery, dau. of John Jeffery and Gertrude, his wife, b. 12th da, 10th mo, 1703.
Andrew Thompson, son of Andrew Thompson and Rebecah, his wife, b. 2nd da, 2nd mo, 1704.
Sarah Mason, dau. of John Mason and Sarah, his wife, b. 2nd da, 2nd mo, 1704.
John Oakford, son of Charles Oakford and Mary, his wife, b. 12th da, 1st mo, 1704.
Susannah Thompson, dau. of William Thompson and Hannah, his wife, b. 26th da, 8th mo, 1704.
Martha Mason, dau. of Thomas Mason and Elizabeth, his wife, b. 12th da, 9th mo, 1704.
George Abbott, son of George Abbott and Mary, his wife, b. 13th da, 10th mo, 1704.
Isabel Collyer, dau. of John Collyer and Elizabeth, his wife, b. 22nd da, 12th mo, 1690.
William Collyer, son of John Collyer and Elizabeth, his wife, b. 15th da, 11th mo, 1692.
Elizabeth Collyer, dau. of John Collyer and Elizabeth, his wife, b. 27th da, 9th mo, 1694.
Sarah Collyer, dau. of John Collyer and Elizabeth, his wife, b. 20th da, 12th mo, 1696.
Percillah Collyer, dau. of John Collyer and Elizabeth, his wife, b. 14th da, 12th mo, 1700.
Benjamin Collyer, son of John Collyer and Elizabeth, his wife, b. 7th da, 12th mo, 1702.
Joseph Stretch, son of Joseph Stretch and Hannah, his wife, b. 16th da, 1st mo, 1704.
James Daniel, son of James Daniel and Jane, his wife, b. 12th da, 8th mo, 1704.
Joseph Hancock, son of John Hancock and Mary, his wife, b. 3rd da, 12th mo, 1704.
Ann Thompson, dau. of James Thompson and Ann, his wife, b. 5th da, 1st mo, 1704.
Martha Collyer, dau. of John Collyer and Elizabeth, his wife, b. 9th da, 1st mo, 1704/5.
Mary Warrick, dau. of Thomas Warrick and Hannah, his wife, b. 12th da, 11th mo, 1704.
Nathaniel Chamness, dau. of Nathaniel Chamnes and Rebeckah, his wife, b. 7th da, 2nd mo, 1705.
Edward Kasbey, son of Edward Kasbey and Elizabeth, his wife, b. 11th da, 3rd mo, 1705.
Isabel Daniel, dau. of James Daniel and Jane, his wife, b. 2nd da, 3rd mo, 1706.
Joseph Mason, son of Thomas Mason and Elizabeth, his wife, b. 14th da, 3rd mo, 1706.
Samuel Mason, son of John Mason and Sarah, his wife, b. 15th da, 3rd mo, 1706.
Josiah White, son of Josiah White and Hannah, his wife, b. 21st

da, 6th mo, 1705.
Daniel Smith, son of Daniel Smith and Dorcas, his wife, b. 16th da, 10th mo, 1705.
Mary Nicholson, dau. of Abel Nicholson and Mary, his wife, b. 1st da, 11th mo, 1705.
Patience Ware, dau. of Joseph Ware and Mary, his wife, b. 12th da, 11th mo, 1705.
Mary Oakford, dau. of Charles Oakford and Margret, his wife, b. 21st da, 1st mo, 1706.
Elizabeth Wiat, dau. of Batholemew Wiat and Sarah, his wife, b. 16th da, 7th mo, 1706.
Hannah Hancock, dau. of John Hancock and Mary, his wife, b. 10th da, 8th mo, 1706.
Mather Kasbey, son of Edward Kasbey and Elizabeth, his wife, b. 28th da, 7th mo, 1706.
Sarah Abbott, dau. of George Abbott and Mary, his wife, b. 16th da, 2nd mo, 1706/7.
Elizabeth Walden, dau. of William Walden and Hannah, his wife, b. 21st da, 3rd mo, 1707.
John Goodwin, son of John Goodwin and Susannah, his wife, b. 29th da, 2nd mo, 1707.
John Thompson, son of James Thompson and Ann, his wife, b. 18th da, 8th mo, 1707.
Sarah Thompson, son of William Thompson and Hannah, his wife, b. 6th da, 9th mo, 1707.
Hester White, dau. of Josiah White and Hannah, his wife, b. 6th da, 10th mo, 1707.
Mary Daniel, dau. of James Daniel and Jane, his wife, b. 20th da, 8th mo, 1707.
Ann Whittan, dau. of James Whittan and Sarah, his wife, b. 12th or 15th da, 10th mo, 1707.
Jonathan Mason, son of Thomas Mason and Elizabeth, his wife, b. 15th da, 11th mo, 1707.
Thomas Thompson, son of Andrew Thompson and Grace, his wife, b. 28th da, 11th mo, 1707.
Sarah Woodnut, dau. of Richard Woodnut and Mary, his wife, b. 10th da, 6th mo, 1708.
Jonathan Hancock, son of John Hancock and Mary, his wife, b. 3rd da, 7th mo, 1708.
Ann Nicholson, dau. of Abel Nicholson and Mary, his wife, b. 15th da, 11th mo, 1707.
Thomas Mason, son of John Mason and Sarah, his wife, b. 28th da, 5th mo, 1708.
Thomas Thompson, son of Andrew Thompson and Grace, his wife, b. 28th da, 11th mo, 1708.
Sarah Woodnut, dau. of Richard Woodnut and Mary, his wife, b. 10th da, 6th mo, 1708.
Jonathan Hancock, son of John Hancock and Mary, his wife, b. 3rd da, 7th mo, 1708.
Ann Nicholson, dau. of Abel Nicholson and Mary, his wife, b. 15th da, 11th mo, 1708.
Thomas Mason, son of John Mason and Sarah, his wife, b. 28th da, 5th mo, 1708.
Susanah Kasby, dau. of Edward Kasbey and Elizabeth, his wife, b.

24th da, 11th mo, 1708.
Sarah Thompson, dau. of Andrew Thompson and Grace, his wife, b. 8th da, 2nd mo, 1709.
Joseph Daniel, son of James Daniel and Jane, his wife, b. 3rd da, 3rd mo, 1709.
Rebeckah Abbott, dau. of George Abbott and Mary, his wife, b. 10th da, 6th mo, 1709.
James Mason, son of Thomas Mason and Elizabeth, his wife, b. 11th da, 6th mo, 1709.
Samuel Collyer, son of John Collyer and Elizabeth, his wife, b. 28th da, 6th mo, 1709.
Richard Goodwin, son of John Goodwin and Susanah, his wife, b. 4th da, 7th mo, 1709.
Joseph Whittan, son of James Whittan and Sarah, his wife, b. 9th da, 9th mo, 1709.
Clement Hall, son of William Hall of Salem and Sarah, his wife, b. 20th da, 6th mo, 1706.
Nathaniel Hall, son of William Hall of Salem and Sarah, his wife, b. 14th da, 9th mo, 1709.
Elizabeth Thompson, dau. of James Thompson and Ann, his wife, b. 3rd da, 12th mo, 1709.
Hannah White, dau. of Josiah White and Hannah, his wife, b. 22nd da, 2nd mo, 1710.
John Nicholson, son of Abel Nicholson and Mary, his wife, b. 8th da, 5th mo, 1710.
Grace Hancock, dau. of John Hancock and Mary, his wife, b. 20th da, 5th Mary, 1710.
Rebeckah Mason, dau. of John Mason and Sarah, his wife, b. 3rd da, 9th mo, 1710.
Mary Thompson, dau. of William Thompson and Hannah, his wife, b. 21st da, 11th mo, 1710.
Sarah Daniel, dau. of James Daniel and Jane, his wife, b. 18th da, 10th mo, 1710.
Elizabeth Stubbines, dau. of Samuel Stubbines and Sarah, his wife, b. 20th da, 12th mo, 1710.
Abraham Thompson, son of Andrew Thompson and Grace, his wife, b. 26th da, 12th mo, 1710.
Mary Goodwin, dau. of John Goodwin and Susanah his wife, b. 1st da, 9th mo, 1710.
George Wamsley, son of Henry Wamsley and Dynah, his wife, b. 1st da, 7th mo, 1702.
Jonathan Wamsley, son of Henry Wamsley and Dynah, his wife, b. 16th da, 10th mo, 1704.
Ann Wamsley, dau. of Henry Wamsley and Dynah, his wife, b. 25th da, 9th mo, 1707.
Henry Stubbines, son of Samuel Stubbines and Sarah, his wife, b. 4th da, 6th mo, 1712.
James Thompson, son of James Thompson and Ann, his wife, b. 26th da, 8th mo, 1712.
Samuel Abbott, son of George Abbott and Mary, his wife, b. 26th da, 6th mo, 1712.
Joshua Thompson, son of Andrew Thompson and Grace, his wife, b. 2nd da, 2nd mo, 1713.
Abigal White, dau. of Josiah White and Hannah, his wife, b. 11th

da, 6th mo, 1713.
Ruth Nicholson, dau. of Abel Nicholson and Mary, his wife, b. 9th da, 9th mo, 1713.
Joseph Goodwin, son of John Goodwin and Susanah, his wife, b. 21st da, 11th mo, 1713.
Rebeckah Thompson, dau. of Thomas Thompson and Sarah, his wife, b. 19th da, 1st mo, 1713/4.
John Smith, son of John Smith and Hannah, his wife, b. 26th da, 12th mo, 1712.
Elizabeth Denn, dau. of John Denn and Elizabeth, his wife, b. 13th da, 12th mo, 1713.
Mary Smart, dau. of Nathan Smart and Deborah, his wife, b. 22nd da, 5th mo, 1714.
Mary Abbott, dau. of George Abbott and Mary, his wife, b. 26th da, 8th mo, 1714.
Rebeckah Thompson, dau. of William Thompson and Hannah, his wife, b. 19th da, 12th mo, 1714.
Elizabeth Daniel, dau. of James Daniel and Isabell, his wife, b. 19th da, 12th mo, 1714.
Thomas Hancock, son of William Hancock and Sarah, his wife, b. 5th da, 12th mo, 1714.
Joseph Woodnut, son of Richard Woodnut and Mary, his wife, b. 5th da, 7th mo, 1697.
Thomas Thompson, son of Andrew Thompson and Grace, his wife, b. 21st da, 7th mo, 1715.
Elizabeth Smart, dau. of Nathan Smart and Deborah, his wife, b. 4th da, 1st mo, 1715.
Joseph White, son of Joseph White, Jr. and Mary, his wife, b. 21st da, 10th mo, 1715.
James Ridley, son of William Ridley and Sarah, his wife, b. 14th da, 4th mo, 1716.
Elizabeth Thompson, dau. of Joseph Thompson and Sarah, his wife, b. 1st da, 8th mo, 1716.
Rebeckah Daniel, dau. of James Daniel and Isabell, his wife, b. 6th da, 9th mo, 1716.
Rebeckah Chamness, dau. of James Chamness and Mary, his wife, b. 3rd da, 11th mo, 1716.
John Goodwin, son of John Goodwin and Susanah, his wife, b. 17th da, 10th mo, 1716.
Samuel Nicholson, son of Abel Nicholson and Mary, his wife, b. 10th da, 12th mo, 1716/7.
James Denn, son of James Denn and Elizabeth, his wife, b. 8th da, 1st mo, 1717.
Rebeckah Hancock, dau. of William Hancock and Sarah, his wife, b. 18th da, 9th mo, 1717.
Rebeckah Thompson, dau. of Andrew Thompson and Grace, his wife, b. 3rd da, 11th mo, 1717/8.
Hannah Smart, dau. of Nathan Smart and Deborah, his wife, b. 23rd da, 12th mo, 1717/8.
Jane Blanchard, dau. of Phillip Blanchard and Mary, his wife, b. 11th da, 3rd mo, 1713.
Elizabeth Blanchard, dau. of Phillip Blanchard and Mary, his wife, b. 20th da, 8th mo, 1716.
Phillip Blanchard, son of Phillip Blanchard and Mary, his wife,

b. 16th da, 12th mo, 1717/8.
John Firth, son of John Firth and Sarah, his wife, b. 3rd da, 7th mo, 1718.
John Daniel, son of James Daniel and Isabell, his wife, b. 25th da, 8th mo, 1718.
Jane Thompson, dau. of Joseph Thompson and Sarah, his wife, b. 7th da, 8th mo, 1718.
Rebeckah Ridley, dau. of William Ridley and Sarah, his wife, b. 4th da, 1st mo, 1718/9.
Jale Darkin, dau. of John Darkin and Sarah, his wife, b. 11th da, 10th mo, 1718.
Naomy Denn, dau. of John Denn and Elizabeth, his wife, b. 19th da, 1st mo, 1718/9.
John Nicholson, son of Abel Nicholson and Mary, his wife, b. 6th da, 3rd mo, 1719.
Mary Chamness, dau. of James Chamness and Mary, his wife, b. 3rd da, 6th mo, 1719.
Benjaman Thompson, son of William Thompson and Hannah, his wife, b. 11th da, 8th mo, 1719.
Piles Smith, son of Samuel Smith and Hannah, his wife, b. 18th da, 10th mo, 1719.
Samuel Smith, son of John Smith and Sarah, his wife, b. 6th da, 12th mo, 1719.
Rebeckah Thompson, dau. of William Thompson and Elizabeth, his wife, b. 25th da, 8th mo, 1720.
William Thompson, son of Joseph Thompson and Sarah, his wife, b. 30th da, 8th mo, 1720.
Jane Hart, dau. of John Hart and Ann, his wife, b. 6th da, 1st mo, 1719/20.
Margret Blanchard, dau. of Phillip Blanchard and Mary, his wife, b. 29th da, 11th mo, 1720.
William Daniel, son of James Daniel and Isabel, his wife, b. 26th da, 1st mo, 1721.
Isaac Smart, son of Nathan Smart and Deborah, his wife, b. 4th da, 2nd mo, 1721.
William Ridley, son of William Ridley and Sarah, his wife, b. 1st da, 5th mo, 1721.
Abraham Thompson, son of Andrew Thompson and Grace, his wife, b. 27th da, 5th mo, 1721.
Thomas Barber, son of Aquilla Barber and Mary, his wife, b. 23rd da, 1st mo, 1706/7.
Hannah Barber, dau. of Aquilla Barber and Mary, his wife, b. 25th da, 9th mo, 1708.
Aquilla Barber, son of Aquilla Barber and Mary, his wife, b. 4th da, 10th mo, 1710.
John Barber, son of Aquilla Barber and Mary, his wife, b. 4th da, 12th mo, 1712.
Daniel Barber, son of Aquilla Barber and Mary, his wife, b. 2nd da, 12th mo, 1714.
Samuel Barber, son of Aquilla Barber and Mary, his wife, b. 16th da, 12th mo, 1716.
Abraham Barber, son of Aquilla Barber and Mary, his wife, b. 16th da, 11th mo, 1718.
Isaac Barber, son of Aquilla Barber and Mary, his wife, b. 29th

da, 3rd mo, 1720/1.
James Chambless, son of James Chambless and Mary, his wife, b. 29th da, 3rd mo, 1721.
Thomas Goodwin, son of John Goodwin and Susannah, his wife, b. 10th da, 6th mo, 1721.
Thomas Hale, son of Thomas Hale and Mary, his wife, b. 7th da, 1st mo, 1718/19.
John Hale, son of Thomas Hale and Mary, his wife, b. 8th da, 4th mo, 1716.
Henry Hale, son of Thomas Hale and Mary, his wife, b. 4th da, 12th mo, 1720/21.
Mary Smith, dau. of Samuel Smith and Hannah, his wife, b. 26th da, 8th mo, 1721.
John Denn, son of John Denn and Elizabeth, his wife, b. 25th da, 7th mo, 1721.
Hannah Huckings, dau. of Roger Huckings and Sarah, his wife, b. 10th da, 10th mo, 1707.
Achsah Huckings, son of Roger Huckings and Sarah, his wife, b. 15th da, 1st mo, 1711/12.
Mary Huckings, dau. of Roger Huckings and Sarah, his wife, b. 24th da, 8th mo, 1709.
Elizabeth Huckings, dau. of Roger Huckings and Sarah, his wife, b. 19th da, 11th mo, 1713.
Susanah Huckings, son of Roger Huckings and Sarah, his wife, b. 12th da, 3rd mo, 1715.
Huldah Huckings, dau. of Roger Huckings and Sarah, his wife, b. 3rd da, 1st mo, 1717/8.
Hindrance Huckings, dau. of Roger Huckings and Sarah, his wife, b. 1st da, 1st mo, 1719.
John Huckings, son of Roger Huckings and Sarah, his wife, b. 9th da, 10th mo, 1722.
Hannah Darkin, dau. of Joseph Darkin and Ann, his wife, b. 18th da, 10th mo, 1722.
Joseph Thompson, son of Joseph Thompson and Sarah, his wife, b. 30th da, 1st mo, 1723.
William Hunt, son of William Hunt and Sarah, his wife, b. 18th da, 4th mo, 1723.
Aaron Daniel, son of James Daniel and Isabel, his wife, b. 21st da, 6th mo, 1723.
William Goodwin, son of John Goodwin and Susanna, his wife, b. 25th da, 8th mo, 1723.
Hannah Vickary, dau. of Edward Vickary and Sarah, his wife, b. 6th da, 5th mo, 1723.
Hannah Smith, dau. of Samuel Smith and Hannah, his wife, b. 21st da, 10th mo, 1723.
Elizabeth Champness, dau. of James Champness and Margeret, his wife, b. 10th da, 5th mo, 1723.
Joshua Morris, son of David Morris and Jane, his wife, b. 3rd da, 10th mo, 1724.
Thomas Woodnut, son of Joseph Woodnut and Rachel, his wife, b. 12th da, 3rd mo, 1724.
Edward Smart, son of Nathan Smart and Deborah, his wife, b. 14th da, 5th mo, 1724.
Martha Thompson, dau. of Joseph Thompson and Sarah, his wife, b.

31st da, 11th mo, 1724.
Isaac Thompson, son of William Thompson and Elizabeth, his wife, b. 20th da, 12th mo, 1724.
Marcy Denn, dau. of John Denn and Lea, his wife, b. 21st da, 1st mo, 1724.
Rebeckah Vickary, dau. of Edward Vickary and Sarah, his wife, b. 13th da, 12th mo, 1725.
Joshua Morris, son of David Morris and Jane, his wife, b. 3rd da, 10th mo, 1723.
Thomas Woodnut, son of Joseph Woodnut and Rachel, his wife, b. 12th da, 3rd mo, 1724.
Edward Smart, son of Nathan Smart and Deborah, his wife, b. 14th da, 5th mo, 1724.
Martha Thompson, dau. of Joseph Thompson and Sarah, his wife, b. 31st da, 11th mo, 1724.
Isaac Thompson, son of William Thompson and Elizabeth, his wife, b. 20th da, 12th mo, 1724.
Marcy Denn, dau. of John Denn and Lea, his wife, b. 21st da, 1st mo, 1724.
Rebeckah Vickary, dau. of Edward Vickary and Sarah, his wife, b. 13th da, 12th mo, 1725.
James Butcher, son of John Butcher and Jane, his wife, b. 10th da, 3rd mo, 1726.
Thomas Hunt, son of William Hunt and Sarah, his wife, b. 30th da, 5th mo, 1726.
Elizabeth Smith, dau. of Samuel Smith and Hannah, his wife, b. 1st da, 7th mo, 1726.
Edward Kasbey, son of Edward Kasbey and Elizabeth, his wife, b. 22nd da, 3rd mo, 1726.
James Thompson, son of William Thompson and Elizabeth, his wife, b. 24th da, 11th mo, 1726.
Sarah Darkin, dau. of Joseph Darkin and Ann, his wife, b. 11th da, 2nd mo, 1726.
Sarah Thompson, dau. of Joseph Thompson and Sarah, his wife, b. 31st da, 5th mo, 1726.
Amos Denn, son of John Denn and Lea, his wife, b. 21st da, 7th mo, 1727.
William Clifton, son of Hugh Clifton and Elizabeth, his wife, b. 31st da, 10th mo, 1727.
Elizabeth Oakford, dau. of Charles Oakford and Esther, his wife, b. 12th da, 4th or 11th mo, 1727.
Richard Hancock, son of Samuel Hancock and Rebeckah, his wife, b. 22nd da, 4th mo, 1727.
Daniel Denn, son of John Denn and Lea, his wife, b. 1st da, 8th mo, 1728.
Thomas Huckings, son of Roger Huckings and Sarah, his wife, b. 28th da, 2nd mo, 1728.
Mary Kasbey, dau. of Edward Kasbey and Elizabeth, his wife, b. 14th da, 1st mo, 1727/8.
John Acton, son of Benjaman Acton and Elizabeth, his wife, b. 31st da, 8th mo, 1728.
Thomas Hunt, son of William Hunt and Sarah, his wife, b. 10th da, 1st mo, 1728/9.
Andrew Thompson, son of William Thompson and Elizabeth, his wife,

b. 4th da, 3rd mo, 1729.
Milisent Waid, dau. of Joseph Waid and Hannah, his wife, b. 29th da, 6th mo, 1729.
Mary Ann Smith, dau. of Samuel Smith and Hannah, his wife, b. 23rd da, 2nd mo, 1729.
Gwen Barrot, dau. of Thomas Barrot and Elizabeth, his wife, b. 6th da, 10th mo, 1726.
Thomas Barrot, son of Thomas Barrot and Elizabeth, his wife, b. 22nd da, 7th mo, 1728.
Grace Thompson, dau. of Joseph Thompson and Sarah, his wife, b. 15th da, 2nd mo, 1730.
Joseph Clifton, son of Hugh Clifton and Elizabeth, his wife, b. 26th da, 12th mo, 1730.
Elihu Hughes, son of Edward Hughes and Hannah, his wife, b. 16th da, 11th mo, 1725.
Tabitha Hughs, dau. of Edward Hughes and Hannah, his wife, b. 29th da, 7th mo, 1729.
Benjaman Hughes, son of Edward Hughes and Hannah, his wife, b. 17th da, 12th mo, 1728.
Joseph Acton, son of Benjamin Acton and Elizabeth, his wife, b. 3rd da, 9th mo, 1730.
Bradway Kasbey, son of Edward Bradway and Elizabeth, his wife, b. 4th da, 10th mo, 1730.
Mary Davis, dau. of John Davis and Elenor, his wife, b. 24th da, 4th mo, 1713.
Phebe Davis, dau. of John Davis and Elenor, his wife, b. 3rd da, 2nd mo, 1716.
Charity Davis, dau. of John Davis and Elenor, his wife, b. 3rd da, 1st mo, 1717/8.
Thomas Davis, son of John Davis and Elenor, his wife, b. 13th da, 11th mo, 1719.
Hannah Davis, dau. of John Davis and Elenor, his wife, b. 15th da, 2nd mo, 1721.
Elizabeth Davis, dau. of John Davis and Elenor, his wife, b. 9th da, 1st mo, 1723.
Marcy Davis, dau. of John Davis and Elenor, his wife, b. 10th da, 6th mo, 1726.
John Davis, son of John Davis and Elenor, his wife, b. 13th da, 5th mo, 1730.
Richard Moss, son of Abraham Moss and Rebeckah, his wife, b. 6th da, 11th mo, 1724/5.
Isaac Moss, son of Abraham Moss and Rebeckah, his wife, b. 18th da, 11th mo, 1726/7.
Hannah Moss, dau. of Abraham Moss and Rebeckah, his wife, b. 14th da, 10th mo, 1730.
Mary Clifton, dau. of Hugh Clifton and Elizabeth, his wife, b. 17th da, 4th mo, 1731.
Leah Denn, dau. of John Denn and Leah, his wife, b. 18th da, 8th mo, 1731.
Bartholomew Wiat, son of Bartholomew Wiat and Elizabeth, his wife, b. 20th da, 5th mo, 1731.
Hannah Siddons, dau. of William Siddons and Mary, his wife, b. 1st mo, 9th da, 1732.
John Thompson, son of William Thompson and Elizabeth, his wife,

b. 29th da, 9th mo, 1732.
Thomas Moss, son of Abraham Moss and Rebeckah, his wife, b. 22nd da, 11th mo, 1732/3.
Sarah Wiat, dau. of Batholomew Wiat and Elizabeth, his wife, b. 6th da, 6th mo, 1733.
Elizabeth Plats, dau. of Jonathan Plats and Jane, his wife, b. 11th da, 6th mo, 1731.
Sarah Mason, dau. of Samuel Mason and Elizabeth, his wife, b. 25th da, 9th mo, 1732.
Elizabeth and Hannah Mason, daus. of Samuel Mason and Elizabeth, his wife, b. 2nd da, 10th mo, 1733.
John Mason, son of Thomas Mason and Sarah, his wife, b. 17th da, 12th mo, 1733.
Elizabeth Hill, dau. of Thomas Hill and Elizabeth, his wife, b. 1st da, 12th mo, 1714.
Thomas Hill, son of Thomas Hill and Elizabeth, his wife, b. 17th da, 4th mo, 1717.
Rebecah Hill, dau. of Thomas Hill and Elizabeth, his wife, b. 13th da, 12th mo, 1719.
Hannah Hill, dau. of Thomas Hill and Elizabeth, his wife, b. 17th da, 9th mo, 1722.
Sarah Hill, dau. of Thomas Hill and Elizabeth, his wife, b. 31st da, 6th mo, 1725.
Benjaman Acton, son of Benjaman Acton and Elizabeth, his wife, b. 15th da, 9th mo, 1733.
Susanna Thompson, dau. of Joseph Thompson and Sarah, his wife, b. 15th da, 6th mo, 1734.
Paul Denn, son of John Denn and Leah, his wife, b. 18th da, 2nd mo, 1734.
James Thomas, son of John Thomas and Ann, his wife, b. 14th da, 12th mo, 1734/5.
Elizabeth Platts, dau. of Jonathan Platts and Jane, his wife, b. 11th da, 6th mo, 1731.
Thomas Platts, son of Jonathan Platts and Jane, his wife, b. 16th da, 6th mo, 1734.
George Abbott, dau. of Samuel Abbott and Hannah, his wife, b. 29th da, 11th mo, 1734/5.
Sarah Siddons, dau. of William Siddons and Mary, his wife, b. 24th da, 5th mo, 1735.
Hannah Thompson, dau. of William Thompson and Elizabeth, his wife, b. 3rd da, 2nd mo, 1735.
Mary Woodnut, dau. of Joseph Woodnut and Rachel, his wife, b. 19th da, 4th mo, 1727.
Hannah Woodnut, dau. of Joseph Woodnut and Rachel, his wife, b. 11th da, 9th mo, 1729.
Richard Woodnut, son of Joseph Woodnut and Rachel, his wife, b. 10th da, 1st mo, 1731/2.
Joseph Woodnut, son of Joseph Woodnut and Rachel, his wife, b. 8th da, 11th mo, 1734/5.
Benjaman Acton, son of Benjaman Acton and Elizabeth, his wife, b. 28th da, 12th mo, 1735/6.
William Abbott, son of Samuel Abbott and Hannah, his wife, b. 4th da, 4th mo, 1737.
Elizabeth Thompson, dau. of William Thompson and Elizabeth, his

wife, b. 9th da, 7th mo, 1737.
Thomas Thompson, son of Samuel Thompson and Edith, his wife, b. 17th da, 6th mo, 1732.
Hannah Thompson, dau. of Samuel Thompson and Edith, his wife, b. 10th da, 1st mo, 1734.
Mary Thompson, dau. of Samuel Thompson and Edith, his wife, b. 10th da, 11th mo, 1735.
Anne Thompson, dau. of Samuel Thompson and Edith, his wife, b. 14th da, 10th mo, 1737.
Jane Hewes, dau. of James Hewes and Jane, his wife, b. 9th da, 8th mo, 1737.
Daniel Thompson, son of Thomas Thompson and Mary, his wife, b. 19th da, 4th mo, 1737.
Sarah Hancock, dau. of Samuel Hancock and Rebeckah, his wife, b. 26th da, 7th mo, 1729.
Easter Hancock, dau. of Samuel Hancock and Rebeckah, his wife, b. 14th da, 4th mo, 1731.
Rebeckah Hancock, dau. of Samuel Hancock and Rebeckah, his wife, b. 24th da, 6th mo, 1734.
Elizabeth Hancock, dau. of Samuel Hancock and Rebeckah, his wife, 24th da, 7th mo, 1736.
Samuel Hancock, dau. of Samuel Hancock and Rebeckah, his wife, 28th da, 6th mo, 1736.
Samuel Acton, son of Benjaman Acton and Elizabeth, his wife, b. 31st da, 6th mo, 1738.
Jane Siddons, dau. of William Siddons and Mary, his wife, b. 1st da, 4th mo, 1738.
Easter Oakford, dau. of Charles Oakford and Easter, his wife, b. 22nd da, 12th mo, 1729/30.
Charles Oakford, son of Charles Oakford and Easter, his wife, b. 17th da, 1st mo, 1731.
Elizabeth Oakford, dau. of Charles Oakford and Easter, his wife, b. 11th da, 2nd mo, 1736.
James Oakford, son of Charles Oakford and Easter, his wife, b. 2nd da, 8th mo, 1738.
Joshua Thompson, son of Thomas Thompson and Mary, his wife, b. 9th da, 12th mo, 1739/40.
James Thompson, son of Thomas Thompson and Edith, his wife, b. 21st da, 11th mo, 1739/40.
Deborah Siddons, dau. of William Siddons and Mary, his wife, b. 30th da, 11th mo, 1739/40.
Jane Platts, dau. of Jonathan Platts and Jane, his wife, b. 22nd da, 12th mo, 1740/1.
Rebeckah Abbott, dau. of Samuel Abbott and Hannah, his wife, b. 26th da, 10th mo, 1740.
John Thompson, son of Thomas Thompson and Mary, his wife, b. 28th da, 4th mo, 1741.
Mary Powel, dau. of John Powel and Sarah, his wife, b. 20th da, 11th mo, 1714.
Sarah Powel, dau. of John Powel and Sarah, his wife, b. 31st da, 10th mo, 1721.
Mary Nicholson, dau. of John Nicholson and Sarah, his wife, b. 15th da, 6th mo, 1741.
Samuel and Edith Thompson, son and dau. of Samuel Thompson and

Edith, his wife, b. 16th da, 1st mo, 1742.
Sarah Thompson, dau. of Joshua Thompson and Sarah, his wife, b. 23rd da, 11th mo, 1733.
Grace Thompson, dau. of Joshua Thompson and Sarah, his wife, b. 23rd da, 11th mo, 1734/5.
Ann Thompson, dau. of Joshua Thompson and Sarah, his wife, b. 6th da, 3rd mo, 1737.
Andrew Thompson, son of Joshua Thompson and Sarah, his wife, b. 29th da, 5th mo, 1739.
Sarah Thompson, dau. of Joshua Thompson and Sarah, his wife, b. 24th da, 12th mo, 1741/2.
Elizabeth Powel, dau. of Jeremiah Powel and Jane, his wife, b. 22nd da, 12th mo, 1736.
Mary Powel, dau. of Jeremiah Powel and Jane, his wife, b. 13th da, 11th mo, 1738.
John Powel, son of Jeremiah Powel and Jane, his wife, b. 5th da, 12th mo, 1740.
Richard Goodwin, son of Joseph Goodwin and Sarah his wife, b. 29th da, 7th mo, 1739.
Phebey Goodwin, dau. of Joseph Goodwin and Sarah, his wife, b. 8th da, 5th mo, 1741.
Joseph Goodwin, son of Joseph Goodwin and Sarah, his wife, b. 8th da, 10th mo, 1742.
Mary Stretch, dau. of Joseph Stretch, b. 11th da, 6th mo, 1704 and Deborah, his wife, b. 2nd da, 5th mo, 1728.
Joseph Stretch, son of Joseph Stretch and Deborah, his wife, b. 3rd da, 9th mo, 1732.
Samuel Stretch, son of Joseph Stretch and Deborah, his wife, b. 8th da, 7th mo, 1735.
Jonathan Stretch, son of Joseph Stretch and Deborah, his wife, b. 9th da, 8th mo, 1737.
Joshua Stretch, son of Joseph Stretch and Deborah, his wife, b. 28th da, 12th mo, 1740.
Martha Stretch, son of Joseph Stretch and Deborah, his wife, b. 21st da, 4th mo, 1742.
Joshua Thompson, son of Thomas Thompson and Mary, his wife, b. 30th da, 7th mo, 1743.
William Siddons, son of William Siddons and Mary, his wife, b. 16 da, 11th mo, 1742/3.
Hannah White, dau. of John White and Elizabeth, his wife, b. 27th da, 5th mo, 1735.
Mary White, dau. of John White and Elizabeth, his wife, b. 9th da, 1st mo, 1738/9.
Joshua Huddy, son of Daniel Huddy and Elizabeth, his wife, b. 8th da, 11th mo, 1735.
Martha Huddy, dau. of Daniel Huddy and Elizabeth, his wife, b. 29th da, 5th mo, 1742.
Nathan Stretch, son of Joseph Stretch and Deborah, his wife, b. 16th da, 7th mo, 1744.
John Oakford, son of John Oakford and Hannah, his wife, b. 4th da, 7th mo, 1734.
Amos Oakford, son of John Oakford and Hannah, his wife, b. 2nd da, 2nd mo, 1738.
Elizabeth Oakford, dau. of John Oakford and Hannah, his wife, b.

16th da, 7th mo, 1741.
Abraham Moss, son of Richard Moss and Rebeckah, his wife, b. 14th da, 12th mo, 1744/5.
Mary Ware, dau. of Joseph Ware and Elizabeth, his wife, b. 22nd da, 12th mo, 1735/6.
Sarah Ware, dau. of Joseph Ware and Elizabeth, his wife, b. 22nd da, 8th mo, 1737.
Hannah Ware, dau. of Joseph Ware and Elizabeth, his wife, b. 4th da, 7th mo, 1739.
Rebeckah Ware, son of Joseph Ware and Elizabeth, his wife, b. 9th da, 11th mo, 1741/2.
Joseph Ware, son of Joseph Ware and Elizabeth, his wife, b. 26th da, 3rd mo, 1744.
Elijah Ware, son of Joseph Ware and Elizabeth, his wife, b. 30th da, 1st mo, 1748.
Rachel Gibson, dau. of Joseph Gibson and Elizabeth, his wife, b. 3rd da, 7th mo, 1721.
Sarah Gibson, son of Joseph Gibson and Elizabeth, his wife, b. 2nd da, 12th mo, 1722/3.
Elizabeth Gibson, dau. of Joseph Gibson and Elizabeth, his wife, b. 27th da, 8th mo, 1724.
Joseph Gibson, son of Joseph Gibson and Elizabeth, his wife, b. 28th da, 3rd mo, 1726.
Dorcas Gibson, dau. of Joseph Gibson and Elizabeth, his wife, b. ? da, 6th mo, 1732.
Ezekiel Siddons, son of William Siddons and Mary, his wife, b. 10th da, 7th mo, 1745.
Samuel Oakford, son of John Oakford and Rebeckah, his wife, b. 4th da, 7th mo, 1733.
Mable Oakford, dau. of John Oakford and Rebeckah, his wife, b. 13th da, 6th mo, 1735.
Sarah Oakford, dau. of John Oakford and Rebeckah, his wife, b. 21st da, 12th mo, 1737/8.
Rebeckah Oakford, dau. of John Oakford and Rebeckah, his wife, b. 17th da, 8th mo, 1741.
Susannah Oakford, dau. of John Oakford and Rebeckah, his wife, b. 2nd da, 2nd mo, 1745.
Mary McNichole, dau. of George McNichole and Rebeckah, his wife, b. 13th da, 8th mo, 1745.
Sarah Keasbey, dau. of Matthew Keasbey and Sarah, his wife, b. 21st da, 10th mo, 1730.
Mary Keasbey, dau. of Matthew Keasbey and Sarah, his wife, b. 24th da, 2nd mo, 1733.
Elizabeth Keasbey, dau. of Matthew Keasbey and Sarah, his wife, b. 2nd da, 12th mo, 1734/5.
John Keasbey, son of Matthew Keasbey and Sarah, his wife, b. 13th da, 9th mo, 1736.
Philip Rice, son of Thomas Rice and Sarah, his wife, b. 16th da, 1st mo, 1739/40.
Hannah Rice, dau. of Thomas Rice and Sarah, his wife, b. 10th da, 5th mo, 1742.
Thomas Thompson, son of Thomas Thompson and Mary, his wife, b. 19th da, 10th mo, 1745.
Milissent Thompson, dau. of Benjamin Thompson and Elizabeth, his

wife, b. 12th da, 6th mo, 1747.
Ebenezer Miller, son of Ebenezer Miller and Sarah, his wife, b. 15th da, 9th mo, 1725.
Hannah Miller, dau. of Ebenezer Miller and Sarah, his wife, b. 20th da, 1st mo, 1728.
Josiah Miller, son of Ebenezer Miller and Sarah, his wife, b. 1st da, 3rd mo, 1731.
Andrew Miller, son of Ebenezer Miller and Sarah, his wife, b. 4th da, 12th mo, 1732/3.
William Miller, son of Ebenezer Miller and Sarah, his wife, b. 13th da, 8th mo, 1735.
John Miller, son of Ebenezer Miller and Sarah, his wife, b. 7th da, 11th mo, 1737/8.
Mark Miller, son of Ebenezer Miller and Sarah, his wife, b. 28th da, 6th mo, 1740.
Sarah Miller, dau. of Ebenezer Miller and Sarah, his wife, b. 17th da, 3rd mo, 1743.
Rebeckah Miller, dau. of Ebenezer Miller and Sarah, his wife, b. 17th da, 5th mo, 1747.
Ezra Firth, son of John Firth and Judith, his wife, b. 24th da, 1st mo, 1744/5.
Rebeckah Thompson, dau. of Joshua Thompson and Elizabeth, his wife, b. 10th da, 6th mo, 1745.
Elizabeth Siddons, dau. of William Siddons and Mary, his wife, b. 20th da, 10th mo, 1747.
Sarah Firth, dau. of John Firth and Judith, his wife, b. 13th da, 9th mo, 1747.
Sarah Thompson, dau. of Thomas Thompson and Mary, his wife, b. 5th da, 9th mo, 1747.
Mary Thompson, dau. of Thomas Thompson and Mary, his wife, b. 2nd da, 9th mo, 1749.
Hannah Thompson, dau. of Benjamin Thompson and Elizabeth, his wife, b. 14th da, 11th mo, 1749/50.
Richard Smith, son of John Smith and Sarah, his wife, b. 10th da, 11th mo, 1743/4.
Hill Smith, son of John Smith and Sarah, his wife, b. 15th da, 4th mo, 1745.
John Smith, son of John Smith and Sarah, his wife, b. 27th da, 11th mo, 1748/9.
Richard Booth, son of Richard Booth and Ann, his wife, b. 21st da, 8th mo, 1739.
Elizabeth Booth, dau. of Richard Booth and Ann, his wife, b. 14th da, 2nd mo, 1742.
Jane Booth, dau. of Richard Booth and Ann, his wife, b. 10th da, 6th mo, 1744.
Ruth Booth, dau. of Richard Booth and Ann, his wife, b. 15th da, 5th mo, 1746.
Sarah Booth, dau. of Richard Booth and Ann, his wife, b. 25th da, 9th mo, 1748.
Rachel Denn, dau. of John Denn and Elizabeth, his wife, b. 30th da, 2nd mo, 1745.
James Denn, son of John Denn and Elizabeth, his wife, b. 19th da, 11th mo, 1746/7.
John Denn, son of John Denn and Elizabeth, his wife, b. 5th da,

3rd mo, 1751.
Edward Siddons, son of William Siddons and Mary, his wife, b. 25th da, 5th mo, 1750.
William Smith, son of Thomas Smith of Manington and Sarah, his wife, b. 31st da, 8th mo, 1741.
David Smith, son of Thomas Smith of Manington and Sarah, his wife, b. 17th da, 7th mo, 1744.
Thomas Smith, son of Thomas Smith of Manington and Sarah, his wife, b. 28th da, 4th mo, 1747.
Hannah Fogg, dau. of Charles Fogg and Hannah, his wife, b. 10th da, 11th mo, 1749/50.
Mary Fogg, dau. of Charles Fogg and Sarah, his wife, b. 11th da, 7th mo, 1753.
Rachel Thompson, son of Joseph Thompson and Mary, his wife, b. 26th da, 1st mo, 1748.
Samuel Thompson, son of Joseph Thompson and Mary, his wife, b. 18th da, 12th mo, 1749/50.
Hannah Thompson, dau. of Joseph Thompson and Mary, his wife, b. 26th da, 1st mo, 1752.
William Thompson, son of Joseph Thompson and Mary, his wife, b. 20th da, 3rd mo, 1754.
David Barber, son of Jacob Barber and Rebeckah, his wife, b. 16th da, 9th mo, 1747.
Jonathan Barber, son of Jacob Barber and Rebeckah, his wife, b. 3rd da, 1st mo, 1750.
Elija Barber, son of Jacob Barber and Rebeckah, his wife, b. 29th da, 10th mo, 1752.
Louisa Barber, dau. of Jacob Barber and Rebeckah, his wife, b. 13th da, 11th mo, 1754.
Grace Thompson, dau. of Thomas Thompson and Mary, his wife, b. 22nd da, 5th mo, 1751.
Elizabeth Firth, dau. of John Firth and Judith, his wife, b. 2nd da, 5th mo, 1751.
John Firth, son of John Firth and Judith, his wife, b. 26th da, 8th mo, 1754.
Isaac Siddons, son of William Siddons and Mary, his wife, b. 13th da, 11th mo, 1754.
Abel Nicholson, son of Samuel Nicholson and Sarah, his wife, b. 24th da, 6th mo, 1744.
Grace Nicholson, dau. of Samuel Nicholson and Sarah, his wife, b. 16th da, 6th mo, 1746.
Rachel Nicholson, son of Samuel Nicholson and Sarah, his wife, b. 1st da, 10th mo, 1750.
Abel Nicholson, son of Samuel Nicholson and Sarah, his wife, b. 8th da, 3rd mo, 1752.
Samuel Nicholson, son of Samuel Nicholson and Sarah, his wife, b. 26th da, 8th mo, 1753.
Thomas Draper, son of Edward Draper and Mary, his wife, b. 21st da, 9th mo, 1747.
Jael Draper, dau. of Edward Draper and Mary, his wife, b. 25th da, 8th mo, 1749.
Rebeckah Draper, dau. of Edward Draper and Mary, his wife, b. 8th da, 9th mo, 1751.
Mary Draper, dau. of Edward Draper and Mary, his wife, b. 16th

da, 2nd mo, 1754.
Cathrine Smart, dau. of Isaac and Ann Smart, b. 6th da, 6th mo, called August, 1750.
Deborah Smart, dau. of Isaac and Ann Smart, b. 27th da, 8th mo, called October, 1751.
Nathan Smart, son of Isaac and Ann Smart, b. 5th da, 10th mo, (n.s.) 1755.
Henry Firth, son of John Firth and Judith, his wife, b. 19th da, 8th mo, 1756.
John Butcher, son of Thomas Butcher and Rachel, his wife, b. 3rd da, 10th mo, 1756.
Griffith Rice, son of Thomas Rice and Sarah, his wife, b. 26th da, 2nd mo, 1747.
Sarah Rice, dau. of Thomas Rice and Sarah, his wife, b. 20th da, 8th mo, 1750.
John Rice, son of Thomas Rice and Sarah, his wife, b. 26th da, 4th mo, 1753.
Samuel Mason, son of Aaron Mason and Abigail, his wife, b. 10th da, 10th mo, 1731.
Jonathan Woodnut, son of Richard Woodnut and Ann, his wife, b. 17th da, 3rd mo, 1731.
Sarah Mason, dau. of Aaron Mason and Abigail, his wife, b. 8th da, 11th mo, 1734.
Henry Woodnut, son of Richard Woodnut and Ann, his wife, b. 4th da, 12th mo, 1735/6.
Richard Woodnut, son of Jonathan Woodnut and Sarah, his wife, b. b. 13th da, 1st mo, 1754.
James Mason Woodnut, son of Jonathan Woodnut and Sarah, his wife, b. 21st da, 11th mo, 1755.
Rebeckah Bradway, dau. of Aaron Bradway and Mary, his wife, b. 19th da, 7th mo, (o.s.) 1746.
Joshua Bradway, son of Aaron Bradway and Mary, his wife, b. 9th da, 9th mo, (o.s.) 1748.
John Firth, son of John Firth and Judith, his wife, b. 5th da, 9th mo, 1757.
Aaron Bradway, son of Aaron Bradway and Mary, his wife, b. 6th da, 11th mo, 1757.
David Fogg, son of Joseph Fogg and Elizabeth, his wife, b. 30th da, 10th mo, 1738.
Ebenezer Fogg, son of Joseph Fogg and Elizabeth, his wife, b. 26th da, 3rd mo, 1741.
Charles Fogg, son of Joseph Fogg and Elizabeth, his wife, b. 29th da, 2nd mo, 1743.
Hannah Fogg, dau. of Joseph Fogg and Elizabeth, his wife, b. 5th da, 12th mo, 1744/5.
Ann Fogg, dau. of Joseph Fogg and Elizabeth, his wife, b. 23rd da, 3rd mo, 1747.
Elizabeth Fogg, dau. of Joseph Fogg and Elizabeth, his wife, b. 1st da, 11th mo, 1749/50.
Holme Fogg, son of Joseph Fogg and Elizabeth, his wife, b. 28th da, 3rd mo, 1752.
Isaac Fogg, son of Joseph Fogg and Elizabeth, his wife, b. 17th da, 3rd mo, 1755.
Rebeckah Fogg, dau. of Joseph Fogg and Elizabeth, his wife, b.

22nd da, 5th mo, 1758.
Ann Fogg, dau. of Joseph Fogg and Elizabeth, his wife, d. 17th da, 7th mo, 1751 aged about 4 years and 4 months.
David Den, son of John Den and Elizabeth, his wife, b. 3rd da, 7th mo, 1756.

John Denn d. 7th da, 9th mo, 1733.

Nathan Stretch, son of Joseph Stretch and Deborah, his wife, b. 16th da, 7th mo, 1744.
Aaron Stretch, son of Joseph Stretch and Deborah, his wife, b. 14th da, 10th mo, 1746.
Rebeckah Stretch, dau. of Joseph Stretch and Deborah, his wife, b. 27th da, 7th mo, 1749.
Elizabeth Stretch, dau. of Joseph Stretch and Elizabeth, his wife, b. 26th da, 6th mo, 1756.
Elizabeth Stewart, dau. of John Stewart and Mary, his wife, b. 27th da, 9th mo, 1735.
Lidya Stewart, dau. of John Stewart and Mary, his wife, b. 16th da, 12th mo, 1737.
Samuel Stewart, son of John Stewart and Mary, his wife, b. 26th da, 12th mo, 1740.
John Stewart, son of John Stewart and Mary, his wife, b. 16th da, 7th mo, 1743.
Mary Stewart, dau. of John Stewart and Mary, his wife, b. 6th da, 1st mo, 1746.
Ann Stewart, dau. of John Stewart and Mary, his wife, b. 14th da, 11th mo, 1748.
James Stewart, son of John Stewart and Mary, his wife, b. 26th da, 3rd mo, 1751.
Melisent Stewart, dau. of John Stewart and Mary, his wife, b. 8th da, 6th mo, 1754.
Joseph Stewart, son of John Stewart and Mary, his wife, b. 1st da, 4th mo, 1758.
William Bradway, son of Jonathan Bradway and Mary, his wife, b. 13th da, 7th mo, 1728.
Rachel Bradway, dau. of Jonathan Bradway and Mary, his wife, b. 11th da, 1st mo, 1735.
Jonathan Bradway, son of Jonathan Bradway and Mary, his wife, b. 17th da, 7th mo, 1735.
Edward Bradway, son of Jonathan Bradway and Susannah, his wife, b. 31st da, 3rd mo, 1741.
Sarah Bradway, dau. of Jonathan Bradway and Susannah, his wife, b. 28th da, 7th mo, 1743.
Nathan Bradway, son of Jonathan Bradway and Susannah, his wife, b. 15th da, 2nd mo, 1746.
Adna Bradway, son of William Bradway and Sarah, his wife, b. 10th da, 11th mo, 1750/1.
William Bradway, son of William Bradway and Sarah, his wife, b. 20th da, 10th mo, 1752.
Mary Bradway, dau. of William Bradway and Sarah, his wife, b. 28th da, 12th mo, 1756.
Elizabeth Pedrick, dau. of Samuel Pedrick and Hester, his wife, b. 7th da, 7th mo, 1752.

Charles Pedrick, son of Samuel Pedrick and Hester, his wife, b. 6th da, 4th mo, 1754.
Sarah Pedrick, dau. of Samuel Pedrick and Hester, his wife, b. 9th da, 7th mo, 1756.
John Ware, son of John Ware and Elizabeth, his wife, b. 16th da, 7th mo, 1752.
Millicent Ware, dau. of John Ware and Elizabeth, his wife, b. 12th da, 10th mo, 1753.
David Ware, son of John Ware and Elizabeth, his wife, b. 5th da, 4th mo, 1755.
Mary Ware, dau. of John Ware and Elizabeth, his wife, b. 27th da, 10th mo, 1756.
Margaret Oakford, dau. of Charles Oakford and Hester, his wife, b. 3rd or 30th da, 11th mo, 1740/1.
Joseph Tindall, son of Benjamin Tindall and Hester, his wife, b. 16th da, 6th mo, 1749.
Mary Tindall, dau. of Benjamin Tindall and Hester, his wife, b. 7th da, 10th mo, 1751.
Hannah Chamneys, dau. of Nethaniel Chamneys and Susannah, his wife, b. 4th da, 8th mo, 1738.
Rebeckah Champneys, dau. of Nethaniel Chamneys and Susannah, his wife, b. 9th da, 4th mo, 1742.
Thomas Test, son of Francis Test and Elizabeth, his wife, b. 22nd da, 9th mo, 1725.
Rachel Test, dau. of Francis Test and Elizabeth, his wife, b. 2nd da, 8th mo, 1727.
Elizabeth Test, dau. of Francis Test and Elizabeth, his wife, b. 18th da, 12th mo, 1731.
Benjamin Test, son of Francis Test and Elizabeth, his wife, b. 14th da, 8th mo, 1734.
John Test, son of Francis Test and Elizabeth, his wife, b. 18th da, 4th mo, 1736.
Ruth Test, dau. of Francis Test and Elizabeth, his wife, b. 10th da, 2nd mo, 1741.
Leatitia Test, dau. of Francis Test and Elizabeth, his wife, b. 20th da, 11th mo, 1742.
Francis Test, son of Francis Test and Elizabeth, his wife, b. 4th da, 2nd mo, 1744.
Abner Test, son of Francis Test and Elizabeth, his wife, b. 23rd da, 8th mo, 1747.
Peter Ware, son of Solomon Ware and Sarah, his wife, b. 25th da, 8th mo, 1741.
Elizabeth Ware, dau. of Solomon Ware and Sarah, his wife, b. 30th da, 9th mo, 1743.
Job Ware, son of Solomon Ware and Sarah, his wife, b. 10th da, 8th mo, 1745.
Hannah Ware, dau. of Solomon Ware and Sarah, his wife, b. 25th da, 7th mo, 1747.
Elisha Ware, son of Solomon Ware and Sarah, his wife, b. 22nd da, 4th mo, 1749/50.
Bathsheba Ware, son of Solomon Ware and Sarah, his wife, b. 5th da, 3rd mo, 1753.
Sarah Ware, dau. of Solomon Ware and Sarah, his wife, b. 5th da, 3rd mo, 1753.

Solomon Ware, son of Solomon Ware and Sarah, his wife, b. 17th
da, 7th mo, 1760.
James Daniel, son of William Daniel and Rebeckah, his wife, b.
17th da, 3rd mo, 1743.
Joseph Daniel, son of William Daniel and Rebeckah, his wife, b.
14th da, 1st mo, 1745.
Thomas Daniel, son of William Daniel and Rebeckah, his wife, b.
23rd da, 6th mo, 1747.
Sarah Daniel, dau. of William Daniel and Rebeckah, his wife, b.
2nd da, 11th mo, 1749.
William Daniel, son of William Daniel and Rebeckah, his wife, b.
25th da, 7th mo, 1753.
John Daniel, son of William Daniel and Rebeckah, his wife, b.
16th da, 10th mo, 1755.
Henry Daniel, son of William Daniel and Rebeckah, his wife, b.
4th da, 12th mo, 1757.
Elizabeth Keasby, dau. of Bradway Keasby and Prudence, his wife,
b. 15th da, 10th mo, 1756.
Edward Keasby, son of Bradway Keasby and Prudence, his wife, b.
5th da, 10th mo, 1760.
Sarah Fogg, dau. of Charles Fogg and Hannah, his wife, b. 10th
da, 5th mo, 1747, and d. sometime in the fall following.
Rachel Fogg, dau. of Charles Fogg and Hannah, his wife, b. 26th
da, 9th mo, 1758.
Mary Fogg, dau. of Charles Fogg and Hannah, his wife, b. and d.
in the first month of 1759.
Charles Fogg, son of Charles Fogg and Hannah, his wife, b. 19th
da, 10th mo, 1760.
Rebeckah Kay, dau. of Joseph Kay and Ann, his wife, b. 2nd da,
5th mo, 1769.
Josiah Kay, son of Joseph Kay and Ann, his wife, b. 12th da, 2nd
mo, 1761.

Richard Wood d. on the 3rd da, 8th mo, 1759 and was interred at
his own burial ground on the 5th da, of same.

Elizabeth Wyat was b. within the verge of Haddonfield Monthly
Meeting 1st da, 11th mo, 1707.

Elizabeth Siddons, dau. of William Siddons and Mary, his wife, d.
14th da, 4th mo, 1759 aged 11 years, 3 months and 14 days.
Isaac Siddons, son of William Siddons and Mary, his wife, d. 27th
da, 4th mo, 1759, aged 4 years 5 months and 14 days.
William Siddons, son of William Siddons and Mary, his wife, d. on
the 10th da, 1st mo, 1760.

John Goodwin, son of William Goodwin and Mary, his wife, b. 19th
da, 6th mo, 1745.
Lewis Goodwin, son of William Goodwin and Mary, his wife, b. 20th
da, 12th mo, 1750/1.
Mary Goodwin, dau. of William Goodwin and Mary, his wife, b. 17th
da, 2nd mo, 1756.
William Goodwin was b. the 18th da, 2nd mo, 1756 at 8 minutes
past 2 in the morning.[The two above births may possibly be

twins.]
Nathan Stretch, son of Joseph Stretch and Deborah, his wife, b. 16th da, 7th mo, 1744.
Aaron Stretch, son of Joseph Stretch and Deborah, his wife, b. 14th da, 10th mo, 1746.
Rebeckah Stretch, dau. of Joseph Stretch and Deborah, his wife, b. 27th da, 7th mo, 1749.
Mellicent Thompson, dau. of Benjamin Thompson and Elizabeth, his wife, b. 12th da, 6th mo, 1747.
Benjamin Thompson, son of Benjamin Thompson and Elizabeth, his wife, b. 18th da, 12th mo, 1756.
Sarah Thompson, dau. of Benjamin Thompson and Elizabeth, his wife, b. 26th da, 3rd mo, 1759.
Rebeckah Thompson, dau. of Joshua Thompson and Elizabeth, his wife, b. 10th da, 6th mo, 1745.
Joseph & Joshua Thompson, sons of Joshua Thompson and Elizabeth, his wife, b. 8th da, 6th mo, 1748.
John Thompson, son of Joshua Thompson and Elizabeth, his wife, b. 17th da, 4th mo, 1752.
Joseph Thompson, son of Joshua Thompson and Elizabeth, his wife, b. 26th da, 3rd mo, 1756.

Elizabeth Thompson, wife of the aforesaid Joshua Thompson d. 29th da, 11th mo, 1759 and was buried at Salem in Friends burying grounds.

Robert Wilson, son of Robert Wilson and Jane, his wife, b. 5th da, 4th mo, 1756.
William Wilson, son of Robert Wilson and Jane, his wife, b. at Salem 30th da, 7th mo, 1757, and d. on the 12th da, 10th mo, following and was buried at Chichester Meeting House in Pa.
William Wilson, son of Robert Wilson and Jane, his wife, b. 3rd da, 3rd mo, 1759.

Prudence Hall, dau. of Clement Hall by Margaret, his wife, b. 29th da, 9th mo, 1746.
Elizabeth Hall, dau. of Clement Hall by Margaret, his wife, d. 14th da, 8th mo, 1749 and was buried 14th da, 8th mo, 1749.
Morris Hall, son of Clement Hall by Margaret, his wife, b. 26th da, 9th mo, 1750 and was buried the 6th da, 11th mo, following.
William Hall, son of Clement Hall by Margaret, his wife, b. 20th da, 2nd mo, 1752 and was buried the 21st da, 9th mo, following.
Clement Hall, son of Clement Hall by Margaret, his wife, b. 13th da, 11th mo, 1753.
Sarah Hall, dau. of Clement Hall by Margaret, his wife, b. 14th da, 4th mo, 1755.
Joseph Hall, son of Clement Hall by Margaret, his wife, b. 5th da, 2nd mo, 1757 and was buried the 17th da of the same month.
Sarah Siddons d. 7th da, 6th mo, 1752.
Jacob Ware, son of John Ware by Elizabeth, his wife, b. 28th da, 8th mo, 1759.
Jedidiah Allen, son of Jedidiah Allen and Elizabeth, his wife, b. 22nd da, 11th mo, 1739.
Hannah Allen, dau. of Preston Carpenter and Hannah, his wife, b.

4th da, 10th mo, 1743. (being the wife of Jedidiah Allen
aforesaid.)
Jedidiah Allen, son of Jedidiah Allen and Ann, his wife, b. 27th
da, 8th mo, 1780.
Hannah Allen, dau. of Jedidiah Allen and Hannah, his wife, b. 3rd
da, 9th mo, 1786.
Mary Ellet, dau. of Charles Ellet and Hannah, his wife, b. 23rd
da, 10th mo, 1782.
William Abbott, b. 4th da, 4th mo, 1737.
Rebecca Abbott, b. 18th da, 2nd mo, 1743.
Samuel Abbott, son of William Abbott and Rebecca, his wife, b.
27th da, 11th mo, 1763.
Children of Samuel Abbott and Mercy, his wife: William Abbott, b.
22nd da, 8th mo, 1792; Rebecca Abbott, b. 29th da, 7th mo,
1794; Hannah Abbott, b. 3rd da, 4th mo, 1796; Sarah Abbott, b.
8th da, 10th mo, 1797, d. 12th da, 1st mo, 1798.

Mercy Abbott, wife of Samuel Abbott, d. 1st da, 2nd mo, 1798.
Sarah Acton, widow of Samuel Acton d. 6th da, 11th mo, 1768.

Elizabeth Ambler, b. 4th da, 5th mo, 1729.
Jedidiah Allen, Jr., son of Jedidiah Allen and Ann, his wife: b.
21st da, 8th mo, 1780.
Lettice Allen, wife of Jedidiah Allen, Jr. b. 22nd da, 11th mo,
1749.
Children of Samuel Austin, b. 22nd da, 11th mo, 1749 and Lydia
Austin, wife of Samuel Austin, b. 27th da, 4th mo, 1760: Sarah
Austin, Jr. b. 27th da, 4th mo, 1788; Samuel Austin, Jr., b.
6th da, 11th mo, 1793.
Children of Samuel Acton and Sarah, his wife: Clement Acton, b.
5th da, 11th mo, 1797; Mary Acton, b. 10th da, 8th mo, 1798;
Isaac Acton, b. 6th da 2nd mo, 1800; Samuel Acton, b. 11th da,
8th mo, 1801.
Children of David Allen, son of Jedidiah Allen, b. 12th da, 2nd
mo, 1742 and Rebekah, dau. of Samuel and Edith Thompson, his
wife, b. ? 10th mo, 1748: Hannah Allen, b. 5th da, 3rd mo,
1767; Mary Allen, b. 26th da, 5th mo, 1768; Ann Allen, b. 28th
da, 1st mo, 1770; Rebekah Allen, b. 21st da, 3rd mo, 1772;
David Allen, b. 21st da, 3rd mo, 1772, d. 10th da, 2nd mo,
1783; Ruth Allen, b. 8th da, 6th mo, 1775, d. 2nd mo, 1796;
Sarah Allen, b. 8th da, 7th mo, 1777, d. 5th da, 8th mo, same
year; Beulah Allen, b. 2nd da, 6th mo, 1779; Samuel Allen, b.
21st da, 10th mo, 1781; Jedidiah Allen, b. 27th da, 8th mo,
1784; David Allen, b. 1st da, 5th mo, 1787; Chumbless Allen, b.
8th da, 9th mo, 1789.

David Allen, parent of the aforesaid children d. 17th da, 3rd mo,
1795.
Rebecca Allen, widow of David Allen, d. 28th da, 7th mo, 1809.

Mary Andrews, wife of Peter Andrews, dau. of Whitten Cripps and
Martha, his wife, b. 31st da, 2nd mo, 1762.
Sarah Acton, wife of Benjamin Acton, dau. of Richard Miller and
Elizabeth, his wife, b. 24th da, 9th mo, 1791.

Children of Joseph Bassett, son of Elisha, Jr. and Mary Bassett,
b. 26th da, 6th mo, 1765 and Mary, his wife, dau. of David and
Rebecca Allen, b. 26th da, 5th mo, 1768: Elisha Bassett, b.
26th da, 1st mo, 1788; Joseph and David Bassett, twins, b. 9th
da, 1st mo, 1790; Hannah Bassett, b. 29th da, 1st mo, 1793;
Rebecca Bassett, b. 3rd da, 4th mo, 1796; Samuel Bassett, b.
18th da, 1st mo, 1799; Benjamin Bassett, b. 23rd da, 5th mo,
1801.
Joshua Bradway, b. 9th da, 11th mo, 1748.
Elizabeth Bates (the elder), b. 20th da, 12th mo, 1736/7.
Esther Brown, b. 3rd da, 6th mo, 1759.
Children of Elgar Brown, b. 2nd da, 7th mo, 1761 and Sarah Brown,
his wife: Ann Brown, b. 13th da, 2nd mo, 1794; Elisha Brown, b.
18th da, 5th mo, 1796; Israel Brown, b. 6th da, 1st mo, 1799;
John Mason Brown, b. 29th da, 2nd mo, 1801.

Sarah Brown, wife of Elgar Brown, d. 21st da, 6th mo, 1801.
Mary Bates, wife of Ezekiah Bates, d. 6th da, 12th mo, 1793.
Children of Ezekiah Bates and Mary, his wife: Catharine Bates, b.
29th da, 9th mo, 1781, d. 26th da, 7th mo, 1784; William Bates,
b. 16th da, 4th mo, 1784, d. 7th mo, 1793; Rebeccah Bates, b.
9th da, 9th mo, 1786, d. 23rd da, 4th mo, 1788; James Oldden
Bates, b. 11th da, 5th mo, 1789; Elizabeth Bates, b. 1st da,
10th mo, 1790; Amos Bates, b. 4th mo, 1792, d. 6th mo, 1793.
Children of Abner Beesley, b. 8th da, 9th mo, 1769 and Mary, his
wife, dau. of John and Susannah Mason, b. 10th da, 3rd mo,
1776: Susannah Beesley, b. 5th da, 5th mo, 1794, d. 2nd da,
10th mo, 1794; Mary Beesley, b. 4th da, 11th mo, 1795; William
Beesley, b. 31st da, 7th mo, 1797; Benjamin Beesley, b. 26th
da, 7th mo, 1799; Thomas Mason Beesley, b. 28th da, 9th mo,
1801.[The record states Mary Mason, the wife's birth year as
1796, earlier records determine the actual year.]
Child of Samuel Bacon and Mary, his wife: Ann Bacon, b. 10th da,
11th mo, 1775.
Children of George Brown, b. 28th da, 3rd mo, 1768 and Mary, his
wife, b. 26th da, 7th mo, 1779: John Miller Brown, b. 21st da,
2nd mo, 1793, d. 8th da, 3rd mo, 1793; Margaret Brown, b. 26th
da, 11th mo, 1794; James Brown, b. 26th da, 8th mo, 1796;
Rebeccah Brown, b. 20th da, 4th mo, 1798; Miller Brown, b. 11th
da, 10th mo, 1801; Mary Brown, b. 20th da, 11th mo, 1803.
Children of Edward Bradway, son of Aron and Sarah Bradway, b. 7th
da, 8th mo, 1761 and Ann, his wife: Grace Bradway, b. 27th da,
4th mo, 1783; Aron Bradway, b. 28th da, 11th mo, 1784.

Ann Bradway, wife of Edward Bradway, d. 18th da, 3rd mo, 1786.

Anna Bradway, the 2nd wife of Edward Bradway, dau. of Christopher
and Rebecca Smith, b. 22nd da, 2nd mo, 1764.
Children of Joseph Brown, son of James and Elizabeth Brown, b.
30th da, 3rd mo, 1770 and Ann, his wife, dau. of David and
Rebecca Allen, b. 21st da, 1st mo, 1770: Rebecca Brown, b. 18th
da, 9th mo, 1795, d. 29th da, 3rd mo, 1799; Joseph Brown, b.
22nd da, 2nd mo, 1797; James Brown, b. 9th da, 3rd mo, 1801;
Elizabeth Brown, b. 22nd da, 6th mo, 1803.

Children of Samuel Brick, son of Joseph and Rebecca Brick, b.
16th da, 11th mo, 1762 and Ann, his wife, dau. of Isaac and Ann
Smart, b. 25th da, 9th mo, 1768: Deborah Brick, b. 30th da, 1st
mo, 1791; Rebecca Brick, b. 17th da, 3rd mo, 1796; Ann Brick,
b. 30th da, 8th mo, 1799; Samuel and Joseph Brick, b. 4th da,
8th mo, 1806.
Child of Joseph Brick and Martha, his wife: Joseph Brick, b. 13th
da, 4th mo, 1784.
Children of John Bacon, b. 8th da, 7th mo, 1759 and Hannah, his
wife, b. 13th da, 10th mo, 1758: Thomas Bacon, b. 27th da 3rd
mo, 1785; Eleanor Bacon, b. 14th da, 9th mo, 1787; Martha
Bacon, b. 9th da, 11th mo, 1789; Lydia Bacon, b. 28th da, 1st
mo, 1792; Hannah Bacon, b. 1st da, 6th mo, 1794; John Bacon, b.
14th da, 2nd mo, 1798; Abner Bacon, b. 14th da, 2nd mo, 1798.
Child of Thomas Bond and Jane, his wife: Jesse Bond, b. 8th da,
10th mo, 1781.
Elizabeth Bond, wife of Jesse Bond, dau. of Samuel and Margaret
Philips, b. 23rd da, 10th mo, 1786.
Mary Craft, wife of John Craft, b. 11th da, 9th mo, 1748.
Joseph Copner, b. 27th da, 7th mo, 1749.
Martha Craig, wife of Samuel Craig and dau. of Isaac and Hannah
Pedrick, b. 21st da, 8th mo, 1780.
Child of Thomas Clement and Elizabeth, his wife: Ruth Clement, b.
7th da, 4th mo, 1779.
William Carpenter, son of Preston Carpenter and Hannah, his wife,
b. 1st da, 10th mo, 1754.
Mary Carpenter, dau. of John Redman and Rachel, his wife, b.
11th(?) da, 1st mo, 1779.
Children of Benjamin Carter and Elizabeth, his wife: Thomas
Carter, b. 14th da, 8th mo, 1799; Restore Carter, b. 13th da,
9th mo, 1801; Rebecca Carter, b. 9th mo, 1st da, 1804; Maria
Carter, b. 27th da, 2nd mo, 1806; Hester Carter, b. 13th da,
5th mo, 1808; Benjamin Carter, b. 2nd da, 7th mo, 1810;
Elizabeth Carter, b. 13th da, 12th mo, 1811.
Children of Richard Dunn, b. 4th da, 1758, d. 9th da, 6th mo,
1803 and Sarah, his wife, b. 20th da, 10th mo, 1764: William
Dunn, b. 12th da, 6th mo, 1789; Rebecca Dunn, b. 6th da, 1st
mo, 1793.
John Denn, Jr. b. 20th da, 8th mo, 1780 and Rhoda Denn, his wife
b. 19th da, 1st mo, 1784.
Children of William and Elizabeth Dunham: Elizabeth Dunham, b.
7th da, 4th mo, 1785; David Dunham, b. 17th da, 8th mo, 1787;
Job Dunham, b. 17th da, 4th mo, 1791.
Children of Aron and Jael Evans: Eleanor Evans, b. 13th da, 11th
mo, 1782; James Evans, b. 10th da, 5th mo, 1794.
Sarah Evans, b. 19th da, 1st mo, 1745/6.
Children of John Ellet and Mary, his wife: Hannah Carpenter
Ellet, b. 22nd da, 11th mo, 1793; Maria Chambless Ellet, b.
29th da, 9th mo, 1795.
Children of Holme Fogg, b. 28th da, 5th mo, 1752 and Lydia, his
wife, b. 7th da, 6th mo, 1756: Joseph Fogg, b. 4th da, 6th mo,
1780; Job Fogg, b. 8th mo, 7th da, 1782, d. 28th da, 8th mo,
1782; William Fogg, b. 16th da, 10th mo, 1783, d. 5th da, 11th
mo, 1783; Mary Fogg, b. 4th da, 2nd mo, 1785; Daniel Fogg, b.

24th da, 9th mo, 1787; Holme Fogg, b. 30th da, 8th mo, 1790, d.
9th da, 10th mo, 1793; Job Fogg, b. 6th da, 8th mo, 1793, d.
16th da, 8th mo, 1798; Holme Fogg, b. 19th da, 8th mo, 1798, d.
10th da, 1st mo, 1799.
Children of Aaron Fogg, son of Charles Fogg and Sarah, his wife,
b. 7th da, 12th mo, 1752 and Hannah, his wife, dau. of David
and Rebecca Allen, b. 5th da, 3rd mo, 1767: Elisha Fogg, b.
12th da, 1st mo, 1786; David Fogg, b. 30th da, 9th mo, 1789;
Rebecca Fogg, b. 7th da, 12th mo, 1792; Ebenezer Fogg, b. 13th
da, 5th mo, 1795; Sarah Fogg, b. 5th da, 6th mo, 1797; Aaron
Fogg, Jr., b. 3rd da, 9th mo, 1799; Thomas Fogg, b. 12th da,
6th mo, 1802.
Children of Jonas Freedland, b. 14th da, 7th mo, 1756; Elizabeth,
his wife, b. 4th da, 4th mo, 1757: Sarah Freedland, b. 3rd da,
12th mo, 1790; Lydia Freedland, b. 28th da, 1st mo, 1793;
Jonathan Freedland, b. 5th da, 7th mo, 1796.
Sarah Potts, the elder, was b. fall of 1735.
Sarah Potts, Jr. her dau., b. 15th da, 1st mo, 1768.
Nathan Keais, an apprentice, b. 10th da, 4th mo, 1781.
Henry Dennis, b. 29th da, 9th mo, 1784.
Children of William Goodwin, Jr. and Elizabeth, his wife, dau. of
Richard Woodnutt and Elizabeth, his wife, b. 14th da, 9th mo,
1757: Mary Morris Goodwin, b. 6th da, 4th mo, 1786; Rachel
Goodwin, b. 25th da, 11th mo, 1787; Elizabeth Goodwin, b. 25th
da, 9th da, 1789; Sarah Goodwin, b. 12th da, 5th mo, 1792;
Abigail Goodwin, b. 1st da, 12th mo, 1793.
William Griscom, son of Andrew and Susanna Griscom, b. 10th da,
11th mo, 1747 and Rachel, his wife, dau. of John and Elizabeth.
Children of John Harris and Esther, his wife: Hepzibah Harris, b.
18th da, 7th mo, 1777; Enoch Harris, b. 23rd da, 11th mo, 1779;
Mark Harris, b. 23rd da, 7th mo, 1781, d. 5th da, 8th mo, 1790
aged 9 years; Samuel Harris, b. 22nd da, 12th mo, 1782; Hannah
Harris, b. 5th da, 12th mo, 1786; Aron Harris, b. 13th da, 3rd
mo, 1789; Mary Harris, b. 5th da, 5th mo, 1791, d. 25th da, 1st
mo, 1795 aged 3 years; Jacob Harris, b. 4th da, 12th mo, 1793,
d. 14th da, 1st mo, 1794; Chalkley Harris, b. 21st da, 10th mo,
1796; Jonathan Harris, b. 11th da, 9th mo, 1799.

Esther Harris, wife of John Harris, d. 25th da, 2nd mo, 1802 aged
45 years.
Abner Harris, d. 8th da, 9th mo, 1783 aged 20 years, son of John
Harris and Ruth, his wife.

Mary Hall, dau. of John and Ann Brick, wife of Nathaniel Hall, b.
10th da, 4th mo, 1730.
Elizabeth Hall, wife of Stephen Hall, dau. of Christopher Smith
and Rebecca, his wife, b. 17th da, 5th mo, 1768, d. 17th da,
2nd mo, 1802.
Stephen Hall, son of Nathaniel Hall and Mary, his wife, b. 24th
da, 3rd mo, 1765.
Joseph Hall, son of Stephen and Elizabeth Hall, b. 11th da, 2nd
mo, 1802.

Esther Hartley, d. 7th da, 5th mo, 1793.

Jane Hews, Sr., dau. of Archabele and Mary Silver, b. 13th da, 10th mo, 1733.

Children of Nathaniel Hall and Mary, his wife: Ann Hall, b. 4th da, 1st mo, 1758, d. 11th da, 9th mo, 1768; Elizabeth Hall, b. 19th da, 5th mo, 1762, d. 2nd da, 9th mo, 1763; Josiah Hall, b. 9th da, 10th mo, 1766; John Hall, b. 9th da, 3rd mo, 1770; Samuel Hall, b. 2nd da, 2nd mo, 1772; Mary Hall, b. 17th da, 4th mo, 1774, d. 12th da, 6th mo, 1775.

Children of Ezekiah Hewes, son of Thomas and Jane Hewes, b. 9th da, 12th mo, 1759 and Elizabeth, his wife, dau. of Benjamin and Ruth Wright, b. 20th da, 3rd mo, 1759: Benjamin Hewes, b. 8th da, 3rd mo, 1788; Jane Hewes, b. 20th da, 7th mo, 1789; Thomas Hewes, b. 2nd da, 9th mo, 1790.

Benjamin Hewes, d. 3rd da, 1st mo, 1789.

Elizabeth Hewes, wife of Ezekiah Hewes, d. 4th da, 10th mo, 1790.

Children of Ezekiah Hewes and Edith, his second wife, dau. of Isaac and Jane Pyle, b. 8th da, 12th mo, 1766: Isaac Hewes, b. 16th da, 12th mo, 1794, d. 24th da, 7th mo, 1795; Hiriam Hewes, b. 13th da, 11th mo, 1796, d. 21st da, 8th mo, 1797.

Children of John Hewes, b. 1st da, 2nd mo, 1754 and Hannah, his wife, dau. of John and Rebecca Page, b. 26th da, 8th mo, 1763: Samuel Hewes, b. 27th da, 11th mo, 1785; Rebecca Hewes, b. 27th da, 5th mo, 1792; John Hewes, b. 4th da, 8th mo, 1792.

John Hewes, (the elder) d. 4th da, 5th mo, 1796.

Joseph Hance, son of Isaac and Mary Hance, b. 21st da, 2nd mo, 1779 and Mary Hance, his wife, b. 1st da, 9th mo, 1783.

Margaret Hall, dau. of Joseph and Prudence Morris, widow of Clement Hall, b. 13th da, 1st mo, 1722/3, d. 21st da, 9th mo, 1786.

Children of Clement Hall, son of Clement Hall and Margaret, his wife, b. 13th da, 11th mo, 1753 and Rebecca, his wife, dau. of Joseph and Ann Key, b. 2nd da, 5th mo, 1759: Joseph Hall, b. 29th da, 3rd mo, 1779, d. 2nd da, 4th mo, 1779; Ann Hall, b. 30th da, 5th mo, 1780; Margaret Hall, b. 19th da, 4th mo, 1782, d. 10th mo, 1784; Rodra Hall, b. 13th da, 1st mo, 1784, d. 30th da, 1st mo, 1784; Astill Hall, b. 13th da, 1st mo, 1784; Margaret Morris Hall, b. 14th da, 6th mo, 1785; Morris Hall, b. 27th da, 3rd mo, 1787; Prudence Hall, b. 1st da, 6th mo, 1789; Sarah Hall, b. 1st da, 7th mo, 1791; Charlotte Hall, b. 2nd da, 1st mo, 1793, d. 4th da, 1st mo, 1793; Deborah Key Hall, b. 23rd da, 2nd mo, 1796; Rebecca Hall, b. 30th da, 6th mo, 1798; Isaac Key Hall, b. 14th da, 8th mo, 1800, d. 10th mo, 1801.

Children of John Haines and Martha, his wife: Lydia Haines, b. 18th da, 9th mo, 1793; Jedidiah Haines, b. 23rd da, 10th mo, 1797; Mary Haines, b. 11th da, 5th mo, 1800; John Haines, b. 9th da, 5th mo, 1802.

Reuben Hillard, b. 21st da, 8th mo, 1769 and Hannah, his wife, b. 17th da, 8th mo, 1779.

Children of Joseph Hall: Hannah Hall, b. 27th da, 9th mo, 1783,
d. 10th mo, 1785; Samuel Hall, b. 18th da, 12th mo, 1784;
Margaret Hall, b. 13th da, 6th mo, 1787; William Hall, b. 30th
da, 1st mo, 1789; Martha Hall, b. 7th da, 6th mo, 1791, d. 11th
mo, 1791; Rebecca Hall, b. 26th da, 8th mo, 1792; Joseph Hall,
b. 11th da, 9th mo, 1794; Ann Hall, b. 30th da, 11th mo, 1796;
Edward Hall, b. 20th da, 5th mo, 1798; James Hall, b. 20th da,
12th mo, 1799; Hannah Hall, b. 18th da, 3rd mo, 1802; Martha
Hall, b. 7th da, 2nd mo, 1804.
Children of Morris Hall and Lidia, his wife, dau. of Jonathan
Potts and Sarah, his wife: Clement Hall, b. 27th da, 8th mo,
1788; David Hall, b. 18th da, 2nd mo, 1790; Sarah Hall, b. 1st
da, 9th mo, 1791; John Hall, b. 9th da, 9th mo, 1793; Lewis
Hall, b. 2nd da, 2nd mo, 1798; Thomas Hall, b. 8th da, 12th mo,
1799, d. 28th da, 9th mo, 1801; Lydia Hall, b. 19th da, 7th mo,
1802, d. 7th da, 9th mo, 1803.
Children of Joshua Jefferis, son of John and Massey Jefferis, b.
6th da, 3rd mo, 1759 and Rebecca, his wife, dau. of Richard and
Hannah Ware, b. 7th da, 8th mo, 1766: Sarah Jefferis, b. 1st
da, 12th mo, 1789; Hannah Jefferis, b. 13th da, 4th mo, 1792;
Richard Ware Jefferis, b. 19th da, 9th mo, 1793.
John Knight, b. 9th da, 6th mo, 1760, Sarah, his wife, b. 24th
da, 7th mo, 1760.
Benjamin Kirby, b. 23rd da, 3rd mo, 1783; Marcy Kirby, b. 11th
da, 8th mo, 1788.
Thomas Lippincott, b. 25th da, 11th mo, 1790.
Abigail Lippincott, wife of Samuel Lippincott and dau. of Thomas
and Ann Lawrice, b. 12th da, 11th mo, 1794.
Ruth Miller, widow of Ebenezer Miller, dec'd., b. 16th da, 1st
mo, 1732.
Children of William Murphey, b. 25th da, 12th mo, 1760; Lettitia
Murphey, his wife, b. 12th da, 12th mo, 1752.
Children of William Craig and Letitia, his wife: Sarah Craig, b.
3rd da, 2nd mo, 1785; Ann Craig, b. 30th da, 1st mo, 1785.
Children of William Murphey and Naomi, his wife: Mahlon Murphey,
b. 19th da, 4th mo, 1787; Noah Murphey, b. 11th da, 11th mo,
1789; Smith Murphey, b. 27th da, 1st mo, 1792, d. 30th da, 8th
mo, 1795.

William Craig, d. 30th da, 9th mo, 1799.
Naomi Murphey, wife of William Murphey, d. 20th da, 12th mo,
1799; William Murphy, husband of Naomi, d. 3rd da, 8th mo,
1803.
Ebenezer Miller, Sr., d. 11th da, 7th mo, 1800; Hannah, his wife,
d. 23rd da, 4th mo, 1792; James Miller, son of Ebenezer and
Hannah Miller, d. 7th da, 12th mo, 1789.
Mark Miller, d. 9th da, 4th mo, 1800.
Children of Mark Miller and Phebe Miller, Sr., b. 8th da, 8th mo,
1749: William Fister Miller, b. 10th da, 1st mo, 1778; Lidia
Miller, b. 4th da, 9th mo, 1780; Rebecca Miller, b. 29th da,
2nd mo, 1782; Phebe Miller, Jr., b. 28th da, 3rd mo, 1788.
Children of Richard Miller, son of Josiah and Leatitia Miller, b.
15th da, 4th mo, 1764 and Elizabeth Wyatt Miller, b. 22nd da,
12th mo, 1766: Leatitia Miller, b. 30th da, 8th mo, 1759; Sarah

Wyatt Miller, b. 24th da, 9th mo, 1791; Josiah Miller, b. 24th da, 8th mo, 1799.

Josiah Miller, son of Josiah and Leatitia Miller, b. 12th da, 12th mo, 1761.

Abraham Miller, son of Joseph and Christina Miller, b. 8th da, 8th mo, 1759 and Elizabeth his wife, b. 12th da, 8th mo, 1759: Samuel Miller, b. 24th da, 11th mo, 1783; William Miller, b. 10th da, 3rd mo, 1786, d. 9th da, 5th mo, 1799; Pyle Smith Miller, b. 18th da, 2nd mo, 1788; Mary Miller, b. 15th da, 3rd mo, 1790.

Children of James and Rebecca Mason: Letitia Mason, b. 21st da, 9th mo, 1775; Ruth Mason, b. 8th da, 6th mo, 1781; Aron Mason, b. 24th da, 12th mo, 1770, d. 6th da, 4th mo, 1802.

Elizabeth Maxwell, widow of John Maxwell, b. 5th da, 9th mo, 1742.

Thomas Mason, son of John and Susannah Mason, b. 7th da, 7th mo, 1772.

Children of Rachel Miller, widow of Andrew Miller, b. 27th da, 8th mo, 1763: Rebecca Miller, b. 25th da, 9th mo, 1784; Daniel Miller, 8th da, 2nd mo, 1788; Sarah Miller, b. 18th da, 10th mo, 1793; Mary Miller, b. 21st da, 2nd mo, 1795.

Children of William Nicholson, Sr., b. 10th da, 1st mo, 1753 and Sarah, his wife, b. 6th da, 1st mo, 1756: Rachel Nicholson, b. 9th da, 1st mo, 1774, d. 1st da, 9th mo, 1777; Millicent Nicholson, b. 3rd da, 8th mo, 1775, d. 1st da, 10th mo, 1777; William Nicholson, Jr., b. 8th da, 3rd mo, 1779; Samuel Nicholson, b. 2nd da, 7th mo, 1781; Sarah Nicholson, b. 16th da, 11th mo, 1783, d. 2nd da, 9th mo, 1784; Daniel Nicholson, b. 19th da, 1st mo, 1786; Ruth Nicholson, b. 30th da, 6th mo, 1788, d. 18th da, 12th mo, 1792; Sarah Nicholson, b. 26th da, 7th mo, 1791; Noah Nicholson, b. 17th da, 1st mo, 1794, d. 2nd da, 3rd mo, 1795; Ann Nicholson, b. 30th da, 3rd mo, 1796.

Daniel Townsend, b. 18th da, 2nd mo, 1753, d. 3rd da, 8th mo, 1788.

Children of William Nicholson, Jr., son of William Nicholson and Sarah, his wife and Elizabeth, his wife, dau. of Joshua and Sarah Thompson, b. 25th da, 12th mo, 1780: Elisha Nicholson, b. 13th da, 10th mo, 1799; Ruth Nicholson, b. 28th da, 9th mo, 1801; Rachel Nicholson, b. 24th da, 11th mo, 1803; Beulah Nicholson, b. 9th da, 1st mo, 1806.

Children of Darkin Nicholson, son of John and Hannah Nicholson, b. 17th da, 6th mo, 1761 and Elizabeth, his wife, dau. of James and Elizabeth Brown, b. 8th da, 7th mo, 1766, d. 22nd da, 9th mo, 1802: Mary Nicholson, b. 8th da, 3rd mo, 1787; Esther Nicholson, b. 6th da, 3rd mo, 1793; James Nicholson, b. 21st da, 3rd mo, 1795; Darkin Nicholson, b. 22nd da, 1st mo, 1798; John Nicholson, b. 12th da, 3rd mo, 1800.

Samuel Nicholson, son of William Nicholson and Sarah, his wife, and Sarah, his wife, b. 3rd da, 10th mo, 1779.

Children of Joseph Pettit, b. 4th da, 5th mo, 1752 and his wife, Sarah, b. 8th da, 10th mo, 1759: Woodnutt Pettit, b. 27th da, 2nd mo, 1781; Rachel Pettit, b. 7th da, 1st mo, 1784; David Pettit, b. 23rd da, 2nd mo, 1786, d. 10th da, 6th mo, 1806; Jonathan Pettit, b. 10th da, 4th mo, 1789; Thomas Pettit, b.

10th da, 6th mo, 1791, d. 9th da, 6th mo, 1806; Mary Pettit, b. 10th da, 8th mo, 1793; Joseph Pettit, b. 13th da, 9th mo, 1801.
Children of Daniel Ridgway and Rachel, his wife: John Ridgway, b. 14th da, 11th mo, 1778; Elizabeth Ridgway, b. 8th da, 1st mo, 1785; Hannah Ridgway, b. 17th da, 12th mo, 1789; Ann Ridgway, b. 12th da, 8th mo, 1793; Job Ridgway, b. 24th da, 2nd mo, 1800.
Children of Joseph Reeve, b. 26th da, 9th mo, 1756 and Martha, his wife, b. 9th da, 8th mo, 1760: Samuel Reeve, b. 2nd da, 1st mo, 1790; Milisent Reeve, b. 31st da, 8th mo, 1792; Thomas C. Reeve, b. 21st da, 1st mo, 1795; Mary Reeve, b. 16th da, 5th mo, 1797; Joseph Reeve, b. 8th da, 9th mo, 1801.
Children of John Redman, b. 22nd da, 8th mo, 1744 and Rachel, his wife, b. 18th da, 12th mo, 1744/5: Mercy Redman, b. 9th da, 9th mo, 1770, d. 18th da, 9th mo, 1789; Rachel Redman, b. 7th da, 12th mo, 1776; Mary Redman, b. 1st da, 1st mo, 1779, Elizabeth Ray, b. 30th da, 12th mo, 1766.
Richard Smith, son of John Smith and Sarah, his wife, b. 10th da, 1st mo, 1743/4 and Rachel, his wife, dau. of Philip Dennis and Lucy, his wife, b. 6th da, 6th mo, 1743: Grace Smith, b. 21st da, 9th mo, 1764, d. 18th da, 4th mo, 1782; Elizabeth Smith, b. 30th da, 1st mo, 1767; Sarah Smith, b. 17th da, 12th mo, 1769; Rachel Smith, b. 13th da, 5th mo, 1773; Prudence Smith, b. 26th da, 2nd mo, 1776; Ann Smith, b. 13th da, 8th mo, 1778; Lucy Smith, b. 13th da, 12th mo, 1780; Martha Smith, b. 30th da, 1st mo, 1784.
Children of Samuel Stewart, b. 26th da, 12th mo, 1740 and Sarah, his wife, b. 30th da, 4th mo, 1746: Rebekah Stewart, b. 7th da, 11th mo, 1766, d. 22nd da, 6th mo, 1770; John Stewart, b. 28th da, 2nd mo, 1769, d. 1st da, 5th mo, 1773; Mary Stewart, b. 16th da, 12th mo, 1770; William Stewart, b. 27th da, 8th mo, 1772, d. 28th da, 12th mo, 1777; Samuel Stewart, b. 23rd da, 5th mo, 1774, d. 24th da, 8th mo, 1800; George Stewart, b. 29th da, 23rd mo, 1776, d. 28th da, 7th mo, 1779; Ann Stewart, b. 22nd da, 8th mo, 1777; Mark Stewart, b. 2nd da, 10th mo, 1779; John Stewart, b. 25th da, 7th mo, 1781, d. 28th da, 12th mo, 1781; Joseph Stewart, b. 7th da, 3rd mo, 1783; Sarah Stewart, b. 11th da, 6th mo, 1786, d. 12th da, 10th mo, 1786; John Stewart, b. 22nd da, 6th mo, 1788.
Mary Hartley, b. 26th da, 9th mo, 1782.
Children of James Simpson, b. ca. 1750 and Hannah Simpson, his wife, b. 21st da, 11th mo, 1763: Benjamin Simpson, b. 12th da, 2nd mo, 1785; Hannah Simpson, b. 19th da, 4th mo, 1787; James Simpson, b. 10th da, 10th mo, 1790; Anna Simpson, b. 10th da, 11th mo, 1792, d. 23rd da, 10th mo, 1795; Samuel and Ann Simpson, twins, b. 21st da, 2nd mo, 1797, Anne d. 24th da, 2nd mo, 1797; Thomas Simpson, b. 11th da, 9th mo, 1799; William Simpson, b. 4th da, 5th mo, 1802.
Children of Benjamin Shourds, b. 7th da, 1st mo, 1753 and Mary, his wife, b. 6th da, 8th mo, 1756: Rachel Shourds, b. 20th da, 3rd mo, 1779; Samuel Shourds, b. 6th da, 9th mo, 1781; Rhoda Shouds, b. 9th da, 1st mo, 1784; William Shourds, b. 15th da, 4th mo, 1786; Mary Shourds, b. 6th da, 4th mo, 1789; Benjamin Shourds, Jr., b. 1st mo, 4th da, 1797.

Children of Zadock Street, b. 28th da, 10th mo, 1751 and Eunice, his wife, b. 13th da, 9th mo, 1751: William Street, b. 10th da, 11th mo, 1775, d. 3rd da, 3rd mo, 1788; Aaron Street, b. 4th da, 5th mo, 1778; John Street, b. 14th da, 3rd mo, 1782; Anna Street, b. 17th da, 8th mo, 1784; Lydia Street, b. 1st da, 1st mo, 1789.
Christopher Smith and Rebecca, his wife: Esther Smith, b. 2nd da, 1st mo, 1775.
Children of David Smith, b. 26th da, 8th mo, 1755 and Hannah, his wife, b. 26th da, 9th mo, 1753: Evi Smith, b. 13th da, 1st mo, 1786; Elizabeth Smith, b. 1st da, 9th mo, 1788; Jonathan Smith, b. 9th da, 3rd mo, 1792.
Aron Street, son of Zadock and Eunice Street and Mary, his wife, dau. of Isaac and Hannah Pedrick, b. 21st da, 8th mo, 1780.
Children of Isaac Smart, son of Nathan and Deborah Smart, b. 4th da, 2nd mo, 1721 (o.s.) and Ann, his wife, dau. of Robert and Ann Wilson, b. 10th da, 4th mo, (o.s.), 21st da, 6th mo, (n.s.), 1733 in Concord, Chester County, PA.: Catharine Smart, b. 6th da, 6th mo, 1750; Deborah Smart, b. 27th da, 8th mo, 1751, d. 24th da, 1st mo, 1800; Nathan Smart, b. 5th da, 10th mo, 1755; Mary Smart, b. 1st da, 10th mo, 1757; Wilson Smart, b. 12th da, 2nd mo, 1759, d. 12th mo, 26th da, 1759; Isaac Smart, b. 2nd da, 3rd mo, 1761; Robert Smart, b. 19th da, 11th mo, 1763, d. 16th da, 4th mo, 1766; Ann Smart, b. 25th da, 11th mo, 1765, d. 3rd mo, 19th da, 1766; Ann Smart, b. 25th da, 9th mo, 1768; Hannah Smart, b. 7th da, 12th mo, 1770; Jane Smart, b. 26th da, 10th mo, 1775, d. 31st da, 10th mo, 1775.
Children of Isaac Smart, and Rebecca, his wife, dau. of John and Mary Thompson, b. 21st da, 8th mo, 1777, m. 1st da, 11th mo, 1797: Anna Smart, b. 5th da, 7th mo, 1798; Nathan Smart, b. 20th da, 4th mo, 1800; John Smart, b. 22nd da, 9th mo, 1802; Mary Smart, Jr., b. 8th da, 5th mo, 1805.
Children of John Stevenson and Amelia, his wife: William Laurice Stevenson, b. 22nd da, 6th mo, 1788; Mary Stevenson, b. 16th da, 9th mo, 1791; Daniel Stevenson, b. 28th da, 3rd mo, 1795; Charles Stevenson, b. 2nd da, 3rd mo, 1797; John Stevenson, b. 6th da, 5th mo, 1803; Emelia Stevenson, b. 8th mo, 1808.
Children of William Smith, son of Thomas Smith and Sarah, his wife, b. 31st da, 10th mo,(o.s.) 1741 and Sarah Chambless, dau. of James Chambless and Sarah, his wife, b. 19th da, 8th mo, (o.s.), 1748: William Smith, b. 26th da, 6th mo, 1780; James Smith, b. 28th da, 11th mo, 1785; Clement Smith, b. 27th da, 9th mo, 1788; Beulah Smith, b. 31st da, 7th mo, 1791; Atilla Smith, b. 10th da, 4th mo, 1796.
Children of Hill Smith, b. 29th da, 6th mo, 1750 and Ann, his wife: John Smith, b. 31st da, 8th mo, 1781; Hill Smith, b. 5th da, 7th mo, 1787. Hill Smith dec'd.
Children of Dorothy Smith, b. 30th da, 7th mo, 1756: Sarah Smith, b. 29th da, 7th mo, 1792; Daniel Smith, b. 23rd da, 4th mo, 1795; Josiah Smith, b. 29th da, 9th mo, 1797.
Rebecca Scoggin, b. 15th da, 9th mo, 1760.
Samuel Shourds, of Benjamin Shourds and Mary, b. 6th da, 9th mo, 1781 and Elizabeth, his wife, dau. of Jacob Ware and Mary, his

wife, b. 26th da, 8th mo, 1781.
Martha Shourds, wife of William Shrouds, b. 10th da, 10th mo, 1791.
Children of John Thompson, son of Joshua Thompson and Elizabeth, his wife, b. 17th da, 4th mo, 1752 and Mary, his wife, dau. of William Bradway and Sarah, his wife, b. 28th da, 12th mo, 1756: Rebecca Thompson, b. 21st da, 8th mo, 1777; Sarah Thompson, b. 12th da, 5th mo, 1779, d. 26th da, 2nd mo, 1791; Ruth Thompson, b. 25th da, 2nd mo, 1781; Ann Thompson, b. 30th da, 7th mo, 1783; John Thompson, b. 31st da, 1st mo, 1786; William Thompson, b. 16th da, 4th mo, 1788; Joseph Thompson, b. 10th da, 9th mo, 1792, d. 9th da, 10th mo, same year.
Sarah Bradway, dau. of James Bradway, b. 27th da, 10th mo, 1791.
Children of Joshua Thompson, son of Andrew and Grace Thompson, b. 19th da, 9th mo, 1767 and Rebeccah, his wife, dau. of David and Rebecca Allen, b. 21st da, 3rd mo, 1772: Grace Thompson, b. 1st da, 3rd mo, 1794, d. 28th da, 10th mo, 1794; Andrew Thompson, b. 12th da, 8th mo, 1795; Ann Thompson, b. 5th da, 5th mo, 1797; Mary Thompson, b. 6th da, 3rd mo, 1799; Rebeccah Thompson, b. 1st da, 9th mo, 1801; David Thompson, b. 4th da, 6th mo, 1803.
Children of William Thompson, son of Joseph Thompson and Mary, his wife, b. 20th da, 3rd mo, 1754 and Mary, dau. of James Evans and Sarah, his wife, b. 15th da, 11th mo, 1756, d. 27th da, 7th mo, 1798: Hannah Thompson, b. 16th da, 8th mo, 1783; James Thompson, b. 20th da, 8th mo, 1787; Sarah Thompson, b. 28th da, 2nd mo, 1790; Mary Thompson, b. 16th da, 3rd mo, 1793, 2nd da, 11th mo, 1799.
Elizabeth Thompson, dau. of Joseph Thompson and Mary, his wife: b. 4th da, 10th mo, 1762.
Jacob Thompson, 4th da, 7th mo, 1777; Mary Thompson, wife of Jacob, b. 26th da, 10th mo, 1782.
Children of Caleb Townsend, b. 5th da, 12th mo, 1765 and Ann, his wife, b. 13th da, 4th mo, 1761: Sarah Townsend, b. 17th da, 9th mo, 1790, d. 14th da, 12th mo, 1796; Beulah Townsend, b. 19th da, 9th mo, 1792; Abigail Townsend, b. 6th da, 1st mo, 1796; Caleb Thompson, b. 17th da, 7th mo, 1798.
Children of Samuel Test, b. 16th da, 1st mo, 1774 and Sarah, his wife, b. 14th da, 10th mo, 1777: Elizabeth Test, b. 31st da, 3rd mo, 1797; Samuel Test, Jr., b. 6th da, 8th mo, 1798; Rachel Test, b. 14th da, 5th mo, 1800, d. same day; John Test, b. 25th da, 2nd mo, 1802; Rachel Test, b. 19th da, 9th mo, 1804.
Joseph Thompson, son of Joshua and Sarah Thompson, b. 27th da, 10th mo, 1774 and Ann Thompson, dau. of John and Susanna Mason, b. 6th da, 9th mo, 1778.
Children of Job Tyler: Benjamin Tyler, b. 7th da, 3rd mo, 1784; Job Tyler, b. 25th da, 11th mo, 1790; Mary Tyler, b. 15th da, 6th mo, 1794; Richard Tyler, b. 2nd da, 2nd mo, 1798.
Hannah Thompson, wife of Aron Thompson and dau. of Charles and Hannah Fogg, b. 10th da, 11th mo, 1749/50.
Child of William and Catharine Tyler: Hannah Gillasphey Tyler, b. 29th da, 8th mo, 1798.
Children of John Wistar, b. 7th da, 5th mo, 1759 and Charlotte, his wife, b. 29th da, 1st mo, 1762: Sarah Wistar, b. 25th da,

11th mo, 1782, d. 6th da, 4th mo, 1794; Mary Wistar, b. 8th da, 4th mo, 1785; Elizabeth Wistar, b. 15th da, 10th mo, 1788, d. 4th mo, 1799; Bartholomew Wistar, b. 25th da, 11th mo, 1790; Cleayton Wistar, b. 23rd da, 2nd mo, 1793; Casper Wistar, b. 4th da, 2nd mo, 1795; Charlotte Wistar, b. 18th da, 6th mo, 1797; Hannah Wistar, b. 12th da, 3rd mo, 1800; Catharine Wistar, b. 27th da, 11th mo, 1802; John Wistar, b. 25th da, 12th mo, 1804.

Hannah Willets, dau. of Amos Willets, b. 18th da, 4th mo, 1790.

Children of Benjamin Wright, the elder, b. 31st da, 1st mo, 1735 (o.s.) and Ruth, his wife, b. 3rd da, 8th mo, 1734: Elizabeth Wright, b. 20th da, 3rd mo, 1759; Stephen Wright, b. 6th da, 10th mo, 1760; Nathan Wright, b. 19th da, 11th mo, 1762; Peter Wright, b. 22nd da, 5th mo, 1766; George Wright, b. 7th da, 4th mo, 1768; Thomas Wright, b. 10th da, 3rd mo, 1772; William Wright, b. 9th da, 10th mo, 1773; Benjamin Wright, b. 27th da, 4th mo, 1777.

Children of Stephen Wright and Priscilla, his wife, dau. of Ebenezer Miller and Ruth, his wife, b. 9th da, 7th mo, 1763: Rebecca Wright, b. 14th da, 11th mo, 1783, d. 27th da, 5th mo, 1791; Sarah Wright, b. 27th da, 4th mo, 1786, d. 23rd da, 10th mo, 1786; Elizabeth Wright, b. 30th da, 9th mo, 1787; Ebenezer Wright, b. 4th da, 11th mo, 1789; Hannah Wright, b. 3rd da, 11th mo, 1791; Ruth Wright, b. 1st da, 6th mo, 1793, 7th da, 9th mo, 1795; Benjamin Wright, b. 16th da, 5th mo, 1798; Lettitia Wright, b. 25th da, 7th mo, 1800.

Thomas Draper, son of Edward Draper and Hannah, his wife, b. 22nd da, 4th mo, 1784.

Jacob Wood, son of Henry Wood and Ruth, his wife, late of Deptford twp, Gloucester County, b. 29th da, 7th mo, 1758 and Hannah, his wife, dau. of Mark Miller and Mary, his wife, b. 31st da, 8th mo, 1768.

Caleb Wood, son of David Wood and Lydia, his wife, late of Woodbury, Gloucester County, b. 16th da, 12th mo, 1786.

Children of William Wilson, b. 3rd da, 3rd mo, 1759 and Ruth, his wife, b. 9th da, 12th mo, 1763, m. 29th da, 11th mo, 1786: Robert Darkin Wilson, b. 30th da, 12th mo, 1787; John Wilson, b. 17th da, 6th mo, 1789; Hannah Wilson, b. 14th da, 2nd mo, 1791; Darkin Wilson, b. 19th da, 8th mo, 1798; William Wilson, Jr. b. 10th da, 4th mo, 1800; Jane Wilson, b. 21st da, 9th mo, 1802.

Jacob Ware, son of John Ware and Elizabeth, his wife, b. 28th da, 8th mo, 1759 and Mary, his wife: Elizabeth Ware, b. 20th da, 8th mo, 1781; Milicent Ware, b. 17th da, 8th mo, 1783.

Children of Jacob Ware and Sarah, his wife, dau. of Andrew Thompson and Grace, his wife, b. 10th da, 1st mo, 1769, d. 31st da, 12th mo, 1799: Sarah Ware, d. 2nd da, 5th mo, 1791; David Ware, b. 25th da, 3rd mo, 1793; Samuel Thompson Ware, b. 25th da, 30th mo, 1794.

Amos Wright living in John Redman's family and son of Thomas Wright and Mary, his wife of Burlington County, b. 3rd da, 6th mo, 1783.

Abigail Warner, dau. of George Warner and Phebe, his wife, b. 19th da, 3rd mo, 1787.

SALEM MONTHLY MEETING 41

Hannah Wilson, Sr., dau. of Robert and Hannah Wilson, b. at Salem 12th da, 6th mo, 1773, d. 17th da, 8th mo, 1803.
Jesse Wilson, b. 14th da, 7th mo, 1773 and Elizabeth Wilson, b. 23rd da, 6th mo, 1781.
Elijah Ware, son of Joseph and Elizabeth, his wife, b. 30th da, 1st mo, (o.s.), 1748 and Mary Tindal, dau. of Benjamin Tindal and Esther, his wife, and wife of Elijah Ware, b. 7th da, 10th mo, (o.s.) 1751: Lydia Ware, b. 21st da, 1st mo, 1772, d. 15th da, 9th mo, 1771.
Children of James Woodnutt, b. 21st da, 12th mo, 1755 and Margaret, his wife, dau. of Preston Carpenter and Hannah, his wife, b. 26th da, 8th mo, 1756: Sarah Woodnutt, b. 28th da, 11th mo, 1777; Jonathan Woodnutt, b. 12th da, 10th mo, 1784; Preston Woodnutt, b. 24th da, 1st mo, 1787; William Woodnutt, b. 7th da, 4th mo, 1792; Margaret Woodnutt, b. 16th da, 8th mo, 1794; Mary Woodnutt, b. 22nd da, 3rd mo, 1797; Martha Woodnut, b. 26th da, 9th mo, 1799.
Children of Preston Woodnut and Rachel, his wife dau. of William Goodwin and Elizabeth, his wife, b. 25th da, 11th mo, 1787.

SALEM MONTHLY MEETING CERTIFICATES OF REMOVAL

Ann Hanby from Nashaminy Monthly Meeting, Bucks County, PA dated 14th da, 12th mo, 1691.
Mary Bannesters from Devenshirehouse Monthly Meeting dated 2nd da, 3rd mo, 1704.
Mary Ellertons from Yorke Monthly Meeting in Old England dated 2nd da, 3rd mo, 1704.
Hugh Copperthwaite from Flushing Monthly Meeting, dated 2nd da, 3rd mo, 1704.
Paul Chandler from Mount Mellick Monthly Meeting in Ireland dated 29th da, 9th mo, 1708.
Robert Lodge and his wife from Philadelphia Monthly Meeting dated 27th da, 3rd mo, 1715.
John Hart from Philadelphia Monthly Meeting dated 27th da, 2nd mo, 1716 accepted.
William Hunt and his wife, Sarah dated 31st da, 10th mo, 1722.
Samuell Worthington and his wife, Sarah dated 31st da, 10th mo, 1722.
Richard Graves and his wife from Burlington Monthly Meeting dated 30th da, 10th mo, 1723.
Joseph Clark from Haddonfield Monthly Meeting, accepted and also acquaints this meeting he intends to go to Maryland, dated 30th da, 10th mo, 1723.
Samuel Rowland and his sister, Abigail from Burlington Monthly Meeting dated 27th da, 11th mo, 1723.
Robart Worthington from Philadelphia Monthly Meeting dated 29th da, 3rd mo, 1727.
Thomas Hodgkins from Shipton Monthly Meeting, dated 12th da, 3rd mo, 1729.
John Thomas from Goshen Monthly Meeting dated PA, 26th da, 4th mo, 1732.
William Shields from Stockton, Durham County, Old England dated

8th da, 12th mo, 1731.
Benjamin Crips dated 28th da, 11th mo, 1733.
Lydia Tomlinson dated 27th da, 3rd mo, 1734.
Mary Crips from Burlington Monthly Meeting dated 1st da, 5th mo, 1734.
Rachel Henshaw from London Bull Monthly Meeting dated 11th da, 12th mo, 1733.
Grace Mason from Middletown Monthly Meeting, Bucks County, PA. dated 29th da, 10th mo, 1735.
William Crabb from Bull and Mouth, London Monthly Meeting dated 9th da, 12th mo, 1735.
Samuel Abbot from Tread Heaven and Tolbutt County Monthly Meeting, MD, dated 28th da, 1st mo, 1736.
Joseph Gibson and his wife from Haddonfield Monthly Meeting dated 31st da, 3rd mo, 1736.
John Jones and wife from Philadelphia Monthly Meeting dated 28th da, 11th mo, 1736.
Roger Brag from Abington Monthly Meeting, Philadelphia County dated 28th da, 1st mo, 1737.
James Holliday from Lurgan Monthly Meeting dated 1st da, 4th mo, 1737.
Thomas Hodgkins and wife from Philadelphia Monthly Meeting dated 28th da, 8th mo, 1737.
Benjamin Acton from Nansemund Monthly Meeting, VA dated 8th da, 4th mo, 1738 and one from Little River Monthly Meeting, NC dated 24th da, 4th mo, 1738.
Joshua Gill from Providence Monthly Meeting dated 27th da, 9th mo, 1738.
Daniel Bradreth and his wife from Egg Harbour Monthly Meeting dated 3rd da, 7th mo, 1739.
Richard Smith and his wife from Chesterfield Monthly Meeting dated 3rd da, 11th mo, 1739/40.
Jacob Townsend and wife from Philadelphia Monthly Meeting dated 28th da, 1st mo, 1740.
John Duell and Thomas Duell and his wife from Abbington Monthly Meeting dated 28th da, 4th mo, 1740.
William Griscom from Chesterfield Monthly Meeting dated 7th da, 6th mo, 1740.
Abraham Moss from Porthmouth Monthly Meeting dated 28th da, 8th mo, 1740.
Benjamin Bispham and wife from Lancashare, Great Brittan Monthly Meeting dated 5th da, 12th mo, 1738, accepted.
Jacob Lippincott and wife from Burlington Monthly Meeting dated 4th da, 3rd mo, 1741.
Archabel Silver and wife from Burlington Monthly Meeting dated 1st da, 4th mo, 1741.
Josiah Key from Haddonfield dated 8th da, 4th mo, 1741.
John Gill from Haddonfield Monthly Meeting dated 9th da, 9th mo, 1741.
Ebenezer Miller from NC dated 24th da, 1st mo, 1742.
Benjamin Lippincott and wife from Burlington Monthly Meeting dated 5th da, 1st mo, 1742.
Robert Hartshorn from Burlington Monthly Meeting dated 5th da, 2nd mo, 1742.

Edward James from Philadelphia Monthly Meeting dated 25th da, 4th
mo, 1742.
George MacNichols from Burlington Monthly Meeting dated 7th mo,
6th da, 1742.
William Grigg from Newark Monthly Meeting dated 2nd da, 8th mo,
1742.
Preston Carpenter from Philadelphia Monthly Meeting dated 29th
da, 8th mo, 1742.
Samuel Abbott from Westbury Monthly Meeting, Long Island dated
27th da, 8th mo, 1742.
Benjamin Tindal from Haddonfield Monthly Meeting dated 8th da,
12th mo, 1742.
Samuel Graves and wife from Kenet Monthly Meeting dated 2nd da,
5th mo, 1743, accepted.
Othniel Tomlinson from Haddonfield Monthly Meeting dated 9th da,
2nd mo, 1744.
Abraham Whitall from Philadelphia Monthly Meeting dated 27th da,
5th mo, 1744.
John Page from Cape May Monthly Meeting dated 14th da, 12th mo,
1744/5.
Abraham Moss from Flushing Monthly Meeting, Long Island dated
27th da, 3rd mo, 1745.
John Oakford from Burlington Monthly Meeting dated 3rd da, 5th
mo, 1745.
Joseph Marriott from Philadelphia Monthly Meeting dated 25th da,
8th mo, 1745.
Jacob Spicer from Haddonfield Monthly Meeting dated 8th da 7th
mo, 1746 to marry.
Jacob Spicer from Haddonfield Monthly Meeting dated 10th da, 6th
mo, 1747.
Preston Carpenter from Philadelphia Monthly Meeting dated 28th
da, 6th mo, 1747.
Thomas Redman from Haddonfield dated 14th da, 7th mo, 1747.
Abraham Humphres from Duck Creek Monthly Meeting, 28th da, 10th
mo, 1747.
Batholomew Wyatt and wife from Philadelphia Monthly Meeting dated
27th da, 9th mo, 1747.
David Jess and Ruth, his wife, from Burlington Monthly Meeting
31st da, 8th mo, 1748.
Isaac Ellis from Haddonfield Monthly Meeting 30th da, 11th mo,
1748.
Joshua Lord from Haddonfield Monthly Meeting, 27th da, 12th mo,
1748.
Samuel Lippincott and wife from Haddonfield Monthly Meeting, 31st
da, 5th mo, 1749.
Joshua Belinger from Haddonfield Monthly Meeting to marry, 30th
da, 8th mo, 1749.
William Haynes and his wife from Haddonfield Monthly Meeting
dated 9th da, 5th mo, 1750.
Lewis Owen from Philadelphia Monthly Meeting dated 30th da, 9th
mo, 1750.
Richard Dawson and his wife from Burlington Monthly Meeting dated
5th da, 9th mo, 1750.
John Page and his wife from Eggharbour Monthly Meeting dated 4th

da, 1st mo, 1751.
Richard Willets and his wife from Little Eggharbor Monthly Meeting dated 12th da, 2nd mo, 1751.
Joseph Hughs from Wilmington Monthly Meeting dated 13th da, 4th mo, 1751.
Francis Hinkley from Wilmington Monthly Meeting dated 8th da, 6th mo, 1751.
Richard Wistar from Philadelphia Monthly Meeting dated 25th da, 8th mo, 1751.
Andrew Griscum from Cape May Monthly Meeting dated 26th da, 2nd mo, 1753 to marry.
Richard Townsend from Egg Harbour Monthly Meeting dated 7th da, 5th mo, 1753.
Joshua Lippincutt from Philadelphia Monthly Meeting dated 24th da, 2nd mo, 1755.
Joseph Hains from Haddonfield Monthly Meeting dated 14th da, 2nd mo, 1755.
Jacob Bell from Philadelphia Monthly Meeting dated 30th da, 6th mo, 1755.
Jonathan Jess from Burlington Monthly Meeting dated 27th da, 10th mo, 1755.
Jonathan Potts, Jr. from Gwinned Monthly Meeting, Philadelphia County dated 30th da, 9th mo, 1755.
Andrew Griscom from Cape May Monthly Meeting dated 2nd da, 8th mo, 1756.
William Bassit from Philadelphia Monthly Meeting dated 24th da, 9th mo, 1756.
Robert Howard, his wife and children from Concord Monthly Meeting, Chester County dated 4th da, 10th mo, 1756.
Benjamin Buffington from the Swansey Monthly Meeting, dated 12th da, 11th mo, 1756.
John Hart from Philadelphia Monthly Meeting dated 28th da, 1st mo, 1757.
Joseph Zanes from Haddonfield Monthly Meeting dated 11th da, 10th mo, 1756.
Samuel Dennis from Haddonfield Monthly Meeting dated 8th da, 8th mo, 1757.
William Cattel from Haddonfield Monthly Meeting dated 10th da, 8th mo, 1757.
Mark Reeve from Portsmouth Monthly Meeting on Road [Rhode] Island dated 30th da, 8th mo, 1757.
Samuel Reynolds from Concord Monthly Meeting, PA. dated 26th da, 12th mo, 1757.
John Summers and wife from Great Egg Harbor Monthly Meeting dated 6th da, 3rd mo, 1758.
Joseph Kay from Haddonfield Monthly Meeting dated 29th da, 5th mo, 1758.
Joseph Wilkinson from Haddonfield Monthly Meeting dated 12th da, 6th mo, 1758 signifying his clearness to marry.
Daniel Tiltons from Chesterfield Monthly Meeting dated 7th da, 7th mo, 1758.
Robert Wilson and his wife from Concord Monthly Meeting, PA dated 3rd da, 10th mo, 1758.
Samuel Ballinger from Haddonfield Monthly Meeting dated 10th da,

12th mo, 1759.
Thomas Thackery and his wife from Haddonfield Monthly Meeting dated 13th da, 8th mo, 1759.
David Townsend from Cape May Monthly Meeting dated 26th da, 5th mo, 1760.
Cornelius Clark from Haddonfield Monthly Meeting dated 11th da, 8th mo, 1760.
Thomas Copperthwaite, Jr. from Haddonfield Monthly Meeting dated 8th da, 9th mo, 1760.
Abel Thomas from Kingwood Monthly Meeting dated 9th da, 10th mo, 1760.
William Bassett from Philadelphia Monthly Meeting dated 9th da, 10th mo, 1760.
John Williams from Shrewsbury Monthly Meeting dated 2nd da, 2nd mo, 1761.
Joseph Clement from Haddonfield Monthly Meeting dated 8th da, 6th mo, 1761.
Thomas Burden from Evesham Monthly Meeting dated 4th da, 11th mo, 1762.
Benjamin Reeve from Philadelphia Monthly Meeting, 26th da, 10th mo, 1761.
Joseph Bacon from the Falls Monthly Meeting, PA dated 1st da, 12th mo, 1762.
Samuel Summers and wife from Eggharbour and Cape May Monthly Meeting dated 2nd da, 5th mo, 1763.
Isaac Summers from Eggharbor and Cape May Monthly Meeting dated 7th da, 3rd mo, 1763.
John Copperthwaite from Evesham Monthly Meeting dated 8th da, 9th mo, 1763.
Richard and Mary Humphreys [Humphries], children of Abraham and Hannah Humphries from Ducks Creek Monthly Meeting dated 24th da, 12th mo, 1763.
William Brown, Jr. and his wife, Rebeckah, from Philadelphia Monthly Meeting dated 28th da, 1st mo, 1764.
Isaac Bassett from Philadelphia Monthly Meeting dated 24th da, 2nd mo, 1764.
Wade Barker dated 24th da, 2nd mo, 1764.
Ebenezer Miller, Jr., his wife, and dau. Hannah, from Haddonfield Monthly Meeting dated 14th da, 5th mo, 1764.
Ezekiel Wright from Chesterfield Monthly Meeting dated 3rd da, 5th mo, 1764.
Sarah Coleson from Philadelphia Monthly Meeting 6th mo, 1764.
Isaac Ward from Haddonfield Monthly Meeting dated 9th da, 7th mo, 1764.
Darius Lippincott from Shrewsberry Monthly Meeting dated 4th da, 4th mo, 1763.
Hugh Hains, his wife and children from Hopewell Monthly Meeting, Frederick County, VA dated 3rd da, 9th mo, 1764.
Isabel Coatsutton from Rights Town Monthly Meeting [Wrightstown] dated 6th da, 4th mo, 1765, inquiry to be made.
Jonathan Faucet, an apprentice from Haddonfield Monthly Meeting, dated 13th da, 5th mo, 1765.
Jacob Hollinshead from Burlington Monthly Meeting dated 3rd da, 6th mo, 1765.

Isaac Wood and his wife, Rebekah from Concord Monthly Meeting, PA. dated 5th da, 6th mo, 1765.
David Evans from Haddonfield Monthly Meeting dated 7th da, 7th mo, 1765.
Catharine Smart, dau. of Isaac Smart from Concord Monthly Meeting, PA dated 7th da, 8th mo, 1765.
John Grinslade from Chesterfield Monthly Meeting dated 5th da, 9th mo, 1765.
Benjamin Reeve and his wife, Ruth, dated 30th da, 11th mo, 1765.
John Miller and his dau. Leatitia from Haddonfield Monthly Meeting dated 9th da, 12th mo, 1765.
Joseph Gibson, Jr. from Haddonfield Monthly Meeting dated 9th da, 12th mo, 1765.
John Stephens from Haddonfield Monthly Meeting dated 9th da, 12th mo, 1765.
Grace Nicholson from Philadelphia Monthly Meeting 30th da, 12th mo, 1765.
Naomy Ballinger and her children from Evesham Monthly Meeting dated 3rd mo, 1766.
Mary Chamnes from Philadelphia Monthly Meeting dated 3rd mo, 1766.
Joseph Harman from Abington Monthly Meeting, PA. dated 28th da, 4th mo, 1766.
Sarah Clark from Kennet Monthly Meeting, PA. dated 4th mo, 1766.
Abil Sleeper from Burlington Monthly Meeting dated 6th mo, 1766.
David Smith from Philadelphia Monthly Meeting dated 9th mo, 25th da, 1767.
Hannah Stretch from Philadelphia Monthly Meeting dated 28th da, 8th mo, 1767.
Cathrine Townsend from Philadelphia Monthly Meeting dated 8th mo, 1767.
Aaron Thompson from Haddonfield Monthly Meeting dated 12th da, 10th mo, 1767.
Margaret Mead, wife of Samuel Mead from Fairfax, Loudon County, VA. for herself and three children: Richard, Ruth and Margaret dated 26th da, 10th mo, 1767.
Sarah Mead from Fairfax Monthly Meeting, Loudon County, VA dated 8th mo, 1767.
Samuel Wright from Falls Monthly Meeting, Bucks County, PA. dated 2nd da, 12th mo, 1767.
Abel Thompson from Chesterfield Monthly Meeting dated 7th da, 1st mo, 1768.
Elizabeth Butler, wife of John Butler from Cape May and Great Eggharbor Monthly Meeting dated 1st da, 2nd mo, 1768.
Elizabeth Duel from Haddonfield Monthly Meeting dated 4th mo, 1768.
Joseph Rookhill from Chesterfield Monthly Meeting dated 5th da, 5th mo, 1768.
Richard Bacon from Philadelphia Monthly Meeting dated 24th da, 6th mo, 1768.
Benjamin Moore, Jr. and his wife, Hannah from Evesham Monthly Meeting dated 4th da, 8th mo, 1768.
Joshua Thompson from Cane Creek Monthly Meeting, NC dated 14th da, 5th mo, 1768.

John Wright from Chesterfield Monthly Meeting dated 6th da, 10th
mo, 1768.
Betty Woodnutt, her two children, Mary and Betty Wilson from
Wilmington Monthly Meeting dated 1st mo, 1769.
William Griscom, Jr. from Haddonfield Monthly Meeting dated 13th
da, 2nd mo, 1769.
William Cowper, his wife, Mary and son, William from Abbington
Monthly Meeting dated 7th da, 2nd mo, 1769.
Job Ridgway, his wife, Mary and children: Elizabeth, Hannah,
Daniel, Ann, Lidia and Beulah from Providence, Chester County
dated 24th da, 3rd mo, 1769.
Samuel Ballinger, his wife and son, Joshua from Evesham Monthly
Meeting dated 6th da, 4th mo, 1769.
Thomas Folwell and his wife, Elizabeth and their three children:
William, Elizabeth and Samuel from Burlington Monthly Meeting
dated 3rd da, 4th mo, 1769.
Caleb Squibb from Providence Monthly Meeting, Chester County
dated 29th da, 5th mo, 1769.
Mary Headly from Wrightstown Monthly Meeting dated 5th mo, 1769.
Samuel Ballenger, wife Elizabeth and son, Joshua from Evesham
Monthly Meeting dated 5th mo, 1769.
Abigail James and her four children: Sarah, Hannah, James and
Mary from Philadelphia Monthly Meeting 5th mo, 1769.
Abraham Shreeve and his wife, Edith and their children:
Elizabeth, Robert, Hope, Marey, Ann, Abraham and Edith dated
1st da, 6th mo, 1769.
Shadlock Pancost, his wife and two children, Isaiah and Jonathan
from Burlington Monthly Meeting dated 4th da, 9th mo, 1769.
Thomas Smith from Philadelphia Monthly Meeting dated 27th da,
10th mo, 1769.
Samuel Ogden from Burlington Monthly Meeting dated 4th da, 12th
mo, 1779.
Richard Humphreys from Abbington Monthly Meeting, PA dated 19th
da, 3rd mo, 1770.
Ruth Wright, wife of Benjamin Wright and her five children:
Elizabeth, Stephen, Nathan, Peter and George from Chesterfield
Monthly Meeting dated 5th mo, 1770.
Mary Humphries from Abinton Monthly Meeting, PA. dated 5th mo,
1770.
Hannah Jessop from Haddonfield Monthly Meeting dated 8th mo,
1770.
Mary Elkinton, wife of Joshua Elkinton and her six children:
Thomas, Joshua, Job, John, Hester and Mary from Evesham Monthly
Meeting dated 10th da, 5th mo, 1770.
Sarah Goodwin from Eggharbor and Cape May Monthly Meeting dated
4th mo, 1770.
Hannah Rockhill from Chesterfield Monthly Meeting dated 12th mo,
1770.
Paul Saunders, wife Elizabeth and their five children: James,
John, Paul, Samuel and Rebecca and his brother, Abraham
Saunders from Burlington Monthly Meeting dated 6th mo, 1770.
Amariah Balinger from Eveshsam Monthly Meeting and Hope, his wife
dated 6th da, 6th mo, 1771.
Levi Jennings, his wife and four children: Hannah, Ann, Levi and

Thomas from Haddonfield Monthly Meeting dated 8th da, 4th mo, 1771.
John Denn from Philadelphia Monthly Meeting dated 29th da, 3rd mo, 1771.
Elizabeth Ballinger from Evesham Monthly Meeting dated 9th da, 5th mo, 1771.
Joshua Thompson and Joseph Oxley from Europe dated 5th mo, 1771.
Samuel Withers from New Garden Monthly Meeting dated 3rd da, 8th mo, 1771.
John Mason from Concord Monthly Meeting, Chester County dated 4th da, 9th mo, 1771.
Mary Oakford from Darby Monthly Meeting dated 1st da, 8th mo, 1771.
Walpole Gregory from Burlington Monthly Meeting dated 7th da, 11th mo, 1771.
Benjamin Wright from Chesterfield Monthly Meeting dated 7th da, 11th mo, 1771.
Joshua Thompson from the quarterly meeting at Salem, New England dated 23rd da, 9th mo, 1771.
Jeremiah Haines, who is an apprentice, from Burlington Monthly Meeting dated 2nd da, 12th mo, 1771.
Mary Gardner and three children: Joseph, Ephraim and James from Haddonfield Monthly Meeting dated 9th da, 12th mo, 1771.
John Redman, Rachel, his wife and children, Mary, Mercy from Haddonfield Monthly Meeting dated 9th da, 3rd mo, 1772.
Joseph Allen and his wife, Hannah and their three children: Martha, Ner and Sarah from Evesham Monthly Meeting dated 5th da, 3rd mo, 1772.
Sarah Clerk from Duck Creek Monthly Meeting held at Little Creek dated 5th mo, 1772.
Meribah Curry from Chesterfield Monthly Meeting dated 5th mo, 1772.
Hannah James from Phila Monthly Meeting dated 6th mo, 1772.
Dennis Daly produced the certificate that he had received to visit Ireland from Cork Monthly Meeting dated 13th da, 1st mo, 1772.
John Taggart from Grange Monthly Meeting, Antrim County dated 31st da, 8th mo, 1772.
Elizabeth Smith from Shrewsbury Monthly Meeting dated 2nd da, 9th mo, 1772.
Joseph Cole from Evesham Monthly Meeting dated 4th da, 6th mo, 1772.
Jonathan Kinsey from Philadelphia Monthly Meeting dated 25th da, 12th mo, 1772, returned to him.
Joseph Pimm from Evesham Monthly Meeting dated 10th da, 12th mo, 1772.
John Ballinger and his wife and children: Esther, Sarah, John, William and Hannah from Evesham Monthly Meeting dated 10th da, 12th mo, 1772.
John Mason from Evesham Monthly Meeting dated 7th da, 1st mo, 1773 along with his parents' consent to his marriage.
Benjamin Clark Cooper and his wife, Ann, from Haddonfield Monthly Meeting dated 12th da, 4th mo, 1773.
John Mason, his wife and children from Concord Monthly Meeting,

PA. dated 7th da, 4th mo, 1773.
Sarah Mason, dau. of John Mason from Concord Monthly Meeting, PA. dated 7th da, 4th mo, 1773.
Isaac Moses from Philadelphia Monthly Meeting dated 24th da, 9th mo, 1773.
Mary Leaver from Nottingham Monthly Meeting in old England dated 17th da, 6th mo, 1773 endorsed by the quarterly meeting of Derby and Nottingham and one from London Monthly Meeting.
Joseph Nixon from Middletown Monthly Meeting, Bucks County dated 3rd da, 2nd mo, 1774.
Joseph Sloan from Haddonfield Monthly Meeting dated 14th da, 3rd mo, 1774.
Isaac Eldridge and his wife, Mary from Haddonfield Monthly Meeting dated 11th da, 4th mo, 1774.
Isaac Stroud and his wife, Lidya from Sadsbury Monthly Meeting, PA dated 23rd da, 3rd da, 1774.
Constantine Jefferies, his wife Patience, and dau. Leatitia, and brother Barzillai, from Haddonfield Monthly Meeting dated 11th da, 8th mo, 1774.
Ann Cowpland, wife of Joshua Cowpland and her four children: Calab, Cadwalader, Sarah and David from Chester Monthly Meeting, PA 25th da, 4th mo, 1774.
Hephsiba Ballenger from Evesham Monthly Meeting dated 4th mo, 1774.
Isaac Eldredge and wife, Mary from Haddonfield Monthly Meeting 4th mo, 1774.
Lidia Stroud from Sedsbury Monthly Meeting, PA. dated 5th mo, 1774.
Constantine Jefferis, wife Patience and dau. Lettita with his brother, Berzillai, a lad from Haddonfield Monthly Meeting dated 5th mo, 1774.
Sarah Hall from Chesterfield Monthly Meeting dated 10th mo, 1774.
Robert Valentine and Joshua Baldwin from Upland Monthly Meeting, PA dated 9th da, 2nd mo, 1775.
Mary Stuart, wife of James Stuart from Haddonfield Monthly Meeting dated 1st mo, 1775.
Benjamin Shourds, a young man, from Haddonfield Monthly Meeting dated 13th da, 2nd mo, 1775.
Nathan Zane from Haddonfield Monthly Meeting dated 3rd da, 4th mo, 1775.
George Matlack from Evesham Monthly Meeting dated 6th da, 3rd mo, 1775.
Isaac Hanes from Shrewsberry Monthly Meeting dated 6th da, 3rd mo, 1775.
Batholomew Eggman and his wife, Elizabeth and two children, Abraham and Sarah dated 9th da, 3rd mo, 1775 from Evesham Monthly Meeting.
Job Ridgeway and his wife, Martha and their six children: Sarah, Jacob, Job, Rebeckah, Martha and Isaac dated 9th da, 3rd mo, 1775 from Evesham Monthly Meeting.
Joshua Thompson from Blackwater Monthly Meeting, VA dated 6th da, 6th mo, 1775.
Peter Townsend from Eggharbour and Cape May Monthly Meeting dated 3rd da, 4th mo, 1775.

Joshua Thompson from Fairfax Monthly Meeting, VA dated 24th da, 6th mo, 1775.
Mary Shephard from Gwynnead Monthly Meeting dated 7th mo, 1775.
Thomson Shourd and her two children, Christopher and Mary from Haddonfield Monthly Meeting 8th mo, 1775.
Susanna Evans and her dau. Elizabeth Burtis from Burlington Monthly Meeting dated 1st mo, 1776.
Hannah Wills from Evesham Monthly Meeting dated 2nd mo, 1776.
Walpole Gregory and wife, Sarah from Northern District Philadelphia Monthly Meeting dated 2nd mo, 1776.
Joseph Crispin and his wife and six children: Margaret, Levy, Roland, Joseph, Hezekiah and Prudence from Evesham Monthly Meeting dated 6th da, 6th mo, 1776.
Mary Bassett from Eggharbour and Cape May Monthly Meeting dated 27th da, 5th mo, 1776.
Mercy Jefferies and her son, Asa, a lad, from Haddonfield Monthly Meeting dated 13th da, 5th mo, 1776.
Mary Gilbert from Philadelphia Monthly Meeting dated 31st da, 5th mo, 1775.
Samuel Blackford from Southern District Philadelphia Monthly Meeting dated 24th da, 7th mo, 1776.
Job Kelly from Burlington dated 1st da, 7th mo, 1776.
Mary Jeffries, Jr. from Haddonfield Monthly Meeting dated 13th da, 5th mo, 1776.
Samuel Sharp from Burlington Monthly Meeting dated 1st da, 7th mo, 1776.
Mary Craft from Shrewsberry Monthly Meeting dated 1st mo, 1777.
Hannah Pederick from Little Eggharbour Monthly Meeting dated 13th da, 3rd mo, 1777.
Davis Bassett, his wife, Mary and two children, Beulah and Josiah and Rebekah White, an ancient, from Philadelphia Monthly Meeting dated 28th da, 3rd mo, 1777.
Elizabeth Andrews from Haddonfield Monthly Meeting dated 14th da, 4th mo, 1777 and her dau. Easter [Esther].
Jeremiah Andrews and his wife and three children: James, Samuel and Josiah from Haddonfield Monthly Meeting dated 14th da, 4th mo, 1777.
Aaron Hews and his family from Philadelphia Monthly Meeting dated 25th da, 4th mo, 1777.
Mary Mason from Southern District Philadelphia Monthly Meeting dated 5th mo, 1777.
David Smith from Little Eggharbour Monthly Meeting dated 12th da, 6th mo, 1777.
Jonathan Gibbs from Burlington Monthly Meeting dated 7th da, 7th mo, 1777.
Phebe Bassett and her two daus., Mary and Abigail, dated 7th mo, 1777.
Joseph Thompson, son of Joshua Thompson from Philadelphia Monthly Meeting dated 25th da, 7th mo, 1777.
Samuel Tonkins from Haddonfield Monthly Meeting dated 8th mo, 1777.
Samuel Huckings from Haddonfield Monthly Meeting dated 8th mo, 12th mo, 1777.
Samuel Paul from Haddonfield Monthly Meeting dated 29th da, 6th

mo, 1778.
Robert Wilson, Jr. from Southern District Philadelphia Monthly
  Meeting dated 22nd da, 4th mo, 1778.
Jedidiah Allen, a youth who is placed as an apprentice at Salem,
  from Chesterfield Monthly Meeting dated 31st da, 8th mo, 1778.
Rebeckah Lewden from Wilmington Monthly Meeting dated 11th da,
  11th mo, 1778.
Deborah Harrison from Chesterfield Monthly Meeting dated 2nd da,
  7th mo, 1778.
Anna Sommers, wife of Jacob Sommers from Eggharbour Monthly
  Meeting dated 7th mo, 1778.
William Shute and his wife, Rachel from Evesham Monthly Meeting
  dated 10th da, 12th mo, 1778.
Josiah Kay produced a certificate from Haddonfield Monthly
  Meeting dated 11th da, 1st mo, 1779.
Barzillai Lippincott, a young man who is placed as an apprentice
  to Salem, from Evesham dated 7th da, 1st mo, 1779.
John Page from Philadelphia Monthly Meeting dated 29th da, 1st
  mo, 1779.
Hannah Smith, wife of David Smith from Little Eggharbour Monthly
  Meeting dated 2nd mo, 1779.
Richard Gibbs and his wife Mary and six children: Hannah,
  Solomon, Enoch, Phebe, Boras and Sarah from Haddonfield Monthly
  Meeting dated 23rd da, 3rd mo, 1779.
Mary Elkinton and her six children: Joshua, Phebe, John, Mary,
  Joseph and Gertrew from Haddonfield Monthly Meeting dated 5th
  da, 10th mo, 1779.
Lucas Gibbs and his apprentice lad, Edmond Wetherly from
  Haddonfield Monthly Meeting dated 14th da, 6th mo, 1779.
Robert Smith, Jr. and Dorothy, his wife and two children,
  Rebeckah and Marmaduke from Eggharbour Monthly Meeting dated
  5th da, 7th mo, 1779.
Meriam Branson from Haddonfield Monthly Meeting dated 7th mo,
  1779.
Ann Hains from Haddonfield Monthly Meeting dated 11th da, 10th
  mo, 1779.
John Ward, a youth placed as an apprentice, from Haddonfield
  Monthly Meeting dated 11th da, 10th mo, 1779.
John Hanse, son of Isaac Hanse from Shrewsberry Monthly Meeting
  dated 4th da, 1st mo, 1779.
Elizabeth Goodwin and her three children: Hester, Elizabeth and
  Joseph Brown from Wilmington Monthly Meeting dated 1st mo,
  1780.
Joseph Pettit from Little Eggharbour Monthly Meeting dated 10th
  da, 2nd mo, 1780.
Jourdan Willis and his wife Hannah, and their dau. Sarah, from
  Eggharbour Monthly Meeting and Cape May dated 3rd da, 4th mo,
  1780.
Joshua Jeffers from Haddonfield Monthly Meeting dated 13th da,
  3rd mo, 1780.
Elizabeth Cowgill from Haddonfield Monthly Meeting dated 5th mo,
  1780.
Joseph Butcher and his wife, Elizabeth, from Evesham Monthly
  Meeting dated 5th mo, 1780.

Samuel Nicholson and his four children, Mary, Sarah, Martha and Mark from Haddonfield Monthly Meeting dated 8th da, 5th da, 1780.
Rachel Carpenter from Northern District Philadelphia Monthly Meeting dated 5th mo, 1780.
Benjamin Webber Oakford from Derby Monthly Meeting dated 31st da, 8th mo, 1780.
Amy Basset from Southern District Philadelphia Monthly Meeting dated 12th mo, 1780.
Giddeon Gibson from Haddonfield Monthly Meeting dated 29th da, 1st mo, 1781.
Ann Wood from Haddonfield Monthly Meeting dated 1st mo, 1781.
Kesiah French from Haddonfield Monthly Meeting dated 4th mo, 1781.
Mark Miller, Pheobe, his wife and five children: Hannah, Mary, William, Ann and Lidia from Haddonfield Monthly Meeting dated 5th mo, 1781.
Josiah Weaver and his wife, Elizabeth, and children, Susannah and Mary from Eggharbour and Cape May Monthly Meeting dated 6th da, 8th mo, 1781.
Joseph Barns from Evesham Monthly Meeting dated 9th da, 8th mo, 1781.
William Lippincott from Haddonfield Monthly Meeting dated 9th da, 7th mo, 1781.
Hezekiah Hews from Falls Monthly Meeting dated 2nd da, 5th mo, 1781.
John Wistar from Philadelphia Monthly Meeting dated 29th da, 6th mo, 1781.
Mark Miller and his wife Phebe and five children: Hannah, Mary, William, Ann and Lidya from Haddonfield Monthly Meeting dated 12th da, 3rd mo, 1781.
Andrew Miller from Haddonfield Monthly Meeting dated 12th da, 3rd mo, 1781.
Mark Nicholson from Haddonfield Monthly Meeting dated 10th da, 2nd mo, 1781.
Sarah Wilson from Concord Monthly Meeting dated 5th mo, 1781.
Joseph Heritage from Haddonfield Monthly Meeting dated 9th da, 7th mo, 1781.
William Lippincott and wife, Elizabeth from Haddonfield Monthly Meeting dated 9th mo, 1781.
Samuel Leeds from Eggharbour Monthly Meeting dated 10th mo, 1781.
Josiah Weaver, Elizabeth, his wife and two children, Susannah and Mary from Little Eggharbor and Cape May Monthly Meeting dated 10th mo, 1781.
Charlotte Wister, wife of John Wister from Chesterfield Monthly Meeting dated 2nd mo, 1782.
Gideon Gibson and his wife, Hannah and son, Joshua from Haddonfield Monthly Meeting dated 8th mo, 4th mo, 1782.
Phebe Bates, and her five children: John, Mercy, Rebeckah, Elizabeth and William from Haddonfield Monthly Meeting dated 13th da, 5th mo, 1782.
Mary Stratton and her dau. Hope, and Elizabeth Test, a child under her care, from Haddonfield Monthly Meeting dated 13th da, 5th mo, 1782.

Deborah Test from Haddonfield Monthly Meeting dated 5th mo, 1782.
Mary Prosser, wife of William and her seven children: William Stephenson, Ann, Uriah, Elizabeth, Benjamin, Mary and Martha from Burlington Monthly Meeting dated 6th da, 5th mo, 1782.
William Matlack and his wife, Mary from Evesham Monthly Meeting dated 6th da 6th mo, 1782.
Beulah Reeve, wife of John Reeve, Jr. from Haddonfield Monthly Meeting dated 6th mo, 1782.
Elgar Brown from Haddonfield Monthly Meeting dated 10th da, 6th mo, 1782.
Azor Lukens from Abbington Monthly Meeting dated 24th da, 6th mo, 1782.
Hezekiah Bates and his wife, Mary and child, Catharine from Haddonfield Monthly Meeting dated 14th da, 10th mo, 1782.
Job Shreve, his wife, Elizabeth and their child, Hannah from Mt. Holly Monthly Meeting 10th mo, 1782.
Sarah Ware, wife of David Ware from Haddonfield Monthly Meeting dated 1st mo, 1783.
James Hanse from Chesterfield Monthly Meeting dated 3rd da, 4th mo, 1783.
Elizabeth Test, dau. of Benjamin Test from Haddonfield Monthly Meeting dated 3rd mo, 1783.
James Jess from Mt. Holly Monthly Meeting dated 5th da, 2nd mo, 1783.
Abigail Lippincott from Evesham Monthly Meeting dated 5th mo, 1783.
Enoch Risley and Peter Dole, who are placed as apprentices from Eggharbour and Cape May Monthly Meeting dated 26th da, 5th mo, 1783.
Gideon Scull from Eggharbour and Cape May Monthly Meeting dated 1st da, 9th mo, 1783.
Thomas Andrews from Haddonfield Monthly Meeting dated 12th da, 4th mo, 1783.
Zachheus Test, wife, Rebecca and son, Benjamin from Haddonfield Monthly Meeting dated 12th da, 4th mo, 1784.
Joseph Ware from Greenwich Monthly Meeting dated 12th da, 6th mo, 1784.
Joseph Lewis, his wife, Mary and four children: William, Ann, Sarah and Jacob dated 13th da, 10th mo, 1783.
Sarah Wetherly and her dau. Sarah from Haddonfield Monthly Meeting 5th mo, 1784.
Ann Fogg, wife of Charles Fogg from Haddonfield Monthly Meeting dated 7th mo, 1784.
Henry Ridgway, his wife, Hannah, and their five children: Elizabeth, Hannah, Rebeccah, Joseph and Mary from Northern District Philadelphia Monthly Meeting dated 24th da, 8th mo, 1784.
William Howey from Evesham Monthly Meeting dated 6th da, 8th mo, 1784.
Rachel Foster, wife of Josiah Foster and their children: Hannah, Mary, Rebecca, Lydia and Rachel from Northern District Philadelphia Monthly Meeting dated 12th mo, 1784.
Lewis Owen from Alloways Creek Monthly Meeting dated 2nd da, 3rd mo, 1785.

Naomi Pedrick and her four children: Hezekiah, Mary, John and Thomas from Chester Monthly Meeting dated 30th da, 18th mo, 1785.
James Atkinson, a minor, placed as an apprentice from Falls Monthly Meeting dated 2nd da, 2nd mo, 1785.
Jedediah Allen and his children: Elizabeth, William, Rachel and Jedediah from Woodbury Monthly Meeting dated 10th da, 5th mo, 1785.
Elizabeth Bates and dau. Rebecca from Haddonfield Monthly Meeting dated 4th mo, 1785.
William Griscom, wife, Rachel and children: John, William, Everatt and Rachel from Greenwich Monthly Meeting dated 27th da, 4th mo, 1785.
Sarah Allen from Evesham Monthly Meeting dated 4th mo, 1785.
Naomi Pedrick from Chester Monthly Meeting, PA, for herself and children: Kesiah, Mary, John and Thomas, dated 5th mo, 1785.
John Smith and his wife, Gulielma Maria and son, Henry Hill Smith from Southern District Philadelphia Monthly Meeting dated 22nd da, 6th mo, 1785.
Mary Standley from Greenwich Monthly Meeting dated 7th mo, 1785.
Isaac and Robert Hewey from Evesham Monthly Meeting dated 10th da, 2nd mo, 1786.
Elizabeth Burrow from Haddonfield Monthly Meeting dated 8th mo, 1785.
Mary Moore from Phila Monthly Meeting dated 4th mo, 1786.
William Smith Dunham, his wife, Elizabeth and four children: Shubal, John, William and Elizabeth dated 5th mo, 1786.
Stephen Wright, his wife Priscilla, and dau. Rebecca from Upper Springfield Monthly Meeting dated 5th da, 4th mo, 1786.
Nathan Lord, Jr. from Woodbury Monthly Meeting dated 9th da, 5th mo, 1786.
Azuba, Kesiah and Sarah Lord from Woodbury Monthly Meeting dated 5th mo, 1786.
Hugh Low for himself and his three daus: Ann, Catharine and Lucy from Southern District Philadelphia Monthly Meeting dated 28th da, 6th mo, 1786.
Jacob Swain from Falls Monthly Meeting, PA dated 8th da, 6th mo, 1785 with an endorsement from Greenwich Monthly Meeting dated 28th da, 6th mo, 1786.
Elizabeth Ware from Greenwich Monthly Meeting dated 26th da, 4th mo, 1786.
John Goodwin from Greenwich Monthly Meeting dated 2nd da, 8th mo, 1786.
Joseph Reeve from Greenwich Monthly Meeting.
William Barber and wife, Ann and child, Isaac from Haddonfield Monthly Meeting dated 9th da, 10th mo, 1786.
William Prosser from Burlington Monthly Meeting, wife and six children: Uriah, Elizabeth, Benjamin, Mary, Martha and John dated 2nd da, 10th mo, 1786.
Elizabeth Lippincott, and her two sons, Charles and Samuel from Haddonfield Monthly Meeting dated 2nd da, 10th mo, 1786.
Elizabeth Freedland from Greenwich Monthly Meeting dated 12th mo, 1786.
Hannah Davis from Eggharbour and Cape May Monthly Meeting dated

1st mo, 1787.
Asa Elkinton from Burlington Monthly Meeting dated 5th da, 3rd mo, 1787.
Ann Veron from Burlington Monthly Meeting dated 4th mo, 1787.
Susanna Ewing from Woodbury Monthly Meeting dated 4th mo, 1787.
Mary Adams from Greenwich Monthly Meeting for herself, and two children, Rebecca and John Townsend dated 5th mo, 1787.
Hannah Acton from Duck Creek Monthly Meeting dated 6th mo, 1787.
Sarah Thompson from Greenwich Monthly Meeting dated 6th mo, 1787.
Sarah Saunders from Woodbury Monthly Meeting dated 7th mo, 1787.
Elizabeth Goodwin from Northern District Monthly Meeting dated 8th mo, 1787.
Lydia Potts from Greenwich Monthly Meeting dated 11th mo, 1787.
William Sheppard from Greenwich Monthly Meeting.
Joseph Brown from Wilmington Monthly Meeting dated 15th da, 8th mo, 1787.
Peter Wright from Woodbury Monthly Meeting dated 13th da, 11th mo, 1787.
William Bradway, a minor who is placed as an apprentice to a non-member from Greenwich Monthly Meeting dated 31st da, 10th mo, 1787.
Joshua Barns from Chester Monthly Meeting dated 27th da, 8th mo, 1787.
John Firth from Chesterfield Monthly Meeting dated 4th da, 12th mo, 1787.
Marjery Woolston from Mt. Holly Monthly Meeting dated 2nd mo, 1788.
Isaac Ward and his wife, Rebeckah and four children: Rebekah, Elizabeth, Gulimarah and Mary from Woodbury Monthly Meeting dated 15th da, 4th mo, 1788.
Sarah Ward from Woodbury Monthly Meeting dated 15th da, 4th mo, 1788.
Hannah Woodnut from Nottingham Monthly Meeting, PA. dated 4th mo, 1788.
Elizabeth Grinslade, for herself and son, John, from Evesham Monthly Meeting dated 9th da, 5th mo, 1788.
Hannah Wells from Evesham Monthly Meeting dated 9th da, 5th mo, 1788.
William Stephenson Prosser from Burlington Monthly Meeting dated 2nd da, 10th mo, 1788.
Ann Prosser from Burlington Monthly Meeting dated 2nd da, 10th mo, 1786[8].
Job Shreeve and his wife and two daus., Abigail and Hannah, from Upper Springfield Monthly Meeting dated 7th da, 5th mo, 1788.
Sarah Lightfoot from Exerter Monthly Meeting dated 27th da, 2nd mo, 1788.
Josiah Hall from Greenwich Monthly Meeting dated 2nd da, 7th mo, 1788.
Deborah Bassett from Shrewsbury Monthly Meeting dated 4th da, 8th mo, 1788.
Hannah Allen, a minor from Burlington dated 4th da, 8th mo, 1788.
Charity Dunlap from Greenwich Monthly Meeting dated 6th da, 10th mo, 1788.
Thomas Ashborn from Little Eggharbour Monthly Meeting to marry

dated 29th da, 10th mo, 1788.
Joshua Thompson, Jr. from Greenwich Monthly Meeting dated 29th da, 10th mo, 1788.
Emmon Bailey from Philadelphia Monthly Meeting dated 31st da, 10th mo, 1788.
Jane Brick from Woodbury Monthly Meeting dated 11th mo, 1788.
Jesse Brown from Woodbury Monthly Meeting dated 13th da, 1st mo, 1789.
William Reeve from Greenwich Monthly Meeting dated 30th da, 3rd mo, 1789.
Ann Stockton, a minor from Burlington Monthly Meeting dated 3rd mo, 1789.
George Warner and his wife, Pheobe and two children, William and Abigail from Greenwich Monthly Meeting dated 25th da, 2nd mo, 1789.
Jacob Sharp, his wife, Jane and four children: Jacob, Anna, Jane and Rebecca from Evesham Monthly Meeting dated 8th da, 5th mo, 1789.
Richard Gibbs, his wife and children: Enoch, Phebe, Burroughs, Sarah, Richard and Edward dated 29th da, 4th mo, 1789.
Solomon Gibbs dated 29th da, 4th mo, 1789.
Abram Silver from Falls Monthly Meeting in Bucks County dated 5th da, 12th mo, 1787.
Elizabeth Miller from Philadelphia Monthly Meeting dated 26th da, 6th mo, 1789.
Grace Thompson from Greenwich Monthly Meeting dated 27th da, 5th mo, 1789.
Ann Lightfoot from Wilmington Monthly Meeting dated 10th da, 6th mo, 1789.
David Lord from Woodbury Monthly Meeting dated 14th da, 4th mo, 1789.
John Dennis from Greenwich Monthly Meeting dated 1st da, 7th mo, 1789.
Jonathan Cowgill, a minor who is placed as an apprentice from Woodbury Monthly Meeting dated 15th da, 9th mo, 1789.
Job Ware from Greenwich Monthly Meeting dated 30th da, 9th mo, 1789.
Thomas Folwell, a minor from Woodbury Monthly Meeting dated 18th da, 10th mo, 1789.
Hannah Allen from Burlington Monthly Meeting dated 11th mo, 1789.
Ruth Scull from Eggharbour Monthly Meeting dated 11th mo, 1789.
Job Brown from Woodbury Monthly Meeting dated 22nd da, 2nd mo, 1790.
Samuel Brick and his wife, Ann from Greenwich Monthly Meeting dated 30th da, 12th mo, 1790.
Elizabeth Haines from Woodbury Monthly Meeting dated 9th da, 2nd mo, 1790.
John Teas and wife, Rachel, and five children: Charles, Rachel, Mary, Martha and John from Darby Monthly Meeting dated 4th da, 1st mo, 1790.
Mary Andrews from Greenwich Monthly Meeting dated 5th mo, 1790.
Bethuel Stratton, a minor placed as an apprentice from Woodbury Monthly Meeting dated 1st da, 12th mo, 1790.
Samuel Test from Greenwich Monthly Meeting dated 24th da, 2nd mo,

1790.
Hannah Acton from Duck Creek Monthly Meeting dated 24th da, 4th mo, 1790.
Andrew Miller, his wife, and two children, Rebecca and Daniel, from Greenwich Monthly Meeting dated 30th da, 8th mo, 1790.
Sarah Hall from Duck Creek Monthly Meeting dated 24th da, 4th mo, 1790.
Naomi Hall from Upper Springfield Monthly Meeting dated 8th da, 9th mo, 1790.
Elisha and Stephen Smith from Southern District Philadelphia Monthly Meeting dated 25th da, 8th mo, 1790.
John Ellet from Woodbury Monthly Meeting dated 12th da, 10th mo, 1790.
Ruth Wood from Haddonfield Monthly Meeting dated 13th da, 12th mo, 1790.
Michael Newbold, a minor, an apprentice from Upper Springfield Monthly Meeting dated 8th da, 12th mo, 1790.
James Wills from Burlington Monthly Meeting dated 7th da, 2nd mo, 1791.
Joseph Crispin, Jr. from Evesham Monthly Meeting dated 8th da, 4th mo, 1791.
John Bacon from Greenwich Monthly Meeting dated 29th da, 6th mo, 1791 and his wife and three children: Thomas, Eleanor and Martha.
Joshua Thompson from Greenwich Monthly Meeting dated 6th da, 29th mo, 1791.
Mary Curry from Wrights Town Monthly Meeting, Bucks County, PA dated 5th da, 7th mo, 1791.
Susanna Newburn and three children: Susannah, William and John, all minors, from Wrights Town Monthly Meeting dated 5th da, 7th mo, 1791.
Grace Haines from Greenwich Monthly Meeting dated 5th da, 10th mo, 1791.
Samuel Chester from this meeting in the 2nd mo, last endorsed from Philadelphia Monthly Meeting dated 7th da, 10th mo, 1791.
Mary Abbott from Haddonfield Monthly Meeting dated 12th da, 12th mo, 1791.
Hannah Pancoast from Burlington Monthly Meeting dated 5th da, 12th mo, 1791.
Mary [Mercy] Abbot from Haddonfield Monthly Meeting dated 5th da, 12th mo, 1791.
Thomas Scattergood produced a minute from Northern District Philadelphia Monthly Meeting dated 3rd da, 1st mo, 1792.
Aaron Briggs from Exeter Monthly Meeting dated 30th da, 11th mo, 1791.
Isaac Ivins and his wife, Hannah and their five children: Barzilla, Thomas, Elizabeth, Mary, Margaret Ann and Hannah from Chesterfield Monthly Meeting dated 7th da, 2nd mo, 1792.
Mahlon Adkinson from Greenwich Monthly Meeting dated 28th da, 3rd mo, 1792.
Mary Hall from Duck Creek Monthly Meeting dated 11th da, 10th mo, 1792.
Nathan Folwell from Woodbury Monthly Meeting dated 13th da, 3rd mo, 1792.

Sarah Potts from Greenwich Monthly Meeting dated 30th da, 5th mo, 1792.
Josiah Stratton, a minor placed as an apprentice from Woodbury Monthly Meeting dated 15th da, 5th mo, 1792.
Rachel Potts from Greenwich Monthly Meeting dated 31st da, 5th mo, 1792.
Thomasin Roberts and her dau. Hester, a minor, from Woodbury Monthly Meeting dated 14th da, 8th mo, 1792.
Samuel Byrnes [Barnes] from Wilmington Monthly Meeting to marry.
Samuel Ellison from Northern District Philadelphia Monthly Meeting dated 28th da, 10th mo, 1792.
Mary Smith from Greenwich Monthly Meeting dated 31st da, 10th mo, 1792.
Mary Silver from Little Eggharbour Monthly Meeting dated 11th da, 10th mo, 1792.
Joshua Hayres from Evesham Monthly Meeting dated 10th da, 8th mo, 1792.
Mary Hall from Duck Creek Monthly Meeting dated 10th da, 11th mo, 1792.
William Pederick, a minor placed as an apprentice from Greenwich Monthly Meeting dated 2nd da, 1st mo, 1793.
John Broadway and his wife, and five children: Beulah, Jonathan, Josiah, Dorcas and Elizabeth from Greenwich Monthly Meeting dated 27th da, 3rd mo, 1793.
Rachel Thompson from Greenwich Monthly Meeting dated 29th da, 5th mo, 1793.
Joshua Howey from Evesham Monthly Meeting dated 5th da, 7th mo, 1793.
Mary Howey from Evesham Monthly Meeting dated 5th da, 7th mo, 1793.
Deborah Howey from Evesham Monthly Meeting dated 5th da, 7th mo, 1793.
John Duell from Woodbury Monthly Meeting dated 10th da, 9th mo, 1793.
John Tuckniss, a minor from Duck Creek Monthly Meeting dated 6th da, 7th mo, 1793.
Samuel Branson from Haddonfield Monthly Meeting dated 10th da, 2nd mo, 1794.
Sarah Silver from Haddonfield Monthly Meeting dated 10th da, 3rd mo, 1794.
Samuel Chester from Philadelphia Monthly Meeting which had been granted to him by Salem due to his returning to Salem.
Mary Acton from Darby Monthly Meeting dated 29th da, 5th mo, 1794.
Elisha Stretch and his wife, Sarah and son, William from Greenwich Monthly Meeting dated 30th da, 4th mo, 1794.
Sarah Jess, a minor from Greenwich Monthly Meeting dated 5th mo, 1794.
Joshua Jeffries and his wife, Rebecca and three children: Sarah, Hannah and Richard Ware from Greenwich Monthly Meeting dated 2nd da, 7th mo, 1794.
Benjamin Griscom, an apprentice from Greenwich Monthly Meeting dated 2nd da, 7th mo, 1794.
Samuel Acton from Chester Monthly Meeting dated 30th da, 6th mo,

1794.
Moses Rulon from Greenwich Monthly Meeting dated 27th da, 8th mo, 1794.
Edith Hews from Concord Monthly Meeting, PA dated 4th da, 6th mo, 1794.
Isaac Gruffyth [Griffith] from Upper Evesham Monthly Meeting dated 11th da, 10th mo, 1794.
Jacob Wood and his nephew, Caleb Wood, a minor from Woodbury Monthly Meeting dated 14th da, 10th mo, 1794.
Samuel Firth from Evesham Monthly Meeting dated 7th da, 11th mo, 1794.
Patience Conrow and her two children, Atkinson and Mary from Evesham Monthly Meeting dated 10th da, 4th mo, 1794.
William Murphy and his wife, Naomi, three children: Mahlon, Neah and Smith from Eggharbour and Cape May Monthly Meeting dated 4th da, 5th mo, 1795.
Caleb Conrow from Evesham Monthly Meeting dated 10th da, 4th mo, 1795.
Job Tyler and his wife, Rachel, and three children: Benjamin, Job and Mary from Greenwich Monthly Meeting dated 29th da, 4th mo, 1795.
Sarah Potts, Jr. from Greenwich Monthly Meeting dated 29th da, 7th mo, 1795.
John Stevenson and his wife, Amelia and three children: William, Mary and Daniel from Chesterfield Monthly Meeting dated 3rd da, 11th mo, 1795.
William Miller from Greenwich Monthly Meeting dated 27th da, 1st mo, 1796.
Mary Tyler from Greenwich Monthly Meeting dated 29th da, 6th mo, 1795.
Lydia Kirby and her two children, Benjamin and Mercy from Greenwich Monthly Meeting dated 29th da, 6th mo, 1796.
Mary Withers from Woodbury Monthly Meeting dated 12th da, 7th mo, 1796.
Lucas Gibbs from Evesham Monthly Meeting dated 8th da, 7th mo, 1796.
Lydia Gibbs, a minor, from Northern District Philadelphia Monthly Meeting dated 20th da, 9th mo, 1796.
Catherine Tomlinson from Haddonfield Monthly Meeting dated 10th da, 10th mo, 1796.
Elizabeth Thompson from Pilesgrove Monthly Meeting dated 22nd da, 12th mo, 1796.
William Craig and his wife, Leatitia, a minister in good esteem and four children: William, Samuel, Sarah and Ann from Pilesgrove Monthly Meeting dated 22nd da, 12th mo, 1796.
Jonathan Griscom from Pilesgrove Monthly Meeting dated 22nd da, 12th mo, 1796.
James Kinsey, Jr. from Pilesgrove Monthly Meeting dated 23rd da, 2nd mo, 1797.
William Barber and his wife, Ann, and four children: Isaac, Burtis, William and Joseph from Pilesgrove Monthly Meeting dated 23rd da, 3rd mo, 1797.
John Gill, Jr. and his son, David, a minor, from Haddonfield Monthly Meeting dated 10th da, 4th mo, 1797.

Thomas Firth from Pilesgrove Monthly Meeting dated 20th da, 4th mo,1797.
Nathan Kous, a minor from Woodbury Monthly Meeting dated 11th da, 4th mo, 1797.
Richard Lamborn from New Garden Monthly Meeting dated 6th da, 5th mo, 1797.
Rebecca Silvers from Pilesgrove Monthly Meeting dated 27th da, 7th mo, 1797.
Rebecca Thompson, a minor from Woodbury Monthly Meeting dated 9th da, 1st mo, 1797.
Richard Reeve from Greenwich Monthly Meeting dated 28th da, 2nd mo, 1798.
Thomas Guest from Northern District Philadelphia Monthly Meeting dated 23rd da, 1st mo, 1798.
Isaac Barber and his wife, Mary and four children: Rebecca, Abraham, Isaac and Jacob from Pilesgrove Monthly Meeting dated 26th da, 4th mo, 1798.
James Stevenson from Upper Springfield Monthly Meeting dated 6th da, 6th mo, 1798.
Margaret Stevenson from Upper Springfield Monthly Meeting dated 6th da, 6th mo, 1798.
Dinah Lamborn from New Garden Monthly Meeting dated 7th da, 7th mo, 1798.
Jesse Townsend and his wife, Judith and two minor children, Josiah and Ketturah from Eggharbour and Cape May Monthly Meeting dated 11th da, 6th mo, 1798.
Joseph Dennis, a minor who is placed as an apprentice from Greenwich Monthly Meeting dated 27th da, 6th mo, 1798.
Amos Wills, a minor who is placed as an apprentice from Greenwich Monthly Meeting dated 27th da, 6th mo, 1798.
Isaac Townsend from Eggharbour and Cape May Monthly Meeting dated 3rd da, 9th mo, 1798.
Eunice Ridgway, a minor from Pilesgrove Monthly Meeting dated 22nd da, 11th mo, 1798.
Elizabeth Nicholson from Greenwich Monthly Meeting dated 30th da, 1st mo, 1799.
Hannah Hart from Southern District Philadelphia Monthly Meeting dated 23rd da, 1st mo, 1799.
Joseph Pettit and his wife, Sarah and their six children: Woodnutt, David, Jonathan, Thomas, Rachel and Mary from Pilesgrove Monthly Meeting dated 21st da, 3rd mo, 1799.
Mary Smart from Woodbury Monthly Meeting dated 9th da, 4th mo, 1799.
William Griscom from Haddonfield Monthly Meeting dated 14th da, 1st mo, 1799.
Rebecca and Richard Wright from Upper Springfield Monthly Meeting dated 5th da, 8th mo, 1799.
Elizabeth Burden from Pilesgrove Monthly Meeting date 20th da, 6th mo, 1799.
Mary Street from Pilesgrove Monthly Meeting dated 23rd da, 5th mo, 1799.
Mary Barber, a minor, placed with a Friend from Greenwich Monthly Meeting dated 27th da, 3rd mo, 1799.
Joseph Allen from Woodbury Monthly Meeting dated 13th da, 8th

mo, 1799.
Jonathan Curtis from Upper Evesham Monthly Meeting dated 6th da, 7th mo, 1799.
William Cooper from Woodbury Monthly Meeting dated 20th da, 12th mo, 1799 to marry.
Hannah Townsend from Pilesgrove Monthly Meeting dated 27th da, 3rd mo, 1800.
John Decow, Jr. from Burlington Monthly Meeting dated 6th da, 1st mo, 1800.
Mary Stanly from Greenwich Monthly Meeting dated 30th da, 4th mo, 1800.
David Smith, wife and three children: Eve, Jonathan and Elizabeth and apprentice, Thomas Weaver from Pilesgrove Monthly Meeting dated 25th da, 5th mo, 1800.
Elias Stratton a minor from Pilesgrove Monthly Meeting dated 22nd da, 5th mo, 1800.
George Brown, his wife, Mary and three children: Margaret, James and Rebecca from Woodbury Monthly Meeting dated 10th da, 6th mo, 1800.
Hannah Hewes and her dau. Rebecca from Pilesgrove Monthly Meeting dated 24th da, 7th mo, 1800.
Martha Craig from Pilesgrove Monthly Meeting dated 24th da, 7th mo, 1800.
Enoch Allen from Woodbury Monthly Meeting dated 12th da, 8th mo, 1800.
Jesse Wilson from Haddonfield Monthly Meeting dated 8th da, 12th mo, 1800.

MARRIAGES FROM SALEM MONTHLY MEETING MINUTES

William Clark of the Whoore Hill on Delaware Bay and Honor Huling, late of Roade Island in New England, her parents present consenting, m. 1st da, 11th mo, 1679.
Charles Begely of Choptank in Talbot County, MD, a tanner and Ann Craver of New Salem in West Jersey, a widdow m. 11th da, 11th mo, 1679.
John Maddock of Salem, yeoman and Scisly Worgan, widow m. 10th da, Dec 1682.
William Cooper of Pine Poynt, Jr. and Mary Bradway, dau. of Edward Bradway m. 8th da, Nov, 1682.
Abraham Strand of Fairfax River, Sissell County, MD and Isabell Deaves of Elsinborough, West Jersey, a spinster m. 7th da, 1st mo, 1683.
Isaac Smart of the twp of New Salem, West New Jersey and Elizabeth Thompson of Elsenborough of aforesaid province, spinster m. 25th da, 2nd mo, 1683.
Joseph Ware of Mummouth River alias Alloways Creek, West New Jersey, husbandman and Martha Becket of the same, spinster m. 30th da, 3rd mo, 1683.
John Beedell [Beethe or Beetle] of Alloways Creek, yeoman and Elizabeth Curier [Currier] of New Salem, spinster accomplished 20th da, 12th mo, 1687.
Richard Robinson of Salem, weaver, and Eliner Prestone of same

town m. 9th da, 7th mo, 1678.
Joseph Reeves of Cohansey, Salem County and Ellin Baggnall of Alloways Creek, having consent of their parents, m. 31st da, 11th mo, 1722.
Frances Test of Salem, wever and Elizabeth Bacon of aforesaid county, having their parents present consenting, m. 3rd da, 12th mo, 1724.
Nathaniell Champness, Jr. of Alloways Creek, Salem County and Susanna Oakford of the same place, having consent of their parents m. 24th da, 9th mo, 1725.
John Brick, Jr. of Gravelly Run, Salem County and Ann Nicholson of Elsinburg, Salem County, having their parents' consent, m. 27th da, 1st mo, 1729.
Joseph Bacon of Cohansey, Salem County and Margret Hancock of Alloways Creek, Salem County, having consent of parents, m. 5th da, 2nd mo, 1733.
John Oakford of Alloways Creek, Salem County and Hannah Colston, dau. of George Colston, dec'd., late of said county, m. last day, 3rd mo, 1733.
John Stuart of Alloways Creek, Salem County and Mary Wade of same place, having consent of relations, m. 1st da, 11th mo, 1734.
Joseph Ware, Jr. of Alloways Creek, Salem County and Elizabeth Blanchard of same place, having consent of parent, m. 7th da, 3rd mo, 1735.
James Daniel of Alloways Creek, Salem County, and Elizabeth Barber of Elsenburgh, Salem County, having their parents' consent, m. 29th da, 7th mo, 1736.
Henry Stubbins of Elsenburgh, Salem County and Rebeckah Daniel, spinster of aforesaid place, having consent of their parents, m. 1st da, 4th mo, 1737.
Charles Davis of Cohansey, Salem County, yeoman and Rachel Dennis of Elsonbourgh, Salem County, having consent of their parents m. 7th da, 9th mo, 1739.
Thomas Smith of Mannenton, Salem County, cordwainer and Sarah Bassett of Pilesgrove, m. 3rd da, 2nd mo, 1740.
Henry Stubbins of Elsenbourgh, Salem County and Mary Vickery of same place m. 24th da, 9th mo, 1742.
Samuel Nicholson of Elsenbourgh, Salem County and Sarah Dennis of same place, m. 23rd da, 1st mo, 1742/3.
John Denn of Alloways Creek, Salem County, yeoman and Elizabeth Bacon of Cohansey, Salem County, having consent of their parents m. 15th da, 9th mo, 1743.
Benjamin Thompson of Alloways Creek, Salem County and Elizabeth Ware of said place, having consent of their parents, m. 4th da, 2nd mo, 1745.
Charles Fogg and Hannah Miller, both of Greenwich twp, Salem County, having consent of their parents, m. 2nd da, 7th mo, 1746.
Benjamin Tyler of Alloways Creek, Salem County and Naomi Denn of Alloways Creek, Salem County, having consent of their relations, m. 3rd da, 7th mo, 1746.
John Barracliff of Salem County and Prudence Bradway of same place, having consent of their parents, m. 7th da, 3rd mo, 1747.

Joseph Thompson of Alloways Creek, Salem County and Mary Condon
of Mannenton, said county, having consent of their parents, m.
9th da, 5th mo, 1747.
John Ware of Salem County, wever and Elizabeth Fogg of same
place, spinster, having consent of relations, m. 13th da, 5th
mo, 1749.
William Bradway of Alloways Creek, Salem County and Sarah Hancock
of same place, having consent of their parents, m. 12th da, 9th
mo, 1750.
John Barricliff of Salem County and Ann Waddington of same place,
having consent of relations m. 28th da, 4th mo, 1750.
Ebenezer Miller, Jr. of Cumberland County and Ruth Wood of same
place, having consent of their parents, m. 5th da, 9th mo,
1751.
Mark Sheppard of Cumberland County and Anne Dennis of same place,
having consent of parents, m. 12th da, 9th mo, 1751.
Charles Fogg of Greenwich, Cumberland County, tanner, and Sarah
Smith of Mannenton, Salem County, m. 20th da, 9th mo, 1752.
John Reeve of Fairfield, Cumberland County, and Elizabeth Brick
of Hopewell, aforesaid county, having consent of their parents
m. 6th da, 12th mo, 1753.
Joseph Stretch of Alloways Creek, Salem County, yeoman, and
Elizabeth Ware, widow of same place, m. 8th da, 5th mo, 1755.
John Barracliff of Stone Creek, Cumberland County and Leatitia
Bacon of Greenwich twp, said county, having parents' consent,
m. 24th da, 4th mo, 1755.
Thomas Butcher of Cumberland County and Rachel Bradway of Salem
County, having consent of their parents, m. 11th mo, 1755.
Jonathan Potts of Greenwich twp, Cumberland County, son of Thomas
Potts and Sarah Clifton, dau. of Hugh Clifton of same place,
having consent of their parents, m. 9th da, 6th mo, 1756.
Richard Hains of Cumberland, Fairfield twp, husbandman and
Elizabeth Test of Alloways Creek, spinster, having consent of
their parents m. 5th da, 8th mo, 1756.
John Sheppard of Cumberland County and Priscilla Wood of said
place, having consent of their parents, m. 11th da, 12th mo,
1756.
Samuel Mason of Mannington twp, Salem County and Hannah Crips of
aforesaid place, having consent of their parents, m. 9th da,
10th mo, 1756.
John Hart of Salem, Salem County and Hannah Chamneys of Alloways
Creek, aforesaid county, having consent of their parents, m.
20th da, 3rd mo, 1757.
Paul Denn of Alloways Creek, Salem County, yeoman and Lidya
Stuart, dau. of John Stewart and Mary, his wife, m. 3rd da,
11th mo, 1757.
Jonathan Stretch of Alloways Creek, Salem County and Hannah Ware
of the same place, having consent of their parents, m. 8th da,
12th mo, 1757.
Samuel Reynolds of Chechester twp, Chester County, PA and Jane
Jones of Salem twp, having parents' consent m. 31st da, 1st mo,
1758.
Jonathan Bradway, Jr. of Alloways Creek, Salem County and
Elizabeth Stewart of same place, having consent of their

parents, m. 20th da, 4th mo, 1758.
Benjamin Test of Alloways Creek, Salem County, son of Francis Test and Elizabeth, his wife and Sarah Dunn, dau. of Zacheus Dunn and Deborah, his wife of aforesaid place, having consent of their parents, m. 31st da, 10th mo, 1758.
Jacob Oakford of Alloways Creek, Salem County and Leah Denn of same place, m. 31st da, 5th mo, 1759.
Samuel Swain of Pens Neck, Salem County and Hannah Pedrick of same place, having consent of their parents, m. 6th da, 9th mo, 1759.
Samuel Hancock of Alloways Creek, Salem County and Rachel Butcher of aforesaid place, having consent of their parents, m. 27th da, 9th mo, 1759.
Whitton Cripps of Mannenton, Salem County and Martha Huddy of same place, having consent of their parents, m. 29th da, 11th mo, 1759.
Daniel Bassett of Pilesgrove, Salem County and Sarah Linch of same place, having consent of their parents, m. 3rd da, 1st mo, 1759.
Samuel Ballinger of Pilesgrove, Salem County and Elizabeth Groaff of Pilesgrove, said county, having consent of their parents, m. 10th da, 1st mo, 1760.
John Van Culin of Pens Neck, Salem County and Margaret Oakford of same place, having consent of their parents, m. 2nd da, 1st mo, 1760.
Benjamin Tyler of Greenwich, Cumberland County and Mary Tomlinson of Fairfield twp, Cumberland County, having consent of their parents, m. 5th da, 3rd mo, 1760.
Abel Silver, son of Archibald and Mary Silver, Pilesgrove, Salem County and Hope Moss, dau. of Abraham and Ann Moss, dec'd. of Elsonburgh, Salem County, having consent of their parents, m. 1st da, 5th mo, 1760.
Josiah Miller of Greenwich twp, Salem County and Laetitia Wood of aforesaid county, having consent of their parents, m. 4th da, 6th mo, 1760.
David Townsend of Cape May County and Elizabeth Brandreth of Salem County, having consent of their parents, m. 2nd da, 7th mo, 1760.
Mark Sheppard of Fairfield twp, Cumberland County and Mary Craven of Greenwich, having consent of their parents, m. 3rd da, 9th mo, 1760.
Joseph Brick of Hopewell twp, Cumberland County and Rebeckah Abbott of Elsenburgh twp, Salem County, having consent of their parents, m. 17th da, 12th mo, 1760.
Edward Bradway of Alloways Creek, Salem County and Elizabeth Waddington of same place, having consent of their parents, m. 1st da, 1st mo, 1761.
Joseph Clement of Haddonfield, Gloucester County and Ann Brick, Jr. of Hopewell twp, Cumberland County, having consent of their parents, m. 1st da, 7th mo, 1761.
Thomas Copperthwaite of Mannenton, Salem County and Mary Willis of Alloways Creek, Salem County, having consent of their parents, m. 26th da, 8th mo, 1761. The rights of the widow's children secured.

John Roberts of Mannenton, Salem County and Mary Mason of same
place m. 15th da, 10th mo, 1761.
Philip Dennis, Jr. of Greenwich twp, Cumberland County and Hannah
Thompson of Alloways Creek, Salem County, having consent of
their parents, m. 4th da, 11th mo,m 1761.
Joseph Stretch, Jr. of Alloways Creek, Salem County and Sarah
Ware of same place, having consent of their parents, m. 5th da,
11th mo, 1761.
Benjamin Reeve of the city of Philadelphia, Pa and Ruth Brick of
Hopewell twp, Cumberland County, having consent of their
parents, m. 28th da, 10th mo, 1761.
Thomas Barber of Pilesgrove, Salem County and Mary Bassett of
same place, widow m. 3rd da, 12th mo, 1761.
John Harris of Alloways Creek, Salem County and Ruth Test of same
place, having consent of their parents, m. 4th da, 2nd mo,
1762.
Richard Smyth of Elsenburgh, Salem County and Susannah Hancock of
same place, widow m. 3rd da, 3rd mo, 1762. The estate of her
former husband to be settled.
Joshua Stretch of Alloways Creek, Salem County and Lidya Dunn of
same place, widow, having consent of their parents, m. 8th da,
4th mo, 1762. Affairs of her child secured.
Thomas Thompson of Alloways Creek, Salem County and Deborah
Oakford of same place, having consent of their parents, m. 28th
da, 4th mo, 1762.
Andrew Thompson of Alloways Creek, Salem County and Elizabeth
Boss of same place, having consent of their parents, m. 28th
da, 7th mo, 1762.
Samuel Dennis of Greenwich, Cumberland County and Elizabeth
Hudson of same place, having consent of their parents, m. 8th
da, 9th mo, 1762.
Richard Smith of Elsenbough, Salem County and Rachel Dennis of
Greenwich, Cumberland County, having consent of their parents,
m. 3rd da, 11th mo, 1762.
William Abbott of Elsenbough, Salem County and Rebeckah Tyler of
the same place, having consent of their parents, m. 2nd da, 2nd
mo, 1763.
Christopher Smith of Mannington, Salem County and Rebeckah
Hancock of Alloways Creek, Salem County, having consent of
their parents, m. 7th da, 4th mo, 1763.
Bradway Keasby of Stow Creek, Salem County and Jane Waddington of
same place, having consent of their parents, m. 5th da, 5th mo,
1763.
James Daniel of Alloways Creek, Salem County and Ruth Sayre of
same place m. 9th da, 6th mo, 1763.
Samuel Nicholson of Elsenburgh, Salem County and Hannah Abbot of
same place, having consent of their parents, m. 5th da, 10th
mo, 1763.
Jacob Townsend of Salem, Salem County and Mary Devenny of
Alloways Creek, having consent of their parents, m. 29th da,
12th mo, 1763.
John Test of Pilesgrove, Salem County and Elizabeth Lippincott of
same place, having consent of their parents, m. 8th da, 3rd mo,
1764.

Richard [Rudy] Dicker of Alloways Creek, Salem County and Esther Hayse of same place, having consent of their parents, m. 31st da, 5th mo, 1764.
Isaac Bassett of Pilesgrove, Salem County and Deborah Dunn, Jr. of same place, having consent of their parents, m. 7th da, 6th mo, 1764.
Isaac Ward of Gloucester County and Rebeckah Cunningham of Greenwich, Cumberland County, having consent of their parents, m. 29th da, 8th mo, 1764.
Thomas Hartley and Susannah Hews of Penns Neck, Salem County, having consent of their parents, m. 28th da, 2nd mo, 1765.
Thomas Borden [Burden] and Amy Silver of Pilesgrove, Salem County, having consent of their parents, m. 7th da, 3rd mo, 1765.
Hugh Pedrick of Greenwich, Cumberland County and Elizabeth Booth of Alloways Creek, Salem, having consent of their parents, m. 28th da, 2nd mo, 1765.
William Hancock, Jr. and Jane Evans of Salem, having consent of their parents, m. 1st da, 5th mo, 1765.
David Allen and Rebeckah Thompson of Salem, having consent of their parents, m. 1st da, 8th mo, 1765.
Joseph Goodwin and Rebeckah Bradway of Salem County, having consent of their parents, m. 9th da, 10th mo, 1765.
John Bacon of Greenwich, Cumberland County and Mary Stewart, Jr. of Alloways Creek, Salem County, having consent of their parents, m. 31st da, 10th mo, 1765.
Samuel Silver of Pilesgrove, Salem County and Rebecca Pedrick of the same place, having consent of their parents, m. 31st da, 10th mo, 1765.
Thomas Barber, Jr. and Abigail Davis, Jr. of Pilesgrove, Salem County, having consent of their parents, m. 6th da, 12th mo, 1765.
Andrew Thompson of Elsenburgh, Salem County and Grace Nicholson of same place, having consent of their parents, m. 1st da, 1st mo, 1766.
Martin Widmayer [Whitemore] of Stow Creek, Cumberland County and Mary Cross of Fairfield twp, said county, m. 9th da, 4th mo, 1766.
Joseph Hermer of Abington, Philadelphia County PA. and Rebeckah Miller of Greenwich, Cumberland County, having consent of their parents, m. 4th da, 6th mo, 1766.
Preston Carpenter of Mannington twp, Salem County and Hannah Mason of same place m. 10th da, 6th mo, 1767.
John Miller of Greenwich, Cumberland County and Margaret Bacon, Jr. of same place, having consent of their parents, m. 2nd da, 9th mo, 1767.
Gabriel Davis of Greenwich, Cumberland County and Sarah Miller, Jr. of same place, having consent of their parents, m. 28th da, 10th mo, 1767.
Daniel Evans of Greenwich, Cumberland County and Jane Brick of same place, having consent of their parents, m. 4th da, 11th mo, 1767.
David Smith of Salem, Salem County and Mary Chamneys of same place, having consent of their parents, m. 23rd da, 12th mo,

1767.
Ezra Firth of Elsenburgh, Salem County and Elizabeth Carpenter of Mannenton, Salem County, having consent of their parents, m. 9th da, 11th mo, 1768.
Samuel Test of Alloways Creek, Salem County and Sarah Stretch of same place m. 10th da, 11th mo, 1768. The rights of the children to be secured.
Daniel Bassett of Pilesgrove, Salem County and Elizabeth Haines of same place, having consent of their parents, m. 10th da, 11th mo, 1768.
John Grinsdale of Pilesgrove, Salem County and Elizabeth Matson of Greenwich, Gloucester County m. 3rd da, 11th mo, 1768.
Aaron Evans of Alloways Creek, Salem County and Elonar Stretch of Alloways Creek, Salem County, having consent of their parents, m. 9th da, 4th mo, 1769.
William Coulson of Pilesgrove twp, Salem County and Deborah Ballinger of same place, having consent of their parents, m. 6th da, 4th mo, 1769.
Benjamin Reeve of Greenwich, Cumberland County and Rachel Tyler of same place, having consent of their parents, m. 26th da, 4th mo, 1769.
John Evans of Alloways Creek, Salem County and Sarah Hancock of same place, having consent of their parents, m. 27th da, 4th mo, 1769.
Joseph Thompson, Jr. of Alloways Creek, Salem and Mary Evans of same place, having consent of their parents, m. 26th da, 4th mo, 1769.
William Oakford of Upper Alloways Creek, Salem County and Rebeckah Moss of same place, having consent of their parents, m. 31st da, 5th mo, 1769.
John Wright [Write] of Pilesgrove, Salem County and Hannah Barber of same place, having consent of their parents, m. 5th da, 10th mo, 1769.
William Oakford, Jr. of Upper Alloways Creek, Salem County and Sarah Coulson of same place, having consent of their parents, m. 6th da, 12th mo, 1769.
Daniel Pedrick of Upper Penns Neck, Salem County and Naomy Hoffman of Pilesgrove, Salem County, having consent of their parents, m. 30th da, 11th mo, 1769.
Samuel Ogden of Pilesgrove, Salem County and Mary Ann Hoffman of same place, having consent of their parents, m. 1st da, 3rd mo, 1770.
Henry Lummis of Upper Alloways Creek, Salem County and Grace Oakford of Alloways Creek, Salem County, having consent of their parents, m. 1st da, 3rd mo, 1770.
John Stewart, Jr. of Alloways Creek, Salem County and Hannah Butcher of same place, having consent of their parents, m. 5th da, 4th mo, 1770.
Abel Hall of Greenwich, Cumberland County and Rebeckah Hermer of same place, having consent of their parents, m. 2nd da, 5th mo, 1770.
Joseph Bacon, a cooper of Greenwich, Cumberland County and Rachel Thompson of Stow Creek, Cumberland County, having consent of their parents, m. 9th da, 5th mo, 1770.

William Miller of Hopewell, Cumberland County and Sarah Dennis of Greenwich, said county, having consent of their parents, m. 30th da, 5th mo, 1770.

William Hancock, Jr. of Elsenburgh, Salem County and Hannah Fogg of Alloways Creek, Salem County, having consent of their parents, m. 3rd da, 10th mo, 1770.

Joseph Lippincott of Pilesgrove, Salem County and Ann Stewart of Alloways Creek, Salem County, having consent of their parents, m. 1st da, 11th mo,

Elijah Ware of Alloways Creek, Salem County and Mary Tindal of same place, having consent of their parents, m. 8th da, 11th mo, 1770.

Aaron Lippincott of Pilesgrove, Salem County and Sarah Hains of same place, having consent of their parents, m. 28th da, 2nd mo, 1771.

Charles Bacon of Alloways Creek, Salem County and Rebeckah Fogg of same place, having consent of their parents, m. 13th da, 5th mo, 1771.

Daniel Huddy of Mannenton Twp, Salem County and Naomi Ballinger of Pilesgrove, Salem County, having consent of their parents, m. 26th da, 6th mo, 1771. The rights of her children are settled.

John Mason of Branddywine Hundered, New Castle County, PA and Susanna Goodwin of Elsenburgh, Salem County, having consent of their parents, m. 2nd da, 10th mo, 1771.

Elihu Pedrick of Penns Neck, Salem County and Mary Ann Barber of Pilesgrove, Salem County, having consent of their parents, m. 3rd da, 10th mo, 1771.

Thomas Hartley of Salem, Salem County and Catherine Townsend of Lower Penns Neck, Said county, having consent of their parents, m. 30th da, 10th mo, 1771.

Lewis Goodwin of Elsenburgh, Salem County and Rebeckah Zane, Jr. of Salem, said county, having consent of their parents, m. 27th da, 11th mo, 1771.

John Smith of Elsenburgh, Salem County and Milisent Ware of Alloways Creek, Salem County, having consent of their parents, m. 28th da, 11th mo, 1771.

William Smith Dunham of Greenwich, Cumberland County and Elizabeth Tyler of same place, having consent of their parents, m. 29th da, 4th mo, 1772.

James Stewart of Alloways Creek, Salem County and Mary Sheppard of Greenwich, Cumberland County, having consent of their parents, m. 5th da, 6th mo, 1772.

George Colson of Pilesgrove, Salem County and Mary Gardner of same place, widow, having consent of their parents, m. 29th da, 10th mo, 1772.

Aaron Evans of Alloways Creek, Salem County and Ann Fogg of same place, having consent of their parents, m. 3rd da, 12th mo, 1772.

John Mason of Evesham, Burlington County and Elizabeth Ballinger, Pilesgrove, Salem County, having consent of their parents, m. 27th da, 1st mo, 1773.

Zacheus Ballinger of Pilesgrove, Salem County and Hope Lippincott of same place, having consent of their parents, m. 4th da, 4th

mo, 1773.
William Griscom, Jr. of Alloways Creek, Salem County and Rachel Denn of same place, having consent of their parents, m. 8th da, 4th mo, 1773.
Joshua Thompson, Jr. of Elsenburgh, Salem County and Sarah Ware of said county, having consent of their parents, m. 7th da, 10th mo, 1773.
Nathan Dunn of Pilesgrove, Salem County and Rhoda Silvers of same place, having consent of their parents, m. 4th da, 11th mo, 1773.
Thomas Daniel of Greenwich, Cumberland County and Elizabeth Denn of same place, having consent of their parents, m. 15th da, 12th mo, 1773.
William Bradway, Jr. of Alloways Creek, Salem County and Mary Ware of same place, having consent of their parents, m. 30th da, 12th mo, 1773.
William Nicholson of Mannington twp, Salem County and Sarah Townsend of same place, having consent of their parents, m. 2nd da, 3rd mo, 1774.
Walpole Gregory of Salem, Salem County and Sarah Barber of Greenwich, Cumberland County m. 13th da, 4th mo, 1774.
Samuel Fogg, Jr. of Lower Alloways Creek, Salem County and Elizabeth Keasby of same place, having consent of their parents, m. 7th da, 4th mo, 1774.
Samuel Withers of Pilesgrove, Salem County and Grace Bassett of same place, having consent of their parents, m. 27th da, 10th mo, 1774.
Zachariah Jess of Pilesgrove, Salem County and Rebeckah Pedrick of same place, having consent of their parents, m. 1st da, 12th, mo, 1774.
Nathan Zane [Zanes] of Upper Greenwich, Gloucester County and Rachel Jennings [Grinnings], having consent of their parents, m. 13th da, 4th mo, 1775.
George Matlack of Moers Town, Burlington County and Sarah Matson of Pilesgrove, Salem County, having consent of their parents, m. 6th da, 4th mo, 1775.
Zadock Street of Elsenburg, Salem County and Eunice Silver of Salem, Salem County m. 5th da, 4th mo, 1775.
David Evans, a taylor of Greenwich, Cumberland County and Mary Sheppard of same place, having consent of their parents, m. 13th da, 8th mo, 1775.
William Colson of Pilesgrove, Salem County and Mary Bassett of same place, having consent of their parents, m. 5th da, 10th mo, 1775.
Joseph Lewis of the twp of Evesham, Burlington County and Mary Haines of Pilesgrove, Salem County, having consent of their parents, m. 6th da, 10th mo, 1775.
Isaiah Stratton of Evesham, Burlington County and Mary Lippincott of Pilesgrove, Salem county, having consent of their parents, m. 2nd da, 11th mo, 1775.
Jonathan Kirby of Pilesgrove, Salem County and Mercy Lippincott of same place, having consent of their parents, m. 9th da, 11th mo, 1775.
William Daniel of Hopewell twp, Cumberland County and Rachel

Bacon of twp of Greenwich, Cumberland County, having consent of their parents, m. 1st da, 11th mo, 1775.
Andrew Griscom of Stow Creek, Cumberland County and Leatitia Tyler of Greenwich, Cumberland County, having consent of their parents, m. 8th da, 11th mo, 1775.
John Harris of Pilesgrove, Salem County and Hester Ballinger of same place, having consent of their parents, m. 7th da, 12th mo, 1775.
Thomas Thompson of Elsenburgh, Salem County and Milliscent Evans of same place, having consent of their parents, m. 3rd da, 4th mo, 1776.
Benjamin Shourds of Upper Penns Neck, Salem County and Mary Silvers of Pilesgrove, Salem County, having consent of their parents, m. 4th da, 4th mo, 1776.
Charles Bacon of Greenwich, Cumberland County and Rebeckah Hall of same place, having consent of their parents, m. 8th da, 5th mo, 1776. The affairs of her children to be secured.
Richard Wistar of the City of Philadelphia, PA, a merchant, son of Casper Wistar late of said city, dec'd. and Catherine, his wife, and Mary Gilbert, widow, dau. of John Bacon late of Cumberland dec'd. and Elizabeth, his wife, having consent of their parents, m. 4th da, 8th mo, 1776. Rights of the children of Mary Gilbert secured.
Holme Fogg of Upper Alloways Creek, Salem County and Lidya Ridgway of Manenton, Salem County, having consent of their parents, m. 28th da, 8th mo, 1776.
John Thompson of Salem, Salem County and Mary Bradway of Lower Alloways Creek, Salem County, having consent of their parents, 10th da, 10th mo, 1776.
Henry Firth of Elsenburgh, Salem County and Sarah Fogg of Alloways Creek, Salem County, having consent of their parents, m. 13th da, 10th mo, 1776.
James Mason Woodnutt of Manenton, Salem County and Margaret Carpenter of the same place, having consent of their parents and guardian, m. 27th da, 11th mo, 1776.
Daniel Ridgeway of Mannenton, Salem County and Rachel Fogg of Alloways Creek, Salem County, having consent of their parents, m. 2nd da, 4th mo, 1777.
Jonathan Stretch of Alloways Creek, Salem County and Elizabeth Fogg of same place m. 3rd da, 4th mo, 1777.
Isaac Hance of Elsenburgh, Salem County and Mary Thompson of Upper Alloways Creek, Salem County, having consent of their parents, m. 29th da, 5th mo, 1777.
Samuel Tonkins of twp of Woolwick, Gloucester County and Mary Carpenter of twp of Mannenton, Salem County, having consent of their parents, m. 29th da, 10th mo, 1777.
David Brown of Greenwich, Gloucester County and Phebe Bassett of Pilesgrove, Salem County, having consent of their parents, m. 27th da, 11th mo, 1777. Rights of her children are secured.
Samuel Dennis of Greenwich, Cumberland County and Mary Stretch of Alloways Creek, Salem County, having consent of their parents, 7th da, 11th mo, 1777.
William Silver of Pilesgrove, Salem County and Rebeckah Page of same place, widow, having consent of their parents, m. 2nd da,

4th mo, 1778. The rights of her children secured.
Samuel Huggins of Pilesgrove, Salem County and Sarah Test of the same place, having consent of their parents, 30th da, 4th mo, 1778.
Samuel Paul of Greenwich, Gloucester County and Elizabeth Butler of Greenwich, Cumberland County m. 1st da, 7th mo, 1778. Rights of her children secured.
David Colson of Pilesgrove, Salem County and Hephzibah Ballinger of the same place, having consent of their parents, m. 8th da, 10th mo, 1778.
William Groff of Woolwich, Gloucester County and Leatitia Test of Pilesgrove, Salem m. 28th da, 1st mo, 1779.
Jonathan Gibbs of Salem, Salem County and Lidya Hancock of Alloways Creek, Salem County, having consent of their parents, m. 29th da, 4th mo, 1779.
James Denn of Lower Alloways Creek, Salem County and Elizabeth Kirby of Pilesgrove, Salem County, having consent of their parents, m. 27th da, 10th mo, 1778.
Aaron Thompson of Elsenburgh, Salem County and Hannah Hancock of the same place, having consent of their parents, 13th da, 6th mo, 1779. The rights of her children secured.
Joseph Pettit of Little Eggharbor, Burlington County and Sarah Bassett of Mannenton, Salem County, having consent of their parents, m. 27th da, 10th mo, 1779. The rights of her children secured.
John Goodwin of Elsenburgh, Salem County and Prudence Hall of the same place, having consent of their parents, 1st da, 3rd mo, 1780.
Paul Cooper of Deptford, Gloucester County and Catharine Smart of Elsenburgh, Salem County, having consent of their parents, m. 29th da, 11th mo, 1780.
Gideon Gibson, Haddonfield and Hannah Bassett accomplished, his father present consenting, m. 29th da, 1st mo, 1781.
Samuel Leeds of Great Eggharbour twp, Gloucester County and Louisa Barber of Pilesgrove, Salem County, having consent of their parents, m. 4th da, 10th mo, 1781.
Joshua Lippincott of Pilesgrove, Salem County and Amey Bassett of the same place, having consent of their parents, 1st da, 2nd mo, 1781.

MARRIAGES FROM SALEM MONTHLY MEETING MINUTES (WOMEN'S)

William Silver and Mary Elkinton m. 2nd da, 2nd mo, 1781.
Amos Kirby and Ann Haines m. 2nd da, 2nd mo, 1781.
Abraham Miller and Elizabeth Smith m. 2nd mo, 1781.
Jonathan Dennis and Naomi Brooks m. 4th mo, 1781.
John Tyler and Abigail Lippincott m. 5th mo, 1781.
Samuel Leeds and Louisa Barber m., her mother present consenting 1st da, 10th mo, 1781.
Benjamin Lippincott, Jr. and Lidya Pimm m. 1st da, 10th mo, 1781.
Henry Barber and Hannah Sommers m. 1st mo, 1782.
Aron Evans and Jail Stretch m. 2nd mo, 1782.
Stephen Wright and Priscilla Miller m. 3rd mo, 1782.

Barzillia Lippincott and Elizabeth Ellett m. 3rd mo, 1782.
Jonathan Kerby and Lydia Tyler m. 4th mo, 1782.
William Carpenter and Elizabeth Wyatt m. 6th mo, 1782.
Edward Bradway and Ann Bowing m. 6th mo, 1782.
James Bradway and Ruth Evans m. 7th mo, 1782.
John Jennings and Mary Ann Hilderbrand m. 9th mo, 1782.
William Goodwin, Jr. and Elizabeth Woodnut m. 10th mo, 1782.
Jeremiah Tracy and Margaret Noblet m. 10th mo, 1782.
William Thompson and Mary Evans m. 1st mo, 1783.
Joseph Hall and Ann Brick m. 2nd mo, 1783.
John Bradway and Abigail Gruff m. 2nd mo, 1783.
Joseph Brick and Martha Reeve m. 3rd mo, 1783.
Edward Draper and Hannah Dicker m. 4th mo, 1783.
Asa Kerby and Hannah Miller m. 10th mo, 1783.
Jethro Lippincott and Phebey Elkington m. 10th mo, 1783.
Ellgar Brown and Sarah Mason m. 10th mo, 1783.
William Colston and Syliva Silver m. 12th mo, 1783.
John Hughs [Hews] and Hannah Page m. 2nd mo, 1784.
Gideon Scull and Sarah James m. 4th mo, 1784.
Isaac Hoffman and Sarah Ridgway m. 12th mo, 1784.
John Davis and Rebecca Silver m. 1st mo, 1785.
Aaron Fogg and Hannah Allen m. 3rd mo, 1785.
Darkin Nicholson and Elizabeth Brown m. 4th mo, 1785.
Seth Silver and Mary Noblet m. 5th mo, 1785.
Jedediah Allen and Hannah Ellet m. 9th mo, 1785.
John Jennings and Mary Reily m. 10th mo, 1785.
Samuel Austin and Lydia Ambler m. 10th mo, 1785.
Isaac Barber and Mary Lippincott m. 4th mo, 1786.
Isaac Ward and Ann Mason m. 5th mo, 1786.
Joseph Bassett and Mary Allen m. 9th mo, 1786.
Mark Bradway and Elizabeth Hartley m. 10th mo, 1786.
William Wilson and Ruth Nicholson m. 11th mo, 1786.
Hezekiah Hewes and Elizabeth Wright m. 12th mo, 1786.
Samuel Smith and Elizabeth Bassett, Jr. m. 1st mo, 1787.
Ephraim Haines and Rebecca Waters m. 2nd mo, 1787.
Joseph Reeve and Martha Carpenter m. 2nd mo, 1787.
Samuel Brick and Anna Smart m. 2nd mo, 1787.
John Ward and Hannah Mason m. 4th mo, 1787.
William Owen and Rachel Summers m. 12th mo, 1787.
William Haines and Susannah Silvers m. 1st mo, 1788.
Morris Hall and Lydia Potts m. 1st mo, 1788.
Arron Thompson and Abigail Page m. 2nd mo, 1788.
Josiah Bassett and Sarah Ellet m. 3rd mo, 1788.
William Matlack and Latitia Haines m. 4th mo, 1788.
Nathan Bassett and Sarah Saunders m. 4th mo, 1788.
John Shepherd and Mary Miller m. 4th mo, 1788.
Ebenezer Miller, Jr. and Hannah Nicholson, Jr. m. 5th mo, 1788.
David Bradway and Hannah Bradway m. 5th mo, 1788.
Thomas Osborn and Rhoda Dunn m. 10th mo, 1788.
Joshua Thompson and Susanna Mason m. 11th mo, 1788.
William Reeve and Latitia Miller m. 3rd mo, 1789.
Job Ware and Grace Thompson m. 11th mo, 1789.
Job Brown and Elizabeth Allen m. 2nd mo, 1790.
John Pimm and Sarah Thompson m. 3rd mo, 1790.

Daniel Bassett, Jr. and Ruth Miller m. 4th mo, 1791.
Mahlon Atkinson and Sarah Smith m. 10th mo, 1791.
Ner Allen and Hope Test m. 10th mo, 1791.
John Grinslade and Rebecca Moore m. 11th mo, 1791.
William Ballenger and Amy Burden m. 1st mo, 1792.
John Ballenger and Hannah MacCall m. 2nd mo, 1792.
John Ellett and Mary Smith m. 4th mo, 1792.
John Haines and Martha Taylor m. 5th mo, 1792.
Jacob Davis and Mary Stratton m. 7th mo, 1792.
Samuel Burnes and Hannah Woodnutt m. 10th mo, 1792.
Samuel Allison and Rachel Smith m. 11th mo, 1792.
John Test and Hannah Allen m. 2nd mo, 1793.
Joshua Thompson and Rebeccah Allen m. 4th mo, 1793.
Joseph Brown and Ann Allen m. 7th mo, 1793.
Samuel Lippencott, Sr. and Mary Hoffman m. 12th mo, 1793.
John Duel and Lydia Lippincott m. 3rd mo, 1794.
Job Ware and Susannah Smith m. 5th mo, 1794.
Moses Ruland and Susannah Hartley m. 10th mo, 1794.
Samuel Acton and Sarah Hall m. 3rd mo, 1796.
Joshua Reeve and Hannah Ware m. 6th mo, 1796.
Lucas Gibbs and Mary Hance m. 7th mo, 1796.
Richard Lambourn and Phoebe Gibbs m. 7th mo, 1796.
William Miller and Susannah Goodwin m. 3rd mo, 1797.
Isaac Smart and Rebecca Thompson m. 10th mo, 1797.
Benjamin Griscom and Susanna Adams m. 11th mo, 1798.
William Wright and Rebecca Silver m. 1st mo, 1799.
Stephen Hall and Elizabeth Smith m. 3rd mo, 1799.
John Gill and Prudence Thompson m. 5th mo, 1799.
William Cooper and Ann Miller m. 12th mo, 1799.
Job Bacon and Ruth Thompson m. 1st mo, 1800.
William Griscom and Ann Stewart m. 11th mo, 1800.

SALEM MONTHLY MEETING MEN'S AND WOMEN'S MINUTES
1676-1800

The men's minutes from 1676 continious through 1800 and the women's minutes from 1763 through 1800 have been combined and edited to conserve space. When the spelling of the names differed, the spelling of the names given by the women's minutes is shown in brackets.

"Some accounts of the first Friends who came over and
settled in Salem, viz. Samuel Nicholson with his wife and
five children transported themselves to America in a ship
called the *Griffin* of London, Robert Griffin, Master who
all arrived in Delaware River in the Province of New
Jersey, 23rd da, 9th mo, 1675 and so to the place now
called New Salem where they did inhabit, also
Edward Wade and Prudence, his wife of the Parish of
Bultolph Aldgate, London came over with the ship *Griffin*.
Robert Griffin, master and brought with them the
following persons as servants, viz: Nethaniel Chamneys
and Nathaniel Chamneys, Jr., Joseph Ware, John Burton and

Francis Smithey, who all arrived in Delaware River and so to New Salem where they inhabited the 23rd da, 9th mo, 1675 and divers others in the same ship. Also

In the year 1677 Andrew Thompson with his wife and children transported himself from the Kingdom of Ireland and landed at Elsenburgh in the province of New Jersey aforesaid with his brother, John Tompson and diverse others on the 22nd da, 12th mo, following.

In the 2nd month 1677, Christopher White and Edward Bradway and their families came from London in the ship called the *Kent*, Gregory Masley, Master who arrived at New Salem in the 7th mo following.

At a meeting the last day of the first month, 1676, it was unaminously agreed that the first second day of the week in every month the Friends of the town of New Salem in Fenwicks Colony do meet together ..."

4th da, 7th mo, 1676. John Spooner produced an acknowledgment condemning his unbecoming language and behavior while on the ship called Griffin.

25th da, 9th mo, 1676. Marriage of Abraham Strand and Rachel Nickholson accomplished.

5th da, 12th mo, 1676. Edward Chamnis reported for marrying out.

7th da, 11th mo, 1676/7. Roger Surkins, his wife and mother reported for neglecting meeting.

4th da, 12th mo, 1677. Difference between John Edridg and John Smith in regards to money owed towards a meeting house is settled.

6th da, 3rd mo, 1678. John Fenwick reported for neglecting meeting.

3rd da, 4th mo, 1678. James Newell reported for neglecting meeting. Edward Wade and Nathan Smart to bring in an account of all marriages, births and deaths to the next meeting.

3rd da, 7th mo, 1678. Marriage of Richard Robinson and Elen Preston accomplished. The condistion [matter][sic] of Samuel Savary to be laid before the court.

2nd da, 4th mo, 1679. John Thomson and Sarah Fairbanks of Elsonburg declare their intentions to marry. Richard Guy, Edward Bradway, Nathan Smart and Edward Wade appointed to seek a convenient place for a meeting house and burial ground.

7th da, 5th mo, 1679. William Penton reported for marrying out.

5th da, 11th mo, 1679. Edward Wade, James Nevill, John Maddocks and George Deacon to speak with Samuel Nicholson, William Penton and Widdow Salter about the price of their houses and plantations in Salem for use as meeting places.

2nd da, 12th mo, 1679. Georg Deackon, John Madocks, Georg Azehead, Henry Jennings to speak with Edward Bradway about the use of his house for a meeting house. Meeting agreed that the weekly meeting be held first at the house of Robert Zane, next at Samuel Nicholson, then Rich Guyes and to continue clockwise. Georg Deacon and Samuel Nicolson to go to John Smith and demand money owed to the meeting which was left in his hand by John Edridge.

2nd da, 6th mo, 1680. John Deen and wife reported for allowing their dau. to marry a non-member.

4th da, 7th mo, 1680. William Waithman and Elizabeth Daniel
declare their intentions to marry. John Deen and wife produced
an acknowledgment of their sorrow in allowing their dau. to
marry a non-member.
A list of subscribers to the purchase of a meeting house: Richard
Guy, Edward Bradway, Edward Wade, John Tomson, Andrew Tomson,
George Deacon, Joseph Maddocks, Richard Robinson, Charles
Bagely, Thomas Woodrofe, Nathan Smarte, Isaac Smarte, Samuel
Wade, Joseph Forrett, Robert Zane, James Newell, William
Wilkinson, Thomas Benson, Will Furedge, Ellen Lewis, Christ.
White, and John Denn.
1st da, 9th mo, 1680. Richard Guy, Georg Haselwood, George
Deacon, Char. Beggerly, Chris. White, Edward Wade, Jo Maddock,
Thomas Woodrofe to speak with Edward Channey and his wife
regarding a piece of land to build a meeting house and a burial
ground. William Waithman ordered to wait until a certificate of
clearness is received from Rode [Rhode] Island to marry.
26th da, 10th mo, 1680. John Smith promised to pay to the meeting
monies lost by John Ethridge to such employees working on the
meeting house. Richard Guy and Edward Wade with the consent of
Friends at Alloways Creek agreed to pay the £5 left to the
meeting by Widow Handcock for the building of a meeting house.
7th da, 12th mo, 1680. William Waithman came to meeting and in an
unsavory manner asked for permission to marry Elizabeth Daniel,
charged the meeting with doing him wrong and breach of contract
because of the certificate not being granted.
6th da, 1st mo, 1681. Ordered that William Waithman come to the
next meeting and bring his certificate. A covenant to be drawn
up for Thomas Woodrofe to take Peter Craven, an orphan to tutor
and bring up.
4th da, 2nd mo, 1681. An indenture to be drawn up between Charles
Begely and Martha Smith and George Deacon to take Peter Craven
to tutor and bring up for eleven years.
2nd da, 3rd mo, 1681. James Newell reported for disorderly
walking.
5th da, 7th mo, 1681. John Foresst reported for his careless
walking.
26th da, 10th mo, 1681. Thomas Benson reported for selling rum
and suffering [allowing] people to have too much to make them
drunk; promised that he would be careful in what liquor he
should sell and take care that no disorder might occur. Ordered
that Robert Zane and Thomas Woodrofe speak with Christ. Sanders
for him to deliver Samuel Ferredge his bed and other things.
30th da, 11th mo, 1681. Henry Chibings and Elizabeth Chattorg
declare their intentions to marry. Thomas Smith reported for
disorderly walking.
11th da, 2nd mo, 1682. Roger Huggins, his wife and her mother
reported for disorderly walking.
26th da, 4th mo, 1682. Thomas Benson reported for writing a
scandalous and invective paper against the Friends and the
government of the province. John Maddock reported for refusing
to remove his family and himself from the widdow Morgan's house
with whom he hath intentions to marry.
28th da, 6th mo, 1682. John Maddock produced an acknowledgement

condemning his moving into the Widow Worgan's house before marriage and agreed he would not live there another night until their marriage.

27th da, 9th mo, 1682. Ordered that Scisila Worgan give a bond of £10 to George Deacon and Thomas Woodrofe for true payment of £5 given by her late deceased husband, Richard Worgan to his nephew James Woran, said bond to be signed and sealed before her marriage.

27th da, 12th mo, 1682. Isabel Deaves, accompanied by Edward Goding, her uncle produced a certificate from Waxford, Ireland.

27th da, 12th mo, 1682. Henry Grubb granted a certificate.

30th da, 5th mo, 1683. Thomas Chanders reported for having raised reports [gossip or questions] between Charles Bageley and John Smith concerning Thomas Craven.

27th da, 6th mo, 1682. Charles Bagely and Martha Smith agreed to leave the ordering and disposing of Thomas Craven, a minor to the meeting.

26th da, 9th mo, 1683. Anthony Dixon and Elizabeth Cammel declare their intentions of marriage.

31st da, 1st mo, 1684. Joseph White, Andrew Thompson and Francis Forest to assist Widow Robbinson in dividing her cattle and putting out her children as she is unable to care for them.

26th da, 3rd mo, 1684. Thomas Chanders reported for neglecting meeting.

27th da, 8th mo, 1684. Roger Huckins and William Rumsey reported for neglecting meeting.

23rd da, 9th mo, 1684. Charles Begley ordered to give better satisfaction and security for the orphan children's portion of Ann, his wife, formerly Craven, which he refuses to do.

30th da, 1st mo, 1685. George Hasselwood reported for neglecting meeting.

A subscription for the purchasing of land for the meeting house was signed as follows: Joseph Maddockes, Edward Bradway, Samuel Carpenter, George Deacon, Christopher White, Henry Jenings, Joseph Thompson, Andrew Thompson, Francis Forrest, Samuel Wade, Edward Wade, Joseph White, Thomas Woodroofe, William Kelley, Isaac Smart, John Smith of Smithfield, John ---, Richard Deane, William Cooper, Roger Carary, Christopher Saunders, William Rumsey, John Smith and Edward Godwin.

27th da, 2nd mo, 1685. Robert Donne is appointed to keep the books for recording of the families. Charles Begley offered to the meeting to make over to Thomas Craven 200 acres of land at £20, given by will to said Thomas, for his portion only, the overplus to go towards the payment of his sister Ann's portion. He also agreed that when he sold his plantation would pay unto Ann Craven the sum of £20 or what comes to her share; accepted. Thomas Craven to choose two persons as his guardians. Robert Stacey, George Hatcheson, Percifful Tole, John Burton and Richard Guy to make inquiry into the expectations put upon by the government for bearing arms. It was also thought that for the time to come that all Friends shall proceed in marriage after the first public hearing and that a paper should be published.

25th da, 3rd mo, 1685. Robert Donne agreed to record the families

of the meeting.
29th da, 4th mo, 1685. Thomas Craven declared that he had chosen his uncle, John Smith and George Deacon to be his guardians, said guardians agreed.
A subscription to again raise money for the meeting house as follows: Edward Bradway, Joseph White, George Deacon, Andrew Thompson, Christopher White, John Thompson, Francis Forrest, Samuel Wade, Henry Jennings, Joseph Ware, William Serrige, Thomas Woodroofe, John Forrest, Samuel Carpenter, Richard Deane, William Kelly, John Thompson, John Ireson and Robert Donne.
25th da, 11th mo, 1685. Roger Carary produced an acknowledgement condemning his fighting with William Batchler.
29th da, 1st mo, 1686. Samuel Carpenter, George Deacon, Thomas Woodrofe, Joseph White, John Thompson and Andrew Thompson to work out an agreement for Edward Bradway and Christopher White regarding their land or the partition of same.
26th da, 5th mo, 1686. Ordered that John Smith of Smithfield send home Peter Craven to his master, George Deacon.
27th da, 7th mo, 1686. A new subscription to furnish the new meeting house: Jonathan Beere, Edward Bradway, John Thompson, Christopher White, Isaac Smart, Andrew Thompson, Thomas Woodroffe, Bartholomew Wiat, Henry Jenings, William Killey, Francis Forrest, John Forrest, Richard Thomson, George Deacon, Joseph White, Edward Wade, Richard Dean, Rudera Moris, Joseph Ware, William Longe, John Smith of Krindall Hill, Robert Caray, Beniamm Knapton, Francis Thomson, Samuel Carpenter, Richard Carpenter. Ann Craven, age 16 years requested Edward Bradway and William Killey to be her guardians.
25th da, 8th mo, 1686. Peter Craven bound as an apprentice to George Deacon for eleven years beginning 4th da, 2nd mo, 1681, John Smith, Edward Wade to be his guardians.
25th da, 5th mo, 1687. William Wilkinson reported for neglecting meeting.
26th da, 7th mo, 1687. William Bradway and Elizabeth Wood declare their intentions of marriage. Christopher Whitton and his wife, being lately deceased leaving four children, two of the children being young. A girl being lame and the boy being bound to John Thompson. Those appointed to look after them for a term of 13 years and at the end of time give the boy £10. Christopher White to take the girl for seven years. Grace Whitton, the eldest dau. to be hired to John Smith of Amwelbury for one year and have for her hire £4 of merchant pay to begin the 29th day of present month. Sarah Whitton, the next eldest dau. is set to William Cooper for three years and a half and at the end of time to have £4.10.
31st da, 8th mo, 1687. A certificate granted for Richard Deane. An agreement to not sell or provide rum to the Indians was signed by the following: Joseph White, Edward Wade, Andrew Thompson, --- Kelly, Christopher White, Anthony Morris, Thomas Woodroofe, Edward Bradway, Henry Jenings, Joseph Ware, Richard Dean, Samuell Wade, Richard Darkin, Francis Forrest, Isaac Smart, Roger Smith, Margaret Dem, George Deacon, Roger Carary, Beniaman Knapton, John Bettle, Matthew Robinson, John Thompson,

John Forrest, Richard Johnson, Jonathan Beere, Benjamin Acton, William Holmes, Bartholomew Wiat, John Maddock, Rothrea Morris, William Cooper, Samuel Nicholson, John Smith, Joseph Brenne [Brown], John Smith of Smithfield, Daniel Smith, Thomas Thompson, John Nickson, Richard Marshall and Edward Goodwin.

26th da, 10th mo, 1687. William Cooper to prepare an indenture for Sarah Whitton. Andrew Thompson to keep the books prepared by Robert Dunn and to continue to record families, births, deaths. Ordered that Christopher Saunders come to the next meeting to settle the differences between himself and Roger Cararary regarding the horse that died or was killed.

26th da, 1st mo, 1688. Thomas Woodroofe to inform the meeting at Chester Monthly Meeting concerning the agreement between Robert Wade and Ann Craven.

28th da, 3rd mo, 1688. Edward Bradway and William Killey chosen by Ann Craven to be her guardians, they to oversee that no wrong be done to her by Robert Wade and his wife.

27th da, 6th mo, 1688. Thomas Woodrofe and Joseph White reported for neglecting meeting. Marriage of George Deacon and Margret Deen accomplished. George Deacon to give bond to Richard Derkin and Andrew Thompson in the sum of £50 in the behalf of James Denn, Darnell Deen, Joseph Deen and Mary Deen before his marriage.

29th da, 8th mo, 1688. William Cooper and his wife reported for their hard usage of Sarah Whitton, their servant.

31st da, 10th mo, 1688. Richard Deane to provide a certificate from Philadelphia Monthly Meeting. A certificate granted for Roger Smith and William Holmes concerning their clearness to marry.

27th da, 11th mo, 1688. Marriage of Richard Deane and Catherin Currier accomplished. Marriage of Ruddea Moris and Jaell Batty accomplished.

24th da, 4th mo, 1689. Marriage of James Denn and Elizabeth Maddocks accomplished.

30th da, 7th mo, 1689. Ann Craven came to meeting and expressed her appreciation for the kindness and care taken of her during her minority, and discharged and released her two guardians, William Killey and Edward Bradway.

28th da, 8th mo, 1689. William Tilar reported for marrying contrary to discipline.

24th da, 12th mo, 1689. John Maddock declared his intentions of marriage to Margarat Kent, of Philadelphia Monthly Meeting and requested a certificate.

31 da, 4th mo, 1690. A certificate granted for Thomas Thompson to marry. Beniamin Acton produced an acknowledgement condemning his selling rum to the Indians.

28th da, 5th mo, 1690. Marriage of William Thompson and Jane Nickson accomplished.

25th da, 6th mo, 1690. John White lately dec'd., brother to Joseph White, in his last will bequeathed to a sister-in-law in England £10.14.

29th da, 7th mo, 1690. Ordered that Thomas Thackera, William Bates and Robert Zanes provide a true account for the estate of John White.

26th da, 11th mo, 1690. Henry Jennings reported for neglecting meeting.
30th da, 1st mo, 1691. Marriage of Henry Hurley and Mary Poppleton accomplished.
28th da, 7th mo, 1691. Joseph Ware granted a certificate to marry Easter Glaves, widow, County of Chester, PA.
30th da, 9th mo, 1691. Beniamin Knapton requested a certificate to marry Ann Hamby of Burlington Monthly Meeting.
25th da, 11th mo, 1691. Marriage of Neale Daniell and Elizabeth Hancock accomplished.
A subscription for the use of printing and other expenses of the meeting was signed by the following: George Deacon, Andrew Thompson, John Maddock, Christopher White, Jonathan Beere, John Thompson, Richard Darkin, John Smith of Krindall Hill, Samuel Wade, Nathaniell Champineys, Joseph Ware, Bartholomew West, Rudera Morris, Mathew Robinson, Samuell Nicholson, Joseph White, Henry Jennings, William Thompson, Neall Daniell, Beniamin Knapton, John Pledger and Edward Bradway.
30th da, 6th mo, 1692. Marriage of George Deacon, Alloways Creek and Susanna Ashton, dau. of Robert Ashton of New Castle County, PA. accomplished.
26th da, 10th mo, 1692. William Kenton produced a certificate to marry from Choptank Monthly Meeting, MD.
30th da, 11th mo, 1692. Marriage of William Kentin, Choptank Monthly Meeting, MD and Mary Cooper of New Salem accomplished.
24th da, 2nd mo, 1693. Marriage of Bartholomew Wieat and Sarah Aston, dau. of Robert Aston of Chelsey, PA. accomplished. Marriage of John Mason and Ann Thompson, dau. of John Thompson, Elsinburgh accomplished.
25th da, 10th mo, 1693. A subscription to help Thomas Woodroofe rebuild his house lost due to fire was signed by the following: John Thompson, John Pledger, Joseph White, Andrew Thompson, Richard Darkin, Isaac Smart, John Scholes, Joseph Ware, Beniamin Knapton, Beniamin Acton, John Mason, Israell Harrison, Rudera Morris, Joseph Nicholason, Samuel Wade, George Deacon, John Maddocks, William Tilar, Edward Wade, Abell, Nicholson, Jonathan Beere, Bartholomew Wieat, Samuell Nicholson, Henry Jennings, Daniell Smith, Edward Godwin, Easter White, Thomas Thompson, Nathaniel Champney and John Smith of Krindaill Hill.
26th da, 12th mo, 1693. Marriage of Israell Harrison and Easter White accomplished. Marriage of Abell Nicholson and Mary Tilar, dau. of William Tilar accomplished.
25th da, 4th mo, 1694. Marriage of William Hall and Sarah Bradway accomplished.
27th da, 6th mo, 1694. John Walker and Elizabeth Abbot, widow declare their intentions of marriage.
26th da, 9th mo, 1694. John Remington and Susannah Bradway declare their intentions of marriage. Hugh Middleton and Mary Kenton declare their intentions of marriage, but Mary Kenton having her first husband's children's portion of his estate and no course of security, it is referred to next meeting.
31st da, 9th mo, 1694. Samuel Wade and Abell Nicholson to inquire as to clearness and that security for Mary Kenton's children be given.

28th da, 11th mo, 1694. Marriage of Jeremiah Powell and Elizabeth Denn accomplished.

24th da, 4th mo, 1695. Marriage of Charles Okeford and Mary Denn accomplished.

28th da, 8th mo, 1695. A subscription for paying for work done on the meeting house was signed as follows: Nathaniell Champney, William Hall Carpenter, Robert Ashton, John Remington, Nathaniell Champneys, Beniamin Knapton, John Smith of Smithfield, Richard Darken, Rudrah Moris, Batholomew Wieat, Thomas Thompson, John Scholes, Samuel Wade, Charles Oakford, John Maddocks, Mathew Robinson, Andrew Thompson, Isaac Smart, George Abbot, William Thompson, Joseph Ware, Abell Nicholson, John Smith, Joseph Nicholson, Edward Kesby, John Mason, John Hancock, Edward Godwinn, William Tyler.

30th da, 10th mo, 1695. Marriage of Richard Marshall and Elizabeth Daniell accomplished. Marriage of Joseph Pledger and Mary Hurley accomplished. Joseph Pledger has given £40 to be paid to Sarah Hurley, dau. of Henry and Mary Hurley when she is married or comes to the age of 18.

27th da, 11th mo, 1695. Joseph Nicholson granted a certificate to marry.

30th da, 1st mo, 1696. Andrew Thompson granted a certificate to marry Mary Sharpley, late widow of Adam Sharpley.

29th da, 2nd mo, 1696. Marriage of Thomas Thompson and Dorothy Duncley accomplished. Dorothy Duncley produced a certificate from Philadelphia Monthly Meeting.

30th da, 9th mo, 1696. Nathaniel Chammes and Rebeckah Woodes declare their intentions to marry.

28th da, 10th mo, 1696. The matter of a certificate for Nathaniel Chammes from Newton Monthly Meeting to be deferred to next meeting. John Mason and Sarey Smith declare their intentions to marry. Sarah Smith proposed to give her children the lot of land and to each child £5 to be paid within one year of her marriage, but the meeting was not in agreement.

25th da, 11th mo, 1697/8. Marriage of Andrew Thompson and Rebeck Pedrick accomplished. A certificate produced from Newton Monthly Meeting for Rebeckah Pedrick.

28th da 1st mo, 1698. Marriage of Josiah White and Hannah Powell accomplished.

27th da, 2nd mo, 1698. John Hugg reported that Joseph White had not fulfilled the award concerning the estate of John White, dec'd.

31st da, 8th mo, 1698. A subscription for the relief of Friends and others in New England was signed by the following: Bartholemew Wiat, Richard Johnson, Edward Godwin, William Thompson, Benimen Knapton, Thomas Thompson, John Hancock, Nathaniel Chamnes, Jr., Daniel Smith, Hester Herrison, Josiah White, John Thompson.

27th da, 12th mo, 1698/9. Daniel Smith and Dorcas Burrell declare their intentions of marriage.

27th da, 1st mo, 1699. Daniel Smith and Dorcas Burrell appeared the second time, but she not bringing her former husband's certificate referred to next meeting. Joseph Eastland and Ann Reeve declare their intentions to marry, but they went away disorderly, were sent for and Ann Reeve returned, referred to the next meeting. The certificate for Dorcas Burrell's former husband was presented, Daniel Smith to pay the Dorcas's child £40 when she comes of age.

29th da, 3rd mo, 1699. A subscription taken to enlarge the meeting house was signed as follows: Richard Marshall, James Danyol, John Smith of Smithfield, John Scools, Nathaniel Chamnes, Jr., Samuell Ward, Richard Johnson, Richard Darkin, and Nathaniel Chamnes.

30th da, 5th mo, 1699. Marriage of William Thompson and Hannah Pedney accomplished. A certificate was produced for Hannah Pedney from New England. Isaac Dutfield, a poor man was reported as being in need of help.

30th da, 8th mo, 1699. A subscription toward the maintenance of the meeting house was signed by the following: John Scools, Joseph White, John Smith of Smithfield, Richard Marchal, Nathan Chamnes, Jr, Samuel Wade, Benamen Knapton, Ed Keasbey, Charles Oackfoard, William Tylor, Abel Nicholson, Wade Oackfoard, Joseph Ware, Hester Herrison, Thomas Thompson.

24th da, 10th mo, 1699. Richard Darkin's name was omitted from the list of subscribers in the 8th month.

29th da, 11th mo, 1699/1700. William Rumsey added to subscription.

26th da, 12th mo, 1699/1700. Mabel Came presented a certificate. Richard Marshall reported for marrying contrary to discipline.

29th da, 1st mo, 1700. Marriage of Samuel Oakfoard and Mabel Came accomplished.

29th da, 2nd mo, 1700. Marriage of Jonathan Smith and Rayns White accomplished.

26th da, 6th mo, 1700. Marriage of James Daniell and Jany Paten accomplished.

30th da, 7th mo, 1700. James Thompson granted a certificate to marry Ann Holingsworth of New Castle Monthly Meeting.

28th da, 8th mo, 1700. Marriage of Edward Godwin and Frances Chandler accomplished. Edward Godwin had formerly obtained a certificate and Frances Chandler produced a certificate from Philadelphia Monthly Meeting.

25th da, 9th mo, 1700. A subscription for the support of the meeting was signed as follows: John Thompson, Batholomew Wiat, Rothrak Moris, Richard Darkin, Thomas Thompson, William Thompson, John Mason, Richard Woodnut, Andrew Thompson, Edward Keasbey, Abell Nicholson, George Abbit, Richard Johnson, Elizabeth Smart, John Smith, John Hancock, William Tylor, Edward Godwin, Benimen Knapton, Josiah White, Nathan Chamnes, Joseph Stretch, John Remington, Daniel Smith, Joseph Ware, Charles Oackefoard, and Sarah, the wife of William Hall.

30th da, 10th mo, 1700. Ordered to pay Richard Darkin £3.1.3 for the relief of Isaac Dustfield.

24th da, 12th mo, 1700. John Scools reported as having died and left his child with the grandmother for two years.

28th da, 5th mo, 1701. Simon Andrews of Philadelphia Monthly Meeting and Hester Harrison declare their intentions of marriage.

25th da, 6th mo, 1701. Jayn Waid reported for marrying contrary to discipline.

29th da, 7th mo, 1701. Simon Andrews produced a certificate of clearness for marriage with Hester Harrison from Philadelphia Monthly Meeting. It was ordered that a agreement be drawn up before the marriage for the security of the children. Joseph Stretch produced an acknowledgement condemning his marrying contrary to discipline.

29th da, 10th mo, 1701. John Freth produced a certificate which was accepted. Richard Johnson and Bartholemew Wiat to demand the £2 which was given to the meeting by the will of John Haselwood.

26th da, 11th mo, 1701. Marriage of Samuel Wade and Marry Powell accomplished.

23rd da, 12th mo, 1701. Marriage of Edward Keasbey and Elizabeth Smart accomplished.

30th da, 1st mo, 1702. Timothy Harst formerly a servant to William Thompson granted a certificate. A certificate granted for John Firth, son of Edward Firth of Stafford to the care of Samuel Burkly of Philadelphia. A certificate granted for Robert Heath.

A list of names of donors for the building of the meeting house as follows: John Thomson, Richard Darkin, William Tylor, Isaac Smart, Bathomolew Wiat, John Smith of Hedgefield, Richard Johnson, Ruthera Morris, William Rumsey, Thomas Thompson, Nathaniel Chamles, Sr., Nathaniel Chamles, Jr., Josiah White, John Hancock, Ben Knapton, William Thompson, Andrew Thomson, Joseph Ware, Edward Goodwin, Joseph White, Esther Harrison, John Mason, John Remington, Wade Oakford, William Bradway, Edward Keasby, Jerimiah Powel, James Whitton, John Maddock's Legacy, William Surrige, William Hall of Salem, John Smith of Smithfield, Daniel Smith, Charles Oakfoard, Samuel Wade, Sr., Esther White, a widow, James Daniel, Abel Nicholson, Richard Woodnut and John Scoles.

Names and gifts of other Friends dwelling in other parts: Samuel Carpenter of Philadelphia, Edward Shipping of same, Sam Jennings of Burlington, Bridget Guy of Burlington, her legacy, Robert Ashton of George's Creek, Thomas Smith of Darby.

25th da, 3rd mo, 1702. William Hall, Alloways Creek, reported for unbecoming behavior. John Firth produced an acknowledgement condemning his accusing Friends of ingravity [insincerity]. James Ridley, wife, Rebeccah and family produced a certificate from Tredhaven (Third Haven) Creek Monthly Meeting, Maryland, dated 25th da, 12th mo, 1701, accepted.

29th da, 4th mo, 1702. Sarah and Hannah Stretch produced a certificate, accepted.

27th da, 5th mo, 1702. William Fleetwood reported for unbecoming conversation produced an acknowledgement that he did not intend to remain a Friend. William Hall of Alloways Creek produced an acknowledgement condemning his behavior and his desire to stay under the care of the Friends. A certificate for Simon Andrews granted.

31st da, 6th mo, 1702. Certificate of Simon Andrews stopped until he give further satisfaction concerning the two children. Ordered that Rothrah Morris pay to Richard Darkin for the

clothing of Isaac Dustfield; to John Toottit for recording the
money paid by Friends for the building of the meeting house and
the disbursements of same.

29th da, 1st mo, 1703. Nathaniel Chamnes came to meeting and paid
the legacy of Prudence Wade. A certificate granted for Hannah
Stretch.

29th da, 2nd mo, 1703. John Hugg, as guardian to William White,
son and heir of John White, dec'd., informed the meeting that
Joseph White, one of the executors of said John White has not
fulfilled the award [bond] of Edward Shippen, Anthony Morris
and Isaac Norris bearing the dated 8th da, 3rd mo, 1699. The
meeting ordered Joseph White pay to William White the sum of
£24.13.8, being the said William White is of age.

31st da, 3rd mo, 1703. William Hall is reported for accusing
Richard Darkin of turning light into darkness and darkness into
light.

27th da, 7th mo, 1703. Ann Epistel reported for wearing red in
the presence of Friends. Cornelius Empson, New Castle and Marey
Richinson, of Windham declare their intention of marriage.
Joseph Brown of Cohansey granted a certificate to Gratious
Street Monthly Meeting in London.

25th da, 8th mo, 1703. Cornelius Empson produced a certificate
from New Castle Monthly Meeting. James Ridley reported for
unbecoming behavior.

27th da, 10th mo, 1703. John Smith of Hedgefield, John Mason and
William Hall of Salem granted certificates. Thomas Graves
reported for neglecting meeting and marrying contrary to
discipline. John Remington and Joseph Rediknap reported for
neglecting meeting.

31st da, 11th mo, 1703. James Ridley produced an acknowledgement
condemning his unbecoming behavior.

28th da, 12th mo, 1703. William Bradway reported for marrying
contrary to discipline. Joseph White informed the meeting that
he had complied with the award and had paid all of the money
plus interest to William White, son and heir to John White.

24th da, 2nd mo, 1704. Joseph White produced an acknowledgement
condemning his sorrow of the words spoken to the yearly
meeting.

2nd da, 3rd mo, 1704. Thomas Graves is to be spoken with again
regarding his disorderly walking both in marriage and
neglecting of meeting. Isaac Sharp produced a certificate from
Samuel Jenings, Samuel Carpenter and Thomas Sharp which
signified that his father had given the consent to the said
marriage.

26th da, 4th mo, 1704. Thomas Graves produced an acknowledgement
desiring his return to Friends and amendment of his
conversation.

31st da, 5th mo, 1704. Rothrah Morris formerly being appointed
the keeper of Friends Boblick stock, his widdow brought in an
account of the remainder of the stock. [The account not given
in original manuscript.] Isaac Sharp produced a certificate
from Newtown Monthly Meeting and made a bond with Thomas
Thompson and Richard Woodnit for the bringing up of the child
without charging the principal of the estate. Marriage of Isaac

Sharp, Newtowne and Margaret Broadwit of this county, accomplished.

28th da, 6th mo, 1704. Daniel Weles produced a certificate from Cape May Monthly Meeting, accepted.

30th da, 8th mo, 1704. A subscription for defraying debts for the meeting house was signed as follows: John Smith of Alloways Creek, James Thompson, Benjamin Knapton, Bartholomew Wiat, John Hancock, Thomas Mason, Thomas Tomson, Edward Goddin, John Smith of Maniton, Nathaniel Chamnies, Ephraim Allen, George Abbit, John Masson, Richard Johnson, Samuel Wade, John Billangly, Joseph Ware, William Thompson, William Tylor, Andrew Thompson, Richard Woodnut, Charles Oackford, John Freth, Edward Casely, Jael Morriss, Abell Nichols, Joseph Rednap, John Remington, Benjamin Acton, Richard Darken, John Hancock, Wade Oackford, James Whitton, Josias Whitton, Joseph Browne, Samuel Woodhouse, Witt Remington, Joseph Stretch, John Tylor, James Daniell, Daniell Smith, Thomas Graves, John Cullyer, William Hall of Land, Isaak Pearson. John Billangey, late belonging to Philadelphia Monthly Meeting produced a certificate.

29th da, 11th mo, 1704. Richard Johnson reported for sitting in court when the oath was tendered.

26th da, 12th mo, 1704. Isaac Pearson produced an acknowledgement condemning his neglecting meeting. Marey Williams produced a certificate from Eggharbor Monthly Meeting.

26th da, 1st mo, 1705. Marriage of Joseph Wair and Marey Williams, late of Eggharbor Monthly Meeting accomplished. Marriage of Charles Oakford and Margaret Write accomplished. Marriage of Thomas Merrion and Rebeck Redknap accomplished. Thomas Worrick and Hannah Engle declare their intentions of marriage. Richard Darkin reported the affairs relating to his mother-in-law's will were not duly executed.

23rd da, 2nd mo, 1705. Thomas Garwood produced a certificate from Burlington Monthly Meeting. Marriage of Thomas Garwood of North Hampton and Margret Hancock accomplished. Marriage of Richard Hancock and Hester Gleaves accomplished.

1st da, 3rd mo, 1705. At the yearly meeting, Richard Johnson produced an acknowledgement condemning his sitting in court when the oath was administered, he promised to do better in future.

25th da, 4th mo, 1705. A subscription to raise funds for necessities was signed by the following: John Thompson, John Smith of Hedgefield, Richard Darkin, Bartholomew Wiat, Richard Johnson, William Thompson, John Mason, Thomas Thompson, Edward Keasbey, John Hancock, James Thompson, John Billings, Dewitt Hewes, Abell Nicholson, John Tylor, Joseph Wair, Isaac Pearson, John Colyer, Josiah White, Richard Woodnut, Daniel Wells, William Remington, Samuel Woodhouse, James Witton, John Smith of Smithfield, John Freth, Georg Abbit, Beniemen Knapton, Nathaniel Chamnes, Epraim Allen, Richard Hancock, Edward Godwin and Thomas Mason.

27th da, 6th mo, 1705. Peter Blecksfield ordered to remove the monument from his wife's grave and all other monuments from the burial grounds before next meeting.

24th da, 7th mo, 1705. A letter was read from Burlington Monthly

Meeting wherein Ann Knapston has charged some of their members
with errers [errors]; referred to next meeting.
29th da, 8th mo, 1705. Marriage of John Goodwin and Susanah
Smith, dau. of John Smith accomplished. Isaac Sharp reported
for making a misstep in his proceedings of his marriage.
31st da, 10th mo, 1705. Isaac Sharp produced a paper alleging
that the bond was not drawn according to the order of the
meeting and refused to sign it. Marriage of Nathaniel Breeden,
of Boston, New England and Sarah Hall, dau. of William Hall of
Salem accomplished, her parents consenting and six of his
Friends. Nathaniel Breeden, produced a certificate from Boston,
New England as his place of abode.
29th da, 11th mo, 1705. John Thompson and Benimen Actton to see
if they can gain security for the child, Prudence Brathwit
which Isaac Sharp was to give to the meeting. Joseph Stretch
reported for neglecting meeting, he produced an acknowledgement
that he does not desire to come to meeting.
25th da, 1st mo, 1706. John Holingsworth, New Castle and Newark
Monthly Meeting and Catrine Tylor of this meeting declare their
intentions of marriage. Daniel Wells reported to be in a
declining condition from the truths of the society. Joseph
Brown granted a certificate to Philadelphia Monthly Meeting.
Andrew Thompson granted a certificate to marry at Darby Monthly
Meeting, PA.
24th da, 2nd mo, 1706. John Remington and wife granted a
certificate to Chester County. Andrew Thompson granted a
certificate to marry.
24th da, 4th mo, 1706. Timothy Brandrith reported as having
married contrary to discipline.
29th da, 5th mo, 1706. A subscription to build a stable was
signed as follows: John Thompson, John Smith of Hedgefield,
Joseph Smith, Richard Hancock, Bar. Wiat, William Heues,
Richard Johnson, John Billings, John Maison, Thomas Thompson,
Daniel Smith, James Thompson, Will Hall, Abel Nicholson, Ben
Acton, John Hancock, Edward Keasbey, Andrew Thompson, Joseph
White, John Lewis, Beniamin Knapton, John Goodwin, Thomas
Maison, Richard Woonut, William Tylor, John Frith, Stephen
Simmons, John Colyer, Richard Darkin, William Thompson, Joseph
Redknap, George Abbot, Nathaniel Chamley, Samuel Wade, James
Chamler, John Thompson, Sr. and Joseph Wore.
26th da, 6th mo, 1706. Marriage John Lewis of Kent County, MD and
Jayel Morris, widow, of Elsinborrow near Salem accomplished.
27th da, 11th mo, 1706. The committee appointed to have a hearing
for Richard Darkin and Ephraim Allen report that Ephraim is to
blame for using unseemly and unsavory words to Richard Darkin
for which he acknowledges his sorrow.
24th da, 12th mo, 1706. Marriage of James Witton and Sarah
Darkin, dau. of Richard Darkin accomplished.
28th da, 5th mo, 1707. Daniel Smith reported for breaking his
word with Nathaniel Breaden. Danniel Wells reported for
marrying contrary to discipline.
25th da, 6th mo, 1707. Railfe Allen of Shroasbury, East Jersey
produced a certificate of clearness to marry with his parents'
consent.

29th da, 7th mo, 1707. Marriage of Railfe Allen of Shroasbury in East Jersey and Margaret Denn of Alloways Creek accomplished.

24th da, 9th mo, 1707. Daniel Smith disowned for giving false information about Friends under his hand.

29th da, 10th mo, 1707. A subscription was signed for raising public stock for the use of the meeting was signed as follows: Richard Johnson, John Thompson, John Lewis, William Hall, Batholomew Wait, Benj Knapton, John Mason, Thomas Thompson, Richard Woodnut, Andrew Thompson, Thomas Mason, Joseph Ware, Sr., George Abbott, Josiah White, Ephraim Allen, James Whitton, John Culleyer, Joseph Readknap, John Thompson, Jr., John Gooding, William Thomson, John Smith of Hedgefield, James Thomson, William Walden, John Freth, Abell Nickolson, Richard Darkin, Edward Keasby, Edward Goodwin, James Daniell, Samuel Stuben, James Chamber, Nathaniel Chamnes and Beniamin Acton.

6th da, 11th mo, 1707. Marriage of Joseph Ware and Elizabeth Waker accomplished.

31st da, 3rd mo, 1708. William Horn produced a certificate from Duck Creek Monthly Meeting.

26th da, 5th mo, 1708. Timothy Brandrith produced an acknowledgement condemning his unbecoming behavior, accepted.

27th da, 7th mo, 1708. William Tylor reported for neglecting meeting.

29th da, 9th mo, 1708. A collection was to be made as following: John Thompson, Richard Johnson, Batholomew Wait, John Lius, John Mason, Thomas Thompson, Edward Keasbey, John Smith of Hedgefield, Will Thompson, Andrew Thompson, James Thompson, Richard Woodnut, Nathan Chamnis, George Abbot, Joseph Ware, John Hancock, Abel Nicholson, Benia Knapton, Josiah White, Thomas Mason, John Goodwin, James Dannil, John Colyer, Beniamen Acton, Will Walden, Samuel Stubins, James Whittin and Richard Darkin.

31st da, 11th mo, 1708. Marriage of Jonathan Smith and Marey Quinton accomplished. William Heues and John Pedrick to appear at next meeting informing the meeting of the reasons why John Belangey should not have a certificate.

30th da, 3rd mo, 1709. Marriage of Philip Blansher and Marey Hancock accomplished.

28th da, 9th mo, 1709. William Sharp granted a certificate. Marriage of Richard Woodnut and Rebeck Ridley accomplished. Marriage of John Ferth and Sarah Boyer accomplished.

27th da, 1st mo, 1710. Marriage of Samuel Stubins and Sarah Smarte accomplished. Samuel Wade reported for neglecting meeting.

29th da, 3rd mo, 1710. Isaac Pearson requested a certificate to marry Hannah Gardenor of Burlington.

A subscription was found to be needful and was signed as follows: John Thompson, Richard Darkin, Bartho Wiat, John Lewis, John Smith, Edward Beasbey, John Mason, Richard Johnson, Thomas Thompson, Thomas Mason, Will Thompson, George Abbot, Abell Nicholson, Samuel Stubins, John Frith, James Thompson, Josiah White, John Colyer, William Walden, James Whitton, Benimen Acton, Benimen Knapton, Joseph Redknap, Andrew Thompson, Isaac Pearson, Richard Woodnut, Joseph Darkin, Jonathan Surrey, John

Smith, Jr., Joseph Smith, John Thompson, Sr., Philip Blansher,
John Surrig, William Tylor, Wade Samuel Oackford, James Daniel,
Nathaniel Chamnes.
29th mo, 11th mo, 1710. A subscription to help the Boston Monthly
Meeting was signed as follows: Richard Darkin, John Smith,
Richard Johnson, Bartholomew Wiat, John Lius, Edward Keasbey,
Thomas Thompson, James Daniel, Richard Woodnut, James Thompson,
George Abbot, John Godwin, John Thompson, William Thompson,
Andrew Thompson, John Maison, Abel Nicholson, Beniamen Knapton,
John Colyer, Josiah White, William Tylor, Wad Sam Oackford,
William Waldren, Samuel Stubins, James Whitton, Thomas Maison,
Beniamen Acton, Nathaniel Chamnes, Joseph Waire, Sr., Joseph
Redknap, Henry Wamsley and John Thompson, Jr.
26th da, 1st mo, 1711. Marriage of William Tylor and Marey Abbot
accomplished.
30th da, 5th mo, 1711. Wade Oackford reported for neglecting to
account for his brothers and sisters' burial. Joseph Wair
reported for neglecting to account for his father's burial.
30th da, 1st mo, 1712. Marriage of John Smith, Jr. and Hannah
Boyer accomplished.
29th da, 7th mo, 1712. Marriage of Henry Hoser of Cisell Monthly
Meeting, MD and Hannah Darkin accomplished, he produced a
certificate from his father-in-law and his own mother of their
consent and a certificate from Cisell Monthly Meeting. Marriage
of John Madox Denn and Elizabeth Bucmaster accomplished.
24th da, 9th mo, 1712. Marriage of Frances Rennols of Chichester
and Elizabeth Acton, dau. of Beniamen Acton of this meeting
accomplished with the parents consenting. Richard Woodnut
presented the meeting with concerns regarding a child left to
him or his wife by Margret Oakford. Wade Samuel Oakford,
executor to said Margret was heard. A copy of the will to be
brought to next meeting.
22nd da, 2nd mo, 1713. Marriage of Thomas Thompson and Sarah
Ridley accomplished.
25th da, 3rd mo, 1713. Marriage of James Chamnis and Marey Ridley
accomplished.
30th da, 9th mo, 1713 Marriage of Henry Wamsley and Elizabeth
Keasbey accomplished.
25th da, 11th mo, 1713. Marriage of William Ridley and Sarah
Frith accomplished. Marriage of James Daniel and Isbell Coyler
accomplished.
31st da, 3rd mo, 1714. Marriage of William Hancock and Sarah
Thompson accomplished.
26th da, 5th mo, 1714. Robert Worthington and wife produced a
certificate from Dublin Monthly Meeting, Ireland, accepted.
31st da, 11th mo, 1714. Joseph White and Mary Smith declare their
intentions of marriage.
A subscription was signed as follows: Richard Darkin, John Smith,
Sr, Richard Johnson, Bartha Wiat, Henry Wamsley, Richard
Woodnut, Georg Abbot, Abel Nicholson, Thomas Mason, Andrew
Thompson, James Daniell, John Colier, John Thompson, John Denn,
John Smith, Jr., Nathan Smart, Jonathan Morris, Joseph White,
Jr., Benimen Knapton, William Hancock, Richard Hancock, James
Chamnes, Will Ridley, Nathaniel Chamnis, Will Thompson and John

Mason.

28th da, 1st mo, 1715. Marriages of Henry Wamsley to Sarah Thompson accomplished. Marriage of John Smith, of Amwelbery to Ann Testt accomplished.

20th da, 2nd mo, 1715. Isaac Shatterwite [Satterthwaite] produced a certificate from Burlington Monthly Meeting of clearness to marry. Marriage of Isaac Shaterwite [Satterthwaite] and Phebey Knapton accomplished.

30th da, 3rd mo, 1715. Marriage of John Frith and Sarah Stubins accomplished after the meeting accepts an acknowledgement from Sarah Marshall condemning the lies she had put forth relating to a child of Sarah Stubins. A bond to be prepared for the legacy of the child.

31st da, 8th mo, 1715. Hannah White reported for marrying contrary to discipline.

28th da, 9th mo, 1715. Hannah White promised she would settle some estate upon her children.

26th da, 10th mo, 1715. Marriage of William Willis and Mary Acton accomplished. Marriage of Joseph Tomson and Sarah Penton accomplished.

27th da, 12th mo, 1715 Richard Darkins and others to assist Jael Lius in settling her outward affairs before marriage.

26th da, 1st mo, 1716. Marriage of John Mason and Jael Luis accomplished.

28th da, 3rd mo, 1716. George Abbit reported for having a bond due to Abraham Bukley; he is to settle as soon as possible.

29th da, 7th mo, 1716. Widdow Hannah White disowned for her evil doings. Wade Oackford produced an acknowledgement condemning his neglect of meeting and keeping a distance from Friends.

29th da, 8th mo, 1716. An accounting of the legacy of Elizabeth Tankersley given by John Smith, executor. Joseph Smith reported for marrying contrary to discipline.

28th da, 11th mo, 1716. Samuel Powell to be spoken to regarding the sum of 40 shillings left to the meeting by John Hazelwood.

24th da, 2nd mo, 1717. Marriage of John Darkins and Sarah Morris accomplished. Reneir Louden and Elizabeth Tindell declare their intentions of marriage.

27th da, 3rd mo, 1717. John Borten produced a certificate for his clearness to marry. Marriage of John Borten and Ann Darnelley accomplished.

26th da, 6th mo, 1717. Friends to discuss with Reneir Louden and Elizabeth Tindell as to why their marriage was not accomplished.

30th da, 7th mo, 1717. Friends meeting with Renier Louden and Elizabeth Tindell report that she did not have the love for him to continue in marriage.

28th da, 8th mo, 1717. Marriage of Joseph Darkins and Ann Mason accomplished.

24th da, 12th mo, 1717. Marriage of John Hart and Ann Buzby accomplished.

A subscription was signed toward an addition to the meeting house as follows: John Smith, Sr., Bartho Wayatt, John Mason, Able Nicholson, Richard Woodnutt, Thomas Mason, Andrew Thompson, George Abbitt, John Smith, Jr., John Darkins, Henry Wamsley,

William Wolden, William Willis, William Thompson, Richard
Johnson, John Hart, James Whitte, William Hancock, John
Goodwin, Robart Worthington, Joseph Darkins, Jonathan Morris,
Joseph Morris, William Smith, Nathan Smart, Joseph White, Roger
Huggins, John Coller, Benja Knapton, Philip Blanshare, Reneir
Louden, William Ridley, John Firth, and Joseph Smith.
31st da, 1st mo, 1718. A committee appointed to divide the land
between Joseph and John Darkins, sons of Richard Darkins,
dec'd.. A certificate granted for Archibald Silver.
26th da, 3rd mo, 1718. James Whitten granted a certificate of
clearness to marry.
29th da, 7th mo, 1718. Marriage of Richard Woodnutt and Grace
Bacon accomplished. Marriage of John Bacon and Elizabeth Sawyer
accomplished. A certificate granted for Robert Lodge.
27th da, 8th mo, 1718. Marriage of Philip Tylor and Rachal
Thompson accomplished.
26th da, 11th mo, 1718. George Deacon has delivered the deed for
the meeting house to the meeting. A committee appointed to
divide the land that was Rothoray Morris' between his sons
according to the will.
23rd da, 12th mo, 1718. Marriage of Samuell Smith, Jr. and Hannah
Hall accomplished.
30th da, 1st mo, 1719. Marriage of John Chanler and Elizabeth
Oakeford accomplished.
22nd da, 2nd mo, 1719. Marriage of John Smith, Jr. and Sarah
Siddon accomplished.
25th da, 3rd mo, 1719. Marriage of Luis Morris and Grace Woodnutt
accomplished.
31st da, 6th mo, 1719. A subscription was signed as follows:
Bartholomew Waytt, Thomas Mason, Jeanes Whitton, John Smith,
Sr, John Mason, Richard Johnson, Able Nicholson, Richard
Woodnutt, Andrew Thompson, Robart Worthington, George Abbitt,
Henry Wamsley, Nathan Smart, John Cullier, William Thompson,
Roger Huggins, Joseph White, Jr., Joseph Cluse, Aquillea
Barbert, John Smith, Jr. William Hancock, Joseph Darkins,
George Garrat's bill paid to Andrew Thompson, William Wolden,
William Willis and William Tyler.
30th da, 9th mo, 1719. Marriage of William Smith and Mary Mason
accomplished. Marriage of William Thompson, Jr. and Elizabeth
Chamlis accomplished.
29th da, 12th mo, 1719 Benjamin Acton, Jr. granted a certificate
to marry.
20th da, 2nd mo, 1720. Marriage of Frances Test and Rebekah Smart
accomplished.
26th da, 7th mo, 1720. Marriage of William Hanby and Mary Pedrick
accomplished.
28th da, 9th mo, 1720. A certificate granted to Auther Boyer to
marry.
26th da, 10th mo, 1720. Marriage of Renier Louden and Easter
Worthington accomplished.
A subscription was signed as follows: John Smith, Bartho Wayatt,
John Mason, Richard Woodnutt, Thomas Mason, Able Nicholson,
Robart Worthington, Andrew Thompson, George Abbitt, William
Wolden, Henry Wamsley, William Willis, Reneir Louden, Jeams

Whitten, John Goodwin, John Den, Nathan Smart, William Coaksly, John Hart, Benj. Anton, Jr., John Smith, Jr, Frances Test, William Hancock, Joseph Darkins, John Mason, Jr, Joseph Morris, Batholomew Wyett, John Darkin, Lewis Morris, Joseph Powes.

30th da, 11th mo, 1720. William Coaksley requested a certificate.

27th da, 12th mo, 1720. A difference between Wade Oakford, Samuel Wade and Able Nicholson regarding the estate of Charles Oakford, dec'd., to be decided by an arbitrator from the meeting.

29th da, 3rd mo, 1721. Richard Woodnutt appointed to care for the graveyard.

26th da, 4th mo, 1721. Marriage of Joseph Test and Ann Jeans accomplished.

31st da, 5th mo, 1721. David Morris produced an acknowledgement condemning his marrying contrary to discipline.

30th da, 8th mo, 1721. Marriage of Joseph Morris and Prudence Broughwhite accomplished.

27th da, 9th mo, 1721. Wade Oakford reported for a complaint made by his servant girl.

25th da, 10th mo, 1721. Marriage of David Morris and Jean Jeffrey accomplished. Wade Oakford refuses to leave the matter of the complaint by his servant girl to the meeting.

26th da, 12th mo, 1721. Daniel Stretch reported for neglecting meeting.

26th da, 1st mo, 1722. John Smith granted a certificate to marry.

28th da, 3rd mo, 1722. Nathaniel Chamles appointed as overseer for Alloways Creek Monthly Meeting. Roger Huggins appointed overseer for Piles Grove Monthly Meeting.

25th da, 4th mo, 1722. Robart Worthington requested a certificate to Philadelphia Monthly Meeting.

30th da, 5th mo, 1722. A certificate was produced for Hugh Clifton.

27th da, 6th mo, 1722. Marriage of Edward Vickrery and Sarah Firth accomplished. Sarah Firth to provide for her two children before the marriage. A certificate granted to Jeams Smith.

24th da, 7th mo, 1722. Marriage of Hugh Clifton and Elizabeth Tindell accomplished.

29th da, 8th mo, 1722. Marriage of Ephraim Worthington and Elizabeth Brick accomplished. Marriage of Joseph Woodnutt and Rachel Craven accomplished.

28th da, 11th mo, 1722. Joseph Allen granted a certificate. Marriage of Joseph Reaves and Elennor Baggnall accomplished. John Darnalley granted a certificate to marry.

26th da, 6th mo, 1723. Marriage of Robart Smith and Elizabeth Wayatt accomplished.

28th da, 8th mo, 1723. Marriage of William Hall and Elizabeth Smith accomplished. Marriage of Philip Denis and Luce Bacon accomplished.

27th da, 11th mo, 1723. A certificate granted to Joseph Clark to Maryland.

24th da, 12th mo, 1723. John Deen granted a certificate to mary. Marriage of Abraham Moss and Rebecca Marshall accomplished.

29th da, 4th mo, 1724. Samuel Worthington and wife granted a certificate.

27th da, 5th mo, 1724. Marriage of Aaron Mason and Abigail Rowland accomplished.
31st da, 6th mo, 1724. Richard Brickham and his wife and children requested a certificate. Marriage of Jeremiah Powell and Vashty Allen accomplished.
28th da, 10th mo, 1724. Marriage of Edward Hewes and Hannah Abbott accomplished.
29th da, 1st mo, 1725. Marriage of Edward Casby and Elizabeth Bradway accomplished.
25th da, 2nd mo, 1725. Marriage of Thomas Barrett and Elizabeth Thomas accomplished.
31st da, 3rd mo, 1725. Marriage of John Bucher and Jean Daniell accomplished. Marriage of Samuel Rowland and Sarah Hall accomplished.
28th da, 4th mo, 1725. Marriage of Joseph Walker and Mary Thomas accomplished. Marriage of John Chandler and Mary Dickinson accomplished.
26th da, 5th mo, 1725. A subscription was signed as follows: John Cullier; George Abbott; James Whitton; Abell Nicholson; James Daniell; Andrew Thompson; William Hunt; John Denn; Samuel Waide; Richard Hancock; Edward Vickery; William Huse; Charles Oakford; Joseph Clows; Isaac Davis; Roger Huggins; Bartho Wyatt, Jr.; Joseph Allen; Benjamin Acton; Hugh Clifton; Stephen Lewis; Bartholomew Wyatt; John Mason; Richard Woodnut; Thomas Mason; Samuel Rowland; David Morris; John Smith; Nathaniel Champness; Joseph Smith; William Thompson, Sr; Lewis Morris; Joseph Morris; Nathan Smart; Jospeh Waide; John Chandler; Ephraim Allen.
27th da, 7th mo, 1725. A legacy of £20 given to the meeting by the will of John Foolett, dec'd. Robert Smith, late of Salem but now of Burlington requested a certificate.
25th da, 8th mo, 1725. A certificate granted for Robert Smith, late of Salem, but now of Burlington Monthly Meeting.
27th da, 10th mo, 1725. Richard Graves appointed grave digger for the graveyard in the future, to have five shillings for each grave dug. Thomas Wright reported for negelecting meeting.
28th da, 12th mo, 1725. William Ridley produced an acknowledgement condemning his drinking strong drink to excess.
34th da, 3rd mo, 1726. Renier Lowden requested a certificate to Philadelphia Monthly Meeting. Abell Nicholson appointed overseer in place of Bartho Wyate, Sr., dec'd.; Richard Hancock appointed overseer for Alloways Creek to assist James Daniell; William Hews appointed overseer for Pilesgrove to assist Roger Huggins.
27th da, 4th mo, 1726. Henery Ballinger granted a certificate.
25th da, 5th mo, 1726. Marriage of Ephraim Allen and Hannah Leonard accomplished.
27th da, 6th mo, 1726. A certificate granted for Renier Lowden. Jael Mason to be spoken to concerning her not allowing Richard Graves to dig graves for her family in the meeting graveyard.
31st da, 8th mo, 1726. Marriage of Charles Oakford and Ester Hancock accomplished.
28th da, 9th mo, 1726. A subscription for the use of the meeting was subscribed as follows: Thomas Mason; Abell Nicholson;

George Abbott; Richard Woodnut; James Daniell; James Whitton; Samuel Waide, Sr.; William Hunt; William Hancock; John Smith; Roger Huggins; John Denn; Bartholomew Wyatt; Edward Hughes; Edward Vickary; Benjamin Acton; Stephen Lewis; Joseph Clows; Jospeh Waide; Joseph Allen; Abell Nicholson; Frances Test; George Abbot, Jr; John Cullier; Hugh Clifton; Lewis Morris; ?William Smith; Edward Casby; William Hall; Daniel Morris; Richard Smith; Nathan Smart; John Darkin; Nathaniel Champness; James Champness; Joseph Ware; Joseph Test; Josiah Wade; Joseph Darkin; Thomas Marshall; Andrew Thompson; David Davis; Joseph Morris; Malachi Davis; Joseph Smith; William Thompson, Jr.; Abraham Moss; Thomas Daniell; Charles Oakford; James Daniell, Jr. and Richard Hancock.

26th da, 10th mo, 1726. Marriage of David Allen and Hannah Champness accomplished.

27th da, 12th mo, 1726. A certificate requested by Abel Nicholson for Josiah Ballenger.

24th da, 2nd mo, 1727. Marriage of Richard Woodnut and Ann Wamsley accomplished. Thomas Anderson and Hannah Hancock declare their intentions of marriage. Robart Worthington requested a certificate. Stephen Lewis granted a certificate.

29th da, 3rd mo, 1727. A subscription for the building of a stable was signed as follows: Thomas Mason; Abell Nicholson; Andrew Thompson; George Abbot; Batho Wyatt; James Whitton; Wiliam Willis; Richard Hancock, Joseph Darkin; Wiliam Hunt; Samuel Waide; James Champness; Abraham Moss; John Smith; David Morris; Lewis Morris; John Cullier; Benjamin Acton; Philip Blanchard; Nathan Smart; Waid Oarkford; Thomas Daniell; Joseph Ware; Joseph Clues; David Davis; John Chandler; Thomas Marshall; Roger Huggins; Edward Casby; John Denn; Hugh Clifton; Thomas Barret; Nathaniel Champness; Joseph Waid; Abel Nicholson, Jr.; Aquilla Barber; George Abbot, Jr.; Isaac Davis; James Daniell; Malachi Davis; Richard Wood; Malachi Davis; William Tyler; John Davis; William Hancock; Josiah White; Philip Denis; John Darkin.

26th da, 4th mo, 1727. Marriage of Jonathan Hughs and Hannah Chandler accomplished. Marriage of James Champness and Hannah Sidden accomplished. Marriage of Samuell Hancock and Rebecca Fog accomplished.

28th da, 6th mo, 1727. Joseph White reported for disorderly walking and neglecting meeting; disowned.

25th da, 7th mo, 1727. Joseph Darkin appointed treasurer in the place of Andrew Thompson, dec'd. Joseph Ward requested a certificate.

27th da, 9th mo, 1727. Marriage of Benjamin Acton and Elizabeth Hill accomplished. A bond to be given to Abel Nicholson by Benjmanin Acton in trust for the children of Elizabeth Hill.

25th da, 10th mo, 1727. A subscription for use of traveling Friends was signed by the following: Thomas Mason; Abel Nicholson; William Hunt; Joseph Darkin; Benjamin Acton; James Champness; Edward Vicary; Malachi Davis; Roger Huggins; John Davis; Joseph Woodnut; Joseph Clews; Bartho Wyate; Richard Smith; Joseph Waide; Joseph Ware; David Morris.

26th da, 12th mo, 1727. Joseph Allen requested a certificate to

Shrewsberry Monthly Meeting.

24th da, 2nd mo, 1728. Marriage of Zachcheus Dunn and Deborah Hughs accomplished. Renier Louden produced a certificate from Philadelphia Monthly Meeting for himself and his wife, accepted.

27th da, 3rd mo, 1728. James Whitton produced an account showing that he had paid the £20 left to the meeting by Bartholomew Wyate.

29th da, 5th mo, 1728. A subscription was signed for the meetings as follows: Thomas Mason; Abel Nicholson; Barth Wyat; Benjamin Acton; Richard Hancock; Waid Oakford; John Denn; Hugh Clifton; Abraham Moss; Joseph Waid; Joseph Clows; John Davis, Malchi Davis; Josiah White; Will Thompson; Roger Huggins; John Oakford; Samuell Waid; William Hunt; John Smith; James Champness; Joseph Darkin; Richard Smith; Nathan Smart; Edward Vickary; George Abott, Jr.; Edward Hughs; James Hughs; James Daniel; Abell Nicholson, Jr.; James Whitton; Stephen Lewis; William Hancock; Joseph Morris; Aron Mason; Edward Casby; David Davis; Richard Wood; Lewis Moris; Joseph Woodnutt; David Morris.

24th da, 12th mo, 1728. Marriage of John Darkin and Elizabeth Bucher accomplished.

31st da, 1st mo, 1729. Marriage of James Allen and Hannah Evans accomplished. Isaac Davis reported for disorderly walking.

23rd da, 2nd mo, 1729. Thomas Moore and Sarah Thompson declare their intentions of marriage.

26th da, 3rd mo, 1729. A certificate granted for Thomas Wright to marry. A certificate granted for Josiah White to Burlington Monthly Meeting.

30th da, 4th mo, 1729. A certificate granted for John Oakford, a shoemaker.

29th da, 5th mo, 1729. John Chandler reported for going out in marriage.

28th da, 6th mo, 1279. The meeting gave judgement that Robart Lodge is too forward to speak as a teacher at the meeting.

27th da, 8th mo, 1729. Marriage of Thomas Daniel and Hannah Butcher accomplished. Marriage of Lewis Howell and Rebeckah Abbot accomplished. Marriage of John Oarkford and Elizabeth Pedrick accomplished. Thomas Moore and Sarah Thompson declare their intentions of marriage.[At a later meeting this marriage contract was cancelled.]

24th da, 9th mo, 1729. Marriages of Thomas Daniell and Hannah Butcher accomplished. Marriage of Lewis Howell and Rebecakah Abbott accomplished. Marriage contracted between Thomas Moore and Sarah Thompson cancelled, Thomas Moore willing to leave Sarah Thompson to marry whomever she desires.

29th da, 10th mo, 1729. Mariage of Joseph Test and Sarah Thompson accomplished. Marriage of Jonathan Plats and Jean Butcher accomplished. John Chandler reported for his disorderly walking. Richard Graves reported for marrying contrary to discipline.

25th da, 11th mo, 1729. Isaac Davis reported for disorderly walking; disowned. John Chandler produced an acknowledgment condemning his disorderly walking.

30th da, 1st mo, 1730. Marriage of Abell Nicholson, Sr. and Isabell Daniel accomplished. Marriage of William Nicholson and Jean Tuft accomplished. Marriage of Clement Hall and Elizabeth Ashton accomplished.

27th da, 5th mo, 1730. Batholomew Wyate granted a certificate. Richard Graves produced an acknowledgement condemning his disorderly walking.

A subscription was signed as follows: James Whitton; Abell Nicholson; Joseph Darkin; Bartho Wyatt; Benjamin Acton; Ruth Hancock; Richard Graves; John Denn; Joseph Woodnut; John Smith; William Hunt; Joseph Morris; Abraham Moss; William Willis; Clement Hall; John Mason; Samuel Waide; David Morris; Edward Casby; Lewis Morris; Stephen Lewis; Edward Vickary; Hugh Clifton; John Davis; David Davis; William Basset; Joseph Clows; James Daniel; Jospeph Waide; Jonathan Hughs; Warwick Rundle; Joseph Daniel; Richard Wood; Richard Smith; Thomas Barret; James Mason; Wiiilam Tyler; John Bacon; Edward Hews; William Hall; John Darkin; Aron Mason; Charles Oakford; Thomas Barber; Nathaniell Champness; Samuel Waid, Jr.; Jerimy Powell; Samuel Worthington.

31st da, 6th mo, 1730. An extract from the Philadelphia yearly meeting forbidding the buying and selling negroes was read and approved.

30th da, 9th mo, 1730. Marriage of Warrnick Rundel and Sarah Rowland accomplished. Marriage of John Evans and Ruth Nicholson accomplished. Marriage of John Jones and Mary Goodwin accomplished.

A subscription was taken to be given to Samuel Dennis who sustained a great loss by fire was signed: Abell Nicholson; James Whitton; Richard Smith; William Hancock; Samuel Waide; Bartholomew Wyatt; Richard Hancock; David Davis; Aron Mason; John Davis; John Denn; Joseph Clows; William Tyler; Stephen Lewis; John Smith; Joseph Woodnut; Richard Wood; Roger Huchins; Abram Moss; Samuel Abbott; James Mason; Edward Vickary; Charles Oakford; Warrick Rundle; Wiliam Basset; Samuel Ward, Jr.; Jerimy Powel; Joseph Daniell; Smuel Hancock; ;Sarah Wyatt; Hannah Abbot; William Hunt; Benjamin Acton; Edward Casby; James Daniell; Edward Huses; Joseph Ward; Joseph Darkin; Joseph Smith; John Waid; Nathan Smart; James Howes.

25th da, 11th mo, 1730. Elizabeth Taylor, wife of Christopher Taylor made a complaint against Clement Hall concerning a bond that he refused to pay. Thomas Hewes produced an acknowledgement condemning his marrying contrary to discipline.

22nd da, 12th mo, 1730. William Will appointed to be overseer in the room of Thomas Mason.

26th da, 5th mo, 1731. Marriage of Joseph Wair and Hannah Barber accomplished.

30th da, 6th mo, 1731. Robert Lodge reported for his disorderly appearance in public; disowned.

27th da, 7th mo, 1731. John Wright and Hannah Daniel declare their intentions of marriage. Thomas Mason and Sarah, his wife produced an acknowledgement of his marrying contrary to discipline.

25th da, 8th mo, 1731. Marriage of Samuell Mason and Elizabeth

Hill accomplished. John Wright did not attend to declare his
intentions of marriage to Hannah Daniel as she is now deceased.
James Daniel granted a certificate to Old England.
27th da, 10th mo, 1731. Marriage of Samuell Thompson and Edith
Tyler accomplished. Marriage of John Pledger, Sr. and Hannah
Champness accomplished. Samuell Ward, Richard Hancock and
William Hancock to see that the children of Hannah Champness
are justly dealt with according to the will of their father and
John Pledger produced a bond for the security.
28th da, 12th mo, 1731. Marriage of William Siddon and Mary Smart
accomplished. Security for the children of James Champness,
husband of Hannah Champness given to the care of William
Hancock.
29th da, 3rd mo, 1732. Marriage of William Nicholson and Rachel
Smith accomplished. Marriage of James Mason and Mary Powel
accomplished.
31st da, 5th mo, 1732. Marriage of John Thomas and Ann Hunt
accomplished. Philip Pedrick requested a certificate to
Haddonfield Monthly Meeting to marry.
25th da, 6th mo, 1732. Rebecca Howell granted a certificate.
27th da, 9th mo, 1732. Nathan Smart appointed as clerk in the
room of John Goodwin.
25th da, 10th mo, 1732. Marriage of John Pledger, Jr. and Mary
Johnson accomplished.
26th da, 1st mo, 1733. Marriage of John White and Elizabeth Denn
accomplished.
30th da, 2nd mo, 1733. James Mason reported for disorderly
walking.
28th da, 3rd mo, 1733. Marriage of John Hendricks and Marcy
Barber accomplished. Edward Huse appointed overseer of
Pilesgrove Monthly Meeting in the room and place of his dec'd.
father.
30th da, 6th mo, 1733. Samuel Abboot requested a certificate to
Haddonfield Monthly Meeting to marry.
24th da, 7th mo, 1733. Marriage of Edward Hughes and Hannah
Barber accomplished. Marriage of Thomas Barber and Ruth Hughes
accomplished.
29th da, 8th mo, 1733. Abel Nicholson and William Willis
appointed as elders.
31st da, 10th mo, 1733. Joseph Dakin appointed in the place of
James Whitton, dec'd. to assist Richard Smith.
28th da, 11th mo, 1733. John Wright granted a certificate. James
Daniell appointed overseer in the place of Richard Hancock.
Isaac Satathwyte and John Pledger to give leave [permission]
for persons to bury their died who do not belong to the meeting
or to deny such.
25th da, 12th mo, 1733. Benjamin Crips requested a certificate to
Burlington Monthly Meeting. Richard Wood and Joseph Reeves
appointed overseer of the Greenwich Monthly Meeting.
25th da, 1st mo, 1734. Marriage of Joseph Tomlinson and Lydia
Wade accomplished.
30th da, 7th mo, 1734. Robert Lodge granted a certificate to
Chester Monthly Meeting.
25th da, 9th mo, 1734. Marriage of Hugh Clifton and Esther

Anderson accomplished. Abraham Moss granted a certificate to Haddonfield Monthly Meeting to marry.

30th da, 10th mo, 1734. John Wright granted a certificate to go to New England.

27th da, 11th mo, 1734. William Shields reported for disorderly walking; disowned. Jeremiah Powell produced an acknowledgement condemning his disorderly walking, accepted.

31st da, 1st mo, 1735. Marriage of Robert Townsend and Mary Tylor accomplished. Marriage of Jeremiah Powell and June Blansher accomplished. Marriage of Beniaman Coller and Elizabeth Hacket Marriage of Joseph Graves and Rebecca Basset accomplished. William Smith reported for his neglecting meeting and other disorders.

26th da, 3rd mo, 1735. Marriage of John Winton and Hannah Barbor accomplished.

28th da, 5th mo, 1735. Samuel Fogg, William Oakeford, Isaac Oakeford, William Willis, Jr., Joseph Smith, William Smith, Matthew Keasby, Edward Joseph, Nathaniel Hancock, Thomas Anderson, and Joshua Thompson all reported for disorderly conduct.

25th da, 6th mo, 1735. A certificate granted for Samuel Mason to Middletown, Bucks County to marry. Jonathan Bradway appointed as overseer at Alloways Creek Monthly Meeting with James Daniel.

24th da, 9th mo, 1735. William Wills, Jr. produced an acknowledgement condemning his outgoing, accepted.

29th da, 10th mo, 1735. Warwick Rundle produced an acknowledgement condemning his conduct in settling his accounts with his creditors. Joshua Thompson produced an acknowledgement condemning his disorderly conduct, accepted.

26th da, 11th mo, 1735. Marriage of Thomas Hodgkins and Mary Sickes accomplished.

23rd da, 12th mo, 1735. Samuel Fogg produced an acknowledgement condemning his disorderly conduct, accepted.

29th da, 1st mo, 1736. Marriage of George Coulson and Elisabeth Barratt accomplished.

31st da, 3rd mo, 1736. Thomas Hodgkins requested a certificate to Philadelphia Monthly Meeting.

26th da, 5th mo, 1736. Marriage of Aquilla Barber and Hannah Huckins accomplished. Thomas Handcock and Hannah Brick declare their intentions of marriage.

30th da, 6th mo, 1736. Marriage of Thomas Thompson and Mary Hains accomplished. Richard Seers requested a certificate.

27th da, 7th mo, 1736. Marriage of Joseph Test and Rachel Tyler accomplished. A certificate granted for Richard Seers. Samuel Abbot requested a certificate to Maryland.

25th da, 8th mo, 1736. Marriage of James Hewes and Jane Lodge accomplished. A certificate granted for Samuel Abbot.

29th da, 9th mo, 1736. A subscription was signed as follows: Abell Nicholson; William Willis; Hugh Clifton; Bartholomew Wyat; Joseph Darkin; Samuel Mason; Abraham Moss; John Pledger; William Hunt; Charles Oakford; James Daniel; Daniel Huddy; Joseph Ware; Jonathan Bradway; Joshua Thompson; Thomas Thompson; Joseph Stretch; Joseph Clows; Samuel Nicholson;

George Coulson; Joseph Gibson; Nathan Smart; Lewis Morris; John
Steward; John Oakford; John Eglenton; Stephen Lewis; Edward
Vickery; Samuel Abbott; Richard Booth; Thomas Hodgkins; Joseph
Morris; Frances Test; Benajmin Acton; William Hall; John Smith;
John Winton; Joseph Godwin; John Pledger, Jr.; Richard Smith;
William Willis, Jr.; John White; John Mason; Henry Stubbins;
Samuel Thompson; James Allen; William Thompson; Nathaniel
Chambles; Samuel Hancock; William Hancock; John Willis; Wiliam
Crabb; Thomas Handcock.
28th da, 12th mo, 1736. The account for Susanah Godwin for taking
care of the meeting house is settled. William Smith disowned
for his disorderly walking.
18th da, 2nd mo, 1737. Marriage of Joseph Darkin and Hannah Allen
accomplished. Marriage of Peter Stretch and Sarah Smith
accomplished. Marriage of Richard Vickery and Phebe Barber
accomplished.
30th da, 3rd mo, 1737. Joseph Smith produced an acknowledgement
condemning his disorderly conduct.
27th da, 4th mo, 1737. Joseph Ware, Sr. appointed overseer at
Alloways Creek Monthly Meeting in the room of James Daniel.
26th da, 7th mo, 1737. Richard Smith requested a certificate to
London.
28th da, 9th mo, 1737. Marriage of Samuel Graves and Margret
Overend accomplished. Philip Denis appointed overseer at
Cohansey Monthly Meeting with Richard Wood.
30th da, 11th mo, 1737. A certificate granted for Ebenezer Miller
to Barbados Monthly Meeting.
29th da, 1st mo, 1738. Marriage of Erasmus Fettors and Rebeckah
Thompson accomplished. Marriage of Richard Booth and Ann Barber
accomplished. Marriage of Henry Apple and Mary Davis
accomplished.
17th da, 2nd mo, 1738. Marriage of Joseph Fogg and Elizabeth
Holmes accomplished. Lydia Fossit granted a certificate. Joseph
Goodwin granted a certificate to Cape May Monthly Meeting to
marry.
A subcription was signed as follows: William Willis; Abel
Nicholson; Jonathan Bradway; Bartholomew Wyat; Abraham Moss;
Charles Oakford; John Pledger; Benjamin Acton; Hugh Clifton;
David Davis; Philip Dennis; Joseph Stretch; Samuel Abbott; Abel
Nicholson, Jr.; Joseph Gibson; Joshua Thompson; Thomas
Thompson; Roger Huchins; John Willis; Henry Stubbins; William
Thompson; Joseph Clows; Joseph Thompson; Samuel Thompson; John
Bacon; Richard Wood; Edward Hews; Samuel Nicholson; Daniel
Huddy; Samuel Hancock; Samuel Fogg; Benjamin Acton; Stephen
Lewis; Joseph Test; Joseph Fogg; Zacheus Dun; Wade Oakford;
William Hunt; James Daniel; John Smith; Edward Vickary; Samuel
Mason; Joseph Goodwin; Lewis Morris; William Hall; Benjamin
Crips.
28th da, 6th mo, 1738. William Smith disowned for his disorderly
conduct.
25th da, 7th mo, 1738. Joseph Smith produced an acknowledgement
condemning his disorderly conduct. Marriage of George Larrance
and Mary Hewes accomplished.
30th da, 8th mo, 1738. Hugh Clifton granted a certificate to

Burlington Monthly Meeting to marry.
25th da, 10th mo, 1738. Help will be provided to Joseph Ware who has met with a great loss due to fire.
26th da, 12th mo, 1738. Joshua Gill requested a certificate to Providence Monthly Meeting, PA. George Coulson produced an acknowledgement condemning his disorderly conduct. Daniel Barber reported for marrying contrary to discipline.
26th da, 1st mo, 1739. Nathaniel Hancock and Leah Denn declare their intentions of marriage. Joshua Gill granted a certificate to Providence Monthly Meeting, PA.
30th da, 2nd mo, 1739. Marriage of James Allen and Elizabeth Street accomplished. The affairs of the children of Elizabeth Street to be decided before the marriage. Marriage of Thomas Rice and Sarah Keasey accomplished. John White to keep the writings of the settlement of Sarah Keasley for her children. William Crabb reported for marrying contrary to discipline and disorderly walking.
28th da, 3rd mo, 1739. Marriage of Solomon Ware and Sarah Stretch accomplished. Nathaniel Hancock and Leah Denn declared that they will not marry each other. Daniel Barber reported for disorderly conduct. William Willis, Jr. produced an acknowledgment condemning his disorderly conduct.
26th da, 4th mo, 1739. Marriage of Edward Vickery and Martha Kidd accomplished. Roger Bragg requested a certificate to Abbington Monthly Meeting. Thomas Thompson appointed clerk in the room of Nathan Smart.
30th da, 5th mo, 1739. Nathaniel Hancock to be taken under the care of the Friends.
27th da, 6th mo, 1739. A certificate granted Thomas Barber and his wife to Center Monthly Meeting. A certificate granted Samuel Barber to Center Monthly Meeting.
A subscription was signed as follows: Abel Nicholson; William Willis; Samuel Abbot; Richard Smith; Abraham Moss; James Daniel; Joseph Gibson; David Davis; Benjamin Acton; Samuel Mason; Jonathan Bradway; Nathan Smart; Benjamin Crips; Samuel Thompson; Ebenezer Miller; Charles Oakford; Roger Huggins; Edward Hawes; William Hunt; Daniel Huddy; Daniel Brandreth; Samuel Fogg; Joseph Clews; Thomas Hodkins; Joseph Thompson; John Bacon; Thomas Thompson; Samuel Hancock, William Thompson; Bartholomew Wiat; William Hall; Clement Hall; John Pledger; Samuel Nicholson; Henry Stubbins; James Hewes; Joshua Thompson; Joseph Stretch; Joseph Eglington; Joseph Steward; Joseph Graves.
27th da, 8th mo, 1739. Marriage of Thomas Hill and Margret Sharp accomplished.
26th da, 9th mo, 1739. William Thompson appointed overseer of the Alloways Creek Monthly Meeting; Joshua Thompson appointed treasurer in the room of Lewis Moore. William Crabb produced an acknowledgment condemning his disorderly conduct.
31st da, 10th mo, 1739. Marriage of Jonathan Bradway and Susanna Oakford accomplished. Marriage of John White and Huldah Huggins accomplished.
31st da, 1st da, 1740. Marriage of Thomas Smith and Sarah Basset accomplished. Marriage of John Barker and Esther Wade

accomplished.
21st da, 2nd mo, 1740. James Allen and wife reported for his disorderly living; disowned.
26th da, 3rd mo, 1740. David Davis appointed overseer of the Pilesgrove Monthly Meeting in the room of Roger Hugins.
30th da, 4th mo, 1740. Hugh Clifton to be treated concerning the way he lives and what he intends to do with his children.
28th da, 2nd mo, 1740. Charles Oakford appointed overseer of Alloways Creek Monthly Meeting in the room of Jonathan Bradway. John Jones reported for his disorderly walking.
28th da, 5th mo, 1740. Hugh Clifton reports that he will put out his children as soon as a paper can be drawn up. Abraham Moss was granted a certificate to Long Island.
23rd da, 7th mo, 1740. Marriage of James Hews and Elizabeth Huggins accomplished. Hugh Clifton reported for neglecting meeting.
A subscription for the New England friend, John Hanson towards his great charge in redeeming his wife and children out of captivity subscribed as follows: Bartholomew Wyatt; Thomas Mason; Abell Nicholson; James Daniell; John Cullier; George Abbot; Richard Hancock; Andrew Thompson; Roger Huggins; William Willis; Joseph Darkin; Nathan Smart; Edward Vickery; Hugh Clifton; Joseph Clows; Stephen Lewis; Joseph Waide; Barthomolew Wyat, Jr.; Josiah White; Abel Nicholson, Jr.; Thomas Daniell; John Goodwin; William Hunt; Samuel Rowland; Richard Woodnut; John Smith; John Denn; Charles Oakford; John Hart; Lewis Morris; William Hughs; David Morris; Moses Barber; Richard Smith.
27th da, 8th mo, 1740. Marriage of William Griscom of Haddonfield and Sarah Davis accomplished. Sarah Griscom granted a certificate. John Jones disowned for his disorderly walking.
29th da, 10th mo, 1740. Marriage of John Nicholson and Sarah Powel accomplished.
30th da, 1st mo, 1741. John Duel appointed overseer for Pilesgrove Monthly Meeting in the room of Edward Hughes, dec'd. Benjamin Acton and Bartholomew Wyat appointed to care for the estate of John White's children and settle it for them.
20th da, 2nd mo, 1741. Marriage of Daniel Huddy and Elizabeth White accomplished. Jonathan Bradway disowned for his disorderly walking. Dobson Wheeler granted a certificate to Kennet & Centre Monthly Meeting. Samuel Mason and Joseph Clowes to go to Hugh Clifton to assist him in his time of need.
25th da, 3rd mo, 1741. David Davis is appointed to stand as an elder. Hugh Clifton to be treated with for his misconduct in his out goings and his affairs.
29th da, 4th mo, 1741. Jonathan Bradway and wife to appeal to the quarterly meeting their disownment.
31st da, 6th mo, 1741. Marriage of Joseph Test and Hannah Darkin accomplished. Samuel Abbott and Joseph Clowes appointed to care for the children's estate of Joseph Darkin, late husband of Hannah Darkin. Jonathan Bradway and his wife, Susannah produced an acknowledgement condemning his disorderly walking.
28th da, 7th mo, 1741. Marriage of Henry Dennis and Grace Bacon accomplished.

26th da, 8th mo, 1741. Ebenezer Miller granted a certificate to North Carolina.
30th da, 9th mo, 1741. Marriage of John Gill and Amie Davis accomplished.
28th da, 10th mo, 1741. Samuel Graves and wife requested a certificate to Center and Kennet Monthly Meeting.
25th da, 11th mo, 1741. Daniel Barber disowned for his disorderly walking.
22nd da, 12th mo, 1741/2. Thomas Davis and Elizabeth Basit declare their intentions of marriage.
24th da, 1st mo, 1742. Thomas Davis and Elizabeth Basit declare their intentions of marriage the 2nd time, but the meeting came to the decision not to allow the marriage as she is the dau. of his first cousin. Marriage of Robert Hartshorn and Hannah Hill accomplished, having their parents' consent. Marriage of Andrew Haze and Elioner Evens accomplished. Marriage of William Daniel and Rebecca Vickary accomplished. A certificate granted for Samuel Graves and his wife.
31st da, 3rd mo, 1742. John Bacon, an elder to sit in the meeting of the ministers and elders.
28th da, 4th mo, 1742. Marriage of Edward James and Rebeckah Satterthwaite accomplished having their parents' consent.
30th da, 6th mo, 1742. A certificate granted to Hannah Hartshorne. A certificate granted to Samuel Abbott. Abraham Moss reported for his disorderly conduct.
27th da, 7th mo, 1742. Bartholomew Wyatt and Benjamin Acton appointed to provide for the estate of Richard Woodnut's children. Benjamin Cullier reported for disorderly practices.
25th da, 8th mo, 1742. Marriage of William Grigg and Anne Woodnut accomplished. Marriage of Henry Stubbins and Mary Vickary accomplished. Marriage of Nathaniel Evens and Elizabeth Ladd accomplished. A certificate granted for Benjamin Lodge to Haddonfield Monthly Meeting to marry. Rebeckah James granted a certificate. Abraham Moss produced an acknowledgement condemning his disorderly practices.
29th da, 9th mo, 1742. Marriage of Preston Carpenter and Hannah Smith accomplished.
31st da, 11th mo, 1742/3. Hannah Carpenter granted a certificate. Edward Vickary spoken to concerning his giving security to Joseph Test.
28th da, 12th mo, 1743. Marriage of Samuel Nicholson and Sarah Denis accomplished.
28th da, 1st mo, 1743. A certificate granted for Anne Gregg.
18th da, 2nd mo, 1743. Marriage of John Smith and Sarah Hill accomplished.
30th da, 3rd mo, 1743. Joshua Garrison requested membership. Ersamus Fetters disowned for his outgoing behavior.
27th da, 4th mo, 1743. Stephen Lewis sent in a paper requesting that Friends help him pay his debt; it was refused.
25th da, 5th mo, 1743. Benjamin Collier disowned for his disorderly behavior.
29th da, 6th mo, 1743. A certificate granted for Joseph Clowes to Burlington Monthly Meeting. A certificate granted for Robert Lodge and his wife to Haddonfield Monthly Meeting.

31st da, 8th mo, 1743. Marriage of George Laraunce and Hannah
Hughes accomplished. Roger Huggens and Jacob Lippincot to
settle the estate of the children of Edward Hughes. Stephen
Lewis ordered to make satisfaction of false charges he made
against Benjamin Acton. Joseph Gibson and Joshua Thompson
appointed overseers of the meeting.
26th da, 10th mo, 1743. Marriage of William Pedrick and Mary
Silver accomplished.
30th da, 11th mo, 1743. John Hendrickson reported for disorderly
conduct.
27th da, 12th mo, 1743. Benjamin Acton disowned for marrying
contrary to discipline.
26th da, 1st mo, 1744. Marriage of James Chambliss and Sarah
Hancock accomplished. Thomas Hancock reported for marrying
contrary to discipline. John Hendrickson disowned for
neglecting meeting and frequenting with the Anabaptists. Isaac
Sharp to be taken under the care of the Friends. John Hunt
reported for marrying contrary to discipline.
30th da, 2nd mo, 1744. Marriage of Richard Moss and Rebekah
Simpson accomplished.
25th da, 4th mo, 1744. Marriage of Othniel Tomlinson and Mary
Marsh accomplished. John Smith made a complaint against John
Thomas concerning an amount of money owed him. James Halliday
reported for his going out in marriage.
30th da, 5th mo, 1744. Thomas Goodwin reported for marrying
contrary to discipline.
27th da, 6th mo, 1744. Isaac Oakford produced an acknowledgement
his disorderly behavior, accepted. Bartholomew Wyatt granted a
certificate to Philadelphia Monthly Meeting.
29th da, 8th mo, 1744. Marriage of Joshua Thompson and Elizabeth
Gibson accomplished. James Chambliss reported for his
disorderly behavior. Thomas Hancock reported for his disorderly
behavior.
26th da, 9th mo, 1744. Marriage of George McNichole and Rebekah
Thompson accomplished. Marriage of William Thompson, Jr. and
Elizabeth Hunt accomplished. Marriage of Thomas Huggins and
Mercy Davis accomplished. Richard Matlack and Prudence Morris
declare their intentions of marriage. Steven Lewis is ordered
to produced an acknowledgement condenming his false accusations
against Hannah Oakford.
31st da, 10th mo, 1744. Samuel Abbott and Joshua Thompson to take
care for Joseph Morris's children's estate. Samuel Atkeson of
Haddonfield Monthly Meeting brought a complaint that Aquilla
Barber owes him money.
28th da, 11th mo, 1745. John Hunt reported for disorderly
behavior. Steven Lewis disowned for refusing to make
satisfaction of charges against Hannah Oakford.
25th da, 12th mo, 1745. Marriage of John Page and Rebekah Bassit
accomplished. James Chambles produced an acknowledgement
condemning his outgoings. Thomas Hancock produced an
acknowledgement condemning his outgoings. Joseph Ware, Jr.
reported for his disorderly behavior.
25th da, 1st mo, 1745. A certificate was granted for Abraham Moss
to Long Island. William Crabb reported for his gaming in his

house.

22nd da, 2nd mo, 1745. Marriage of Aaron Daniel and Rebekah Test accomplished. Marriage of John Barber and Rebekah Norberry accomplished. Rebekah Page granted a certificate.

27th da, 3rd mo, 1745. John Hunt reported for his going out in marriage. Joseph Ware, Jr. reported for his disorderly practices.

24th da, 4th mo, 1745. Thomas Goodwin reported for his outgoings. John Firth reported for his outgoings.

26th da, 6th mo, 1745. James Halliday produced an acknowledgement condemning his going out in marriage. Henry Dennis and wife granted a certificate to Philadelphia Monthly Meeting. Frances Test appointed as overseer for Alloways Creek Monthly Meeting.

30th da, 7th mo, 1745. John Hunt produced an acknowledgement condemning his going out in marriage.

28th da, 8th mo, 1745. Marriage of Joseph Marriott and Mary Smith accomplished, his father's consent in writing.

25th da, 9th mo, 1745. John Firth produced an acknowledgement condemning his outgoing in marriage and other disorders. Thomas Goodwin produced an acknowledgement condemning his going out in marriage. William Goodwin produced an acknowledgement condemning his going out in marriage and other disorders. A committed appointed to find funds to help the family of John Bacon who has sustained a fire.

27th da, 11th mo, 1745. Joseph Ware, Jr. disowned for his misconduct. Daniel Huddy made a complaint against John Chandler for money owed him.

24th da, 12th mo, 1745. Edward Tyley and Margrett Graves declare their intentions of marriage. Daniel Huddy reported that John Chandler had made satisfaction on the money owed. Thomas Thompson appointed to dig graves in the room of Richard Graves.

31st da, 1st mo, 1746. A certificate granted for Mary Marriott. Daniel Huddy and Thomas Thompson to go to Elizabeth Hall to see if her time of 7 years is up or not in the meeting house.

21st da, 2nd mo, 1746. Marriage of Edward Tyley and Rebekah Graves accomplished. [Evidently a mistake in the original records. see 12th mo, 1745.]

28th da, 5th mo, 1746. Marriage of Samuel Pedrick and Tabitha Hews accomplished, his parents' consent in writing. Clemant Hall and William Hancock, Jr. reported for going out in marriage.

25th da, 6th mo, 1746. Marriage of Benjamin Tyler and Naomi Denn accomplished. William Hancock, Jr. disowned for going out in marriage.

27th da, 8th mo, 1746. Marriage of Jacob Spicer and Mary Lippincott accomplished, his parents' consent in writing. Joseph Thompson granted a certificate to Burlington Monthly Meeting to marry. Isaac Barber produced an acknowledgement condemning his going out in marriage.

24th da, 9th mo, 1746. Marriage of Jacob Barber and Rebekah Hunter accomplished. Hugh Clifton sent in a complaint against Thomas Rice and the other two Friends which had his estate in their hands that they would not come to a settlement with him.

29th da, 10th mo, 1746. The Friends appointed to speak to Thomas

Rice concerning the estate of Hugh Clifton have not completed
it due to the death of Benjamin Eaton. Grace Mason granted a
certificate. Joseph Gibson, Jr. granted a certificate to
Haddonfield Monthly Meeting.
26th da, 11th mo, 1746. Marriage of Edward Draper and Mary Barber
accomplished. Joseph Gibson made a complaint on behalf of
Casper Whister that Edward Vickery owed him a sum of money.
23rd da, 12th mo, 1746. William Test to be taken under the care
of the Friends.
20th da, 2nd mo, 1747. Marriage of John Barraclift and Prudence
Bradway accomplished, his father's consent in writing.
25th da, 3rd mo, 1747. Marriage of Thomas Bacon and Elonar Dare
accomplished. Henry Appel and wife granted a certificate to
Philadelphia Monthly Meeting. Samuel Pedrick and his wife
granted a certificate to Wilmington Monthly Meeting. John
Oakford disowned for abusing his father and brothers.
29th da, 4th mo, 1747. John Oakford appeared at the meeting and
requested an appeal which was granted.
28th da, 7th mo, 1747. Marriage of Thomas Redman and Mercy Davis
accomplished. Marriage of Philip Tyler and Mercy Denn
accomplished.
26th da, 8th mo, 1747. Benjamin Bispham granted a certificate to
Burlington Monthly Meeting.
30th da, 9th mo, 1747. Testimony to be prepared for Elonar
Chamblis.
28th da, 10th mo, 1747. Marriage of Abraham Humphres and Hannah
Smart accomplished, with parents' consent in writing. Edward
Vickery to receive some assistance due to his loss by a great
fire.
28th da, 1st mo, 1748. A certificate granted for Hannah Humphres.
Edward Tyley and wife produced an acknowledgement condemning
their disorders. Hannah Wittakars produced a acknowledgement
condemning her disorders. Sarah Goodwin reported for her
disorders.
18th da, 2nd mo, 1748. William Ridley reported for going out in
marriage. Clemant Hall reported for going out in marriage and
other disorders.
27th da, 4th mo, 1748. Clemant Hall disowned for going out in
marriage and other disorders.
25th da, 5th mo, 1748. Testimony to be drawn against Rebekah
Hayns was prepared and read. A certificate was granted for
Abraham Moss and his dau. to Philadelphia Monthly Meeting.
Testimony to be prepared against Charity Smith.
26th da, 7th mo, 1748. Marriage of Benjamin Tindall and Esther
Oakford accomplished.
30th da, 11th mo, 1748. Marriage of Isaac Ellis and Mary Shivers
accomplished.
27th da, 12th mo, 1748. Marriage of Joshua Lord, Jr. and Hannah
Lippincott accomplished.
27th da, 1st mo, 1749. Marriage of William Haynes and Sarah
Lippincott accomplished. John Eglington reported for removing
from the meeting without a certificate.
17th da, 2nd mo, 1749. Aaron Bradway to be taken under the care
of the Friends.

26th da, 4th mo, 1749. A certificate granted for David Bacon to Philadelphia Monthly Meeting. Certificate granted for Hannah Lord and Sarah Haynes. Steven Willis and others reported for their disorders. William Ridley reported for his disorders.

31st da, 5th mo, 1749. John Eglington disowned for neglecting meeting and removing without a certificate. It is agreed that none be buried in the Salem burial grounds except Friends in unity with the meeting.

25th da, 7th mo, 1749. A certificate granted for Aaron Silver to Haddonfield Monthly Meeting to marry. A certificate granted for Isaac Smart to Concord Monthly Meeting to marry. William Ridley produced an acknowledgment condenming his disorders. John Stewart made a complaint against Richard Moss that he is unwilling to comply with his father's will. Steven Willis produced an acknowledgment condemning his disorders.

30th da, 8th mo, 1749. Marriage of Joshua Ballenger and Naomi Dunn accomplished. Marriage of William Chandler and Abigail Mason accomplished, care is to be taken for the estate of Abigail Mason's children by her former husband. Marriage of Joseph Noblit and Lettitia Oakford accomplished. William Oakford reported for his going out in marriage.

27th da, 9th mo, 1749. Mary Dennis granted a certificate to Philadelphia Monthly Meeting. Naomi Ballinger granted a certificate.

25th da, 10th mo, 1749. Richard Moss produced an acknowledgement that he will comply with his father's will.

29th da, 11th mo, 1749/50. James Halliday disowned for marrying contrary to discipline.

26th da, 12th mo, 1749. Edward Tyley requested a certificate to Haddonfield Monthly Meeting.

30th da, 2nd mo, 1750. Elisha Bassitt produced a acknowledgement condemning his outgoings.

28th da, 3rd mo, 1750. Thomas Graves granted a certificate to Philadelphia Monthly Meeting.

30th da, 5th mo, 1750. Overseers of Alloways Creek reported that a proposal of marriage for Samuel Pedrick and Esther Oakford was not to be allowed. The overseers of Cohansie Monthly Meeting reported that a proposal of marriage for Jacob Garrison and Elonar Smith was not to be allowed. [See 7th mo, 1750 minutes.]

27th da, 6th mo, 1750. A certificate granted to Benjamin Hughs to Wilmington Monthly Meeting.

24th da, 7th mo, 1750. Jacob Garrison produced his parents' consent to marriage. Marriage of Jacob Garrison and Elonar Smith accomplished. A certificate granted for Daniel Bassit to Haddonfield Monthly Meeting to marry. Samuel Fogg produced an acknowledgement condeming his disorders.

29th da, 8th mo, 1750. Marriage of Joseph Reeves and Milisant accomplished.

26th da, 9th mo, 1750. Marriage of Andrew Hayse and Esther Chandler accomplished.

31st da, 10th mo, 1750. A certificate granted for Jacob Lippincoat, Jr. to Burlington Monthly Meeting to marry. Samuuel Fogg disowned for his disorders. John Acton, Joseph Acton and

Joseph Test, Jr. reported for marrying contrary to discipline.
25th da, 1st mo, 1751. Marriage of Jospeh Gibson and Jane Platts accomplished. Joseph Test, Jr. produced an acknowledgement condemning his going out in marriage. Jospeh Graves disowned for taking a wife contrary to discipline. Rebeckah Daniels reported for her disorderly practices.
22nd da, 2nd mo, 1751. A complaint was made against Edward Draper on behalf of Benjain Bispham about an amount of money owed.
27th da, 3rd mo, 1751. Marriage of Lewis Owen and Susannah Jones accomplished. John Test produced an acknowledgement condemning his going out in marriage, not sufficient returned to him. A complaint was made against David Jess about an sum of money owed to Jacob Lippincoat, Jr.
24th da, 4th mo, 1751. A complaint was made against Thomas Rice of an amount he owes to Joseph Hughs, a Friend from Wilmington Monthly Meeting.
29th da, 5th mo, 1751. Jonah Platts and Sarah Stretch declare their intentions of marriage. Inquiry to be made into the care of the children of Sarah Stretch. Able Silver produced an acknowledgement condemning his disorders.
26th da, 6th mo, 1751. Nathan Sheppard and Mark Sheppard received under the care of the Friends. Friends appointed to inquire of Jonah Platts' clearness to marry find that he will not comply with his father's will in respect to land left him and his younger brother. Samuel Pedrick disowned by the Wilmington Monthly Meeting. A complaint made against Edward Draper of money he owes Jonathan Zane of Philadelphia.
28th da, 8th mo, 1751. Marriage of Richard Smith and Deborah Brandreth accomplished.
25th da, 9th mo, 1751. Marriage of Richard Wistar and Sarah Wyatt accomplished. Piles Smith reported for going out in marriage and disorderly conduct. William Crabb is reported for having removed to Concord Monthly Meeting without a certificate. Samuel Tyler disowned for marrying contrary to discipline. Thomas Hancock and William Siddon reported for neglecting meeting.
27th da, 1st mo, 1752 [n.s.] formerly called the 11th mo. Isaac Oakford and Benjamin Thompson appointed overseers of the Alloways Creek Monthly Meeting.
24th da, 2nd mo, 1752. Marriage of Richard Vickary and Hannah Chandler accomplished.
30th da, 3rd mo, 1752. John Test produced an acknowledgement condemning his going out in marriage. A certificate was granted for Joseph Hughes to take a wife at Wilmington Monthly Meeting. John Acton disowned for his disorderly conduct.
20th da, 4th mo, 1752. John Test granted a certificate to marry at Philadelphia Monthly Meeting. Certificates granted for Jael Morris and Elizabeth Mason.
25th da, 5th mo, 1752. A certificate requested for Othniel Tomlinson to Concord Monthly Meeting in Chester County, PA.
29th da, 6th mo, 1752. Friends appointed for Othniel Tomlinson find that the circumstances forbid the granting of a certificate until he settles his affairs.
31st da, 8th mo, 1752. A certificate granted for Richard Wistar

to Philadelphia Monthly Meeting.
27th da, 11th mo, 1752. William Crab sent in an acknowledgement condemning his misconduct.
29th da, 1st mo, 1753. Marriage of Samuel Test and Ann Thompson accomplished. Marriage of Jonathan Woodnut and Sarah Mason accomplished. Alloways Creek Monthly Meeting reported that John Winton did not discharge his just debts.
26th da, 2nd mo, 1753. James Bucher reported for marrying contrary to discipline. A certificate granted for Elizabeth Hall, her children and her son, William.
26th da, 3rd mo, 1753. Marriage of Andrew Griscum and Mary Bacon accomplished. Mary Reeves granted a certificate to remove to Philadelphia Monthly Meeting.
30th da, 4th mo, 1753. Othniel Tomlinson and his wife granted a certificate.
30th da, 7th mo, 1753. James Bucher produced an acknowledgement condemning his disorders, accepted. Aaron Daniel disowned for marrying contrary to discipline. Joseph Acton disowned for marrying contrary to discipline.
24th da, 9th mo, 1753. John Dennis appointed overseer of Alloways Creek Monthly Meeting in place of Joseph Ware.
29th da, 10th mo, 1753. Marriage of Andrew Miller and Rachel Basit accomplished, their parents present and giving consent.
25th da, 3rd mo, 1754. Marriage of Richard Wood, Jr. and Hannah Davis accomplished.
22nd da, 4th mo, 1754. David Jess reported for neglecting to discharge his just debts or satisfy his creditors.
24th da, 6th mo, 1754. A certificate granted for Nathan Shepard to Philadelphia Monthly Meeting. Richard Vickary reported for neglecting to discharge his just debts.
29th da, 7th mo, 1754. Marriage of John Nicholson and Hannah Darkin accomplished. The meeting was informed that widdow Martha Vickary was in need because of a fire.
26th da, 8th mo, 1754. Marriage of Joseph Test and Hannah Pledger accomplished. A certificate was granted for Francis Hinkle to Concord Monthly Meeting, Chester County, PA.
28th da, 10th mo, 1754. Pile Smith disowned for marrying contrary to discipline to one of another society.
25th da, 11th mo, 1754. John Shepard received under the care of the Friends.
30th da, 12th mo, 1754. Phillip Tyler disowned for marrying contrary to discipline and by a Presbyterian priest.
27th da, 1st mo, 1755. Marriage of Savery Goslin and Isabel Kidd accomplished.
24th da, 2nd mo, 1755. Marriage of John Chandler and Hannah Anderson accomplished. Thomas Bucher received under the care of the Friends.
21st da, 4th mo, 1755. Marriage of Bradway Caesby and Prudence Sayre accomplished. Marriage of Thomas Brown, Jr. and Mary Reeve accomplished. A committee appointed to enquire whether Joseph Ware's s children have any estate left them by their father and settle before the marriage. John Hopman received under the care of the Friends. Samuel Lippincott appointed overseer in the room of David Davis, deceased at Pilesgrove

Monthly Meeting.
26th da, 5th mo, 1755. Samuel Abbot is chosen clerk of the meeting. Joshua Thompson is appointed as an elder of the Salem Monthly Meeting. John Frith to transcribe births of children into a bound book.
30th da, 6th mo, 1755. Samuel Pedrick produced an acknowledgement condemning the liberties he had taken in the world and going out in marriage.
25th da, 8th mo, 1755. Joseph Test appointed overseer of the Salem Monthly Meeting in the room of Joseph Gibson.
27th da, 10th mo, 1755. Marriage of Thomas Butcher and Rachel Bradway accomplished. David Davis granted a certificate to Burlington Monthly Meeting to marry. Samuel Dennis granted a certificate to Haddonfield Monthly Meeting. Mark Reeve appointed elder of the Greenwich Monthly Meeting.
24th da, 11th mo, 1755. Marriage of Richard Woodnut and Elizabeth Hall accomplished. Testimony against Hannah Jones to be prepared.
23rd da, 2nd mo, 1756. A certificate granted for Samuel Nicholson to Duck Creek and Little Creek Monthly Meeting to marry. Charles Fogg appointed overseer of Salem Monthly Meeting in place of Joseph Test, dec'd. Samuel Stretch disowned for marrying contrary to discipline to his first cousin.
22nd da, 3rd mo, 1756. The meeting determined that the controversy between Samuel Nicholson and the heirs of John Smith, dec'd. shall be settled as follows: Samuel Nicholson is to deliver the deed of property awarded him in a law suit to the heirs of John Smith and is to not build a house on the disputed land.
31st da, 5th mo, 1756. Marriage of Jonathan Potts, son of Thomas Potts and Sarah Clifton, dau. of Hugh Clifton accomplished. Richard Hayns produced a certificate to Haddonfield Monthly Meeting for himself and his family, but returned the certificate as he remains in vincity. David Jess granted a certificate to Burlington Monthly Meeting.
28th da, 6th mo, 1756. Marriage of Daniel Huddy and Rachel Nicholson accomplished. Inquiry made regarding the rights of the children of Rachel Nicholson find it satisfactory. A certificate requested for Richard Hains and children. Inquiry into the affairs of Richard Hains and children found that there are some questionable actions of two of the sons, Anthony and Richard. Satisfaction to be made before a certificate will be granted. John Stewart made a complaint against the executors of Joseph Ware concerning a bond not being paid.
26th da, 7th mo, 1756. Marriage of Daniel Huddy and Rachel Nicholson accomplished. Anthony Hains produced an acknowledgement condemning his going out in marriage and other disorders. William Hancock reported for his disorderly conduct and abusing the overseers at Alloways Creek Monthly Meeting.
7th da, 8th mo, 1756. William Smith, son of Richard Smith of County of Cumberland, disowned for going out in marriage.
27th da, 9th mo, 1756. Marriage of Thomas Hews and Jane Silver accomplished. Caleb Lipincott granted a certificate to Burlington Monthly Meeting to marry. Thomas Rice produced an

acknowledgement that he will pay Henry Dennis the sum of money owed.

29th da, 11th mo, 1756. Marriage of Aaron Bradway and Grace Thompson accomplished. Joseph Reeve appointed overseer for the Greenwich Monthly Meeting.

27th da, 12th mo, 1756. Marriage of John Davis and Elizabeth Graves accomplished. William Hancock disowned for his neglect and refusal to make satisfaction for his disorderly conduct and behavior.

31st da, 1st mo, 1757. Thomas Rice disowned for neglecting to pay his just debts on time. John Chandler reported for neglecting to pay his just debts.

28th da, 2nd mo, 1757. Marriage of William Pedrick and Lidya Faucet accomplished. Marriage of Isaac Thompson and Hannah Hews accomplished.

28th da, 3rd mo, 1757. Marriage of Nethaniel Hall and Mary Brick accomplished. Michael Pedrick produced an acknowledgement condemning his going out in marriage. A complaint made by John Brick against Susannah Hancock of refusing to discharge a debt due him.

25th da, 4th mo, 1757. The rights of the child of Hannah Hews by her former husband were secured. Marriage of Zebede Basset and Rachel Hews accomplished. Marriage of Lewis Owen and Prudence Willis accomplished.

30th da, 5th mo, 1757. Elizabeth Waddington reported for going out in marriage. Elizabeth Test recovered under the care of the Friends.

25th da, 7th mo, 1757. William and John Robert received the care of the Friends. Joseph Zane produced a acknowledgement condemning his misconduct. Ebenezer Miller, Jr. appointed clerk in the room of Samuel Abbott.

29th da, 8th mo, 1757. Marriage of Christopher Smith and Ann Oakford accomplished. William Cattel produced an acknowledgement condemning his past misconduct.

25th da, 9th mo, 1757. Jacob Bell requested a certificate to Philadelphia Monthly Meeting. Richard Vickery disowned for going out in marriage.

31st da, 10th mo, 1757. Marriage of Samuel Test and Lidya Allen accomplished. Jacob Bell granted a certificate to Philadelphia Monthly Meeting. The overseers at the Salem Monthly Meeting reported that Samuel Mason has purchased a Negro.

26th da, 12th mo, 1757. Samuel Bassett produced an acknowledgement condemning his going out in marriage.

30th da, 1st mo, 1758. Marriage of John Mason and Ann Hall accomplished. John Freeth reported for delaying to pay Grace Smith of Philadelphia a sum of money owed. Richard Willits reported for unbecoming behavior.

27th da, 2nd mo, 1758. A certificate was granted for Jane Reynolds to Concord Monthly Meeting.

23rd da, 3rd mo, 1758. Marriage of Jonathan Bradway, Jr. and Elizabeth Stewart accomplished. John Vanculin to be taken under the care of the Friends.

The following Friends are appointed to record births, burials and marriages: Joshua Thompson and Samuel Nicholson for Salem

Monthly Meeting; Samuel Lippincott and John Duell for Piles
Grove Monthly Meeting; John Denn and Frances Test for Alloway
Creek Monthly Meeting and Mark Reeve and Benjamin Tyler for
Greenwich Monthly Meeting.
24th da, 4th mo, 1758. Jonathan Jess granted a certificate to
Burlington Monthly Meeting. John Hall granted a certificate to
Duck's and Little Creek's Monthly Meeting, PA. John Miller
granted a certificate to Haddonfield Monthly Meeting.
29th da, 5th mo, 1758. Marriage of Joseph Kay and Ann Thompson
accomplished, having his parents' consent. Richard Willets
produced an acknowledgement condemning his misconduct. Mark
Reeve and Ebenezer Miller, Jr. ordered to write to Chesterfield
Monthly Meeting regarding Daniel Tilton who refuses to give his
certificate to meeting. Clark Smith disowned for going out in
marriage. Samuel Nicholson, Joshua Thompson and John Stewart to
settle with widow of Thomas Hancock regarding the meeting house
lease.
26th da, 6th mo, 1758. Thomas Goodwin reported for having bought
a negro woman.
31st da, 7th mo, 1758. Marriage of Joseph Wilkinson and Hannah
Walker accomplished. A difference between William Oakford and
Isaac Oakford regarding land conveyed to be settled by the
meeting.
28th da, 8th mo, 1758. Milliscent Reeve appointed as elder of the
women's meeting.
2nd da, 10th mo, 1758. Aaron Evans to be taken under the care of
the Friends.
30th da, 10th mo, 1758. Ephraim Hains granted a certificate to
Haddonfield Monthly Meeting. Daniel Tiltons produced an
acknowledgement condemning his disorderly conduct.
27th da, 11th mo, 1758. Marriage of Joseph Stretch, Jr. and Sarah
Fogg accomplished. Joseph Thompson appointed overseer of
Alloways Creek Monthly Meeting in place of Isaac Oakford.
25th da, 12th mo, 1758. Marriage of Aaron Bradway and Sarah Ralph
accomplished. The rights of the children of Sarah Ralph have
been secured. Greenwich Monthly Meeting informed the meeting
that Jonathan Sheppard requested membership.
29th da, 1st mo, 1759. John Duel requested to be excused from
service of overseer of Pilesgrove Monthly Meeting. A
contribution is to be collected to help Friend Richard Smith
whose house had burned. John Denn appointed an elder for
Alloways Creek Monthly Meeting.
26th da, 2nd mo, 1759. The committee advises John Test to accept
the legacy and interest offered by John Mason which he accepts.
30th da, 4th mo, 1759. Ebenezer Miller, Jr. appointed overseer of
Greenwich Monthly Meeting in the room of Philip Dennis.
28th da, 5th mo, 1759. William Oakford disowned for refusing to
abide with the decision of the meeting regarding his
differences with Isaac Oakford.
25th da, 6th mo, 1759. Thomas Craven received under the care of
the Friends.
27th da, 8th mo, 1759. Marriage of Samuel Swain and Hannah
Pedrick accomplished. Samuel Lippincott appointed elder of
meeting. The committee appointed to collect memorials of the

decease of ministers and elders produced the following list: James Daniel, John Colier, John Denn, Richard Hancock, Mary Wade, William Willis, David Davis, Elizabeth Wiat, Abel Nicholson, John Bacon, Elizabeth Nicholson, Thomas Duel, Rachel Potts.

29th da, 10th mo, 1759. Thomas Bare reported for allowing his son to be bound to a non-member. George Colson reported for allowing his brother to be bound to a non-member. Nethaniel Hancock received under the care of the Friends.

31st da, 12th mo, 1759. Thomas Huchings [Huckins] produced an acknowledgement condemning his disorderly conduct and neglecting meeting.

28th da, 1st mo, 1760. Esther Stretch reported for breaking up the meeting at Alloways Creek Monthly Meeting.

25th da, 2nd mo, 1760. A certificate was granted for John Hart and his wife to Philadelphia Monthly Meeting. William Bradway appointed as overseer for Alloways Creek Monthly Meeting. Samuel Vickery reported as gone as a solider in the military.

31st da, 3rd mo, 1760. Josiah Kay granted a certificate to Haddonfield Monthly Meeting.

28th da, 4th mo, 1760. Jacob Oakford and wife reported for breaking up a meeting at Salem. David Smith, a lad, bound apprentice to a Friend in Philadelphia granted a certificate.

26th da, 5th mo, 1760. Martin Whitmore received under the care of the Friends.

30th da, 6th mo, 1760. A certificate to Philadelphia Monthly Meeting granted for William Bassett and Isaac Bassett, a minor. Alloways Creek Monthly Meeting reported that Sarah Vickery, a poor orphan child was likely to become chargeable because of convulsive fits. The deed for Alloways Creek held by Samuel Abbott who is in a declining state of health and Nethaniel Chamneys who is in a very advanced age to be conveyed to other Friends.

28th da, 7th mo, 1760. John Chandler reported for not paying his just debts.

25th da, 8th mo, 1760. John Brick granted a certificate to marry at Haddonfield Monthly Meeting. Frances Test appointed an elder in the place of John Deen, late deceased, and Sarah Bradway appointed as a woman elder.

6th da, 10th mo, 1760. Samuel Vickery disowned for his disorderly conduct. Henry Woodnutt reported for his going out in marriage. A certificate granted for Anthony Haines to Hopewell Monthly Meeting, VA. Samuel Pedrick requested a certificate to Wilmington Monthly Meeting. Cornelius Clark reported for marrying a non-member.

27th da, 10th mo, 1760. Cornelius Clark informed the meeting that he had made acknowledgement to other Friends meetings.

29th da, 12th mo, 1760. James Holiday reported for neglecting meeting and marking someone else's hogs and being sued by law. Elisha Bassett, Jr. and Samuel Lippincott, Jr. reported for marrying contrary to discipline.

26th da, 1st mo, 1761. Joseph Bacon, an apprentice to a Friend at Bristol, Falls Monthly Meeting, PA. granted a certificate. A certificate was granted for Ruth Brick to Haddonfield Monthly

Meeting.
23rd da, 2nd mo, 1761. John Duel, Jr. granted a certificate to marry at Evesham Monthly Meeting. Elisha Basset produced an acknowledgement condemning his marrying out. Samuel Lippincott, Jr. produced an acknowledgement condemning his going out in marriage to a non-member. Samuel Pedrick, who requested a certificate is deceased.
30th da, 3rd mo, 1761. A certificate was granted for Aaron Oakford to marry at Darbe Monthly Meeting, PA. Daniel Tilton produced an acknowledgement condemning going out in marriage and former misconduct. Rudick Dicker received under the care of the Friends.
26th da, 4th mo, 1761. Jacob Davis granted a certificate to marry at Evesham Monthly Meeting. Samuel Ballinger and wife granted a certificate to Evesham Monthly Meeting. Aaron Oakford granted a certificate to Philadelphia Monthly Meeting. William Graoff to be taken under the care of the Friends. Memorials were produced for Samuel Abbott and Elizabeth Daniel, lately deceased.
25th da, 5th mo, 1761. Elisha Bassett disowned for being concerned with military service. Testimony to be read against James Haliday for breaking up a public meeting. Samuel Lippincott, Jr. produced an acknowledgement condemning his marrying contrary to discipline. Mary Siddon and family granted a certificate to Philadelphia Monthly Meeting. A certificate requested for Thomas Smith, a young lad bound as an apprentice to Joshua Pancoast of Philadelphia Monthly Meeting.
27th da, 7th mo, 1761. Henry Woodnutt reported for marrying contrary to discipline to a non-member.
31st da, 8th mo, 1761. It is reported that the following Friends are qualified in the Commission of the peace and are subject to the administration of oaths: Preston Carpenter, Elisha Bassett and Nethaniel Chamneys. Also reported that Ebenezer Miller is qualified as Commission of the Judge of the Court. Cornelius Clark disowned for marrying contrary to discipline.
5th da, 10th mo, 1761. Nethaniel Chamneys produced an acknowledgement that he will lay down his commission as soon as he could. Preston Carpenter agreed to lay down his commission. Ebenezer Miller informed the meeting that he stood in respect to his commission. Charity Dunlap produced an acknowledgement condemning her misconduct. Mark Reeve granted a certificate to Evesham Monthly Meeting to marry. Henry Woodnutt produced an acknowledgement condemning his misconduct.
26th da, 10th mo, 1761. Elisha Bassett informed the meeting he intended to get clear of his commission as soon as he could. William Bassett granted a certificate to marry at Evesham Monthly Meeting. John Butler, Jr. requested to come under the care of the Friends.
30th da, 11th mo, 1761. A certificate granted for Samuel Bacon, son of Margaret Bacon, an apprentice to David Bacon of Philadelphia.
22nd da, 2nd mo, 1762. Ebenezer Miller, Jr., his wife and child granted a certificate to Haddonfield Monthly Meeting.
5th da, 3rd mo, 1762. Philip Dennis, Jr. appointed to receive the records of clerk, Ebenezer Miller, Jr. A certificate granted

for William Griscom, son of Andrew Griscom, a youth, bound as apprentice to William Griscom at Haddonfield Monthly Meeting.

26th da, 4th mo, 1762. Josiah Miller appointed clerk in the room of Ebenezer Miller, Jr. Richard Booth left a legacy of £6 to the support of the poor at Alloways Creek. Joshua Thompson requested a certificate to West River yearly meeting.

28th da, 6th mo, 1762. John Stewart appointed overseer for Alloways Creek Lower Monthly Meeting in the room of Frances Test, lately deceased.

30th da, 8th mo, 1762. Richard Hains, Jr. reported for moving without a certificate. Anthony Hains reported that he has not produced a certificate since his return. Elisha Bassett and Preston Carpenter reported for having administered oaths.

4th da, 10th mo, 1762. David Davis granted a certificate to Haddonfield Monthly Meeting to marry. Philip Dennis appointed overseer for Greenwich Monthly Meeting in place of Ebenezer Miller, Jr.

29th da, 11th mo, 1762. Joseph Bacon to be taken under the care of the Friends.

4th da, 3rd mo, 1763. John Brick and wife requested a certificate to Evesham Monthly Meeting.

30th da, 5th mo, 1763. John Stewart is appointed elder for Alloways Creek Monthly Meeting; William Bradway appointed as a minister.

25th da, 7th mo, 1763. John Reeve appointed overseer in the room of Joseph Reeve, dec'd.

29th da, 8th mo, 1763. Samuel Ayars received under the care of the Friends. Mary Allen produced an acknowledgment condemning her going out in marriage, accepted. Hannah Silver disowned.

31st da, 10th mo, 1763. The overseers to write to the former meeting John Brick belonged to regarding a matter between he and his sister before granting a certificate. Mary Wyatt [Wiat], formerly White, and Rains White reported for marrying contrary to discipline; disowned. Hannah Stretch to Philadelphia Monthly Meeting. Mary Deviny received under the care of the Friends. Rachel Hilman produced an acknowledgement condemning her going out in marriage.

26th da, 12th mo, 1763. Benjamin Test appointed overseer of Pilesgrove Monthly Meeting in the place of Samuel Lippincott.

30th da, 1st mo, 1764. James and William Pedrick granted certificates to Abbington Monthly Meeting.

27th da, 2nd mo, 1764. Andrew Miller requested a certificate to Haddonfield Monthly Meeting. Margaret Hall appointed clerk of the women's meeting in the place of Hannah Nicholson.

2nd da, 3rd mo, 1764. The affair between John Brick and his sister settled, therefore a certificate granted for John Brick, his wife, Abigail, and son, John, to Haddonfield Monthly Meeting. William Silver produced an acknowledgement condemning his former misconduct. John Thomson reported for having neglected paying his just debts. Isaac Moss, being placed as an apprentice at Philadelphia Monthly Meeting, requested a certificate.

30th da, 4th mo, 1764. A certificate granted for Andrew Miller and his son, Andrew. Isaac Bassett granted a certificate.

Richard Humphreys granted a certificate to go as an apprentice at Philadelphia Monthly Meeting. Sarah Stretch, formerly Smith, reported for going out in marriage. Benjamin Thompson appointed as elder for Salem Preparative Meeting. Samuel Swain, his wife and children requested a certificate to Falls Monthly Meeting, PA. Hester Davies appointed in the place of Mary Lippincott as overseer for the women's meeting at Pilesgrove.
28th da, 5th mo, 1764. Mary Bacon granted a certificate to Philadelphia Monthly Meeting.
25th da, 6th mo, 1764. Richard Bacon, who is put as an apprentice to Philadelphia requested a certificate. A certificate requested for John Denn, who is put as an apprentice to Philadelphia. Samuel Barber reported for going out in marriage and marrying by a hireling minister. Mary Lippincott, dau. of Joseph Lippincott granted a certificate to Burlington Monthly Meeting. Rebecah Coningum received under the care of the Friends. Mary Champlis granted a certificate to Philadelphia Monthly Meeting.
30th da, 7th mo, 1764. Barbara Huggins now Barber and Rachel White now Campbell disowned for going out in marriage. Mary Huggins disowned for going with her dau. to a hireling minister to marry. Samuel Barber reported for going out in marriage. Anthony Hains reported for refusing to produce a certificate from Hopewell Monthly Meeting, VA. Wade Barber reported for having a certificate from Philadelphia Monthly Meeting but refusing to bring it to the meeting.
27th da, 8th mo, 1764. Darius Lippincott reported for having a certificate but failing to produce it to the meeting. Sarah Adams, late Bradway, reported for going out in marriage (being married by a Baptist teacher). Sarah Beard reported for going out in marriage. John Thompson reported for neglecting to pay his just debts. Anthony Hains disowned for refusing to produced a certificate from Hopewell Monthly Meeting, VA. Sarah Vaughan reported as going out in marriage some years ago.
29th da, 10th mo, 1764. Jemima Thompson, formerly Hews, reported for going out in marriage; disowned. Catharine Smart, dau. of Isaac Smart and his wife, Ann granted a certificate to Concord Monthly Meeting. Sarah Bradway appointed in the place of Elizabeth Denn as overseer at women's meeting at Alloways Creek. Elizabeth Kent reported for going out in marriage. Rebecca Ward granted a certificate to Concord Monthly Meeting.
26th da, 11th mo, 1764. Samuel Swain, his wife and two sons, Isaac and Jacob granted a certificate to Falls Monthly Meeting. Elizabeth Oakford now Kent reported for going out in marriage.
31st da, 12th mo, 1764. Thomas Hartley to be taken under the care of the Friends. Samuel Lippincott appointed as a minister. John Lawrence treated for going out in marriage. Joseph Pledger reported for neglecting meeting and going out in marriage contrary to discipline. John Hews reported for going out in marriage contrary to discipline. Jane Evins requested to come under the care of the Friends. Hannah Lawrance reported for going out in marriage.
28th da, 1st mo, 1765. Sarah Vickery, now Bilderback, reported for going out in marriage. Hannah Sharp, now Delany, reported

for going out in marriage to her first cousin; disowned. John Van Culan reported for going out in marriage with his wife's first cousin. Elizabeth Summers reported for going out in marriage.

25th da, 2nd mo, 1765. Grace Sharp received under the care of the Friends. Catharine Townsend granted a certificate to Philadelphia Monthly Meeting.

1st da, 4th mo, 1765. John Lawrence reported for going out in marriage. Henry Woodnutt reported for going out in marriage. Frances Test reported for marrying contrary to discipline. Jacob Davis appointed as an elder at Pilesgrove. Mary Savig reported for going out in marriage.

29th da, 4th mo, 1765. David Allen of Mannenton received under the care of the Friends. Nathan Dunn requested a certificate to Egg Harbour and Cape May Monthly Meeting. Mary Tylar received under the care of the Friends.

27th da, 5th mo, 1765. Mary Savage formerly Chandler reported for going out in marriage; disowned. Wade Barker disowned for disorderly walking. Mark Miller granted a certificate to Haddonfield Monthly Meeting. Elizabeth Duel requested a certificate to Haddonfield Monthly Meeting. Elenor Whitteur and Abigail Davis received under the care of the Friends.

24th da, 6th mo, 1765. Certificate for Isabel Coatsutton accepted. Deborah Thompson, formerly Siddon, reported for going out in marriage; disowned. Mary Cross received under the care of the Friends.

29th da, 7th mo, 1765. A certificate granted for Josiah Burroughs and his wife, Sarah, to Rahway Monthly Meeting. Joseph Smith, son of John Smith, reported for marrying contrary to discipline to his first cousin, Mary Hall, dau. of William Hall. Benjamin Eaton reported for marrying contrary to discipline to a non-member. Philip Rice reported for marrying contrary to discipline to a non-member. Josiah Miller requested to be released from the service of clerk. Esther Stretch reported for going out in marriage. Mary Smith reported for going out in marriage.

2nd da, 8th mo, 1765. Benjamin Eaton produced an acknowledgement condemning his going out in marriage. Stephen Mullford sent a letter requesting assistance towards the maintenance of Rachel Barrot, a poor idiot, an account of her legacy to be prepared. Ebenezer Miller, Jr. recommended as a minister. Hannah Nicholson appointed overseer for the Salem Monthly Meeting in place of Sarah Goodwin.

28th da, 10th mo, 1765. Testimony against Philip Rice to be prepared. Benjamin Eaton produced an acknowledgement condemning going out in marriage, disowned. Aaron Stretch reported by the Alloways Creek Monthly Meeting that he had married contrary to discipline to a non-member.

25th da, 11th mo, 1765. Hannah Dickensen [Dixon], formerly Smith, reported for marrying out; disowned.

30th da, 12th mo, 1765. The care of Rachel Barrot is given to the community. John Barns to be taken under the care of the Friends, but a committee to inquire into his marriage with his first cousin. William Smith reported for going out in marriage

to Sarah Chamneys. Rachel Patterson [Peterson], formerly
Vickery, reported for going out in marriage; disowned.
24th da, 2nd mo, 1766. Pilesgrove Monthly Meeting reported that
George Lawrence neglected meeting. Ann Tyler produced an
acknowledgement condemning her going out in marriage.
3rd da, 3rd mo, 1766. Meeting to inquire of Mannington Twp. for a
certificate for Rachel Barrott.
28th da, 4th mo, 1766. Sarah Thompson, now Hancock, and Sarah
Nicholson, now Smith, reported for going out in marriage; both
disowned.
26th da, 5th mo, 1766. John Barns produced an acknowledgement
condemning his marrying his first cousin.
30th da, 6th mo, 1766. Bartholomew Wyatt, Jr. produced an
acknowledgement of condemnation. A certificate granted to Sarah
Clark to Kennet Monthly Meeting. Elizabeth Davis produced an
acknowledgement condemning her going out in marriage.
28th da, 7th mo, 1766. Renier Holingshead granted a certificate
to Haddonfield Monthly Meeting.
27th da, 10th mo, 1766. A certificate was produced for Rachel
Barrott and placed in the care of Elisha Bassett, one of the
magistrates of Pilesgrove Twp. William Willis reported for
neglecting meeting and refusing to pay an amount of money due
to Thomas Copperthwaite. Peter Stretch reported for going out
in marriage to a non-member.
24th da, 11th mo, 1766. William Goodwin proposed as overseer at
Salem in place of Joshua Thompson. Aaron Allen reported for
neglecting meeting, disorderly life and conversation. Mary
McNichols, now McFarlin, reported for going out in marriage to
a non-member; disowned.
29th da, 12th mo, 1766. John Thompson, son of Joshua Thompson, an
apprentice to William Dawson, granted a certificate to
Philadelphia Monthly Meeting. Joshua Lippincott granted a
certificate to Haddonfield Monthly Meeting. John Evans received
under the care of the Friends. Sarah Bowen reported for going
out in marriage.
26th da, 1st mo, 1767. John Mason and his dau. Sarah granted a
certificate to Concord Monthly Meeting, PA.
23rd da, 2nd mo, 1767. Mark Reeve appointed as a minister.
Richard Wood appointed as an elder for Greenwich Monthly
Meeting. Rebeckah Mills, formerly Daniel, and Temperance Tyler,
now Watson, reported for going out in marriage and other
disorders; disowned. Mary Cade, formerly Barber, reported for
going out in marriage and other disorders; disowned. Eloner
Stretch received under the care of the Friends. A memorial was
read for Hannah Brick, dau. of John and Ann Brick.
30th da, 3rd mo, 1767. Joseph Gibson, a minor, granted a
certificate to Haddonfield Monthly Meeting.
27th da, 4th mo, 1767. Joseph Kay granted a certificate for
himself, wife and three children: Rebeckah, John and Isaac and
Aaron Thompson, his wife's brother, to Haddonfield Monthly
Meeting. Joseph Gibson, the elder, granted a certificate to
Haddonfield Monthly Meeting. Lidia Shute reported for going out
in marriage.
25th da, 5th mo, 1767. David Davis is recommended as an elder at

Pilesgrove Monthly Meeting. Lydia Shute, formerly Barber, reported for going out in marriage. Susannah King requested a certificate to Philadelphia Monthly Meeting. Elizabeth Hains appointed elder at Pilesgrove Monthly Meeting. Sarah Bowen, formerly Daniel, reported for going out in marriage with a non-member; disowned.

27th da, 7th mo, 1767. Jonathan Stretch appointed overseer at Alloways Creek Preparative Meeting in the place of William Bradway. Anna Pedrick, formerly Dawson, reported for going out in marriage; disowned.

31st da, 8th mo, 1767. A certificate was granted for Joshua Thompson. Sarah Coperthwaite, late Meed, reported for going out in marriage and other disorders.

5th da, 10th mo, 1767. An account was given to the meeting the upkeep of Rachel Barrott and one from John Barber for the upkeep of Sarah Vickery. It was agreed upon that Negroes both free and bound should have the liberty to attend a meeting. A certificate was produced for Hannah Stretch, she to be visited to inquire as to the delay of bringing the certificate to meeting. A testimony against Lettisha Hogbeen(?) was presented; disowned.

30th da, 11th mo, 1767. Isaac Barber agreed to keep Rachel Barrott for one year. Martha Crips reported for neglecting meeting and other disorders.

28th da, 12th mo, 1767. Hannah Stretch reported for her neglecting meeting and other disorders; disowned.

29th da, 2nd mo, 1768. A complaint was produced that the children of Stephen Willis were concerned about the estate of their father now in the hands of the father-in-law. William Willis, Jr. reported for going out in marriage to a non-member. Zacheus Dunn requested a certificate to visit friends at Cape May Monthly Meeting.

29th da, 3rd mo, 1768. Whitton Cripps reported for horse racing, gaming and other indecent and unbecoming practices; disowned. Samuel Wright granted a certificate. William Oakford produced an acknowledgement condemning his former misconduct.

4th da, 4th mo, 1768. Ann Dawson disowned for her misconduct.

30th da, 5th mo, 1768. Benjamin Thompson appointed to sign papers of disownment. Greenwich Preparative meeting proposed John Bacon as an overseer for Greenwich Monthly Meeting in the place of Philip Dennis, dec'd. Ruth Allen reported for going out in marriage. Mary Crips reported for disorderly conduct and neglecting meeting.

27th da, 6th mo, 1768. Sarah Adams produced an acknowledgement condemning her going out in marriage.

25th da, 7th mo, 1768. Joseph Thompson moved from the Alloways Creek Monthly Meeting, requested to be released as overseer. Sarah Pedrick requested a certificate to Haddonfield Monthly Meeting.

29th da, 8th mo, 1768. Jonathan Woodnutt granted a certificate to Wilmington Monthly Meeting. William Brown reported for fraudulent dealings in his debts. John Reeve proposed as elder for Greenwich Monthly Meeting.

3rd da, 10th mo, 1768. Mary Page, now Wallace, reported for going out in marriage; disowned. Hannah Allen, formerly Howard, reported for going out in marriage; disowned. Lidya Dawson granted a certificate to the Falls Monthly Meeting, Bucks County, PA. Frances Test produced an acknowledgement condemning his misconduct in marrying contrary to discipline.

31st da, 10th mo, 1768. Jacob Evans, his wife, Mary and children: Susanah, Milicent, Levi, Nathaniel, Amy and David, to be taken under the care of the Friends. Ruth Allen, formerly Nicholson, treated for her going out in marriage; disowned. Alloways Creek Monthly Meeting reported Nathan Stretch for going out in marriage. Pilesgrove Monthly Meeting reported Thomas Burden was likely to fall short of discharging his debts.

28th da, 11th mo, 1768. Aaron Evans received under the care of the Friends. Benjamin Test reported for unbecoming behavior. Rebeckah Evans, formerly Stretch, reported for her out going in marriage, disowned. Hannah Elliott, late Carpenter, reported for going out in marriage. Rebeckah Evans reported for going out in marriage; disowned.

26th da, 12th mo, 1768. Martha Divine received under the care of the Friends. Amy Baker reported for going out in marriage; disowned.

30th da, 1st mo, 1769. John Cowperthwaite granted a certificate to Woodbridge Monthly Meeting. Jene Booth granted a certificate to Philadelphia Monthly Meeting.

27th da, 2nd mo, 1769. Isaac Woodward [Ware] and Rebeckah, his wife granted a certificate to Haddonfield Monthly Meeting. Ezekiel Siddon reported for disorderly conduct. Mary Humphries granted a certificate to Abington Monthly Meeting.

4th da, 4th mo, 1769. Thomas Copperthwaite reported for going out in marriage to a non-member. Hannah Elliot produced an acknowledgement condemning her going out in marriage.

24th da, 5th mo, 1769. Mary Clark produced an acknowledgement condemning her going out in marriage. Rachal Jenings received under the care of the Friends. Mary Allen received under the care of the Friends. Priscilla Shepperd appointed as overseer in the room of Lucy Dennis for Greenwich Monthly Meeting.

28th da, 8th mo, 1769. Thomas Goodwin requested a certificate to marry at Great Eggharbor Monthly Meeting. Hannah Bucher received under the care of the Friends.

1st da, 10th mo, 1769. Thomas Cowperthwaite disowned for his misconduct. Elisha Bassett and Robert Howart reported for continuing to administer oaths.

27th da, 11th mo, 1769. Meeting refused Henry Lummas to come under the care of Friends. Elisha Basset informed the meeting that he would not administer the oath and would lay down his commission. Robert Howard signified he would be more cautious and would lay down his commission. Benjamin Lippincott appointed overseer for Pilesgrove Monthly Meeting.

25th da, 12th mo, 1769. Testimony against John Cripps for going out in marriage, neglecting meeting, horse racing and other disorders, was approved. Charles Elliott to be taken under the care of the Friends. John Gamster and Dennis Daley to be taken under the care of the Friends. Hannah Couldon, now Kirby, reported for going out in marriage. Caleb Squibb requested a

certificate to Chester Monthly Meeting.
29th da, 1st mo, 1770. William Brown reported for defraud in not giving up his affects. Samuel Winton reported for going out in marriage.
26th da, 2nd mo, 1770. Rhody Silver received under the care of the Friends.
2nd da, 4th mo, 1770. Caleb Squibb granted a certificate to Chester Monthly Meeting, PA. John Lanning received under the care of the Friends. Mary Rockhill received under the care of the Friends.
30th da, 4th mo, 1770. Benjamin Tyler appointed as elder. Thomas Graves requested a certificate to Philadelphia Monthly Meeting. Mary Swain received under the care of the Friends.
28th da, 5th mo, 1770. A certificate granted for Joseph Thompson, son of Joshua Thompson, who is placed as an apprentice to Philadelphia Monthly Meeting. Edward Hall and wife, Hester, late Willis, reported for going out in marriage. John Jones disowned for leaving his master, to whom he was put as apprentice, in a disreputable manner. Elizabeth Ballenger granted a certificate to Evesham Monthly Meeting.
25th da, 6th mo, 1770. The Friends refused Charles Bacon membership. Betty Woodnut granted a certificate for herself and her three children: Mary and Betty Wilson and Hannah Woodnut, to Wilmington Monthly Meeting.
30th da, 7th mo, 1770. Patience Huggins, now Lowderback, reported for going out in marriage; disowned. Sarah White, now Armbruster, reported for marrying out; disowned. Thomas Thompson, son of Thomas Thompson, reported for going out in marriage. Sibil Sleeper returned to Burlington Monthly Meeting with an endorsement on her certificate.
27th da, 8th mo, 1770. James Tyler produced an acknowledgement condemning his unbecoming behavior, he is to bring the names and births of his children for recording.
1st da, 10th mo, 1770. William Cooper granted a certificate for himself, wife and two children, William and Magdalene, to Philadelphia Monthly Meeting. James Hews, Jr. and his wife, Sarah, late Page, reported for going out in marriage; disowned. Mary Oakford granted a certificate to Derby Monthly Meeting. Elizabeth Somers produced an acknowledgement condemning her going out in marriage.
26th da, 11th mo, 1770. Greenwich Monthly Meeting reported that Benjamin Reeve appointed in the place of John Reeve as overseer. Joshua Thompson appointed treasurer in the place of Thomas Goodwin, who at this time stands under the censure of the meeting.
31st da, 12th mo, 1770. Testimony against Grace Lummis produced. Elizabeth Grinsley, and her children, Hepzibah, Sarah and Mary Matson, by her former husband Mathias Matson, received under the care of the Friends.
28th da, 1st mo, 1771. William Cripps reported for his misconduct. Mary Humphries granted a certificate to Duck Creek Monthly Meeting. Naomy Lippincott, late Tyley, reported for going out in marriage; disowned.
25th da, 2nd mo, 1771. An endorsement to be made for Samuel

Ballinger and his wife's certificate to Evesham Monthly
Meeting. Rebecca Fogg received under the care of the Friends.
2nd da, 4th mo, 1771. The charge of fraud against William Brown
against his creditors was unfounded, therefore a certificate to
Philadelphia granted for him, his wife and children.
29th da, 4th mo, 1771. Elisha Davis, a young man, son of Thomas
Davis, received under the care of the Friends. Exeter Monthly
Meeting appointed Abel Thompson as a minister. Pilesgrove
proposed Hester Davis as an elder at that meeting. Sarah Barber
disowned for her disorderly conduct. Esther Davis appointed as
elder for Pilesgrove Monthly Meeting. Rachal Spark, late
Sommers, reported for going out in marriage; disowned.
27th da, 5th mo, 1771. James Mason, Rebecca, his wife and
children: Elizabeth, Reeve and Letitia Miller, received under
the care of the Friends. Rebecca Diviny produced an
acknowledgement condemning her going out in marriage.
24th da, 6th mo, 1771. James Mason and wife produced the ages of
their children to the meeting. Anthony Sharp, a young lad, who
is an apprentice requested a certificate to Philadelphia
Monthly Meeting. Alloways Creek Monthly Meeting reported that
Richard Smith and his cousin, John Smith, requested help to
settle the differences concerning land. Eunice Silver requested
to come under the care of the Friends.
29th da, 7th mo, 1771. Preston Carpenter granted a certificate
for his son, Thomas Carpenter, who is placed as an apprentice
to a merchant at Philadelphia Monthly Meeting. Neomy
Lippincott, formerly Tyler, reported for going out in marriage.
26th da, 8th mo, 1771. A memorial was produced for Mary
Lippincott, dec'd., a elder at the Pilesgrove Monthly Meeting.
Dennis Daly granted a certificate to go to Ireland to see his
father.
30th da, 9th mo, 1771. Susannah Mason, late Goodwin, granted a
certificate to Concord Monthly Meeting.
28th da, 10th mo, 1771. Mary Todd, formerly Sharp, reported for
going out in marriage; disowned. Thomas Graves reported for
going away in a disorderly manner and neglecting to satisfy his
creditors.
30th da, 12th mo, 1771. William Smith Dunham recieved under the
care of the Friends. Isaac Barber produced an account for the
keeping of Rachel Barrott.
27th da, 1st mo, 1772. Mary Butcher produced an acknowledgement
condemning her former misconduct. Judah Townsend reported for
going out in marriage. Rachel Bassett granted a certificate for
herself and her dau. Amy to Philadelphia Monthly Meeting.
24th da, 2nd mo, 1772. Joseph Tindall reported for going out in
marriage. A certificate granted for David Davis, his wife, Mary
and their four children: Samuel Coles, Joseph, Mary and Jacob
to Haddonfield Monthly Meeting. Rebekah Barnes, wife of John
Barnes, produced an acknowledgement condemning her going out in
marriage.
30th da, 3rd mo, 1772. Anthony Sharp granted a certificate to
Philadelphia Monthly Meeting. Judah Thompson produced an
acknowledgement condemning his going out in marriage.
27th da, 4th mo, 1772. Thomas Smith and his wife, Hannah,

reported for going out in marriage; disowned. Ralph Allen requested to come under the care of the Friends. Richard Hains, Jr. reported for neglecting meeting, going away and leaving his family and his creditors in a disreputable condition. Thomas Draper, a young man, reported for having gone away in debt and without a certificate. Aaron Dawson reported for going out in marriage. Hannnah Jesop granted a certificate to Haddonfield Monthly Meeting.

25th da, 5th mo, 1772. Sarah David [Davis] received under the care of the Friends.

29th da, 6th mo, 1772. Nathan Bradway reported for having gone out in marriage. Lidia Dawson granted a certificate to Falls Monthly Meeting.

31st da, 8th mo, 1772. John Stephens reported for neglecting meeting. Samuel Bassett's children, Davis and Ann received under the care of the Friends. Anna Fogg received under the care of the Friends. Richard Dawson and wife, Lidia requested a certificate to Haddonfield Monthly Meeting.

26th da, 10th mo, 1772. Mary Acton, formerly Oakford, reported for having gone out in marriage. Elizabeth Fogg received under the care of the Friends. Letitia Miller appointed as overseer for the Salem Preparative Meeting. Mary Acton, late Oackford, reported for going out in marriage; disowned.

30th da, 11th mo, 1772. Mary Philpott, formerly Evans, reported for going out in marriage; disowned.

25th da, 1st mo, 1773. Jane Grantland, formerly Booth, reported for having gone out in marriage. Richard Humphreys reported for having removed from the meeting and gone out in marriage. Prudence Dennis appointed overseer for Greenwich Monthly Meeting.

22nd da, 2nd mo, 1773. Robert Howard reported for administering the oath, he said he would lay it down as soon as he could. Preston Carpenter reported for administering the oath, he agreed he would do it no further. John Nicholson reported for administering the oath, he said he had only done it once and did not intend to do it again. Pilesgrove Preparative Meeting proposed Daniel Bassett as an elder. An account given from Pilesgrove for doctoring and nursing Jesse Winton. Hannah Kerby produced an acknowledgement condemning her going out in marriage.

1st da, 4th mo, 1773. Richard Kirby and his children: Jonathan, Amos and Samuel, received under the care of the friends. Elizabeth Mason, late Ballenger, granted a certificate to Evesham Monthly Meeting. Sarah Stuart, wife of Samuel Stuart, and her children received under the care of the Friends.

26th da, 4th mo, 1773. Robert Howard produced an acknowledgement of his intention to lay down his commission as magistrate. Paul Sanders and family granted a certificate to Duck Creek Monthly Meeting. Salem Preparative Meeting proposed Josiah Miller as overseer for that meeting.

31st da, 5th mo, 1773. Elisha Bassett reported that he had resigned as a magistrate in any new matter. Thomas Wharton of Philadelphia proposed the paying the annual sum of £10 for the support of Rachel Barrot and that she be placed with her half

sister, the wife of Richard Kirby.
28th da, 6th mo, 1773. Rebecca Page, Jr. granted a certificate to Wilmington Monthly Meeting. Sarah Pierpoint received under the care of the Friends.
30th da, 8th mo, 1773. Testimonies for deceased friends: Elizabeth Test, Zacchas Dunn, and his wife Deborah, were read.
4th da, 10th mo, 1773. Samuel Fogg, Jr. received under the care of the friends. Testimony against Robert Howard regarding his remaining a magistrate read and approved.
25th da, 10th mo, 1773. Leatitia Craig, formerly Noblit, reported for going out in marriage to a non-member. John Lanning reported for marrying contrary to discipline to a non-member. Lewis Reaford, a young man, produced a certificate from Grange, Kingdom of Ireland.
29th da, 11th mo, 1773. Richard Mead reported for marrying contrary to discipline.
27th da, 12th mo, 1773. John Barnes appointed in the place of Jacob Davis as overseer.
31st da, 1st mo, 1774. Pilesgrove Monthly Meeting requested help in paying the expenses for Abner Test's stay in the hospital at Philadelphia. Joshua Stretch granted a certificate to Haddonfield Monthly Meeting.
28th da, 2nd mo, 1774. Jesse Bacon and Sarah, late Pierpoint, reported for going out in marriage; disowned.
4th da, 4th mo, 1774. William Folwell, son of Thomas Folwell, an apprentice to Philadelphia Monthly Meeting granted a certificate. Moses Dawson reported for going out in marriage. Mary Elkenton granted a certificate to Haddonfield Monthly Meeting for herself and her children: Thomas, Esther, Joshua, Job, John, Mary, Joseph and Gertrude. Mary Draper granted a certificate to Evesham Monthly Meeting.
25th da, 4th mo, 1774. Alloways Creek Monthly Meeting reported that Richard Smith, Sr. had purchased a negro man.
30th da, 5th mo, 1774. Richard Humphreys produced an acknowledgement condemning his misconduct in marrying a non-member. Rachel Wynkoop, late Sharp, reported for marrying out; disowned.
25th da, 7th mo, 1774. Joseph Cole reported for disorderly conduct. Lidya Dawson, now Cowgill, reported for her going out in marriage; disowned. Isaac Oakford reported for marrying contrary to discipline. Mary Silver received under the care of the Friends. Martah Bacon, late Divine, reported for going out in marriage. Prudence Smith, late Barrowcliff, reported for going out in marriage.
29th da, 8th mo, 1774. Philadelphia Monthly Meeting appointed Samuel Nicholson, William Goodwin and Joseph Brick to take the proper care of Rachel Bassett's rights which are unjustly detained from her by her brother-in-law. Thomas Carpenter reported for going out in marriage.
31st da, 10th mo, 1774. Rebeckah Hancock, formerly Ware, reported for going out in marriage. James Stewart granted a certificate to marry at Haddonfield Monthly Meeting. Samuel Sharp, a youth who is placed as an apprentice to Burlington Monthly Meeting, granted a certificate.

28th da, 11th mo, 1774. Thomas Carpenter reported for going out in marriage. Lidia Cogle, late Dawson, reported for going out in marriage; disowned. Anna Morrison, late Noblet, reported for going out in marriage; disowned. Rebeckah Hancock, late Ware, reported for going out in marriage; disowned.
26th da, 12th mo, 1774. Benjamin Lippincott requested to be released from the station of overseer. Zadock Street, a young man, received under the care of the friends. A committee to be appointed to inquire into the Negroes kept in bondage beyond the limit of time prescribed by law. Jane Hughs granted a certificate to Falls Monthly Meeting, PA.
30th da, 1st mo, 1775. Walpole Gregory and wife, Sarah, granted a certificate to Northern District Philadelphia Monthly Meeting. Eloner Davis received under the care of the Friends. Ann Ridway, dau. of Mary Ridgway, granted a certificate to Burlington Monthly Meeting.
27th da, 2nd mo, 1775. A memorial read for Mary Thompson, wife of Joseph Thompson, died 21st da, 1st mo, 1775.
24th da, 4th mo, 1775. William Abbott, Leatitia Miller and Rebeckah Abbott nominated for elders at Salem Monthly Meeting. Sarah Roan, formerly Hall, reported for going out in marriage to a non-member; disowned. Edward Siddons reported for going out in marriage with a non-member. Greenwich Monthly Meeting appointed Benjamin Reeve as a minister.
29th da, 5th mo, 1775. Sarah Booth, now Drake, reported for going out in marriage; disowned. Sarah Matlack granted a certificate to remove with her husband to Evesham Monthly Meeting.
31st da, 7th mo, 1775. Judiah Allen and his children received under the care of the Friends. Anthony Sharp and John Stephens, both from Pilesgrove Monthly Meeting, reported for bearing arms and being concerned in learning the art of war. Ruth Barracliff, now Shinto, reported for going out in marriage; disowned. Mary Thompson received under the care of the Friends. Rachel Zanes granted a certificate to Haddonfield Monthly Meeting.
28th da, 8th mo, 1775. John Page, a youth, being placed as an apprentice, granted a certificate to Philadelphia. Mary Butcher, wife of Job Butcher, received under the care of the Friends.
30th da, 10th mo, 1775. Jonathan Kinsey treated for neglecting of meeting, joining in military preparations and bearing arms.
25th da, 12th mo, 1775. Thomas Thompson, son of Abraham Thompson received under the care of the Friends. Richard Hains, Jr., a young man, reported for enlisting in the military and going away in service, disowned. Edward Bradway appointed in the place of John Stewart as overseer at Lower Alloways Creek Monthly Meeting.
29th da, 1st mo, 1776. Sarah Ware, formerly Adams, reported for going out in marriage; disowned. Bershebe Ballenger granted a certificate to Evesham Monthly Meeting. Sarah Ballenger granted a certificate to Evesham Monthly Meeting.
26th da, 2nd mo, 1776. Testimony against Hugh Haines and his wife, Naomi for marrying contrary to discipline to a first cousin; disowned. Daniel Bassett, Jr. granted a certificate to

Eggharbour and Cape May Monthly Meeting in order to marry. John
Jennings produced a certificate from Warrington Monthly
Meeting, PA.
1st da, 3rd mo, 1776. Deborah Bassett appointed in the place of
Hester Davis as overseer for Pilesgrove.
29th da, 4th mo, 1776. Greenwich Monthly Meeting nominate
Elizabeth Reeve and Priscilla Sheppard as elders. Hannah Dennis
appointed in the place of Prudance Dennis as overseer for
Greenwich Monthly Meeting.
"A list of overseers belonging to Salem Monthly Meeting such as
were under the appointment 5th mo, 1776 with the names of such
as were appointed to this present year 1784 1st mo, the time of
revising and transcribing the minutes.
For Salem: Charles Fogg, released; William Goodwin, released and
since continued; Josiah Miller, released; Andrew Thompson,
dec'd.; David Allen, John Redman.
For Pilesgrove: Benjamin Test, released; John Barns; Joseph
Lippincott, dec'd.; John Redman, released; Samuel Ogden.
For Alloways Creek: Jonathan Stretch, released; Edward Bradway,
Aaron Evans, released; Joshua Thompson, Jr.
For Greenwich: John Bacon, Benjamin Reeves, released; William
Miller, released; Richard Wood."
27th da, 5th mo, 1776. Charles Fogg requested to be released as
overseer of Salem Monthly Meeting. Joseph Lippincott appointed
in place of Benjamin Test as overseer of Pilesgrove Monthly
Meeting. Thomas Followay, and wife, Elizabeth and children:
Elizabeth, Samuel, Nathan, John and Thomas granted a
certificate to Haddonfield Monthly Meeting. Phebe Bassett and
her two children, Mary and Abigail, granted a certificate to
Evesham Monthly Meeting.
24th da, 6th mo, 1776. Mary Townsend, now Adams, reported for
going out in marriage; disowned. Nathan Bradway produced an
acknowledgement condemning his misconduct in going out in
marriage. Jonathan Kinsey disowned for neglecting meeting and
being concerned in military ways. Mary Hancock, late Goodwin,
reported for going out in marriage. Ruth Miller appointed as
overseer in the place of Rebecca Abbott for Salem Preparative
Meeting.
29th da, 7th mo, 1776. Hill Smith and wife, Ann, reported for
going out in marriage. Thomas Hancock reported for going out in
marriage. William Miller appointed in the place of Benjamin
Reeve as overseer at Greenwich.
26th da, 8th mo, 1776. John Roberts and William Oakford to be
treated with regarding the keeping of slaves. Mary Lewis
requested a certificate to Evesham to live with her husband.
Jonathan Hains disowned for enlisting in the military and going
away in the army. Joel Daniel disowned for enlisting in the
military and going away in the army. Jacob Barber disowned for
enlisting in the military and going away in the army.
30th da, 9th mo, 1776. Thomas Hancock and Mary, his wife,
reported for going out in marriage. Peter Amler and Elizabeth,
his wife, and two daus., Lidya and Sarah, received under the
care of the Friends.
28th da, 10th mo, 1776. Isaac Pedrick requested a certificate to

marry at Little Eggharbour Monthly Meeting. Joshua Eaton disowned for enlisting in the military and going away in the army. Abraham Sanders disowned for enlisting in the military and going away in the army.

25th da, 11th mo, 1776. Mary Gilbert, now Wistar, granted a certificate to Philadelphia Monthly Meeting.

27th da, 1st mo, 1777. Mary White reported for neglecting meeting.

24th da, 2nd mo, 1777. Prudence Ireland, formerly Bacon, reported for going out in marriage; disowned.

31st da, 3rd mo, 1777. John Redman appointed overseer at Pilesgrove Monthly Meeting.

28th da, 4th mo, 1777. Rebekah Mills produced an acknowledgement condemning her going out in marriage to a non-member. An account was brought for money put out for the care of Hannah Chandler.

26th da, 5th mo, 1777. Elijah Cattell disowned for enlisting in the military and going away in the army. Tamson [Thomason] Shourds granted a certificate for herself, her two children, Christopher and Mary, to Chesterfield Monthly Meeting. Rebeckah McPeak formerly Huckings reported for going out in marriage; disowned. James Daniel, dec'd. has left an legacy of land and money to the meeting.

6th da, 10th mo, 1777. A memorial was read for James Daniel, an ancient and worthy Friend.

25th da, 8th mo, 1777. Jonathan Waddington received under the care of the friends. Eleanor Ashton formerly Garrison reported for going out in marriage. Edward Bradway nominated as elder for Alloways Creek Monthly Meeting, Aaron Evans nominated as overseer in the place of Jonathan Stretch. Mary Stretch received under the care of the Friends.

27th da, 10th mo, 1777. Ann Hains granted a certificate to Haddonfield Monthly Meeting. Zachery Jess and wife Rebekah requested a certificate to Evesham Monthly Meeting. Isabel Goslin reported for neglecting meeting and other disorders. Sarah Willis reported for neglecting meeting.

24th da, 11th mo, 1777. Charles Fogg reported for selling two of his negro girls for such a number of years and under such circumstances as renders their case little better than slaves. Zacheriah Jess and Rachel, his wife, granted a certificate to Evesham Monthly Meeting.

29th da, 12th mo, 1777. Sarah Willis reported for neglecting meeting. Isabel Gosling reported for neglecting meeting.

26th da, 1st mo, 1778. Charles Fogg informed the meeting that one of the negro girls had been released. Abraham Miller, a young man, received into the care of the friends. Samuel Gosling reported for enlisting in the military and going away in the army; disowned. Jacob Summers granted a certificate to Eggharbour Monthly Meeting to marry.

23rd da, 2nd mo, 1778. Aaron Silvers produced an acknowledgement condemning his former conduct.

30th da, 3rd mo, 1778. Ephraim Hains, Jr. for enlisting in the military as a substitute; disowned.

A testimony of Margaret Hall, clerk, is as follows: "As this book

is scrabled and some leaves torn out in the first of the Record
and many in the last of the book, and three meetings minutes
intirely gone in this place, I must inform all who may have the
looking over this book, that it was done by the British Troops
when at Salem, in the 3rd mo, 1778 and under the command of
Mawhood, they got into the meeting house and broke open a chest
where this book was and abused it as may be seen... I could not
be easy without leaving this testimony least it should be
thought to be done through the carelessness of the clerk."

27th da, 4th mo, 1778. Mary Tonkins [Thompkins] granted a
certificate to Haddonfield Monthly Meeting. A certificate was
granted for Phebe Brown, and her two daus., Mary and Abigail
Bassett, to remove with her husband to Haddonfield Monthly
Meeting. Bartholomew Wyatt appointed clerk in the place of
Ebenezer Miller. Mary Evens received under the care of the
Friends.

25th da, 5th mo, 1778. Richard Ware and children received under
the care of the Friends. John Daniel disowned for removing to
the city of Philadelphia without a certificate. Elizabeth Denn,
Jr. granted a certificate to Philadelphia Monthly Meeting.
William Goodwin, an overseer of Salem, requested to be
released, Andrew Thompson to take his place.

27th da, 7th mo, 1778. Mary Swain granted a certificate to
Evesham Monthly Meeting. Sarah Jones, formerly Hall, reported
for going out in marriage.

31st da, 8th mo, 1778. Sarah Ware produced an acknowledgement
condemning her misconduct. Mary Bassett produced an
acknowledgement condemning her going out in marriage, she
requested that her children: Hannah, Joseph and David, be taken
under the care of the Friends. Sarah Waddington, formerly
Bradway, reported for going out in marriage; disowned. Sarah
Jones late Hall reported for going out in marriage; disowned.

5th da, 10th mo, 1788. Elizabeth Paul granted a certificate to
Haddonfield for herself and her three children: Richard,
Elizabeth and Hannah Butler. Sarah Ware's acknowledgement
accepted, she is received back into membership.

30th da, 11th mo, 1778. Francis Dawson reported for his
misconduct. Sarah Bassett received under the care of the
Friends. Isaac Stroud requested a certificate for himself and
his family to Wilmington Monthly Meeting. A certificate was
granted for David Smith to Little Eggharbour Monthly Meeting to
marry.

28th da, 12th mo, 1778. Clement Hall reported for going out in
marriage.

25th da, 1st mo, 1779. William Noblet reported for neglecting
meeting and frequenting taverns and places of diversion, and
being in the military.

22nd da, 2nd mo, 1779. Hannah Hodge produced an acknowledgement
condemning her misconduct in going out in marriage; accepted.
Rebeckah Hall, late Kay, and her husband, Clement, reported for
going out in marriage; disowned.

5th da, 4th mo, 1779. William Noblit reported for his disorderly
conduct. Elizabeth Smith, a young woman received under the care
of the Friends. Hester Davis and Deborah Bassett recommended as

ministers by Pilesgrove Preparative Meeting. John Smith and Sarah, his wife, reported for going out in marriage, she being first cousin to his first wife; disowned. Barzillai Jefferies granted a certificate to Haddonfield Monthly Meeting. A certificate granted for Shadlock Pancocast and his four children. Josiah Lawrence reported as having been unexpectedly released from jail in Cumberland by a non-member who paid the demands against him. John Jennings reported as being confined in Salem jail for refusing to pay military fines, released by a non-member who paid the demands.

31st da, 5th mo, 1779. Isaac Stroud, wife Lidia, and three children: Thomas, Mary and Elizabeth, granted a certificate to Wilmington Monthly Meeting. Charles Bacon and wife, Elizabeth, late Fogg, reported for marrying contrary to discipline; disowned. A certificate granted for Mary Stratton to Haddonfield Monthly Meeting. A certificate granted for Mary Matson to Evesham Monthly Meeting.

28th da, 6th mo, 1779. Hannah Stretch, a widow, received under the care of the Friends with her two children, Samuel and Luke. Ann Hilderman, late Hains, reported for going out in marriage; disowned. Jonas Freedland requested to come under the care of the Friends. Grace Bassett, late Sharp, reported for going out in marriage.

26th da, 7th mo, 1779. Judiah Allen requested a certificate to Haddonfield Monthly Meeting. David Allen appointed in the place of Josiah Miller overseer of Salem.

30th da, 8th mo, 1779. Grace Bassett, formerly Sharp, reported for going out in marriage and owning a slave for life; disowned. A testimony for Ann Reeve, deceased, the dau. of Mark and Hannah Reeve, was read.

4th da, 10th mo, 1779. A certificate granted for Deborah Harrison to Chesterfield Monthly Meeting. A certificate granted for Benjamin Test to Haddonfield Monthly Meeting. Lewis Owen, lately died intestate, left children, therefore a committee appointed to care for them and the estate.

25th da, 10th mo, 1779. Jonas Freeland received into care of the Friends. Benjamin Cripps reported for attending horse racing, active in military services and going out in privateering; disowned. A certificate granted for William Goodwin to Wilmington Monthly Meeting to marry. Job Butcher requested to come under the care of the Friends. Job Kelly reported for going out in marriage. Beulah Brown, late Bassett, reported for going out in marriage. Hephsiba Kelly, late Matson, reported for going out in marriage. Rebecca Fogg reported for neglecting meeting.

29th da, 11th mo, 1779. Mary Colson appointed overseer at Pilesgrove Monthly Meeting in place of Deborah Bassett. Elizabeth Hackett, formerly Nicholson, reported for going out in marriage; disowned. Judiah Allen and his children: Samuel, William and Rachel, granted a certificate to Haddonfield Monthly Meeting. James Barber reported for going out in marriage.

27th da, 12th mo, 1779. Job Kelly and wife reported for marrying out; disowned. Lewis Goodwin and wife, Rachel, formerly

Nicholson, reported for marrying out; disowned. Elizabeth
Bacon, an elder of Greenwich Monthly Meeting, died 2nd da, 10th
mo, 1779. John Ware reported for going out in marriage.
31st da, 1st mo, 1780. Hannah Clark received under the care of
the Friends. A certificate granted for Benjamin Test and his
children: Zacheus, Deborah, Elizabeth and David, to Haddonfield
Monthly Meeting. A certificate for Aaron Hews, his wife, and
children, Lidya and Sarah, was granted to Hopewell Monthly
Meeting, VA.
3rd da, 4th mo, 1780. Richard Kirby and his sons: Samuel, Asa and
Amos have withdrawn their requests for certificates. John
Grinslade, wife and two children, John and Elizabeth, granted a
certificate to Haddonfield Monthly Meeting. William Lippincott
granted a certificate to Haddonfield to marry. Thomas
Cowperthwaite, a youth, granted a certificate to Chesterfield
Monthly Meeting. Elizabeth Sharp, Jr. reported for her dress
and deviating from the Friends' truths; disowned. Rebecca Fogg
reported for neglecting meeting; disowned.
24th da, 4th mo, 1780. Samuel Smith, a young man, requested to
come under the care of the Friends. An account for keeping
Sarah Vickery for one year was given to the meeting.
Testification against Rebeckah Fogg to be prepared.
29th da, 5th mo, 1780. William Lippincott granted a certificate
to Haddonfield Monthly Meeting. Richard Butler, a youth,
granted a certificate to Haddonfield Monthly Meeting. Richard
Wood appointed in the place of John Bacon as overseer at
Greenwich Monthly Meeting.
26th da, 6th mo, 1780. Richard Kirby gave an account of keeping
Rachel Barrot for four years which was paid. Samuel Chester
requested to come under the care of the Friends. Giddeon Gibson
requested a certificate to Haddonfield Monthly Meeting. Hannah
Wells granted a certificate to Evesham Monthly Meeting.
31st da, 7th mo, 1780. Joseph Pimm and his wife, Hannah, and
their five children: Joseph, Elizabeth, Levi and Teresa
[Tharasa], received into the care of the Friends. Lida Pimm,
dau. of Joesph and Hannah Pimm, received under the care of the
Friends. Samuel Chester received into the care of the Friends.
Gideon Gibson produced a certificate which the clerk is
directed to endorse.
28th da, 8th mo, 1780. Asher Powner [Pounder] received into the
care of the Friends. Daniel Ridgway reported for meeting and
assembling with others with clubs to recover property
distrained [detained] for fines. Sarah Firth reported for
neglecting meeting and giving way to her turbulent temper;
disowned. Naomy Brooks received under the care of the Friends.
2nd da, 10th mo, 1780. Sarah Hollinshead, formerly Rice, reported
for going out in marriage; disowned.
30th da, 10th mo, 1780. Richard Wood, Jr. granted a certificate
to marry at Haddonfield Monthly Meeting. Sarah Firth reported
for neglecting meeting and other disorderly conduct. Samuel
Blackford requested a certificate. William Bassett reported for
privateering; disowned.
27th da, 11th mo, 1780. Joseph Barns requested a certificate to
Evesham Monthly Meeting. The endorsement for Samuel Blackford's

certificate was granted. John Redman appointed clerk of the meeting.

25th da, 12th mo, 1780. Samuel and Mark Cowperthwaite, two sons of Thomas Cowperthwaite, granted a certificate to Evesham Monthly Meeting. William Goodwin appointed overseer for Salem Monthly Meeting. Joshua Thompson appointed overseer for Alloways Creek in the place of Aaron Evans.

29th da, 1st mo, 1781. Catharine Cooper granted a certificate to Haddonfield Monthly Meeting. Elonar Davis granted a certificate to Haddonfield Monthly Meeting. Ann Smith, dau. of Joseph Smith, requested to come under the care of the friends. Levi Jennings requested a certificate for himself and his two sons, Levi and Thomas to Haddonfield Monthly Meeting. Elizabeth Carpenter, late Ware, reported for going out in marriage; disowned.

2nd da, 4th mo, 1781. A certificate granted for Hannah and Anna Jennings to Haddonfield Monthly Meeting. A certificate granted for Hannah Gibson to Haddonfield Monthly Meeting to live with her husband. Jacob Andrews requested a certificate to Philadelphia Monthly Meeting. Mary House [Houseman] produced an acknowledgement condemning her going out in marriage; accepted. An account from Charity Dunlap for keeping Sarah Vickery for one year was presented and paid.

28th da, 5th mo, 1781. Mary Acton produced an acknowledgment condemning her going out in marriage; accepted. Leatitia Craig produced an acknowledgement condemning her going out in marriage; accepted. Esther Vickery reported for misconduct; disowned.

25th da, 6th mo, 1781. Mary Hilderbrand requested to be taken under the care of the Friends. Ruth Coombs, formerly Mead, reported for going out in marriage; disowned.

30th da, 7th mo, 1781. Hannah Fogg reported for going out in marriage; disowned.

7th da, 8th mo, 1781. Meeting refused Mary Ann Hilderbrand to come under the care of the Friends. Rachel Sayre [Sears] received into the care of the Friends. Jemimah Clever, formerly Draper, reported for going out in marriage; disowned.

1st da, 10th mo, 1781. John Wistar granted a certificate to Chesterfield Monthly Meeting to marry.

29th da, 10th mo, 1781. Ruth Wright appointed as overseer in the place of Ruth Miller. It is reported that Joseph Bacon, dec'd. had left a legacy to the meeting.

26th da, 11th mo, 1781. Louisa Leeds [Lavisey Ledes] granted a certificate to Eggharbour and Cape May Monthly Meeting. Jacob Ware reported for going out in marriage.

31st da, 12th mo, 1781. John Wright, his wife, Hannah and three children: Isaac, Joseph and Mary, granted a certificate to Haddonfield Monthly Meeting. Hannah Green, late Thackery, reported for going out in marriage.

28th da, 1st mo, 1782. Jacob Ware produced an acknowledgement condemning his marrying contrary to discipline. A certificate granted for Isaac and Edward Sharp who are placed as apprentices to Philadelphia.

25th da, 2nd mo, 1782. A certificate granted for Robert Smith,

Rachel [Dorothea], his wife, and children, Rebeckah and
Marmaduk to Eggharbour and Cape May Monthly Meeting. A
certificate granted for Daniel Pedrick, his wife, Neomy, and
children, Kesiah and Mary, to Providence Monthly Meeting.
Testimony against Millisant Mason read and approved.
25th da, 3rd mo, 1782. John Reeve, Jr. granted a certificate to
Haddonfield Monthly Meeting to marry. Josiah Kay granted a
certificate to Haddonfield Monthly Meeting. Ann Bowen requested
to come under the care of the Friends. Sarah Wilson granted a
certificate to Concord Monthly Meeting, PA. Ann Bowing received
under the care of the Friends.
29th da, 4th mo, 1782. Mary Ann Hilderbrand received in the care
of Friends. Hannah Stewart appointed in the place of Sarah
Bradway as overseer for Alloways Creek Monthly Meeting. Davis
Bassett and Samuel Ogden appointed as overseers at Pilesgrove
Monthly Meeting.
27th da, 5th mo, 1782. Jeremiah Tracey received under the care of
the Friends. Sarah Allen and child granted a certificate to
Evesham Monthly Meeting. Elizabeth Allen granted a certificate
to Haddonfield Monthly Meeting. Rachel Mackleray, late Haines,
reported for going out in marriage. Ruth Evans received under
the care of the Friends. Samuel Nicholson, his wife and four
children: Mary, Sarah, Martha and Samuel, granted a certificate
to Haddonfield Monthly Meeting. Abel Nicholson produced an
acknowledgement condemning his misconduct. Mary Bacon appointed
in the place of Hannah Dennis as overseer at Greenwich Monthly
Meeting. Elizabeth Allen, dau. of Jedediah Allen, granted a
certificate to Haddonfield Monthly Meeting.
24th da, 6th mo, 1782. Mary Acton and two children, Samuel and
John, granted a certificate to Derby Monthly Meeting. An
account from Charity Dunlap sent in for the care of Sarah
Vickery for one year. Barzillai Lippincott and wife, Elizabeth,
granted a certificate to Haddonfield Monthly Meeting. Rachel
Muckleroy, late Haines, reported for going out in marriage;
disowned.
29th da, 7th mo, 1782. Joshua Elkinton disowned for neglecting
meeting, going to sea in an armed vessel and being concerned in
a taking a prize manifests. A certificate granted for Caleb,
Sarah and David Chew Copeland, the orphan children of Joshua
Copeland, to Chester Monthly Meeting. George Warner, Jr.
received under the care of the Friends. Phebe Warner received
under the care of the Friends. Joshua Barnes requested a
certificate to Chester Monthly Meeting in PA.
26th da, 8th mo, 1782. David Ware granted a certificate to
Haddonfield Monthly Meeting to marry.
30th da, 9th mo, 1782. Keziah French granted a certificate to
Northern District Philadelphia Monthly Meeting.
28th da, 10th mo, 1782. Joseph Heritage granted a certificate to
Haddonfield Monthly Meeting. Joseph Busom granted a certificate
to Chesterfield Monthly Meeting. Elisha Davis reported for
going out in marriage.
25th da, 11th mo, 1782. Elizabeth Somers, dau. of John Somers who
lives with Sarah Goodwin, received under the care of Friends.
Abigail Groaff requested to come under the care of the Friends.

Leatitia Hains reported for neglecting meeting and disorderly walking; disowned. Joseph Brick appointed in the place of Andrew Thompson, dec'd.

27th da, 1st mo, 1783. Anna Morrison produced an acknowledgement condemning her going out in marriage; accepted. William Goodwin, Jr. and his wife, Elizabeth, requested a certificate to Northern District Philadelphia Monthly Meeting. Elizabeth Huggings reported for withdrawing herself from the Friends. Hannah Smith, wife of Thomas Smith, produced an acknowledgement condemning her going out in marriage.

24th da, 2nd mo, 1783. John Bacon appointed in the place of William Miller as overseer at Greenwich Monthly Meeting.

31st da, 3rd mo, 1783. The two children of Leatitia Craig, wife of William Craig, received under the care of the Friends. Andrew Miller granted a certificate to Eggharbour and Cape May Monthly Meeting to marry. Elizabeth Test, dau. of John Test, granted a certificate to Burlington Monthly Meeting.

28th da, 4th mo, 1783. Hannah Smith produced an acknowledgement condemning her going out in marriage; accepted. Rachel Griscom appointed in the place of Hannah Stewart, dec'd., as overseer at Alloways Creek. Sarah Davis granted a certificate to Philadelphia Monthly Meeting. Rachel Tiler, late Sears, reported for going out in marriage. Ann Evans requested to come under the care of the Friends.

25th da, 5th mo, 1783. Alloways Creek Monthly Meeting reported that Peter Townsend for going out in marriage; disowned.

30th da, 6th mo, 1783. James Jess disowned for his misconduct. John Elkinton, a minor, who is placed as an apprentice to Haddonfield Monthly Meeting, granted a certificate. Joseph Barns granted a certificate to Evesham Monthly Meeting.

6th da, 10th mo, 1783. John Hews received under the care of the Friends.

27th da, 10th mo, 1783. Elizabeth Maxwell received under the care of the Friends. Elizabeth Huckings treated for neglecting meeting and other disorders; disowned. Isaac Nixon, grandson of Mary Thompson, received under the care of the Friends.

24th da, 11th mo, 1783. Elizabeth Cowgill granted a certificate to Haddonfield Monthly Meeting. Phebe Dewel [Duel] and a child granted a certificate to Evesham Monthly Meeting.

29th da, 12th mo, 1783. James Tyler, Jr. reported for going out in marriage to a non-member; disowned. Mary Stanley [Standley] received under the care of the Friends.

26th da, 1st mo, 1784. A certificate was granted for Samuel Brick to Philadelphia Monthly Meeting.

23rd da, 2nd mo, 1784. Hannah Dewell granted a certificate to Haddonfield Monthly Meeting.

29th da, 3rd mo, 1784. Mary Prosser and her children: William Stephenson, Ann, Uriah, Elizabeth, Benjamin, Mary and Martha Prosser, granted a certificate to Burlington Monthly Meeting. Charles Fogg granted a certificate to Haddonfield Monthly Meeting to marry. Phebe Coney, late McNichol, reported for going out in marriage; disowned. William Thompson and wife reported for going out in marriage; disowned.

26th da, 4th mo, 1784. Walpole Gregory granted a certificate to

SALEM MONTHLY MEETING   131

Haddonfield Monthly Meeting. Azor Lukins granted a certificate
to Haddonfield Monthly Meeting. William Barber granted a
certificate to Chesterfield Monthly Meeting. George Warner,
wife Phebe, and child William granted a certificate to
Greenwich Monthly Meeting. Sarah Peterson, late Gosling,
reported for going out in marriage; disowned. Isaac Taylor and
Martha Carpenter declare their intentions of marriage, he to
provide a certificate at next meeting. The account for Sarah
Vickery to be settled. Inquiry to be made concerning the
placement of Mary Cattel to Jane Morrow. John Bacon, dec'd.,
had left a legacy to the meeting.
31st da, 5th mo, 1784. Hannah Smith, wife of Thomas Smith granted
a certificate to Southern District Philadelphia Monthly
Meeting. Disposition of Martha Carpenter prevented the second
declaration of marriage. Gideon and Elizabeth Stratton,
children of Mary Stratton, received under the care of the
Friends. The meeting will pay for the care of Mary Cattel. John
Somers produced an acknowledgement condemning his going out in
marriage.
28th da, 6th mo, 1784. Isaac Taylor and Martha Carpenter appeared
and her father informed the meeting that she had changed her
mind about marrying. Hill Smith and wife produced an
acknowledgement condemning their going out in marriage;
accepted. Mary Riley received under the care of the Friends.
26th da, 7th mo, 1784. Isaac Taylor reported as going away from
these parts to the sea. Rebeccah Lownsberry requested to come
under the care of the friends.
30th da, 8th mo, 1784. Job Shreeve and wife granted a certificate
to Springfield Monthly Meeting. Mary [Mercy] Shreeve granted a
certificate to Philadelphia Monthly Meeting. Accounts for the
care of Mary Cattell from Jane Morrow and Sarah Vickery from
Charity Dunlap settled. Joseph Brown requested a certificate to
Wilmington Monthly Meeting.
4th da, 10th mo, 1784. Sarah Weatherby produced a certificate for
herself and her dau. to Haddonfield with an endorsement which
was read and accepted.
29th da, 11th mo, 1784. John Ellett, a minor, placed as an
apprentice to Haddonfield Monthly Meeting granted a
certificate.
28th da, 2nd mo, 1785. Esther [Hester] Silver, late Andrews,
reported for going out in marriage; disowned. Seth Silvers
received under the care of the Friends. William Thompson
granted a certificate to Woodbury Monthly Meeting.
2nd da, 4th mo, 1785. Samuel Austin received under the care of
the Friends. Henry Ridgway requested a certificate for himself,
his wife, and five children to Burlington Monthly Meeting.
25th da, 4th mo, 1785. John Jennings appointed minister. Stephen
Wright, wife Priscilla, and dau. Rebecca granted a certificate
to Springfield Monthly Meeting. Zaccheus Test, wife Rebecca,
and son Benjamin granted a certificate to Woodbury Monthly
Meeting. Mary Stratton and dau. Hope granted a certificate to
Mt. Holly Monthly Meeting. Peter Wright granted a certificate
to Woodbury Monthly Meeting.
30th da, 5th mo, 1785. Elizabeth Somers granted a certificate to

Gwynned Monthly Meeting. Henry Ridgway, Hannah his wife and children: Hannah, Rebecca, Joseph and Mary, requested a certificate to Burlington Monthly Meeting.

27th da, 6th mo, 1785. Hannah Wainman, late James, reported for going out in marriage; disowned.

29th da, 8th mo, 1785. Henry Ridgway requested that the certificate be delayed at the present. Amariah Ballinger reported for not fulfilling his contracts in business.

3rd da, 10th mo, 1785. Ralph Allen received under the care of the Friends. A certificate was granted for John Firth to Chesterfield Monthly Meeting. Deborah Test reported for disorderly conduct and reproachful manner; disowned.

31st da, 10th mo, 1785. Hannah Rockhill granted a certificate to Philadelphia Monthly Meeting. John Balinger, Jr. reported for marrying contrary to discipline.

28th da, 11th mo, 1785. Hannah Keasbey, late Brick, treated with for going out in marriage; disowned.

26th da, 12th mo, 1785. Mary Clarke granted a certificate to Wilmington Monthly Meeting. Daniel Bassett, Jr. appointed in the place of John Barnes as overseer at Pilesgrove Monthly Meeting.

30th da, 1st mo, 1786. A certificate granted for Henry Ridgway, his wife and children to Burlington Monthly Meeting. Elizabeth Sommers, a child, granted a certificate to live with her father, John Sommers, at Eggharbour and Cape May Monthly Meeting. A certificate was granted for Susannah Ewen [Hewings] to Woodbury Monthly Meeting. Aaron Bradway reported for going out in marriage. Jacob Ware requested that his two daus., Mary and Miliscent, be taken under the care of the Friends. Joseph Smith produced an acknowledgement condemning his going out in marriage.

27th da, 2nd mo, 1786. Ann Thomas, late Smith, reported for going out in marriage to a non-member; disowned. Mary Lippincott received under the care of the Friends.

27th da, 3rd mo, 1786. Joseph Butcher granted a certificate for himself, his wife Elizabeth and two children, Prudence and Samuel, and an apprentice lad, Ephraim Garner, to Haddonfield Monthly Meeting. John Hopman reported for marrying contrary to discipline.

24th da, 4th mo, 1786. John Smith granted a certificate for himself and his wife, Gulielma Maria, to Evesham Monthly Meeting. Mary Duel granted a certificate to Woodbury Monthly Meeting. Richard Dicker granted a certificate to Greenwich Monthly Meeting to marry. Sarah, an infant dau. of Leititia Craig, received under the care of the Friends.

31st da, 7th mo, 1786. A certificate was granted for Rachel Foster and her daus. Rebecca, Lydia and Rachel to Evesham Monthly Meeting. A certificate was granted for Hannah and Mary Foster to Evesham Monthly Meeting. Samuel Chester reported for going out in marriage; disowned. An account was produced from Charity Dunlap for the upkeep of Sarah Vickery. Elizabeth Test requested a certificate to Southern District Philadelphia Monthly Meeting. Hester Hartley received under the care of the Friends. Ann Mason, late Ward, granted a certificate to

Woodbury Monthly Meeting.
28th da, 8th mo, 1786. David Davis granted a certificate to
Eggharbour Monthly Meeting to marry. Elizabeth Test withdrew
her request for a certificate. Jesse Bacon requested a
certificate to Greenwich Monthly Meeting. Mary Andrews late
Cripps produced an acknowledgement condemning her going out in
marriage; accepted.
2nd da, 10th mo, 1786. A certificate granted for Jonas Freedland
to Greenwich Monthly Meeting. Hester [Ester] Hartley received
under the care of the Friends. Sarah Wray, late Haines,
reported for going out in marriage; disowned.
2nd da, 9th mo, 1786. Rebecca Vickery reported for going out in
marriage; disowned.
27th da, 11th mo, 1786. Hannah Allen, dau. of Joseph Allen
granted a certificate to Burlington Monthly Meeting. Joseph
Crispin, Jr. who is placed as an apprentice at Evesham Monthly
Meeting requested a certificate.
25th da, 12th mo, 1786. Jemima Ballinger, formerly Haines,
reported for going out in marriage; disowned. Rebecca Waters
produced an acknowledgement condemning her going out in
marriage.
29th da, 1st mo, 1787. Elizabeth Bradway, late Hartley, granted a
certificate to Greenwich Monthly Meeting.
26th da, 2nd mo, 1787. Hannah Willis and her son, Silas, granted
a certificate to Eggharbour and Cape May Monthly Meeting. Mary
Andrews granted a certificate. Joseph Pettit, wife and children
requested a certificate to Burlington Monthly Meeting.
2nd da, 4th mo, 1787. Joseph Pettit withdrew his request for a
certificate. Elizabeth Smith granted a certificate to
Eggharbour and Cape May Monthly Meeting. Elizabeth Borton
reported for going out in marriage.
30th da, 4th mo, 1787. A certificate granted for Jeremiah Tracy
to Greenwich Monthly Meeting. A certificate granted for
Elizabeth Smith, late Bassett, to Eggharbour and Cape May
Monthly Meeting.
28th da, 5th mo, 1787. Sarah Pedrick and her four children:
Mirabe, Hester, Jesse and Elizabeth received into the care of
the Friends. A certificate granted for John Hance, son of Isaac
Hance, to Greenwich Monthly Meeting.
25th da, 6th mo, 1787. Mary Smith received into the care of the
Friends. John Ware [Ward] and wife, Hannah, granted a
certificate to Haddonfield Monthly Meeting. Joseph Sloan
granted a certificate to Haddonfield Monthly Meeting. Sarah
Hewes [Hews], formerly Oakford, reported for going out in
marriage; disowned. Priscilla Boggs requested to come under the
care of the Friends.
30th da, 7th mo, 1787. Charity Dunlap requested a certificate to
Greenwich. Sarah Vickery to stay under the care of Charity
Dunlap. Elizabeth Borton produced an acknowledgement condemning
her going out in marriage; accepted. The account of the estate
of Joseph Bacon was received.
24th da, 9th mo, 1787. Joseph Ware and Sarah Thompson declare
their intentions of marriage.
29th da, 10th mo, 1787. Thomas Norris received under the care of

the Friends. Mary Ballinger, wife of John, received under the care of the Friends.

26th da, 11th mo, 1787. A certificate granted for Samuel Brick and wife, Ann, to Greenwich Monthly Meeting. A certificate granted for Elizabeth Borton to Evesham Monthly Meeting. John Ballinger requested that his son, Daniel, be taken under the care of the Friends. Dorcas Pidgeon late Dawson treated with for marrying contrary to discipline; disowned.

31st da, 12th mo, 1787. A certificate was granted for Rebecca Ware to Greenwich Monthly Meeting. Elizabeth Jervis [Gervas] reported for going out in marriage; disowned. David Smith requested a certificate for himself, his wife Hannah and three children: Daniel, Mary and Evi, to Eggharbour and Cape May Monthly Meeting. Rebecca Ware granted a certificate to Greenwich Monthly Meeting.

28th da, 1st mo, 1788. Mary Bassett proposed as a minister at Pilesgrove Monthly Meeting.

25th da, 2nd mo, 1788. Jedediah Dawson treated for marrying contrary to discipline; disowned. A certificate granted for Elizabeth Ware to Greenwich Monthly Meeting with an endorsement.

30th da, 3rd mo, 1788. Hannah Acton granted a certificate to Duck Creek Monthly Meeting. Solomon Gibbs, son of Richard Gibbs requested a certificate to Greenwich Monthly Meeting. Abigal Mount produced an acknowledgement that she no longer desires to be a member; disowned. Thomas Norris and Meriam Branson declare their intentions of marriage.

28th da, 4th mo, 1788. Richard Gibbs granted a certificate for himself, his wife and six children: Enoch, Phebe, Burroughs, Sarah, Richard and Edward, to Greenwich Monthly Meeting.

26th da, 5th mo, 1788. Hugh Haines and his wife, Hannah, produced an acknowledgement condemning their going out in marriage, they being first cousins.

30th da, 6th mo, 1788. The acknowledgement condemning their going out in marriage of Clement Hall and his wife, and three children: Ann, Margaret and Morris; accepted. Ebenezer Miller, Jr. produced an acknowledgement condemning his misconduct in attending a place of diversion. An account was produced from Charity Dunlap informing of the death of Sarah Vickery. Meriman Smith reported for being at a horse race and allowing his animal to run. Naomi Haines produced an acknowledgement condemning her misconduct; accepted. Mary Pimm, late Test, reported for going out in marriage; disowned.

27th da, 7th mo, 1788. William Craig received into the care of the Friends. Certificates granted for Mary Stanley, Hannah Bradway and Mary Sheppard to Greenwich Monthly Meeting.

25th da, 8th mo, 1788. Hannah Firth granted a certificate to Woodbury Monthly Meeting. Davis Bassett, an elder at Pilesgrove died aged 61; also Mary Bassett, a minister of the aforesaid meeting. George Colson appointed in the room of Davis Bassett.

6th da, 10th mo, 1788. Jesse Bacon granted a certificate to Greenwich Monthly Meeting. William Harris reported for being charged with fighting.

27th da, 10th mo, 1788. William Harris disowned. Hannah Ridgway granted a certificate for herself and children: Elizabeth, Hannah, Rebecca, Joseph, Mary and Henrietta, to Mt. Holly Monthly Meeting. Asa Elkington and Leatitia Lippincott declare their intentions of marriage.

29th da, 12th mo, 1788. Levi Evans reported for marrying contrary to discipline.

26th da, 1st mo, 1789. Susanna Thompson and children: Mary, Ann, Elizabeth and John Mason, granted a certificate to Greenwich Monthly Meeting.

23rd da, 2nd mo, 1789. Mary Moore granted a certificate to Third Haven Monthly Meeting, MD. Richard Miller produced an acknowledgement condemning his going out in marriage. Amariah Ballanger reported for neglecting to comply with his just debts or engagements. Jacob Thackery reported for marrying his first cousin and marrying by a priest.

30th da, 3rd mo, 1789. Levi Evans produced an acknowledgement condemning his misconduct; disowned. Joseph Pettit granted a certificate for himself, his wife Sarah and three children: Woodnut, Rachel and David to Haddonfield Monthly Meeting. Edward Bradway produced an acknowledgement condemning his going out in marriage. John Barns appointed overseer for Pilesgrove Monthly Meeting. William Stephenson Prosser reported for neglecting meeting.

25th da, 5th mo, 1789. A certificate was granted for Rebecca Barber to Eggharbor and Cape May Monthly Meeting. A certificate was granted for Hugh Low to Southern District Philadelphia Monthly Meeting. A certificate was granted for Ann, Catharine and Lucy Lowe to Southern District Philadelphia Monthly Meeting. Marian Ogden appointed overseer for Pilesgrove Monthly Meeting. A certificate granted for Leatitia Reeve to Greenwich Monthly Meeting. Testimony prepared for Martha Allen.

27th da, 7th mo, 1789. Magery Woolster granted a certificate to Mt. Holly Monthly Meeting. Sedons Linsey requested to come under the care of Friends.

31st da, 8th mo, 1789. Samuel Silver's children: William, Rebecca, Samuel and Archibald, received under the care of the Friends. Ruth Silver received under the care of the Friends. Mary Colson appointed by Pilesgrove as an elder.

5th da, 10th mo, 1789. John Elkinton granted a certificate to Greenwich Monthly Meeting. Gideon Gibson and his children, Daniel and Gideon, granted a certificate to Woodbury Monthly Meeting. Jacob Haines granted a certificate to Woodbury Monthly Meeting to marry.

26th da, 10th mo, 1789. Joseph Gardiner granted a certificate to Evesham Monthly Meeting to marry. Samuel Firth, a minor who is placed as an apprentice, granted a certificate to Evesham Monthly Meeting. Jesse Bacon granted a certificate to Baltimore Monthly Meeting, MD. William Daniel reported for marrying contrary to discipline and refusing to take the friends' advice in settle a dispute. Elizabeth Allen received under the care of the Friends. A proposal was made and agreed that the women's meeting should in the future inform the men's meeting prior to disowning a Friend. Elizabeth Shreeve reported for leaving her husband in a disorderly manner but has returned to him. Mary

Holmes reported for going out in marriage; disowned.
30th da, 11th mo, 1789. William Smith and wife produced an acknowledgement condemning their going out in marriage and request that their children be taken under the care of the Friends.
28th da, 12th mo, 1789. Mary Holmes, late Houseman, reported for going out in marriage; disowned. Ameriah Ballenger treated for neglecting meeting and neglecting to comply with his paying his just debts.
25th da, 1st mo, 1790. Elizabeth Clement and dau. Ruth received under the care of the Friends.
22nd da, 2nd mo, 1790. Rachel Shute and three children: Isaac, Hannah, and Samuel granted a certificate to Evesham Monthly Meeting. Phoebe Warner appointed as a minister. Sarah Thorne produced an acknowledgement condemning her going out in marriage. Sarah Smith and her dau. Sarah received under the care of the Friends.
26th da, 4th mo, 1790. James Simpson, his wife Hannah and children, Benjamin and Hannah, received under the care of the Friends. A certificate granted for Joseph Garner to Evesham Monthly Meeting. A certificate was granted for Rhoda Osborn and her children, Josiah and Nathan, to Eggharbour Monthly Meeting. A certificate granted for Deborah Dunn and Phoebe Osborn to Eggharbour Monthly Meeting. A certificate granted for Naomi Peddrick [Pedrick] and her son, Daniel, to Greenwich Monthly Meeting. Elizabeth Borough [Boroughs] granted a certificate to Greenwich Monthly Meeting. Elizabeth Brown granted a certificate to Woodbury Monthly Meeting. Samuel Chester produced an acknowledgement condemning his going out in marriage. Mark Nicholson treated for neglecting to comply with a contract.
31st da, 5th mo, 1790. A certificate was granted for Grace Ware to Greenwich Monthly Meeting. Job Shreeve and wife produced an acknowledgement condemning their disorderly conduct.
28th da, 6th mo, 1790. Deborah Nielson reported for going out in marriage; disowned. Edward Draper reported for going out in marriage, disowned. Jane Cassady, late Barber, reported for going out in marriage.
26th da, 7th mo, 1790. The two minor sons of Thomas Clement received under the care of the Friends. Amariah Ballenger treated for neglecting to fulfill his debts; disowned. Sarah Thorne granted a certificate to Chesterfield Monthly Meeting. Sarah Risley reported for going out in marriage.
30th da, 8th mo, 1790. Joshua Thompson, an elder, died 6th da, 3rd mo, 1790 and Dorothy Davis an ancient Friend, testimony read. Isaac Hovey reported as marrying contrary to discipline.
4th da, 10th mo, 1790. Peter Dole produced an acknowledgement condemning his marrying contrary to discipline. Emmor Bailey granted a certificate to Bradford Monthly Meeting, PA. James Wood granted a certificate to Haddonfield Monthly Meeting to marry. Thomas Davis requested a certificate to Eggharbour and Cape May Monthly Meeting to marry. Isaac Smart treated for neglecting to settle his debts owed to Elgar Brown. Enoch Risley reported for marrying contrary to discipline and

removing without a certificate.
25th da, 10th mo, 1790. Thomas Davis granted a certificate to
Eggharbour and Cape May Monthly Meeting to marry. Isaac Howey
produced an acknowledgement. John Knight received under the
care of the Friends. Rebecca Lippincott, formerly McNichols,
treated for going out in marriage. Elizabeth Cole, formerly
Pimm, treated for going out in marriage.
29th da, 11th mo, 1790. Jacob Hoffman reported for marrying
contrary to discipline.
31st da, 1st mo, 1791. Jane Cassady, late Barber, produced an
acknowledgement condemning her going out in marriage; accepted.
Jacob Ridway and wife produced an acknowledgement condemning
their going out in marriage.
28th da, 2nd mo, 1791. Enoch Risley reported for marrying
contrary to discipline and removing without a certificate;
disowned. Levi Pimm, a minor placed as an apprentice to Evesham
Monthly Meeting granted a certificate. John Duel, a minor who
has lived with his guardian at Woodbury Monthly Meeting,
granted a certificate. Samuel Chester granted a certificate to
Philadelphia Monthly Meeting. William McNichols treated with
for going out in marriage; disowned.
28th da, 3rd mo, 1791. Jacob Ridgway and Kezia, his wife disowned
for going out in marriage. David Evans, Mary, his wife and
children: John, David, Benjamin, Joseph, Nathan, Isaac and
Sarah granted a certificate to Greenwich Monthly Meeting. Jane
Sharp recommended as minister.
30th da, 5th mo, 1791. Jane Cassady granted a certificate to
Woodbury Monthly Meeting. John Dunham, a minor granted a
certificate to Evesham Monthly Meeting. Elijah Ware appointed
in the place of Mark Miller as overseer of Salem Monthly
Meeting. Ezekiah Bates treated for neglecting to pay a debt due
Jacob Davis as an executor; also he stands bound for one not in
membership with the Friends.
25th da, 7th mo, 1791. Lydia Daniel, late Hancock, reported for
going out in marriage; disowned. Rebeckah Wright, late Ridgway,
reported for going out in marriage; disowned. Ann Stockton
granted a certificate to Greenwich Monthly Meeting. Elihu
Pedrick appointed in the place of Daniel Bassett, Jr. as
overseer of Pilesgrove Monthly Meeting.
29th da, 8th mo, 1791. Aaron Thompson, wife and two children,
Rebecca and Ann, granted a certificate to Woodbury Monthly
Meeting. Benijah Dunn, a minor granted a certificate to Little
Eggharbor Monthly Meeting. Solomon Gibbs produced an
acknowledgement condemning his misconduct of indisputably
leaving his parents and joining a military expedition against
the Indians.
26th da, 9th mo, 1791. Nathan Bassett, wife and children: Hannah,
Elizabeth and Ann, granted a certificate to Woodbury Monthly
Meeting. George Abbot granted a certificate to Haddonfield
Monthly Meeting to marry. Solomon Gibbs disowned for his
disorderly conduct. Samuel Abbot requested a certificate to
Haddonfield Monthly Meeting to marry.
31st da, 10th mo, 1791. Lydia Kirby and children, Benjamin and
Mercy, minors granted a certificate to Greenwich Monthly

Meeting. Josiah Abbott reported for going out in marriage; disowned. Mahlon Adkinson informed the meeting that he had left his certificate at home, other friends testified that a certificate had been granted from Greenwich Monthly Meeting. William Lippincott reported for neglecting to pay a debt due a Friend. Robert Howey and Neomy Coleston declare their intentions of marriage.

28th da, 11th mo, 1791. A memorial for our ancient friend, Dorothy Davis, was read. Hannah McCatts [McCall] received under the care of the Friends. Richard Barnes reported for going out in marriage.

26th da, 12th mo, 1791. Mark Street granted a certificate to Greenwich Monthly Meeting. Ruth Scull granted a certificate to Eggharbour and Cape May Monthly Meeting. Thomas Hartly, a minor, granted a certificate to Greenwich Monthly Meeting. Sarah Webb, late Sharp, reported for going out in marriage. A testimony given from Jacob Davis for his mother, Dorotha Davis, dec'd.

30th da, 1st mo, 1792. Richard Barnes produced an acknowledgement condemning his going out in marriage; disowned. Joseph Haines reported for going out in marriage; disowned.

27th da, 2nd mo, 1792. John Tees [Teas], Rachel his wife, and children: Charles, Rachel, Mary, Martha and John, granted a certificate to Northern District Philadelphia Monthly Meeting. Isaac Nixon, a minor placed as an apprentice, granted a certificate to Woodbury Monthly Meeting. Sarah Webb produced an acknowledgement condemning her going out in marriage, accepted. Sarah Adkinson [Atkinson], late Davis, produced an acknowledgement condemning her going out in marriage; disowned. Martha Taylor received under the care of the Friends. Sarah Bevan, late Lord, reported for going out in marriage; disowned.

2nd da, 4th mo, 1792. Naomi Hall granted a certificate to Evesham Monthly Meeting. Sarah Ward granted a certificate to Woodbury Monthly Meeting. Sarah Lord, late Eggman, reported for going out in marriage; disowned.

30th da, 4th mo, 1792. Hannah Roberts, late Basset, reported for going out in marriage; disowned.

25th da, 6th mo, 1792. Joseph Lewis, wife Mary, and children: William, Hannah, Joseph and John, granted a certificate to Northern District Philadelphia Monthly Meeting. [Men's minutes state there were five children, but only four named.]

30th da, 7th mo, 1792. Seth Silver granted a certificate to Little Eggharbour Monthly Meeting to marry. Rebeccah Ward granted a certificate to Haddonfield Monthly Meeting. Elizabeth Groaf, late Test, reported for going out in marriage to a non-member; disowned.

27th da, 8th mo, 1792. Richard Smith, Jr. granted a certificate to Greenwich Monthly Meeting to marry. Mark Haines treated for marrying contrary to discipline. A proposal of marriage between Samuel Burnes and Hannah Woodnut is prevented at this time due to the indisposition of the young woman.

29th da, 10th mo, 1792. Rebeccah Jennings, a minor granted a certificate to Woodbury Monthly Meeting. Mary Springer, late Pederick, reported for going out in marriage to a non-member;

disowned.
26th da, 11th mo, 1792. Mark Haynes, disowned for his misconduct. Charles Ellott, a minor placed as an apprentice granted a certificate to Philadelphia Monthly Meeting.
31st da, 12th mo, 1792. Peter Dole granted a certificate to Greenwich Monthly Meeting. Mary Harker, late James, reported for going out in marriage; disowned. Rebecca Pew, late Goslin, reported for going out in marriage; disowned.
28th da, 1st mo, 1793. Abigail Howey, wife of Isaac Howey, received under the care of the Friends with her two children, Mary and Benjamin. Jonathan Cowgill granted a certificate to Woodbury Monthly Meeting. A certificate requested for Naome Hall.
25th da, 2nd mo, 1793. A certificate granted for Hannah Burnes to Wilmington Monthly Meeting. A certificate which had been granted for Naomi Hall and her son to Evesham Monthly Meeting was not forwarded, her son now being dead, another certificate to Chesterfield Monthly Meeting granted. William Thompson's children: Hannah, James and Sarah, received under the care of the Friends. Thomason Roberts and her dau. Esther requested a certificate to Woodbury Monthly Meeting.
1st da, 4th, mo, 1793. Thomason Roberts and her dau. withdrew the request for a certificate. Rachel Ellison [Allison or Atkinson] granted a certificate to Southern District Philadelphia Monthly Meeting.
27th da, 5th mo, 1793. Mary Cammel, late Elkinton, reported for going out in marriage; disowned. Gideon Stratton, a minor placed with a Friend, granted a certificate to Evesham Monthly Meeting.
29th da, 7th mo, 1793. Ann Swinny, late Bassett, reported for going out in marriage; disowned.
26th da, 8th mo, 1793. Preston Firth granted a certificate to Northern District Philadelphia Monthly Meeting. Samuel Chester and Jonathan Gibbs granted a certificate to Philadelphia Monthly Meeting. William Griscom, Jr., a minor placed as an apprentice, granted a certificate to Haddonfield Monthly Meeting.
30th da, 9th mo, 1793. Peter Borden reported for going out in marriage; disowned.
28th da, 10th mo, 1793. Abraham Silver granted a certificate.
25th da, 11th mo, 1793. Nathan Folwell granted a certificate to Woodbury Monthly Meeting. Rachel Higby, late Potts, reported for going out in marriage, she has since left the meeting to go to Pennsylvania. Josiah Weaver and children: Susannah, Mary, Thomas, Ann and Elizabeth, requested a certificate to Eggharbor Monthly Meeting.
30th da, 12th mo, 1793. Charity Dunlap requested assistance of the Friends to take care of her property.
31st da, 2nd mo, 1794. Ezekiah Hews granted a certificate to Concord Monthly Meeting, PA to marry. William Bradway treated for neglecting meeting. Rachel Griscom appointed in the place of Ruth Wright as overseer.
28th da, 4th mo, 1794. Elizabeth Thompson, Sr. received under the care of the Friends. James Adkinson disowned for his

misconduct. William Bradway disowned for neglecting meeting. Mahlon Adkinson, Sarah his wife, son Richard, and their apprentice, Joshua Reeve, granted a certificate to Mt. Holly Monthly Meeting.

26th da, 5th mo, 1794. Sarah Hammett, late Gibbs, reported for marrying contrary to discipline; disowned.

30th da, 6th mo, 1794. John Griscom granted a certificate to Burlington Monthly Meeting. Elizabeth Fogg, a minor, granted a certificate to Haddonfield Monthly Meeting.

28th da, 7th mo, 1794. Samuel Stewart, Jr. granted a certificate. Joseph Lewis and his family had a certificate from Philadelphia but had not produced it to the meeting.

29th da, 9th mo, 1794. Susanna Ware granted a certificate to Haddonfield Monthly Meeting.

27th da, 10th mo, 1794. Hannah Wilson received under the care of the Friends.

24th da, 11th mo, 1794. Abraham Eggman disowned for marrying contrary to discipline.

29th da, 12th mo, 1794. Hannah Wills granted a certificate to Evesham Monthly Meeting. Grace Smith late Haines reported for going out in marriage; disowned. Rachel Highby late Potts reported for going out in marriage and removing to a distant part of the county; disowned. Phebe Miller appointed as elder. David Allen appointed as elder. Josiah Weaver and children: Susanna, Mary, Thomas, Ann and Elizabeth granted a certificate to Eggharbour Monthly Meeting.

26th da, 1st mo, 1795. Thomas Andrews granted a certificate to Woodbury Monthly Meeting. Susanna Rulon [Ruland] granted a certificate to Greenwich Monthly Meeting. Elizabeth Thompson granted a certificate to Pilesgrove Monthly Meeting.

30th da, 3rd mo, 1795. Stephen Smith, a minor, granted a certificate to Northern District Philadelphia Monthly Meeting. Abraham Swain granted a certificate to Middletown Monthly Meeting, Bucks County, PA. John Hancock granted a certificate to Southern District Philadelphia Monthly Meeting. Abraham Miller reported for neglecting to pay his just debts.

27th da, 4th mo, 1795. A certificate granted for Lydia Gibbs to Northern District Philadelphia Monthly Meeting. A certificate was granted for Job Shreeve, wife Elizabeth, and four children: Abigail, Job, Elizabeth and Thomas, to Springfield Monthly Meeting. Lydia Gibbs granted a certificate to Evesham Monthly Meeting. Sarah Smith, late Ambler, reported for marrying contrary to discipline; disowned.

25th da, 5th mo, 1795. Burrough Gibbs by his father produced an acknowledgement condemning his conduct in horse racing and running a foot race; disowned. Abner Briggs granted a certificate to Northern District Philadelphia Monthly Meeting. Michael Newbold granted a certificate to Southern District Philadelphia Monthly Meeting. James Wood, wife, and two children, Richard and Beulah, and apprentice, John Tuckniss, granted a certificate to Northern District Philadelphia Monthly Meeting. A certificate granted for John Hancock to Philadelphia Monthly Meeting returned to meeting as he remains in the area.

29th da, 6th mo, 1795. Mary Smith of Salem appointed in the place

of Rebecca Abbott as overseer. Thomas Folwell granted a
certificate to Philadelphia Monthly Meeting.
27th da, 7th mo, 1795. James Hanse granted a certificate to
Greenwich Monthly Meeting. Mary Withers granted a certificate
to Woodbury Monthly Meeting.
31st da, 8th mo, 1795. Joseph Reeve appointed overseer in the
place of David Allen, dec'd. William Wilson treated for being
in the practice of administering the oath. Mary Tyler received
under the care of the Friends.
26th da, 10th mo, 1795. David Evans granted a certificate to
Greenwich Monthly Meeting. William Pederick granted a
certificate to Greenwich Monthly Meeting. Ezekiah Bates
disowned for committing an assault. Elizabeth Hancock, late
Ware, disowned for marrying contrary to discipline to a man
whose former wife was her first cousin; disowned.
30th da, 11th mo, 1795. John James dec'd. has left a legacy to
the meeting.
28th da, 12th mo, 1795. Griffith Owen granted a certificate to
Haddonfield Monthly Meeting. Isaac Griffith granted a
certificate to Philadelphia Monthly Meeting. Samuel Nicholson,
dec'd. has left a legacy to the meeting. Joseph Lewis, wife
Mary and five children: William, Hannah, Ann, Joseph and John,
produced a certificate to Northern District Philadelphia
Monthly Meeting dated 7th mo, 1792, but not given to that
meeting, requested a certificate to Pilesgrove Monthly Meeting.
25th da, 1st mo, 1796. John Firth, Jr. produced an
acknowledgement condemning his going out in marriage; disowned.
29th da, 2nd mo, 1796. John Pimm and dau. Mary, a minor,
requested a certificate to Pilesgrove Monthly Meeting.
26th da, 3rd mo, 1796. Mary Aborn received under the care of the
friends. Isaac Griffith requested that his certificate be
changed to Horsham Monthly Meeting. Mark Miller, Jr. requested
a certificate to Philadelphia Monthly Meeting.
27th da, 6th mo, 1796. William Sheppard requested a certificate
to Greenwich Monthly Meeting. Rachel Tindall, late Thompson,
reported for marrying contrary to discipline; disowned.
25th da, 7th mo, 1796. Isaac Hance, a minor who is placed as an
apprentice, granted a certificate to Pilesgrove Monthly
Meeting.
29th da, 8th mo, 1796. Mary Gibbs and her dau. Martha Hanse, a
minor, granted a certificate to Evesham Monthly Meeting.
31st da, 10th mo, 1796. Samuel Test reported for marrying
contrary to discipline; disowned. Sarah Potts, Jr. granted a
certificate to Southern District Philadelphia Monthly Meeting.
28th da, 11th mo, 1796. Hannah Reeve, late Ware, granted a
certificate to Greenwich Monthly Meeting.
26th da, 12th mo, 1796. Rachel Griscom appointed an elder. Nathan
Lord granted a certificate to Duck Creek Monthly Meeting.
27th da, 3rd mo, 1797. A certificate was granted for Elizabeth
Cripps to Darby Monthly Meeting.
24th da, 4th mo, 1797. Sarah Bevin produced an acknowledgement
condemning her going out in marriage; accepted. George Abbott
and wife granted a certificate to Southern District
Philadelphia Monthly Meeting. Ann Bacon received under the care

of the Friends.

26th da, 6th mo, 1797. John Goodwin, a minor, granted a certificate to Philadelphia Monthly Meeting. Mark Hartly granted a certificate to Southern District Philadelphia Monthly Meeting with his guardian.

30th da, 10th mo, 1797. A certificate granted for Sarah Beven to Duck Creek Monthly Meeting.

27th da, 11th mo, 1797. Thomas Firth granted a certificate to Northern District Philadelphia Monthly Meeting.

26th da, 2nd mo, 1798. Samuel Firth reported for removing with a certificate. John Redman requested to be released as clerk.

30th da, 4th mo, 1798. Mary Smart granted a certificate to Woodbury Monthly Meeting.

25th da, 6th mo, 1798. Samuel Stewart appointed in the place of John Thompson as overseer. Richard Dunn and his wife, Sarah and their two minor children requested to come under the care of the Friends.

30th da, 7th mo, 1798. Friends appointed to visit Richard Dunn and his family reported that the time has not come to allow them membership.

24th da, 9th mo, 1798. Mary Withers [Weathers] informed the meeting that she had joined the Methodist society and did not desire to retain her right; disowned.

29th da, 10th mo, 1798. Hepzebeth Gibbs, late Harris, produced an acknowledgement condemning her marrying contrary to discipline; disowned.

26th da, 11th mo, 1798. Elizabeth Dunham, and her three children: Elizabeth, David and Job, granted a certificate to Greenwich Monthly Meeting. William Nicholson granted a certificate to Greenwich Monthly Meeting to marry. George Wright granted a certificate to Upper Springfield Monthly Meeting to marry.

25th da, 2nd mo, 1799. Aaron Street granted a certificate to Pilesgrove Monthly Meeting to marry. Joseph Hall treated for neglecting to pay a just debt. John James, dec'd., has left a legacy to the meeting. A legacy from Samuel Nicholson, dec'd. is ready to be paid.

25th da, 3rd mo, 1799. Patience Conrow granted a certificate to Mt. Holly Monthly Meeting. A certificate granted for Mary Conrow to Burlington Monthly Meeting.

27th da, 4th mo, 1799. Calebe Conrow disowned for his misconduct.

27th da, 5th mo, 1799. Richard Dunn and Sarah, his wife, and their two children, William and Rebecca, received under the care of the Friends. John Gill, his wife Prudence, and son David granted a certificate to Pilesgrove Monthly Meeting.

29th da, 7th mo, 1799. Samuel Acton granted a certificate for himself, his wife, Sarah, and their two minor children, Clement and Mary, to Haddonfield Monthly Meeting. Elizabeth Dunham returned the certificate for herself and her three children from Greenwich, she having moved back before having the opportunity to present the certificate.

26th da, 8th mo, 1799. Elizabeth Black, late Smith, reported for going out in marriage; disowned. Mary Acton granted a certificate to Haddonfield Monthly Meeting.

30th da, 9th mo, 1799. Elizabeth Maxwell [Maxfield] granted a

certificate to Greenwich Monthly Meeting.
28th da, 10th mo, 1799. Mary Thompson appointed in the place of Phebe Miller as overseer.
25th da, 11th mo, 1799. Isaac Townsend granted a certificate to Pilesgrove Monthly Meeting to marry.
30th da, 12th mo, 1799. Thomas Guest reported for marrying contrary to discipline to a non-member of our society; disowned.
27th da, 1st mo, 1800. William Abbott, an elder, died 4th da, 12th mo, 1799 aged 63 years. A certificate was granted for Samuel Lippincott to Northern District Philadelphia Monthly Meeting and one for Charles Lippincott to Horsham Monthly Meeting.
24th da, 2nd mo, 1800. Jonathan Crispin granted a certificate to Pilesgrove Monthly Meeting. A certificate was granted for Samuel Craig to Pilesgrove Monthly Meeting to marry.
1st da, 3rd mo, 1800. Job Tyler treated for neglecting to settle a difference with a Friend. Ann Cooper granted a certificate to Woodbury Monthly Meeting.
28th da, 4th mo, 1800. Isaac Barber, his wife, Mary, and children: Rebecca, Mary Ann, Abraham, Isaac and Jacob, granted a certificate to Pilesgrove Monthly Meeting. Samuel Firth who some time ago left without a certificate, reported as settling at Charlestown and has married contrary to discipline. Ruth Bacon granted a certificate to Greenwich Monthly Meeting.
30th da, 6th mo, 1800. Hannah Acton, late Woodnutt, reported for marrying contrary to discipline to a non-member; disowned.
8th da, 7th mo, 1800. John Smith disowned for his disorderly conduct. Joseph Hanse granted a certificate to Philadelphia Monthly Meeting. Rachel Carpenter Ellet granted a certificate to Woodbury Monthly Meeting. Rebecca Thompson granted a certificate to Darby Monthly Meeting. Rachel Hall, late Shourds, reported for marrying contrary to discipline; disowned.
29th da, 9th mo, 1800. Elizabeth Mason received under the care of the Friends. Elizabeth Ray, late Burden, reported for having gone out in marriage to a non-member. Mary Hunt, late Carpenter, reported for having gone out in marriage; disowned.
27th da, 10th mo, 1800. Joseph Copner requested to come under the care of Friends.
24th da, 11th mo, 1800. Jael Smith, late Nicholson, reported for marrying contrary to discipline to a man whose former wife was her half-sister. Sarah Hammitt received under the care of the Friends.
29th da, 12th mo, 1800. Sarah Hammet granted a certificate to Redstone Monthly Meeting, PA.

BIRTHS AND BURIALS FROM PILESGROVE MONTHLY MEETING
(Salem Monthly Meeting Record Book)

Children of Samuel Lippincott, son of Freedom and Elizabeth
Lippincott, b. 12th da, 12th mo, 1728 and Abigail, wife of said
Samuel Lippincott, dau. of Joseph and Mary Bates, b. 20th da,
1st mo, 1722: Joseph Lippincott, b. 20th da, 8th mo, 1747;
Samuel Lippincott, b. 25th da, 12th mo, 1752; Joshua
Lippincott, b. 8th da, 7th mo, 1755; Mercy Lippincott, b. 24th
da, 9th mo, 1757; Abigail Lippincott, b. 6th da, 12th mo, 1759;
Elizabeth Lippincott, b. 17th da, 11th mo, 1762.
Children of George McNickols, son of Daniel McNickols and
Margaret, and Rebeckah his wife: Hannah McNickols, b. 1st da,
5th mo, 1747; William McNickols, b. 1st da, 5th mo, 1749; Phebe
McNickols, b. 6th da, 6th mo, 1751; Nethaniel McNickols, b.
12th da, 12th mo, 1753; Isaac McNickols, b. 14th da, 3rd mo,
1756; John McNickols, b. 25th da, 4th mo, 1758; Andrew
McNickols, b. 24th da, 12th mo, 1760; Rebeckah McNickols, b.
19th da, 7th mo, 1764.
Children of Daniel Bassett, b. 29th da, 5th mo, 1722 and Mary,
his wife, b. 5th da, 12th mo, 1728: Daniel Bassett, b. 17th da,
9th mo, 1753; Mary Bassett, b. 17th da, 5th mo, 1756
Children of Zacheus Dunn, b. 2nd da, 12th mo, 1698/9 and Deborah,
his wife, b. 10th da, 2nd mo, 1708: Naomi Dunn, b. 6th da, 11th
mo, 1728/9; Sarah Dunn, b. 30th da, 11th mo, 1730/1; John Dunn,
b. 26th da, 10th mo, 1732; Mary Dunn, b. 22nd da, 9th mo, 1735;
Isaac Dunn, b. 2nd da, 12th mo, 1737/8; Nathan Dunn, b. 25th
da, 12th mo, 1742/3; Deborah Dunn, b. 6th da, 4th mo, 1756;
John Dunn, b. 25th da, 10th mo, 1747.

John, Mary and Isaac Dunn d. the same day with the bloody flux.
John and Isaac Dunn were buried in one day in the 6th mo, 1745.
John Dunn, the 8th child d. the 6th da, 11th mo, 1747.

Children of Isaac and Elizabeth Sharp: Mary Sharp, b. 2nd da, 6th
mo, 1744; Hannah Sharp, b. 8th da, 7th mo, 1746; Sarah Sharp,
b. 9th da, 9th mo, 1750; Anthony Sharp, b. 3rd da, 11th mo,
1752; Rachel Sharp, b. 27th da, 2nd mo, 1754; Samuel Sharp, b.
4th da, 5th mo, 1756; Margaret Sharp, b. 21st da, 8th mo, 1758.
Children of William Hains, son of Nathan Hains and his wife,
Sarah, b. 5th da, 1st mo, 1726: Sarah Hains, b. 17th da, 10th
mo, 1752; Mary Hains, b. 24th da, 1st mo, 1754; Ann Hains, b.
3rd da, 6th mo, 1755; Susannah Hains, b. 4th da, 10th, mo,
1756; Jacob Hains, b. 1st da, 5th mo, 1758; William Hains, b.
20th da, 10th mo, 1759.
John Duel, son of John Duel and Hannah, his wife, b. 25th da, 3rd
mo, 1732.
Children of Aquilla Barber and Hannah, his wife: Hannah Barber,
b. 12th da, 1st mo, 1739; Susannah Barber, b. 28th da, 1st mo,
1741; Sarah Barber, b. 4th da, 6th mo, 1744; Liddy Barber, b.
22nd da, 1st mo, 1746; Aquilla Barber, b. 17th da, 5th mo,
1759; James Barber, b. 13th da, 2nd mo, 1752.

Aquilla Barber, d. 26th da, 11th mo, 1764 aged 87 and was buried in Friends burying grounds at Pilesgrove.

Children of Isaac Barber and Jane, his wife: Hannah Barber, b. 12th da, 12th mo, 1750/1; Mary Ann Barber, b. 12th da, 12th mo, 1753/4; Sarah Barber, b. 9th da, 1st mo, 1754; Isaac Barber, Barber, b. 6th da, 2nd mo, 1756; Henry Barber, b. 1st da, 4th mo, 1758; William Barber, b. 18th da, 2nd mo, 1761; Jane Barber, b. 21st da, 4th mo, 1763.

Jane Barber, the elder d. 13th da, 9th mo, 1789 aged 63 years.
William Hains, d. 29th da, 5th mo, 1769 aged 33 years 2 months 13 days.

Children of James Hews and Elizabeth, his wife: Susannah Hews, b. 18th da, 5th mo, 1741; James Hews, b. 26th da, 9th mo, 1743; Jemima Hews, b. 24th da, 11th mo, 1756.
Children of Benjamin Lippincott and Hope, his wife: Elizabeth Lippincott, b. 27th da, 9th mo, 1742; Aaron Lippincott, b. 27th da, 5th mo, 1749; Mary Lippincott, b. 23rd da, 6th mo, 1752; Hope Lippincott, b. 27th da, 7th mo, 1754; Benjamin Lippincott, b. 17th da, 8th mo, 1757.
Children of William Cattell and Ann, his wife: Elijah Cattell, b. 27th da, 7th mo, 1751; Mary Cattell, b. 24th da, 9th mo, 1757.
Child of David Davis and Dorothy, his wife, b. 19th da, 11th mo, 1693/4: David Davis, b. 31st da, 10th mo, 1730; Jacob Davis, b. 22nd da, 4th mo, 1734.
Abigail Davis, wife of the aforesaid David Davis was b. 20th da, 9th mo, 1734.
Children of Joseph Thompson and Mary, his wife: Prudence Thompson, b. 24th da, 4th mo, 1756; Mary Thompson, b. 12th da, 8th mo, 1758; Rebeckah Thompson, b. 2nd da, 11th mo, 1760.
Children of Samuel Hancock and Rachel, his wife: Rebeckah Hancock, b. 2nd da, 7th mo, 1760; Easter Hancock, b. 10th da, 1st mo, 1763; Prudence Hancock, b. 10th da, 2nd mo, 1765; Richard Hancock, b. 10th da, 6th mo, 1767.
Children of Daniel Huddy and Elizabeth, his wife: Martha Huddy, b. 29th da, 5th mo, 1742; Daniel Huddy, b. 15th da, 6th mo, 1747. Elizabeth Huddy, mother of the aforesaid children d. 22nd da, 6th mo, 1755.
Children of William Nicholson and Rachel, his wife: Ruth Nicholson, b. 1st da, 2nd mo, 1748; William and Rachel Nicholson, twins b. 10th da, 12th mo, 1753.

Elizabeth Daniel, wife of James Daniel of Alloways Creek, d. 30th da, 10th mo, 1760 of a pleuritic disorder.
Hannah Winton, sister to the aforesaid Elizabeth Daniel and wife of John Winton, of Pilesgrove, d. 5th da, 12th mo, 1760.
Joseph Reeve of Greenwich, d. 4th da, 1st mo, 1763 in the small pox plague.
Jane Wilson, wife of Robert Wilson of Salem, d. 10th da, 3rd mo, 1765.

Children of John Page and Rebecca, his wife: Sarah Page, b. 14th da, 10th mo, 1745; James Page, b. 3rd da, 11th mo, 1747; Mary

Page, b. 14th da, 11th mo, 1749; Rachel Page, b. 7th da, 2nd mo, 1752; Rebeckah Page, b. 3rd da, 8th mo, 1754; John Page, b. 4th da, 8th mo, 1760; Rachel Page, b. 28th da, 12th mo, 1765.
Children of John Hoffman: Neomy Hoffman, b. 11th da, 9th mo, 1750; Mary Anne Hoffman, b. 19th da, 10th mo, 1752; Elizabeth Hoffman, b. 22nd da, 12th mo, 1755; Isaac Hoffman, b. 14th da, 10th mo, 1762; John Hoffman, b. 7th da, 5th mo, 1765; Jacob Hoffman, b. 3rd da, 12th mo, 1767.

Henry Stubbins, d. 7th da, 6th mo, 1761 and was buried at Salem.
Richard Booth, d. 8th da, 11th mo, 1760.
Elizabeth Colson, d. 31st da, 1st mo, 1758, aged 54 years.
George Colson, d. 3rd da, 2nd mo, 1758, aged 54 years.
Jonathan Colson, d. 21st da, 3rd mo, 1759 aged 19 years.

Children of Edward Draper and Mary, his wife: Amy Draper, b. 10th da, 6th mo, 1756; Jemime Draper, b. 27th da, 10th mo, 1758.
Children of Benjamin Test and Sarah, his wife: Sarah Test, b. 11th da, 1st mo, 1761; Zaceheus Test, b. 23rd da, 9th mo, 1762; Deborah Test, b. 17th da, 12th mo, 1764; Benjamin Test, b. 25th da, 7th mo, 1769.
Children of Andrew Miller and Rachel, his wife: Mary Miller, b. 21st da, 4th mo, 1755, d. 25th da, 8th mo, 1768; William Miller, b. 12th da, 12th mo, 1756, died 13th da, 2nd mo, 1757; Rachel Miller, b. [no date], d. 27th da, 9th mo, 1758; Andrew Miller, b. 12th da, 11th mo, 1760.

Rachel Miller, the elder d. 16th da, 11th mo, 1760, aged 28 years.

James Bradway, son of William Bradway and Sarah, his wife, b. 13th da, 10th mo, 1762.
Children of Aaron Bradway and Sarah, his wife: Sarah Bradway, b. 26th da, 1st mo, 1760; Edward Bradway, b. 7th da, 8th mo, 1761; Hannah and Thomas Bradway, b. 23rd da, 3rd mo, 1764.
Children of Jacob Davis and Esther, his wife: Hannah Davis, b. 30th da, 4th mo, 1762; David Davis, b. 19th da, 8th mo, 1763; Jacob Davis, b. 5th da, 6th mo, 1765; Thomas Davis, b. 13th da, 3rd mo, 1768.
Children of Abel Silver and Hope of Pilesgrove, his wife: Silviah [Silvia] Silver, b. 24th da, 9th mo, 1762; Hope Silver, b. 14th da, 5th mo, 1779.
Children of Joseph Brick and Rebeckah, his wife: Samuel Brick, b. 16th da, 11th mo, 1762; Ann Brick, b. 7th da, 2nd mo, 1765; Hannah Brick, b. 7th da, 6th mo, 1768.
Child of Charles Fogg by Sarah, his wife: Aaron Fogg, b. 7th da, 12th da, 1762.
Children of Mark Reeve and Hannah, his wife: Josiah Reeve, b. 23rd da, 9th mo, 1762; Ann Reeve, b. 29th da, 2nd mo, 1764; Mark Reeve, b. 30th da, 8th mo, 1765; William Reeve, b. 11th da, 12th mo, 1766; George Reeve, b. 19th da, 8th mo, 1769.
Children of Josiah Miller and Leatitia, his wife: Josiah Miller, b. 12th da, 12th mo, 1761; Richard Miller, b. 15th da, 4th mo, 1764; Ebenezer Miller, 1st da, 2nd mo, 1766, d. the 7th week of

his age; John Miller, b. 8th da, 2nd mo, 1767; Leatitia Miller, b. 1st da, 6th mo, 1769; Mark Miller, b. 28th da, 12th mo, 1774.
Children of John Harris and Ruth, his wife: David Harris, b. 1st da, 11th mo, 1762; Abner Harris, b. 27th da, 2nd mo, 1764; William Harris, b. 27th da, 8th mo, 1765; Leatitia Harris, b. 22nd da, 3rd mo, 1767; John Harris, b. 26th da, 10th mo, 1769; Isaac Harris, b. 28th da, 12th mo, 1770; Nathan Harris, b. 16th da, 7th mo, 1772, d. 20th da, 1st mo, 1773; Ruth Harris, b. 18th da, 7th mo, 1774.
Children of John Sheppard and Priscilla, his wife of Greenwich: Rachel Sheppard, b. 31st da, 7th mo, 1762; Mary Sheppard, b. 4th da, 11th mo, 1764; John Sheppard, b. 29th da, 1st mo, 1757; Richard Wood Sheppard, b. 8th da, 11th mo, 1771; Sarah Sheppard, b. 22nd da, 8th mo, 1775; Moses Sheppard, b. 3rd da, 2nd mo, 1777.
Children of Philip Dennis and Hannah, his wife: Edward Dennis, b. 13th da, 2nd mo, 1763; John Dennis, b. 20th da, 10th mo, 1764; Mary Dennis, b. 13th da, 4th mo, 1767; Philip Dennis, b. 26th da, 7th mo, 1769; Hannah Dennis, b. 20th da, 1st mo, 1772.
Children of Nathaniel Hancock and Hannah, his wife: William Hancock, b. 6th da, 10th mo, 1756; Joseph Hancock, b. 25th da, 11th mo, 1761.
Children of William Daniel and Rebeckah, his wife: Jael Daniel, b. 10th da, 10th mo, 1759; Edmund Daniel, b. 14th da, 1st mo, 1762.
Child of Thomas Brown and Mary, his wife: Thomas Brown, b. 10th da, 8th mo, 1760.
Children of John Ware and Elizabeth, his wife: Hannah Ware, b. 17th da, 10th mo, 1761; Elizabeth Ware, b. 2nd da, 3rd mo, 1763; Job Ware, b. 16th da, 1st mo, 1766; Sarah Ware, b. 11th da, 4th mo, 1769.
John Davis, son of John and Elizabeth Davis, b. 21st da, 4th mo, 1762.

John Davis, the elder, d. 11th da, 3rd mo, 1763.

Child of Thomas Graves, and Rebecca, his wife: Thomas Graves, b. 8th mo, 1742.
Children of Edward Bradway and Elizabeth, his wife: David Bradway, b. 27th da, 11th mo, 1761; Edward Bradway, b. 22nd da, 12th mo, 1767; Waddington Bradway, b. 15th da, 1st mo, 1770; Elizabeth Bradway, b. 22nd da, 1st mo, 1774; Adna Bradway, b. 16th da, 2nd mo, 1777.
Children of Joseph Thompson and Mary, his wife: Elizabeth Thompson, b. 4th da, 10th mo, 1762; Sarah Thompson, b. 7th da, 12th mo, 1764.
Children of Joseph Stretch and Sarah, his wife: Jael Stretch, b. 17th da, 7th mo, 1762; Martha Stretch, 10th da, 11th mo, 1765.
Children of Christopher Smith and Ann, his wife: Oakford Smith, b. 30th da, 2nd mo, 1759; Ann Smith, b. 23rd da, 12th mo, 1763; Abigail Smith, b. 26th da, 1st mo, 1765.
Children of Richard Smith of Elsonborugh and Rachel, his wife: Grace Smith, b. 21st da, 9th mo, 1764; Elizabeth Smith, b. 30th

da, 1st mo, 1767; Sarah Smith, b. 17th da, 12th mo, 1769; Rachel Smith, b. 13th da, 5th mo, 1773; Prudence Smith, b. 26th da, 2nd mo, 1776.
Children of David Davis and Martha, his wife: Samuel Coles Davis, b. 26th da, 10th mo, 1764; Joseph Davis, b. 15th da, 6th mo, 1766; Mary Davis, b. 2nd da, 3rd mo, 1768; Jacob Davis, b. 31st da, 4th mo, 1770.
Child of Isaac Bassett and Deborah, his wife: Deborah Bassett, b. 17th da, 3rd mo, 1765.

David Barber, son of Jacob Barber and Rebeckah, his wife, d. 17th da, 10th mo, 1767.
Jacob Barber, son of Aquilla Barber and Mary, d. 4th da, 5th mo, 1765.
Hannah Davis, dau. of Jacob Davis and Esther, his wife, d. 13th da, 6th mo, 1765.
Jacob Davis, son of Jacob Davis and Esther, his wife, d. 19th da, 11th mo, 1767.

Children of John Test and Elizabeth, his wife from Pilesgrove: Mary Test, b. 30th da, 5th mo, 1765; Elizabeth Test, b. 10th da, 9th mo, 1767; Hope Test, b. 18th da, 11th mo, 1769; John Test, b. 12th da, 11th mo, 1771; Martha Test, b. 19th da, 9th mo, 1774.
Children of Samuel Test and Lydia, his wife from Alloways Creek: Dorcas Test, b. 31st da, 10th mo, 1758; Isaac Test, b. 3rd da, 8th mo, 1761.

Lidya Test, wife of Samuel Test, d. 11th da, 1st mo, 1765 and was buried at Salem.

Children of Samuel Test and Sarah, his wife: Joseph Test, b. 21st da, 10th mo, 1769; Lidya Test, b. 17th da, 11th mo, 1771.
Children of Joshua Stretch and Lidya, his wife from Alloways Creek: Job Stretch, b. 6th da, 12th mo, 1763; Millisent Stretch, b. 17th da, 8th mo, 1766; Elisha Stretch, b. 17th da, 12th mo, 1768.

Lidya Stretch, wife of Joshua Stretch above mentioned, d. 5th da, 5th mo, 1772.

Child of John Mason and Ann, his wife from Elsenburgh: Sarah Mason, b. 24th da, 6th mo, 1763.
Children of Thomas Thompson and Deborah, his wife from Alloways Creek: Isaac Thompson, b. 25th da, 6th mo, 1763; Samuel Thompson, b. 27th da, 9th mo, 1764; Aaron Thompson, b. 18th da, 8th mo, 1766.
Children of Richard Dicker and Esther, his wife from Salem: Hannah Dicker, b. 19th da, 6th mo, 1765; Lidya Dicker, b. 19th da, 5th mo, 1768; Elizabeth Dicker, b. 30th da, 5th mo, 1771.
Child of John Barber and Jane, his wife: John Barber, b. 22nd da, 4th mo, 1764.
Deborah Thompson, wife of Thomas Thompson, d. 29th da, 11th mo, 1768.

Sarah Goodwin, wife of Thomas Goodwin d. 5th da, 10th mo, 1765 aged 41 years and about 10 months.
Sarah Goodwin, the 2nd wife of aforesaid Thomas Goodwin d. 25th da, 5th mo, 1783 aged 53 years and about 2 months.
Sarah Ware, widow of Solomon Ware d. 17th da, 11th mo, 1765.
Hannah Ware, dau. of Solomon Ware and Sarah, his wife, d. 7th da, 11th mo, 1765.
Job Ware, son of Solomon Ware and Sarah, his wife d. 19th da, 12th mo, 1765.
Abigail Hoffman, dau. of John Hoffman and Mary, his wife d. 24th da, 2nd mo, 1760.

Children of Jonathan Stretch and Hannah, his wife from Alloways Creek: Sarah Stretch, b. 8th da, 9th mo, 1759; David Stretch, b. 25th da, 5th mo, 1762; Deborah Stretch, b. 1st da, 4th mo, 1764; Mark Stretch, b. 7th mo, 9th mo, 1766; Elizabeth Stretch, b. 26th da, 5th mo, 1769; Rebeckah Stretch, b. 18th da, 12th mo, 1771; Jonathan Stretch, b. 12th da, 3rd mo, 1774 and d. 27th da, 5th mo, following; Hannah Stretch, b. 11th da, 21st mo, 1778.
Child of Joseph Kay and Ann, his wife: Isaac Kay, b. 22nd da, 8th mo, 1765.
Children of Richard Hains and Elizabeth, his wife: Ephraim Hains, b. 4th da, 3rd mo, 1758; Elizabeth Hains, b. 18th da, 9th mo, 1759; Leatitia Hains, b. 4th da, 5th mo, 1761; Mary Hains, b. 7th da, 4th mo, 1763; Susannah Hains, b. 11th da, 10th mo, 1764; Grace Hains, b. 19th da, 5th mo, 1766; Beulah Hains, b. 20th da, 10th mo, 1768; Deborah Hains, b. 30th da, 6th mo, 1769.

Abigail Bassett, wife of Elisha Bassett of Pilesgrove, d. 30th da, 12th mo, 1770, aged 70 years.

Child of Thomas Hartley and Susannah, his wife: Elizabeth Hartley, b. 12th da, 12th mo, 1765.
Children of Thomas Hartley by Catharine, his wife: Susannah Hartley, b. 3rd da, 10th mo, 1772; Sarah Hartley, b. 30th da, 3rd mo, 1774, d. 27th da, 5th mo, 1775; Thomas Hartley, b. 13th da, 7th mo, 1775.
Children of Clement Hall and Margaret, his wife: Joseph Hall, b. 19th da, 11th mo, 1760; Morris Hall, b. 13th da, 10th mo, 1762; Margaret Hall, b. 18th da, 1st mo, 1765 and buried the 16th da, 10th mo, of same year.
Child of William Hancock and Jane, his wife: Lydia Hancock, b. 19th da, 4th mo, 1766.
Children of Nathan Dunn and Ann, his wife: Rebeckah Dunn, b. 27th da, 6th mo, 1766 and d. 30th da, 9th mo, 1767; Zacheus Dunn, b. 24th da, 10th mo, 1768.
Children of Samuel Hancock and Rachel, his wife: Samuel b. 25th da, 3rd mo, 1772.
Child of William Bradway and Sarah, his wife: Samuel Bradway, 28th da, 2nd mo, 1766.

Esther Hancock, dau. of Samuel and Rachel Hancock, d. 22nd da,

9th mo, 1769 in the 7th year of her age.

Children of Hugh Pedrick and Elizabeth, his wife: Hannah Pedrick, b. 4th da, 6th mo, 1766 and d. 8th da, 9th mo, following; Richard Pedrick, b. 16th da, 10th mo, 1767; James Pedrick, b. 22nd da, 10th mo, 1769; Philip Pedrick, b. 13th da, 10th mo, 1771; William Pedrick, b. 11th da, 6th mo, 1774; Rebeckah Pedrick, b. 17th da, 8th mo, 1776; Elizabeth Pedrick, b. 7th da, 12th mo, 1778; Susannah Pedrick, b. 4th da, 12th mo, 1781.

Children of William Abbott and Rebeckah, his wife: Samuel Abbott, b. 27th da, 11th mo, 1763; George Abbott, b. 27th da, 9th mo, 1765; Josiah Abbott, b. 23rd da, 9th mo, 1768.

Jane Gibson, wife of Joseph Gibson, d. 26th da, 11th mo, 1766 of a cancer in her face.

Jane Barber, dau. of Isaac Barber and Jane, his wife, d. 12th da, 4th mo, 1766 aged near 3 years.

Hannah Brick, dau. of John Brick and Ann, his wife, d. 22nd da, 4th mo, 1766 after a lingering illness aged 24 years.

Mary Bradway, wife of Jonathan Bradway, d. 23rd da, 8th mo, 1738 aged about 38 years.

Jonathan Bradway, d. 3rd mo, 1765 aged 66 years.

Samuel Bradway, son of William Bradway and Sarah, his wife, d. 17th da, 2nd mo, 1767.

Solomon Ware, Jr., d. 10th da, 12th mo, 1766.

Child of Aaron Daniel and Elizabeth, his wife: David Daniel, b. 4th da, 3rd mo, 1749.

Children of Jonathan Bradway and Elizabeth, his wife: John Bradway, b. 23rd da, 3rd mo, 1759; Mark Bradway, b. 27th da, 11th mo, 1763; Jonathan Bradway, b. 24th da, 2nd mo, 1766; Mary Bradway, b. 12th da, 4th mo, 1768; Adna Bradway, b. 25th da, 4th mo, 1770; William Bradway, b. 9th da, 10th mo, 1772.

Joseph Stretch, d. 1st da, 1st mo 1767; Joseph Stretch, Jr., d. 6th da, 5th mo, 1767.

Philip Dennis, d. 15th da, 2nd mo, 1768 aged 66 years.

Elisha Ware, d. 1st da, 2nd mo, 1769.

Sarah Keasbey, dau. of Bradway Keasbey and Jane, his wife, d. 15th da, 5th mo, 1764.

Margaret Bacon, an elder of Greenwich Monthly Meeting, d. 29th da, 1st mo, 1769 aged 55 years.

Hannah Brown, dau. of Thomas Brown and Mary, his wife, d. 22nd da, 8th mo, 1771 aged 15 years and 5 months.

John Evans, d. 28th da, 4th mo, 1770.

Children of Martin Widmayer and Mary, his wife: Virgin Widmayer, b. 3rd da, 2nd mo, 1767; Mary Widmayer, b. 20th da, 8th mo, 1769; Hannah Widmayer, b. 11th da, 3rd mo, 1773.

Child of Benjamin Reeve and Ruth, his wife: Hannah Reeve, b. 24th da, 11th mo, 1766, d. 16th da, 3rd mo, 1767.

Ruth Reeve, wife of Benjamin Reeve, d. 25th da, 2nd mo, 1767.
Hannah Duel, wife of John Duel of Pilesgrove, d. 14th da, 5th mo,

1767 aged 77 years.
Susannah Hartley, wife of Thomas Hartley, d. 14th da, 3rd mo, 1768 aged 26 years 7 months.
Eleanor Evans, wife of Aaron Evans, d. 23rd da, 11th mo, 1770.

Child of Isaac Bassett and Deborah, his wife: Abigail Bassett b. 19th da, 7th mo, 1768.
Children of David Allen and Rebeckah, his wife: Hannah Allen, b. 5th da, 3rd mo, 1767; Mary Allen, b. 26th da, 5th mo, 1768; Ann Allen, b. 28th da, 1st mo, 1770; Rebeckah Allen and David Allen, b. 21st da, 3rd mo, 1772; Edith Allen, b. 8th da, 5th mo, 1775; Beulah Allen, b. 2nd da, 6th mo, 1779; Samuel Allen, b. 21st da, 10th mo, 1781; Jedidiah Allen, b. 27th da, 8th mo, 1784.
Child of William Hancock, Jr. and Jane, his wife: Thomas Hancock, b. 30th da, 11th mo, 1768, d. 28th da, 9th mo, 1769. Jane Hancock, wife of William Hancock, Jr., d. 16th da, 4th mo, 1769 aged 21 years and 9 months.
Child of Joseph Hermer and Rebeckah, his wife: Joseph Hermer, b. 5th da, 3rd mo, 1767. Joseph Hermer, the elder, d. 25th da, 10th mo, 1767.
Child of Charles Ellet and Sarah, his wife: Elizabeth Ellet, b. 30th da, 9th mo, 1761.
Children of Charles Ellet and Hannah, his wife: John Ellet, b. 3rd da, 2nd mo, 1769; Sarah Ellet, b. 15th da, 11th mo, 1770; Thomas Ellet, b. 2nd da, 3rd mo, 1772; Samuel Ellet, b. 16th da, 1st mo, 1774, d. 15th da, 7th mo, 1774; William Ellet, b. 3rd da, 7th mo, 1775; Charles and Hannah Ellet, b. 4th da, 3rd mo, 1777, Hannah d. the same day; Hannah Ellet, b. 3rd da, 1st mo, 1779, d. 12th da, 8th mo, following; Rachel Ellet, b. 12th da, 9th mo, 1780; Mary Ellet, b. 23rd da, 10th mo, 1782.
Children of Jacob Townsend and Mary, his wife: Richard Townsend, b. 16th da, 11th mo, 1766; Rebeckah Townsend, b. 5th da, 12th mo, 1769; John Townsend, 6th da, 1st mo, 1772.
Children of Joseph Rockhill and Mary, his wife: Robert Rockhill, b. 3rd da, 3rd mo, 1756; Hannah Rockhill, b. 1st da, 2nd mo, 1761; Samuel Rockhill, b. 6th da, 10th mo, 1762; Lida Rockhill, b. 28th da, 6th mo, 1766; Clement Rockhill, b. 1st mo, 11th mo, 1768; Mary Rockhill, b. 4th da, 3rd mo, 1776.
Children of Andrew Thompson and Grace, his wife: Joshua Thompson, b. 19th da, 9th mo, 1767; Sarah Thompson, b. 20th da, 1st mo, 1769; Grace Thompson, b. 12th da, 2nd mo, 1771; Rachel Thompson, b. 7th da, 5th mo, 1773; Samuel Thompson, b. 21st da, 1st mo, 1776, was buried 24th of the same; Samuel Thompson, b. 23rd da, 5th mo, 1777.
Children of James Tyler and Martha, his wife: James Tyler, b. 11th da, 1st mo, 1755; Ruth Tyler, b. 29th da, 6th mo, 1760.

Mary Silver, wife of Archibald Silver, d. 3rd da, 11th mo, 1767, aged 66; Archibald Silver, d. 11th da, 2nd mo, 1772, aged 78.
Adna Bradway, son of William Bradway and Sarah, his wife, d. 7th da, 2nd mo, 1770 aged 20 years.
Nethaniel Chamneys, d. 14th da, 3rd mo, 1767.
Esther Tindall, d. 17th da, 12th mo, 1767 aged 16.

Children of John Grinslade and Elizabeth, his wife: Elizabeth
Grinslade, b. 23rd da, 10th mo, 1769; John Grinslade, b. 8th
da, 9th mo, 1771.
Children of Mathias Matson and Elizabeth, his wife: Hapzibah
Matson, b. 29th da, 9th mo, 1755; Sarah Matson, b. 22nd da, 2nd
mo, 1757; Mary Matson, b. 24th da, 10th mo, 1764.
Children of Isaac Summers and Elizabeth, his wife: Isaac Summers,
b. 20th da, 8th mo, 1767; Elizabeth Summers, b. 20th da, 8th
mo, 1769.[This entry was crossed out in the original record.]
Children of James Mason and Rebeckah, his wife: Ann Mason, b.
17th da, 8th mo, 1762; Melissa Mason, b. 1st da, 8th mo, 1764;
Barrott Mason, b. 15th da, 9th mo, 1766; Hannah Mason, b. 17th
da, 11th mo, 1768; Aaron Mason, b. 24th da, 12th mo, 1770;
Sarah Mason, b. 7th da, 3rd mo, 1773; Rebeckah Mason, b. 29th
da, 6th mo, 1774; Leatitia Mason, b. 21st da, 9th mo, 1776;
John Mason, b. 27th da, 10th mo, 1778; Ruth Mason, b. 8th da,
6th mo, 1781; Mary Mason, b. 27th da, 6th mo, 1784.
Children of Levi Jennings and Sarah, his wife: Hannah Jennings,
29th da, 1st mo, 1760; Ann Jennings, b. 27th da, 3rd mo, 1762;
Levi Jennings, b. 15th da, 5th mo, 1764; Thomas Jennings, b.
15th da, 11th mo, 1766.

James Mason, d. 22nd da, 8th mo, 1799 aged 67 lacking one day.
Rebecca Mason, widow of James Mason d. 19th da, 9th mo, 1799 aged
59 years lacking 6 weeks.
Amos Oakford, d. 24th da, 10th mo, 1765.
John Oakford, d. 1st da, 3rd mo, 1771.
Hannah Oakford, d. 7th da, 4th mo, 1771.
Richard Hancock, son of Samuel Hancock by Rachel, his wife, d.
12th da, 3rd mo, 1773.
Andrew Griscom, d. 3rd da, 4th mo, 1773 aged 62 years.
William Bassett, d. 22nd da, 1st mo, 1769.

Children of Paul Saunders and Elizabeth, his wife: James
Saunders, b. 22nd da, 10th mo, 1763; John Saunders, b. 14th da,
5th mo, 1765; Paul Saunders, b. 28th da, 8th mo, 1767; Samuel
Saunders, b. 29th or 30th da, 4th or 5th mo, 1769 [this is a
copy of date as given in original]; Rebeckah Saunders, b. 29th
da, 4th mo, 1771.
Children of William Bassett and Phebe, his wife: Mary Bassett, b.
18th da, 9th mo, 1762; Abigail Bassett, b. 6th da, 9th mo,
1766.
Jacob Andrews, son of said Phebe by her former husband, Samuel
Andrews b. 10th da, 9th mo, 1755.
Children of John Hoffman and Mary, his wife: Jonathan Hoffman, b.
28th da, 7th mo, 1771; Samuel Hoffman, b. 22nd da, 1st mo,
1776.
Children of William Hancock, Jr. and Hannah, his wife: William
Hancock, b. 4th da, 7th mo, 1771, d. 10th da of same; John
Hancock, b. 24th da, 4th mo, 1773; Elizabeth Hancock, b. 17th
da, 7th mo, 1776.
Children of Benjamin Reeve and Rachel, his wife: Benjamin Reeve,
b. 6th da, 4th mo, 1770; James Reeve, b. 1st da, 4th mo, 1772;

Richard Reeve, b. 14th da, 5th mo, 1774; Joshua Reeve, b. 21st
da, 11th mo, 1775; George Reeve, b. 14th da, 9th mo, 1780.
Child of Thomas Huckins and Mercy, his wife: Samuel Huckins, b.
4th da, 8th mo, 1756.
Note: Isaac Test, son of Samuel Test by Lidya, his wife, being
set to watch the team whilst his father was unloading a load of
hay being near the horse's head, one of them bit of the flesh
part and stripped half way along the back part of his left ear
in the 8th mo, 1769 being near the age of 8 years.
Children of Jacob Davis and Hester, his wife: Josiah Davis, b.
24th da, 10th mo, 1770; James Davis, b. 21st da, 2nd mo, 1773;
Esther Davis, b. 18th da, 5th mo, 1778.
Children of Joseph Lippincott and Ann, his wife: Mary Lippincott,
b. 6th da, 11th mo, 1771; Lidya Lippincott, b. 1st da, 2nd mo,
1775.
Children of David Smith and Hannah, his wife: Daniel Smith, b.
25th da, 3rd mo, 1780; Mary Smith, b. 20th da, 12th mo, 1783.
Child of Benjamin Test and Sarah, his wife: David Test, b. 22nd
da, 9th mo, 1771.
Children of Christopher Smith and Rebeckah, his wife: Rebeckah
Smith, b. 13th da, 12th mo, 1766; Elizabeth Smith, b. 17th da,
5th mo, 1768; John Smith, b. 27th da, 12th mo, 1770; Susannah
Smith, b. 18th da, 12th mo, 1771; Esther Smith, b. 3rd da, 1st
mo, 1774.
Children of Abel Silver and Hope, his wife: Rebeckah Silver, b.
11th da, 7th mo, 1765; Susannah Silver, b. 8th da, 8th mo,
1767; Archibald Silver, b. 23rd da, 5th mo, 1769; Abraham
Silver, b. 15th da, 10th mo, 1771; Mary Ann Silver, b. 17th da,
2nd mo, 1774; James Silver, b. 20th da, 6th mo, 1776.
Children of Hugh Pedrick and Elizabeth, his wife: James Pedrick,
b. 22nd da, 10th mo, 1769; Philip Pedrick, b. 13th da, 10th mo,
1771. [This entry was crossed out of original record.]

Jonathan Bradway, d. 19th da, 11th mo, 1772.
Adna Bradway, son of Jonathan Bradway, d. 23rd da, 1st mo, 1773.
Mary Stewart, wife of James Stewart, d. 24th da, 2nd mo, 1773.
Jacob Townsend, d. 4th da, 9th mo, 1772, aged 37 years.

Children of John Barns, b. 1st da, 1st mo, 1741 and Rebeckah, b.
4th da, 1st mo, 1737, his wife: Joseph Barns, b. 27th da, 9th
mo, 1759; Sarah Barns, b. 12th da, 9th mo, 1761; John Barns, b.
13th da, 10th mo, 1763; Joshua Barns, b. 19th da, 7th mo, 1766;
Richard Barns, b. 20th da, 7th mo, 1769; Hepzebah Barns, b.
27th da, 7th mo, 1771; Ephraim Barns, b. 15th da, 6th mo, 1774;
Samuel Barns, b. 26th da, 8th mo, 1778; Elizabeth Barnes, b.
13th da, 5th mo, 1780.
Children of David Evans and Jane, his wife: John Evans, b. 7th
da, 9th mo, 1768; Ann Evans, b. 8th da, 4th mo, 1770, d. 18th
da, 10th mo, 1772; Elizabeth Evans, b. 5th da, 2nd mo, 1772.
Child of David Evans and Mary, his wife: John Evans, b. 5th da,
5th mo, 1776.
Children of Samuel Bassett and Ann, his wife: Grace Bassett, b.
16th da, 3rd mo, 1756; William Bassett, b. 4th da, 2nd mo,
1758; Samuel Bassett, b. 30th da, 8th mo, 1760; Morris Bassett,

b. 31st da, 4th mo, 1763; Davis Bassett, b. 3rd da, 8th mo, 1765; Ann Bassett, b. 5th da, 1st mo, 1770.
Children of William Adams and Sarah, his wife: John Adams b. 20th da, 12th mo, 1773; Susannah Adams b. 19th da, 2nd mo, 1773.
Child of Joseph Bacon by Rachel, his wife: Margaret Bacon b. 8th da, 9th mo, 1771.
Children of Benjamin Wright and Ruth, his wife: Elizabeth Wright, b. 20th da, 3rd mo, 1759; Stephen Wright, b. 6th da, 10th mo, 1760; Nathan Wright, b. 19th da, 11th mo, 1762; Peter Wright, b. 22nd da, 5th mo, 1766; George Wright, b. 7th da, 4th mo, 1768; Thomas Wright, b. 10th da, 3rd mo, 1772; William Wright, b. 9th da, 10th mo, 1773; Benjamin Wright, b. 27th da, 4th mo, 1777.
Child of Bartholomew Wyatt and Mary, his wife: Elizabeth Wiatt, b. 12th da, 3rd mo, 1763.
Children of Abel Hall by Rebeckah, his wife: Ebenezer Hall, b. 11th da, 4th mo, 1771; Mark Hall, b. 26th da, 2nd mo, 1773.

Abel Hall, d. 26th da, 9th mo, 1773 age 26 years.
Bartholomew Wyatt, d. 23rd da, 1st mo, 1770 aged near 72 years.
Edith Thompson, d. 13th da, 2nd mo, 1773, widow of Samuel Thompson, dec'd.
Job Ridgway, d. 21st da, 2nd mo, 1773 aged 53 years and 5 months.
John Ware of Lower Alloways Creek, d. 12th da, 5th mo, 1773 aged 53 years 2 months.
Mary Widmayer, d. 26th da, 4th mo, 1773 aged 29 years.
Mary Griscom, d. 27th da, 2nd mo, 1774 aged 56 years.
Joshua Stretch, d. 24th da, 4th mo, 1774 aged near 34 years.
Jane Evans, wife of David Evans, d. 29th da, 1st mo, 1774.
Ruth Harris, wife of John Harris, d. 1st da, 8th mo, 1774.
John Taggart, d. 26th da, 11th mo, 1774.
Rebeckah Deviney, d. 16th da, 2nd mo, 1775 aged 68 years.
Aaron Barracliff, son of John Barracliff by Leatitia, his wife, d. 13th da, 6th mo, 1775 aged 18 years and 5 months.
John Firth, d. 5th da, 4th mo, 1776.
Benjamin Thompson, d. 29th da, 6th mo, 1775.
Milliscent Thompson, dau. of Benjamin Thompson, d. 23rd da, 6th mo, 1776.

Children of Samuel Ogden and Mary Ann, his wife: Mary Ogden, b. 13th da, 6th mo, 1771; Esther Ogden, b. 15th da, 2nd mo, 1773; Joseph Ogden, b. 4th da, 8th mo, 1775.
Children of Charles Bacon and Rebeckah, his wife: Rebeckah Bacon, b. 4th da, 4th mo, 1773; Charles Bacon, b. 7th da, 10th mo, 1777. Rebeckah Bacon, wife of Charles Bacon d. 18th dam, 12th mo, 1777 aged 33 years.
Children of Isaac Summers and Elizabeth, his wife: Isaac Summers, b. 20th da, 8th mo, 1767; Elizabeth Summers, b. 20th da, 8th mo, 1769; Jacob Summers, b. 22nd da, 10th mo, 1771; Rebeckah Summers, b. 2nd da, 1st mo, 1774; David Summers, b. 28th da, 3rd mo, 1777.
Children of Thomas Thackery and Elizabeth, his wife: Hannah Thackery, b. 13th da, 9th mo, 1754; William Thackery, b. 27th da, 12th mo, 1756; Stephen Thackery, b. 24th da, 1st mo, 1760;

Jacob Thackery, b. 27th da, 11th mo, 1763; Joseph Thackery, b.
20th da, 10th mo, 1765; Thomas Thackery, b. 14th da, 1st mo,
1771.

Elizabeth, wife of Thomas Thackery, d. 30th da, 10th mo, 1774
aged 45 years.

Children of Ezra Firth and Elizabeth, his wife: Preston Carpenter
Firth, b. 25th da, 10th mo, 1769; John Firth, b. 28th da, 10th
mo, 1771; Samuel Firth, b. 14th da, 10th mo, 1773; Thomas
Firth, b. 14th da, 2nd mo, 1776.
Child of John Smith and Milliscent, his wife: John Smith, b. 4th
da, 2nd mo, 1774.
Child of Samuel Withers and Grace, his wife: Mary Withers, b. 2nd
da, 10th mo, 1775.
Children of William Griscom and Rachel, his wife: John Griscom,
b. 27th da, 9th mo, 1774; William Griscom, b. 8th da, 8th mo,
1777; Samuel Griscom, b. 22nd da, 1st mo, 1780, d. 11th da, 3rd
mo, 1780; Everatt Griscom, b. 24th da, 12th mo, 1781; Rachel
Griscom, b. 24th da, 8th mo, 1784.
Child of Zacheus Ballinger and Hope, his wife: Jacob Ballinger,
b. 16th da, 9th mo, 1775.
Children of John Mason and Susannah, his wife: William Mason b.
13th da, 1st mo, 1774; Mary Mason, b. 10th da, 3rd mo, 1776.
Child of Aaron Evans and Ann, his wife: Prudence Evans, b. 10th
da, 11th mo, 1773.

Milliscent Smith, wife of John Smith, d. 11th da, 6th mo, 1777.
Sarah Fogg, wife of Charles Fogg, d. 21st da, 3rd mo, 1776 aged
56.
Andrew Thompson of Alloways Creek, d. 15th da, 1st mo, 1775.
Elizabeth Thompson, wife of said Andrew Thompson, d. 21st da, 1st
mo, 1775.
John Taggart, d. 26th da, 11th mo, 1774.
Abraham Shreeve, d. 17th da, 5th mo, 1775.
Edith Shreeve, dau. of Abraham Shreeve, d. 20th da, 11th mo,
1774.
Hope Shreeve, dau. of Abraham Shreeve, d. 27th da, 4th mo, 1776.
Robert Shreeve, son of Abraham Shreeve, d. 22nd da, 5th mo, 1776
aged 17 years.
Catharine Hartley, wife of Thomas Hartley, d. 26th da, 4th mo,
1776 aged 29 years and 6 months.
John Miller, son of Josiah Miller and Leatitia, his wife, d. 29th
da, 6th mo, 1773.
Josiah Davis, son of Jacob Davis, d. 1st da, 2nd mo, 1776.
James Davis, son of Jacob Davis, d. 16th da, 2nd mo, 1776.
Naomy Huddy, d. 6th da, 11th mo, 1775.
Thomas Right, son of Benjamin Wright, d. 13th da, 8th mo, 1775.
Hannah Stretch, wife of Jonathan Stretch, d. 18th da, 12th mo,
1775.
Ann Bassett, wife of Samuel Basset, d. 26th da, 3rd mo, 1776.
Edith Thompson, wife of Benjamin Thompson, d. 2nd da, 10th mo,
1775.

Child of Andrew Thompson and wife: Elizabeth Thompson, b. 9th da, 7th mo, 1777.
Children of Benjamin Clark Cooper and Ann, his wife: Mary Cooper, b. 6th da, 12th mo, 1773, d. 5th da, 11th mo, 1774; James Cooper, b. 17th da, 2nd mo, 1775; William Cooper, d. 16th da, 8th mo, 1776; Deborah Cooper, b. 30th da, 10th mo, 1778; Samuel Cooper, b. 8th da, 11th mo, 1780.
Children of John Bacon and Mary, his wife: John Bacon, b. 11th da, 10th mo, 1766; Job Bacon, b. 2nd da, 10th mo, 1768; Ann Bacon, b. 17th da, 6th mo, 1772; Elizabeth Bacon, b. 6th da, 1st mo, 1776.
Children of George Colson and Mary, his wife: Mary Colson, b. 13th da, 8th mo, 1774; George Colson, b. 13th da, 4th mo, 1776; Asa Colson, b. 6th da, 1st mo, 1778; David and Jonathan Colson, b. 1st da, 5th mo, 1780, David d. 16th da, 10th mo, following.
Children of Thomas Hartley: Samuel Hartley, b. 1st da, 2nd mo, 1777; Mary Hartley, b. 26th da, 10th mo, 1782; Mark Hartley, b. 27th da, 10th mo, 1784.

Mary Goodwin, wife of William Goodwin of Elsenburgh, Salem County, d. 3rd da, 4th mo, 1776.
Samuel Hancock, d. 21st da, 3rd mo, 1776.
James Daniel, d. 18th da, 3rd mo, 1776 aged 72 years 3 months 26 days.
Samuel Withers, d. 7th da, 10th mo, 1776.
Joseph Thompson, d. 15th da, 6th mo, 1776.
John McNichols, Jr., d. 2nd da, 1st mo, 1777.
William Thackery, d. 18th da, 6th mo, 1776.
Nethaniel Hancock, d. 3rd da, 6th mo, 1776.
William Hancock, son of Nethaniel Hancock, d. 4th da, 2nd mo, 1776.
Hannah Rockhill, dau. of Joseph and Mary Rockhill, d. 2nd da, 4th mo, 1777 aged 17 years.
Ann Lippincott, wife of Joseph Lippincott, d. 7th da, 4th mo, 1777.
Milliscent Smith, wife of John Smith, d. 11th da, 6th mo, 1777.
Rachel Nicholson, dau. of William Nicholson, d. 1st da, 9th mo, 1777.
Milliscent Nicholson, dau. of William Nicholson, d. 1st da, 10th mo, 1777.
Ebenezer Miller of Greenwich, Cumberland County, d. 6th da, 2nd mo, 1774.
Ann Evans, wife of Aaron Evans, d. 11th da, 4th mo, 1778 aged 28 years.
Joseph Thompson, son of Joshua Thompson, d. 23rd da, 3rd mo, 1778 aged 22 years and buried at Salem.

Children of William Nicholson and Sarah, his wife: Rachel Nicholson, b. 9th da, 11th mo, 1774; Milliscent Nicholson, b. 3rd da, 8th mo, 1776; William Nicholson, b. 8th da, 3rd mo, 1779, and since died; Samuel Nicholson, b. 2nd da, 7th mo, 1781; William Nicholson, b. 16th da, 11th mo, 1783.

Sarah Nicholson, d. 2nd da, 9th mo, 1784.

Sarah Nicholson, b. 26th da, 7th mo, 1791.
Ruth Nicholson, d. 18th da, 12th mo, 1792.
Daniel Nicholson, b. 19th da, 1st mo, 1786.

Children of William Dunham and Elizabeth, his wife: Shobal
Dunham, b. 27th da, 5th mo, 1773; John Dunham, b. 7th da, 4th
mo, 1775; William Dunham, b. 28th da, 12th mo, 1776.
Child of Jedidah Allen and Mary, his wife: Samuel Allen, b. 12th
da, 11th mo, 1762.
Children of Jedidah Allen and Ruth, his wife: Elizabeth Allen, b.
11th da, 9th mo, 1768; William Allen, b. 24th da, 1st mo, 1770;
Rachel Allen, b. 12th da, 8th mo, 1771.
Children of Isaac Stroud and Lidya, his wife: Thomas Stroud, b.
2nd da, 11th mo, 1774; Mary Shroud, b. 30th da, 9th mo,
Elizabeth Stroud, b. 16th da, 10th mo, 1778.
Children of Zadock Street and Eunice, his wife: William Street,
b. 10th da, 11th da, 1775; Aaron Street, b. 4th da, 1st mo,
1778; John Street, b. 14th da, 3rd mo, 1782; Anna Street, b.
17th da, 8th mo, 1784; Lydia Street, b. 1st da, 1st mo, 1789;
William Street, b. 3rd da, 3rd mo, 1788.
Children of William Bradway and Mary, his wife: Sarah Bradway, b.
12th da, 6th mo, 1775; Anna Bradway, b. 13th da, 2nd mo, 1780.
Children of Benjamin Moore and Hannah, his wife: Rebeckah Moore,
b. 3rd da, 2nd mo, 1769; Josiah Moore, b. 31st da, 7th mo,
1770; Chalkey Moore, b. 30th da, 10th mo, 1773; Mary Moore, b.
8th da, 5th mo, 1776.
Children of Samuel Fogg and Prudence, his wife: Elijah Fogg, b.
12th da, 6th mo, 1775; Prudence Fogg, b. 19th da, 4th mo, 1777.
Children of John Miller and Margaret, his wife: Joseph Miller, b.
16th da, 6th mo, 1768; Mary Miller, b. 26th da, 7th mo, 1770;
John Miller, b. 3rd da, 3rd mo, 1772; William Miller, b. 5th
da, 4th mo, 1774; Isaac Miller, b. 21st da, 5th mo, 1776.
Children of Joshua Thompson and Sarah, his wife: Joseph Thompson,
b. 27th da, 10th mo, 1774; John Thompson, b. 3rd da, 8th mo,
1776; Elizabeth Thompson, b. 13th da, 11th mo, 1778, d. 1st da,
2nd mo, 1779.

Charles Davis, d. 3rd da, 9th mo, 1778 aged 71 years 6 months.
Elizabeth Evans, dau. of David Evans and Jane, his wife, d. 12th
da, 8th mo, 1778.
George Reeve, son of Mark Reeve and Hannah, his wife, d. 31st da,
7th mo, 1778 aged 4 years.
Ann Reeve, dau. of same parents d. 12th da, 8th mo, 1778 aged 14
years 5 months.
Joseph Lippincott, son of Samuel and Abigail Lippincott, d. 25th
da, 9th mo, 1778 aged 31 years and 2 weeks.
Mercy Kerby Lippincott, dau. of Samuel and Abigail Lippincott, d.
11th da, 10th mo, 1778 aged 21 years 2 weeks 3 days.
John Barber, d. 18th da, 11th mo, 1776 aged 56.
Rebeck Barber, d. 8th da, 2nd mo, 1778 aged 53 years.
James Silver, son of Abel and Hope Silver, d. 19th da, 8th mo,
1778 aged 2 years.
Archibald Silver, son of above parents d. 22nd da, same mo, same
year, aged 9 years and 3 months.

Mary Ann Silver, dau. of same parents d. 26th da, same mo, aged 4 years and 5 months.
Elizabeth Bacon, wife of Charles Bacon, d. 16th da, 11th mo, 1778, aged 27 years.
Jonathan Stretch, d. 31st da, 12th mo, 1778 aged 41 years.
Benjamin Test, son of Benjamin Test d. 29th da, 7th mo, 1778.
Sarah Test, wife of Benjamin Test d. 15th da, 8th mo, 1778 aged 47 years.
Elizabeth Hains, dau. of Elizabeth Hains, d. 3rd da, 8th mo, 1778 aged 18 years.

Children of Aaron Lippincott and Sarah, his wife: Deborah Lippincott, b. 16th da, 8th mo, 1772; John Lippincott, b. 11th da, 1st mo, 1774; Hope Lippincott, b. 14th da, 3rd mo, 1777; Elizabeth Lippincott, b. 13th da, 1st mo, 1781; Benjamin Lippincott, b. 14th da, 10th mo, 1782.
Children of John Wright and Hannah, his wife: Isaac Wright, b. 14th da, 11th mo, 1774; Joseph Wright, b. 21st da, 12th mo, 1777; Mary Wright, b. 5th da, 5th mo, 1780.
Children of Daniel Pedrick and Naomi, his wife: Keziah Pedrick, b. 1st da, 6th mo, 1771; Mary Pedrick, b. 25th da, 5th mo, 1773; John Pedrick, b. 1st da, 10th mo, 1777.
Child of Jonathan Kirby and Mercy, his wife: Samuel Kirby, b. 8th da, 8th mo, 1776.
Child of Jacob Ware and Naomi, his wife: Richard Ware, b. 2nd da, 3rd mo, 1744.
Children of Richard Ware and Hannah, his wife: Rebeckah Ware, d. 7th da, 8th mo, 1766; Elizabeth Ware, b. 16th da, 10th mo, 1771; Hannah Ware, d. 28th da, 6th mo, 1774.
Child of John Thompson and Sarah, his wife: Rebeckah Thompson, b. 21st da, 8th mo, 1777.
Children of John Thompson and Mary, his wife: Sarah Thompson, b. 12th da, 5th mo, 1779; Ruth Thompson, b. 25th da, 2nd mo, 1781; Ann Thompson, b. 30th da, 7th mo, 1783; John Thompson, b. 31st da, 1st mo, 1786; William Thompson, 16th da, 4th mo, 1788.
Children of Andrew Griscom and Leatitia, his wife: Benjamin Griscom, b. 26th da, 7th mo, 1776; Andrew Griscom, b. 9th da, 5th mo, 1778.
Child of David Smith and Hannah, his wife: Joseph Smith, b. 13th da, 1st mo, 1786.
Children of Thomas Thompson and Milliscent, his wife: Jacob Thompson, b. 14th da, 7th mo, 1777; Abraham Thompson, b. 8th da, 5th mo, 1781; Edith Thompson, b. 22nd da, 9th mo, 1783.
Children of Benjamin Shrouds and Mary, his wife: Thomas Shrouds, b. 7th da, 1st mo, 1777; Rachel Shrouds, b. 20th da, 3rd mo, 1779; Samuel Shrouds, b. 6th da, 9th mo, 1781; Rhoda Shrouds, b. 19th da, 1st mo, 1784; William Shrouds, b. 15th da, 4th mo, 1786.
Children of Daniel Bassett, Jr. and Mary, his wife: Gideon Scull Bassett, b. 30th da, 3rd mo, 1777; Mary Bassett, b. 8th da, 2nd mo, 1779; Daniel Bassett, b. 31st da, 8th mo, 1781, d. 7th da, 12th mo, 1782; David Bassett, b. 17th da, 11th mo, 1783; Mark Bassett, b. 6th da, 4th mo, 1786.
Michael Pedrick, d. 27th da, 8th mo, 1776 aged 69 years.

Mary Dennis, wife of Samuel Dennis, d. 27th da, 1st mo, 1780.
Samuel Dennis, son of aforesaid Samuel and Mary Dennis, b. 12th
  da, 9th mo, 1779 and d. 26th da, 1st mo, 1780.
Rebeckah Silver, wife of William Silver and dau. of Elisha
  Bassett, d. 17th da, 3rd mo, 1779 aged 55 years.
Josiah Lawrence d. 24th da, 7th mo, 1776 aged 34 years.
Grace Thompson, wife of Andrew Thompson, d. 13th da, 1st mo, 1779
  aged 33 years.
Elizabeth Bacon, d. 16th da, 11th mo, 1778 aged 27 years.
Isaac Summers, d. 25th da, 12th mo, 1778.
Thomas Shrouds, b. 23rd da, 11th mo, 1778.
Gideon Scull Bassett, d. 6th da, 10th mo, 1779 aged 2 years 6
  months, 6 days.
Everatt Griscom, d. 15th da, 5th mo, 1780 aged 34 years.
Mark Sheppard d. 16th da, 5th mo, 1780 aged 52 years.
Samuel Fogg d. 18th da, 2nd mo, 1778 aged 33 years.
William Mason, son of John Mason, d. 25th da, 11th mo, 1776.
Hannah Ellett, dau. of Charles Ellet and Hannah, his wife, d.
  12th da, 9th mo, 1779.
Sarah Gregory, wife of Walpole Gregory, d. 18th da, 6th mo, 1780
  aged 32 years.
Mary Butcher, wife of Job Butcher, d. 7th da, 1st mo, 1781 aged
  39 years.
Joseph Stuart, d. 29th da, 8th mo, 1782 aged 24 years.

Children of Richard Gibbs and Mary, his wife: Richard Gibbs, b.
  23rd da, 5th mo, 1779; Mary Gibbs, b. 1st da, 12th mo, 1781.
Child of Walpole Gregory and Sarah, his wife: Samuel Gregory, b.
  8th da, 28th da, 1778.
Children of Thomas Daniel and Elizabeth, his wife: Joseph Daniel,
  b. 20th da, 12th mo, 1774; Thomas Daniel, b. 15th da, 4th mo,
  1776; Edmond Daniel, b. 12th da, 8th mo, 1777; Sarah Daniel, b.
  28th da, 3rd mo, 1779, d. 26th da, 4th mo, following.
Children of Isaac Hance and Mary, his wife: Joseph Hance, b. 21st
  da, 2nd mo, 1779; Isaac Hance, b. 30th da, 8th mo, 1781; Martha
  Hance, b. 8th da, 1st mo, 1784; William Hance, b. 23rd , 6th
  mo, 1786.
Children of Benjamin Clark Cooper and Ann, his wife: William
  Cooper, b. 16th da, 8th mo, 1776; Deborah Cooper, b. 30th da,
  10th mo, 1778; Samuel Cooper, b. 8th da, 11th mo, 1780. [This
  entry crossed out in original record.]
Children of Mark Sheppard and Mary, his wife: Thomas Sheppard, b.
  12th da, 11th mo, 1764; Sarah Sheppard, b. 2nd da, 5th mo,
  1769; William Sheppard, b. 7th da, 2nd mo, 1772; Josiah
  Sheppard, b. 5th da, 4th mo, 1774.
Children of Isaac Pedrick and Hannah, his wife: Phebe Pedrick, b.
  16th da, 10th mo, 1777; Mary Pedrick, b. 21st da, 8th mo, 1780.
Children of Nathan Dunn and Rhoda, his wife: Deborah Dunn, b. 9th
  da, 2nd mo, 1775; William Dunn, b. 11th da, 11th mo, 1777;
  Josiah Dunn, b. 19th da, 10th mo, 1779; Rachel Dunn, b. 5th da,
  1st mo, 1781; Nathan Dunn, b. 11th da, 11th mo, 1782.
Children of David Colson and Hepzibah, his wife: Jonathan Colson,
  b. 28th da, 10th mo, 1779; David Colson, b. 27th da, 5th mo,
  1782.

Mary Gibbs, dau. of Richard and Mary Gibbs, d. 15th da, 9th mo, 1784.
Nathan Smart d. 5th da, 9th mo, 1756 aged 66 years.
Deborah Smart, d. 28th da, 8th mo, 1762 aged 73.
Jonathan Bradway, son of Jonathan Bradway, d. 1st da, 2nd mo, 1778.

Children of Jonathan Gibbs: Edward Gibbs, b. 17th da, 6th mo, 1781, d. 31st da, 10th mo, following; Lydia Gibbs, dau. of Jonathan b. 5th da, 12th mo, 1786.
Children of James Denn and Elizabeth, his wife: Ann Denn, b. 12th da, 7th mo, 1779; Elizabeth Denn, b. 19th da, 5th mo, 1781.
Child of Joseph Lippincott and Amey, his wife: Joseph Lippincott b. 21st da, 11th mo, 1781.
Children of James Stewart and Mary, his wife: Sarah Stewart, b. 27th da, 7th mo, 1776, d. 25th da, 1st mo, 1778; John Stewart, b. 7th da, 2nd mo, 1778; Amariah Stewart, b. 5th da, 7th mo, 1779; William Stewart, b. 24th da, 5th mo, 1781.

Joseph Rockhill, d. 21st da, 12th mo, 1780 aged 56 years and 5 months.
John Hoffman, d. 12th da, 11th mo, 1780 aged 55 years.
Rebeckah Brick, wife of Joseph Brick, d. 16th da, 11th mo, 1780 aged 39 years 11 months.
Martha Test, dau. of John and Elizabeth Test, d. 27th da, 10th mo, 1780 aged 6 years.
Joseph Stewart, son of James Stewart and Mary, his wife, b. 2nd da, 2nd mo, 1773, d. 17th da, 6th mo, 1780.
Sarah Miller, wife of William Miller, d. 14th da, 4th mo, 1782 aged 49 years 2 months.
William Oakford, d. 30th da, 7th mo, 1778 aged 33 years.
Jonathan Bradway, son of Jonathan Bradway, d. 1st da, 2nd mo, 1778.
Hope Silver, wife of Abel Silver, d. 4th da, 11th mo, 1781 aged 42 years 9 months.
Andrew Thompson, son of Joshua Thompson and Sarah, his wife d. 15th da, 8th mo, 1782 aged 43 years and 3 months, buried at Salem.
Hester or Easter Dicker, wife of Richard Dicker, d. 28th da, 1st mo, 1782 aged 49 years and 11 months.
Elizabeth Andrews, widow of Isaac Andrews d. 9th da, 5th mo, 1778 aged 59 years 3 months.
Joseph Fogg, d. 6th da, 12th mo, 1774 aged 52 years.
Elizabeth Hancock, dau. of William Hancock and Hannah, his wife, d. 12th da, 4th mo, 1782 aged 5 years and 3 months.
William Silver, d. 1st da, 2nd mo, 1787 aged 57 years.

Children of Isaac Smart and Ann, his wife: Mary Smart, b. 1st da, 10th mo, 1757; Wilson Smart, b. 20th da, 12th mo, 1759, d. 26th day of same; Isaac Smart, b. 2nd da, 3rd mo, 1761; Robert Smart, b. 19th da, 11th mo, 1763, d. 16th da, 4th mo, 1766; Ann Smart, b. 25th da, 11th mo, 1765, d. 19th da, 3rd mo, 1766; Anna Smart, b. 25th da, 9th mo, 1768; Hannah Smart, b. 7th da, 12th mo, 1770; Jane Smart, b. 26th da, 10th mo, 1775, d. 31st

da, 10th mo, 1775.
Children of William Oakford and Sarah, his wife: Elizabeth
Oakford, b. 29th da, 7th mo, 1771; Hannah Oakford, b. 14th da,
2nd mo, 1779.
Children of John Acton and Mary, his wife: Samuel Acton, b. 31st
da, 10th mo, 1772; John Acton, b. 23rd da, 10th mo, 1774.
Children of Abraham Miller and Elizabeth, his wife: Hannah White
Miller, b. 25th da, 1st mo, 1782; William Miller, b. 10th da,
3rd mo, 1786, d. 9th da, 5th mo, 1799.

Pyle Smith Miller, d. 18th da, 9th mo, 1799.

Children of William Thompson and Mary, his wife: Hannah Thompson,
b. 16th da, 8th mo, 1783; James Thompson, b. 20th da, 8th mo,
1787; Sarah Thompson, b. 28th da, 2nd mo, 1790.
Children of Jeremiah Andrews and Ann, his wife: James Andrews, b.
24th da, 10th mo, 1771; Samuel Andrews, b. 2nd da, 10th mo,
1773; Josiah Andrews, b. 6th da, 3rd mo, 1775; Elizabeth
Andrews, b. 26th da, 8th mo, 1778.
Children of Joseph Bacon and Rachel, his wife: Mary Bacon, b. 5th
da, 3rd mo, 1778; John Bacon, b. 10th da, 7th mo, 1780.
Children of Holm Fogg and Lidya, his wife: Joseph Fogg, b. 4th
da, 6th mo, 1780; Job Fogg, b. 8th da, 7th mo, 1782, d. 28th
da, 8th mo, 1782; Mary Fogg, b. 4th da, 2nd mo, 1785; Daniel
Fogg, b. 24th da, 9th mo, 1787; Holmes Fogg, b. 30th da, 8th
mo, 1790, d. 9th da, 10th mo, 1793; Job Fogg, b. 6th da, 8th
mo, 1793.
Child of George Warner and Phebe, his wife: William Warner, b.
21st da, 9th mo, 1779.
Children of Seth Silver and Mary, his wife: Anna Silver, b. 20th
da, 3rd mo, 1786; Leatitia Silver, b. 6th da, 5th mo, 1788.
Children of John Stewart and Hannah, his wife: Mylasent Stewart,
b. 4th da, 10th mo, 1771, d. 6th da, 9th mo, 1772; James
Stewart, b. 10th da, 10th mo, 1773; Thomas Stewart, b. 5th da,
2nd mo, 1783, d. 18th da of the same. Hannah Stewart, the
mother d. 20th da, 2nd mo, 1783 aged 30 years and 18 days.
Children of Jourdan Willis and Hannah, his wife: Sarah Willis, b.
1st da, 9th mo, 1774; Silas Willis, b. 25th da, 5th mo, 1779; a
dau., b. 12th da, 6th mo, d. the 7th da, of same month
following.
Children of John Jennings and Mary Ann, his wife: Rebeckah
Jennings, b. 23rd da, 7th mo, 1783. Mary Ann Jennings, d. 29th
da, 7th mo, 1783 aged 31 years 2 months.
Child of Jeremiah Tracey and Margaret, his wife: Margaret Tracey,
b. 17th da, 8th mo, 1783.
Children of Joseph Pettit and Sarah, his wife: Rachel Pettit, b.
7th da, 1st mo, 1784; David Pettit, b.23rd da, 2nd mo, 1786.

Margaret Hancock, dau. of Nethaniel Hancock and Hannah, his wife,
d. 9th da, 9th mo, 1777.
Hannah Hancock, dau. of above said parents d. 17th da, of the
same month.
Edward Bradway, son of Edward Bradway and Elizabeth, his wife, d.
24th da, 9th mo, 1777.

Joseph Barber, d. 8th da, 2nd mo, 1783.
Samuel Test, d. 24th da, 3rd mo, 1783 aged 55 years.
Elizabeth Shreeve, dau. of Abraham and Edith Shreeve, d. 10th da, 2nd mo, 1777 aged 19 years.
Ann Shreeve, dau. of above parents, d. 19th da, said month, 1777.
Rachel Dunn, dau. of Nathan Dunn and Rhoda, his wife, d. 2nd da, 11th mo, 1781.
Nathan Dunn, d. 19th da, 12th mo, 1782 aged 39 years.
David Bacon, son of Joseph Bacon and Rachel, his wife, d. 24th da, 7th mo, 1783 aged 8 years 6 months.
Mary Bacon, dau. of Joseph and Rachel Bacon, d. 25th da, 7th mo, 1783 aged 5 years 4 months.
Susannah Gibbs, dau. of Jonathan Gibbs and Lidya, his wife, b. 28th da, 4th mo, 1783, d. 14th da, 7th mo, following being 2 months 16 days.
Margaret Tracy, wife of Jeremiah Tracy, d. 25th da, 8th mo, 1783 aged 23 years 8 months 11 days.
Ann Morrison, wife of Matthew Morrison, d. 6th da, 3rd mo, 1784 aged 28 years 8 months 21 days.
Mary Thompson, widow of Joseph Thompson, d. 23rd da, 1st mo, 1784 aged 59 years.
Charles Fogg of Alloways Creek, d. 22nd da, 12th mo, 1783 aged 64 years.
John Adams, son of William Adams, d. 6th da, 12th mo, 1784 aged 19 years.

Children of Stephen Wright and Priscilla, his wife: Rebeckah Wright, b. 14th da, 11th mo, 1783; Sarah Wright, b. 27th da, 4th mo, 1786, d. 23rd da, 10th mo, following; Elizabeth Wright, b. 30th da, 9th mo, 1787.
Children of Asa Kirby and Hannah, his wife: Ebenezer Kirby, b. 28th da, 7th mo, 1784, d. 17th da, 11th mo, following.
Children of Edward Draper and Hannah, his wife: Thomas Draper, b. 22nd da, 4th mo, 1784; Rebecca Draper, b. 4th da, 4th mo, 1788;
Children of Joseph Brick and Martha, his wife: Joseph Brick, b. 13th da, 8th mo, 1785.

Hannah Draper, wife of Edward Draper, d. 12th da, 4th mo, 1788.
Rebeckah Pedrick, d. 12th da, 2nd mo, 1784.
Richard Townsend, son of Jacob and Mary Townsend, d. 6th da, 11th mo, 1783 aged 16 years 11 months 22 days.
Ann Thompson, dau. of Thomas Thompson and Millicent, his wife, d. 3rd da, 1st mo, 1782 aged 2 years 9 months.
Abigail Smith, dau. of Christopher Smith and Rebeckah, his wife, d. 11th da, 8th mo, 1785 aged 20 years 5 months 15 days.
Asa Colson, son of George Colson and Mary, his wife, d. 3rd da, 9th mo, 1784 aged 7 years.
Hannah Oakford, dau. of William Oakford and Sarah, his wife, d. 21st da, 12th mo, 1783 aged 5 years.
Preston Carpenter, d. 20th da, 10th mo, 1785 aged 64 years 11 mo, 22 days.
Bartholomew Wyatt, d. 19th da, 6th mo, 1786 aged 54 years 11 months.

Children of William Carpenter and Elizabeth, his wife: Mary Wyatt Carpenter, b. 26th da, 6th mo, 1783; Hannah Carpenter, b. 27th da, 5th mo, 1785, d. 30th da, 11th mo, 1785.

Elizabeth Carpenter, wife of William Carpenter, d. 11th da, 1st mo, 1790 aged 26 years 10 months.
Lydia Gibbs, wife of Jonathan Gibbs, d. 10th da, 11th mo, 1791 aged 43 years 6 months.
William Stretch, son of Elisha Stretch and Sarah, his wife, d. 28th da, 3rd mo, 1794.

Children of William Griscom and Rachel, his wife: John Griscom, b. 27th da, 9th mo, 1774; William Griscom, b. 8th da, 8th mo, 1777; Everatt Griscom, b. 24th da, 12th mo, 1781; Rachel Griscom, b. 24th da, 8th mo, 1784; Samuel Griscom, b. 2nd da, 4th mo, 1787; David Griscom, b. 21st da, 10th mo, 1789.
Children of James Mason Woodnutt and Margaret, his wife: Sarah Woodnutt, b. 28th da, 11th mo, 1777; Hannah Woodnutt, b. 16th da, 1st mo, 1780; Thomas Woodnutt, b. 30th da, 7th mo, 1782; Jonathan Woodnutt, b. 12th da, 10th mo, 1784; Preston Woodnutt, b. 24th da, 1st mo, 1787; Elizabeth Woodnutt, b. 19th da, 9th mo, 1789.

Elizabeth Ridgeway d. 28th da, 8th mo, 1798.
Hannah Ridgway, her sister, d. 28th da, 8th mo, 1798.

BIRTHS AND DEATHS OF PILESGROVE MONTHLY MEETING
(Pilesgrove records)

Child of William and Anna Adams of Greenwich: William Adams, b. 3rd da, 6th mo, 1779.
Children of John Atkinson b. 1st da, 8th mo, 1756 and Elizabeth, his wife, b. 10th da, 8th mo, 1768 of Greenwich: Esther Atkinson, b. 5th da, 4th mo, 1799; Elizabeth b. 26th da, 8th mo, 1800; John Atkinson, b. 19th da, 3rd mo, 1802; Cabel Atkinson, b. 1st da, 11th mo, 1803; Samuel Atkinson, b. 14th da, 1st mo, 1805; Eli Atkinson, b. 14th da, 7th mo, 1806; Hannah Atkinson, b. 27th da, 3rd mo, 1808; George Atkinson, b. 26th da, 10th mo, 1810; John Atkinson, the 2nd, b. 12th da, 3rd mo, 1814.
Child of Enoch and Anne Allen of Woolrich: Samuel C. Allen, b. 28th da, 7th mo, 1792.
Rebecca Allen, b. 24th da, 9th mo, 1775.
James Andrews, b. 25th da, 12th mo, 1798.
Child of Isaac Barber and Mary: Isaac Barber, b. 29th da, 7th mo, 1792.
Child of John and Hannah Ballinger of Pilesgrove: Mary Ballinger, b. 10th da, 1st mo, 1798.
Children of Isaac and Mary Barber: Isaac Barber, b. 19th da, 4th mo, 1796; Mary Ann Barber, b. 29th da, 6th mo, 1798; Jane Barber, b. 8th da, 10th mo, 1800.
Children of Nathan and Sarah Basset of Pilesgrove: Hannah Basset, b. 19th da, 12th mo, 1789; Ann and Elizabeth Basset, b. 19th

da, 12th mo, 1790; Deborah Basset, b. 18th da, 2nd mo, 1793; Josiah Basset, b. 4th da, 7th mo, 1795; Mary Basset, b. 25th da, 8th mo, 1797; Sarah Basset, b. 14th da, 10th mo, 1799; Beulah Basset, b. 11th da, 7th mo, 1801; Ruth Basset, b. 17th da, 11th mo, 1803.

Children of Henry and Hannah Barber: Jane Barber, b. 3rd da, 1st mo, 1783; Sarah Barber, b. 24th da, 10th mo, 1784; John Barber, b. 20th da, 11th mo, 1786; William Barber, b. 24th da, 8th mo, 1788; Henry Barber, b. 26th da, 12th mo, 1790; Samuel Barber, b. 1st da, 7th mo, 1792; William Barber, the 2nd, b. 26th da, 12th mo, 1795; Isaac Barber, b. 12th da, 8th mo, 1797; Isaiah Barber, b. 15th da, 9th mo, 1798; Jacob Barber, b. 1800; Rachel Barber, b. 12th da, 8th mo, 1802; George Barber, b. 25th da, 1st mo, 1805.

Children of Zacheus and Hope Ballinger: Jacob Ballinger, b. 16th da, 9th mo, 1775; Joshua Ballinger, b. 8th da, 3rd mo, 1781; Mary Ballinger, b. 1st mo, 9th mo, 1783; Isaac Ballinger, b. 7th da, 1st mo, 1786; Naomi Ballinger, b. 18th da, 10th mo, 1789; Benjamin Ballinger, b. 8th da, 8th mo, 1792; Josiah Ballinger, b. 22nd da, 9th mo, 1801.

Children of Joseph and Mary Davis of Pilesgrove: David Davis, b. 8th da, 8th mo, 1789; Martha C. Davis, b. 30th da, 3rd mo, 1791; Amos Davis, b. 22nd da, 1st mo, 1793; Ann H. Davis, b. 3rd da, 9th mo, 1807.

Children of Thomas and Esther Davis: Samuel Davis, b. 19th da, 3rd mo, 1797; Jacob Davis, b. 28th da, 8th mo, 1798; Martha Davis, b. 23rd da, 6th mo, 1800; Mary Ann Davis, b. 13th da, 5th mo, 1802; Josiah Davis, b. 28th da, 7th mo, 1804; Esther Davis, b. 14th da, 9th mo, 1805; Thomas Wilkins Davis, b. 13th da, 4th mo, 1808; Richard Davis, b. 21st da, 1st mo, 1811; Esther Davis, 2nd b. 8th da, 6th mo, 1813; Sarah Davis, b. 3rd da, 3rd mo, 1818.

Child of David and Hannah Davis: Hannah S. Davis, b. 1st da, 9th mo, 1789.

Children of John and Lydia Duell: Ann Duell, b. 7th da, 12th mo, 1794; Joseph D. Duell, b. 22nd da, 10th mo, 1796; Samuel Duell, b. 17th da, 7th mo, 1798; John Duell, b. 16th da, 1st mo, 1801; Phebe Duell, b. 11th da, 8th mo, 1803; Joshua Duell, b. 31st da, 1st mo, 1806.

Abigail Duell, dau. of William and Phebe Bassett, b. 6th da, 9th mo, 1766, wife of Gabriel Davis.

Children Hezekiah Eastlake, son of Restore and Anne Eastlack, b. 4th da, 2nd mo, 1762 and Anne his wife: Thomas Eastlack, b. 2nd da, 7th mo, 1792; John Eastlack, b. 31st da, 7th mo, 1794; Charles Eastlake, b. 15th da, 2nd mo, 1800; Rhoda Eastlack, b. 26th da, 3rd mo, 1797; Rachel Eastlack, b. 3rd da, 10th mo, 1802.

Children of Asa and Martha Engle: Levi Engle, b. 28th da, 5th mo, 1797; Joseph Engle, b. 8th da, 9th mo, 1797; Mary Engle b. 16th da, 4th mo, 1800; Joshua Engle, b. 25th da, 8th mo, 1804; Josiah Engle, b. 13th da, 1st mo, 1807; Charles Engle, b. 25th da, 7th mo, 1809; Martha Engle, b. 3rd da, 2nd mo, 1812.

Children of Jacob and Elizabeth Haines of Pilesgrove: Samuel Haines, b. 16th da, 8th mo, 1790; Joel Haines, b. 25th da, 9th

mo, 1794; Ann Haines, b. no date.
Children of William and Susannah Haines of Pilesgrove: Hope
Haines, b. 26th da, 2nd mo, 1789; Elizabeth Haines, b. 2nd da,
3rd mo, 1792,
Children of Isaac and Abigail Howey of Woolrich: Mary Howey, b.
8th da, 2nd mo, 1790; Benjamin Howey, b. 18th da, 1st mo, 1792;
Rebecca Howey, b. 12th da, 2nd mo, 1794; Isaac Howey, b. 19th
da, 2nd mo, 1798; Ann Howey, b. 9th da, 12th mo, 1799; Hope
Howey, b. 11th da, 11th mo, 1801; Martha Howey, b. 17th da, 2nd
mo, 1806.
Children of Robert and Naomi Howey of Woolrich: Isaac Howey, b.
6th da, 8th mo, 1792; Deborah Howey, b. 11th da, 9th mo, 1794;
Elizabeth Howey, b. 29th da, 7th mo, 1796; William Howey, b.
30th da, 3rd mo, 1798.
Thomas Iredell, b. 9th da, 4th mo, 1778 and his wife, Sybble of
Woolrich.
Children of Thomas and Rachel Jennings of Pilesgrove: Hannah
Jennings, b. 28th da, 8th mo, 1797; Levi Jennings, b. 19th da,
12th mo, 1799.
Asa Kirby, b. 29th da, 11th mo, 1794 and Hannah, his wife of
Pilesgrove.
Children of Caleb and Hannah Lippincott of Woolrich: Elizabeth
Lippincott, b, 12th da, 6th mo, 1764; Lettitia Lippincott, b.
28th da, 10th mo, 1766, m. Asa Elkinton; Mary Lippincott, b.
27th da, 11th mo, 1768; Hannah Lippincott, b. 25th da, 10th mo,
1770; Ann Lippincott, b. 6th da, 7th mo, 1781; Deborah
Lippincott, b. 28th da, 3rd mo, 1783; Samuel Lippincott, b. 9th
da, 1st mo, 1785; Elizabeth Lippincott, b. 8th da, 12th mo,
1786; Hannah Lippincott, b. 13th da, 12th mo, 1788; Thomas
Lippincott, b. 25th da, 11th mo, 1790; Mary Lippincott, b. 26th
da, 11th mo, 1792; William Lippincott, b. 1795.
Child of Samuel and Mary Lippincott: Caleb Lippincott, b. 25th
da, 4th mo, 1795.
Children of Benjamin and Hannah Moore of Woolrich: Chalkley
Moore, b. 30th da, 10th mo, 1773; Mary Moore, b. 8th da, 5th
mo, 1776; Hannah Moore, b. 15th da, 9th mo, 1778; Elizabeth
Moore, b. 5th da, 11th mo, 1780; Benjamin Moore, b. 5th da, 8th
mo, 1783; Rachel Moore, b. 3rd da, 11th mo, 1785; Asa Moore, b.
18th da, 6th mo, 1788; Jacob Moore, b. 1st da, 7th mo, 1790.
Children of William and Mary Mulford of Woolrich: Elizabeth B.
Mulford, b. 8th da, 8th mo, 1794; Deborah Mulford, b. 6th da,
1st mo, 179?; Mary Ann Mulford, b. 12th da, 1st mo, 1802;
Martha B. Mulford, b. 19th da, 12th mo, 1810.
Children of Joshua and Rachel Moore of Woolrich: Thomas Moore, b.
29th da, 9th mo, 1773; Sybbl Moore, b. 8th da, 2nd mo, 1778;
Samuel Moore, b. 12th da, 5th mo, 1780; Priscilla Moore, b. 1st
da, 1st mo, 1784; Mary Moore, b. 18th da, 11th mo, 1785;
Kiturah Moore, b. 28th da, 12th mo, 1788; Hannah Moore, b. 15th
da, 4th mo, 1791; Rebecca Moore, b. 31st da, 10th mo, 1794;
Atlantic Moore, b. 29th da, 1st mo, 1796.
Children of Samuel and Mary Ann Ogden of Woolrich: Mary Ogden, b.
13th da, 6th mo, 1771; Esther Ogden, b. 15th da, 2nd mo, 1773;
Joseph Ogden, b. 4th da, 8th mo, 1775; Martha Ogden, b. 2nd da,
2nd mo, 1779; Hannah Ogden, b. 29th da, 6th mo, 1781; Ann

EARLY CHURCH RECORDS OF SALEM COUNTY

Ogden, b. 22nd da, 11th mo, 1783; Samuel Ogden, b. 22nd da, 7th mo, 1787; Samuel Ogden, b. 27th da, 4th mo, 1790; John Ogden, b. 20th da, 6th mo, 1792; David Ogden, b. 19th da, 2nd mo, 1796.
Child of Joshua and Ann Owen: Sydney Owen, b. 26th da, 9th mo, 1797.
Children of Isaac and Hannah Pedrick of Pennseck: Phebe Pedrick, b. 16th da, 10th mo, 1771; Mary and Martha Pedrick, b. 21st da, 8th mo, 1780; Ann Pedrick, b. 24th da, 4th mo, 1783; Lydia Pedrick, b. 23rd da, 4th mo, 1788; Hannah Pedrick, b. 15th da, 7th mo, 1790; William Pedrick, b. 9th da, 12th mo, 1792.
Children of William and Elizabeth Perkins of Woolrich: Ann Perkins, b. 6th da, 11th mo, 1785; Rachel Perkins, b. 24th da, 3rd mo, 1787; Mary Perkins, b. 15th da, 5th mo, 1788; Sarah Perkins, b. 30th da, 12th mo, 1789; Benjamin Perkins, b. 16th da, 10th mo, 1792; Elizabeth Perkins, b. 11th da, 6th mo, 1794; Zibbiah Perkins, b. 22nd da, 3rd mo, 1796; Hannah Perkins, b. 22nd da, 3rd mo, 1799; Lettice Jane Perkins, b. 16th da, 3rd mo, 1801.
Aaron Pancoast, son of Aaron and Hannah Pancoast, b. 10th da, 1st mo, 1779 and Anne Cooper Pancoast, dau. of Amos and Sarah Cooper, b. 20th da, 7th mo, 1784.
Ann Ridgway, b. 22nd da, 9th mo, 1790; Naomi Ridgway, b. 4th da, 10th mo, 1792; Martha Ridgway, b. 27th da, 1st mo, 1795; Job Ridgway, b. 21st da, 9th mo, 1797; Phebe Ridgway, b. 22nd da, 11th mo, 1799.
Isaac Ridgway, son of Job and Martha Ridgway, b. 27th da, 7th mo, 1772 and Teresa Pimm Ridgway, dau. of Joseph and Hannah Pimm, b. 3rd da, 1st mo, 1778.
Charlotte Ridgway, b. 11th da, 2nd mo, 1799.
Children of John Somers and first wife of Pennsneck: Sarah Somers, b. 29th da, 1st mo, 1784; Tabitha Somers, b. 5th da, 3rd mo, 1786; Deborah Somers, b. 23rd da, 3rd mo, 1788; John Somers, b. 4th da, 9th mo, 1792.
Child of Abraham and Sarah Silver of Pilesgrove: Sarah Knight Silver, b. 17th da, 11th mo, 1794.
Children of Abraham and Elizabeth Silver of Pilesgrove: Mary Silver, 4th da, 11th mo, 1795; Adna Silver, b. 18th da, 12th mo, 1800; Josiah Silver, b. 11th da, 1st mo, 1803; Elizabeth Bradway Silver, b. 20th da, 2nd mo, 1805.
Children of Jacob and Ann Somers of Pennsneck: James Somers, b. 29th da, 10th mo, 1799 [sic]; John Somers, b. 4th da, 7th mo, 1781; Hannah Somers, b. 27th da, 12th mo, 1783; Richard Somers, b. 12th da, 12th mo, 1786; Guli Elma Somers, b. 4th da, 8th mo, 1788; Phebe Somers, b. 13th da, 8th mo, 1791; Jacob Somers, b. 20th da, 3rd mo, 1794; Ann Somers, b. 2nd da, 6th mo, 1799.
Children of John and Deborah Somers of Pennsneck: William Somers, b. 11th da, 12th mo, 1796; Elwood Somers, b. 12th da, 12th mo, 1797; Chalkley Somers, b. 7th da, 5th mo, 1799.
Children of Gideon and Sarah Scull of Pilesgrove: Abigail Lawrence Scull, b. 29th da, 4th mo, 1785; Abigail Scull, b. 14th da, 9th mo, 1786; James Scull, b. 24th da, 11th mo, 1788; Gideon Scull, b. 22nd da, 10th mo, 1790; Paul Scull, b. 9th da, 9th mo, 1792; Offley Scull, b. 4th da, 12th mo, 1794; Sarah

Scull, b. 11th da, 3rd mo, 1797; David Scull, b. 8th da, 12th
mo, 1797; Hannah Scull, b. 21st da, 9th mo, 1802.
Children of William and Rebecca Silver of Pilesgrove: Elizabeth
Silver, b. 20th da, 1st mo, 1799; Samuel Silver, b. 17th da,
3rd mo, 1801; Hephzibah Silver, b. 27th da, 6th mo, 1803;
Martha Ann Silver, b. 30th da, 10th mo, 1805; William B.
Silver, b. 14th da, 2nd mo, 1808; Joseph E. Silver, b. 24th da,
8th mo, 1810; Horatio D. Silver, b. 17th da, 2nd mo, 1813;
Phebe E. Silver, b. 7th da, 8th mo, 1816.
Children of John and Hannah Test of Pilesgrove: Elizabeth Test,
b. 11th da, 2nd mo, 1794; Sarah Test, b. 14th da, 8th mo, 1795;
Joseph Test, b. 29th da, 6th mo, 1797; Thomas Test, b. 5th da,
2nd mo, 1799; Hannah Test, b. 14th da, 2nd mo, 1801; John Test,
b. 27th da, 2nd mo, 1803; Lettitia Test, b. 25th da, 7th mo,
1804; Clayton Test, b. 3rd da, 1st mo, 1807; Mary Test, b. 1st
da, 7th mo, 1808; Elenore Ann Test, b. 8th da, 4th mo, 1810.
Beulah Tatum b. 23rd da, 8th mo, 1784.

DEATHS FROM PILESGROVE MONTHLY MEETING

Isaac Barber of Pilesgrove, d. 30th da, 12th mo, 1792 nearly 72
years of age.
Mary Ballinger, widow of John Ballinger, d. 28th da, 10th mo,
1794 near 74 years of age.
Mary Ballinger, wife of John Ballinger, d. 1st da, 3rd mo, 1790
near 27 years of age.
William Barber d. 8th da, 10th mo, 1789.
Isaac Barber, son of Henry and Hannah Barber, d. 12th da, 8th mo,
1797.
Jonathan Colson, son of David and Hepseah Colson, of Pilesgrove
d. 29th da, 1st mo, 1799.
Hepsabah Colson, widow of David Colson of Pilesgrove, d. 23rd da,
12th mo, 1799 near 45 years of age.
Hannah Davis, wife of David Davis of Pilesgrove, d. 14th da, 1st
mo, 1789 near 27 years of age.
Children of Joseph and Mary Davis: Amos Davis, d. 18th da, 3rd
mo, 1795, 2 years 2 mo, 26 das; David Davis, d. 26th da, 12th
mo, 1795 age 6 years 7 mo, 18 das.
Joseph Lipincott Duel, d. 7th da, 2nd mo, 1799.
Sarah Silvers, wife of Abraham Silvers of Pilesgrove d. 26th da,
11th mo, 1794, age 23 years, 5 mos.

MARRIAGES OF PILESGROVE MONTHLY MEETING

Peter Burden of Pilesgrove, Salem County and Elizabeth Allin of
same place m. 27th da, 11th mo, 1794.
Samuel Lippincott of Woolwich, Gloucester County, yeoman and Mary
Ogden of same place, m. 29th da, 1st mo, 1795.
Chalkley Moore of Woolwich, Gloucester County and Mary Colson of
Pilesgrove, Salem County m. 5th da, 2nd mo, 1795.
John Somers of Upper Pennsneck, Salem County and Deborah
Lippincott of Woolrich, Gloucester County m. 3rd da, 3rd mo,

1796.
Caleb Pancoast of Greenwich, Gloucester County and Deborah Dunn of Pilesgrove, Salem County, m. 1st da, 3rd mo, 1796.
Joshua Evans, Jr. of Newtown, Gloucester County and Rebecca Somers of Pilesgrove, Salem County m. 28th da, 4th mo, 1796.
Thomas Davis of Pilesgrove, Salem County and Esther Ogden of Woolrich, Gloucester County, m. 2nd da, 6th mo, 1796.
John Lippincott of Woolrich, Gloucester County and Hannah Moore, Jr. of same place m. 2nd da, 3rd mo, 1797.
Nathan Ball of the city of Philadelphia, PA., son of John and Sarah Ball, dec'd. late of Darby in Pennsylvania, and Atlantick Allen, dau. of Joseph Allen and Hannah, of Woolrich, Gloucester County m. 27th da, 4th mo, 1797.
John Pimm of Pilesgrove, Salem County and Sarah Allen, Woolrich, Gloucester County m. 13th da, 11th mo, 1797.
Isaac Ridgway of Woolwich, Gloucester County, son of Job Ridgway and Martha, his wife of same place, dec'd. and Terase Pimm of Pilesgrove, Salem County m. 3rd da, 5th mo, 1798.
Aaron Street of Mannington, Salem County and Mary Pedrick of Upper Pennsneck, Salem County, m. 27th da, 3rd mo, 1799.
Elisha Davis of Pilesgrove, Salem County, son of Thomas and Elizabeth Davis of Pilesgrove and Hannah Ballinger, of same place dau. of Edward Clark, dec'd. and Mary his wife of Upper Pennsneck, Salem County m. 2nd da, 5th mo, 1799.
Isaac Townsend of Mannington, Salem County, son of Isaac Townsend and Keturah, his wife of the Upper Precinct of the county of Cape May, dec'd. and Hannah Ogdon, dau. of Samuel Ogdon and Mary Ann, his wife of Woolrich, Gloucester County, m. 2nd da, 1st mo, 1800.
Samuel Craig of Upper Alloways Creek,, Salem County, son of William Craig, dec'd. and Letticia his wife of the same place and Martha Pedrick, dau. of Isaac Pedrick and Hannah, his wife of Upper Pennsneck, Salem County, m. 2nd da, 4th mo, 1800.
Enoch Allen of Woolwich, Gloucester County and Ann Kirby of Upper Pennsneck, Salem County m. 7th da, 5th mo, 1800.
Thomas Moore of Greenwich, Gloucester County, son of Joshua Moore and Rachel, his wife and Mary Allen of Woolwich, same county, dau. of Joseph Allen and Hannah, his wife m. 5th da, 11th mo, 1800.
Joshua Lynch of Upper Pennsneck, Salem County and Rachel Owen of Woolwich, Gloucester County m. 5th da, 11th mo, 1800.
Joshua Lippincott of Woolwich, Gloucester County, son of Joshua Lippincott and Rebecca his wife of aforesaid place and Esther Davis of Pilesgrove, Salem County, dau. of Jacob Davis and Esther, his wife m. 27th da, 11th mo, 1800.

PILESGROVE MONTHLY MEETING MEMBERS BY REQUEST

Peter Mounce, b. 16th da, 10th mo, 1793 and Ann Mounce, b. 11th da, 11th mo, 1792 of Woolrich by request.
Edward Hanes, b. 24th da, 9th mo, 1792 of Pilesgrove became a member by request.

PILESGROVE MONTHLY MEETING MINUTES
1794-1800

A meeting to be held at Pilesgrove was established at the
quarterly meeting held at Haddonfield on 21st da, 3rd mo, 1794.
The first meeting was held the 24th da, 4th mo, 1794. Elders
appointed were: Daniel Bassett, Jacob Davis, Elizabeth Bassett,
Mary Colson and Ann Somers. Deborah Basset and Jane Sharp
appointed ministers. Friends appointed as overseers being:
Samuel Ogden, John Barnes and Elihu Pederick. Daniel Bassett,
Jr. was appointed clerk for the meeting.
22nd da, 5th mo, 1794. A certificate was granted for Asa Elkinton
and wife to Abington Monthly Meeting, PA. A certificate was
granted for Sarah Willis to Eggharbour and Cape May Monthly
Meeting.
26th da, 6th mo, 1794. A certificate was produced from Woodbury
Monthly Meeting for Ann Stewart dated 15th da, 4th mo, 1794.
24th da, 7th mo, 1794. Sarah, Tabitha, Deborah and John Somers,
children of John Somers received under the care of the Friends.
Rebecca Holson reported for marrying contrary to discipline.
Rebecca Barnes requested to be released from the station of
overseer.
21st da, 8th mo, 1794. A certificate was produced from
Haddonfield Monthly Meeting for Jacob Davis dated 8th da, 11th
mo, 1794. Ruth Haines requested a certificate to Evesham
Monthly Meeting.
20th da, 11th mo, 1794. A certificate granted for Ruth Haines to
Evesham Monthly Meeting.
? da, 12th mo, 1794. John Howey produced a certificate from
Evesham Monthly Meeting dated 10th da, 10th mo, 1794. Lettiatia
Craig recommended as minister.
22nd da, 1st mo, 1795. Jacob Davis, Jr. and Rebecca Sommers
declare their intentions of marriage, parents present
consenting. Rebecca Pederick received under the care of the
Friends.
19th da, 2nd mo, 1795. Jacob Davis, Jr. and Rebecca Sommers
inform the meeting that the decline to continue their
declaration of marriage. Elizabeth Thompson produced a
certificate from Salem Monthly Meeting dated 26th da, 1st mo,
1795.
26th da, 5th mo, 1795. A certificate was granted to Mary
Lippincott to Burlington Monthly Meeting. A certificate from
Upper Evesham Monthly Meeting dated 11th da, 4th mo, 1795 for
Joshua Owen and Ann, his wife and nine children: Jesse, Sarah,
Prudence, David, Joshua, Joseph, Elizabeth, Benjamin and
Rowland. A certificate from Woodbury Monthly Meeting for Joseph
Stettet and Sarah, his wife and their six children: Woodnut,
David, Jonathan, Thomas, Rachel and Mary dated 11th da, 4th mo,
1795. A certificate from Woodbury Monthly Meeting for Elizabeth
Morgan and her five children: David, Hannah, Jonathan ... a
certificate ... Rebecca Wright produced an acknowledgement
condemning her going out in marriage. Gertrude Medarey late
Elkinton reported for going out in marriage; disowned. Lucy
Dawson received under the care of the Friends.

6th mo, 1795. A certificate from Woodbury Monthly Meeting for
Nathan Bassett, his wife Sarah and their four children: Hannah,
Anna, Elizabeth and Deborah dated 14th da, 4th mo, 1795. A
certificate from Woodbury Monthly Meeting for Hannah Fisher
dated 9th da, 6th mo, 1795. Sarah Cade formerly Haines reported
for going out in marriage. Jacob Ridgway and his wife produced
an acknowledgement condemning their going out in marriage.
23rd da, 7th mo, 1795. Ephraim Barnes granted a certificate to
Wilmington Monthly Meeting. John Pederick, a minor granted a
certificate to Greenwich Monthly Meeting. A certificate from
Little Eggharbor Monthly Meeting for Thomas Osborne, wife and
their five children: Nathan, Dunn, Phebe, Palmyra and Rhoda
dated 11th da, 6th mo, 1795. A certificate from Little
Eggharbour Monthly Meeting for Elizabeth Ivey dated 9th da, 4th
mo, 1795.
24th da, 9th mo, 1795. William Prosser disowned for paying
military fines. Isaac Pedrick appointed in the place of Elihu
Pedrick as overseer. Jonathan Hoffman reported for going out in
marriage and is guilty of unchastity behavior by having a child
too soon after marriage.
25th da, 2nd mo, 1796. Jonathan Hoffman produced an
acknowledgement condemning his going out in marriage and having
a child too soon after marriage. Marriage of John Somers and
Deborah Lippincott accomplished, their parents present
consenting. A certificate for Joseph Lewis, Mary his wife and
five children: William, Hannah, Ann, Joseph and John to
Philadelphia Monthly Meeting dated 7th mo, 1792, which he is
returning to this meeting, accepted.
3rd mo, 1796. Caleb Pancoast produced a certificate from Woodbury
Monthly Meeting. James Kinsey, Jr. produced a certificate from
Burlington Monthly Meeting dated 7th da, 2nd mo, 1796. Hannah
Ballinger produced an acknowledgement her misconduct.
4th mo, 1796. Joshua Evans produced a certificate from
Haddonfield Monthly Meeting.
5th mo, 1796. A certificate from Woodbury Monthly Meeting for
Benjamin Carter, his wife Rebeckah, and their two children:
Benjamin and Mary dated 12th da, 4th mo, 1796. A certificate
for William Stratton, a minor from Woodbury Monthly Meeting
dated 12th da, 4th mo, 1796. A certificate for John Pimm and
dau. Mary from Salem Monthly Meeting dated 25th da, 4th mo,
1796. A certificate from Ephraim Barnes from Wilmington Monthly
Meeting dated 13th da, 1st mo, 1796. Sarah Kirby formerly
Barnes reported for going out in marriage. Mary Green produced
a certificate dated 3rd da, 5th mo, 1796. Miles Pedrick
requested to come under the care of the Friends.
25th da, 6th mo, 1796. John Bradway., wife and children granted a
certificate to Greenwich Monthly Meeting. It is reported that
there is a difference between Jacob Davis, exec. of the will of
Isaac Somers, dec'd. and Joshua Evans, Jr. regarding some
interest owed. Joshua Haines requested a certificate to
Woodbury Monthly Meeting. A certificate from Benjamin Heritage,
his wife and three minor children from Woodbury Monthly Meeting
dated 15th da, 8th mo, 1797. A certificate from Evesham Monthly
Meeting for Asa Engle, Martha, his wife and their infant son,

Levi dated 11th da, 8th mo, 1797. The overseer reported that
there was a dispute in a matter of interest between William
Groff and Isaac Eldridge. Friends of the neighborhood of
Mullica Hill requested to hold a meeting in their schoolhouse.
11th mo, 1797. Susanna Mishner late Newman reported for going out
in marriage; disowned. A certificate requested for Elizabeth
Stratton to Mt. Holly Monthly Meeting.
21st da, 12th mo, 1797. A certificate from Samuel Pine and wife
and their infant from Evesham Monthly Meeting dated 6th da, 9th
mo, 1797.
25th da, 1st mo, 1798. Peter Borden treated with for frequenting
of taverns and drinking to excess; disowned.
22nd da, 3rd mo, 1798. Isaac Barber requested a certificate for
himself, his wife and five children to Salem Monthly Meeting.
21st da, 4th mo, 1798. Isaac Barber, his wife, Phebe and his four
children: Rebekah, Abraham, Isaac and Jacob Barber granted a
certificate to Salem Monthly Meeting. A certificate from
Woodbury Monthly Meeting for Hezekiah Eastlack, his wife and
their minor children, John and Rhoda from Woodbury Monthly
Meeting dated 11th da, 4th mo, 1798. A certificate for Thomas
Lippencott and Abigail, his wife, and their infant dau. Julia
Ann, from Evesham Monthly Meeting dated 4th da, 6th mo, 1798.
Samuel Ogden requested to be released from overseer of
Pilesgrove preparative meeting.
21st da, 5th mo, 1798. William Elliott reported for going out in
marriage; disowned. Waity Parker late Roberts reported for
going out in marriage; disowned. Daniel Bassett, Jr. requested
a certificate for himself, his wife and three children to
Haddonfield Monthly Meeting. Mary Bassett requested a
certificate to Haddfonfield Monthly Meeting.
4th da, 7th mo, 1798. Daniel Bassett, Jr., his wife and three
children: David, Hannah and Elizabeth granted a certificate to
Haddonfield Monthly Meeting. Mary Bassett granted a certificate
to Haddonfield Monthly Meeting. John Lewis reported for
neglecting meeting and neglecting to take his certificate;
disowned.
23rd da, 8th mo, 1798. A certificate from Woodbury Monthly
Meeting for Elisabeth Perkins dated 10th, 7th mo, 1798. A
certificate from Haddonfield Monthly Meeting for Mary Weaver
dated 9th da, 7th mo, 1798.
25th da, 10th mo, 1798. Joshua Howey reported for going out in
marriage; disowned. Martha Nicholason treated with for taking
what was not her own.
24th da, 11th mo, 1798. Unis Ridgway requested a certificate to
Salem Monthly Meeting. Elizabeth Owen late Prosser reported for
going out in marriage.
27th da, 12th mo, 1798. Samuel Ogden and Mary Ann, his wife
appointed elders for the meeting. Martin Green and his four
children: Lewis, Hannah, Mary and Anthony received under the
care of the friends. Joshua Lynch received under the care of
the friends. Elijha Davis produced an acknowledgement
condemning his neglecting of meeting and going out in marriage.
Mary Howey late Prosser reported for going out in marriage and
having a child too soon after marriage; disowned.

29th da, 1st mo, 1799. Grace Bassett produced an acknowledgement condemning her going out in marriage; accepted. 11th da, 2nd mo, 1799. Abigail Irvin late Bassett reported for going out in marriage; disowned. Ann Springer late Sharp reported for going out in marriage; disowned. Elias Stratton from Haddonfield Monthly Meeting dated 5th da, 11th mo, 1795.
21st da, 3rd mo, 1799. Joseph Pettet, his wife, Sarah and their six minor children: Woodnut, David, Jonathan, Thomas, Rachel and Mary granted a certificate to Salem Monthly Meeting. David Sommers reported for going out in marriage; disowned. Nathan Basset and Samuel Ogden to write to Burlington Monthly Meeting to inform them of the manner in which Benjamin Prosser left this meeting.
23rd 5th mo, 1799. Mary Street granted a certificate to Salem Monthly Meeting. A certificate for Thomas Enoch and Mary, his wife, Mary from Woodbury Monthly Meeting dated 4th da, 9th mo, 1799. A certificate for Thomas Enoch from Woodbury Monthly Meeting dated 4th da, 9th mo, 1799. John Smith of Burlington complained against Frances Bogs for neglecting to pay off a note of debt.
20th da, 6th mo, 1799. Elizabeth Borden granted a certificate to Salem Monthly Meeting. A certificate for Frances Eastlack from Woodbury Monthly Meeting dated 11th da, 6th mo, 1799.
25th da, 7th mo, 1799. A certificate for John Gills, his wife, Prudence from Salem Monthly Meeting dated 22nd da, 6th mo, 1799. A complaint has been made by Joshua Owen against Henry Barber for neglecting to pay an obligation.
22nd da, 8th mo, 1799. Charity Dixon reported for going out in marriage; disowned. A certificate for Margaret Sharp from Evesham Monthly Meeting dated 7th da, 5th mo, 1799.
26th da, 9th mo, 1799. James Wills treated with for neglecting meeting and the payment of military fines; disowned.
24th da, 10th mo, 1799. Sarah Wilkins produced a copy of a minute from Evesham Monthly Meeting dated 10th da, 4th mo, 1799 for the purpose of visiting Friends. Benjamin Prosser produced an acknowledgement condemning his misconduct. Hannah Ballenger reported for having a child in an unmarried state; disowned.
26th da, 12th mo, 1799. Frances Boggs gave encouragement of repaying the debit he owed. A certificate granted for Benjamin Prosser to Burlington Monthly Meeting. Thomas Ogdon and children: Phebe, Palmira and Rhoda granted a certificate to Little Eggharbour Monthly Meeting. A certificate for James Whiteall from Philadelphia Monthly Meeting dated 25th da, 6th mo, 1799.
23rd da, 1st mo, 1800. Grace Bassett granted a certificate. A certificate for Stephen Heritage from Woodbury Monthly Meeting dated 14th da, 1st mo, 1800.
20th da, 2nd mo, 1800. Ephraim Barnes reported for going out in marriage; disowned. A certificate for Hannah Thanney and her infant dau. Elizabeth from Haddonfield Monthly Meeting dated 12th da, 1st mo, 1800. Hannah Townsend requested a certificate to Salem Monthly Meeting.
27th da, 3rd mo, 1800. William Perkins and his eight children: Ann, Rachel, Mary, Sarah, Benjamin, Elizabeth, Zebiah and

Hannah received under the care of the friends. A certificate for Jonathan Smith, his wife and their three minor children: Daniel, Joshua and Elizabeth from Little Eggharbour Monthly Meeting dated 13th da, 3rd mo, 1800.

24th da, 4th mo, 1800. Elizabeth Looy granted a certificate to Little Eggharbour Monthly Meeting. Enoch Allen produced a certificate from the meeting he belongs declaring his clearness to marry. Elias Stratton requested a certificate to Salem Monthly Meeting. Jacob Ridgway from Upper Evesham Monthly Meeting dated 3rd mo, 1800. William Howey granted a certificate to Woodbury Monthly Meeting.

22nd da, 5th mo, 1800. David Smith granted a certificate for himself, his wife, Hannah and three children, also Thomas Weaver, a minor to Salem Monthly Meeting. A certificate for Isaac Barber, his wife, Mary and five children: Rebecca, Mary Ann, Abraham, Isaac and Jacob from Salem Monthly Meeting dated 23rd da, 4th mo, 1800. Joshua Haines, sometime ago was granted a certificate to Woodbury Monthly Meeting, but has not removed from the area, to be visited.

26th da, 6th mo, 1800. Joshua Owen, a minor granted a certificate to Greenwich Monthly Meeting. Grace Bassett granted a certificate to Philadelphia Monthly Meeting. Benjamin Test from Greenwich Monthly Meeting dated 28th da, 5th mo, 1800.

24th da, 7th mo, 1800. A certificate for Jonathan Griffin and wife from Salem Monthly Meeting dated 24th da, 2nd mo, 1800. Mary Wright late Ridgway reported for going out in marriage; disowned. Hannah Hews and her dau. Rebeccah granted a certificate to Salem Monthly Meeting. Martha Craig granted a certificate to Salem Monthly Meeting.

25th da, 10th mo, 1800. Abigail Howey appointed in the place of Mary Ann Ogden as overseer.

20th da, 11th mo, 1800. Joseph Moore reported for going out in marriage, disowned. Jacob Davis, Jr. and wife, Elizabeth produced an acknowledgement condemning their going out in marriage. Mark Ridgway reported for being guilty of horse racing staking his wife as a wager on the occasion; disowned. A certificate for Stephen Thackery, a minor from Haddonfield Monthly Meeting dated 9th da, 11th mo, 1800.

25th da, 12th mo, 1800. Heziah Grueth late Griffin reported for going out in marriage; disowned.

BIRTHS AND BURIALS BELONGING TO GREENWICH MONTHLY MEETING
(Salem Monthly Meeting records)

Children of John Bacon and Elizabeth, his wife: Thomas Bacon, b. 29th da, 6th mo, 1721; John Bacon, b. 30th da, 11th mo, 1724; Elizabeth Bacon, b. 31st da, 10th mo, 1726; David Bacon; b. 14th da, 1st mo, 1729; Martha Bacon, b. 4th da, 5th mo, 1731; Mary Bacon, b. 17th da, 8th mo, 1733; Job Bacon, b. 16th da, 10th mo, 1735.

Children of Joseph Reeve and Elenor, his wife: Mark Reeve, b. 28th da, 12th mo, 1723; Joseph Reeve, b. 5th da, 7th mo, 1725; John Reeve, b. 5th da, 1st mo, 1730; Mary Reeve, b. 15th da, 7th mo, 1734; Benjamin Reeve, b. 2nd da, 7th mo, 1737.

Joseph Reeve, the elder, d. 25th da, 9th mo, 1748.
John Bacon, the elder, d. 10th da, 1st mo, 1755, aged 56 years and 10 months. He was an elder.

Children of Richard Wood and Priscilla, his wife: Jane Wood, b. 18th da, 4th mo, 1723; Richard Wood, b. 18th da, 11th mo, 1728; Leatita Wood, b. 5th da, 2nd mo, 1730; Ruth Wood, b. 16th da, 1st mo, 1732; Priscilla Wood, b. 4th da, 1st mo, 1734.

Children of Philip Dennis and Lucy, his wife: Martha Dennis, b. 15th da, 7th mo, 1724; Prudence Dennis, b. 19th da, 9th mo, 1726; Philip Dennis, b. 19th da, 11th mo, 1731; Grace Dennis, b. 7th da, 7th mo, 1740; Rachel Dennis, b. 6th da, 4th mo, 1742; Elizabeth Dennis, b. 29th da, 5th mo, 1747; Jonathan Dennis, b. 4th da, 6th mo, 1750; Martha Dennis, b. 7th dam, 12th mo, 1760.

Children of John Brick and Ann, his wife: Mary Brick, b. 10th da, 2nd mo, 1730; Elizabeth Brick, b. 4th da, 3rd mo, 1732; John Brick, b. 10th da, 11th mo, 1733; Joseph Brick, b. 24th da, 3rd mo, 1735; Ann Brick, b. 23rd da, 1st mo, 1738; Hannah Brick, b. 8th da, 3rd mo, 1741; Ruth Brick, b. 1st da, 10th mo, 1742; Jean Brick, b. 10th da, 3rd mo, 1743.

John Brick, the elder d. 23rd da, 1st mo, 1758.
Joseph Bacon, d. 26th da, 11th mo, 1757.
Naomy Tyler, d. 15th da, 2nd mo, 1758 aged 39 years.

Child of Joseph Bacon and Mary, his wife: Edmond Bacon, b. 12th da, 12th mo, 1725.

Children of Joseph Bacon and Margaret, his wife: Esther Bacon, b. 23rd da, 7th mo, 1735; Margaret Bacon, b. 20th da, 2nd mo, 1737; Deborah Bacon, b. 22nd da, 10th mo, 1738; Joseph Bacon, b. 24th da, 5th mo, 1741; Prudence Bacon, b. 21st da, 12th mo, 1744; Richard Bacon, b. 14th da, 12th mo, 1746; Samuel Bacon, b. 20th da, 5th mo, 1747; Jesse Bacon, b. 28th da, 5th mo, 1749; Elizabeth Bacon, b. 30th da, 5th mo, 1751.

Children of Samuel Dennis and Ann, his wife: Joseph Dennis, b. 15th da, 10th mo, 1718; Elizabeth Dennis, b. 20th da, 3rd mo, 1724; Ann Dennis, b. 14th da, 3rd mo, 1729; Dorcas Dennis, b. 6th da, 12th mo, 1730/31; Samuel Dennis, b. 12th da, 2nd mo, 1732; Sarah Dennis, b. 8th da, 12th mo, 1733/4.

Gabriel Davis, son of Charles Davis by Rachel, his wife, b. 22nd da, 5th mo, 1743.
Rachel Miller, dau. of Andrew Miller by Rachel, his wife, b. 17th da, 4th mo, 1758.
Children of Thomas Bacon and Elonar, his wife: Charles Bacon, b. 18th da, 1st mo, 1748; Rachel Bacon, b. 20th da, 10th mo, 1753; Dorcas Bacon, b. 20th da, 8th mo, 1756.
Children of John Reeve and Elizabeth, his wife: John Reeve, b. 3rd da, 11th mo, 1754; Eleonar Reeve, b. 15th da, 6th mo, 1757; Peter Reeve, b. 1st da, 2nd mo, 1759.
Children of Richard Wood and Hannah, his wife: Richard Wood, b. 7th da, 2nd mo, 1755; James Wood, b. 30th da, 8th mo, 1765.
Children of Joseph Reeve and Millisent, his wife: Samuel Reeve, b. 22nd da, 6th mo, 1751; Martha Reeve, b. 29th da, 11th mo, 1754; Joseph Reeve, b. 26th da, 9th mo, 1756.
Children of Benjamin Tyler and Naomy, his wife: Elizabeth Tyler, b. 28th da, 2nd mo, 1748; Rachel Tyler, b. 12th da, 7th mo, 1751; John Tyler, b. 1st da, 2nd mo, 1753; Leatitia Tyler, b. 9th da, 11th mo, 1755.
Children of Benjamin Tyler and Mary, his wife: Job Tyler, b. 20th da, 11th mo, 1760; Lydia Tyler, b. 30th da, 7th mo, 1763; Hannah Tyler, b. 15th da, 2nd mo, 1765; Benjamin Tyler, b. 30th da, 10th mo, 1771.
Children of John Barracliff and Ann, his wife: Prudence Barracliff, b. 16th da, 5th mo, 1751; Ruth Barracliff, b. 7th da, 4th mo, 1753.
Children of John Barracliff and Laetitia, his wife: Aron Barracliff, b. 9th da, 2nd mo, 1757; George Barracliff, b. 13th da, 1st mo, 1761.
Children of Ebenezer Miller and Ruth, his wife: Hannah, b. 14th da, 4th mo, 1753; Ebenezer Miller, b. 18th da, 1st mo, 1761 and d. 16th da, 2nd mo, following; Priscilla Miller, b. 9th da, 7th mo, 1763; Ebenezer Miller, 2nd son, b. 18th da, 8th mo, 1766; Sarah Miller, b. 12th da, 11th mo, 1768; Ruth Miller, b. 23rd da, 4th mo, 1772.
Children of Mark Sheppard and Ann, his wife: Mary Sheppard, b. 21st da, 6th mo, 1752.
Children of Richard Haines and Agnes, his wife: Joseph Haines, b. 23rd da, 7th mo, 1722; Anthony Hains, b. ? da, 1st mo, 1726; Ephraim Hains, b. 23rd da, 7th mo, 1733; Richard Hains, b. 3rd da, 5th mo, 17??; Rebeckah Hains, b. 4th da, 1st mo, 1737.[The blanks are in the original record.]
Children of Joseph Hains and Ann, his wife: Reuben Hains, b. 24th da, 10th mo, 1750; Joseph Hains, b. 20th da, 9th mo, 1751; Agnes Haines, b. 11th da, 9th mo, 1753; Naomy Haines, b. 16th da, 1st mo, 1755.

Margaret Hall, dau. of Clement Hall by Margaret, his wife, b. 18th da, 1st mo, 1765 and buried the 16th da, 10th mo, following.

Children of Anthony Hains and Jemima, his wife: Rebeckah Hains, b. 6th da, 10th mo, 1754; Anthony Hains, b. 3rd da, 11th mo, 1756.

Child of Richard Hains and Elizabeth, his wife: Ephraim Hains, b. 2nd da, 3rd mo, 1758. [This entry crossed out in original records.]

Child of Jonathan Potts and Sarah, his wife: Elizabeth Potts, b. 4th da, 4th mo, 1757.

Children of Andrew Griscom and Susannah, his wife: Sarah Griscom, b. 8th da, 7th mo, 1742, d. 5th da, 7th mo, 1762; Everat Griscom, b. 1st da, 6th mo, 1746; William Griscom, b. 10th da, 11th mo, 1747.

Children of Andrew Griscom and Mary, his wife: Mary Griscom, b. 16th da, 12th mo, 1753, d. 25th da, 9th mo, 1762; Andrew Griscom, b. 21st da, 11th mo, 1755; Deborah Griscom, b. 29th da, 4th mo, 1758.

John Denn, d. 10th da, 10th mo, 1759.
John Chandler, Jr., d. 7th da, 12th mo, 1765.
Josiah Chandler, d. 8th da, of the same aged 23 years.
John Chandler, Sr., d. 18th da, 3rd mo, 1766 aged 73 years.
Susannah Bradway, d. 28th da, 12th mo, 1767.

FRIESBURG EMANUEL LUTHERAN CHURCH

BAPTISMS

Children bapt. at Cohansie, beginning in 1749.

The following seven children were bapt. by Peter Brunnholtz:
Friederich Fries of Jacob and Anna Margaretha, b. Oct. 12, 1748, bapt. May 25, 1749. Sponsors: Friedrich Tendelsbeck and his wife.
Elisabeth Trollinger of Gabriel and Margaretha, b. Dec. 16, 1748, bapt. May 25, 1749. Sponsors: Friedrich Tendelsbeck and Margretha his wife, Michael Dillshoever and Maria Elisabeth his wife.
Johan Jacob Meyer of Leonhard and Cathrina, b. May 4, 1749, bapt. May 25, 1749. Sponsors: Jacob Fries and his wife.
Maria Hahn of Jurg and Christina, b. Nov. 13, 1748, bapt. May 25, 1749. Sponsors: Leonhard Mayer, Anna Barbara wife of Johan Kanus.
Anna Cathrina of Michael and Anna Maria, b. Sept. 16, 1748, bapt. May 25, 1749. Sponsors: Philip Mintz and Anna Cathrina his wife.
Daniel Wentzel of Johan Wilhelm, Cath., and Anna Maria, b. 4 months before, bapt. May 25, 1749. Sponsors: Carl Sauder, Reformed, and Maria Dorothea MacKascen.
Maria Dorothea Mackaschen of William and Maria Dorothea, b. May 4, 1748, bapt. May 25, 1749. Sponsors: Johan Wilhelm Wentzel and Anna Maria his wife, Christian Nazel and Anna Margretha his wife.

Maria Cathrina Herpe of Michael and Margrethe, b. Jan. 6, 1750, bapt. May 23, 1750. Sponsors: Michael Muller and his wife.
Christina Hochschild of Justus and Magdalena, b. March 21, 1750, bapt. May 23, 1750. Sponsors: Diedrich Rheinhard, Ref. and Mrs. Christ. Hochschild.
Johannes Gauger of Conrad and Anna Barbara, b. Feb. 17, 1750, bapt. May 23, 1750. Sponsor: Johannes Kueper, single.
Jonathan Hahn of Ludwig and Cathrina, b. Oct. 11, 1749, bapt. May 23, 1750. Sponsors: Johannes Stamm, Ref., and Cathrina his wife, Luth., Jacob Fries and Margretha his wife, Ref.
Maria Cathrina Stam of Johannes and Cathrina, b. March 10, 1750, bapt. May 23, 1750. Sponsors: Ludwig Hahn and Cathrina his wife and Michael Born and Anna Maria his wife.
Cathrina Graemeu of Mathias, Cath[olic], and Anna Margreth, Luth., b. Aug. 15, 1749, bapt. May 23, 1750. Sponsors: Johannes Stamm, Ref., Jacob Utzen's wife Maria Cathrina, Ref., and Ludwig Hahn's wife Cathrina.
Johan Jacob Heppel of Nicolas and Maria Barbara, b. March 24, 1750, bapt. May 23, 1750. Sponsors: Jacob Utz, Jacob Fries, Mrs. Anna Maria Born and Mrs. Maria Elizabeth Decker.
Anna Elizabeth Ridmann of Johan Andreas and Anna Barbara, b. Oct. 31, 1749, bapt. May 23, 1750. Sponsors: Adam Reis, Anna Nessin, single servant and Mrs. Maria Elisabeth Crattinger.
Christian Dillshoever of Michael and Maria Elisabeth, b. May 7,

1750, bapt. May 24, 1750. Sponsors: Christian Nazel and
Margretha his wife.
Wilhelm Sauder of Wilhelm, Ref., and Cathrina, Luth., b. Feb. 25,
1750, bapt. May 24, 1750. Sponsors: Hans Wilhelm Wentzel and
Anna Maria his wife.
Michael Kniest of Johannes, Ref., and Barbara, Luth., b. May 13,
1750, bapt. May 24, 1750. Sponsors: Michael Born and Anna
Maria his wife, not yet anything.
Margretha Drollinger of Gabriel and Margretha, b. Sept. 14, bapt.
April 20, 1745. Sponsors: Andreas Welde and Margretha
Coellischen.
Maria Elisabetha Hohenshildt of Adam and Anna Elisabetha, b. July
20, 1744, bapt. Aug. 2, 1744. Sponsors: Elias Beitelman and
Maria Elisabetha his wife, and Anna Elisabetha wife of Adam
Hohenshilt.
Gabriel Drollinger of Gabriel and Margaretha, b. Jan. 25, 1751,
bapt. July 24, 1751. Sponsors: The parents themselves.
Elisabetha Zobel of Georg Adam and Eva Ursula, b. xbr: 23, 1750,
bapt. July 24, 1751. Sponsors: Adam Hochschild and Elisabetha
his wife.
Johann Georg Friess of Jacob and Anna Margaretha, Ref., b. 3 7br:
1750, bapt. July 24, 1751. Sponsors: Friderich Denttelsbek
and Margaretha his wife.
Anna Margaretha Meyer of Joh: Leonhard and Eva Catharina, b. 23
xbry 1750, bapt. July 24, 1751. Sponsors: Jacob Friess and
Anna Margaretha his wife.
David Hahn of Georg and Christina, b. 25, 8bry 1750, bapt. July
24, 1751. Sponsors: Ludwig Hahn and Chatarina his wife.
Maria Hahn of Michael and Catharina, b. ---, bapt. by
Schoolmaster, act of emergency and affirmed by pastor, March
1751. Sponsors: Michael Born and Anna Maria his wife.
Barbara Krumreim of Georg Leonhard and Barbara, b. 5 7bry 1751,
bapt. by Anna Maria, wife of Michael Born in emergency same
day. Sponsors: Zusana Grismeyerin, widow, and Christina,
Philipp Sauter's wife, both addicts to the Catholic Religion.
Margaretha Stamm of Johannes and Catharina, b. 22 9bry 1751,
bapt. by Schoolmaster Aberle in emergency March 20, 1752.
Sponsors: Margaretha, wife of Jacob Friess.
Louisa Falck of Simon and Elisabetha, b. Jan. 2, 1752, bapt. June
16 same year. Sponsors: Louisa, single dau. of Adam
Hohenshild and Adam Hohenshildther, father.
Johann Jacob Meyerer of Jacob and Anna Margaretha, b. ---, bapt.
June 16, this year. Sponsors: Jacob Meyerer and Anna
Margaretha.
Johann Adam Heppel of Niclaus and Maria Barbara, b. April 10,
1752, bapt. June 16 this year. Sponsors: Adam Hohenshild,
Catharina, wife of Ludwig Hahn, Michael Schrottner and Agnesa
Dorothea, wife of Schoolmaster Aberle.
Johann Jacob Dillshoeffer of Michael and Maria Elisabetha, b. 27
xbry 1751, bapt. June 17, this year. Sponsors: Jacob Friess
and Margretha his wife.
Johannes Schmick of Joh: Philipp and Sovia Elisabetha, b. May 1,
1751, bapt. June 17, this year. Sponsor: Johannes Luz.
Maria Margaretha Gratinger of Christian and Maria Louisa, b. May

17, 1752, bapt. June 17 this year. Sponsors: Georg Krumrein, Maria Louisa wife of Michel Dillshoeffer and Anna Margareth wife of Adam Reiss.
Maria Catharina Kinny of Bartolome and Maria, single, b. 3 8bry 1751, bapt. June 17, 1752. Sponsors: Philipp Muenz and Maria Catharina his wife.
Johann David Hausser of Christoph and Regina, b. April 3, 1751, bapt. June 17, 1752. Sponsors: Conrad Israel Aberle and Maria Magdalena, David Hammen's wife.
Johann Heinrich Fries of Jacob and Margaretha, b. Dec. 21, 1752, bapt. July 1, 1753. Sponsors: Friederich Tendelsbeck and Anna Margretha his wife.
Friederich Trollinger of Gabriel and Anna Margretha, b. June 17, 1753, bapt. July 1 same year. Sponsors: Friederich Tendelsbeck and Anna Margretha his wife.
Daniel Dilshoefer of Michael and Maria Elisabeth, b. March 15, 1753, bapt. July 1, 1753. Sponsors: Christian Nassel and Anna Margretha his wife.
Anna Margaretha Stamme of Johannes and Charlotte, b. Feb. 22, 1753, bapt. July 1, 1753. Sponsors: Jacob Friess and Margaretha his wife.
Elisabeth Hahn of Michael and Catharina, b. Feb. 25, 1753, bapt. July 1, 1753. Sponsors: Christian Kradinger and wife, and Ludwig Hahn.
Johann Juerg Meyer of Leonhard and Catharina, b. March 18, 1753, bapt. July 1 same year. Sponsor: Hans Juerg Kaucher.
Abraham Krumreyn of Juerg and Barbara, b. Jan. 4, 1753, bapt. July 1 this year. Sponsors: Abraham Zimmermann, Christian Kradinger and Mrs. Margretha Reis.
Jacob Ross of Juerg and Catharina, b. Dec. 14, 1752, bapt. July 1, 1753. Sponsors: Michael Schrotner and Ester his wife and Mrs. Anna Ross, widow.
Catharina Margaretha Braun of Martin, b. Sept. 18, 1752, bapt. July 1, 1753. Sponsors: Michael Schrotner and Ester his wife.
Johannes Schmidt of Christian and Appellona, b. May 22, 1753, bapt. July 1 same year. Sponsors: Johannes Stamme and Charlotte his wife.
--- Maier of Jacob and Elisabeth, b. Dec. 26, 1752, bapt. July 1, 1753. Sponsors: Heinrich Rodgeb and his wife.
Eva Michler of Jost and Catharina, b. April 8, 1753, bapt. July 1 same year. Sponsors: Simon Walter and Eva his wife.
Jacob Kaucher of Conradt and Barbara, b. Nov. 3, 1752, bapt. July 1, 1753. Sponsors: Hans Juerg Kaucher and Maria Appellona his wife.
Martha Juliana Probe of Johann Heinrich and Catharina Hedewig, b. Dec. 4, 1753 and because child very weak bapt. by Schoolmaster J. C. Kuhlemann. Sponsors: Martha Master Aebt's wife Engl. and Magdalena Juliana wife of Schoolmaster Kuhleman.
Elisabeth Kuntz of Isaac and Sophia Augusta, b. April 5, 1754, bapt. June 9 same year. Sponsors: Leonhard Wilfort and Kunigunda his wife.
Anna Catharina Ramelton of Marius and Barbara Herbstler, single, b. Nov. 15, 1753, bapt. June 9, 1754. Sponsors: Christoph Kuhleman, Schoolmaster and Anna Catharina Linter, widow.

EARLY CHURCH RECORDS OF SALEM COUNTY

Peter Walter of Simon and Eva, b. March 19, 1754, bapt. June 9 same year. Sponsors: Peter Doffel and Margretha wife of Michael Herb.

Catharina Walter of Carl and Maria Margretha, b. 11 8br 1752, bapt. June 9, 1754. Sponsors: Master Taylor Schwaille and Anna Catharina wife of Master Mich Mueller.

Elisabeth Diestler of Johann Wilh. and Anna Margareta, b. May 8, 1754, bapt. June 9 same year. Sponsors: Leonhard Wilford and Mrs. Elisabeth Falck.

Elisabeth Falck of Simon and Elisabeth, b. Jan. 6, 1754, bapt. June 9 same year. Sponsors: Hans Juerg Schneider and Loysa Hochschild, spinster dau. of Adam Hochschild.

The 2 children below were bapt. by the Rev. Caspar Ruebel, Reformed Pastor:

Johannes Mueller of Heinrich and Schena, b. May 11, 1754, bapt. June 28 same year. Sponsors: Heinrich Rothgeb and Barbara his wife.

Heinrich Rothget of Heinrich and Barbara, b. June 18, 1754, bapt. dito 28 same year. Sponsors: Heinrich Mueller and Schena his wife.

The 3 children below were bapt. by the Rev. Peter Brunnholtz, Lutheran Pastor:

Johann Adam Zimmermann of Abraham and Anna, b. Oct. 14, 1754, bapt. dito 27 same year. Sponsors: Adam Reiss and Margreta his wife, and Melchior Ruh and Barbara his wife.

Maria Elizabeth Schwam of Johann and Maria Elisabeth, b. Oct. 21, 1754, bapt. Oct. 27 same year. Sponsors: Adam Reiss and Margreta his wife.

Anna Catharina Nasel of Christian and Margreta, b. 17 8br 1754, bapt. 27 8br same year. Sponsors: Johann Juerg Beghold, Mrs. Anna Zimmermann, and Mrs. Catharina Mueller.

The below registered five children were bapt. by the Reverende Mr. Heinz Elmann, Lutheran Parson:

Catharina Hahn of Johann and Elisabeth, b. May 9, 1754, bapt. March 2, 1755. Sponsors: The Rev. Parson Mathias Heinzelmann and Anna Margreta, wife of Jacob Fries and the parents themselves.

Johann Adam Stamm of Johannes and Charlotte, b. Dec. 18, 1754, bapt. March 2, 1755. Sponsors: Jacob Fries and Anna Margreta his wife and Adam Schaeffer and Margreta his wife.

Johann Simon Mejer of Leonhard and Catharina, b. Nov. 2, 1754, bapt. March 2, 1755. Sponsors: Jacob Fries and Anna Margreta his wife.

Maria Catharina Johnson of Paul and Elisabeth, b. Feb. 6, 1755, bapt. March 2 this year, d. March 10 this year. Sponsors: His brother's wife, Mrs. Barbara Johnson.

Elisabeth Schmidt of Johann and Maria Barbara, b. Jan. 4, 1755, bapt. March 2 same year. Sponsors: Juerg Reimar and Mrs. Maria Barbara, widow.

The following baptisms by the Reverend Mr. Reubel, Reformed

Minister:
Margareta Barbara Braun of Martin and Margreta, b. March 13, 1755, bapt. May 3, same year. Sponsors: Michael Schrotner and Ester Margreta his wife, and Adam Mensch and Barbara his wife.
Anna Maria Fries of Jacob and Anna Margreta, b. March 4, 1755, bapt. May 4, same year. Sponsors: Friederich Dendelsbeck and Anna Margreta his wife.
Georg Adam Kradinger of Christian and Elisabeth, b. Nov. 13, 1754, bapt. May 4, 1755. Sponsors: Adam Reis, Juerg Krumrein and Barbara his wife.
Johann Wilhelm Schmick of Philip and Elisabeth Magdalena, b. Dec. 2, 1754, bapt. May 4, 1755. Sponsors: Johannes Lotz and the mother herself.
Johann Christian Krumrein of Juerg and Barbara, b. Jan. 22, 1755, bapt. May 4 same year. Sponsors: Christian Kradinger and Elisabeth his wife.
Elisabeth Maurer of Jacob and Elisabeth, b. March 10, 1755, bapt. May 4 same year. Sponsors: Parents themselves.
Maria Barbara Zobel of Adam and Eva Ursula, b. April 13, 1755, bapt. May 4 same year. Sponsors: Johann Schmidt and Maria Barbara his wife.

The following registrations beginning with the Baptism of the wife of Hinrich Foerster, the taylor and her dau. and ending with the baptisms of twelve other children bear witness to the administration of the Sacrament by the Reverend Johann Friederich Handshuch, pastor on the twentieth day of June:
Miriam Foerster, wife of Hinrich, 25 years of age, bapt. June 20, 1756 and Elisabeth Foerster of Hinrich and Miriam, b. Sept. 12, 1755, bapt. June 20, 1756. Sponsors: Miriam - Hinrich Gonrath; Elisabeth - Mrs. Eva Phocer.
Michael Jahnson of Peter and Barbara, b. April 15, 1756, bapt. June 20 same year. Sponsor: Michael Mueller.
Andreas Mensch of Joh: Adam and Barbara, b. April 9, 1756, bapt. June 20 same year. Sponsor: Andreas Brandner.
Maria Margaretha Faber of Hinrich and Maria Elisabeth, b. Nov. 29, 1755, bapt. June 20, 1756. Sponsors: Johannes Dendelsbeck and Mrs. Maria Elisabeth Foerster.
Johannes Georg Noll of Johannes and Maria, b. Jan. 28, 1756, bapt. June 20 same year. Sponsors: Georg Krumrein and Barbara his wife.
Johannes Doffel of Wilhelm and Catharina, b. July 15, 1755, bapt. June 20, 1756. Sponsor: Peter Doffel.
Maria Hahn of Johannes and Elisabeth, b. March 9, 1756, bapt. June 20 same year. Sponsors: Michael Mueller and Catharina his wife.
Maria Barbara Uetzner of Jacob and Magdalena, b. Jan. 6, 1756, bapt. June 20 same year. Sponsors: Henrich Rothgeb and Barbara his wife.
Johann Jacob Hahn of George and Christina, b. Oct. 4, 1755, bapt. June 20, 1756. Sponsor: Mrs. Margretha Fries.
Catharina Kauger of Conrath and Anna Barbara, b. Nov. 10, 1755, bapt. June 20, 1756. Sponsors: Hinrich Faber and Elisabeth his wife and Mrs. Catharina Ross.

Elisabeth Schneider of Georg and Margretha, b. April 25, 1756,
bapt. June 20 same year. Sponsors: Johannes Schimph and
Elisabeth his wife.
Andreas Kraemer of Mathias and Anna Margratha, b. May 22, 1756,
bapt. June 20 same year. Sponsor: Andreas Brandner.
Jacob Friederich M'casson of William and Maria Dorothea, b. Jan.
19, 1756, bapt. June 20 same year. Sponsors: Christian
Friederich Krauss and Mrs. Margretha Fries.

The following children were bapt. by the Swedish Pastor, the
Reverend Lydenius:
Michael Langenbach of Paul and Elisabeth, b. 11 7br 1756, bapt.
Feb. 22, 1757. Sponsors: Michael Mueller, Jun. and Margretha
his wife.
Johannes Philip Schmick of Philip and Catharina Magdalena, b. 18
7br 1756, bapt. Feb. 22, 1757. Sponsors: Johannes Lotz and
the mother herself.
--- Foerster of Hinrich and Miriam, b. ---, bapt. ---.
Sponsors: Johannes Horn and Margretha, legitimate dau. of
Jacob Fries.

The following children were bapt. by the Reformed minister, the
Reverend Mr. Stoy:
Maria Margretha Rammel of Jacob and Magdalena, b. July 24, 1756,
bapt. April 17, 1757. Sponsors: Christoph Koch and Margretha
his wife.
Philip Schimph of Johannes and Elisabeth, b. Dec. 20, 1756, bapt.
April 17, 1757. Sponsors: Philip Schimph and Catharina,
spinster.
Adam Ramster of Joh: Georg and Margaretha, b. March 8, 1757,
bapt. April 17, 1757. Sponsors: Adam Mensch and Barbara his
wife.
Charlotte Wuster of Michael and Anna, b. March 20, 1757, bapt.
April 17 same year. Sponsors: Johannes Stamm and Charlotta
his wife.

The following children were bapt. by the Lutheran Pastor, the
Rev. Handschue:
Catharina Schmidt of Johannes and Barbara, b. Feb. 10, 1757,
bapt. April 30 same year. Sponsor: Mrs. Catharina Teyckert.
Juliana Margretha Fischer of Georg and Margretha, b. Feb. 27,
1757, bapt. April 30 same year. Sponsors: Christoph Kuhlemann
and Magdalena Juliana.
Maria Meier of Leonhard and Catharina, b. Feb. 3, 1757, bapt.
April 30 same year. Sponsors: George Kaucher and Maria his
wife.

The following children were bapt. by the Reverend Pastor Stoy:
Maria Catharina Janson of Paul and Elisabeth, b. Aug. 30, 1757,
bapt. April 2, 1758. Sponsors: Michael Mueller, Senr., and
Catharina his wife.
Johann Michael Mueller of Michael, Jr. and Margretha, b. Dec. 12,
1757, bapt. April 2, 1758. Sponsors: Michael Mueller, Sr. and
Catharina his wife.

Maria Catharina Janson of Peter and Barbara, b. Nov. 18, 1757,
bapt. April 2, 1758. Sponsors: Mich: Mueller, Sr. and
Catharina his wife.
Johann Henrich Nolle of Johannes and Anna Maria, b. Jan. 2, 1758,
bapt. April 2 same year. Sponsors: Georg Krumrein and
Henrich, single.
Christian Damerus of Peter and Anna Maria, b. Dec. 6, 1757, bapt.
April 2, 1758. Sponsors: Christian Schmidt and Appelona his
wife.
Elisabeth Hoffmann of Johannes and Anna Margretha, b. Aug. 12,
1757, bapt. April 2, 1758. Sponsors: Georg Kaucher and Anna
Elisabeth his dau.
Anna Maria Rothgeb of Henrich and Barbara, b. May 12, 1757, bapt.
April 2, 1758. Sponsors: Friederich Dendelsbeck and Margretha
his wife.
Anna Margretha Wentzel of Johann Wilhelm and Anna Maria, b. March
1, 1758, bapt. April 2 same year. Sponsors: Adam Schaeffer
and Margretha his wife.
Anna Eva Phozer of Adam and Eva, b. March 26, 1758, bapt. April 2
same year. Sponsors: Abraham Zimmermann and Anna his wife.
Johann Philip Flack and Susanna Flack (twins) of Simon and
Elisabeth, b. May 1, 1757, bapt. April 2, 1758. Sponsors:
Philip Junge and Louisa his wife, Adam Valentin, single, and
Mrs. Maria Elisabeth Wagner.
Johann Philip Fries of Jacob and Margretha, b. June 29, 1757,
bapt. Feb. 26, 1758. Sponsor: Philip Sauter.
Johann Philip Junge of Philip and Louisa, b. Aug. 7, 1757, bapt.
Feb. 26, 1758. Sponsors: Philip Schmich and Elisabeth
Magdalena his wife.
Charlotta Stamm of Johannes and Charlotta, b. June 29, 1757,
bapt. Feb. 26, 1758. Sponsors: Joh: Wilhelm Wentzel and
Margaretha wife of Jacob Fries.
Andreas Gelloper of Benjamin and Maria, b. Nov. 1, 1757, bapt.
Feb. 26, 1758. Sponsors: Andreas Brandner and Susanna his
wife.

The following children were bapt. by Lutheran Pastor, The Rev.
Handschue:
Johann Georg Schimph of Johannes and Elisabeth, b. May 13, 1758,
bapt. June 24 same year. Sponsors: Joh: Georg Schneider and
Margretha his wife.
Margretha Kaucher of Conrath and Anna Barbara, b. May 11, 1758,
bapt. June 24 same year. Sponsors: Leonhard Meier and
Catharina his wife.
Anna Maria Faber of Henrich and Elisabeth, b. March 5, 1758,
bapt. June 24 same year. Sponsors: Adam Maurer and Anna
Margretha his wife.
Johann Melchior Hitzler of Peter and Margretha, b. April 19,
1758, bapt. June 24 same year. Sponsors: Melchior Zimmermann,
Deobald Schwenk and Catharina Jacob, all three single.
Johannes Hoeltzel of Georg Friederich and Elizabeth, b. March 30,
1758, bapt. June 24 same year. Sponsors: Johannes Schnitzer
and Anna Barbara his wife.
Johannes Hahn of Johannes and Elisabeth, b. May 10, 1758, bapt.

June 24 same year. Sponsors: Jacob Fries and Margretha his wife.

The following children were bapt. by the Lutheran Parson, The Rev. Mr. Schrenck:

Simon Rammel of Jacob and Magdalena, b. Jan. 10, 1759, bapt. June 24 same year. Sponsors: Simon Martini and Catharina his wife.

Johannes Johnson of Peter and Bargara, b. March 25, 1759, bapt. June 24 same year. Sponsors: Hans Michael Muller and Maria Catharina his wife.

Johann Carl Walter of Carl and Margaretha, b. Dec. 3, 1758, bapt. June 24, 1759. Sponsors: Joh: Heinrich Stertz and Mrs. Magdalena Foerster.

Peter Doffel of Wilhelm and Catharina, b. May 1759, bapt. June 24 same year. Sponsors: Peter Doffel and his wife.

Jacob Kraemer of Matthias and Margretha, b. 11 8br 1758, bapt. June 24, 1759. Sponsors: Jacob Kasar and Maria Eva his wife.

Susanna Mensch of Adam and Barbara, b. April 11, 1759, bapt. June 24 same year. Sponsors: Andreas Brandner and Susanna his wife.

Maria Barbara Brandner of Andreas and Susanna, b. 9 7br 1758, bapt. June 24, 1759. Sponsors: Adam Mensch and Barbara his wife.

Johann Peter Falck of Simon and Elisabeth, b. May 23, 1759, bapt. June 24 same year. Sponsors: Philip Junge and Louise his wife.

Johannes Stamm of Johannes and Charlotta, b. May 20, 1759, bapt. June 24 same year. Sponsors: Hans Michael Mueller and Maria Catharina his wife.

Michael Thueringer of Johannes and Catharina, b. 22 7br 1758, bapt. June 24, 1759. Sponsors: Melchior Zimmermann, Johann Kantz and Mrs. Anna Thueringer.

Abraham Ross of Matthias and Margretha, b. April 28, 1759, bapt. June 24 same year. Sponsors: Abraham Zimmermann and Anna his wife.

Johannes Schmidt of Johannes and Maria Barbara, b. Jan. 13, 1759, bapt. June 24 same year. Sponsors: The parents themselves.

Wilhelm Seiler of Zacharias and Maria, b. Aug. 6, 1758, bapt. June 24, 1759. Sponsor: Wilhelm Wagner.

Friederich Reinhard Schmick of Philip and Elisabeth Magdalena, b. Aug. 26, 1758, bapt. June 24, 1759. Sponsors: Philip Junge and Louisa his wife.

Johann Georg Uetzner of Jacob and Magdalena, b. May 6, 1759, bapt. June 24 same year. Sponsors: Henrich Rothgeb and Barbara his wife.

Catharina Winckler of Margretha Winckler, spinster, b. Aug. 11, 1758, bapt. June 24, 1759. Sponsors: Catharina, Peter Johnson, Serv:

The following children were bapt. by the Reformed minister, The Rev. Mr. Steiner:

Johann Peter Fries of Jacob and Margretha, b. July 29, 1759, bapt. Aug. 21 same year. Sponsors: The parents themselves.

Johannes Hoffmann of Johann and Johanna Margretha, b. Aug. 17,

1758, bapt. Aug. 21, 1759. Sponsors: The parents themselves.
Johann Henrich Conrath of Charlotta, widow of Henrich Conrath, deceased, b. July 26, 1759, bapt. Aug. 21 same year. Sponsors: Georg Krumrein and Barbara his wife.

The following children were bapt. by the Lutheran Parson, The Rev. Mr. Hanschue on the 25th of June 1760:
Georg Hammer of Georg and Anna, b. March 2, 1760, bapt. June 25 same year. Sponsors: Zacharias Seiler and Maria his wife.
Jacob Wilhelm Fuchs and Isaac Fuchs (twins) of Joh: Friederich and Sophia Margretha, b. Oct. 13, 1759, bapt. June 25, 1760. Sponsors: Hans Wilhelm Wentzel, Abraham Zimmermann and Anna his wife, and Deobald Schoch.
Johannes Schneider of Georg and Margretha, b. 13 8br 1759, bapt. June 25, 1760. Sponosrs: Johannes Schimph and Elizabeth his wife.
Maria Catharina Mueller of Michael, Jr. and Margretha, b. April 20, 1760, bapt. June 25 same year. Sponsors: Hans Michael Mueller, Sr. and Catharina his wife.
Catharina Maria Kirman of Marcus and Maria Elisabeth, b. Jan. 25, 1760, bapt. June 15 same year. Sponsors: Bodo Otto Dr. and Catharina Dorothea his wife.
Michael Janson and Philip Janson (twins) of Paul and Elisabeth, b. Jan. 17, 1760, bapt. June 25 same year. Sponsors: Peter Janson and Barbara his wife.
Johann Adam Tamerus of Peter and Maria, b. April 30, 1760, bapt. June 25 same year. Sponsors: Christian Schmidt and Adam Saul and Margretha.
Johannes Fischer of Georg and Margretha, b. May 24, 1760, bapt. June 25 same year. Sponsors: Johannes Schimph and Elisabeth his wife.
Peter Sauter of Johannes and Margretha, b. ---, bapt. June 25 same year. Sponsors: Jacob Fries, Jr. and Miss Elisabeth Aebel, single.
Elisabeth Meier of Leonhard and Catharina, b. June 14 this year, bapt. June 25 same year. Sponsors: Johann Kaumann and Eva Maria his wife.
Elisabeth Graff of Georg and Anna Barbara, b. Aug. 17, 1759, bapt. June 25, 1760. Sponsors: Michael Ross and Elisabeth his wife.
Johann Adam Braun of Martin and Margretha, b. March 21, 1760, bapt. June 25 same year. Sponsors: Michael Schrotner and Esther Margretha his wife and Adam Mensch and Barbara his wife.
Catharina Carl of Martin and Catharina, b. March 10, 1760, bapt. June 25 same year. Sponsors: Wilhelm Schoch and Catharina Jacobi his wife.
Anna Catharina Hoeltzel of Georg Fried: and Elisabeth, b. Feb. 15, 1760, bapt. June 25 same year. Sponsors: Johannes Ifft and Anna Catharina his wife.

At the Lumber Mill were bapt. by the Rev. Mr. Handtschue of June 26, 1760:
Agnesa Bauer of Joh: Michael and Susanna Salome b. May 29, 1760.

Sponsors: Johannes Licht and Agnesa his wife.
Jacob Coster of Johannes and Jacobina b. Aug. 15, 1759.
   Sponsors: Jacob Schleich and Mrs. Elisabeth Hoffmann.
Georg Weiser of Joh: Georg and Catharina b. April 6, 1760.
   Sponsors: Georg Blume and Elisabeth his wife and Mrs.
   Catharina Pfeil.
Georg Wahl of Gottfried and Christina b. March 25, 1759.
   Sponsors: Georg Blume and Elisabeth his wife.

The following children were bapt. by the Rev. Mr. Steiner Nov. 13, 1760:
Johannes Gellhoefer of Benjamin and Maria b. 13 8br 1760.
   Sponsors: Johannes Lotz and Maria his wife.
Johann Heinrich Schmick of Philip and Elisabeth Magdalena b. 27 8br 1760. Sponsors: Johannes Lotz and Maria his wife.
Johann Adam Fister of Adam and Christina b. 4 8br 1760.
   Sponsors: Michael Schrotner and Esther Margretha his wife, and Johann Walcker and Margretha his wife.
Anna Maria Jung of Philip and Louisa b. May 25, 1760. Sponsors: Johannes Lotz and Maria his wife.
Anna Margretha Hahn of Johann and Elisabeth b. Sept. 20, 1760.
   Sponsors: Jacob Fries and Margretha his wife.
Johann Georg Prindesholtz of Adam and Anna Maria b. 4 7br 1760.
   Sponsors: The parents themselves.

Bapt. by the Rev. Mr. Steiner May 17, 1761:
Friederich Marcus Kirmann of Marcus and Maria Elisabeth b. April 27, 1761. Sponsors: Bodo Otto Dr. and Catharina Dorothea his wife.
Georg Graff of Jacob and Margretha b. July 3, 1760. Sponsors: Georg Rotgeb and Mrs. Anna Margretha Fries.
Anna Margretha Graff of Peter and Margretha b. Dec. 3, 1760.
   Sponsors: Adam Schaeffer and Margretha his wife.
Anna Maria Uetzner of Jacob and Magdalena b. November 12, 1760.
   Sponsors: Heinrich Rotgeb and Barbara his wife and Georg his son.
Johannes Mueller of Georg and Susanna b. April 2, 1761. Sponsors Hans Mich: Mueller, Sr. and Catharina his wife.
Georg Jacob Martin of Simon and Catharina b. May 14, 1761.
   Sponsors: Jacob Rammel and Magdalena his wife, Joh: George Kautz, and Anna Thueringer, both single.
Johann Hinrich Faber of Heinrich and Maria Elisabeth b. Aug. 29, 1760. Sponsors: Johannes Dendelsbeck and Francisca Margretha his wife.
Magdalena Schmitt of Johannes and Barbara b. Jan. 1, 1761.
   Sponsors: Jacob Uetzner and Anna Magdalena his wife.
Anna Elisabeth Horn of Johannes and Christina b. April 10, 1761.
   Sponsors: Andreas Roth and Anna Elisabeth Emmel, single.
Margretha Kraemer of Mathias and Margretha b. Dec. 30, 1760.
   Sponsors: Johannes Sauter and Margretha his wife.
Anna Regina Eichhorn of Jacob and Regina b. Nov. 16, 1760.
   Sponsors: Johann Walther and Margretha his wife.
Johann Paul Reiffschneider of Egidius and Margretha b. 29 7br 1760. Sponsor: Paul Janson.

Anna Elizabeth Remel of Georg and Catharina b. March 18, 1761.
Sponsors: Georg Mebold and Christina his wife.
Anna Regina Albrecht of Johann and Catharina b. Aug. 8, 1760.
Sponsors: Andreas Brandner and Susanna his wife.
Johann Heinrich Wesemeier of Christoffer and Helena b. Feb. 14, 1761. Sponsors: Henrich Urich and Barbara his wife.
Maria Elisabeth Seiler of Zacharias and Maria b. Feb. 24, 1761.
Sponsors: Johannes Schimph and Elizabeth his wife.
Isaac Reser of Adam and Catharina b. May 11, 1761. Sponsors: Joh: Schimph and Elizabeth his wife.

And on Oct. 27, 1761, by C. M. Wrangel, Superviser of the Swedish Lutheran Church in America:
Philip Henrich Hoffecker of Henrich and Margaretha b. Sept. 7, 1761. Sponsors: Philip Sauder and Christina Sauder.
Elisabeth Janson of Peter and Barbara b. ---. Sponsors: Hans Michael Mueller and Catharina his wife.
Johan Georg Metzger of Georg and Ledi b. Feb. 1, 1761. Sponsors: Gottlieb Kauffmann and the parents themselves.

The following children were bapt. April 25, 1762, by the Rev. Steiner:
Elisabeth Braun of Martin and Margretha b. April 4, 1762.
Sponsors: Michael Schrotner and Esther Margretha his wife, and Adam Mensch and Barbara his wife.
Matthaeus Linck of Johannes and Maria b. March 24 ct. year.
Sponsor: Matthias Wullfort, single.
Catharina Krumrein of Georg and Barbara b. Jan. 2, 1762.
Sponsors: The parents themselves.
Juliana Muller of Michael, Jr. and Margretha b. Nov. 9, 1761.
Sponsors: The parents themselves.
Maria Elisabeth Dendelsbeck of Johannes and Francisca b. Feb. 20 ct. year. Sponsors: Heinrich Faber and Friedr. Dendelsbeck.
Johann Georg Rammel of Jacob and Magdalena b. Nov. 31, 1761.
Sponsors: H. Georg Mecklin and A. Maria Barbara his wife.
Andreas Uetzner of Jacob and Magdalena b. March 26 ct. year.
Sponsors: The parents themselves.
Sara Elisabeth Schimph of Philip and Elisabeth b. Nov. 4, 1761.
Sponsors: Johannes Schimph and Elisabeth his wife.
Johannes Marderstick of Johann and Catharina b. March 13 ct. year. Sponsors: Johannes Lotz and Anna Maria his wife.

The following children were bapt. by his Reverency, The Mr. Parson Muehlenberg, on the 13th day of June 1762:
Johann Georg Schnitzer of Johannes and Barbara b. March 28, 1762.
Sponsors: Joh: Georg Schneider and his wife.
Friederich Faber of Heinrich and Maria Elisabeth b. April 24, ct. year. Sponsors: Friederich Dendelsbeck and Margretha his wife.
Margretha Janson of Paul and Elisabeth b. April 9 ct. year.
Sponsors: Adam Schaeffer and Margretha his wife.
Christina Hahn of Georg and Christina b. July 30, 1760.
Sponsors: The parents themselves.
Anna Magdalena Schmidt of Johann and Barbara b. May 29, 1762.

Sponsors: Jacob Uetzner and Magdalena his wife.
Maria Elisabeth Hoeltzel of Friederich and Maria Elisabeth b.
Jan. 7, 1762. Sponsors: The parents themselves.
Maria Christina Reser of Adam and Maria Elisabeth b. May 7, 1762.
Sponsors: Johannes Schimph and Elisabeth his wife.

Anno 1763 on the 7th of Aug. again by His Eminency the Rev.
Muehlenberg the following children were bapt.:
Anna Maria Albrecht of Johann and Catharina b. Oct. 4, 1762.
Sponsors: Zacharias Seiler and Maria his wife.
Elisabeth Karll of Georg Martin and Catharina b. Aug. 13, 1762.
Sponsors: Nicolaus Olbers and Catharina Mueller, both single.
Johann Adam Kautz of Joh: Georg and Barbara b. March 25, 1763.
Sponsors: Adam Fix and Elisabeth his wife.
Johann Peter Tamerus of Peter and Anna Maria b. Jan. 2, 1763.
Sponsors: Adam Pistrau and Christina his wife.
Paul Langenbach of Paul and Elisabeth b. Aug. 22, 1762.
Sponsors: Michael Miller, Jr. and Margretha his wife.
Benjamin Gellhoeffer of Benjamin and Maria b. 17 xbr 1762.
Sponsors: Adam Mensch and Barbara his wife.
Johannes Horn of Johann and Christina b. April 19, 1763.
Sponsors: Andreas Roth and Elisabeth Emlin, both single.
Elisabeth Fries of Jacob and Margretha b. June 20, 1763.
Sponsors: The parents themselves.
Andreas Hahn of Johann and Elisabeth b. Jan. 16, 1763. Sponsors:
Jacob Fries and Margretha his wife.
Johann Friederich Lotz of Johann and Anna Maria b. Dec. 9, 1762.
Sponsor: Friederich Fuchs.
Anna Maria Carner of Martin (the mother dead) b. Jan. 8, 1762.
Sponsors: Joh: Kaumann and Eva his wife.
Johannes Hinrichs of Peter and Maria b. Oct. 9, 1762. Sponsors:
Johannes Hinrich and his wife.
Johann Adam Prindesholtz of Adam and Maria b. Dec. 8, 1762.
Sponsor: Georg Prindesholtz, single.
Peter Mensch of Adam and Barbara b. May 6, 1763. Sponsors:
Benjamin Gellhoeffer and Maria his wife.
Elisabeth Ifft of Johannes and Catharina b. Jan. 29, 1763.
Sponsors: Friederich Hoeltzel and Elisabeth his wife.
Catharina Seiler of Zacharias and Anna Maria b. April 20, 1763.
Sponsors: Johann Albrecht and Catharina his wife.
Matthaeus Zimmermann of Melchior and Magdalena b. Dec. 11, 1762.
Sponsors: Matthaeus Ross and Johanna his wife.

Anno 1764 on May 11th the following children were bapt. by His
Eminency the Rev. Wiksell, M. V. D., at Rac and Pensneck:
Jacob Janson of Peter and Barbara b. Jan. 21, 1764. Sponsor:
Jacob Miller, single.
Susanna Miller of Michael, Jr. and Anna Margretha b. Dec. 7,
1763. Sponsors: The parents themselves.
Elisabeth Maurer of Adam and Anna Margretha b. Oct. 23, 1763.
Sponsors: Henrich Faber and Elisabeth his wife.
Heinrich Stertz of Heinrich and Margretha b. Nov. 13, 1763.
Sponsors: Adam Saul and Margretha his wife.
Susanna Gauger of Georg and Maria b. Nov. 3, 1763. Sponsors:

Heinrich Faber and Elisabeth his wife.
Johann Hinnin of Johann and Maria Elisabeth b. March 1, 1764.
Sponsors: Adam Schaeffer and Margretha his wife.
Wilhelm Doffel of Wilhelm and Catharina b. Oct. 6, 1763.
Sponsor: Peter Doffel.
Barbara Kraemer of Matthaeus and Margretha b. Aug. 7, 1763.
Sponsors: Adam Mensch and Barbara his wife.
Elisabeth Kirmann of Marcus and Elisabeth b. Oct. 2, 1763.
Sponsors: Bodo Otto Dr. and Dorothea Catharina his wife.
Matthaeus Klein of Maria (Jacob's widow) b. March 31, 1764.
Sponsors: Matthaeus Blenninger and Catharina his wife.
Rebecca Dendelsbeck of Johannes and Francisca b. ---. Sponsors: Heinrich Faber and Elisabeth his wife.
--- Remmel of Georg and Catharina b. Oct. 25, 1763. Sponsors: Georg Mebold and Christina his wife.
Anna Margretha Linck of Johannes and Maria b. March 31, 1764.
Sponsors: Michael Wulfort and Margretha his wife.
Margretha Schimph of Philip and Elisabeth b. Oct. 19, 1763.
Sponsors: Georg Fischer and Margretha.
Eva Elisabeth Hoeltzel of Friederich and Elisabeth b. Dec. 26, 1763. Sponsors: Joh: Jacob Roder and Anna Catharina his wife.
Johann Peter Hinrich of Peter and Eva Maria b. Dec. 16, 1763.
Sponsors: The parents themselves.
Joh: Adam Hoffecker of Heinrich and Margretha b. Sept. 15, 1763.
Sponsors: Adam Schaeffer and Margretha his wife.
Margretha Uetzner of Jacob and Magdalena b. April 23, 1764.
Sponsors: The parents themselves.
Catharina Barbara Wuster of Michael and Catharina b. April 22, 1764. Sponsors: Adam Mensch and Barbara his wife.
Georg Ross of Matthaeus and Hanna b. Feb. 10, 1764. Sponsors: Georg Meier, single and Philip Wentzel, single.
Georg Adam Reser and Anna Maria Reser (twins) of Adam and Catharina b. Feb. 10, 1764. Sponsors: Georg Fischer and Margretha his wife, and Johann Schnitzer and Barbara his wife.
Georg Wesemeier of Christoph and Helena b. Jan. 27, 1764.
Sponsors: H. Georg Mecklin and A. Maria Barbara his wife.
Johann Georg Marderstick of Johannes and Catharina b. Nov. 25, 1763. Sponsors: I. Georg Meier and Ann Elisabeth Hinrich, both single.
Michael Koch of Michael and Maria Margretha Hartmann (have engendered outside of matrimony) b. Dec. 22, 1763. Sponsors: Johannes Seiser and Ann Maria his wife and Mrs. Anna Breitinger.
Elizabeth Butcher of George b. May 22, 1763. Sponsors: The parents themselves.
Anna Rosina Hollsheid of Johan and Maria Margaretha b. March 11, 1764. Sponsors: The parents themselves.
Johann Adam Brandner of Andreas and Susannah b. Feb. 9, 1764.
Sponsors: Adam Mensch and Barbara his wife.
Johannes Faber of Henry and Elisabeth b. June 2, 1764. Sponsors: Johannes Dentelspeck and his wife.

On 28 Aug. 1764, the following children were bapt. by Rev. Mr. Wicksell:

Regina Schitsher of Johannes and Anna Barbara b. July 1, 1764.
Sponsors: The parents themselves.
Anna Maria Knarry of Lorentz and Anna Maria b. July 22, 1764.
Sponsors: Mrs. Catharina Miller and Nicholaus Olbers.
Margareth Fistar of Adam and Mrs. Christina b. July 7, 1764.
Sponsors: Johannes Walker, Margareth Waker and Easter Schrodner.

Oct 14th 1764 bapt. by Rev. Mr. Parson Wicksell:
Philip Schneider of George b. ---. Sponsors: The parents themselves.
Susannah Beesly of Jacob b. ---. Sponsors: Susannah Brandner and Andreas Brandner.
Johannes Lutz of Johann and Anna Maria b. Sept. 25, 1764.
Sponsors: Frederich Tox and Anna Maria his wife.
Anna Catharina Herman of Friederich and Barbara b. Sept. 12, 1764. Sponsors: George Ramel and Catharina his wife.
Johann Friederich Efft of John and Maria Catharina b. Aug. 9, 1764. Sponsors: Joh: Fried: Pillgrim and Anna Maria his wife.
Maria Miller of George and Susannah b. Sept. 25, 1764. Sponsor: Mrs. Maria Miller.

Anno 1764 Dec. 18th again by His Reverency the Mr. Parson Wicksell, the following children were bapt.:
Johann Willhellm Schimp of Johannes and Elisabeth b. Dec. 9, 1764. Sponsors: The parents themselves.
Elisabeth Johnson of Paul and Elisabeth b. Aug. 31, 1764.
Sponsors: Hans. Michl: Miller and Catharina his wife.
Hans George Kauffman of Gotlieb and Christina b. Nov. 15, 1764.
Sponsors: Hans George Couch and Anna his wife.
Juliana Fuchs of Friederich and Anna Maria b. 27 8br 1764.
Sponsors: Christoph Kuhlemann and Magdalena Juliana his wife.
Heinrich Moslet of Friederich and Elisabeth b. Aug. 23, 1763.
Sponsors: Heinrich Faber and Joh: Dendelsbeck and wife.
Maria Barbara Breunesholtz of Adam and Maria b. Jan. 16, 1765.
Sponsors: Ulrich Dreudinger and Anna his wife.
Maria Elisabeth Horn of Johan and Christina b. March 19, 1765.
Sponsors: Adam Saul and Maria Eliesabeth his wife.
Johannes Albreith of Johan and Catharina b. March 2, 1765.
Sponsors: The parents themselves.
Georg Saejler of Zacharias and A. Maria b. April 13, 1765.
Sponsors: George Fischer and Margretha his wife.
Catharina Raemel of Jacob and Magdalena b. March 22, 1765.
Sponsors: Simon Maertin and Catharina his wife.
Falentin Bleiniger of Matias and Catharina b. March 26, 1765.
Sponsors: Falentin B. Reiling and Margretha his wife.
Margaretha Eaemmel of Peter R. and Elisabeth b. Feb. 26, 1765.
Sponsors: Fallentin Rheiling and Margretha his wife.
Catharina Carl of Maertin and Catharina b. Nov. 8, 1764.
Sponsors: William Schack and Catharina his wife.
Maria Catharina Bauer of Ehrhard and Magdalena b. April 15, 1765.
Sponsor: Mrs. Maria Catharina Miller.
Catharina Scack of Wilhelm and Catharina b. March 15, 1765.
Sponsors: The parents themselves.

Elisabeth Hahn of Johann and Elisabetha b. May 15, 1765.
Sponsors: Jacob Fries and Margretha his wife.
Catharina German of Marx and Elisabeth b. March 26, 1765.
Sponsors: Bodo Otto and Catharina his wife.
Maria Barbara Gelbhoeffer of Benjamin and Maria b. July 2, ---.
Sponsors: Adam Mensch and M. Barbara his wife.
Elisabeth Merthensbeck of Johan and Elisabeth b. July 26, 1765.
Sponsors: Peter Sauder and Elisabeth his wife.
Benjamin Mensch of Adam and M. Barbara b. Sept. 15, 1765.
Sponsors: Benjamin Gelbhoeffer and Maria his wife.
Rosina Margretha Wolport of Matias and Catharina b. Sept. 15,
1765. Sponsors: Michael Wolport and Rosina Margreth his wife.
Lorentz Upman of Andreas and Abertin b. Oct. 2, 1765. Sponsors:
Lorentz Upman and Margretha his wife.
Christina Maurer of Adam and A. Margretha b. Aug. 27, 1765.
Sponsors: The parents themselves.
Maria Catharina Rheil of Heinrich and Susanna b. Oct. 2, 1765.
Sponsor: Miss Maria Catharina Stam, single.
Margretha Dandelsbaecher of Ludwig and Catharina b. Sept. 1,
1765. Sponsor: Margretha Rothgeb, single.
Heinrich Hoffaecker of Heinrich and Margareth b. Oct. 18, 1765.
Sponsors: Adam Schaeffer and Margretha his wife.
Maria Frieas of Jacob and A: Margretha b. Jan. 2, 1766.
Sponsors: The parents themselves.
Maria Dorothea Hoelzel of Friederich and Elisabeth b. Dec. 12,
1765. Sponsors: Daniel Straueb and Mrs. Catharina Roth.
Joh: Martin Rempel of Georg and Anna Catharina b. Dec. 7, 1765.
Sponsors: Martin Wolff and M. Elisabetha his wife.
Joh: Georg Brandner of Andreas and Susanna b. March 18, 1766.
Sponsors: Paul Janson and Eliesabeth his wife.
Elenora Catharina Bluemlein of Chistop and Margretha b. March 3,
1766. Sponsor: Catharina Wolpert, single.
Christina Miller of Michael and Margretha b. Nov. 13, 1765.
Sponsors: The parents themselves.
Anna Maria Fries of Jacob, Junor and Eliesabeth b. March 23,
1766. Sponsor: Margretha Friess, single.
Christina Fix of Adam and Elisabeth b. Sept. 10, 1766. Sponsors:
Georg Kautz and Anna his wife.
Anna Barbara Kautz of Joh: and Anna b. Oct. 10, 1765. Sponsors:
Adam Fix and Elisabeth his wife.
Elisabeth Ross of Michael and Eliesabeth b. Nov. 2, 1765.
Sponsors: The parents themselves.
Philip Schimp of Philip and Elisabeth b. Jan. 17, 1765.
Sponsors: The parents themselves.
Johanns Thueringer of Joh: and M: Catharina b. March 18, 1766.
Sponsors: Abraham Zimerman and Anna his wife.
Daniel Janson of Peter and Barbara b. Jan. 14, 1766. Sponsors:
Joh: Michael Miller and Maria Catharina his wife.
Jacob Ross of Matias and Johanna b. June 3, 1766. Sponsors: The
parents themselves.
Johannes Hochscheid of Joha: and Margretha b. Dec. 25, 1765.
Sponsors: The parents themselves.
Johannes Fucks of Friederich and A: Maria b. June 8, 1766.
Sponsors: Joh: Luetz and Anna Maria his wife.

Susanna Coelsch of Philip and Margretha b. Sept. 8, 1765.
  Sponsors: The parents themselves.
Susanna Bechler of Simon and Margretha b. May 27, 1766.
  Sponsors: Georg Miler and Susanna his wife.
Wilhelm Shneider of Georg and Margretha b. March 4, 1766.
  Sponsors: The parents themselves.
Susanna Miller of Georg and Susanna b. Sept. 9, 1766. Sponsors:
  The parents themselves.
Anna Margretha Heintz of Peter and Liesabeth b. Dec. 22, 1765.
  Sponsors: Georg Kautz and Anna his wife.
Johannes Meyer of Georg and Elisabeth b. July 20, 1766.
  Sponsors: Johannes Wacker and Margretha his wife.
Johannes Hitschner of Peter and Barbara b. Dec. 15, 1765.
  Sponsor: Thoedorus Wenzel, single.
Johannes Ackerman of Philip and Eliesabeth b. Oct. 5, 1766.
  Sponsors: Michael Miller and Anna Maria his wife.
Anna Maria Barbara Freysemeier of Christian and Helena b. Nov.
  18, 1766. Sponsors: Johan Georg Naeglin and Anna Maria his
  wife.
Maria Chatarina Witscher of Herman and Charlotha Lowisa b. Feb.
  13, 1767. Sponsors: Joh: Michael Miller and Maria Catharina
  his wife.
Magdalena Zimerman of Melchor and Magdalena b. April 25, 1765.
  Sponsors: Johannes Lutz and Maria his wife.
Fomas Langenbach of Paul and Elisabeth b. May 31, 1767.
  Sponsors: Michael Miler and Margratha his wife.
Adreas Schimp of Joh: and Elisabeth b. Feb. 18, 1767. Sponsors:
  Georg Fischer and Margretha his wife.
Barbara Hoelzel of Friederich and Elisabeth b. Oct. 17, 1767.
  Sponsors: Joh: Schnizer and Barbara his wife.
Johnnes Kreemer of Matias and Catharina b. Oct. 16, 1767.
  Sponsors: Joh: Saeuder and Margretha his wife.
Johanna Nefft of Joh: and Catharina b. Jan. 15, 1767. Sponsors:
  J. Georg Straeub and Johanna Pilgram, both single.
Jacob Printesholz of Adam and Maria b. Sept. 28, 1767. Sponsors:
  Jacob Fries, Jun. and Elisabeth his wife.
J: Adam Wolff of Heinrich and Elisabeth b. Sept. 5, 1767.
  Sponsors: Adam Saul and Margretha his wife.
Catharina Martin of Simon and Catharina b. Feb. 9, 1767.
  Sponsors: Catrina Miller, single.
Marcus Rheiel of Heinrich and Susanna b. 5th 1767. Sponsor:
  Georg Wilhelm Stamm.
Johanna Miller of Michael, Jr. and Margretha b. Sept. 25, 1767.
  Sponsors: The parents.
A. Christina Schimp of Philip and Elisabeth b. March 17, 1767.
  Sponsors: Georg Meopold and Christina his wife.
Catharina Rothgeb of Georg and Sallome b. July 28, 1767.
  Sponsors: Theodor Wentzel and Catharina Hittshener, both
  single.
J. Philip Miller of Georg and Susanna b. Sept. 17, 1767.
  Sponsors: Philip Sauder and Mrs. Catharina Wolpert.
J: Jacob Hahn of Johan and Elisabeth b. Sept. 19, 1767.
  Sponsors: Jacob Friess and Margretha his wife.
Susanna Dendelsbeck of Johannes and Elisabeth b. June 11, bapt.

July 3. Sponsors: Georg Miller and Susanna his wife.
Jacob Materstich of Johannes and Catharina b. April 14, bapt.
July 3. Sponsors: Jacob Schultz and Anna Pilgram, both
single.

On July 3, 1768 the following children were bapt. by Rev. Mr.
Parson Shultz:
Anna Maria Laudeschlegel of Joh: Michael and Elisabeth b. March
17, 1765. Sponsors: Georg Fischer and Margretha his wife.
Johan Georg Laudenslegel of Joh: M: and Elizabeth b. Feb. 17,
1767. Sponsors: Georg Fisher and Margretha his wife.
Joha Schoch of William and Catharina b. Jan. 24, 1768. Sponsors:
The parents themselves.
Susanna Roth of Andreas and Angnes b. Sept. 18, 1767. Sponsors:
Georg Miler and Susanna his wife.
Adam Maurer of Adam and Cath: b. Feb. 12, 1768. Sponsors: Adam
Saul and Margreth his wife.
Wilhelm Schneider of Georg and A: M: b. Dec. 16, 1767. Sponsors:
The parents themselves.
Leonhard Coelsh of Philip and Margretha b. Nov. 12, 1767.
Sponsors: The parents themselves.
Anna Margretha Noll of Joh: and Anna Maria b. Nov. 22, 1767.
Sponsors: Joh: Micha: Jordan and A: Margretha his wife.
Joh: Martin Hittschner of Jacob and Magdalena b. April 24, 1768.
Sponsors: The parents themselves.
J: Georg Straeub of Bastian and Regina b. April 2, 1768.
Sponsors: Georg Straeub and Johanna Pilgram, both single.
Peter Hitschner of Peter and Barbara b. June 13, 1768. Sponsors:
Peter Emmel and Elisabeth his wife.
Sara German of Marx and Elisabeth b. March 26, 1767. Sponsors:
Mathaias Wolport and Catharina.
Anna Margretha Carrl of Martin and Catharina b. March 12, 1768.
Sponsors: The parents themselves.

On April 29, 1770 the following children were bapt. by Rev. Mr.
Parson Schulz:
George Friederich Hoelzel of Friederich and Elisabeth b. Dec. 4,
1769. Sponsors: Friederich Hoffman and Eva his wife.
Christian Stenger of Christian and Salome b. Jan. 13, 1770.
Sponsors: Lorentz Crym and Mrs. Catharina Rotter.
Eva Margretha Wolff of Heinrich and Elizabeth b. Sept. 20, 1769.
Sponsors: Adam Saul and Eva Margretha his wife.
Daniel Frollinger of Gabriel and Margaretha b. Jan. 25, 1769.
Sponsors: The parents themselves.
Jonathan Hahn of Johan: and Elisabeth b. Nov. 1, 1769. Sponsors:
Jacob Friess, the old one, and Anna Margretha his wife.
Maria Margretha Wolpert of Matthias and Catharina, b. Dec. 15,
1770, batpized Dec. 25. Sponsors: George Wolpert and Maria
Magdalena his wife.
Johann Jacob Wolpert of Matthias and Catharina, b. Jan. 23, 1768,
bapt. Easter 1768. Sponsors: George Wolpert and Maria
Magdalena his wife.
Joh: Georg Wolpert of Georg and Maria Magdal, b. Oct. 11, 1770,
bapt. Nov. 1770. Sponsors: Jacob Hiltshner and Mrs. Carolina

Wolpert.
Joh: Georg Linck of Johannes and Anna Maria b. Oct. 10, 1765, bapt. Nov. --, 1765. Sponsors: Joh: Georg Wolpert and Mar: Ma. his wife.

1771:
Catharina Barbara Kammerer of Joh: Georg and Barbara b. 15 weeks today, bapt. April 28. Sponsors: Henrich Shanes and Mrs. Salome Stenger.
Wilhelm Carl of Martin and Catharina b. July 6, bapt. Sept. 1, 1771. Sponsors: Wilhelm Schog and Catharina his wife and father of the child.
Henrich Dendelsbacher of Johann Ludwig and Catharine b. June 28, 1770, bapt. Sept. 1, 1771. Sponsors: Wilhelm Schog and Catharina his wife and father of the child.
Susanna Rosina Schmidt of Abraham (d. 1766, and his wife remarried since early of this year to Johann Ludew Stom who has the child bapt.) and Margaretha b. Feb. 1, 1766, bapt. Sept. 1, 1771. Sponsors: Joh: Heinr. Reil and Susanna his wife.
George Muller of Jacob and Catharina b. Sept. 17, bapt. Oct. 14, 1771. Sponsors: George Muller and Susanna his wife.
Dewald Knery of Lorenz and Anna Mar b. Sept. 15, bapt. Oct. 14, 1771. Sponsors: Dewald Leman and Jul. Klein.
--- Muller of Mich. and Cathar. b. Sept. 13, bapt. Oct. 14, 1771. Sponsors: Cath. Mueller and Hers. Weber.
Joh Jacob Duelshefer (procreated outside the bonds of Matrimony) of George and Miss Cath. Kraemer (who in tears promised to me her father to amend her life whereto God may grant his Grace) b. June 16, bapt. Oct. 14, 1771. Sponsors: Jacob Duelshefer and Charl. Kraemer.
Georg Muller of Georg and Susanna b. Nov. 13, bapt. Jany. 26, 1772. Sponsors: Georg Friess and father of the child.
Elisabeth Sauder of Johannes and Margaretha b. Dec. 20, bapt. Jany. 26, 1772. Sponsors: Georg Muller and Susanna his wife.
Philipp Tillshoefer of Johannes and Mariana b. Nov. 7, bapt. Jany. 26, 1772. Sponsors: Philipp Sauder and Christ. Sauder his wife.
Friedrich Boehmer of Friedr. and Catharina Elisabetha b. Jany. 10, bapt. Jany. 26, 1772. Sponsors: Johannes Sauder and Margaretha his wife.
Johann Jacob Fuchs of Johann Friedr. and Anna Maria b. Dec. 29, bapt. Jany. 26, 1772. Sponsors: Johann Lud. Danzenbacher and Catharina his wife.
Mary Magdalena Rothgeb of George and Salome b. April 11, 1771, bapt. ---.

1772:
Catharina Schaefer of Johannes and Margreta, Reformed, b. May 1, bapt. June 20, 1772. Sponsors: F. Friedrich Boehm, Refnd. Schoolm. and Catharina Elisabeta his wife.
Louisa Stenger of Adam and Catharina, Lutheran, b. Feb. 6, 1772, bapt. June 21, 1772. Sponsors: Salomon Stenger and Queen his wife.
Johan Henrich Schnid of Philip and Elisabet b. March 28, 1772,

bapt. June 21, ---. Sponsors: The parents themselves.
Anna Maria Holscheit of Johannes and Margaretha b. March 23, bapt. June 21. Sponsors: The parents themselves.
Johan Jacob Lantenschlaeger of Michael and Elisabeth, Lutheran, b. ---, 1772, bapt. June 21, 1772. Sponsors: Georg Fischer and Anna Margaretha his wife.
Elisabet Roth of Andreas and Agnes b. Apr. 24, 1772, bapt. June 21, 1772. Sponsors: Catharina Halter, spinster.
Margaretha Hoelzer of Friedr. and Elisabet b. Jan. 23, 1772, bapt. June 21, 1772. Sponsors: The parents themselves.
Jacob Sauder of Johan and Margaret b. May 6, 1772, bapt. June 21, ---. Sponsors: Jacob Duelshefer and Elisabet Frolickheimer.
Susanna Woolf of Henry and Elisabet b. March 13, 1772, bapt. June 21, ---. Sponsors: The parents themselves.
Sebastian Shimpf of Johannes and Elisabet b. July 5, bapt. July 19, 1772. Sponsor: Sebastian Hinderle.
Johannes Sauder of Philip and Christine b. June 24, bapt. July 19, 1772. Sponsors: Johannes Duelshefer and Mariana his wife.
Jonathan Hahn of Georg and Apollonia b. Sept. 9, 1771, bapt. Aug. 16, 1772. Sponsors: The parents.
Margareta Strauch of Joh: and Regina b. Oct. 30, 1771, bapt. Aug. 16, 1772. Sponsors: Jac. Kobel and Anna Barbara his wife.
Margareta Kaendel of Henr. and Anna Maria b. Aug 5, 1772, bapt. Aug 16, 1772. Sponsors: Adam Mauerer and Maria Catharina his wife.
Daniel Heier of Conrad and Christian b. June 20, bapt. Aug. 16, 1772. Sponsors: Theobald Ziegler and Mrs. Magdalena Hutschner.
Samuel Wenzel of Philipp and Elisabeth b. April 18, bapt. Aug. 16, 1772. Sponsors: Father's brother and his mother, Mrs. Benzler.
Rosina Margaretha Emmel of Martin, Reform, and Rosina, Cath., b. Aug 13, 1772, bapt. Sept. 13. Sponsors: Hartman Emmel, grandfather, and Margaretha his wife.
Johannes Ritter of the supposed to be father, Michael Ritter, and the mother the wife of Johannes Lotz in adultery, b. ---, bapt. Aug. 17, 1772. Sponsors: Johannes Schimp and Mrs. Appolonia Schmidt.
Johannes Tendelspeck of Johannes and Elisabet, b. Oct. 8, 1772, bapt. Nov. 15, 1772. Sponsors: Philip Fries, Jun. and Catharina Janson.
--- Wuckert of Wilhelm and wife b. ---, bapt. ---.
Johan Fries of Johan Georg and Catharina (mensis tempestive aiunt at the proper time and month they say), b. March 15, 1773, bapt. April 18 ct. yr. Sponsors: Johan Herche and wife, sister of Mr. Jacob Fries wife as Grandmother.
Jacob Strenger of Salomon and Guin, b. Dec. 5, 1772 and bapt. Dec. 19, emergency and confirmed May 23, 1773. Sponsors: Leonard Bauer and his wife.

The below recorded 8 children were bapt. by me while paying a vist to this congregation, Henry Muehlenberg, Jun., Lutherian Minister:
Louise Jung of Philip and Louise, b. April 21, 1773, bapt. May

23. Sponsors: Louise Falk, single and Daniel Stenger.
Rosina Margaret Wolpert of Peter and Sophia, b. May 2, 1773, bapt. May 23. Sponsors: Mrs. Rosina Marg. Wolpert, the grandmother.
Joh Michael Salgeyer of Jeremias and Elisabet, b. April 28, 1773, bapt. May 23. Sponsors: Joh Michael Wolpert and Rosina Maria his wife.
Daniel Hahn of Joh: and Elisabet, b. April 30, 1773, bapt. May 23. Sponsors: Jacob Fries, Sen. and Marg. his wife.
John Georg Fries of Jacob, Jun. and Elis, b. May 1, 1773, bapt. May 23. Sponsors: John Friedr Fries.
Jacob Hoch of Andreas and Christine, b. May 8, 1773, bapt. May 23. Sponsors: The parents.
Margaret Schaefer of Jacob and Cath., b. April 26, 1773, bapt. May 23. Sponsors: Andreas Mensch and Charlotte Kraemer, single.
Marcus Koch of Rudolph and Sarah, b. Feb. 1, 1773, bapt. May 24. Sponsors: Marcus Kerman and Elisabeth his wife.

1773:
Leonard Bauer of Conrad and Margareta, b. Sept. 23, bapt. Oct. 3. Sponsors: Leonard Bauer and Carolina his wife.
Johann Georg Rotter of Theobald and Elisabeth, b. May 21, bapt. Oct. 3. Sponsor: Johann Georg Mebold.
Johannes Wolpert of Georg and Maria Magdalena, b. Aug. 29, bapt. Oct. 3. Sponsors: Michael Wolpert and Rosina Margareta his wife.
Georg Friedrich Hofmann of Georg Friedrich and Eva, b. Aug. 12, 1771, bapt. Oct. 3, 1773. Sponsor: Louise Hoelzel.
Anna Remel of Georg and Anna Catharina, b. July 24, bapt. Oct. 3. Sponsors: Mrs. Anna Christine Mebold and the parents of the child.
Margareta Sauder of Simon and Margareta, b. July 26, bapt. Oct. 3. Sponsors: Grandparents of Jacob Fries and Margareta his wife.
Elisabeth Sturz of Georg and Barbara, b. June 12, bapt. Oct. 4. Sponsors: Henrich Faber and Maria Magdalena his wife.
Jacob Klober of --- and wife, about 1/2 yr.old, bapt. Oct. 31, 1773. Sponsors: Adam Maurer and Mar Cath Fort.
Maria Catharina Fort of Jam: and Maria Cath, b. ---, bapt. Oct. 31, 1773. Sponsors: Father and mother of the child and Joh P. Dott.
Johannes Wulpert of Joh: Marth and Catharin, b. ---, bapt. Nov. 28, 1773. Sponsors: Johannes Schmid and Mrs. Maria Fischer.
Johann Georg Sauder of Philip and Christina, b. Oct. 11, bapt. Nov. 28, 1773. Sponsors: Georg Gauker and Maria his wife.
Johann Georg Arner of Georg and wife, b. Oct. 17, bapt. Nov. 28, 1773. Sponsors: Math. Pleninger and Catharina his wife.
Susanna Ross of Math: and Susanna, b. Nov. 30, bapt. Dec. 26, 1773. Sponsors: The parents themselves.

1774:
Johann Georg Bender of Johan Georg and Margretha, b. Nov. 9, 1773, bapt. Feb. 27, 1774. Sponsors: Daniel Staenger and

Louise Fulk.
Johann Michael Schneider of Johan Georg and Anna Margareta, b.
Feb. 2, 1774, bapt. ---. Sponsors: The parents themselves.
Johann Georg Kauz of Johann Georg and Anna, b. Nov. 28, 1773,
bapt. April 25, 1774. Sponsors: Adam Fix, Elder in Congr.,
and Elisabeth his wife.
Johann Georg Miller of Michael and Catharina, b. March 13, bapt.
April 25, 1774. Sponsors: Daniel Stenger and Susa Queen his
wife.
Susanna Kaendel of Henrich and Anna Maria, b. April 5, bapt.
April 25, 1774. Sponsors: Christoph Brech and Susanna his
wife.
Andreas Hofmann of Friedr and Eva Maria, b. April 2, bapt. April
25, 1774. Sponsors: Christoph Wacker and Juliane his wife.
Lorenz Kneri of Lorenz and Anna Maria, b. Dec. 5, 1773, bapt.
April 25, 1774. Sponsor: Salomo Stenger.
Catharina Muller of George, Elder of the Congr., and Susanna, b.
Nov. 29, 1773, bapt. April 25, 1774. Sponsors: Jacob Muller
and Catharina his wife.
Johannes Stamm of Joh: Ludw: and Anna Margareta, b. May 12, 1774,
bapt. May 23, 1774. Sponsors: Johannes Herrige and Mrs.
Margareta Stamm.
Henrich Carl of Martin and Catharina, b. March 3, 1774, bapt. May
23, 1774. Sponsors: Adam Maurer and Maria Catharina his wife.
Richard Lautenschlaeger of Joh: Michael and Elisabeth, b. March
22, 1774, bapt. May 23, 1774. Sponsors: Richard Cryford and
Johanna Cryford.
Johanna Schlesmann of Christoph and Catharina, b. April 15, 1774,
bapt. May 23, 1774. Sponsors: Richard Cryford and Johanna
Cryford. Witness: Job: C. Leps.
Johannes Schmidtlein of Balthasar and Catharina, b. June 23,
bapt. same month 26. Sponsors: Jacob Hutschner and Magdalena
his wife.
Daniel Schog of Wilhelm and Catharina, b. June 8, bapt. same
month 26. Sponsors: Theobald Lehmann and Eva his wife.
Johan Georg Hayer of Conrad and Christine, b. July 8, 1774, bapt.
July 24, 1774. Sponsors: Joh Georg Rogeb and Salome his wife.
Maria Elisabet Brenesholz of Georg and Maria, b. June 3, 1774,
bapt. July 24, 1774. Sponsors: Adam Brenesholz and Maria his
wife.
Louisa Bechtler of Simon and Margareta, b. Sept. 22, bapt. same
month 25. Sponsors: Philipp Jung and Louisa his wife.
Johannes Zigler of Theobald and Magdalena, b. Sept. 11, bapt.
same 25. Sponsors: Jacob Hutschner and Magdalena his wife.
Philip Fries of Johan Georg and Catherine, b. Nov. 14, 1774,
bapt. Nov. 20, 1774. Sponsor: Mr. Jacob Fries, Sen.
Barbara Mueller of Jacob and Catherine, b. Oct. 17, 1774, bapt.
Nov. 20. Sponsors: Adam Mensch and Barbara his wife.
Hans Peter Wolpert of Peter and Sophia, b. Jany. 1, 1778, bapt.
May 3 ct. yr. Sponsors: Hans Michael Wolpert and Maria
Fischer, both single.

1775:
Samuel Janson of Peter and Barbara, b. April 18, 1775, bapt. May

28, 1775. Sponsor: Catherine Mueller, widow.
Maria Straup of Sebastian (is dead) and Rahel, b. Oct. 5, 1774, bapt. May 28. Sponsors: Johannes Ift and Anna Catherine his wife.
Johannes Duelshoever of Jacob and Elis, b. Feb. 27, 1775, bapt. May 28. Sponsors: Joh Duelshoever and Maria his wife.
Anna Elisabet Dreher of Andr and Anna Marie, b. Dec. 15, 1774, bapt. May 28. Sponsors: Friedr Breitinger and Anna his wife.
David Schimpf of Johan and Elis., b. April 3, 1775, bapt. May 28. Sponsors: David Ott, the Mr. School, and Mrs. Elisabet Schneider.
Susanne Schuetz of Joseph and Louise, b. Feb. 19, 1775, bapt. May 28. Sponsors: Georg Mueller and Susanne his wife.
Rosina Roth of Andr. and Cath., b. Oct. 19, 1774, bapt. May 28. Sponsors: Arbanus Weidenmeyer and Magdalene his wife.
Juliana Wucker of Wilhelm and Barb, b. March 29, bapt. May 28. Sponsors: Christoph Wucker and Juliana his wife.
Johannes Fries of Jacob, Jun. and Elis., b. Jany. 25, 1775, bapt. May 28, 1775. Sponsors: Joh. Herche and Mrs. Halter.
Hans Jacob Sehler of Zachar. and Anna Maria, b. Nov. 20, 1774, bapt. May 28. Sponsors: Jacob Mueller and Cath. his wife.
Catherine Koch of Rudy and Sarah, b. May 10, 1775, bapt. May 28, 1775. Sponsor: Catherine Wolpert.
Leonard Schaefer of Conrad and Elisabeth, b. July 1, bapt. Aug. 27, 1775. Sponsors: Leonard Bauer and Carolina his wife.
Adam Wenzel of Theodorus and Eva, b. Aug. 3, bapt. Aug. 27, 1775. Sponsors: Adam Fix and Elisabeth his wife.
Salomo Staenger of Salomo and Queen, b. June 16, bapt. Aug. 27, 1775. Sponsors: Daniel Staenger and Mrs. Eva Forcer.
Johann Balthasar Schmidt of Balthasar and Catharine, b. Aug. 10, bapt. same mo. 27, 1775. Sponsors: The parents themselves.
Georg Gaeck of David and Margaretha, b. Aug. 22, bapt. Sept. 24. Sponsors: Adam Saul and Margaretha his wife.
Johann Matthey Fisher of Georg and Elisabeth, b. Aug. 20, bapt. Sept. 24. Sponsors: Matthey Wulpert and Catharina his wife.
Jacob Heuer of Conrad and Christina, b. Aug. 23, bapt. Sept. 24. Sponsors: Jacob Hitschner and Magdalena his wife.
Johannes Diel of Georg and Anna Margareta, b. Sept. 17, bapt. same month 24. Sponsors: Jacob Miller and Catharina his wife.
Johannes Wulpert of Georg and Catharina, b. ---, bapt. Sept. 24. Sponsor: Peter Wulpert.
Elisabeth Kammer of Georg and Catharina, b. Nov. 20, 1775, bapt. Dec. 31, 1775. Sponsors: Christian Temerus and Mrs. Elisabeth Schneider.
Daniel Schneider of Georg and Anna Margaretha, b. Sept. 20, 1775, bapt. Dec. 31 s. yr. Sponsor: The father himself.
Jacob Sauder of Johannes and Margaretha, b. Nov. 18, bapt. Dec. 31, 1775. Sponsor: Jacob Mueller.
Johann Martin Kuhlemann of Christoph and Anna Maria, b. Nov. 11, 1775, bapt. Dec. 31, 1775. Sponsors: Martin Hauck and Margaretha Meir, both single.

1776:
Elisabeth Dillshoefer of Johannes and Mariana, b. Nov. 29, 1775,

bapt. Jany. 1, 1776. Sponsors: Jacob Dillshoefer and
Elisabeth his wife.
Carolina Christina Bauer of Conrad and Anna Margaretha, b. Nov.
27, 1775, bapt. Jany. 1, 1776. Sponsors: Leonhard Bauer and
Carolina his wife.
Susanna Hoch of Andreas and Christina, b. Dec. 10, 1775, bapt.
Jany. 14, 1776. Sponsor: Susanna Mensch.
Johannes Fosker of Georg and Salome, b. Nov. 6, 1775, bapt. Feb.
11, 1776. Sponsors: Balthasar Schmid and Catharina his wife.
Anna Maria Brechner of Christoph and Susanna, b. Jany. 29, 1776,
bapt. Feb. 11 same year. Sponsors: Henrich Candle and his
wife.
Anna Margaretha Sauther of Peter and Margaretha, b. Jany. 1,
1776, bapt. March 10 s. yr. Sponsors: Johannes Sauther and
Margaretha his wife.
Elisabeth Ziegler of Theobald and Magdalena, b. Feb. 12, 1776,
bapt. March 10 s. yr. Sponsors: Mrs. Anna Barara Hitschner
and father of the child.
Margaretha Schott of Fridrch. and Susanna, b. Jany. 9, 1776,
bapt. March 10 s. yr. Sponsors: Daniel Stinger and Eva
Fartzen.
Margaretha Stamm of Wilhelm and Sophia, b. March 27, 1776, bapt.
April 7 s. yr. Sponsors: Andreas Usinger and Mrs. Margaretha
Stamm.
Adam Miller and Margaretha Miller (twins) of Michael and
Catharina, b. April 23, bapt. June 2, 1776. Sponsors: Daniel
Stenger, Mrs. Catharina Miller, Henrich Weber and Mrs.
Margaretha Stamm.
Johann Nicolaus Hector of Caspar and Maria, b. April 8, 1776,
bapt. June 2 same yr. Sponsors: Joh. Nicolaus Wid and Maria
his wife.
Hanna Wentzel of Carl and Catharina, b. March 16, 1776, bapt.
June 2 s. yr. Sponsors: Valentin Fortscher and Anna Barbara
Fix, both single.
Rosina Maria Fuchs of Friederich and Anna Maria, b. Jany. 29,
1776, bapt. June 2 s. yr. Sponsors: Johannes Schmidt and
Rosina his wife.
Eva Rosina Wolpert of Mathias and Catharina, b. May 16, 1776,
bapt. June 2 s. yr. Sponsors: Joh. Michael Wolpert and Rosina
Catharina his wife.
Peter Schimpf of Phil. and Elis., b. May 23, 1776, bapt. June 30,
1776. Sponsors: Phil. Schimpf, Jun. and Maria Fischer, sing.
Margar Week of Mich. and Marg., b. May 3, 1776, bapt. June 30.
Sponsors: Marg. Schott and brother-in-law Philip.
Maria Magdal Hilgert of Henr. and Salome, b. June 6, bapt. June
30, 1776. Sponsors: Friedr Kroneberger and his wife.
Marg. Stamm of Joh. Ludw. and Marg., b. April 12, 1776, bapt.
June 30. Sponsors: Valent. Thomas and Mrs. Margar. Stamm.
Magdalene Wolpert of Peter and Magd., b. June 13, bapt. June 30.
Sponsors: Georg Wolpert and Magd. his wife.
Matthias Herdman of Johannes and Maria, b. April 6, bapt. Aug.
25, 1776. Sponsors: Matthias Kraemer and Marg: Catharina.
Francisca Margaretha Raemmel of Georg and Anna Cathr., b. March
19, 1776, bapt. Aug. 25 s. yr. Sponsors: Johannes Dendelspeck

and Elisabetha his wife.
Elisabetha Frevel of Joh: and Anna Marg:, b. July 26, bapt. Aug. 25. Sponsors: Conrad Schaeffer and Elisabetha his wife.
Salomon Herge of Johannes and Barbara, b. Aug. 2, 1776, bapt. 25 ditto. Sponsors: Salomon Stenger and Gwin his wife.
Andreas Posthumus Drehert of Andreas and Maria Margar (his wife left behind), b. Sept. 6, 1776, bapt. Nov. 17 this year. Sponsors: Andreas Mensch and Dorothea Schwab, both single.
Catharina Kautz of Georg and wife, b. Nov. 6, 1776, bapt. 17 ditto this year. Sponsors: Adam Fix and Elisabetha his wife.

1777:
Joh. Henrich Fries of Joh: Fried: and Catharina, b. April 6, 1777, bapt. 16 ditto. Sponsors: Peter Janson and his wife.
Elisabeth Hitschner of Jacob, Jr. and Christina, b. July 15, bapt. Aug. 5, 1777. Sponsors: Jacob Hitschner and Mrs. Barbara Fix.
Joh. Georg Stenger of Salomon and Guin, b. Oct. 3, 1777, bapt. May 3, 1778. Sponsors: Joh. Georg Blumer and Elisabetha his wife.
Johannes Schmidt of Johannes and Rosina, b. Aug. 15, 1776, bapt. Aug. 13, 1777. Sponsors: The parents themselves.
Georg Van Lahnen of Jacob, local schoolmaster, and Johanna Maria, b. Aug. 13, 1777, bapt. on the 22 ditto 1777. Sponsors: Georg Seitz and wife in Philadelphia.
Maria Friess of Jacob, Sen. and Dorcas, b. Feb. 22, 1776, bapt. by the English preacher, Enoch Green. Sponsors: The parents themselves.
Anna Fries, of Jacob, Sen. and Dorcas, b. Sept. 1, 1777, bapt. by the English preacher, Nehemiah Green. Sponsors: The parents themselves.

1778:
Elisabeth Kaendel of Henrich and Anna Maria, b. Oct. 2, bapt. Nov. 22, 1778. Sponsors: Jacob Huetschner and Elisabeth his wife.
Margareta Kaek of David and Margareta, b. May 24, 1777, bapt. Nov. 22, 1778. Sponsors: Adam Saul and Margareta his wife.
Catharina Maria Pilgram of Francis and Catharina, b. Dec. 25, 1776, bapt. Nov. 22, 1778. Sponsors: Johannes Hahn and Elisabeth his wife.
Charlotte Stam of Wilhelm and Sophia, b. Oct. 24, bapt. Nov. 22, 1778. Sponsors: Andreas Usinger and Mrs. Margareta Stamm.
Hanna Bacon of Lott and Barbara, b. Sept. 22, bapt. Nov. 22, 1778. Sponsors: Jacob Hutschner and Magdalena his wife.
Johannes Hartmann of Johann and Anna Maria, b. July 8, 1778, bapt. Nov. 22, 1778. Sponsors: Georg Kammerer and Catharina his wife.
Johannes Auz of Georg and Barbara, b. Oct. 28, 1776, bapt. Nov. 22, 1778. Sponsors: Ge Schenermann and his wife.
Johannes Michael Rotter of Theobald and Maria Elisabeth, b. Oct. 21, bapt. Nov. 22, 1778. Sponsors: Jacob Miller and Cathar. his wife.
Johann Georg Hahn of Jacob and Catharina, b. July 1, bapt. Nov.

22, 1778. Sponsors: Georg Schneider and Margareta his wife.
Maria Catharina Stamm of Johann Ludew. and Margareta, b. July 23, bapt. Nov. 22. Sponsors: Michael Muller and Catharina his wife.
Rosina Maria Schmidt of Johannes and Rosina, b. Feb. 26, bapt. Nov. 22. Sponsors: Georg Miller and Maria Apollonia.
Johann Matthias Wolpert of Matthias and Magdalena, b. Oct. 24, bapt. Nov. 23. Sponsors: Michael Wolpert, Sen. and Rosina Margareta his wife.
Michael Bossard of Johannes and Dorothea Schumacher, a single maiden, b. Oct. 10, bapt. Nov. 23, 1778. Sponsors: Michael Wolpert, Jun. and Maria his wife.
Hanna Nestler of Joh. Gottfried and Rahel, b. Aug. 15, 1777, bapt. May 24, 1778. Sponsors: George Kautz and Anna his wife.

1779
Below named 25 children were all at once bapt. by me during my vist on Sept. 26 of this year. The two last ones have not had as yet their children transcribed. J. C. Kunze, Ev. - Luth. Preacher:
Elizabeth Schuz of Joseph and Louisa, b. June 8, bapt. Sept 26. Sponsors: Adam Fix and Elisabeth his wife.
Johann Jacob Ochsenbecher of Henrich and Catharina, b. Jan. 4, bapt. Sept. 26. Sponsors: Michael Makre and Mrs. Sophia Stenger.
Johann Usinger of Andreas and Margareta, b. Sept. 23, bapt. Sept. 26. Sponsors: Michael Miller and Catharina his wife.
Jacob Bauer of Conrad and Anna Margareta, b. July 9, bapt. Sept. 26. Sponsors: Jacob Miller and Catharina his wife.
Conrad Schaefer of Conrad and Elisabeth, b. Nov. 19, 1776, bapt. Sept. 26, 1779. Sponsors: Conrad Heier and Christine his wife.
Christina Heier of Conrad and Christina, b. May 4, bapt. Sept. 26. Sponsors: Johannes Heppener and Mrs. Anna Maria.
Michael Dielshoefer of Johannes and Mariana, b. May 18, bapt. Sept. 26. Sponsor: Georg Miller.
Anna Maria Wenzel of Wilhelm and Elisabeth, b. Dec. 14, 1776, bapt. Sept. 26, 1779. Sponsors: Georg Schneider and Margareta his wife.
Elisabeth Wenzel of Theodorus and Eva, b. Aug. 5, bapt. Sept. 26. Sponsors: Daniel Stenger and Eva his wife.
Wilhelm Bender of Georg and Margareta, b. May 19, bapt. Sept. 26. Sponsors: Georg Kauz and Anna his wife.
Johannes Zimmermann of Adam and Catharina, b. Dec. 14, 1776, bapt. Sept. 26, 1779. Sponsors: Conrad Schafer and Elisabeth his wife.
Hanna Hoch of Andreas and Christina, b. Dec. 4, 1778, bapt. Sept. 25, 1779. Sponsors: The parents themselves.
Andreas Janson of Michael and Susanna, b. Sept. 17, bapt. Sept. 26. Sponsors: Adam Mensch and Barbara his wife.
Maria Magdalena Auz of Georg and Barbara, b. Feb. 6, bapt. Sept. 26. Sponsors: Henrich Faber and Maria Magdalena his wife.
Catharina Schmidt of Balthasar and Catharina, b. May 12, bapt. Sept. 26. Sponsors: Georg Hitchner and Mrs. Elisabeth Hofmann.

Anna Barbara Rothkep of Georg and Salome, b. Feb. 18, bapt. Sept.
    26. Sponsors: Father and Mrs. Barbara Rothkepp.
Christina Dilsheofer of Jacob and Elisabeth, b. Feb. 11, bapt.
    Sept. 26. Sponsors: Parents.
Anna Elisabeth Hector of Caspar and Maria, b. Dec. 18, 1778,
    bapt. Sept. 26, 1779. Sponsors: Christian Raiser and Anna
    Elisab. his wife.
Elisabeth Fries of Jacob, Sen. and Dorcas, b. Aug. 16, bapt.
    Sept. 26. Sponsors: The parents themselves.
Johann Henrich Fries of Jacob, Jun. and Elisabeth, b. March 16,
    bapt. Sept. 26. Sponsors: Parents.
Elisabeth Fries of Friedrich and Catharina, b. July 18, bapt.
    Sept. 26. Sponsors: Peter Janson and Barbara his wife.
Philipp Serger of Johann and Catharina, b. June 4, bapt. sept.
    26. Sponsors: Philipp Sauder and Christina his wife.
Georg Fries of Johann Georg and Catharina, b. Sept. 24, 1778,
    bapt. Sept. 26, 1779. Sponsor: Georg Miller.
--- Wolpert of Georg and Maria, b. ---, bapt. ---. Sponsors:
    Michael Wolpert, Jun. and his wife.
--- Fischer of Georg and wife, b. ---, bapt. ---. Sponsors:
    Georg Wolpert and his wife.

1780
The below entered children have been bapt. by me today the 21 day
of May 1780. J. H. Ch. Helmuth, Ev. Luth. Preacher in
Philadelphia:
Johannes Hofmann of Johannes and Margaretha, b. June 15, 1779,
    bapt. the 21 ditto. Sponsors: The parents themselves.
Joh Heinrich Schmidt of Johannes and Rosina, b. Dec. 29, 1779,
    bapt. March 25, 1780. Sponsors: The parents themselves.
Andreas Miller of Jacob and Catharina, b. Dec. 1, 1779, bapt. May
    21, 1780. Sponsors: Adam Mensch and Barbara his wife.
Johann Sauder of Joh. and Maria, b. July 7, 1779, bapt. May 21,
    1780. Sponsors: Jacob Miller and Catharina his wife.
Margareta Sauder of Peter and Maria, b. Dec. 29, 1779, bapt. May
    21, 1780. Sponsors: Johann Schimp and Elisabeth his wife.
Jacob Bakon of Loth and Barbara, b. Jany. 25, 1779, bapt. May 21,
    1780. Sponsors: Jacob Hitzner and Magdalena his wife.
Joh. Georg Fuchs of Johann Frid. and Anna Maria, b. Nov. 23,
    1779, bapt. May 21, 1780. Sponsors: Joh. Georg Macklin and
    Anna Maria his wife.
Christina Sauder of Phil. and Christina, b. Jany. 12, 1779, bapt.
    May 21, 1780. Sponsors: Simon Sauder and Elisabeth his wife.
Susanna Brechner of Christoph and Susanna, b. Dec. 2, 1779, bapt.
    May 21, 1780. Sponsors: Michael Monie and Mrs. Susanna
    Sauder.
Susanna Watson of John and Maria, b. March 6, 1778, bapt. May 21,
    1780. Sponsors: Georg Miller and Susanna his wife.
Johann Watson of John and Maria, b. Sept. 4, 1779, bapt. May 21,
    1780. Sponsors: Johann Frevel and Margareta his wife.
Wilhelm Ross of Adam and Phoebe, b. Oct. 21, 1779, bapt. May 21,
    1780. Sponsors: Adam Saul and Margareta his wife.
Jeany Sieglin of Georg and Jeany, b. Dec. 7, 1778, bapt. May 21,
    1780. Sponsor: Margareta Eff.

Joh. Georg Kammerer of Johann Georg and Cath., b. March 29, 1780, bapt. May 21. Sponsors: Georg Hitschner and Mrs. Margareta Dendelspeck.
Elisabeth Hitschner of Jacob and Elisabeth, b. May 4, bapt. May 21, 1780. Sponsors: Jacob Mohsholder and Elisabeth his wife.
Elisabeth Strenger of Daniel and Eva, b. Jany. 3, 1779, bapt. May 21, 1780. Sponsors: Carl Wenzel and Catharina his wife.
Sibylla Strenger of Daniel and Eva, b. June 5, 1777, bapt. June 24. (This child was bapt. in the Reformed Church by Rev. P. Wack.) Sponsors: Salomon Strenger and Quinney his wife.
Elisabeth Schmueck of Phil and Elisabeth, b. Nov. 7, 1779, bapt. May 21, 1780. Sponsors: Peter Emmel and Elisabeth his wife.
Maria Barbara Schott of Fridrich and Susanna, b. Dec. 8, 1779, bapt. May 21, 1780. Sponsors: The parents themselves.
Salome Sehler of Zacharias and Anna Maria, b. March 17, bapt. May 21, 1780. Sponsors: Johann Delzhefer and Maria his wife.
Anna Maria Weck of Michael and Anna Cath., b. Feb. 23, bapt. May 21, 1780. Sponsors: Joh. Nic. Weck and Mrs. Anna Maria Noll.

These 12 bapt. April 29, 1781 by Johann Christoph Kunze:
Johannes Rudolf of Ludewich and Catharina, b. Oct. 4, bapt. Nov. 5, 1780. Sponsors Johannes Horn and Margareta his wife.
Anna Margareta Raempster of Friedrich and Juliana, b. Sept. 25, bapt. Nov. 5, 1780. Sponsors: Marcus Kerrmann and Elisabeth his wife.
Johannes Schuz of Jost, Cathol., and Elisabeth, NB, not yet confirmed but promised to become Luth. confirmed, b. March 25, 1780, bapt. Nov. 5, 1780. Sponsors: Johannes Heopfner and Susanna Wauk.
Johann Catharina Hector of Caspar and Maria, b. Dec. 15, 1780, bapt. April 29, 1781, by Schoolmaster here. Sponsors: Johann Christian Breymann and Catharina his wife.
Johann Henrich Johnson of Michael and Susanna, b. April 20, bapt. April 29, 1781. Sponsors: Peter Mensch and Mrs. Elisabeth Johnson.
Johannes Schaefer of Conrad and Elisabeth, b. Jany. 11, bapt. April 29, 1781. Sponsors: Johannes Rick and Maria his wife.
Anna Margareta Heier of Conrad and Christiana, b. Nov. 20, 1780, bapt. April 29. Sponsors: Philipp Schimpf and Mrs. Anna Margar Hutschner.
Wilhelm Schmick of Wilhelm and Anna Maria, b. March 7, bapt. April 29, 1781. Sponsors: Leonard Bauer and Carolina his wife.
John Polnell of Charles, Engl., and Nancy, NB, both as yet not bapt., but the Godparents have vowed in to the hands of the elders and mine to bring this child to Church to be nurtured therein, b. April 20, bapt. April 29, 1781. Sponsors: Friedrich Hofmann and Eva his wife.
Johann Philipp Brass of Adam and Philippina, b. March 18, bapt. April 29, 1781. Sponsors: Johann Philipp Saul and Elisabeth his wife.
Christina Fries of Jacob and Elisabeth, b. March 5, bapt. April 29. Sponsors: The parents themselves.
David Hess of Johannes and Margareta, b. Aug. 15, 1780, bapt.

April 29, 1781. Sponsors: Theobald Sicherer and Magdalena his wife.
William Rhoder of Thomas and Margareta, mother English and not confirmed but the sponsors pledged to bring this child to Church to be nurtured therein, b. Oct. 11, bapt. April 29. Sponsors: Andreas Kraemer and Mrs. Susanna Sauder.
Henrich Hartmann of Henrich and A. Maria, b. July 3, 1780, bapt. April 29, 1781. Sponsors: Martin Ott and Margareta his wife.
Anna Margareta Leutenberger of Eberhard and Elisabeth, b. Jany. 13, bapt. April 29. Sponsors: The parents.

These nine children were bapt. by me on May 20, 1781. J. H. Ch. Helmuth:
Georg Schmidt of Johann and Rosina, b. March 16, bapt. May 20, 1781. Sponsors: Georg Miller and Susanna his wife.
Joh Phil Schmueck of Phil and Elisabeth, b. May 11, bapt. May 20, 1781. Sponsors: Conrad Schaeffer and Elisabeth his wife.
Jacob Dilsheffer of Joh. and Maria Anna, b. Jany. 11, bapt. May 20, 1781. Sponsors: Jacob Miller and Catharina his wife.
Elisabeth Sauter of Simon and Elisabeth, b. Nov. 19, 1780, bapt. May 20, 1781. Sponsors: Georg Miller and Susanna his wife.
Joh. Heinrich Oxenbecher of Heinrich and Christina, b. April 27, bapt. May 20, 1781. Sponsors: Heinrich Kendel and Anna Maria his wife.
Margareta Sauter of Johann and Margareta, b. Jany. 1, bapt. May 20, 1781. Sponsors: Jacob Miller and Catharina his wife.
Elisabeth SchmidtHeine of Balthasar and Catharina, b. May 1, bapt. May 20, 1781. Sponsors: Jacob Hitschner and Elisabeth his wife.
Catherina Ziegler of Theobald and Magdalena, b. May 3, bapt. May 20, 1781. Sponsors: Balthasar Schmidt and Catharina his wife.
John Cox of Caspar and Martha, b. March 26, bapt. May 20. Sponsors: Adam Maurer and Mrs. Anna Margar. Fuchs.

1781:
Johann Michael Linck of Johannes and Sophia, b. June 16, 1781, bapt. Aug. 28, 1781. Sponsors: Johann Michael Wolpert and Rosina Margaretha his wife.

These 12 children were bapt. by me Oct. 28, 1781. Johann Christoph Kunze, Preacher at Philadelphia:
Johannes Miller of Jacob and Catharina, b. Sept. 29, bapt. Oct. 28, 1781. Sponsors: Johannes Hahn and Elisabeth his wife.
Maria Magdalena Bakon of Loth and Anna Barbara, b. July 31, bapt. Oct. 28, 1781. Sponsors: Jacob Hitschner and Maria Magdalena his wife.
Elisabeth Bender of Georg and Margareta, b. July 22, bapt. Oct. 28, 1781. Sponsors: Georg Kauz and Anna his wife.
Hanna Dillshoefer of Jacob and Elisabeth, b. July 3, bapt. Oct. 28, 1781. Sponsors: Andr Hitschner and Mrs. Charlotte Fix.
Johannes Schuz of Joseph and Louisa, b. May 25, bapt. Oct. 28, 1781. Sponsors: Johannes Miller and Mrs. Anna Mar. Falk.
Margaretha Fries of Jacob, Sen. and Dorcas, b. July 14, 1781, bapt. July 16, 1781, by Engl. Minister Skenk. Sponsors: The

parents themselves.
Hanna Fries of Friedrich and Catharina, b. May 21, bapized Oct. 28, 1781. Sponsors: Peter Johnson and Barbara his wife.
Elisabeth Koek of David and Margareta, b. Aug. 29, bapt. Oct. 28. Sponsors: Philipp Saul and Elisabeth his wife.
David Staengel of Salomo and Queen, b. July 9, bapt. Oct. 28. Sponsors: Valentin Phorcer and Sophia his wife.
Margareta Heft of Johannes and Margareta, b. Aug. ---, bapt. Oct. ---, 1781. Sponsors: Johannes Horn and Margareta his wife.
Matthias Zimmermann of Adam and Catharina, b. Sept. 6, bapt. Oct. 28, 1781. Sponsors: Matthias Scheuermann and Barbara his wife.
Johannes Hoch of Andreas and Christina, b. Sept. 10, bapt. Oct. 28, 1781. Sponsors: Johannes Hahn and Elisabeth his wife.
--- Emmel of Peter and Elisabeth, b. June 12, bapt. Oct. 28. Sponsors: Joseph Schuz and Louisa his wife.

178
One married man, Lad Bakon, about 30 years of age, b. in Hockin Township, Cumberland County, and all of the Confirmants of the year of 1782 were bapt. by me on the 16th day of June all together. Johann Christoph Kunze, Ev. Luth. Preacher, at Philadelphia:
Margareta Wenzel of Philipp and Anna Barbara, b. April 13, bapt. June 16. Sponsors: Adam Fix and Elisabeth his wife.
Johannes Dielshoefer of Johannes and Mariana, b. May 27, bapt. June 16. Sponsors: Johannes Sauder and Margareta his wife.
Elisabeth Miller of Michael and Catharina, b. Nov. 29, 1781, bapt. June 16. Sponsors: Michael Miller and Anna Maria his wife.
Margareta Saul of Philipp and Elisabeth, b. March 7, bapt. June 16. Sponsors: Johann Adam Saul and Margareta his wife.
Johannes Noll of Henrich and Susanna, b. Feb. 4, bapt. June 16. Sponsors: Friedrich Fries and Catharina his wife.
Maria Elisabeth Biel of Georg and Elisabeth, b. Nov. 23, 1781, bapt. June 16. Sponsors: Johann Sofrer and Maria Elisabeth his wife.
Wilhelm Wenzel of Wilhelm and Elisabeth, b. Aug. 20, bapt. June 16. Sponsors: Georg Kammer and Catharina his wife.
Margareta Bitter of Henrich and Elisabeth, b. 6 mos. ago, bapt. June 16. Sponsors: Georg Schneider and Margareta his wife.
Anna Maria Wenzel of Theodorus and Eva, b. April 16, bapt. June 16. Sponsors: Johannes Miller and Mrs. Charlotte Fix.
Anna Maria Rothkap of Georg and Salome, b. Dec. 13, 1781, bapt. June 16. Sponsors: Michael Mony and Mrs. Anna Maria Hitschner.
Rosina Carolina Wolpert of Hans Michael and Maria, b. Nov. 1, 1781, bapt. June 16. Sponsors: Martin Immel and Rosina his wife.
Theobald Rotter of Simon and Elisabeth, b. Oct. 8, bapt. June 16. Sponsors: Adam Mensch and Barbara his wife.
Johann Peter Bauer of Conrad and Anna Margareta, b. Jany. 4, bapt. June 16. Sponsors: Peter Mensch and Mrs. Elisab. Schimpf.

Wilhelm Sauder of Peter and Maria, b. April 29, bapt. June 16.
Sponsors: Theobald Rotter and Elisabeth his wife.
Sara Brenesholz of Adam and Maria (deceased), b. Jany. 7, bapt.
June 16. Sponsors: Philipp Schimpf, Sen., and Elisabeth his wife.
Lydia Hahn of Jacob and Catharina, b. Oct. 16, bapt. June 16.
Sponsors: Jacob Miller and Catharina his wife.
Johannes Caspar Hofmann of Johannes and Elisabeth, b. Dec. 12,
bapt. June 16. Sponsors: Caspar Hector and Anna Catharina his wife.
Catharina Stamm of Wilhelm and Sophia, b. May 16, 1781, bapt.
June 16. Sponsors: Michael Miller and Catharina his wife.
Susanna Hitchner of Georg and Mariana, b. July 25, 1782, bapt.
Sept 22. Sponsors: Mrs. Susanna Miller and Geo. Hitchner, the father.
Wilhelm Schuetz of Joh: Jost and Elisabeth, b. Dec. 15, 1781,
bapt. Sept. 22, 1782. Sponsors: Peter Kroneneberger and spinster Barbara and Narten.

By Heinrich Mueller, Ev. Luther. Preacher at Colestown and Longa Commings in this state:
Joh: Adam Rudolph of Ludewig and Catharina, b. Nov. 25, 1782,
bapt. Dec. 29. Sponsors: Adam Saul and Margaretha his wife.
Elisabeth Herp of Michael and Charlotta, b. Nov. 3, bapt. Dec.
29. Sponsors: Philip Saul and Elisabeth his wife.
Hanna Kautz of Geo. and Anna, b. Sept. 14, bapt. Dec. 29.
Sponsors: Geo. Benter and Margaretha his wife.
Johannes Schmueck of Willh: and Anna Maria, b. Nov. 17, bapt.
Dec. 29. Sponsors: Joh: Hebner and Margaretha Emmel, spinster.
Maria Sergio of Johann and Catharina, b. Dec. 17, bapt. 29 ditto.
Sponsors: Nicolaus Fitzeran and Maria his wife.
Magdalena Hitchner of Jacob and Elisabeth, b. Oct. 15, bapt. Dec.
29. Sponsors: Jacob Hitchner and Magdalena his wife, the Grandparents.
Johannes Heyer of Conrad (deceased) and Christina, b. Nov. 28,
bapt. Dec. 29. Sponsors: Jacob Hitchner and Magdalena, his wife, the Grandparents.
Susanna Miller of Johannes and Mrs. Magdalena Fuchs, b. Sept. 9,
bapt. Dec. 29. Sponsors: Geo. Kautz and Anna his wife.
Heinrich Kendel of Heinr. and Anna Maria, b. Sept. 28, bapt. Dec.
29. Sponsor: Heinr. Saul.

By. Henr. Helmuth, Evangel. Luth. preacher in Philadelphia, 1783:
Elisabeth Pilgrim of Francys and Catharina, b. March 26, bapt.
June 29, 1783. Sponsors: Johann Hahn and Elisabeth his wife.
Johann Peter Friess of Jacob and Elisabeth, b. Jany. 30, bapt.
June 29, 1783. Sponsors: The parents themselves.
Georg Paris of Peter and Susanna, b. March 30, bapt. June 29,
1783. Sponsors: Georg Kauz and Hanna his wife.
Joh: Jacob Ziegler of Theobald and Magdalena, b. Jany. 21, bapt.
June 29, 1783. Sponsors: Jacob Hitschner and Magdalena his wife.
Elisabeth Schaeffer of Conrad and Elisabeth, b. Nov. 28, 1782,

bapt. June 29, 1783. Sponsors: Philipp Schmueck and Elisabeth Margareta his wife.
Anna Friess of Fridr. and Catharina, b. June 26, bapt. June 29, 1783. Sponsors: Gabr. Janson and Barbara his wife.
Catharina Bellincker of Johann and Elisabeth, b. Oct. 1, 1782, bapt. June 29, 1783. Sponsors: Mathaeus Bleninger and Catharina his wife.
Susanna Remster of Fridr. and Juliana, b. Dec. 3, 1782, bapt. June 29, 1783. Sponsors: Peter Mensch and Mrs. Margareta Haehns.
Margareta Hector of Caspar and Maria, b. May 27, bapt. June 29, 1783. Sponsors: Joh. Nicol. Wick and Margareta his wife.
Johann Balthasar Heine of Balth. Schmidt and Catharina, b. Feb. 6, 1783, bapt. June 29, 1783. Sponsors: Georg Rohkep and Salome his wife.
Phoebe Fries of Jacob, Sen.? and Dorcas, b. May 25, bapt. 25 same month 1783 by the Engl. Preacher Mr. S. Kenck. Sponsors: The parents themselves.

1784
By Joh. Christ. Kunze, Pr. in Philadelphia:
Johann Henrich Wolpert of Johann Michael and Maria, b. June 19, bapt. Feb. 29, 1784. Sponsors: Johannes Rick and Sarah his wife and Sarah his dau.
Magdalena Hitschner of Georg and Mariana, b. Oct. 24, bapt. Feb. 29, 1784. Sponsors: Theobald Sickler and Magdalena his wife.
Jacob Bender of Georg and Margareta, b. Feb. 18, bapt. 29 same month 1784. Sponsors: Georg Kauz and Barbara his wife.
Israel Beeden of Lat and Barbara, b. Sept. 22, bapt. Feb. 29, 1784. Sponsors: Georg Hitschner and Maria his wife.
Henrich Frebel of Johann and Anna Margareta, b. Oct. 9, bapt. March 1. Sponsors: Henrich Hilliard and Salome his wife.
Catharina Hahn of Andreas and Sarah, b. Oct. 17, 1783, bapt. March 1, 1784. Sponsors: Johannes Hahn and Elisabet his wife.
Elisabet Leidenberger of Eberhard and Elisabet, b. July 25, 1783, bapt. March 1, 1784. Sponsors: Friedrich Lachs and Mrs. Elisab. Hofmann.
David Kake of David and Margareta, b. Sept. 18, 1783, bapt. March 1, 1784. Sponsors: Adam Saul and his mother.
Anna Barbara Hoeppener of Johannes and Anna Maria, b. Dec. 20, bapt. March 1. Sponsors: Friedrich Mark and Mrs. Anna Barbara Kauz.
Elisabeth Rotter of Johann and Maria Elisabeth, b. Nov. 16, 1783, bapt. June 13, 1784. Sponsors: Joh. Schimp and Elisabeth his wife.
Johann Georg Schuetz of Johann Johst. and Elisabeth, b. Dec. 30, 1783, bapt. June 13, 1784. Sponsors: Georg Schnitzer, Mathias Scheuermann and Barbara his wife.
Johann Adam Saul of Philipp and Elisabeth, b. March 6, bapt. June 13. Sponsors: Johann Adam Saul and Margareta.
Elisabeth Hahn of Johann, Junior and Catharina, b. Dec. 20, 1783, bapt. June 13. Sponsors: Joh. Hahn, Senior and Elisabeth his wife.
Anna Maria Seal of Benjamin (father) and Jacob Rammel (2nd

husband) and Ann, b. Dec. 17, 1781, bapt. June 13, 1784. Sponsors: Johann Adam Saul and Margareta his wife.
Margareta Noll of Heinr. and Susanna, b. March 31, bapt. June 13. Sponsor: Mrs. Margareta Sauter.
Jacob Friess of Philipp and Maria, b. March 8, bapt. June 6 by Rev. Mr. Weiberg. Sponsors: Jacob Friess and Dorcas his wife.
Juliana Sauter of Peter and Maria, b. Dec. 8, 1783, bapt. June 13, 1784. Sponsors: Christoph Wucher and Judith his wife.
Joh. Georg Maurer of Johann and Catharina, b. Aug. 25, 1783, bapt. June 13, 1784. Sponsors: Heinr. Candel and Anna Maria his wife.
Elisabeth Wolpert of Michael and Elisabeth, b. April 21, bapt. June 13. Sponsor: Rosina Emmelson.

1785
The following 10 children were bapt. by Joh. Friederich Schmidt, Evangel. Luth. preacher in Germantown and Philadelphia:
Jacob Weck of Joh. Nicolaus, Jun. and Margarethe, b. Aug. 19, 1784, bapt. Sept. 4, 1785. Sponsors: Jacob Marsholder and Elisabeth.
Susanna Mensh of Peter and Christine, b. March 28, bapt. Sept. 4. Sponsors: Michael Johnson and Susanna his wife.
Catharine Rammel of Simon and Christina, b. Aug. 4, bapt. Sept. 4. Sponsors: Baltzer Schmidt and Catharine his wife.
Maria Margarethe Frevel of Johannes and Margarethe, b. Aug. 7, bapt. Sept. 4. Sponsors: Conrad Fromm and Maria Margarethe his wife.
Matthias Rother of Thomas and Margarethe, b. Sept. 11, 1783, bapt. Sept 4. Sponsors: Mathias Creamer and Margarethe his wife.
Jacob Hitchner of Jacob, Jun. and Elisabeth his wife, b. July 5, bapt. Sept. 4. Sponsors: Jacob Hitschner, Sen. and Magdalene his wife.
Christine Dilshaefer of Johannes and Mariane, b. July 10, 1784, bapt. Sept. 4. Sponsors: Friderich Fries and Catharine his wife.
Joh. Georg Stutz of Joh. Georg and Barbara, b. July 5, bapt. Sept. 4. Sponsors: The parents.
Andreas Hartmann of Johannes and Anne Maria, b. July 8, bapt. Sept. 4. Sponsor: Andreas Craemer.
Ludwig Rudolph of Ludwig and Catharine, b. Nov. 15, 1784, bapt. Sept. 4. Sponosrs: Johannes Horn and Margarethe his wife.

Christine Rammel of Simon and Christine, b. Oct. ---, 1784, bapt. Oct. 21, 1784, emergency baptism by Schoolmaster L. Ilgen. Sponsors: The parents of the child.
Sara Fries of Jacob, Sr. and Dorcas, b. Jany. 1, 1786, bapt. Jany. 10, 1786 by the Engl. Parson Skank. Sponsors: The parents of the child.

On the 7th Sunday after Trinity, 1786, July 30. Heinrich Helmuth, Evangel. Luth. Preacher at Philadelphia:
Bodo Kerrmann of Fridrich and Margareta, b. Jany. 24, 1786, bapt. July 30. Sponsors: The parents themselves.

FRIESBURG EMANUEL LUTHERAN CHURCH 209

Philipp Wolbert of Joh. Michael and Maria Cath., b. Sept. 23, 1785, bapt. July 30. Sponsors: Philipp Schimpf and Mrs. Sarah Rick.
Catharina Jung of Philipp and Margareta, b. Feb. 5, 1786, bapt. July 30. Sponsors: Ludw. Tanzbecher and Cathar. his wife.
Isaak Schuez of Joh. Georg and Elisabeth, b. Feb. 19, 1786, bapt. July 30. Sponsors: Phil. Schimpf and Elizab his wife.
Johann Kelly of Georg and Elisabeth, b. May 8, 1786, bapt. July 30. Sponsors: Joh. Schempf and Elisab. his wife.
Hanna Bellinger of Joh. and Elisabeth, b. Aug. 24, 1785, bapt. July 30. Sponsors: Fridr. Schott and Susanna his wife.
Ludwig Wilh Ehsenbeck of Christoph Wilhelm and Cath., b. March 29, 1786, bapt. July 30. Sponsors: Ludwig Illgen and Anna Barbara his wife.
Anna Catharina Ifft of Joh. and Margareta, b. April 3, 1786, bapt. July 30. Sponsors: The parents themselves.
Christina Johnson of Michael and Susanna, b. Sept. 31, 1785, bapt. July 30. Sponsors: Peter Mensch and Christina his wife.
Susanna Hinne of Adam and Elisab., b. Feb. 27, 1786, bapt. July 30. Sponsors: Beniamin Mensch and Mrs. Susanna Tennelsberg.
Peter Vozen of Joh. Val. and Sophia, b. Dec. 30, 1785, bapt. July 30. Sponsors: Franz Stenger and Mrs. Maria Fix.
Maria Schmidt of Johann and Rosina, b. July 4, 1785, bapt. July 30. Sponsors: Jacob Schwaab and Maria Reichard.
Adam Painter of Georg and Margareta, b. Jany. 27, 1786, bapt. July 30. Sponsors: Georg Kauz and Anna his wife.
Christina Stenger of Daniel and Eva, b. March 4, 1786, bapt. July 30. Sponsors: Ludw. Illgen and Anna his wife.
Philipp Stenger of Philipp and Dorothea, b. Aug. 19, 1784, bapt. July 30. Sponsors: Jacob Schwaab.
Fridrich Stenger of Philipp and Dorothea, b. June 12, 1786, bapt. July 30. Sponsors: Fridrich Kerrmann and Margar. his wife.
Elisabeth Hizner of Andr. and Sarah, b. Sept. 25, 1785, bapt. July 30. Sponsor: Elisab. Schimpf.
Isaak Bakon of Loth and Barbara, b. Jany. 29, 1786, bapt. July 30. Sponsors: Martin Hitschner and Mrs. Cath. Rothgeiber.
Anna Maria Hector of Caspar and Anna Maria, b. Oct. 3, 1785, bapt. July 30. Sponsors: Anna Maria Miller and Franz Pilgrim.
Heinrich Roth of Thomas and Margar, b. April 22, 1786, bapt. July 30. Sponsors: Heinrich Breida and Sarah Loyd.
Samuel Peterson of Andr. and Anna Maria, b. Dec. 27, 1780, bapt. July 30. Sponsors: Joh. Adler and Anna Barbara his wife.
Joh Sterz of Heinrich and Nancy, b. Dec. 31, 1785, bapt. July 30. Sponsors: Joh. Adler and Anna Barbara his wife.
Hanna Ilgen of Lewis and Barbara, b. April 11, 1786, bapt. June 28. Sponsors: The parents themselves.
Elisabeth Bernhard of Georg and Elisabeth, b. April 18, 1880, bapt. July 30. Sponsors: Georg Merckel and Maria his wife.
Sarah Sicken of Beniamin and Charlott, b. April 8, 1779, bapt. July 30. Sponsor: Mrs. Margareta Bremer.
Margareta Friess of Philipp and Maria, b. Dec. 26, 1785, bapt. July 30. Sponsors: Jacob Friess, Senr. and Dorcas his wife.
Maria Brenersholz of Adam and Barbara, b. June 21, 1786, bapt. July 30. Sponsors: Carl Wenzel and Catharina his wife.

Anna Margareta Schmueck of Phil. and Elisabeth, b. Oct. 21, 1785, bapt. July 30. Sponsors: Joseph Herrmann and Anna Maria his wife.
Lydia Friess of Fridrich and Catharina, b. Sept. 11, 1785, bapt. July 30. Sponsors: The parents themselves.
Maria Tilshefer of Jacob and Susanna, b. Feb. 21, bapt. July 30. Sponsors: Ludw. Illgen and Anna his wife.
Maria Catharina Humschier and Maria Cath., b. April 17, 1786, bapt. July 30. Sponsors: The parents themselves.
Christina Tanzenbecher of Ludwig and Catharina, b. Dec. 21, 1785, bapt. July 30. Sponsors: The parents themselves.
Wilhelm Stamm of Wilhelm and Sophia, b. May 12, 1785, bapt. July 30. Sponsors: Michael Miller and Maria Catharina his wife.
Wilhelm Miller of Michael and Maria Catharina, b. April 26, 1786, bapt. July 30. Sponsors: Wilhelm Stamm and Sophia his wife.
Barbara Remster of Fridr. and Juliana, b. Jany. 31, 1786, bapt. July 30. Sponsor: Barbara Mensch.

On April 29, 1787, the following children were bapt. Friedrich Schmidt, Evangel. Luth. Preacher at Philadelphia:
Johann Adam Saul of Henrich and Maria, b. Sept. 27, 1786, bapt. April 29. Sponsors: Adam Saul and Margrethe his wife.
Elisabeth Ramel of Jacob and Anne, b. Sept. 30, 1786, bapt. April 29. Sponsors: Adam Saul and Margrethe his wife.
Jacob Schuetz of Joseph and Louise, b. Aug. 25, 1786, bapt. April 29. Sponsors: Jacob Delshoefer and Susanna his wife.
Martin Rammel and Maria Magdalena Rammel (twins) of Simon and Christina, b. March 1, bapt. April 29. Sponsors: Martin Hitschner, Pier Schmidt, Georg Reichert and Magdalen Rammel.
Jacob Hitschner of Georg and Maria, b. Oct. 10, 1786, bapt. April 29. Sponsors: Jacob Hitschner and Magdalene his wife.
Susanna Kammerer of Georg and Catharine, b. April 22, bapt. April 29. Sponsors: Andreas Mensch and Susanna Denelspeck.
Christina Hitschner of Andreas and Sara, b. March 12, bapt. April 29. Sponsors: Simon Rammel and Christine his wife.
Georg Delshoefer of Johannes and Mariane, b. Sept. 5, 1786, bapt. April 29. Sponsors: Georg Kautz and Anna his wife.
Johannes Wentzel of Carl and Catharine, b. Nov. 6, 1786, bapt. April 29. Sponsors: Parents.
David Wentzel of Daniel and Maria, b. March 16, bapt. April 29. Sponsors: Benjamin Mensch and Mariane Fix.
Jacob Hoepner of Johannes and Anna Maria, b. Sept. 11, 1786, bapt. April 29. Sponsors: Jacob Hitschner, Jun. and Elisabeth his wife.
Anna Maria May of Johannes and Margrethe, b. Jany. 27, bapt. April 29. Sponsors: Henrich Saul and Anna Maria his wife.
Georg Mueller of Johannes and Magdalene, b. Sept. 8, 1786, bapt. April 29. Sponsors: Ditorius Wentzel and Eva his wife.
Catharina Henckel of Henrich and Anna Maria, b. April 8, bapt. April 29. Sponsors: Henrich Ochsenberger and Christine his wife.
Johannes Weck of Joh. Nicoluas and Margrethe, b. Nov. 2, 1786, bapt. April 29. Sponsors: Joh. Dendelspeck and mother of the child.

Johannes Hahn of Andreas and Sara, b. Aug. 30, 1786, bapt. April 29. Sponsors: Parents.
Johannes Hahn of Johannes and Catharine, b. Jany. 5, ----, bapt. April 29. Sponsors: Grandparents.
Andreas Rothgaep of Georg and Salome, b. June 17, 1786, bapt. April 29. Sponsors: Andreas Hitschner and Elisabeth his wife.
Michael Noll of Henrich and Susanne, b. Sept. 28, 1786, bapt. April 29. Sponsors: Jacob Mueller and Catharine his wife.
Adam Friess of Jacob and Elisabeth, b. Jany. 30, bapt. April 29. Sponsors: Adam Printesholz and Elizabeth his wife.
Sara Kautz of Adam and Barbara, b. 5 month April 17, bapt. April 29. Sponsors: Georg Kautz and Anne his wife.
Joh. Jacob Hoffman of Johannes and Anne Margrethe, b. Aug. 5, 1786, bapt. April 29. Sponsors: Jacob Hitschner and Elisabeth his wife.

The following were bapt. June 8, 1788, Friedrich Schmidt, Ev. Luth. Precher at Philadelphia:
Thomas Schaefer of Conrad and Elisabeth, b. Nov. 28, 1787, bapt. June 8. Sponsors: Parents.
Catharine Janson of Michael and Susanna, b. March 31, bapt. April 5. Sponsor: Andreas Mensch.
Adam Schimp of Johannes and Charlotte, b. Feb. 8, bapt. June 8. Sponsors: Johannes Schimp and Elizabeth his wife, Grandparents.
Georg Ott of Martin and Margrethe, b. April 24, bapt. June 8. Sponsors: Georg Rothkap and Salome his wife.
Johann Adam Ziegler of Dewald and Magdalene, b. Dec. 23, 1787, bapt. June 8. Sponsors: Parents.
Johannes Paris of Peter and Susanna, b. Sept. 11, 1787, bapt. June 8. Sponsors: Joh. Georg Keller and Elisabeth his wife.
Johannes Henne of Adam and Elisabeth, b. May 18, bapt. June 8. Sponsors: Adam Saul and Margrete his wife.
Samuel Wolpert of Peter and Sophia, b. Dec. 19, 1786, bapt. June 8. Sponsors: Parents.
Henrich Kerman of Friedrich and Margrete, b. March 1, bapt. June 8. Sponsors: Henrich Saul and Maria his wife.
Peter Dietrich of Jacob and Rosine, b. Nov. 14, 1781, bapt. June 8. Sponsor: Christian Schaefer.
Maria Dietrich of Jacob and Rosine, b. Jany. 28, 1784, bapt. June 8. Sponsor: Catharine Mueller.
Margrete Dietrich of Jacob and Rosine, b. Feb. 24, 1786, bapt. June 8. Sponsor: Elisabeth Keller.
Andreas Scheidner of Philip and Louise, b. March 25, bapt. June 8. Sponsors: Andreas Usinger and Catharine Rammel.
Barbara Saul of Philip (dead) and Elisabeth, b. Oct. 17, 1787, bapt. June 8. Sponsors: Adam Saul and Margrete his wife.
Elisabeth Hahn of Andreas and Sara, b. Jan. 13, bapt. June 8. Sponsors: Johannes Hahn and Elisabeth his wife.
Daniel Hahn of Jacob and Elisabeth, b. April 15, bapt. June 8. Sponsors: Joh. Hahn and Elisabeth his wife.
Johannes Schneider of Peter and Margrete, b. July 12, 1787, bapt. June 8. Sponsors: Johannes Schimp and Charlotte his wife.
Ester Meyers of Christoph and Sara, b. March 31, 1787, bapt. June

8. Sponsors: Johann Hahn and Margrete his wife.
Philip Demaeris of Adam and Maria, b. May 10, bapt. June 8.
 Sponsors: Philip Henckel and Barbara his wife.
Samuel Stretsch of Thomas and Anne Maria, b. Feb. 17, 1787, bapt.
 June 8. Sponsors: Jacob Friess and Elisabeth his wife.
Hanna Thomas of Valentin and Elisabeth, b. Dec. 31, 1787, bapt.
 June 8. Sponsors: Andreas Schimp and Hanna Heft his wife.
Daniel Wenzel of Theodor and Eva, b. Aug. 10, 1787, bapt. June 8.
 Sponsors: Adam Kautz and Barbara his wife.
Jacob Wolpert of Joh. Michael and Maria, b. Oct. 22, 1787, bapt.
 June 8. Sponsors: Jacob Hitschner and Elizabeth his wife.
Margrete Jung of Philip and Margrete, b. March 16, bapt. June 8.
 Sponsors: Philip Schimp and Maria his wife.
Joh. Georg Hamscher of Johannes and Maria Catherine, b. Feb. 13,
 bapt. June 8. Sponsors: Georg Hitschner and Maria his wife.
Jonathan Schmid of Wilhelm and Anne Maria, b. March 5, 1787,
 bapt. June 8. Sponsors: Martin Hitschner and Catherine
 Bigler.
Jeremias Bacon of Loth. and Barbara, b. Oct. 7, 1787. Sponsors:
 Parents.
Maria Magdalene Ilgen of Ludwig A. W. and Anne Barbara, b. Oct.
 12, 1787, bapt. June 8. Sponsors: Georg Kautz and Anne his
 wife.
Sara Sauter of Simon and Elisabeth, b. March 31, bapt. June 8.
 Sponsors: Parents.
Daniel Hartman of Johannes and Anne Maria, b. Nov. 24, 1787,
 bapt. June 8. Sponsors: Parents.
Susanna Hecktor of Casper and Anne Maria, b. April 28, bapt. June
 8. Sponsors: Henrich Kendel and Susanna his dau.
Simon Dilshoefer of Johannes and Mariana, b. March 28, bapt. June
 8. Sponsors: The parents.
Richard Shelden of Odel and Margrete, b. April 10, 1787, bapt.
 June ---. Sponsors: Balzer Schmidt and Catharine his wife.
Ester Shelden of Odel and Margrete, b. June 10, 1785, bapt. June
 8. Sponsor: Maria Maises?
Joh. Georg Ochseberger of Henrich and Maria Christine, b. Sept.
 27, 1787, bapt. June 8. Sponsor: Georg Reichert.
Joseph Herman of Joseph and Maria, b. Feb. 17, bapt. June 8.
 Sponsors: Parents.
Johann Bellinger of John and Elisabeth, b. June 17, 1787, bapt.
 June 8. Sponsors: Johanns Horn and Margrethe his wife.
John McGee of Abraham and Elisabeth, b. March 21, bapt. June 8.
 Sponsors: Johannes Schimp and Charlotte his wife.
Anna Dixon of George and Anna Barbara, b. May 4, bapt. June 8.
 Sponsors: Parents.
Elisabeth Rudolph of Ludwig and Catharine, b. Sept. 10, 1786,
 bapt. June 8. Sponsors: Peter Kroneberger and Margrete his
 wife.
Hanna Schmidt of Philip and Elisabeth, b. Dec. 28, 1787, bapt.
 June 8. Sponsors: Valentin Thomas and Elisabet his wife.
Moritz Pilgrim of Franz and Pescheby, b. April 19, 1787, bapt.
 June 8. Sponsors: Peter Mensch and Christine his wife.
David Bender of Georg and Margrete, b. March 16, bapt. June 8.
 Sponsors: Georg Kautz and Anne his wife.

Georg Howel of George and Elisabeth Johnson, b. Feb. 7, 1786, bapt. June 8. Sponsor: The mother.
Elisabeth Friess of Philip and Mary, b. Dec. 14, 1787, bapt. June 8, 1788. Sponsors: Jacob Friess, Sen. and Dorcas his wife.
Friedrich Friess and Catharine Friess (twins) of Friedrich and Catharine, b. May 29, bapt. June 8. Sponsors: The parents.
Friedrich Schott of Friedrich and Susanna, b. May 16, 1787, bapt. June 8. Sponsors: The parents.

The following children were bapt. Oct. 31 and Nov. 1, 1789 by Heinrich Helmuth, Evangel. Luth. Preacher at Philadelphia.
Oct. 31, 1789:
Elizabeth Schuetz of Johann Jost and Elisabeth, b. June 14, 1788, bapt. Oct. 31, 1789. Sponsors: Joseph Schuetz and Louisa his wife.
Johann Georg Schuetz of Joseph and Louisa, b. Oct. 25, 1788, Oct. 31, 1789. Sponsors: Johann Georg Schimpf and Anna Maria his wife.
Catharina Rudolph of Ludwig and Catharina, b. Aug. 12, 1788, bapt. Oct. 31, 1789. Sponsors: Johann Horn and Margareta his wife.
Deamy Pilgramm of Franz and Bershabey, b. Feb. 28, 1789, bapt. Oct. 31, 1789. Sponsor: Catharina Mueller, widow.
Margareta Schmueck of Wilhelm and Anna Maria, b. May 28, 1789, bapt. Oct. 31. Sponsors: Peter Croneberger and Margareta his wife.
Elisabeth Schimpf of Georg and Anna Maria, b. Aug. 2, 1788, bapt. Oct. 31, 1789. Sponsors: Johann Schimpf and Elisabeth his wife.
David Jung of Adam and Maria, b. March 30, 1789, bapt. Oct. 31, 1789. Sponsors: The parents themselves.
Isaack Bacon of Loth and Barbara, b. June 19, 1789, bapt. Oct. 31, 1789. Sponsors: The parents themselves.
Fridrich Saul of Heinrich and Anna Maria, b. Nov. 27, 1788, bapt. Oct. 31, 1789. Sponsors: Fridrich Kehrmann and Margareta his wife.
Adam Rothkaepp of Georg and Salome, b. Feb. 22, 1788, bapt. Oct. 31, 1789. Sponsors: The parents themselves.
Martin Ziegler of Theobald and Magdalena, b. Sept. 20, bapt. Oct. 31, 1789. Sponsors: Martin Huetschner and mother of the child.
Johann Ludwig Tenzenbecher of Ludwig and Catharina, b. March 12, bapt. Oct. 31, 1789. Sponsors: The parents themselves.
Johann Georg May of Johann and Margareta, b. ---, bapt. Oct. 31, 1789. Sponsors: The parents themselves.
Adam Mensch of Andreas and Catharina, b. Jany. 25, bapt. Oct. 31, 1789. Sponsors: Adam Saul and Margareta his wife.
Wilhelm Ehrig of Michael and Sarah, b. March 22, bapt. Oct. 31, 1789. Sponsors: Georg Miehl and Elisabeth his wife.
Johann Huetschner of Jacob and Elisabeth, b. Sept. 4, 1788, bapt. Oct. 31, 1789. Sponsors: Johann Nicolaus Weil and Margareta his wife.
Carl Brennesholz of Adam and Barbara, b. April 13, bapt. Oct. 31, 1789. Sponsors: Carl Wenzel and Catharina his wife.

Elisabeth Weil of Johann Nicolaus and Margareta, b. Oct. 5, 1789, bapt. Oct. ·31. Sponsors: Jacob Huetschner and Elisabeth his wife.
Johann Heppner of Johann and Anna Maria, b. July 6, 1788, bapt. Oct. 31, 1789. Sponsors: Johann Heppner and Anna Maria his wife.
Anna Maria Heppner of Johann and Anna Maria, b. Sept. 6, 1789, bapt. Oct. 31, 1789. Sponsors: The parents themselves.
Elisabeth Ehbrecht of Heinrich and Sarah, b. Oct. 25, 1788, bapt. Oct. 31, 1789. Sponsors: The parents themselves.
Adam Schott of Fridrich and Susanna, b. Aug. 2, bapt. Oct. 31, 1789. Sponsors: The parents themselves.
Hanna Huetschner of Andreas and Sarah, b. Sept. 27, 1788, bapt. Oct. 31, 1789. Sponsors: The parents themselves.
Richard Bender of Ludwig and Margareta, b. Oct. 16, 1788, bapt. Oct. 31. Sponsors: Georg Keller and Elisabeth his wife.
Daniel Mensch of Peter and Christina, b. Dec. 10, 1788, bapt. Oct. 31, 1789. Sponsors: The parents themselves.
Elizabeth Mensch of Beniamin and Hanna, b. April 19, bapt. Oct. 31, 1789. Sponsors: The parents themselves.
Daniel Delshoefer of Jacob and Susanna, b. Sept. 14, 1788, bapt. Oct. 31, 1789. Sponsors: The parents themselves.
Georg Huetschner of Georg and Mariane, b. Dec. 25, 1788, bapt. Oct. 31, 1789. Sponsors: The parents themselves.
Georg Huetschner of Georg and Mariane, b. Dec. 25, 1788, bapt. Oct. 31, 1789. Sponsors: The parents themselves.
Georg Serger of Peter and Catharina, b. Sept. 8, 1789, bapt. Oct. 31. Sponsors: Ludwig Tanzebecher and Catharina his wife.
Elisabeth Fischer of Johann and wife, b. April 9, 1788, bapt. Oct. 31, 1789. Sponsors: Johann Schimpf and Elisabeth his wife.
Maria Kautz of Adam and Barbara, b. Aug. ---, 1788, bapt. Oct. 31, 1789. Sponsors: The parents themselves.

Nov. 1, 1789:
Margareta Borges of Peter and Susanna, b. Oct. 10, bapt. Nov. 1, 1789. Sponsors: Adam Saul and Margareta his wife.
Christina Rammel of Simon and Christina, b. Nov. 20, 1788, bapt. Nov. 1, 1789. Sponsors: Jacob Schwaab and Christina Schmidt.
Simon Uhsingers of Andreas and Catharina, b. Sept. 14, bapt. Nov. 1, 1789. Sponsors: Simon Rammel and Christina his wife.
Jacob Watson of John and Maria, b. Aug. 13, 1788, bapt. Nov. 1, 1789. Sponsors: Adam Ridsch and Catharina Monny his wife.
Margareta Miller of Johann and Magdalena, b. April 3, 1789, bapt. Nov. 1. Sponsors: The parents themselves.
Thomas Radyn of Thomas and Margareta, b. Oct. 25, 1788, bapt. Nov. 1, 1789. Sponsors: The mother herself.
Johann Georg Riemster of Fridrich and Juliana, b. Nov. 4, 1788, bapt. Nov. 1, 1789. Sponsors: The parents themselves and John George Remster.
Georg Taylor of Peter and Margareta, b. Sept. 27, 1788, bapt. Nov. 1, 1789. Sponsors: Georg Schimpf and Anna Maria his wife.
Anna Maria Taylor of Peter and Margareta, b. Feb. 19, bapt. Nov.

1, 1789. Sponsor: Anna Maria Andreas.
Johann Friess of Philipp and Maria, b. Oct. 10, bapt. Nov. 1, 1789, and d. Oct. 31, 1811, burried in the God's Acre about a half a mile above Woodbury. Sponsors: Jacob Friess, Senior and Dorcas his wife.

The following children were bapt. by Heinrich Helmuth, Evangel. Luth. Preacher at Philadelphia on June 6, 1790:
Anna Maria Schimp of Georg and Anna Maria, b. Nov. 4, 1789, bapt. June 5. Sponsors: The parents themselves.
Philipp Jung of Philipp and Margareta, b. Feb. 26, bapt. June 5. Sponsors: Ludwig Tanzeberger and Catharina his wife.
Elisabeth Illgen of Ludwig and Anna Barbara, b. April 26, bapt. June 5. Sponsors: The parents themselves.
Johann Samuel Ehsenbeck of Wilhelm and Catharina, b. Sept. 29, 1789, bapt. June 5. Sponsor: Jacob Schwab.
Anna Janson of Jacob and Margareta, b. Nov. 23, 1789, bapt. June 5. Sponsors: The parents themselves.
Anna McKee of Abraham and Elisabeth, b. May 2, bapt. June 5. Sponsors: Phil. Schimp and Elisabeth his wife.
Johann Adam Schuetz of Joh. Johst and Elisabeth, b. Feb. 17, bapt. June 6. Sponsors: Joh. Adam Kautz and Barbara his wife.
Johann Reichhard of Joh. and Anna, b. March 19, bapt. June 6. Sponsors: Balthasar Reichhard and Hanna his wife.
Sarah Wenzel of Theodorus and Eva, b. Feb. 18, bapt. June 6. Sponsors: The parents themselves.
Sarah Keller of Georg and Elisabeth, b. Feb. 24, bapt. June 6. Sponsors: The parents themselves.
Thomas Chew of Richard and Susanna, b. May 16, 1786, bapt. June 6, 1790. Sponsors: Adam Manch and Anna Maria his wife.
Robert Chew of Richard and Susanna, b. Feb. 6, 1788, bapt. June 6, 1790. Sponsors: Christian Roeser and Elisab. his wife.
Susanna Chew of Richard and Susanna, b. Sept. 6, 1789, bapt. June 6, 1790. Sponsors: Jacob Manch and Susanna his wife.
Johann Kroneberger of Peter and Margareta, b. Feb. 27, bapt. June 6. Sponsors: Joh. Horn and Margar. his wife.
Sarah Weiss of Sickel and Elisabeth, b. Oct. 14, 1789, bapt. June 6. Sponsors: Johann Adler and Barbara his wife.
Sarah Wolpert of Joh. Peter and Sophia, b. April 6, 1789, bapt. June 6. Sponsors: Johann Frevle and Margare his wife.
Susanna Rammel of Jacob and Anna, b. May 3, 1789, bapt. June 6. Sponsor: Elisabeth Roeser.
Mathias Huetschner of Andreas and Sarah, b. Feb. 14, bapt. June 6. Sponsors: Jacob Huetschner and Magdalena his wife.
Hanna Scheitner of Phil. and Louise, b. Nov. 4, 1789, bapt. June 6. Sponsor: Elisabeth Weiss.
Margareta Hahn of Jacob and Elisabeth, b. March 23, bapt. June 6. Sponsors: Johann Hahn and Elisabeth his wife.
Maria Hahn of Andreas and Sarah, b. March 19, bapt. June 6. Sponsors: The grandparents.
Georg Fischer of Johann and Magdalena, b. Jany. 14, bapt. June 6. Sponsors: Joh. Georg Rothkepp and Salome his wife.
Margareta May of Johann and Margareta, b. March 13, bapt. June 6. Sponsors: The parents themselves.

EARLY CHURCH RECORDS OF SALEM COUNTY

Elisabeth Shimp of Phil., Jun. and Elisabeth, b. Jany. 3, bapt. June 6. Sponsors: Phil. Schimpp and the parents themselves.
Johann Kammerer of Georg and Catharina, b. Feb. 28, bapt. June 6. Sponsors: The parents themselves.
Johann Candel of Heinrich and Anna Maria, b. March 12, bapt. June 6. Sponsors: Johann Adler and Barbara his wife.
Sarah Stretsch of Thomas and Anna Maria, b. Dec. 6, 1789, bapt. June 6. Sponsors: Jacob Friess and Dorcas his wife.
Wilhelm Schneider of Peter and Margareta, b. Feb. 20, bapt. June 6. Sponsors: Phil. Schimp and Elisabeth his wife.

The following children were bapt. on October 22 and 23, 1791, by Heinrich Helmuth, Preacher in Philadelphia:
Catharina Thomas of Valentin and Elisabeth, b. April 25, bapt. Oct. 22. Sponsors: The parents themselves.
Daniel Schimp of Georg and Anna Maria, b. Sept. 7, bapt. Oct. 22. Sponsors: The parents themselves.
Margareta Hitschner of Jacob and Elisabeth, b. Feb. 28, bapt. Oct. 22. Sponsors: The parents themselves.
Anna Maria Ziegler of Theobald and Magdalena, b. May 26, bapt. Oct. 22. Sponsor: The mother herself.
Susanna Peter of Georg and Margareta, b. Feb. 20, bapt. Oct. 22. Sponsors: The parents themselves.
Carl Wenzel of Carl and Catharina, b. Oct. 5, bapt. Oct. 22. Sponsors: The parents themselves.
Hanna Schimp of Johann and Charlotte, b. Jany. 21, bapt. Oct. 22. Sponsors: The parents themselves.
Elisabeth Sorge of Peter and Catharina, b. April 3, bapt. Oct. 22. Sponsors: The parents themselves.
Gabriel Paris of Peter and Susanna, b. Aug. 25, bapt. Oct. 22. Sponsors: The parents themselves.
Johann Kautz of Adam and Barbara, b. Sept. 29, 1790, baptizd Oct. 22. Sponsors: Georg Kautz and Anna his wife.
Martin Hitschner of Georg and Maria Anna, b. Dec. 12, 1790, bapt. April 22 by the Schoolmaster. Sponsors: The parents themselves.
Joh. Georg Tillshefer of Jacob and Susanna, b. Sept. 10, 1790, bapt. Oct. 22. Sponsors: Joh. Georg Kautz and Anna his wife.
Sarah Ehrig of Michael and Sarah, b. Nov. 9, 1790, bapt. Oct. 22. Sponsors: Joh. Rick and Sarah his wife.
Anna Sauder of Simon and Elisabeth, b. Oct. 8, 1790, bapt. Oct. 22. Sponsor: The mother herself.
Joh. Heinrich Schmueck of Wilhelm and Anna Maria, b. Sept. 6, 1790, bapt. Oct. 22. Sponsors: Valentin Thomas.
Christian Mensch of Andreas and Catharina, b. Feb. 12, bapt. Oct. 22. Sponsors: Peter Mensch and Christine.
Catharina Frevel of Johann and Margareta, b. July 11, 1790, bapt. Oct. 22. Sponsors: The parents themselves.
Sarah Friess of Jacob and Elisabeth, b. June 15, bapt. Oct. 22. Sponsor: The mother herself.
Andreas Remster of Fridr. and Juliana, b. Sept. 6, bapt. Oct. 22. Sponsors: Andreas Mensch and Catharina his wife.
Hanna Johnson of Johann and Catharina, b. Feb. 9, bapt. Oct. 22. Sponsors: The parents themselves.

Sarah Margareta Emmel of Martin and Rosina, b. Oct. 22, 1790, bapt. Oct. 22. Sponsors: Margareta Wolpert and Martin Hitschner.
Zacharias Jordan of Adam and Catharina, b. May 25, bapt. Oct. 22. Sponsors: Margareta Wolpert and Martin Hitschner.
David Schiets of Joseph and Louisa, b. March 8, bapt. Oct. 23. Sponsor: The mother herself.
Elisabeth Jung of Adam and Maria, b. Feb. 20, bapt. Oct. 23. Sponsors: The parents themselves.
Albrecht Pilgramm of Franz and Algeby, b. Sept. 6, bapt. Oct. 23. Sponsors: The parents themselves.
Maria Reichard of Joh. Georg and Anna, b. March 10, bapt. Oct. 23. Sponsors: The parents themselves.
Jacob Ehbrecht of Heinrich and Sarah, b. Sept. 29, bapt. Oct. 23. Sponsors: The parents themselves.
Michael Janson of Michael and Susanna, b. June 26, 1790, bapt. Oct. 23. Sponsors: The parents themselves.
Henrich Woodsise of John and Maria, b. Oct. 17, 1790, bapt. Oct. 23. Sponsors: David Halton and Catharina Weckler.
Margareta Schneider of Georg and Elisabeth, b. July 18, bapt. Oct. 23. Sponsors: Maria Magdalena Anderson.
Maria Mensch of Beniamin and Anna, b. Aug. 15, bapt. Oct. 23. Sponsors: The parents themselves.
Elisabeth Hinney of Adam and Elisabeth, b. Aug. 6, bapt. Oct. 23. Sponsors: Joh. Nicol. Wick and Margar. his wife.
Jonathan Hahn of Johann and Catharina, b. May 31, 1790, bapt. Oct. 23. Sponsors: Joh. Hahn and Elisabeth his wife.
Joh. Phil. Huetschner of Andreas and Sarah, b. July 19, bapt. Oct. 23. Sponsors: Phil. Schimp and Elisab. his wife.
Wilhelm Mayer of Christoph and Sarah, b. Nov. 17, 1789, bapt. Oct. 23, 1791. Sponsors: Johann Horn and Margareta his wife.

The following children were bapt. on June 8 and 9, 1793, by Heinrich Helmuth, Preacher at Philadelphia:
Johann Holzseite of Johann and Maria, b. Sept. 5, 1792, bapt. June 8, 1793. Sponsors: Joh. Horn and Margareta his wife.
Susanna Janson of Michael and Susanna, b. Oct. 29, 1792, bapt. June 8, 1793. Sponsors: Jacob Savary and Susanna his wife.
Anna Maria Schmueck of Wilhelm and Anna Maria, b. March 26, 1793, bapt. June 8, 1793. Sponsors: Phil. Schimpp and Elisabeth his wife.
Johann Schimpp of Georg and Anna Maria, b. March 8, 1793, bapt. June 8. Sponsors: Johann Schimpp and Elisabeth his wife.
Jacob Schimpp of Phil. and Catharina, b. Oct. 28, 1792, bapt. June 8, 1793. Sponsors: Jacob Rothgab and Anna Barbara his wife.
Anna Maria Sauder of Phil. and Christina, b. Dec. 5, 1788, bapt. June 8, 1793. Sponsors: David Geck and Margareta his wife.
Margareta Fuchs of Johann and Christina, b. Feb. 17, 1793, bapt. June 8, 1793. Sponsors: ----.
David Emmel of Martin and Rosina-Carolina, b. April 3, 1793, bapt. June 8. Sponsors: Johann Schimpp and Elisabeth his wife.
Beniamin Mensch of Andreas and Catharina, b. Dec. 7, 1792, bapt.

June 8. Sponsors: The parents themselves.
Anna Margareta Ilgen of Ludwig and Anna Barbara, b. April 6, 1793, bapt. June 8. Sponsors: Georg Kautz and Anna his wife.
Heinrich Wulbert of Maria (illegitimate), b. March 3, 1792, bapt. Jany. --, 1793, by Mr. Ilgen. Sponsors: Mathias Wulbert and Catharina his wife.
Margareta Ziegler of Theobald and Magdalena, b. April 2, 1793, bapt. June 8. Sponsors: The parents themselves.
Sarah Biber of Jacob and Maria, b. Jany. 25, 1787, bapt. June 8, 1793. Sponsors: Mrs. Elisabeth Margareta Stein.
Adam Jung of Adam and Maria, b. March 16, 1793, bapt. June 8. Sponsors: The parents themselves.
Margareta Hitschner of Georg and Mariana, b. Dec. 28, 1792, bapt. June 8. Sponsors: The parents themselves.
Lydia Schimpp of Johann Wilhelm and Maria Magdal, b. Dec. 4, 1792, bapt. June 8, 1793. Sponsors: The parents themselves.
Catharina Wenschel of Carl and Catharina, b. April 1, 1793, bapt. June 8. Sponsors: The parents themselves.
Maria Horn of Johann and Catharina, b. Sept. 3, 1792, bapt. June 8, 1793. Sponsors: Joh. Horn and Anna Maria his wife.
Joh. Georg Husinger of Andreas and Catharina, b. Nov. 13, 1791, bapt. June 8, 1793. Sponsors: Joh. Georg Rammel and Jean his wife.
Simon Rammel of Simon and Christina, b. Jany. 27, 1792, bapt. June 8, 1793. Sponsors: The parents themselves.
Philipp Scheidner of Phil. and Louisa, b. March 1, 1792, bapt. June 8, 1793. Sponsors: Georg Hitschner and Mariana his wife.
Ludwig Serger of Peter and Catherine, b. Feb. 13, 1793, bapt. June 8. Sponsors: Ludwig Danzebecher and Catherina his wife.
Joseph Schuetz of Johann Johst and Elizabeth, b. Jany. 21, 1792, bapt. June 8, 1793. Sponsors: The mother herself.
Joh. Fridrich Hitschner of Jacob and Elisabeth, b. Feb. 2, 1793, bapt. June 8. Sponsors: The parents themselves.
Susanna Schimpp of Andreas and Margareta, b. Aug. 31, 1792, bapt. June 8. Sponsors: The parents themselves.
Margareta Weck of Joh. Nicol. and Margareta, b. Aug. 31, 1792, bapt. June 8. Sponsor: Margareta Schaeffer.
Johann May of Johann and Margareta, b. April 3, 1792, bapt. June 8. Sponsors: The parents themselves.
Sarah Tilzhefer of Jacob and Susanna, b. March 28, 1792, bapt. June 8. Sponsors: The parents themselves.
Juliana Hepner of Johann and Anna Maria, b. Feb. 1, 1793, bapt. June 8. Sponsors: Jacob Hitschner and Magdalena his wife.
Mathias Hepner of Johann and Anna Maria, b. July 12, 1791, bapt. June 8. Sponsors: Andr. Hitschner and Sarah his wife.
Anna Maria Fuchs of Fridrich and Anna Maria, b. July 1, 1792, bapt. June 8. Sponsors: Georg Mecklin and Mrs. Anna Maria Fuchs.
Jacob Faasemeyer of Georg and wife, b. March 22, 1789, bapt. June 8. Sponsors: Jac. Tilzhefer and wife.
Christina Faasemeyer of Georg and wife, b. April 21, 1790, bapt. June 8. Sponsors: The parents themselves.
Georg Faasemeyer of Georg and wife, b. April 22, 1792, bapt. June 8. Sponsors: Georg Mecklin and wife.

Peter Janson of Joh. and Catharina, b. April 29, 1793, bapt. June 8. Sponsor: Barbara Janson.
Anna Friess of Phil. and Maria, b. April 9, 1792, bapt. June 8, 1793. Sponsors: The parents themselves.
Jacob Kandler of Heinrich and Anna Maria, b. Sept. 12, 1792, bapt. June 8, 1793. Sponsors: Jacob Massholder and Catharina his wife.
Susanna Keller of Georg and Elisabeth, b. Oct. 10, 1792, bapt. June 8, 1793. Sponsor: Elisab. Schimpp.
Margareta Saul of Heinr. and Maria, b. May 22, 1793, bapt. June 8. Sponsors: Adam Saul and Margar his wife.
Maria Chew of Richard and Susanna, b. Sept. 12, 1791, bapt. June 8, 1793. Sponsor: Maria Saul.
Adam Kautz of Adam and Barbara, b. March 24, 1793, bapt. June 8. Sponsors: Georg Kautz and Anna his wife.
Sarah Hahn of Johann and Catharina, b. Jany. 29, 1792, bapt. June 8, 1793. Sponsors: Johann Hahn and Elisabeth his wife.
Maria Schott of Fridrich and Susanna, b. Nov. 15, 1791, bapt. June 8, 1793. Sponsors: The parents themselves.
Anna Maria Janson of Jacob and Margareta, b. Jany. 18, 1792, bapt. June 8, 1793. Sponsors: The parents themselves.
Anna Wentzel of Theodor and Eva, b. June 12, 1792, bapt. June 8, 1793. Sponsors: The parents themselves.
Elisabeth Stamm of Wilhelm and Maria, b. Dec. 25, 1792, bapt. June 9. Sponsors: The parents themselves.
Johann Sorger of Jacob and Susanna, b. May 27, 1791, bapt. June 9, 1793. Sponsors: Johann Sorger and Susanna his wife.
Nancy Sorger of Jacob and Susanna, b. May 21, 1793, bapt. June 9. Sponsor: Catharina Sorger.
Hanna Reichert of Johann Georg and Anna, b. Jany. 12, 1793, bapt. June 9. Sponsors: Balthasar Reichert and Hanna his wife.
Johann Kehrmann of Fridrich and Hanna, b. Feb. 1, 1792, bapt. June 9, 1793. Sponsors: Johann Adler and Barbara his wife.
Andreas Saul of Adam and Maria, b. Jany. 9, 1792, bapt. June 9, 1793. Sponsors: Andreas Mensch and Catharina his wife.
Lydia Mensch of Peter and Christina, b. Jany. 22, 1793, bapt. June 8. Sponsors: The parents themselves.
Nancy Schmidt of Philipp and Elisabeth, b. April 8, 1792, bapt. June 9, 1793. Sponsors: The parents themselves.
Maria Fischer of Johann and Magdalena, b. Feb. 28, 1792, bapt. June 9, 1793. Sponsors: Johann Schimpp and Anna Maria.
Michael Manne of Jacob and Margareta, b. March 16, 1793, bapt. June 9. Sponsors: Georg Reichert and Anna his wife.
Catharina Ehrig of Michael and Sarah, b. Dec. 31, 1792, bapt. June 9, 1793. Sponsor: The mother herself.
Johann Hahn of Joh. Jac. and Elisabeth, b. Aug. 10, 1790, bapt. June 9, 1793. Sponsors: Joh. Hahn and Elisabeth his wife.
Margareta Meyer of Christopher and Sarah, b. July ---, 1792, bapt. June 9, 1793. Sponsors: Johann Hahn and Elisabeth his wife.
Christina Hector of Caspar and Anna Maria, b. May 19, 1793, bapt. June 9, 1793. Sponsor: Christina Ochsenbecker.
Sarah Hahn of Andreas and Sarah, b. May 1, 1792, bapt. June 9, 1793. Sponsors: Johann Hahn and Elisabeth his wife.

The following children were bapt. Oct. 25 and 26, 1794, by J. H.
Ch. Helmuth, Preacher in Philadelphia:
Andreas Rammel of Simon and Christina, b. Sept. 17, 1793, bapt.
Oct. 25. Sponsors: The parents themselves.
Johann Reuer of Daniel and Margareta, b. Sept. 28, bapt. Oct. 25.
Sponsors: the parents themselves.
Elisabeth May of Johann and Margareta, b. Jany. 31, bapt. Oct.
25. Sponsors: Jacob Hitschner and Magdalena his wife.
Georg Baton of Loth and Anna Barbara, b. March 27, bapt. Oct. 25.
Sponsors: Georg Reuer and Mrs. Anna Barbara Baton.
Daniel Paris of Peter and Susanna, b. Aug. 28, 1793, bapt. Oct.
25. Sponsors: The parents themselves.
Elisabeth Fuchs of Fridrich and Anna Maria, b. June 7, bapt. Oct.
25. Sponsors: Georg Muehl and Mrs. Anna Elisabeth Rotter.
Johann Schoch of Jacob and Christine, b. Oct. ---, 1793, bapt.
Oct. 25. Sponsors: The parents themselves.
Elisabeth Schneider of Peter and Margareta, b. Sept. 5, 1793,
bapt. Oct. 25. Sponsors: Phil. Schimpf and Elisabeth his
wife.
Johann Hitschner of Georg and Mariana, b. Sept. 20, 1793, bapt.
Oct. 25. Sponsors: The parents themselves.
Philipp Remster of Fridrich and Juliana, b. May 3, bapt. Oct. 25.
Sponsors: Philipp Gonklin and Barbara his wife.
Philipp Rick of Philipp and Louisa Jung, b. April 1, bapt. Oct.
25. Sponsors: Philipp Schimpp and Anna Maria his wife.
Maria Saul of Adam and Maria, b. Aug. 1, 1793, bapt. Oct. 26.
Sponsors: The parents themselves.
Johann Schoch of Jacob and Christina, b. Oct. 29, 1793, bapt.
Oct. 26. Sponsors: The parents themselves.
Elisabeth Kerrmann of Fridrich and Catharine, b. Aug. 12, bapt.
Oct. 26. Sponsors: Georg Keller and Elisabeth his wife.
Wilhelm Janson of Jacob and Margareta, b. Aug. 17, bapt. Oct. 26.
Sponsors: The parents themselves.
Wilhelm Schott of Fridrich and Susanna, b. Aug. 17, bapt. Oct.
26. Sponsors: The parents themselves.
Elisabeth Thomas of Valentin and Elisabeth, b. Jany. 29, bapt.
Oct. 26. Sponsors: The parents themselves.

The following children were bapt. on November 18, 1794, by Ludwig
Ilgen, Schoolmaster in Cohensie at that time - act of
emergency:
Lydia Wulpert of Peter and wife, b. Sept. 15, 1791, bapt. Nov.
18, 1794. Sponsors: The parents themselves.
Susanna Wulpert of Peter and wife, b. June 3, 1793, bapt. Nov.
18, 1794. Sponsors: The parents themselves.
Samuel Jordan of Adam and Catharina, b. June 13, 1793, bapt. Nov.
18, 1794. Sponsors: The parents themselves.

The following children were bapt. on Nov. 14 and 15, 1795, by
Heinr. Helmuth, Preacher in Philadelphia:
Catharina Pilgramm of Franz and Bathsaba, b. May 12, bapt. Nov.
14. Sponsors: The parents.
Sarah Schimpf of Georg and Anna Maria, b. Feb. 2, bapt. Nov. 14.

Sponsors: Philipp Schimpf and Elisabeth his wife.
Susanna Mensch of Andreas and Catharina, b. Nov. 21, 1794, bapt.
  Nov. 14. Sponsors: Michael Janson and Susanna his wife.
Daniel Janson of Michael and Susanna, b. Jany. 24, bapt. Nov. 14.
  Sponsors: Andreas Mensch and Catharina his wife.
Anna Maria Noll of Heinr. and Susanna, b. Jany. 18, bapt. Nov.
  14. Sponsors: The parents.
Susanna Paris of Peter and Susanna, b. Jany. 28, bapt. Nov. 14.
  Sponsors: The parents.
David Weck of Joh. Nicolaus and Margareta, b. Sept. 25, bapt.
  Nov. 14. Sponsors: David Kehk and Margare his wife.
Jacob Rammel of Joh. Georg and Regina, b. Aug. 9, bapt. Nov. 14.
  Sponsors: The parents.
David Hitschner of Jacob and Elisabeth, b. Feb. 8, bapt. Nov. 14.
  Sponsors: The parents.
Elisabeth Coombs of Joel and Elisabeth, b. Oct. 9, bapt. Nov. 14.
  Sponsor: The mother.
Georg Kautz of Adam and Barbara, b. April 13, bapt. Nov. 14.
  Sponsors: Georg Kautz and Anna his wife.
Hanna Hahn of Johann and Catharina, b. Sept. 16, 1793, bapt. Nov.
  14. Sponsor: Elisabeth Hahn.
Maria Hahn of Johann and Catharina, b. April 30, bapt. Nov. 14.
  Sponsor: Johann Hahn.
Elisabeth Bacon of Loth and Barbara, b. Sept. 16, bapt. Nov. 14.
  Sponsor: Mother of the child.
Elisabeth Schimpf of Sebastian and Catharina, b. Sept 12, bapt.
  Nov. 14. Sponsor: Elisabeth Schimpf.
Jacob Hahn of Jacob and Elisabeth, b. May 24, 1793, bapt. Nov.
  15. Sponsors: Joh. Hahn and Elisabeth his wife.
Hanna Schimpf of Andreas and Margareta, b. Dec. 20, 1794,
  baptized Nov. 15. Sponsors: Theodor Wenzel and Eva his wife.
Salome Schimpf of Phil. and Catharina, b. Dec. 19, 1794, bapt.
  Nov. 15. Sponsors: Joh. Georg Rothkerb and Salome his wife.
Hanna Jung of Adam and Maria, b. Aug. 24, 1794, bapt. Nov. 15.
  Sponsors: The parents.
Wilhelm Schoch of Jacob and Christina, b. Nov. 22, 1794, bapt.
  Nov. 15. Sponsors: The parents.
Christian Hess of Tobias and Maria, b. Aug. 7, 1794, bapt. Nov.
  15. Sponsors: Christian Schaeffer and Maria his wife.
David Keller of Georg and Elisabeth, b. May 5, bapt. Nov. 15.
  Sponsors: The parents.
Georg Hinne of Adam and Susanna, b. Sept. 13, 1794, bapt. Nov.
  15. Sponsors: David Kehk and Margareta his wife.
Elisabeth Holzscheld of Johann and Maria, b. Aug. 10, 1794, bapt.
  Nov. 15. Sponsors: David Kehk and Margareta his wife.
Anna Maria Manny of Jacob and Margareta, b. Nov. 26, 1794, bapt.
  Nov. 15. Sponsor: Maria Manny.
Margareta Painter of Georg and Margareta, b. April 14, bapt. Nov.
  15. Sponsor: The mother of the child.
Susanna Ziegler of Theobald and Magdalena, b. July 25, bapt. Nov.
  15. Sponsors: The parents.
Johann Fischer of Johann and Magdalena, b. Feb. 1, 1794, bapt.
  Nov. 15. Sponsors: The parents.
Catharina Sterge of Johann and Elisabeth, b. Aug. 23, 1793, bapt.

Nov. 15. Sponsors; Georg Kammer and the mother of the child.
Johann Sterge of Johann and Elisabeth, b. Aug. 31, bapt. Nov. 15.
Sponsors: The parents.

The following children were bapt. on Nov. 5 and 6, 1796, by
  Johann Friedrich Schmidt, Lutheran Preacher at Philadelphia:
Henrich Rammel of Simon and Christina, b. Dec. 23, 1795, bapt.
  Nov. 5, 1796. Sponsors: The parents.
David Delshoefer of Jacob and Susanna, b. Nov. 14, 1795, bapt.
  Nov. 5. Sponsors: The parents.
David Mensch of Peter and Christina, b. Nov. 13, 1795, bapt. Nov.
  5. Sponsors: The parents.
Elisabeth Mueller of Matthias and Susanna, b. Jany. 5, 1796,
  bapt. Nov. 5. Sponsors: The parents.
Wilhelm Schimpf of Wilhelm and Maria Magdalena, b. March 13,
  1796, bapt. Nov. 5. Sponsors: The parents.
Margaretha Mensch of Benjamin and Hanna, b. Aug. 22, 1793, bapt.
  Nov. 5. Sponsors: The parents.
Ludwig Bender of Ludwig and Margareth, b. Sept. 22, 1795, bapt.
  Nov. 5. Sponsors: Michael Janson and Susanna his wife.
Richard Johnson of Johann and Catharina, b. Nov. 21, 1795, bapt.
  Nov. 5. Sponsors: The parents.
Sara Schmick of Wilhelm and A. Maria, b. July 28, 1796, bapt.
  Nov. 5. Sponsors: Johannes Adler and Barbara his wife.
James Eff of Friedrich and Susanna, b. April 6, 1794, bapt. Nov.
  5. Sponsors: Johann Adler and Barbara his wife.
Johann Christoph Wilhelm Ilgen of Ludwig Albrecht Wilhelm and A.
  Barbara, b. Dec. 7, 1795, bapt. Nov. 5. Sponsors: The
  parents.
Margarethe Kerman of Friedrich and Catharina, b. Dec. 28, 1795,
  bapt. Nov. 6. Sponsors: Henrich Saul and A. Maria his wife.
Margaretha Heins of Georg and Patience, b. Aug. 8, 1796, bapt.
  Nov. 6. Sponsors: Friedrich Remster and Juliana his wife.
Johannes Dendelspeck of Johann and Christina, b. Oct. 16, 1795,
  bapt. Nov. 6. Sponsors: The parents.
Elisabeth Hepner of Johann and A. Maria, b. Nov. 8, 1794, bapt.
  Nov. 6. Sponsors: Jacob Hitschner and Elisabeth his wife.
A. Maria Meyer of Daniel and Margarethe, b. Feb. 6, 1796, bapt.
  Nov. 6. Sponsor: A. Maria Kendel.
Hanna Schmick of Philip and Elisabeth, b. June 10, 1796, bapt.
  Nov. 6. Sponsors: The parents.
Philip Jung of Henrich and Elisabeth, b. Oct. 24, 1793, bapt.
  Nov. 6. Sponsor: Philip Schimpf.
Margarethe Jung of Henrich and Elisabeth, b. Dec. 25, 1795, bapt.
  Nov. 6. Sponsor: Margarethe Dillshoeff.
Jacob May of Johannes and Margarethe, b. Jany. 28, 1796, bapt.
  Nov. 6. Sponsors: The parents.
Rosanna Connor of Patrick and Barbara, b. April 2, 1796, bapt.
  Nov. 6. Sponsors: The parents.
Elisabeth Sauter of Georg and Catharina, b. Oct. 16, 1796, bapt.
  Nov. 6. Sponsors: Henrich Oth and Elisabeth his wife.
Henrich Thomas of Valentin and Elisabeth, b. Sept. 19, 1796,
  bapt. Nov. 6. Sponsors: The parents.
Hesekiel Hahn of Andreas and Sara, b. Dec. 16, 1793, bapt. Nov.

FRIESBURG EMANUEL LUTHERAN CHURCH 223

6, d. Sept. 10, 1817. Sponsors: Johann Hahn and Elisabeth his wife.
Margarethe Horn of Johannes and Catharina, b. Jany. 25, 1795, bapt. Nov. 6. Sponsors: Peter Kronberger and Margarethe his wife.
Margarethe Hitschner of Andreas and Sara, b. June 1, 1794, bapt. Nov. 6. Sponsors: Philip Schimpf and Elisabeth his wife.
Christina Hitschner of Andreas and Sara, b. Sept. 15, 1796, bapt. Nov. 6. Sponsor: Sara Rothkoep.
Elisabeth Hahn of Jacob and Elisabeth, b. April 30, 1796, bapt. Nov. 6. Sponsors: Johann Hahn and Elisabeth his wife.

The following children were bapt. on May 5 and 6, 1798, by H. Helmuth:
Georg Schimp of Georg and Anna Maria, b. July 15, 1797, bapt. May 5. Sponsors: The parents.
Andreas Mensch of Andreas and Catharina, b. Aug. 28, 1797, bapt. May 5. Sponsors: The parents.
Nancy Itschner of Martin and Anna Maria, b. Aug. 1, 1797, bapt. May 5. Sponsors: The parents.
Magdalena Hepner of Johann and Anna Maria, b. Nov. 27, 1796, bapt. May 5. Sponsors: Jacob Itschner and Magdalena his wife.
Peter Janson of Daniel and Juliana, b. Jany. 4, bapt. May 5. Sponsors: The parents.
Hanna Bilgramm of Franz and Berseba, b. Dec. 24, 1797, bapt. May 5. Sponsors: Johann Hahn and the parents.
Philipp Jung of Adam and Maria, b. Nov. 21, 1797, bapt. May 5. Sponsors: The parents.
Margareta Schimp of Johann and Charlotta, b. Aug. 19, 1797, bapt. May 5. Sponsors: The parents.
Elisabeth Mickel of Josua and Rosina, b. Feb. 2, 1797, bapt. May 5. Sponsors: Joseph Staut and Rosina his wife.
Catharina Illgen of Ludwig and Barbara, b. Dec. 7, 1797, bapt. May 5. Sponsor: Catharina Schimp.
Johann Schimp of Sebastian and Catharina, b. July 2, 1797, bapt. May 5. Sponsors: The parents.
Sarah Janson of Michael and Susanna, b. July 15, 1797, bapt. May 6. Sponsor: The mother of the child.
Johann Schimp of Wilhelm and Maria Magdal, b. Oct. 15, 1797, bapt. May 5. Sponsors: Joh. Schimp and Charlotta his wife.
Rebecca Delshefer of Jacob and Susanna, b. Jany. 27, bapt. May 5. Sponsors: Joh. Schimp and Charlotta his wife.
Nancy Delshefer of Elisabeth (illegitimate), b. March 25, 1797, bapt. May 3. Sponsors: Jacob Delshefer and Susanna his wife.
Susanna Hitschner of Jacob and Elisabeth, b. Nov. 14, 1797, bapt. May 5. Sponsors: The parents.
Johann Hefft of Friedr. and Susanna, b. June 7, 1797, bapt. May 5. Sponsors: Johann Adler and Anna Barbara his wife.
Georg Keller of Georg and Elisabeth, b. May 20, 1797, bapt. May 5. Sponsors: The parents.
Adam Kautz and Anna Kautz (twins) of Adam and Barbara, b. July 28, 1791, bapt. May 5. Sponsors: Georg Kautz and Anna his wife.
James Clement of James and Jean, b. Sept. 4, 1797, bapt. May 5.

Sponsor: Margareta Cronenberger.
Peter Paris of Peter and Susanna, b. March 13, 1797, bapt. May 5. Sponsors: The parents.
Catharina Schoch of Daniel and Anna Maria, b. Aug. 5, 1797, bapt. May 5. Sponsors: The parents.
Margareta Saul of Johann Adam and Anna Maria, b. Aug. 14, 1797, bapt. May 5. Sponsors: Andreas Mensch and Catharina his wife.
Anna Maria Dendelspeck of Johann and Christina, b. Jany. 23, bapt. May 5. Sponsors: Joh. Adam Saul and Anna Maria his wife.
Catharina Tanzebecher of Georg and Maria, b. May 2, bapt. May 5. Sponsors: Ludw. Tanzenbecher and Catharina his wife.
Susanna Sarge of Peter and Catharina, b. Oct. 17, 1796, bapt. May 5. Sponsor: Margareta Tanzenbecher.
Johann Fuchs and Margareta Fuchs (twins) of Friedr. and Anna Maria, b. March 31, 1797, bapt. May 5. Sponsor: The mother of the children.
Margareta Schimpp of Philipp and Catharina, b. April 8, bapt. May 6. Sponsors: Georg Rothkepp and Salome his wife.
Jacob Scheuermann of Mathias and Margareta, b. Jany. 14, bapt. May 6. Sponsors: The parents.
David Schoch of Jacob and Christina, b. Sept. 7, 1797, bapt. May 6. Sponsors: The parents.
Georg Miller of Johann and Sarah, b. July 27, bapt. May 6. Sponsors: Georg Schimp and Maria his wife.
Archebald Mensch of Beniamin and Anna, b. Sept. 20, bapt. May 6. Sponsors: The parents.
Beniamin Remster of Friedr and Juliana, b. May 1, 1797, bapt. May 6. Sponsors: Beniamin Mensch and Hanna his wife.
Christina Pfeiler of David and Susanna, b. April 9, bapt. May 6. Sponsors: Jacob Dilshefer and Susanna his wife.
Anna Elisabeth Meyer of Christoph and Sarah, b. Aug. 17, bapt. May 6. Sponsors: Valentin Thomason and Anna Elisab. his wife.
Christina Heuer of Daniel and Margareta, b. Nov. 24, 1797, bapt. May 6. Sponsors: Simon Rammel and Christina his wife.
Johann Saul of Heinrich and Maria, b. June 22, 1797, bapt. May 6. Sponsors: Adam Saul and Margareta his wife.
Johann Georg Starke of Johann and Elisabeth, b. Feb. 21, bapt. May 6. Sponsor: Joh. Georg Kammer.
Jacob Dillshefer of Philipp and Margareta, b. Feb. 5, 1797, bapt. May 6. Sponsors: Jacob Dilshefer and Susanna his wife.
Anna Schimp of Andreas and Margareta, b. Sept. 12, 1797, bapt. May 6. Sponsors: The parents.
Simon Horn of Johann and Catharina, b. March 28, bapt. May 6. Sponsors: Margareta Bechler.
Margareta Henne of Adam and Susanna, b. March 23, 1796, bapt. May 6. Sponsors: David Kehk and Margareta his wife.
Anna Maria Henne of Adam and Susanna, b. Jany. 23, bapt. May 6. Sponsors: David Kehk and Margareta his wife.

The following children were bapt. on May 3 and 4, 1800, by Christian Endress, Evang. Luth. Preacher in Frankfurt:
Elisabeth Schoch of Daniel and Anna Maria, b. Feb. 13, 1800, bapt. May 3. Sponsors: The parents.

Johannes Holscheid of Johannes and Maria, b. April 15, 1798, bapt. May 3. Sponsors: David Kahk and Margarethe his wife.
Matthias Hitschner of Jacob and Elisabeth, b. Dec. 15, 1799, bapt. May 3. Sponsors: The parents.
Matthias Mueller of Matthias and Susanna, b. July 31, 1798, bapt. May 3. Sponsors: The parents.
Sarah May of Johannes and Margarethe, b. Aug. 16, 1798, bapt. May 3. Sponsors: The parents.
Catharina Fuchs of Friedrich and Anne Marie, b. Feb. 23, 1800, bapt. May 3. Sponsors: The parents.
Maria Hitschner of Martin and Maria, b. May 28, 1799, bapt. May 3. Sponsors: The parents.
Margaretha Jansen of Daniel and Juliana, b. Feb. 14, 1800, bapt. May 3. Sponsor: Mrs. Margarethe Bechler.
Johann Georg Thomas of Valentin and Elisabeth, b. Feb. 18, 1799, bapt. May 3. Sponsors: The parents.
Hanna Paris of Peter and Susanna, b. July 17, 1799, bapt. May 3. Sponsors: The parents.
Johann Georg Schmidt of Philip and Elisabeth, b. May 21, 1798, bapt. May 3. Sponsors: The parents.
Elisabeth Kautz of Adam and Barbara, b. March 14, 1800, bapt. May 3. Sponsors: The father and Anna Kautz.
Johann Heinrich Huest of Johann Fr. and Susanna, b. July 15, 1799, bapt. May 3. Sponsors: Henrich Kendel and Anna Maria Kendel.
Johannes Jansen of Johannes and Catharina, b. July 21, 1798, bapt. May 3. Sponsors: The parents.
Enoch Schimpf of Johannes and Charlotte, b. Nov. 16, 1799, bapt. May 3. Sponsors: The parents.
Georg Schimpf of Sebastian and Catherine, b. Aug. 17, 1799, bapt. May 3. Sponsors: The parents.
David Schimpf of Andreas and Margarethe, b. Feb. 10, 1800, bapt. May 3. Sponsors: The parents.
Richard Hahn of Johannes and Catherine, b. Aug. 6, 1798, bapt. May 3. Sponsors: The grandparents Johannes Hahn and Elisabeth.
Jonathan Hahn of Jonathan and Elisabetha, b. Jany. 12, 1799, bapt. May 3. Sponsors: The grandparents Johannes Hahn and Elisabeth.
Anna Maria Weck of Johann Nicolaus and Margareth, b. March 20, 1799, bapt. May 3. Sponsors: The parents.
Anna Mensch of Peter and Christina, b. Aug. 21, 1799, bapt. May 3. Sponsors: The parents.
Martin Weibel of Jesse and Elisabeth, b. Feb. 28, 1800, bapt. May 4. Sponsors: Daniel Schoch and Anna Maria his wife.
Friedrich Kermann of Friedrich and Catharina, b. Aug. 17, 1798, bapt. May 4. Sponsors: The parents.
Peter Bender of Ludwig and Margaretha, b. March 10, 1800, bapt. May 4. Sponsors: Johann Schimpf and Charlotte his wife.
Anna Maria Fuchs of Johannes and Christine, b. Sept. 15, 1799, bapt. May 4. Sponsors: Daniel Schoch and Anna Maria his wife.
Johann Georg Connover of Wilhelm and Barbara, b. Sept. 11, 1798, bapt. May 4. Sponsors: Georg Rothkopf and Salome his wife.
Wilhelm Connover of Wilhelm and Barbara, b. Feb. 11, 1800, bapt.

May 4. Sponsors: Georg Rothkopf and Salome his wife.
Margaretha Dillsheber of Philip and Margaretha, b. March 9, 1799, bapt. May 4. Sponsors: The parents.
Philip Schimpf of Philip and Catharina, b. Feb. 11, 1800, bapt. May 4. Sponsors: The parents.
Ezechiel German of Ruben and Elisabeth, b. Dec. 14, 1798, bapt. May 4. Sponsor: Cath. Fries.
Christina Henne of Adam and Susanna, b. Oct. 5, 1799, bapt. May 4. Sponsors: Simon Rammel and Christina his wife.
Joseph Mickel of Josua and Rosina, b. Dec. 10, 1799, bapt. May 4. Sponsors: Grandparents Joseph Staut and Rosina his wife.
Don Hahn of Andreas and Sarah, b. June 21, 1798, bapt. May 4. Sponsors: Johann Hahn and Elisabeth his wife, Grandparents.
Jonathan Hahn of Jacob and Elisabeth, b. March 6, 1800, bapt. May 4. Sponsors: Johann Hahn and Elisabeth his wife, Grandparents.
Jacob Seigre of Peter and Catharina, b. May 2, 1799, bapt. May 4. Sponsors: Jacob Danzebecher and Hanna his wife.
Jacob Dendelsbeck of Johann and Christina, b. Dec. 27, 1799, bapt. May 4. Sponsors: Jacob Hitschner and Elisabeth his wife.
Samuel Schneider of Peter and Elisabeth, b. Nov. 9, 1798, bapt. May 4. Sponsors: Peter Croneberger and Elisabeth his wife.
Catharina Sauder of Georg and Catharina, b. April 22, 1799, bapt. May 4. Sponsors: Martin Ott and Margaretha his wife.
Martin Ott of Henrich and Elisabeth, b. Oct. 26, 1799, bapt. May 4. Sponsors: Martin Ott and Margaretha his wife.
Wilhelm Heins of Georg and Patience, b. May 21, 1799, bapt. May 4. Sponsors: Johann Adler and Anna Barbara his wife.

Bapt. June 1, 1800, by Christn. Endress:
Andreas Kast of Jacob and Anna Barbara b. March 28, 1798. Sponsors: The parents.
Mariana Rotter of Jacob and Latitia b. Aug. 13, 1796. Sponsors: Grandparents, Elisabeth Rotter and the father.
Michael Rotter of Jacob and Latitia b. March 29, 1798. Sponsors: Grandparents, Elisabeth Rotter and the father.
Mariana Rotter of Jacob and Latitia b. Dec. 16, 1799. Sponsors: Grandparents, Elisabeth Rotter and the father.
Philip Platz of Philip and Elizabeth b. Sept 12, 1799. Sponsors: The parents.

Bapt. July 6, 1800, by Christn Endress:
Hannah Brennesholz of Henrich and Philippine b. April 26, 1797. Sponsors: Jacob Rothkap and Barbara his wife.
Jacob Brennesholz of Henrich and Philippine b. Oct. 4, 1799. Sponsors: Jacob Rothkap and Barbara his wife.
Jacob Fries Lummus of Wilhelm, D. M. D. and Elisabeth b. June 1, 1800. Sponsors: Jacob Fries and Dorcas his wife.

Bapt. Aug. 3, 1800, by J. H. Ch. Helmuth, D. D.:
Jacob Schneider of Peter and Elisabeth b. June 19, 1800. Sponsors: The parents.
Louisa Jung of Adam and Maria b. June 17, 1800. Sponsors: The

parents.
Anna Mueller of Johann and Sarah b. Sept. 4, 1799. Sponsors: Peter Mensch and Christina his wife.
Philippina (Phebe) Mensch of Benjamin and Hanna b. April 15, 1800. Sponsors: The parents.

Bapt. Oct 5, 1800, by Christn Endress:
Abijah Scholl of Wilhelm and Margaretha b. Jany. 26, 1800. Sponsors: David Kehk and Margaretha his wife, the grandparents.

Bapt. Nov. 2, 1800:
Daniel Hahn of Jonathan and Elisabeth b. Oct. 10, 1800. Sponsors: Johannes Hahn and Elisabeth his wife, the grandparents.
Henrich Danzenberger of Georg and Maria b. Sept. 15, 1800. Sponsors: The parents themselves.

Bapt. Dec. 17, 1800:
Joseph Mensch of Andreas and Cathar. b. Oct. 29, 1800. Sponsors: Joseph Staut and Rosina his wife.

Bapt. Dec. 25, 1800:
Simon Bechler of Christian and Susanna b. July 31, 1800. Sponsors: Ludwig Danzenbecher and Catharina his wife.

Bapt. Febry. 2, 1801:
Johann Henrich German of Ruben and Elisabeth b. Oct. 2, 1800. Sponsor: Catharina Fries.

Bapt. March 1, 1801:
Ludwig Danzenbecher of Jacob and Hanna b. Dec. 30, 1800. Sponsors: Ludwig Danzenbecher and Catharina his wife, the grandparents.
Jacob Caspar of Lorenz and Susanna b. March 22, 1798. Sponsors: Ludwig Danzenbecher and Catharina his wife.
Georg Pfeiler of Johann and Margaretha b. Jany. 14, 1797. Sponsor: Barbara Connor.
Heinrich Serger of Johan and Margaretha b. Nov. 23, 1800. Sponsors: Heinrich Ott and Elisabetha his wife.

Bapt. April 5, 1801, Easter:
Elisabeth Schoch of Jacob and Christina, b. March 2, 1801. Sponsors: The parents.
Johann Mueller of Friederich and Elisabetha, b. Feb. 18, 1801. Sponsors: Johann Frevel and Margaretha his wife, great grandparents.
Enoch Wenzel of Adam and Barbara, b. Jany. 18, 1801. Sponsors: The mother.

Bapt. May 3, 1801:
David Kerman of Friedrich and Catharina b. Sept. 20, 1800. Sponsors: David Kehk and Margaretha his wife.
Catharina Hahn of Johannes and Catharina b. June 19, 1800.

EARLY CHURCH RECORDS OF SALEM COUNTY

Sponsors: Johannes Hahn and Elisabeth his wife, the grandparents.
Susanna Heyer of Daniel and Margarethe b. Dec. 19, 1800. Sponsors: The parents.

Bapt. June 7, 1801:
Jacob Dilsheber of Jacob and Susanna b. July 31, 1800. Sponsors: The parents.

Bapt. July 26, 1801:
Anna Schoch of Wilhelm and Anna b. Oct. 5, 1800. Sponsors: Jacob Schoch and Christina his wife.

Bapt. Aug. 30, 1801, by C. E.:
Elisabeth Kast of Jacob and Anna Barbara b. Dec. 5, 1800. Sponsors: The parents.

Bapt. Oct. 25, 1801, by Christn. Endress:
Jacob Dilsheber of Jacob and Susanna, b. July 31, 1800. Sponsors: The parents.

Children bapt. on April 30 and May 1, 1803, by J. F. Schmidt, Preacher in Philadelphia:
Simon String of David and Louise, b. Aug. 25, 1799, bapt. April 30. Sponsor: The mother.
Joseph Litle of William and Nancy, b. Jany. 6, 1800, bapt. May 1. Sponsors: Joh. Nie. Waks and wife.

Bapt. Oct. 18, 1806:
Maria German Friess (wife of Philip Friess) of John and Mary b. Feb. 12, 1765.

BURIALS

Register of those to whom interment was accorded in honest way and Christian rite:

Dec. 27, 1750. Conradt Israel, b. at Bentzneck, Dec. 18th this year the local schoolmaster's Conradt Israel Aberle's honestly procreated son.
Sept. 13, 1751. Barbara, Georg Leonhardt Krumrein's honestly procreated little dau.
Sept. 16 this year. Anna, Gottfried Lauerer's wife.
Nov. 3, 1751. Johann Georg Balz, the local master tailor.
Feb. 19, 1752. Hanns Martin, son of Hs. Martin Halter, Master at the Glassworks.
Aug. 5, 1752. Ludwig Hahn's little dau., Charlotta, of this place.
Aug. 13, 1752. Theobald Knopp of single state.
Same day. Johannes, Christian Asel' at the Glassworks honestly procreated son, single.
22 7 brx 1752. Sovia Elisabetha, wife of the sacristan Philipp Schmuenker.
July 27, 1753. Anna Margretha, nee Johnson, step-dau. of Michael

Mueller.
Sept. 8, 1753. Michael Bach, a married servant.
Sept. 11, 1753. Michael Dilshoefer a local planter.
Same day. Christian Mich: Dilshoefer's child at the same time buried with his father.
Dec. 22, 1753. Johann Jacob, Leonhard Meyer's honestly procreated son.
Oct. 8, 1753. Sabina Hammer a servant woman.
Dec. 22, 1753. Johann Jacob, Leonhard Meyer's honestly procreated son.
Jany. 24, 1754. Daniel, youngest son of first marriage of the remarried Mrs. Dilshoefer, now Schwaemle.
Feb. 29, 1754. Johann Juerg Koelsch inhabitant of this congregation.
May 17, 1754. Anna Elisabeth, master Adam Hohenschild's wife.
Sept. 4, 1754. Johann Adam Hohenschild a planter.
Nov. 26, 1754. Maria, wife of Simon Meyer, resident of Cohacken.
Dec. 22, 1754. The Glassblower Hans Martin Halter's wife called Catharina.
Feb. 11, 1755. Eva, wife of Simon Walter, weaver and local resident.
June 4, 1755. The tailor Michael Schwaille's wife, called Catharina.
Sept. 1755. Jurg Hoff, servant of Philip Sauter.
March 21, 1756. Jacob Fries' honestly procreated dau. Anna Maria.
April 21 Same Year. Johann Schwaemle's wife called Elisabetha.
April 14, 1765. Simon Dilshoeffer, Michael Dilshoeffer's legitimate son.
Aug. 11, 1765. Bodo Otto's wife Catharina.
Nov. 9, 1765. Adam Maurer's wife Christina and one child.
Nov. 20, 1765. Otto Crocelius' wife Ottilia.
Nov. 2, 1765. Peter Sauder's wife Elisabeth.
Dec. 31, 1765. Johann Hahn's matrimonially procreated dau. A: Margrta.
Jan. 8, 1766. Jacob Fries matrimonially procreated dau. Maria.
July 10, 1766. Matias Wolport's little dau. and same date a little dau. of the old Hans Link.
July 27, 1766. Johan Georg Koelsch's wife named Margretha.
Sept. 6, 1766. Matias Ross' little son.
Sept. 13, 1766. Heinrich Wolff's little dau.
Sept. 18, 1766. Georg Miller's little dau.
Oct. 4, 1766. Georg Abla's wife.
Nov. 5, 1766. Friederich Dendelsbecke.
Dec. 1, 1766. Adam Fistar's little dau.
Dec. 3, 1766. Adam Maurer's wife.
Dec. 5, 1766. Peter Borion, servant of Michael Miller.
Dec. 10, 1766. Peter Heintz.
March 2, 1767. Abraham Zimmerman's wife Anna.
March 2, 1767. Joh: Dendelsbeck's little dau.
April 18, 1767. Martin Wolff.
May 22, 1767. Christian Bender.
July 31, 1767. Friederich Herrmann.
Sept. 23, 1767. Friederich Hoeltzel's little dau.

EARLY CHURCH RECORDS OF SALEM COUNTY

Sept. 30, 1767. Joh: Martin Halter.
Oct. 5, 1767. Daniel Straub.
Nov. 7, 1767. Johan Lutz's little son.
Nov. 10, 1767. Vallentin Reihling, Councilman.
Jany. 21, 1768. Nicolaus Oelbers, Bookkeeper with Mr. Richard Wistar.
Elisabet a dau. of Jacob Hitchner and his wife.
Nov. 15, 1772. Magdalena b. 1758, d. Nov. 13, 1772 with high fever buried Nov. 15 by Henr. Muhlenberg, Jun.

Mr. Jacob Fries' wife b. Dec. 11, 1723 in Germany and the name given Anna Margaretha d. Dec. 4, 1774 and was buried on the 6th of this by his Reverency the Parson Mr. Heinrich Muehlenberger.
Mr. Jacob Fries' dau. b. June 20, 1763 receiving in Holy Baptism the name Elisabetha, d. Dec. 10, 1777 and was buried on the 12th inst. by me Jacob Van Lahnen aged 14 years, 5 months and 20 days.
Mr. Simon Sauder's wife, a dau. of Mr. Jacob Fries, b. Feb. 5, 1744 receiving in Holy Baptism the name Anna Margaretha, d. April 27, 1778 and was buried on the 28th ditto in the Reformed Cemetery, aged 34 years 2 months and 22 days.
Johann Heinrich Fries, son of Jacob Fries was b. Dec. 21, 1752, d. July 12, 1778 and was buried on the 14th ditto by me Jacob Van Lahnen, aged 25 years 6 months and 20 days.
Johann Georg, legitimate son of Mr. Jacob Fries, was b. Sept. 3, 1750, d. May 8, 1780, aged 29 years 3 months and 25 days and was buried on May 10th.
Peter, legitimate son of Mr. Jacob Fries, was b. July 29, 1759, d. June 7 and was buried on the 9th aged 20 years 10 months and 7 days.

The following persons were buried by me, Christian Breymann, the temporary local schoolmaster:
Maria Catharina Maurer, wife of Mr. Adam Maurer, given age about 50 years, d. March 5 and was buried March 7, 1781.
A child named Daniel Gerdrick was b. Dec. 22, 1779, and d. March 26 and was buried March 27, 1781.
Mr. Georg Mueller, Trustee of this congregation, b. July 1, 1738, d. on May 29, and was buried July (?) 1, 1781.
Christina Hoyer, dau. of Mr. Conrad Hoeyer was b. May 5, 1779, d. on June 19 and was buried on June 20, 1781.
David Koeck of Cath: Religion, son of Mr. David Koeck was b. March 14, 1779, d. on 27th and was buried on June 28, 1781.
Johannes Adler, son of Mr. Johannes Adler, was b. Aug. 4, 1780, d. July 7 and was buried July 8, 1781.
Jacob Dilshoever, son of Mr. Johannes Dilshoever, was b. Jan. 11, 1781, d. July 11 and was buried July 13, 1781.
Philipp Fries, son of Joh: Georg Fries deceased, b. Nov. 14, 1774, d. Aug. 22 and was buried Aug. 24, 1781.
Mr. Georg Mepold was b. in Anno 1700 in Germany, d. Nov. 8 and was buried Nov. 10, 1781.
Mr. Henrich Faber was b. in the year 1721 in Germany, d. Dec. 3 and was buried Dec. 4, 1781.
Anna Margaretha Toffel, widow of Mr. Peter Toffel, deceased, was

b. on July 17, 1721 in Leisel-Heim, Palatinate, d. Dec. 27 and
   was buried Dec. 28, 1781.
Anna Wulpert, dau. of Mr. Peter Wulpert, b. Jany. 28, 1782, d.
   Feb. 12 and was buried Feb. 14, 1782.
Henrich Faber was b. in Germany in the month of Jan. 1771, d.
   Dec. 3, 1781 and was buried Dec. 5 same year.
Johanne married to Monrohe was b. in Germany in the electorate of
   Hanover, d. Jan. 18 and was buried Jany. 19, 1782.
Anna Margaretha, married to Peter Toffel, was b. in the
   Palatinate July 17, 1721, d. Dec. 27 and was buried on the 29,
   1781.
Mrs. Elisabeth Dilshoever was b. Jany. 1, 1754 in America, d.
   March 12 and was buried the 13th, 1782.
Joh: Nicolaus Weck, son of Mr. Joh: Nicol: Weck, Junior, was b.
   March 14, 1782, d. March 19 and was buried March 20, 1782.
Conrad Hoyer was b. 1744 in Germany, d. May 30 and was buried May
   31, 1782.
Anna, wife of Georg Meopald, was b. in the Palatinate on June 25,
   1712, d. May 4 and was buried May 6, 1782.
William Sauther, a son of Mr. Peter Saugher, was b. April 29,
   1782, d. Oct. 21 and was buried Oct. 23, 1782.
Mr. Matthias Miller was b. in Margraviate Baden Baden in the year
   1732, d. Jany. 21 and was buried 23rd, 1783.
Adam Mueller, a son of Mr. Michael Miller, was b. April 23, 1776,
   d. the 11th and was buried the 13th of April, 1783.
Anna Margaretha, wife of Mr. Conrad Bauer, was b. in Germany, d.
   the 10th and was buried Aug. 12, 1782.
Mr. Adam Fix, Elder of the church, was b. in Dunzenheim in Alsace
   Jan. 8, 1720, d. on Jan. 15 and was buried on the 17th S. M.
   1783.
Carolina Christina Bauer, dau. of Mr. Conrad Bauer, was b. Nov.
   27, 1775, d. on the 16th and was buried on Feb. 18, 1783.
Johannes Soeffner was b. at Pfaffenhofen in Wuertenberg on Dec.
   21, 1726, d. March 20 and was buried on the 22nd, 1783.
Elisabeth Soeffner, wife of Johannes Soeffner, was b. at Flambora
   in the Palatinate, d. May 17 and was buried May 18, 1783.
Phoebe, legitimate dau. of Mr. Jacob Fries, Senior, was b. May
   25, 1783, d. May 27 and was buried May 28, 1783, aged 1 day and
   17 hours.
Johann Adam Jansen, legitimate son of Mr. Michael Jansen, was b.
   May 20, d. July 8 and was buried July 9, 1783, aged 7 weeks.

Register of persons who were buried by me, the temporary local
   schoolmaster, Luois Ilgen:
Jacob Fries, Phillipp Fries' legitimate son, was b. March 8, d.
   Sept. 13 and was buried Sept. 15, 1784, aged 6 months and 6
   days.
Heinerich Frewel, Johannes Frewel's legitimate son, was buried
   Sept. 30, 1784, aged 1 year less 9 days.
Johannes Noll, Hendrick Noll's legitimate son, d. Oct. 1 and was
   buried Oct. 2, 1784, aged 2 years, 7 months and 19 days.
Georg Gauger was b. in Germany May 12 Anno 1704, d. Oct. 6 and
   buried on Oct. 8, 1784 in the local God's acre aside of
   Immanuel's church, aged 80 years, 4 months, 3 weeks and 1 day.

Israel Baken, legitimate son of Lot Baken, was b. on Oct. 11, 1783, d. Oct. 6 and was buried Oct. 8, 1784.
Maria Dillzhoefer, a little dau. of Jacob Dilshoefer was b. Aug. 23, 1783, d. Oct. 10 and was buried Oct. 12, 1784.
Elisabeth Johnson, legitimate dau. of Paul Johnson, was b. Aug. 31, 1764, d. Oct. 19, 1784 and was buried Oct. 21, 1784, aged 20 years, 1 month and 18 days.
Catharina Rammel, Simon Rammel's legitimate little dau., was b. Sept. 11, 1784, d. Oct. 25 and was buried Oct. 26, 1784.
Anna Fries, Friedrich Fries matrimonially procreated dau., was b. June 26, 1783, d. Oct. 26 and was buried on Oct. 28, 1784, aged 1 year and 4 months.
Georg Straub, John Straub's legitimate son, was b. April 2, 1768, d. Oct. 15 and was buried Oct. 17, 1784, aged 16 years, 7 months and 12 days.
Anna Hammer was b. in Germany under Wuertemberg's ruler, d. Dec. 1 and was buried Dec. 3, 1784.
Adam Maurer, native of the Margraviate Anspach and the village Doeckingen at Heidenheim by Hanekamm d. and was buried in the month of May 1785.
Johann George Preus, a native of the Duchy of Wuertemberg, d. and was buried in the year 1785.
Catharina Cundermann, an old woman, who had been supported for quite a while by the township and whom Jacob Miller had ordered to be buried at his expense d. and was buried in 1785.
Dewald Rotter d. and was buried 1785.
Anna Barbara Kautz (by second marriage) Mann, nee Wuertz, of the Margraviate Hessen - Darmstadt and village Hohenlingen, d. and was buried in the month of Sept., 1785, aged 79 years and 9 months.
Catharina Margaretha Rosina Wulperth d. and buried in 1785.
Maria Magdalena Cronenberger, nee Leidinger, a native of Imperial Lands in the County of Falckenstein, d. and buried in the year 1785.
Johann Michael Wulperth d. and buried in the year 1785.
Catharina Plenninger, a native of the duchy of Wuertemberg, d. and buried here in 1785.
Marcus Kermann, a native of the village Kehlen by Strassburg, d. and buried in the year 1785, aged 54 years.
Ludwig Albrecht Wilhelm Ilgen's (local schoolmaster) matrimonially procreated little dau. Hanna, b., d. and buried the very same year 1786.
Friedrich Schott's matrimonially procreated little dau. Susanna d. and buried 1786.

Persons buried during the year 1798:
George Kautz, July 9, aged 63 years.
Theobald Rutter, Aug. 12th.
Adam Saul, Junr., ditto 14th killed by cedar tree.
George Link, Aug. 21, drowned in Alloways Creek.
Catharina Rutter, Sept. 20th.
George Keller, 8br. the 19th.
Francis Pilgram the same month (?).

In the year 1799:
John Heft, Jan. 14th.

March 24, 1801:
Jacob Fries for many years an Elder and Benefactor of the Emanuel's Church and Congregation was b. Feb. 17 old style, A. D. 1715, procreated in his first marriage eleven children (of whom two sons survived him) and in his second matrimony six daus., of whom yet four are alive. He d. old and weary of life on March 21, 1801 and was buried on the 24th of the same month, aged 86 years and 21 days. C. Endress.

Elisabeth Fries, dau. of Philip and Mary Fries, d. on Sunday Sept. 28, 1823, about four o'clock in the afternoon, aged 35 years, 9 months and 14 days.
Philip Fries, Esq. was b. June 29, 1757 and d. Sept. 18, 1832, aged 75 years, 2 months and 20 days.

PRESBYTERIAN CONGREGATION AT PILESGROVE

Beginning April 30th, 1741

The Church Covenant -- set our names here-unto ...

Isaac Van Meter and Hannah, his wife; Henry Van Meter, their son; Sarah Van Meter, their dau.
Cornelius Nieukirk (in copy Nieu Kirk) and Rachel, his wife; Abraham Nieukirk, their son (in copy Nieu Kirk).
Barnet du Bois, who died Jan. - -- and Jacominihee, his wife.
Lewis DuBois and Margaret, his wife; Anna, their dau.
Garret du Bois and Margaret, his wife.
John Miller.
Mary Moor, widow.
Francis Tully and Hannah, his wife.
Jeremiah Garrison and Mary, his wife.
Eleazer Smith and Mary, his wife.
William Alderman and Abigail, his wife.
John Rose and Mary, his wife.
Simon Sparks and Jane, his wife; Thomas Sparks, their son; Elizabeth Sparks, their dau.
Richard Sparks and Elizabeth, his wife.
John Craig and Mary, his wife.
Sarah Carr.
William Miller.
Mary Sherry.
Nathan Tarbel.
Priscilla Tully.
Hugh Moore and Hanna, his wife.
Phebe Conklin, Robert Tully's wife.
Peter Hess.
James Dunlap and Elisabeth, his wife. (Debarred both June 12, 1742 for breaking their marriage and the duties relating therewith and un-Christian behavior in words and actions.)
Jacob du Bois, Jr.
Joshua Garrison and Sarah, his wife.
Joost Miller.

Records of Church Discipline
Elizabethe Dunlap - James Dunlap - Robert Holbrook - Harman Richman - Isaac Van Meter - Obariah Lloyd - Barnet du Bois - William Alderman - Abraham Nieukirk - Joseph Topy.

Admissions to Church Communion

David Garrison and Mary, his wife.
Christiana, wife of Joost Miller.
Rebekah, wife of Henry VanMeter, Jr.
Isabel, wife of Francis Dunlap.
Samuel Bishop.
John Richman.
Jacob du Bois.
Solomon du Bois and David du Bois, sons of Barnet du Bois.
Janitie Nieukirk, dau. of Cornelius Nieukirk.
Hannah Rose, dau. of John Rose.
Henry VanMeter, Sr. and Mary, his wife.
Samuel Purviance and Mary, his wife.
David Reeve and Zeruish, his wife.
Martha, wife of Arthur Davis.
Jane, wife of James Bilderback.

Robert Holbrook.
Elizabeth Wright, of Penns Neck.
Dorothy Dickison.
Joseph VanMeter.
Samuel Hannah and Abigail, his wife.
George Prawner, a Switser.
Nathan Bateman.
James Currey.
Thomas Stonebanks.
James Davis and Mary, his wife from Deerfield.
Elizabeth, wife of Benjamin Harding.
Judith Grimes, wife of William G.
Elizabeth Gilman and Susanna Gilman, two sisters, young women.
William Grimes, deposed.
Mathew duBois.
Mary, wife of Samuel Bishop.
Anna Davies, wife of Daniel Davies.
Ann, wife of William Foster.
Elizabeth, wife of Charles Dalton.
Jonathan du Bois.
John DuBois.

Ann Henry.
Mary Ollinger.
Phebe, wife of William Stratton.
Bethina, a negro maid.
Joseph Tame, debarred.
Martha, wife of Aldon Abbit. (By a letter from the Church In Huntington upon Long Island.)
Mary Johnson.
Matthew Jones.
William Foster.
Mary Richman, Sr., widow.
Ann Snag, widow.
Mary Moor, widow, by a certificate from Mr. Chas. Tennent.
Hannah Gilman.
Elizabeth du Bois, dau. of Lewis duBois.
Benjamin Davies, by the Rev. Mr. Elmer's certificate.
Joseph Abbit.
Francis Thomson and Ann, his wife.
Hannah, wife of Joseph VanMeter.
David VanMeter.
Ann, wife of James Dunlap, Jr.

Baptisms

1740
From May 1st to Aug. 10th:
Priscilla Tully, a grown young woman.
Hannah Fair, a married woman.
Thebe Tully, dau. of Francis and Hannah.
John Garrison, son of David and Mary.
Mary Macclang, dau. of James and Ann.
Gamaliel Garrison, son of Jeremiah and Mary.
Elizabeth Rose, dau. of John and Mary.
Tabitha, Susanna and Abigail Alderman, daus. of William and Abigail.
Martha and Rebekah Smith, daus. of Eleazer and Mary.

Aug. 17th:
John, Sarah, Jane and Daniel Garrison, children of Arthur and Sarah.
Mary Sherry, wife of Samuel.
Samuel, Sarah, Ruampence Sherry, children of Samuel and Mary.

Aug. 24th:
Aner and Phebe Jagger, daus. of Jonathan and Elizabeth.

Aug. 31st:
Nathan, Mary, John, Zuhariah, Sarah, Ephraim and Anna Shaw, children of Nathan and Mary of Deerfield.

Oct. 22d:
Elizabeth, wife of James Dunlap.
Ephraim, her son by a former husband.

Nov. 30th:
Jeremiah Wood and Juhaniah, his son.

1741
Jan. 25th:
Richard Ogden, son of John and Hannah.
Robert Maule and Eleanor Maule, his dau. (These were bapt. at Deerfield.)

April 9th:
Catharine Miller, dau. of John and Margaret.

April 12th:
Fetters VanMeter, son of Henry and Mary.

April 26th:
Elizabeth, Mary and Martha Craig, children of John and Mary.

April 30th:
Francis and John Dunlap, sons of Francis.

May 1st:
John Mulford, a grown person.

May 12th:
Hester Lloyd, dau. of Obadiah.

May 16th:
Joanna Puriance, dau. of Samuel.

May 17th:
Rebekah and Jeremiah Paruin, children of Jeremiah of Deerfield.

May 24th:
Ann Bleu, dau. of John and Elizabeth.

June 7th:
Mary Harris, dau. of Isaac and Mercy of Deerfield.

June 21st:
David Wescote, son of Davis and Rachel of Deerfield.

July 6th:
Jane Whitcraft, dau. of John and Ann.
Sarah Evis, dau. of George and Elizabeth.
Andrew Moffett, son of Samuel and Mary. (The last two were bapt. at the house of Walter Lloyd in Gloucester.)

July 26th:
Bartholomew Garrett, a grown person.
Abraham Haas, son of Peter.

Aug. 23d:
Mary Miller, dau. of Joost and Christiana.

Aug. 30th:
Israel Wharton, son of John and Barcheba Woolsey.

Oct. 11th:
Abigail Garrison, dau. of Jeremiah and Mary.

Oct. 25th:
Ann Humphrey, dau. of John and Rachel at the Great Valley.

Nov. 1st:
Elizabeth Jagger, dau. of Jonathan and Elizabeth.

Nov. 15th:
Rebekah Smith, dau. of Eleazer and Mary.

Dec. 19th:
Barbara Forrest, dau. of John and Ann.

1742
Jan. 24th:
William Alderman, son of
  William and Abigail.

Jan. 31st:
John Brooks, a grown young man
  of Deerfield.
John Bishop, son of Samuel and
  Mary.

Feb. 28th:
Jane McKeen, dau. of John.

March 7th:
Samuel DuBois, son of Lewis and
  Margaret.

March 28th:
John, son of Heymun and
  Elizabeth.

April 4th:
William Cyrrey, son of James.
Elizabeth Garrison, dau. of
  Joshua and Sarah.

April 25th:
Sarah Nieukirk, dau. of
  Cornelius and Rachel.

May 2d:
Azubah Tully, dau. of Francis
  and Hannah.

June 6th:
Hannah Garrison, dau. of John
  and Amey.

June 12th:
Elizabeth Hamilton, wife of
  Archibald.
James Craig, son of John and
  Mary.

June 13th:
Abigail Foster, dau. of
  Jeremiah and Patient.

June 20th:
Mary Carle, dau. of ---.
Annanias Shaw, son of Nathan.

July 4th:
Sarah DuBois, dau. of Garret
  and Margaret.

Aug. 22d:
Abigail Rose, dau. of John and
  Mary.

Sept. 26th:
Isaac VanMeter, son of Henry
  Jr. and Rebekah, his wife.

Oct. 31st:
Benjamin Woolsey, son of John
  and Bersheba at Deerfield.
Mary Foster, dau. of ---.

Dec. 26th:
Thomas Dunlap, son of Francis
  and Isabel.

1743
Jan. 16th:
Mary VanMeter, dau. of Henry
  and Mary.

Jan. 30th:
Joel Garrison, son of Jeremiah.
David and Rachel Jagger,
  children of David and
  Martha.

Feb. 5th:
Joseph Garrison, son of David
  and Mary.

March 17th:
Jane Marshoh, dau. of John and
  Elizabeth at Woodbury.

March 20th:
Rhode, an Indian girl on her
  actual profession of the
  Christian Faith.

March 27th:
Daniel David, son of Arthur and
  Martha of Deerfield.

April 14th:
Benjamin Maule at Deerfield.
Sarah, John, Hannah, Lydia and
  Benjamin Maule, children of
  the said Benjamin.

Isaac Garrison, son of Isaac
and Hannah.
Miriam Garrison, dau. of
Benjamin and Tamson.

April 17th:
Sara-Ann Jackson, wife of
James.
Joseph Jackson, son of James
and Sara-Ann.

April 24th: Susanna Conkelyn,
dau. of Gideon and
Priscilla.
William ---, son of a man
living near Mannington, S.C.
(name forgotten).

May 1st:
Rebekah Richman, dau. of John
and Sarah.
Abijhai, Sarah, Othniel and
Rachel Davies, children of
James and Mary at Deerfield.

May 15th:
Naomi Bishop, dau. of Samuel
and Mary.

May 22d:
Rachel Garrison, dau. of
Benjamin and Tamson.

July 31st:
John, Thomas, Richard, James,
William, Joseph and Mary
Stonebanks, children of
Thomas and Mary.

Sept. 13th:
Thomas Nichols.
David and Christiana Nichols,
children of Thomas.

Sept. 20th:
Joseph Barber, son of Nathaniel
and Jane.

Oct. 3d:
Hester Harris, dau. of Isaac
and Mercy at Deerfield.

Oct. 9th:
Mary Garrison, dau. of Isaac
and Hannah.

Nov. 20th:
Henry Seeley, son of Henry and
Mary of Deerfield.

Nov. 24th: Elizabeth Grimes,
dau. of William and Judith.

1744
Jan. 1st:
Mary Towe, dau. of Joseph and
Hannah.

Jan. 22d:
Elizabeth Alderman, dau. of
William and Abigail.

Feb. 5th:
Henry Miller, son of Joost and
Christiana.

Feb. 29th:
Mary Puriance, dau. of Samuel
and Mary.

March 11th:
Samuel Craig, son of John and
Mary.

April 8th:
Jacob Craig, son of John and
Margaret.

April 14th:
Anna Davies, wife of Daniel.
Broadway, Amon, Uriah and
Joseph Davies, children of
Daniel and Anna. These were
bapt. at Deerfield some time
before this date.

April 15th:
Priscilla Sherry, dau. of
Samuel and Mary.
Hannah Davies, dau. of Daniel
and Anna.
Damaris Moor, dau. of Moses and
Elizabeth.

April 22d:
Eleazer Smith, son of Eleazer and Mary.
John Wescote, son of David and Rachel.

April 28th:
Samuel ---, son of --- widow (name forgotten).

April 29th:
Elizabeth, a servant child of Nehemiah Vial of Greenwich.

May 6th:
Joanna Davies, dau. of James and Mary.
Amey Foster, dau. of ---.
John Carle, son of John and Catherine.

May 13th:
Elizabeth Deton, wife of Charles.

July 8th:
John Jagger, son of Jonathan and Elizabeth.

July 22d:
Moses Hill, son of Aaron.
Jemima Jagger, dau. of David and Mary.

July 29th:
Joseph and John Richardson, sons of Edward and Jane of Cohansey.

Aug. 12th:
Mary Bishop, dau. of Samuel and Mary.
Margaret Pine, dau. of Lazarus and Mary.

Sept. 2d:
Sarah Timvell, dau. of William and Mary.

Sept. 23d:
Phebe Garrison, dau. of Benjamin and Tamzon.

Nov. 11th:
Samuel Tully, son of Francis and Hannah.
James and Samuel Thomson, sons of James and Eupho.
Benjamin VanMeter, son of Henry and Mary.

1745
Feb. 17th:
Aaron Dunlap, son of Francis and Issabel.

Feb. 24th:
Abigail Garrison, dau. of Jeremiah and Mary.

April 6th:
Aaron Stratton, son of William and Phebe.

April 14th:
Elizabeth Tame, dau. of Joseph and Hannah.

April 21st:
Elizabeth Stonebanks, dau. of Thomas and Mary.

June 9th:
Joel Ogden, son of Jonathan and Hannah.
Ezekiel Rose, son of John and Elizabeth.

June 16th:
Mary Dunlap, dau. of Francis and Rebekah.

July 28th:
Jedikiah Moor, son of Nathaniel Jr.

Aug. 17th:
Bethina, a negro maid of John Johnson.

Oct. 12th:
Hannah Seeley, dau. of Henry and Mary.
Jane Barkley, dau. of James and Susanna at Penns Neck.

Nov. 17th:
Isaac Richman, son of John and Sarah.

1746
Jan. 5th:
Robert Currie, son of James.

Jan. 26th:
Arthur Davies, son of Daniel and Anna.

Feb. 2d:
Mary Grimes, dau. of William and Judith.

March 8th:
Sarah Alderman, dau. of William and Abigail.
William Foster, an adopted child of William and Ann.

March 30th:
Susanna Purviance, dau. to Samuel and Mary.

April 6th:
Mary Sherry, dau. of Samuel and Mary.
David Garrison, son of Joshua and Sarah.

April 20th:
Jonathan Jagger, son of Jonathan and Elizabeth.

April 25th:
Simon Marshall, son of John and Elizabeth at Woodbury.

April 27th:
Sarah Bishop, dau. of Samuel and Mary.
Elizabeth Miller, dau. of Joost and Christiana.
Elisabeth Davies, dau. of James and Mary.

May 10th:
Samuel Hannah, son of Samuel and Abigail.
Thomas Mayhew, a grown man.

May 29th:
Elizabeth Smith, dau. of Eleazer and Mary.

June 8th:
Abinidab Wescote, son of David and Rachel.

June 26th:
Samuel and Hannah Smith, children of John and Mary.

July 20th:
Isaac Brown, son of John.

July 24th:
David Tame, son of Joseph and Hannah.

July 27th:
Uriah Mayhew, son of Thomas and Hannah.

July 31st:
Melicent Tarbel, dau. of Nathan and Elizabeth.

Aug. 17th:
Levi Davies, son of Arthur and Hester.
William and Elizabeth Thomson, twin children of James and Eupho.

Aug. 24th:
John Simvell, son of William and Mary.

Sept. 6th:
William Foster, an old man.

Sept. 7th:
Hannah Garrison, dau. of Isaac and Hannah.

Oct. 12th:
Jonathan Garrison, son of Benjamin and Tomson.
Rebekah Maule, dau. of Benjamin.

Oct. 16th:
Thomas Sagel, son of Ann, widow.

Oct. 26th:
Zabulan Pierson, son of Ajabel
and Mary.

Nov. 30th:
Rachel Carle, dau. of John and
Catherine.

Dec. 7th:
Sarah Craig, dau. of John and
Mary.

1747
Jan. 25th:
Phebe Garrison, dau. of
Jeremiah and Mary.

Feb. 15th:
William Robinson, son of John
and Mary.

April 26th:
Deborah Jagger, dau. of David
and Martha.

May 3d:
Abraham Miller, son of John and
Margaret.

May 31st:
Deborah Seeley, dau. of David
and Mary.

June 14th:
Benjamin Abbit, son of Aldon
and Martha.

June 21st:
Samuel Conkelyn, son of Gideon
and Priscilla.

Aug. 2d:
Mary Tully, dau. of Francis and
Hannah.

Aug. 13th:
Sarah Lumley, wife of Edward.
Rebekah and John Lumley,
    children of Edward and
    Sarah. These were bapt. at
    Allaways Creek.
Jane Canada, a widow.
James and Patrick Canada, sons
    of Jane.

Sept. 6th:
Francis Dunlap, son of Francis
and Isabel.

Sept. 26th:
Aaron Alderman, son of William
and Abigail.

Oct. 4th:
Samuel Stonebanks, son of
Thomas and Mary.

Nov. 1st:
Edward Lumley, son of Edward
and Sarah.

Nov. 15th:
Robert Tully, a grown person.
Abraham Tarbel, son of Nathan
and Elizabeth.

1748
Jan. 3d:
Elizabeth Nieukirk, dau. of
Abraham and Ann.

March 10th:
Mary Haglin, a grown young
woman.

March 13th:
Margaret Simvell, dau. of
William and Mary.

March 27th:
Bathsheba Dunlap, dau. of James
and Ann.

April 10th:
Jacob Van Meter, son of Henry
Sr. and Mary, his wife.

April 24th:
Margaret Puruiance, dau. of
Samuel and Mary.

May 22d:
Catherine Millar, dau. of Joost
and Christiana.
Phebe Sherry, dau. of Samuel
and Mary.

May 23d:
Bathsheba Dunlap, dau. of Francis and Rebekah.

May 26th:
Israel Mayhew, son of Thomas and Hannah.

May 29th:
Eunice Jagger, dau. of Jonathan and Elizabeth.

June 5th:
Hannah Tame, dau. of Joseph and Hannah (alias Tossy).
Jenit Cam, dau. of John and Mary.

June 23d:
Sarah Smith, dau. of Eleazer and Mary.

July 31st:
John Garrison, son of Jeremy and Mary.

Aug. 28th:
Sarah Longs, a grown young woman.

Sept. 4th:
Samuel Bishop, son of Samuel and Mary.

Oct. 30th:
Hannah Davies, dau. of Daniel and Anna.
Hester Davies, dau. of James and Mary.

1749
March 19th:
Abigail Garrison, dau. of Benjamin and Tomson.
Gideon Tully, son of Robert and Phebe.

March 26th:
Abraham Carle, son of John and Catherine.

April 16th:
Mary Dunlap, dau. of James and Ann.

April 30th:
Abigail Maule, dau. of Benjamin.

May 4th:
Mary Thomson, dau. of Francis and Ann.

May 14th:
Richard Graham, son of William and Judith (alias Grimes).

May 21st:
Abraham Richman, son of John and Sarah.
Mary Jayner, dau. of Peter and Jane.

May 28th:
Anna Tully, dau. of Francis and Hannah.

June 1st:
James Hannah, son of Samuel and Abigail.

July 9th:
William Hamilton, son of Archibald and Ann.
Euphan Robinson, dau. of John and Mary.

July 16th:
Elizabeth, Henry and Sarah Vanmeter, children of Joseph and Hannah.

Sept. 3d:
Dorothy Jagger, dau. of David and Martha.

Sept. 17th:
Keturah Tarbel, dau. of Nathan and Elizabeth.

Sept. 24th:
Jacob Sauther, son of Charles.

Oct. 29th:
Rachel duBois, dau. of Jacob and Janitie.

Nov. 5th:
William McKinne, son of
  Barnabas and Ann.

Nov. 12th:
Andrew Puruiance, son of Samuel
  and Mary.

1750
Jan. 14th:
Mary Alderman, dau. of William
  and Abigail.

March 11th:
Jacob Duffel, son of William
  and Catherine.

April 1st:
Margaret Currie, dau. of James.

April 5th:
Mary Moore, wife of Richard.

April 22d:
Isaac VanMeter, son of Joseph
  and Hannah.

May 6th:
Catherine Mira, dau. of Jacob
  and Margaret.
Elizabeth Miller, dau. of John
  and Margaret.
Benjamin Seley, son of David
  and Mary.

May 20th:
Hannah Garrison, dau. of
  Jeremiah and Mary.

June 17th:
Rebekah Nieukirk, dau. of
  Abraham and Ann.

Aug. 26th:
Sarah Tossy, dau. of Joseph and
  Hannah.

Oct. 28th:
Elias Craig, son of John and
  Mary.
Rachel Miller, dau. of Joost
  and Christiana.

Nov. 18th:
William Simvell, son of William
  and Mary.

Marriages

1740
Dec. 30th: Isaac Garrison to
  Hannah Bennet.

1741
Jan. 13th: John Conor to
  Hannah Denn.
Feb. 17th: John Forrest to Ann
  Davies.
Feb. 25th: Samuel Hannah to
  Abigail Preston of
  Deerfield.
Sept. 15th: Patrick Carrol to
  Elizabeth McCarty.

1742
Jan. 4th: Enoch Wilson to
  Lydia ---.
Jan. 5th: John Marshal to
  Elizabeth Sparks.
Jan. 27th: John Richman to
  Sarah VanMeter.

Feb. 6th: John Miller to Sarah
  Dickinson.
July 12th: Joseph Tame to
  Hannah Brown.
Sept. 27th: Nicholas Current
  to Mary Powel.
Dec. 18th: John Nichols to Ann
  Deaton.
       William Nichols to
  Leuretia Widdish.
Dec. 31st: Amos Weeks to
  Deborah Nealson.

1743
June 21st: John Plummer to
  Athey Henry.
Sept. 20th: John Robinson to
  Mary Thomson.
Dec. 6th: Arthur Davies to
  Hester Preston (of
  Deerfield).

1744

May 18th: Francis Dunlap to Rebekah Hunter.
July 2d: Ebenezer Parvin to Phebe Rusel (of Deerfield).
Aug. 16th: James Wood to Margaret Booth (of Cohansey).
Joseph Nealy to Elizabeth Booth (of Cohansey).
Dec. 4th: Archibald Grimes to Margaret McGoogan.
Dec. 21st: Laban Longstaff to Ann Hewit.

1745

Jan. 28th: Richard Hammon to Ann Turner.
April 28th: Joseph VanMeter to Hannah Veal.
May 13th: Thomas Mayhew to Hannah Rose.
Sept. 30th: Daniel Weatherby to Mary Cox.
Oct. 3d: Nathan Tarbel to Elizabeth Robinson.
Oct. 16th: Abdon Abbit to Elizabeth Blew.
Nov. 25th: Samuel Elwell to Susanna Elwell.
Dec. 18th: David Seely to Mary Richman.
Dec. 23rd: Abraham Nieukirk to Ann Richman.

1746

Jan. 7th: Hezekiah Shaw to Hannah Buck.
Feb. 18th: Daniel McCleese to Abigail Lumby.
Feb. 24th: Moses Clemens to Mary Lot (free negroes).
Dec. 18th: Archibald Hamilton to Ann Robeson.

1747

Feb. 16th: George Hans to Patience Loper.
June 3d: Jacob DuBois, Sr. to Janetie Nieukirk.
June 10th: William Sauther to Catherine Powlson.
Nov. 24th; Leonard Mire to Catherine Fisher.

1748

Jan. 11th: Anthony Nelson to Phebe Elwell.
Christopher Stump to Mary Long.
Feb. 2d: Francis Thomson to Ann Craig.
Feb. 23d: John Leonard Caarns to Margaret Hea.
May 31st: Gadfreed Richard to Catherine Garrison.
June 30th: Christian Narthel to Margaret Shoot.
March 23d: Robert Tully to Phebe Conkelyn.
Aug. 18th: Benjamin Davies to Ann Foster.
Aug. 24th: Tonias Paulson to Mary Lang.
Dec. 27th: Barnabas McKinne to Ann Henry.

1749

Feb. 7th: John Kinish to Barbara Barn.
March 23d: Thomas Haynes to Jane Brown.
May 30th: John LeCroy to Bridget Darby.
May 31st: Dennis Hart to Ann Clark.
Oct. 19th: John Gillespie to Elizabeth Lord.
Nov. 14ath: John Elericht to Elizabeth Haglin.

1750

May 9th: Jacob DuBois, Jr. to Mary Aligger.
Sept. 26th: George Blew to Eleanor Maule.
Oct. 29th: James Ship to Sarah Cullyar.
Nov. 24th: David Marinus to Ann duBois.

N.B. Mr. Evans arrived at ---- Congregation May 1, 1740 and died Feb. 4, 1751.

Baptisms by John Clark, N. D. M.

Amanda Fish of Enos and Esther, b. Nov. 9, 1805, bapt. May 16, 1806.
Sherry Gaston of David and Elizabeth, b. Sept. 10, 1793, bapt. June 11, 1806.
Lydia Gaston of David and Elizabeth, b. Dec. 27, 1795, bapt. June 11, 1806.
Rhoda Gaston of David and Elizabeth, b. July 17, 1799, bapt. June 11, 1806.
John Gaston of David and Elizabeth, b. April 20, 1801, bapt. June 11, 1806.
Richard Parker of Richard and Hannah, b. June 19, 1794, bapt. Aug. 14, 1806.
Elizabeth Parker of Richard and Hannah, b. Sept. 7, 1794, bapt. Aug. 14, 1806.
John Parker of Richard and Hannah, b. Aug. 20, 1796, bapt. Aug. 14, 1806.
Samuel Parker of Richard and Hannah, b. Feb. 14, 1800, bapt. Aug. 14, 1806.
Julian Parker of Richard and Hannah, b. Nov. 1, 1802, bapt. Aug. 14, 1806.
Rachel Wood of Jeremiah and Sarah, b. Oct. 6, 1793, bapt. Oct. 19, 1806 (adult).
Thomas Brick Wood of ---, b. July 1, 1795, bapt. Oct. 19, 1806.
Isaiah Wood of ---, b. July 25, 1797, bapt. Oct. 19, 1806.
Charles Wood of ---, b. Jan. 17, 1799, bapt. Oct. 19, 1806.
Mariah Richman Wood and Josiah Brick Wood, b. Oct. 9, 1801, bapt. Oct. 19, 1806.
Abigail Whitaker of Recompence and Rachel, b. Dec. 6, 1800, bapt. Oct. 19, 1806.
Enoch More Whitaker of ---, b. Oct. 29, 1802, bapt. Oct. 19, 1806.
Hannah Lecok Whitaker of ---, b. Feburary 9, 1805, bapt. Oct. 19, 1806.
Elizabeth Nieukirk of Matthew and Mary, b. Sept. 9, 1789, bapt. Oct. 19, 1806.
Barshaba Nirukirk of ---, b. Nov. 25, 1792, bapt. Oct. 19, 1806.
Ann Nirukirk of ---, b. March 7, 1795, bapt. Oct. 19, 1806.
Sarah Nieukirk of ---, b. May 14, 1800, bapt. Oct. 19, 1806.
James VanMeter of Samuel and Susannah, b. in 1792, bapt. Jan. 26, 1807.
Lydia VanMeter of Samuel and Susannah, b. March 11, 1794, bapt. Jan. 26, 1807.
Samuel VanMeter of Samuel and Susannah, b. Jan. 25, 1795, bapt. Jan. 26, 1807.
Adam VanMeter of Samuel and Susannah, b. March 10, 1796 (sic), bapt. Jan. 26, 1807.
Richard VanMeter of Samuel and Susannah, b. Jan. 29, 171600 (in ms), bapt. Jan. 26, 1807.
Catherine VanMeter of Samuel and Susannah, b. Decembr 18, 1803, bapt. Jan. 26, 1807.
Nancy Elwell of --- and Nancy, b. Aug. 15, 1798, bapt. April 5, 1807.

Cynthey Reeves of William and Elizabeth, b. Aug. 24, 1796, bapt.
    July 12, 1807.
Ester Reeves of ---, b. July 11, 1800, bapt. July 12, 1807.
Rachel Reeves of ---, b. June 5, 1803, bapt. July 12, 1807.
Mary Reeves of ---, b. Jan. 31, 1805, bapt. July 12, 1807.
Nancy Madera of Christopher and Elizabeth, b. Aug. 4, 1791, bapt.
    July 12, 1807.
David Madera of ---, b. Jan. 21, 1797, bapt. July 12, 1807.
John Madera of ---, b. Jan. 12, 1800, bapt. July 12, 1807.
Margaret Lithens of Enos and Mary, b. Oct. 19, 1800, bapt. July
    14, 1807.
Daniel Lithens of ---, b. Feb. 11, 1802, bapt. July 14, 1807.
Rachel Nieukirk of Matthew and Catherine, b. Feb. 7, 1787, bapt.
    July 14, 1807.
Hannah Nieukirk of ---, b. March 4, 1768, bapt. July 14, 1807.
Christiana Neiukirk of ---, b. Sept. 17, 1796, bapt. July 14,
    1807.
Benjamin Nieukirk of ---, b. Dec. 18, 1794, bapt. July 14, 1807.
Robert Murphy of Samuel and Elizabeth, b. May 27, 1800, bapt.
    July 14, 1807.
John Burrough of Benjamin and Judith, b. in 1795, bapt. July 12,
    1807.
Jonathan Burrough of ---, b. in 1801, bapt. July 12, 1807.
Benjamin Burrough of ---, b. in 1799, bapt. July 12, 1807.
Hannah Burrough of ---, b. in 1803, bapt. July 12, 1807.
Rebeckah Craigg (Craigh) of Abram and Sally, b. Oct. 27, 1791,
    bapt. Dec. 6, 1807.
John Craigg of ---, b. Jan. 4, 1794, bapt. Dec. 6, 1807.
Mary Craigg of ---, b. Jan. 26, 1799, bapt. Dec. 6, 1807.
Elizabeth Craigg of ---, b. July 7, 1801, bapt. Dec. 6, 1807.
Abner Craigg of ---, b. Dec. 8, 1804, bapt. Dec. 6, 1807.
Uphain Frun (dau.) of Wemen and Ann, b. July 7, 1797, bapt. Dec.
    6, 1807.
Sarah Rose of Abraham and Catherine, b. Dec. 9, 1792, bapt. Feb.
    17, 1808.
Phebe Rose of ---, b. Oct. 9, 1794, bapt. Feb. 17, 1808.
William Rose of ---, b. March 25, 1796, bapt. Feb. 17, 1808.
Rebekah Rose of ---, b. Aug. 15, 1807, bapt. Feb. 17, 1808.
Elizabeth Rose of ---, b. April 6, 1798, bapt. Feb. 17, 1808.
John Rose of ---, b. Sept. 12, 1800, bapt. Feb. 17, 1808.
Abraham Rose of ---, b. Dec. 19, 1802, bapt. Feb. 17, 1808.
Eliza Rose of ---, b. Feb. 24, 1805, bapt. Feb. 17, 1808.

   The Rev. John Clark removed from the Church at Pittsgrove on
the 20th day of April ---- one thousand eight hundred and
eight, from which time until the ordination of the Rev. George
W. Janvier took place, which was on the 13th day of May Anno.
D. 1812, there was not any regular record of the Baptisms in
the church to be had on account of the ordinances being
performed by different ministers, and that the Clerk of
Sessions not being furnished with names, etc. no entry could
be made as to the time of baptism or by whom administered, and
those which were known are as follows:

PRESBYTERIAN CONGREGATION AT PILESGROVE   247

The children of Matthew Nieukirk, Jr., and Mary his wife:
Elizabeth, b. Sept. 9, 1789, Bathsheba, b. Nov. 25, 1792, Ann, b.
March 7, 1795, Sarah, b. May 14, 1800, Matthew, b. March 8,
1814 (son of Elizabeth, his wife)
Nathaniel Reeve Nieukirk, b. July 22, 1817.

The children of John VanMeter and Elizabeth his wife:
Mary VanMeter,
Joseph Neley VanMeter, William Alderman VanMeter,
Thomas VanMeter, Elizabeth VanMeter, Rebeckah VanMeter, John
VanMeter.

The children of Abnor Craig and Sarah his wife:
Rebeckah Craig, b. Oct. 29, 1791, John Craig, b. Jan. 4, 1794,
Abnor Penton Craig, b. Oct. 20, 1796 and departed this life
Dec. 25, 1797.
Mary Craig, b. Jan. 26, 1799, Elizabeth Craig, b. July 7, 1801,
Abnor Craig, b. Dec. 8, 1804, Martha Craig, b. March 26, 1810.

The children of Thomas Harding and Lydia his wife:
Catherine Harding, b. July 28, 1797, Benjamin Harding, b. Dec.
25, 1798, John Harding, b. June 8, 1800, Ann Harding, b. Sept.
29, 1801, Rachel Harding, b. Dec. 13, 1803, Elizabeth Harding,
b. June 21, 1805, Thomas Harding, b. Dec. 6, 1808, Henry
Harding, b. Feb. 18, 1811 - bapt. Dec. 1812, by Rev. Geo. W.
Janvier.

The children of Benjamin Burroughs and Judith his wife:
Susanna Burroughs, b. Jan. 12, 1786, Mary Burroughs, b. June 8,
1788, James Burroughs, b. July 20, 1790, Cornelius Burroughs,
b. June 9, 1793, John Burroughs, b. July 21, 1795, Benjamin
Burroughs, b. Oct. 3, 1797, Jonathan Burroughs, b. May 4,
1801, Hannah Burroughs, b. June 29, 1803 - bapt. June 1807 by
Rev. John Clark.

The children of Jeremiah Wood and Sarah his wife:
Rachel Wood, b. Oct. 8, 1793, Thomas B. Wood, b. July 1, 1795,
Isaiah Wood, b. July 25, 1797, Charles Wood, b. Jan. 17, 1799,
Mariah R. Wood, b. Oct. 9, 1801, Josiah B. Wood, b. Oct. 9,
1801, Sarah Wood, b. July 25, 1807, Rebeckah Wood, b. April 4,
1809, John Wood, b. April 4, 1809, Elizabeth Wood, b. July 3,
1813.

The children of Isaac Johnson and Mary his wife:
Harriet Johnson, b. Oct. 3, 1796, Betsey Johnson, b. April 18,
1798, Isaac Johnson, b. Oct. 1, 1799, Amelia Johnson, b. Oct.
16, 1801, Mary Johnson, b. March 15, 1804, Sarah Johnson, b.
Sept. 18, 1805 - bapt. in 1808.
John Johnson, b. March 5, 1810, Samuel E. Johnson, b. May 19,
1812 - bapt. in 1812.
Emme Ann Johnson, William Johnson, Franklin Johnson.

The children of Eleazer Mayhew and Sarah his wife:
John Mayhew, b. May 31, 1776, Stanford Mayhew, b. April 27,

EARLY CHURCH RECORDS OF SALEM COUNTY

1779 - Bapt. by Rev. N. Greenman.
Rebecca Mayhew, b. Sept. 9, 1783 and departed this life Sept. 9, 1808, Eleazer Mayhew, b. Dec. 13, 1785, Benjamin Mayhew, b. April 3, 1788 - Bapt. by Rev. William Schenck.
Catherine Mayhew, b. July 19, 1790, Isaac Mayhew, b. June 20, 1792, Elam Mayhew, b. Sept. 28, 1794, Jacob Mayhew, b. July 26, 1798 - Bapt. by I. Foster.

The children of Enos Fish and Esther his wife:
Elizabeth Fish, b. July 11, 1795, John Fish, b. April 5, 1797, Joseph Fish, b. May 29, 1799, Sarah Fish, b. Feb. 13, 1801, Catherine Fish, b. June 8, 1803, Amanda Fish, b. Nov, 9, 1805 and d. July 10, 1806, Hannah Fish, b. Nov. 7, 1807, Tryphena Fish, b. May 4, 1810, Amanda Fish, b. Dec. 4, 1812, Esther Fish, b. ---.

The children of William Reave and Elizabeth his wife:
Cynthey Reave, b. Aug. 1, 1798, Esther Reave, b. July 11, 1800, Rachel Reave, b. June 5, 1803, Mary V. Reave, b. Jan. 31, 1805, Eliza Ann Reave, b. Aug. 26, 1809 and departed this life Oct. 5, 1813, William Reave, b. Decmember 12, 1811.

The children of John Murphey and Mary his wife:
Rachel Murphey, b. Jan. 31, 1798, bapt. by the Rev. Geo. W. Janvier on June (ad) 5, 1814, Phebe Murphey, b. Jan. 21, 1800, John and Mary Murphey, b. June 17, 1804.

The children of Rev. Nathaniel Todd and --- his wife:
Named Mary Cleveland Todd and Elizabeth Green Todd and bapt. at Woodbury in the County of Gloucester on the 3d Sabbath in Aug. 1813 by the Rev. George W. Janvier;
Elizabeth, above named, departed this life in the month of Sept. following.

Samuel Van Meter, b. Sept. (ad) 7, 1767.
Susannah, his wife, b. Oct. 2, 1771.
James VanMeter, son of Samuel and Susannah, b. June 14, 1792, Lydia VanMeter, b. May 16, 1794, Adam VanMeter, b. March 10, 1796, Samuel VanMeter, b. Jan. 25, 1796 (sic), Richard VanMeter, b. Jan. 23, 1802, Catherine VanMeter b. Dec. 17, 1803, Susannah VanMeter, b. April 30, 1807, died Oct. 20, 1822, Mary Ann VanMeter, b. Jan. 12, 1809, Nancy VanMeter, b. Nov. 28, 1810.

Joel Elwell and Elizabeth his wife were married March 18, 1788.
James Elwell, son of the above, b. Jan. 4, 1789, Abraham Elwell, b. Aug. 5, 1790, Mary Elwell, b. July 16, 1792, and departed this life Sept. 29, 1813, Hannah Elwell, b. May 28, 1795, John H. Elwell, b. Dec. 2, 1797, Margaret Elwell, b. March 25, 1801, Elizabeth Elwell, b. May 3, 1803, Joel Elwell, b. June 24, 1806. This family removed to the Western Country.

The children of David Gartin and Elishebe his wife:
Sherry Garton, b. Sept. 10, 1793, Lydia Garton, b. Dec. 27, 1795,

Rhoda Garton, b. July 17, 1799, John Garton, b. Sept. 20,
1801, Furman Garton, b. March 17, 1808, Rebeckah Garton, b.
Oct. 25, 1817.

The children of Abraham Albertson and Elizabeth his wife:
Mary Albertson, b. Feb. 14, 1796, Sarah Albertson, b. April 1,
1798, Esther Albertson, b. Nov. 5, 1800, David Albertson, b.
Jan. 12, 1803, Elizabeth Albertson, b. Aug. 27, 1805, Benjamin
Archer Albertson, b. Feb. 28, 1810, Abraham Albertson, Jr., b.
Sept. 18, 1812, Hannah Albertson, b. Feb. 3, 1809, died March
22, 1809.

John Richer and Mary, his first wife's children. Mary the wife
of John Richer departed this life ---.
Catherine, b. June 6, 1776, Jacob Richer, b. April 3, 1778.

John Richer and Mary, the present wife, were joined together in
the Holy Bands of Matrimony on March 5 Anno D. 1782 by the
Rev. William Schenck:
Loas Richer (dau.), b. May 22, 1784, Polly Richer, b. Feb. 28,
1787, Annah Richer, b. Sept. 10, 1788, Elizabeth Richer, b.
April 23, 1790, David Richer, b. Oct. 6, 1791.

EARLY CHURCH RECORDS OF SALEM COUNTY

NEW JERSEY MARRIAGE LICENSES
(from New Jersey court records)

Note: The date given is the date that the license was issued.

Joseph Gregory, Salem County, Esquire, and Elizabeth Bowell of Philadelphia, widow m.: Jan 6, 1727.

Joseph Stretch, Salem County, and Deborah Smith of same, spinster m.: Mar 9, 1727.

John Manaring, Salem County, husbandman, and Elizabeth Hendrickson of same, spinster m.: Mar 14, 1727.

Isaac Garrawn, Salem County, cordwainer, and Elizabeth Lawrence of same, spinster m.: March 24, 1727.

John Ellwell, Salem County, carpenter, and Rachel Garrason of same, spinster (marginal heading reads Elwell and Garretson) m.: March 24, 1727.

Note: The year 1727 for the next four entries, is probably correct, even though it is described as the first year of George II, who did not assume the throne until June 10, 1727, the news reaching America some weeks later. This would make the year 1728, but it is set forth that the licenses were granted by Governor Burnet who served only until April 24, 1728. It seems probable that the licenses were delivered in 1727 by some official in Salem County, who delayed sending in his report and that the recording was not done until after the accession of George II, at which time a clerical error was made in entering the year of the sovereign's rein.

Samuel Read, Salem County, cooper, and Elizabeth Eglington (Eglinton in marginal heading) of same, spinster m.: May 4, 1727. (See above note)

John Fry, Salem County, bricklayer, and Mary Brathwart of same, spinster m.: May 4, 1727. (See note above)

Thomas Hughs, Salem County, yeoman, and Mary Pedrick, spinster m.: May 11, 1727.(See note above)

Andrew Paget, Salem County, weaver, and Elizabeth Craford of same, spinster m.: Jun 10, 1727.(See note above)

Henry Vanmeter, Salem County, yeoman, and Sarah Ellwell of same, spinster m.: Sept 4, 1727.

David Wiggins, Salem County, cordwainer, and Rebeccah Griffin of same, spinster m.: Nov 23, 1727.

John Burgin, Cohansey, Salem County, yeoman, and Margate Steel (Steele in marginal heading) of same, widow m.: Jul 31, 1728.

John Oakford, Alloways Creek, Salem County, cordwainer, and Rebecca Pittman, spinster m.: Oct 6, 1732.

Charles Campbell, Salem County, Gent., and Jane McKnight m.: Dec 1, 1732.

Thomas More, Salem, Salem County, yeoman, and Elizabeth Ford, widow m.: Jan 17, 1732.

Joshua Thompson, Salem County, carpenter, and Sarah Hill, spinster m.: Apr 13, 1733.

Edward Sanghurst, Salem County, Gent., and Edisha Crow of same, widow m.: May 16, 1733.

Josiah Fithian, Cohansey, Salem County, yeoman, and Mary Johnson
of same, widow m.: Jun 2, 1733.
Isaac Hudson, Salem, Salem County, yeoman, and Rachel Weaten
(Wheaten in heading) of same, spinster m.: Jun 11, 1733.
Thomas French, Salem County, Gent., and Isabel Mason of same,
widow m.: Jul 13, 1733.
John Turner, Alloways Creek, Salem County, yeoman, and Hannah
Hall, spinster m.: Sept 1, 1733.
John Hampton, Gloucester County, husbandman, and Ann Devall of
Pilesgrove, Salem County, spinster m.: Jan 12, 1736.
Andrew Holsten, Salem County, yeoman, and Elizabeth Royall, widow
Aug 21, 1736.
Nicholas Ridgeley, Salem County, Gent., and Mary Vining of same
county, widow m.: Dec 23, 1736.
John Stretch, Salem County, and Esther Hancock of same, spinster
m.: May 7, 1751.
Hans Rudolph, Philadelphia, mariner, and Ann Eaton of Salem,
Salem County, spinster m.: Jun 3, 1736.
Charles Hopkins, Salem County, weaver, and Ann Green of same,
widow m.: Jun 12, 1736.
Jeremiah Wood, from Long Island, shoemaker, and Catherine Lloyd
of Salem County, widow m.: Jul 2, 1736.
John Hampton, Gloucester County, husbandman, and Ann Devall of
Pilesgrove, Salem County, spinster m.: Jan 12, 1736.
Andrew Holsten, Salem County, yeoman, and Elizabeth Royall, widow
m.: Aug 21, 1736.
Nicholas Ridgeley, Salem County, Gent., and Mary Vining of same
county, widow m.: Dec 23, 1736.
Edward Lummis, Morris's River, Salem County, yeoman, and Margaret
Elmor of Cohanzy, Salem County m.: 1737.
George Bowin, Salem County, labourer, and Charity Davis of same
m.: Aug 26, 1738.
Jeremiah Smith, Philadelphia, ship carpenter, and Magdalen Keen
of Salem County m.: Sept 10, 1738.
Samuel Mclanning, Salem County, blacksmith, and Mary Worldin of
Esinborough township, spinster m.: Dec 31, 1741.
John Lewis, Salem County, and Ruth Roberts of same, spinster m.:
Jan 13, 1741.
Josiah Rolse, Salem County, yeoman, and Hannah Darkin, spinster,
dau. of Joseph Darkin, late of same place m.: May 6, 1742.
Francis Palmer, City of Philadelphia in county of Hunterdon
(sic), and Eleanor Hollinshead of Salem County, Gentlewoman
m.: Feb 10, 1742.
John Lewis, Salem County, farmer, and Ruth Roberts of same,
spinster m.: Jan 13, 1741.
Edward Bully, Salem County, yeoman, and Ann Brooks of same,
spinster m.: Dec 3, 176?.
Jacob Richmond, Salem County, yeoman, and Catharine Malson
(Matson), Gloucester County m.: Feb 22, 1736.
Joseph Brick, Salem County, yeoman, and Elizabeth Cairle of same,
spinster m.: Apr 1, 1736.
William Tyler, Salem County, yeoman, and Elizabeth Thomson of
same, spinster m.: Jun, 1737.
Joshua Brick, Salem County, yeoman, and Ruth Rumsy of same,

spinster m.: Jul 25, 1737.
George Miller, Pilesgrove, Salem County, cooper, and Sarah Rumsy of Salem County, spinster m.: Aug 22, 1737.
Samuel Barns, Salem county, yeoman, and Sarah Hollinshead, spinster, dau. of John Hollinshead, Esq. m.: May 20, 1738.
Seger Garison, Salem County, yeoman, and Susanna Huckings, spinster, dau. of Roger Huckings of same, yeoman m.: May 20, 1738.
Peter Cock, Gloucester County, shoemaker, and Beata Lock of Salem County m.: Jan 5, 1738.
Thomas Robinson, Philadelphia, merchant, and Sarah Mason of Salem, widow m.: Jan 29, 1738.
Wm. Crabb, Salem County, cooper, and Mary Morgan of Salem Town, tayloress m.: Apr 6, 1739.
Benjamin Cross, Salem County, blacksmith, and Virgin Besly of same m.: Sep 25, 1739.
Anthony Casparson, Salem County, and Elizabeth Redstreak of same, widow m.: Oct 15, 1739.
Charles Rumsey, Salem County, weaver, and Susanna Dickson of same, spinster m.: Nov 1, 1739.
Thomas Flanegan, Salem County, yeoman, and Elizabeth Smith of same, spinster m.: Dec 1, 1739.
Wm. Barker, Salem County, bricklayer, and Elizabeth Gregory of same, spinster m.: Jan 7, 1739.
Joshua Bradway, Allaways Creek, Salem County, Gent., and Hannah Wiggins of same, spinster m.: Mar 6, 1739.
James Dunlap, Salem County, Gentleman, and Elizabeth Worthington m.: Mar 14, 1731.
Ephraim Friend of Pens Neck, Salem County, yeoman, and Bridgitta Senecks of Salem County, spinster m.: Jun 5, 1731. [sic]
Bryant Conelly, Salem County, yeoman, and Dorothea Bull of same, spinster m.: Jul 27, 1731.
Samuel Morgan, Salem County, yeoman, and Elizabeth Davies, spinster m.: Sep 10, 1731.
Joseph Zaines (Zane), Salem and Rebeccah Hill of same, spinster m.: Dec 17, 1750.
John Eastlack, Jr., Gloucester County, and Elizabeth Read of Salem County, spinster m.: May 29, 1751.

INDEX

-A-

ABBIT, Abdon, 244
  Aldon, 235, 241
  Benjamin, 241
  George, 81, 84, 88
  Joseph, 235
  Martha, 235, 241
ABBITT, George, 88, 89
ABBOOT, Samuel, 95
ABBOT, Elizabeth, 79
  Georg, 87
  George, 80, 85, 86, 87, 92, 99, 137
  Hannah, 94
  Marey, 87
  Rebeckah, 93
  Samuel, 42, 96, 98, 107
ABBOTT, Benjamin, 9
  George, 9, 10, 11, 12, 13, 14, 19, 86, 91, 92, 93, 141, 150
  Hannah, 10, 19, 20, 30, 65, 91
  Josiah, 138, 150
  Mary, 9, 10, 11, 12, 13, 14, 57
  Mercy, 30, 57
  Rebecca, 30, 123, 141
  Rebeckah, 13, 20, 64, 122, 150
  Samuel, 13, 19, 20, 30, 43, 94, 97, 99, 100, 101, 108, 110, 111, 150
  Sarah, 12, 30
  William, 19, 30, 65, 122, 143, 150
ABERLE, Agnesa
  Dorothea, 178
  Conrad Israel, 179
  Conradt Israel, 228
ABORN, Mary, 141
ACKERMAN,
  Eliesabeth, 192
  Johannes, 192

Philip, 192
ACTON, Beniamen, 86, 87
  Beniamin, 78, 79, 86
  Benimen, 86
  Benjaman, 19, 20
  Benjamin, 10, 17, 18, 30, 42, 78, 84, 89, 91, 92, 93, 94, 97, 98, 99, 100, 101
  Christiana, 10
  Clement, 30, 142
  Elizabeth, 10, 17, 18, 19, 20, 87
  Hannah, 55, 57, 134, 143
  Isaac, 30
  John, 17, 104, 129, 161
  Joseph, 18, 104, 106
  Joshua, 10
  Lidia, 10
  Mary, 10, 30, 58, 88, 120, 128, 129, 142, 161
  Samuel, 20, 58, 73, 129, 142, 161
  Sarah, 30, 142
ADAMS, Anna, 163
  John, 154, 162
  Mary, 55, 123
  Sarah, 113, 116, 122, 154
  Susanna, 73
  Susannah, 154
  William, 154, 162, 163
ADKINSON, James, 139
  Mahlon, 57, 138, 140
  Richard, 140
  Sarah, 138, 140
ADLER, Anna Barbara, 209, 223, 226
  Barbara, 215, 216, 219, 222
  Joh., 209
  Johann, 215, 216, 219, 222, 223,

226
  Johannes, 222, 230
AEBEL, Elisabeth, 185
AEBT, Engl, 179
  Martha, 179
ALBA, Georg, 229
ALBERTSON, Abraham, 249
  Benjamin Archer, 249
  David, 249
  Elizabeth, 249
  Esther, 249
  Hannah, 249
  Mary, 249
  Sarah, 249
ALBRECHT, Anna
  Maria, 188
  Anna Regina, 187
  Catharina, 187, 188
  Johann, 187, 188
ALBREITH, Catharina, 190
  Johannes, 190
  John, 190
ALDERMAN, Aaron, 241
  Abigail, 234, 235, 237, 238, 240, 241, 243
  Elizabeth, 238
  Mary, 243
  Sarah, 240
  Susanna, 235
  Tabitha, 235
  William, 234, 235, 237, 238, 240, 241, 243
ALIGGER, Mary, 244
ALLEN, Aaron, 115
  Ann, 30, 31, 151
  Anne, 163
  Atlantick, 168
  Beulah, 30, 151
  Chumbless, 30
  David, 31, 33, 39, 66, 92, 114, 123, 126, 140, 141, 151
  Edith, 151
  Elizabeth, 29, 54,

72, 129, 135, 157
Enoch, 61, 163, 168, 172, 173
Ephraim, 84, 85, 86, 91
Epraim, 84
Hannah, 29, 30, 33, 48, 55, 56, 72, 73, 97, 117, 133, 151, 168
James, 93, 97, 98, 99
Jedediah, 54, 72, 129
Jedidiah, 30, 51, 151, 157
Jedidian, 29
Joseph, 48, 60, 90, 91, 92, 133, 168
Judiah, 122, 126
Lettice, 30
Lidya, 108
Martha, 48, 135
Mary, 30, 31, 72, 112, 117, 151, 157, 168
Ner, 48, 73
Rachel, 54, 126, 157
Railfe, 85, 86
Ralph, 120, 132
Rebecca, 30, 31, 33, 39, 163
Rebeccah, 39, 73
Rebeckah, 151
Rebekah, 30
Ruth, 30, 116, 117, 157
Samuel, 126, 151, 157
Samuel C., 163
Sarah, 48, 54, 129, 168
Vashty, 91
William, 54, 126, 157
ALLIN, Elizabeth, 167
John, 3
ALLISON, Rachel, 139
Samuel, 73
AMBLER, Elizabeth, 30

Lydia, 72
Sarah, 140
AMLER, Elizabeth, 123
Lidya, 123
Peter, 123
Sarah, 123
ANDERSON, Esther, 96
Hannah, 106
Hester, 10
Maria Magdalena, 217
Simon, 10
Thomas, 10, 92, 96
ANDREAS, Anna Maria, 215
ANDREWS, Ann, 161
Easter, 50
Elizabeth, 50, 160, 161
Esther, 50, 131
Hester, 131
Isaac, 160
Jacob, 128, 152
James, 50, 161, 163
Jeremiah, 50, 161
Josiah, 50, 161
Mary, 30, 56, 133
Peter, 30
Phebe, 152
Samuel, 50, 152, 161
Simon, 81, 82
Thomas, 53, 140
ANTON, Benjamin, 90
APPEL, Henry, 103
APPLE, Henry, 97
ARNER, Johann Georg, 196
ASBUY, Hannah, 5
ASEL, Christian, 228
Johannes, 228
ASH, Jane, 3
ASHBORN, Thomas, 55
ASHTON, Eleanor, 124
Elizabeth, 94
Robert, 6, 79, 80, 82
Susanna, 79
ASTON, Robert, 79
Sarah, 79
ATKESON, Samuel, 101
ATKINSON, Cabel, 163

Eli, 163
Elizabeth, 163
Esther, 163
George, 163
Hannah, 163
James, 54
John, 163
Mahlon, 73
Rachel, 139
Samuel, 163
Sarah, 138
AUSTIN, Lydia, 30
Samuel, 30, 72, 131
Sarah, 30
AUZ, Barbara, 200, 201
Georg, 200, 201
Johannes, 200
Maria Magdalena, 201
AYARS, Samuel, 112
AZEHEAD, Georg, 74

-B-

BACH, Michael, 229
BACON, Abner, 32
Ann, 31, 141, 156
Barbara, 200, 212, 213
Charles, 68, 70, 118, 126, 154, 158, 175
David, 104, 111, 162, 174
Deborah, 174
Dorcas, 175
Edmond, 174
Eleanor, 32, 57
Elisabeth, 221
Elizabeth, 62, 126, 127, 156, 158, 159, 174
Elonar, 175
Esther, 174
Grace, 89, 99
Hanna, 200
Hannah, 32
Isaack, 213
Jeremias, 212
Jesse, 121, 133, 134, 135, 174
Job, 73, 174
John, 32, 57, 66,

89, 94, 97, 98, 100, 102, 110, 116, 123, 127, 130, 131, 156, 161, 174
Joseph, 45, 62, 67, 110, 112, 128, 133, 154, 161, 162, 174
Leatitia, 63
Loth, 213, 221
Loth., 212
Lott, 200
Luce, 90
Lydia, 32
Margaret, 66, 111, 150, 154, 174
Martha, 32, 57, 121, 174
Mary, 31, 106, 113, 129, 156, 161, 162, 174
Prudence, 124, 174
Rachel, 70, 154, 161, 162, 175
Rebeckah, 154
Richard, 46, 113, 174
Ruth, 143
Samuel, 31, 111, 174
Sarah, 121
Thomas, 32, 57, 103, 174, 175
BAGELEY, Charles, 76
BAGELY, Charles, 76
BAGGNALL, Elennor, 90
Ellin, 62
BAGLEY, Charles, 75
BAILEY, Emmon, 56
Emmor, 136
BAKEN, Israel, 232
Lot, 232
BAKER, Amy, 117
BAKON, Anna Barbara, 204
Barbara, 202, 209
Isaak, 209
Jacob, 202
Lad, 205
Loth, 202, 204, 209
Maria Magdaleana, 204
BALDWIN, Joshua, 49
BALINGER, Amariah, 47
John, 132
BALL, John, 168
Nathan, 168
Sarah, 168
BALLANGER, Amariah, 135
BALLENGER, Amariah, 136
Ameriah, 136
Bershebe, 122
Elizabeth, 47, 118, 120
Hannah, 171
Hephsiba, 49
John, 73
Joshua, 47, 104
Josiah, 92
Samuel, 47
Sarah, 122
William, 73
BALLINGER, Amariah, 132
Benjamin, 164
Daniel, 134
Deborah, 67
Elizabeth, 48, 68
Esther, 48
Hannah, 48, 163, 168, 170
Henery, 91
Hephzibah, 71
Hester, 70
Hope, 155, 164
Isaac, 164
Jacob, 155, 164
Jemima, 133
John, 48, 134, 163, 167
Joshua, 47, 164
Josiah, 164
Mary, 134, 163, 164, 167
Naomi, 68, 104, 164
Naomy, 46
Samuel, 44, 47, 64, 111, 119
Sarah, 48
William, 48
Zacheus, 68, 155, 164
BALZ, Johann Georg, 228
BANNESTERS, Mary, 41
BARBARA, Abraham, 173
Isaac, 173
Jacob, 173
Maria, 180
Mary, 173
Mary Ann, 173
Rebecca, 173
BARBER, Abraham, 15, 60, 143, 170, 172
Ann, 54, 59, 97, 172
Aquilla, 15, 92, 96, 101, 144, 148
Burtis, 59
Daniel, 15, 98, 100
David, 24, 148
Elija, 24
Elizabeth, 62
George, 164
Hannah, 15, 67, 94, 95, 144, 145, 164, 167
Henry, 71, 145, 164, 167, 171
Isaac, 15, 54, 59, 60, 72, 102, 116, 119, 143, 145, 150, 163, 164, 167, 170, 172
Isaiah, 164
Jacob, 24, 60, 102, 123, 143, 148, 164, 170, 172
James, 126, 144
Jane, 136, 137, 145, 148, 150, 164, 238
John, 15, 102, 116, 148, 157, 164
Jonathan, 24
Joseph, 59, 162, 238
Liddy, 144
Louisa, 24, 71
Lydia, 116
Marcy, 95

Mary, 15, 60, 103, 115, 143, 148, 163, 172
Mary Ann, 68, 143, 145, 163
Moses, 99
Nathaniel, 238
Phebe, 97
Rachel, 164
Rebecca, 135, 143, 172
Rebeccca, 60
Rebeck, 157
Rebeckah, 24, 148
Rebekah, 170
Samuel, 15, 113, 164
Sarah, 69, 119, 144, 145, 164
Susannah, 144
Thomas, 15, 65, 66, 94, 95, 98
Wade, 113
William, 54, 59, 131, 145, 164, 167
BARBERT, Aquillea, 89
BARBOR, Hannah, 96
BARE, Thomas, 110
BARKER, John, 98
Wade, 45, 114
William, 252
BARKLEY, James, 239
Jane, 239
Susanna, 239
BARN, Barbara, 244
BARNES, Ephraim, 170, 171
John, 119, 121, 132, 169
Joshua, 129
Rebecca, 169
Rebeckah, 119
Richard, 138
Samuel, 58
Sarah, 170
BARNS, Ann, 153
David, 153
Elizabeth, 153
Ephraim, 153
Hepzebah, 153
Jane, 153
John, 114, 123, 135, 153
Joseph, 52, 127, 130, 153
Joshua, 55, 153
Mary, 153
Rebeckah, 153
Richard, 153
Samuel, 153, 252
Sarah, 115, 153
BARRACLIFF, Aaron, 154
Ann, 175
Aron, 175
George, 175
John, 62, 154, 175
Laetitia, 175
Leatitia, 154
Prudence, 175
Ruth, 122, 175
BARRACLIFT, John, 103
BARRATT, Elisabeth, 96
BARRET, Thomas, 92, 94
BARRETT, Thomas, 91
BARRICLIFF, John, 63
BARROT, Elizabeth, 18
Gwen, 18
Rachel, 114, 127
Thomas, 18
BARROTT, Rachel, 115, 116, 119, 120
BARROWCLIFF, Prudence, 121
BASIT, Elizabeth, 100
Rachel, 106
BASSET, Amy, 52
Ann, 163
Beulah, 164
Deborah, 164, 169
Elisha, 111
Elizabeth, 163
Hannah, 163
Josiah, 164
Mary, 164
Nathan, 163, 171
Rebecca, 96
Ruth, 164
Sarah, 98, 163, 164
William, 94
Zebede, 108
BASSETT, Abigail, 50, 123, 125, 149, 151, 152, 164, 171
Amey, 71
Amy, 119
Ann, 120, 137, 139, 153, 154, 155
Anna, 170
Benjamin, 31
Beulah, 50, 126
Daniel, 64, 67, 73, 120, 122, 132, 144, 158, 169, 170
David, 125, 158, 170
Davis, 50, 120, 129, 134, 154
Deborah, 55, 123, 125, 126, 148, 151, 170
Elisha, 31, 110, 111, 112, 115, 117, 120, 149, 159
Elizabeth, 72, 133, 137, 169, 170
Gideon, 158
Gideon Scull, 159
Grace, 69, 126, 153, 171, 172, 173
Hannah, 31, 71, 125, 137, 138, 170
Isaac, 45, 66, 110, 112, 148, 151
Joseph, 31, 72, 125
Josiah, 50, 72
Mark, 158
Mary, 31, 50, 65, 69, 123, 125, 134, 144, 152, 158, 170
Morris, 153
Nathan, 72, 137, 170

INDEX

Phebe, 50, 70, 123, 152, 164
Rachel, 119, 121
Rebecca, 31
Rebeckah, 159
Samuel, 31, 108, 120, 153, 155
Sarah, 62, 71, 125, 170
William, 45, 110, 111, 127, 152, 153, 164
BASSIT, Rebekah, 101
William, 44
BASSITT, Elisha, 104
BATCHLER, William, 77
BATEMAN, Nathan, 235
BATES, Abigail, 144
Amos, 31
Catharine, 31, 53
Elizabeth, 31, 52, 54
Ezekiah, 31, 137, 141
Hezekiah, 53
James Oldden, 31
John, 52
Joseph, 144
Mary, 31, 53, 144
Mercy, 52
Phebe, 52
Rebecca, 54
Rebeccah, 31
Rebeckah, 52
William, 31, 52, 78
BATON, Anna Barbara, 220
Georg, 220
Loth, 220
BATTY, Jaell, 6, 78
Richard, 6
BAUER, Agnesa, 185
Anna Margareta, 201, 205
Anna Margaretha, 199, 231
Carolina, 196, 198, 199, 203
Carolina Christina, 199, 231
Conrad, 196, 199,
201, 205, 231
Ehrhard, 190
Jacob, 201
Joh. Michael, 185
Johann Peter, 205
Leonard, 195, 196, 198, 203
Leonhard, 199
Magdalena, 190
Margareta, 196
Maria Catharina, 190
Susanna Salome, 185
BEARD, Sarah, 113
BEASBEY, Edward, 86
BECHLER, Christian, 227
Margareta, 224
Margarethe, 225
Simon, 227
Susanna, 227
BECHTLER, Louisa, 197
Margareta, 197
Simon, 197
BECKET, Martha, 61
BEEDELL, John, 61
BEEDEN, Barbara, 207
Israel, 207
Lat, 207
BEERE, Abell, 79
Jonathan, 77, 78, 79
Nicholson, 79
BEESLEY, Abner, 31
Benjamin, 31
Mary, 31
Susannah, 31
Thomas Mason, 31
William, 31
BEESLY, Jacob, 190
Susannah, 190
BEETHE, John, 61
BEETLE, Esther, 2
Hester, 2
John, 2, 61
BEGELY, Charles, 61, 75
BEGGERLY, Char., 75
Charles, 75
BEGHOLD, Johann Juerg, 180
BEGLEY, Ann, 76
Charles, 76
BEITELMAN, Elias, 178
Maria Elisabetha, 178
BELANGEY, John, 86
BELCHER, Margretha, 192
Simon, 192
Susanna, 192
BELINGER, Joshua, 43
BELL, Jacob, 44, 108
BELLINCKER, Catharina, 207
Elisabeth, 207
Johann, 207
BELLINGER, Elisabeth, 209, 212
Hanna, 209
Joh., 209
Johann, 212
John, 212
Joseph, 212
Maria, 212
BELLOES, Mathias, 5
BENDER, Christian, 229
David, 212
Elisabeth, 204
Georg, 201, 204, 207, 212
Jacob, 207
Johan, 196
Johann Georg, 196
Ludwig, 214, 222, 225
Margareta, 201, 204, 207, 214
Margareth, 222
Margaretha, 225
Margrete, 212
Margretha, 196
Peter, 225
Richard, 214
Wilhelm, 201
BENNET, Hannah, 243
BENSON, Thomas, 75
BENTER, Geo., 206
Margaretha, 206
BENZLER, Mrs., 195
BERKET, John, 3
Martha, 3
BERNHARD, Elisabeth,

209
Georg, 209
BESLY, Virgin, 252
BETTLE, John, 77
BEVAN, Sarah, 138
BEVEN, Sarah, 142
BEVIN, Sarah, 141
BIBER, Jacob, 218
  Maria, 218
  Sarah, 218
BIEL, Elisabeth, 205
  Georg, 205
  Maria Elisabeth, 205
BIGLER, Catherine, 212
BILDERBACK, James, 234
  Jane, 234
BILGRAMM, Berseba, 223
  Franz, 223
  Hanna, 223
BILLANDEY, John, 84
BILLANGLY, John, 84
BILLINGS, John, 84
BISHOP, John, 237
  Mary, 235, 237, 238, 239, 240, 242
  Naomi, 238
  Samuel, 234, 235, 237, 238, 239, 240, 242
  Sarah, 240
BISPHAM, Benjamin, 42, 105
BISPHAM, Benjamin, 103
BITTER, Elisabeth, 205
  Henrich, 205
  Margareta, 205
BLACK, Elizabeth, 142
BLACKFORD, Samuel, 50, 127
BLANCHARD,
  Elizabeth, 14, 62
  Jane, 14
  Margret, 15
  Mary, 14, 15
  Philip, 14, 15, 92
BLANSHARE, Philip, 89
BLANSHER, June, 96
  Philip, 86, 87
BLECKSFIELD, Peter, 84
BLEINIGER,
  Catharina, 190
  Falentin, 190
  Matias, 190
BLENINGER,
  Catharina, 207
  Mathaeus, 207
BLENNINGER,
  Catharina, 189
  Matthaeus, 189
BLEU, Ann, 236
  Elizabeth, 236
  John, 236
BLEW, Elizabeth, 244
  George, 244
BLIDERBACK, Sarah, 113
BLUEMLEIN, Chistop, 191
  Elenora Catharina, 191
  Margretha, 191
BLUME, Elisabeth, 186
  Georg, 186
BLUMER, Elisabetha, 200
  Joh. Georg, 200
BOEHM, Catharina Elisabeta, 194
  F. Friedrich, 194
BOEHMER, Catharina Elisabetha, 194
  Friedr., 194
  Friedrich, 194
BOGGS, Frances, 171
  Priscilla, 133
BOND, Elizabeth, 32
  Jane, 32
  Jesse, 32
  Thomas, 32
BOOTH, Ann, 23
  Elizabeth, 23, 66, 244
  Jane, 23, 120
  Jene, 117
  Richard, 23, 97, 112, 146
  Ruth, 23
  Sarah, 23, 122
BORDEN, Elizabeth, 171
  Peter, 139, 170
  Thomas, 66
BORGES, Margareta, 214
  Peter, 214
  Susanna, 214
BORION, Peter, 229
BORN, Anna Maria, 177, 178
  Michael, 177, 178
BOROUGH, Elizabeth, 136
BOROUGHS, Elizabeth, 136
BORTEN, John, 88
BORTON, Elizabeth, 133, 134
BOSS, Elizabeth, 65
BOSSARD, Johannes, 201
  Michael, 201
BOWELL, Elizabeth, 250
BOWEN, Ann, 129
  Sarah, 115, 116
BOWIN, George, 251
BOWING, Ann, 72, 129
BOYER, Auther, 89
  Hannah, 87
  Sarah, 86
BRADRETH, Daniel, 42
BRADWAU, Jonathan, 160
BRADWAY, Aaron, 25, 103, 108, 109, 132, 146
  Adna, 26, 147, 150, 151, 153
  Ann, 31
  Anna, 31, 157
  Aron, 31
  David, 72, 147
  Edward, 3, 7, 26, 31, 64, 72, 74, 75, 76, 77, 78, 79, 122, 123, 124, 135, 146, 147, 161
  Elizabeth, 7, 8, 9, 91, 133, 147, 150, 161

INDEX

Grace, 31
Hannah, 3, 72, 134, 146
Henry, 74
James, 39, 72, 146
John, 72, 150, 170
Jonathan, 9, 26, 63, 96, 97, 98, 99, 108, 150, 153
Joshua, 25, 31, 252
Mark, 72, 150
Mary, 3, 25, 26, 39, 61, 70, 150, 157
Nathan, 26, 120, 123
Prudence, 62, 103
Rachel, 26, 63, 107
Rebeckah, 25, 66
Samuel, 149, 150
Sarah, 3, 7, 26, 31, 39, 79, 110, 113, 125, 129, 146, 149, 150, 151, 157
Susanna, 3
Susannah, 26, 79, 99, 176
Thomas, 146
Waddington, 147
William, 7, 8, 9, 26, 39, 55, 63, 69, 77, 82, 83, 110, 112, 116, 139, 140, 146, 149, 150, 151, 157
BRAG, Roger, 42
BRAGG, Roger, 98
BRANDETH, Elizabeth, 64
BRANDNDER, Andreas, 190
  Susannah, 190
BRANDNER, Andreas, 181, 182, 183, 184, 187, 189, 191
  Joh. Georg, 191
  Johann Adam, 189
  Maria Barbara, 184
  Susanna, 183, 184, 187, 191
  Susannah, 189
BRANDRETH, Daniel, 98
  Deborah, 104
BRANDRITH, Timothy, 86
BRANSON, Meriam, 51, 134
  Samuel, 58
BRASS, Adam, 203
  Johann Philipp, 203
  Philippina, 203
BRATHWART, Mary, 250
BRAUN, Catharina Margaretha, 179
  Elisabeth, 187
  Johann Adam, 185
  Margareta Barbara, 181
  Margreta, 181
  Margretha, 185, 187
  Martin, 179, 181, 185, 187
BREADEN, Nathaniel, 85
BRECH, Christoph, 197
  Susanna, 197
BRECHNER, Anna Maria, 199
  Christoph, 199, 202
  Susanna, 199, 202
BREIDA, Heinrich, 209
BREITINGER, Anna, 189, 198
  Friedr, 198
BREMER, Margareta, 209
BRENERSHOLZ, Adam, 209
  Barbara, 209
  Maria, 209
BRENESHOLZ, Adam, 197, 206
  Georg, 197
  Maria, 197, 206
  Maria Elisabet, 197
  Sara, 206
BRENNE, Joseph, 78
BRENNESCHOLZ, Jacob, 226
BRENNESHOLZ, Adam, 213
  Barbara, 213
  Carl, 213
  Hannah, 226
  Henrich, 226
  Philippine, 226
BREUNESHOLTZ, Adam, 190
  Maria, 190
  Maria Barbara, 190
BREYMANN, Catharina, 203
  Christian, 230
  Johann Christian, 203
BRICK, Abigail, 112
  Ann, 32, 33, 56, 64, 72, 115, 134, 146, 150, 174
  Deborah, 32
  Elizabeth, 63, 90, 174
  Hannah, 96, 112, 115, 132, 146, 150, 174
  Jane, 56, 66
  Jean, 174
  John, 33, 62, 108, 110, 112, 115, 150, 174
  Joseph, 32, 64, 72, 121, 130, 146, 160, 162, 174, 251
  Joshua, 251
  Martha, 32, 162
  Mary, 33, 108, 174
  Rebecca, 32
  Rebeckah, 146, 160
  Ruth, 65, 110, 174
  Samuel, 32, 56, 72, 130, 134, 146
BRICKMAN, Richard, 91
BRIDGMAN, Robert, 3
BRIGGS, Aaron, 57
  Abner, 140
BRITTON, Thomas, 3
BROADWAY, Beulah, 58
  Dorcas, 58

Elizabeth, 58
John, 58
Jonathan, 58
Josiah, 58
BROADWIT, Margaret, 84
BROOKS, Ann, 251
John, 237
Naomi, 71
Naomy, 127
BROOTH, Margaret, 244
BROUGHWHITE,
Prudence, 90
BROWN, Abigail, 125
Ann, 31
Beulah, 126
David, 70
Elgar, 31, 53, 136
Elisha, 31
Elizabeth, 31, 36, 72, 136
Ellgar, 72
Esther, 31
George, 31, 61
Hannah, 150, 243
Isaac, 240
Israel, 31
James, 31, 36, 61
Jane, 244
Jesse, 56
Job, 56
John, 240
John Miller, 31
John Mason, 31
Joseph, 31, 55, 78, 83, 131
Margaret, 31, 61
Mary, 31, 61, 125, 147, 150
Miller, 31
Phebe, 125
Rebecca, 31, 61
Rebeccah, 31
Rebeckah, 45
Sarah, 31
Thomas, 106, 147, 150
William, 45, 116, 118, 119
BROWNE, Joseph, 84
BRUNNHOLTZ, Peter, 176, 177, 180
BUCHER, Elizabeth, 93
Hannah, 117
James, 106
John, 91
BUCK, Hannah, 244
BUCKLEY, Abraham, 88
BUCMASTER,
Elizabeth, 87
BUFFINGTON,
Benjamin, 44
BULL, Dorothea, 252
BULLY, Edward, 251
BURDEN, Amy, 73
Elizabeth, 60, 143
Peter, 167
Thomas, 45, 66, 117
BURGIN, John, 250
BURKELL, Frances, 3
BURKLY, Samuel, 82
BURNES, Hannah, 139
Samuel, 73, 138
BURNHAM, Elizabeth, 5
Ralph, 5
Richard, 5
BURRELL, Dorcas, 80, 81
BURROUGH, Benjamin, 246
Hannah, 246
John, 246
Jonathan, 246
Judith, 246
BURROUGHS, Benjamin, 247
Cornelius, 247
Hannah, 247
James, 247
John, 247
Josiah, 114
Judith, 247
Mary, 247
Sarah, 114
Susanna, 247
BURROW, Elizabeth, 54
BURTIS, Elizabeth, 50
BURTON, John, 2, 73, 76
BURWELL, Dorcas, 9
Moses, 9
BUSOM, Joseph, 129

BUSSE, Margret, 3
Paul, 3
BUTCHER, Elizabeth, 51, 132, 189
George, 189
Hannah, 67, 93
James, 17
Jane, 17
Jean, 93
Job, 122, 126, 159
John, 17, 25
Joseph, 51, 132
Mary, 119, 122, 159
Prudence, 132
Rachel, 25, 64
Samuel, 132
Thomas, 25, 63, 107
BUTLER, Elizabeth, 46, 71
Hannah, 125
John, 46, 111
Richard, 127
BUZBY, Ann, 88
BYRNES, Samuel, 58

-C-
CAARNS, John
Leonard, 244
CADE, Mary, 115
Sarah, 170
CAESBY, Bradway, 106
CAIRLE, Elizabeth, 251
CAM, Jenit, 242
John, 242
Mary, 242
CAME, Mabel, 81
CAMMEL, Elizabeth, 76
Mary, 139
CAMPBELL, Charles, 250
Rachel, 113
CANADA, James, 241
Jane, 241
Patrick, 241
CANDEL, Anna Maria, 208, 209, 216
Heinr., 208, 209
Heinrich, 216
Johann, 216
CANDLE, Henrich, 199

INDEX 261

CARARARY, Roger, 78
CARARY, Roger, 76, 77
CARAY, Christopher, 6
　Elizabeth, 6
　Margret, 6
　Mary, 6
　Rachel, 6
　Robert, 77
　Roger, 6
CARL, Catharina, 185, 190, 194, 197
　Henrich, 197
　Maertin, 190
　Martin, 185, 194, 197
　Wilhelm, 194
CARLE, Abraham, 242
　Catherine, 239, 241, 242
　John, 239, 241, 242
　Mary, 237
　Rachel, 241
CARNER, Anna Maria, 188
　Martin, 188
CARPENTER,
　Elizabeth, 67, 128, 163
　Hannah, 29, 32, 41, 100, 117, 163
　Margaret, 41, 70
　Martha, 72, 131
　Mary, 32, 70, 143
　Mary Wyatt, 163
　Preston, 29, 32, 41, 43, 66, 100, 111, 112, 119, 120, 162
　Rachel, 52, 143
　Richard, 77
　Samuel, 76, 77, 82, 83
　Thomas, 119, 121, 122
　William, 32, 72, 163
　William Hall, 80
CARR, Sarah, 234
CARRL, Anna Margretha, 193

Catharina, 193
　Martin, 193
CARROL, Patrick, 243
CARTER, Benjamin, 32, 170
　Elizabeth, 32
　Hester, 32
　Maria, 32
　Mary, 170
　Rebecca, 32
　Rebeckah, 170
　Restore, 32
　Thomas, 32
CASBY, Edward, 91, 92, 93, 94
CASELY, Edward, 84
CASPAR, Jacob, 227
　Lorenz, 227
　Susanna, 227
CASPARSON, Anthony, 252
CASSADY, Jane, 136, 137
CATTEL, Mary, 131
　William, 44, 108
CATTELL, Ann, 145
　Elijah, 124, 145
　Mary, 131, 145
　William, 145
CHAMBER, James, 86
CHAMBLES, James, 101
　Nathaniel, 97
CHAMBLESS, James, 16, 38
　Mary, 16
　Sarah, 38
CHAMBLIS, Elonar, 103
CHAMBLISS, James, 101
CHAMLER, James, 85
CHAMLES, Charles, 82
　Nathaniel, 82, 90
CHAMLEY, Nathaniel, 85
CHAMLIS, Elizabeth, 89
CHAMMES, Nathaniel, 80
CHAMNES, James, 87
　Mary, 46
　Nathaniel, 80, 81, 83, 84, 86, 87
CHAMNESS, Elizabeth,

9
　Hannah, 10
　James, 14, 15
　Mary, 14, 15
　Nathaniel, 9, 10, 11
　Rebeckah, 9, 10, 11, 14
CHAMNEYS, Hannah, 27, 63
　Mary, 66
　Nathaniel, 73
　Nathaniel, 27, 73, 110, 111, 151
　Rebeckah, 27
　Sarah, 114
　Susannah, 27
CHAMNIES, Nathaniel, 84
CHAMNIS, Edward, 74
　James, 87
　Nathan, 86
　Nathaniel, 87
CHAMPINEYS,
　Nathaniell, 79
CHAMPLIS, Mary, 113
CHAMPNESS, Elenor, 8
　Elizabeth, 16
　Hanah, 95
　Hannah, 92
　James, 8, 16, 92, 93, 95
　Margeret, 16
　Mary, 8
　Nathaniel, 8, 91, 92, 94
　Nathaniell, 62
CHAMPNEY, Elizabeth, 7
　Mary, 7
　Nathaniel, 7, 79
　Nathaniell, 2, 80
CHAMPNEYS,
　Nathaniel, 2
　Nathaniell, 80
CHANDERS, Thomas, 76
CHANDLER, Esther, 104
　Frances, 81
　Hannah, 92, 104, 124
　John, 91, 92, 93, 102, 106, 108, 110, 176

Josiah, 176
Mary, 114
Paul, 41
William, 104
CHANLER, John, 89
CHANNEY, Edward, 75
CHATTORG, Elizabeth, 75
CHESTER, Samuel, 57, 58, 127, 132, 136, 137, 139
CHEW, Maria, 219
  Richard, 215, 219
  Robert, 215
  Susanna, 215, 219
  Thomas, 215
CHEW COPELAND,
  David, 129
  Sarah, 129
CHIBINGS, Henry, 75
CHURCH, Arthur, 5
  Elizabeth, 5
CLARK, Ann, 244
  Cornelius, 45, 110, 111
  David, 127
  Deborah, 127
  Edward, 168
  Elizabeth, 127
  Hannah, 127
  John, 246, 247
  Joseph, 41, 90
  Mary, 117, 168
  Sarah, 46, 115
  William, 61
  Zacheus, 127
CLARKE, Mary, 132
CLEMENS, Moses, 244
CLEMENT, Elizabeth, 32, 136
  James, 223
  Jean, 223
  Joseph, 45, 64
  Ruth, 32, 136
  Thomas, 32, 136
CLERK, Sarah, 48
CLEVER, Jemimah, 128
CLEWS, Joseph, 92, 98
CLIFTON, Elizabeth, 17, 18
  Hugh, 17, 18, 63, 90, 91, 92, 93, 94, 95, 96, 97,
99, 102, 103, 107
  Joseph, 18
  Mary, 18
  Sarah, 63, 107
  William, 17
CLOWES, Joseph, 99, 100
CLOWS, Joseph, 91, 92, 93, 94, 96, 97, 99
CLUSE, Joseph, 89
COAKSLEY, William, 90
COAKSLY, William, 90
COATSUTTON, Isabel, 45, 114
COCK, Peter, 252
COELLISCHEN,
  Margaretha, 178
COELSCH, Margretha, 192
  Philip, 192
  Susanna, 192
COELSH, Leonhard, 193
  Margretha, 193
  Philip, 193
COGLE, Lidia, 122
COLE, Elizabeth, 137
  Joseph, 48, 121
COLES, Samuel, 119
COLESON, Sarah, 45
COLESTON, Neomy, 138
COLIER, John, 87, 110
COLLER, Beniaman, 96
  John, 89
COLLIER, Benjamin, 100
COLLYER, Benjamin, 11
  Elizabeth, 11, 13
  Isabel, 11
  John, 11, 13
  Martha, 11
  Percillah, 11
  Samuel, 13
  Sarah, 11
  William, 11
COLSON, Asa, 156, 162
  David, 71, 156, 159, 167
  Elizabeth, 146
George, 68, 110, 134, 146, 156, 162
  Hepseah, 167
  Hepzibah, 159
  Jonathan, 146, 156, 159, 167
  Mary, 126, 135, 156, 162, 167, 169
  William, 69
COLSTON, George, 62
  Hannah, 62
  William, 72
COLYER, John, 84, 85, 86, 87
CONDON, Mary, 63
CONELLY, Bryant, 252
CONEY, Phebe, 130
CONINGUM, Rebecah, 113
CONKELYN, Gideon, 238, 241
  Phebe, 244
  Priscilla, 238, 241
  Samuel, 241
  Susanna, 238
CONKLIN, Phebe, 234
CONNOR, Barbara, 222, 227
  Patrick, 222
  Rosanna, 222
CONNOVER, Barbara, 225
  Johann Georg, 225
  Wilhelm, 225
CONOR, John, 243
CONRATH, Johann Henrich, 185
CONROW, Atkinson, 59
  Caleb, 59
  Calebe, 142
  Mary, 59, 142
  Patience, 59, 142
COOMBS, Elisabeth, 221
  Joel, 221
  Ruth, 128
COOPER, Amos, 166
  Ann, 48, 143, 156, 159
  Anne, 166
  Benjamin Clark,

48, 156, 159
Catharine, 128
Deborah, 156, 159
Hannah, 7
James, 156
Magdalene, 118
Mary, 7, 79, 156
Paul, 71
Samuel, 156, 159
Sarah, 7, 166
William, 7, 61,
  73, 76, 77, 78,
  118, 156, 159
COPELAND, Joshua,
  129
COPERTHWAITE, Sarah,
  116
COPNER, Joseph, 32,
  143
COPPERTHWAITE, Hugh,
  41
  John, 45
  Thomas, 45, 64,
    115, 117
COSTER, Jacob, 186
  Jacobina, 186
  Johannes, 186
COUCH, Anna, 190
  Hans George, 190
COULDON, Hannah, 117
COULSON, George, 96,
  97, 98
  Sarah, 67
  William, 67
COWGILL, Elizabeth,
  51, 130
  Jonathan, 56, 139
  Lidya, 121
COWPER, Mary, 47
  William, 47
COWPERTHWAITE, John,
  117
  Mark, 128
  Samuel, 128
  Thomas, 117, 127,
    128
COWPLAND, Ann, 49
  Cadwalader, 49
  Calab, 49
  David, 49
  Joshua, 49
  Sarah, 49
COX, Caspar, 204
  John, 204

Martha, 204
Mary, 244
COYLER, Isabell, 87
CRAB, William, 106
CRABB, Wiliam, 97
  William, 42, 98,
    101, 104, 252
CRAEMER, Andreas,
  208, 209
CRAFORD, Elizabeth,
  250
CRAFT, John, 32
  Mary, 32, 50
CRAFTOS, Martha, 1
CRAIG, Abnor, 247
  Abnor Penton, 247
  Ann, 35, 59, 244
  Elias, 243
  Elizabeth, 236,
    247
  Jacob, 238
  James, 237
  John, 234, 236,
    237, 238, 241,
    243, 247
  Leatitia, 59, 121,
    128, 130
  Leititia, 132
  Letitia, 35
  Lettiatia, 169
  Letticia, 168
  Margaret, 238
  Martha, 32, 61,
    172, 173, 236,
    247
  Mary, 234, 236,
    237, 238, 241,
    243, 247
  Rebeckah, 247
  Samuel, 32, 59,
    143, 168, 238
  Sarah, 35, 59,
    241, 247
  William, 35, 59,
    130, 134, 168
CRAIGG, Abner, 246
  Abram, 246
  Elizabeth, 246
  John, 246
  Mary, 246
  Rebeckah, 246
  Sally, 246
CRAIGH, Abner, 246
  Abram, 246

Elizabeth, 246
John, 246
Mary, 246
Rebeckah, 246
Sally, 246
CRATTINGER, Maria
  Elizabeth, 177
CRAVEN, Ann, 77, 78
  Mary, 64
  Peter, 75, 77
  Rachel, 90
  Thomas, 76, 77,
    109
CRAVER, Ann, 61
CREAMER, Margarethe,
  208, 209
  Mathias, 208, 209
CRIPPS, Benjamin,
  126
  Elizabeth, 141
  John, 117
  Martha, 30
  Mary, 30, 133
  Whitten, 30
  Whitton, 64, 116
  William, 118
CRIPS, Benjamin, 42,
  95, 97, 98
  Hannah, 63
  Martha, 116
  Mary, 42, 116
CRISPIN, Hezekiah,
  50
  Jonathan, 143
  Joseph, 50, 57,
    133
  Levy, 50
  Margaret, 50
  Prudence, 50
  Roland, 50
CROCELIUS, Ottilia,
  229
  Otto, 229
CRONEBERGER,
  Elisabeth, 226
  Margareta, 213
  Peter, 213, 226
CRONENBERGER,
  Margareta, 224
  Maria Magdalena,
    232
CROSS, Benjamin, 252
  Mary, 66, 114
CROW, Edisha, 250

CRYFORD, Johanna, 197
   Richard, 197
CRYM, Lorentz, 193
CULLEYER, John, 86
CULLIER, Benjamin, 100
   John, 89, 91, 92, 99
CULLYAR, Sarah, 244
CULLYER, John, 84
CUNDERMANN,
   Catharina, 232
CUNNINGHAM,
   Rebeckah, 66
CURIER, Elizabeth, 61
CURRENT, Nicholas, 243
CURREY, James, 235
CURRIE, James, 240, 243
   Margaret, 243
   Robert, 240
CURRIER, Catherin, 78
   Elizabeth, 61
CURRY, Mary, 57
   Meribah, 48
CURTIS, Jonathan, 61
CYRREY, James, 237
   William, 237

-D-

DAGGER, John, 6
DAKIN, Joseph, 95
DALEY, Dennis, 117
DALTON, Charles, 235
   Elizabeth, 235
DALY, Dennis, 48, 119
DAMERUS, Anna Maria, 183
   Christian, 183
   Peter, 183
DANDELSBAECHER,
   Catharina, 191
   Ludwig, 191
   Margretha, 191
DANIEL, Aaron, 16, 102, 106, 150
   David, 150
   Edmond, 159
   Edmund, 147
   Elizabeth, 14, 75, 111, 145, 150, 159
   Hannah, 94, 95
   Henry, 28
   Isabel, 11, 15, 16
   Isabell, 14, 15, 94
   Jael, 147
   James, 10, 11, 12, 13, 14, 15, 16, 28, 62, 65, 82, 87, 93, 94, 95, 96, 97, 98, 110, 124, 145, 156
   Jane, 10, 11, 12, 13
   Joel, 123
   John, 15, 28, 125
   Joseph, 13, 28, 94, 159
   Lydia, 137
   Mary, 12
   Rebeckah, 14, 28, 62, 115, 147
   Sarah, 13, 28, 116, 159
   Thomas, 10, 28, 69, 93, 159
   William, 15, 28, 69, 100, 135, 147
DANIELL, Elizabeth, 80
   James, 81, 84, 86, 87, 91, 92, 94, 95, 99
   Joseph, 94
   Neale, 79
   Neall, 79
   Sarah, 91
   Thomas, 92, 93, 99
DANIELS, Rebeckah, 105
DANNIL, James, 86
DANYOL, James, 81
DANZEBECHER,
   Catherina, 218
   Hanna, 226
   Jacob, 226
   Ludwig, 218
DANZENBACHER,
   Catharina, 194
   Johann Lud., 194
DANZENBECHER,
   Catharina, 227
   Hanna, 227
   Jacob, 227
   Ludwig, 227
DANZENBERGER, Georg, 227
   Henrich, 227
   Maria, 227
DARBY, Bridget, 244
DARE, Elonar, 103
DARKEN, Richard, 80, 84
DARKIN, Ann, 7, 9, 16, 17
   Hannah, 7, 16, 87, 99, 106, 251
   Jale, 15
   John, 7, 15, 90, 92, 93, 94
   Joseh, 92
   Joseph, 7, 16, 17, 86, 92, 93, 94, 96, 97, 99, 251
   Richard, 7, 9, 77, 79, 81, 82, 83, 84, 85, 86, 87
   Sarah, 15, 17, 85
DARKINS, John, 88, 89
   Joseph, 88, 89, 90
   Richard, 88, 89
DARNALLEY, John, 90
DARNELLEY, Ann, 88
DAVID, Arthur, 237
   Daniel, 237
   Martha, 237
   Sarah, 120
DAVIES, Abijhai, 238
   Amie, 100
   Amon, 238
   Ann, 243
   Anna, 235, 238, 240, 242
   Arthur, 240, 243
   Benjamin, 235, 244
   Broadway, 238
   Daniel, 235, 238, 240, 242
   Elisabeth, 240
   Elizabeth, 252
   Hannah, 238, 242
   Hester, 113, 240, 242
   James, 238, 239,

240, 242
Joanna, 239
Joseph, 238
Levi, 240
Mary, 238, 239, 240, 242
Othniel, 238
Rachel, 238
Sarah, 238
Uriah, 238
DAVIS, Abigail, 66, 114, 145
Amos, 164, 167
Ann H., 164
Arthur, 234
Charity, 18, 251
Charles, 62, 157, 175
David, 92, 93, 94, 97, 98, 99, 100, 106, 107, 110, 112, 115, 119, 133, 145, 146, 148, 164, 167
Dorotha, 138
Dorothy, 136, 138, 145
Elenor, 18
Elijha, 170
Elisha, 119, 129, 168
Elizabeth, 18, 115, 147, 168, 172, 173
Elonar, 128
Eloner, 122
Esther, 119, 146, 148, 153, 164, 168
Gabriel, 66, 164, 175
Hannah, 18, 54, 106, 146, 148, 167
Hannah S., 164
Hester, 119, 123, 153
hester, 125
Isaac, 91, 92, 93
Jacob, 73, 111, 114, 119, 137, 138, 145, 146, 148, 153, 155, 164, 168, 169, 170, 172, 173
James, 153, 155, 235
John, 18, 72, 92, 93, 94, 108, 147
Joseph, 119, 148, 164, 167
Josiah, 153, 155, 164
Jospeh, 119
Malachi, 92
Malchi, 93
Marcy, 18
Martha, 148, 164, 234
Martha C., 164
Mary, 18, 97, 119, 148, 164, 167, 235
Mary Ann, 164
Mercy, 101, 103
Phebe, 18
Rachel, 175
Richard, 164
Samuel, 164
Samuel Cole, 119
Samuel Coles, 148
Sarah, 99, 120, 130, 138, 164
Thomas, 18, 100, 119, 136, 137, 146, 164, 168
Thomas Wilkins, 164
DAWSON, Aaron, 120
Ann, 116
Anna, 116
Dorcas, 134
Francis, 125
Jedediah, 134
Lidia, 120, 122
Lidya, 117, 121
Lucy, 169
Moses, 121
Richard, 43, 120
William, 115
DEACKON, Georg, 74
DEACON, Francess, 3
George, 3, 74, 75, 76, 77, 78, 79, 89
DEAN, Richard, 77
DEANE, Richard, 76, 77
DEANER, Richard, 78
DEATON, Ann, 243
DEAVES, Isabel, 76
Isabell, 61
DECKER, Maria Elizabeth, 177
DECOW, John, 61
DEEN, John, 74, 75, 90, 110
Joseph, 78
Margaret, 78
Mary, 78
DELANEY, Hannah, 113
DELSCHOEFER, Susanna, 210
DELSHEFER, Elisabeth, 223
Jacob, 223
Nancy, 223
Rebecca, 223
Susanna, 223
DELSHOEFER, Daniel, 214
David, 222
Georg, 210
Jacob, 210, 214, 222
Johannes, 210
Mariane, 210
Susanna, 214, 222
DELZHEFER, Johann, 203
Maria, 203
DEM, Margaret, 77
DEMAERIS, Adam, 212
Maria, 212
Philip, 212
DEN, David, 26
Elizabeth, 26
John, 26, 90
DENDELSBACHER, Catharina, 194
Henrich, 194
Johann Ludwig, 194
DENDELSBECK, Anna Margreta, 181
Christina, 226
Elisabeth, 192
Francisca, 187, 189
Francisca Margretha, 186
Friederich, 181, 183, 187

Friedr., 187
Jacob, 226
Joh., 229
Johann, 226
Johannes, 181,
  186, 187, 189,
  192
John., 190
Margretha, 183,
  187
Maria Elisabeth,
  187
Rebecca, 189
Susanna, 192
DENDELSBECKE,
  Friederich, 229
DENDELSPECK, Anna
  Maria, 224
  Christina, 222,
  224
  Elisabeth, 200
  Joh., 210
  Johann, 222, 224
  Johannes, 199, 222
  Margareta, 203
DENELSPECK, Susanna,
  210
DENIS, Philip, 90,
  92, 97
  Sarah, 100
DENN, Amos, 17
  Ann, 160
  Daniel, 17
  Elizabeth, 5, 14,
  15, 16, 23, 69,
  80, 95, 113, 125,
  160
  Hannah, 243
  James, 5, 14, 23,
  71, 78, 160
  John, 14, 15, 16,
  17, 19, 23, 26,
  32, 48, 62, 75,
  87, 91, 92, 93,
  94, 99, 109, 110,
  113, 176
  John Maddock, 5
  John Madox, 87
  Lea, 17
  Leah, 18, 19, 64,
  98
  Marcy, 17
  Margaret, 5, 86
  Mary, 80
Mercy, 103
Naomi, 62, 102
Naomy, 15
Paul, 19, 63
Rachel, 23, 69
Rhoda, 32
DENNIS, Ann, 174
  Anne, 63
  Dorcas, 174
  Edward, 147
  Elizabeth, 174
  Grace, 174
  Hannah, 123, 129,
  147
  Henry, 33, 99,
  102, 108
  John, 56, 147
  Jonathan, 71, 174
  Joseph, 60, 174
  Lucy, 37, 117, 174
  Martha, 174
  Mary, 104, 147,
  159
  Philip, 37, 65,
  97, 109, 111,
  112, 116, 147,
  150, 174
  Prudance, 123
  Prudence, 120, 174
  Rachel, 37, 62,
  65, 174
  Samuel, 44, 65,
  70, 94, 107, 159,
  174
  Sarah, 62, 68, 174
DENTELSPECK,
  Johannes, 189
DENTTELSBEK,
  Friederich, 178
  Margaretha, 178
DERKIN, Richard, 78
DETON, Charles, 239
  Elizabeth, 239
DEVALL, Ann, 251
DEVENNY, Mary, 65
DEVINEY, Rebeckah,
  154
DEVINY, Mary, 112
DEWEL, Phebe, 130
DEWELL, Hannah, 130
DICKENSEN, Hannah,
  114
DICKER, Easter, 160
  Elizabeth, 148
Esther, 148
Hannah, 72, 148
Hester, 160
Lidya, 148
Richard, 66, 132,
  148, 160
Rudick, 111
Rudy, 66
DICKINSON, Mary, 91
  Sarah, 243
DICKISON, Dorothy,
  235
DICKSON, Susanna,
  252
DIEL, Anna
  Margareta, 198
  Georg, 198
  Johannes, 198
DIELSHOEFER,
  Johannes, 201,
  205
  Mariana, 201, 205
  Michael, 201
DIESTLER, Anna
  Margareta, 180
  Elisabeth, 180
  Johann Wilh., 180
DIETRICH, Jacob, 211
  Margrete, 211
  Peter, 211
  Rosine, 211
DILLSHEBER,
  Margaretha, 226
  Philip, 226
DILLSHEFER, Jacob,
  224
  Margareta, 224
  Philipp, 224
  Susanna, 224
DILLSHEOFER,
  Elisabeth, 198,
  199
  Jacob, 199
  Johannes, 198
  Mariana, 198
DILLSHOEFER,
  Elisabeth, 204
  Hannah, 204
  Jacob, 204
DILLSHOEFF,
  Margarethe, 222
DILLSHOEFFER, Johann
  Jacob, 178
  Maria Elisabetha,

INDEX

178
Maria Louisa, 179
Michael, 178
Michel, 179
DILLSHOEVER,
  Christian, 177
Maria Elisabeth,
  176, 177
Michael, 176, 177
DILLZHOEFFER, Jacob,
  232
Maria, 232
DILSCHOEVER, Jacob,
  230
Johannes, 230
DILSHAEFER,
  Christine, 208,
  209
Johannes, 208, 209
Mariane, 208, 209
DILSHEBER, Jacob,
  228
Susanna, 228
DILSHEFER, Jacob,
  224
Susanna, 224
DILSHEFFER, Anna
  Maria, 204
Jacob, 204
Joh., 204
Maria Anna, 204
DILSHEOFER,
  Christina, 202
Elisabeth, 202
Jacob, 202
DILSHOEFER,
  Christian Mich.,
  229
Daniel, 179, 229
Johannes, 212
Maria Elisabeth,
  179
Mariana, 212
Michael, 179, 229
Mrs., 229
Simon, 212
DILSHOEFFER,
  Michael, 229
Simon, 229
DILSHOEVER,
  Elisabeth, 231
DIVINE, Martah, 121
Martha, 117
DIVINY, Rebecca, 119

DIXON, Anna, 212
Anna Barbara, 212
Anthony, 76
Charity, 171
George, 212
Hannah, 114
DOFFEL, Catharina,
  181, 184, 189
Johannes, 181
Peter, 180, 181,
  184, 189
Wilhelm, 181, 184,
  189
DOLE, Peter, 53,
  136, 139
DONNE, John, 77
Robert, 76
DOTT, Joh P., 196
DRAKE, Sarah, 122
DRAPER, Amy, 146
Edward, 24, 40,
  72, 103, 104,
  105, 136, 146,
  162
Hannah, 40, 162
Jael, 24
Jemimah, 128
Jemime, 146
Mary, 24, 121, 146
Rebecca, 162
Rebeckah, 24
Thomas, 24, 40,
  120, 162
DREHER, Andr., 198
Anna Elisabet, 198
Anna Marie, 198
DREHERT, Andreas,
  200
Andreas Posthumus,
  200
Maria Margar, 200
DREUDINGER, Anna,
  190
Ulrich, 190
DROLLINGER, Gabriel,
  178
Margaretha, 178
DU BOIS, Anna, 234
Barnet, 234
David, 234
Elizabeth, 235
Garret, 234
Jacob, 234
Jacominihee, 234

John, 235
Jonathan, 235
Lewis, 234, 235
Margaret, 234
Mathew, 235
Solomon, 234
DUBOIS, Ann, 244
Garret, 237
Jacob, 244, 242
Janitie, 242
Lewis, 237
Margaret, 237
Rachel, 242
Samuel, 237
Sarah, 237
DUEL, Elizabeth, 46,
  114
Hannah, 144, 150
John, 73, 99, 109,
  111, 137, 144,
  150
Joseph Lippincott,
  167
Mary, 132
Phebe, 130
Thomas, 110
DUELL, Abigail, 164
Ann, 164
John, 42, 58, 109,
  164
Joseph D., 164
Joshua, 164
Lydia, 164
Phebe, 164
Samuel, 164
Thomas, 42
DUELSCHOEVER, Elis,
  198
Jacob, 198
Joh, 198
Johannes, 198
Maria, 198
DUELSHEFER, Georg,
  194
Jacob, 194, 195
Joh Jacob, 194
Johannes, 195
Mariana, 195
DUFFEL, Catherine,
  243
Jacob, 243
William, 243
DUN, Zacheus, 97
DUNAHM, David, 32

Elizabeth, 32
Job, 32
William, 32
DUNCLEY, Dorothy, 80
DUNHAM, David, 142
  Elizabeth, 54,
    142, 157
  Job, 142
  John, 54, 137
  Shobal, 157
  Shubal, 54
  William, 54, 157
  William Smith, 54,
    68, 119
DUNLAP, Aaron, 239
  Ann, 235, 241, 242
  Bathsheba, 241,
    242
  Charity, 55, 111,
    128, 129, 131,
    132, 133, 134,
    139
  Elisabeth, 234
  Elizabeth, 236
  Elizabethe, 234
  Ephraim, 236
  Francis, 234, 236,
    237, 239, 241,
    242, 244
  Isabel, 234, 237,
    241
  Issabel, 239
  James, 234, 235,
    236, 241, 242,
    252
  John, 236
  Mary, 239, 242
  Rebekah, 239, 242
  Thomas, 237
DUNN, Ann, 149
  Benijah, 137
  Deborah, 64, 66,
    121, 136, 144,
    159, 168
  Isaac, 144
  John, 144
  Josiah, 159
  Lidya, 65
  Mary, 144
  Naomi, 104, 144
  Nathan, 69, 114,
    144, 149, 159,
    162
  Rachel, 159, 162

Rebecca, 32, 142
Rebeckah, 149
Rhoda, 72, 159,
  162
Richard, 32, 142
Robert, 78
Sarah, 32, 64, 142
William, 32, 142,
  159
Zacchas, 121
Zachcheus, 93
Zacheus, 116, 144,
  149
DUSTFIELD, Isaac,
  81, 83
DUTFIELD, Isaac, 81

-E-
EAEMMEL, Elisabeth,
  190
  Margaretha, 190
  Peter R., 190
EASTLACK, Frances,
  171
  Hezekiah, 170
  John, 170, 252
  Rhoda, 170
EASTLAKE, Anne, 164
  Charles, 164
  Hezekiah, 164
  John, 164
  Rachel, 164
  Restore, 164
  Rhoda, 164
  Thomas, 164
EASTLAND, Joseph, 80
EATON, Ann, 251
  Benjamin, 103, 114
  Joshua, 124
EDRIDG, John, 74
EDRIDGE, John, 74
EDWARDS, Thomas, 3
EFF, Friedrich, 222
  James, 222
  Margareta, 202
  Susanna, 222
EFFT, Johann
  Friederich, 190
  John, 190
  Maria Catharina,
    190
EGGMAN, Abraham, 49,
  140
  Batholomew, 49

Elizabeth, 49
Sarah, 49, 138
EGLENTON, John, 97
EGLINGTON,
  Elizabeth, 250
  John, 103, 104
  Joseph, 98
EGLINTON, Elizabeth,
  250
EHBRECHT, Elisabeth,
  214
  Heinrich, 214, 217
  Jacob, 217
  Sarah, 214, 217
EHRIG, Catharina,
  219
  Michael, 213, 216,
    219
  Sarah, 213, 216,
    219
  Wilhelm, 213
EHSENBECK, Cath.,
  209
  Catharina, 215
  Christoph Wilhelm,
    209
  Johann Samuel, 215
  Ludwig Wilh, 209
  Wilhelm, 215
EICHHORN, Anna
  Regina, 186
  Jacob, 186
  Regina, 186
ELDRDIGE, Isaac, 170
ELDREDGE, Isaac, 49
  Mary, 49
ELDRIDGE, Isaac, 49
  Mary, 49
ELERICHT, John, 244
ELKENTON, Esther,
  121
  Gertrude, 121
  Job, 121
  John, 121
  Joseph, 121
  Joshua, 121
  Mary, 121
  Thomas, 121
ELKINGTON, Asa, 135
  Phebey, 72
ELKINTON, Asa, 55,
  165, 169
  Gertrude, 169
  Gertruew, 51

Hester, 47
Job, 47
John, 47, 51, 130, 135
Joseph, 51
Joshua, 47, 51, 129
Lettitia, 165
Mary, 47, 51, 71, 139
Phebe, 51
Thomas, 47
ELLERTONS, Mary, 41
ELLET, Charles, 30, 151
Elizabeth, 151
Hannah, 30, 72, 151
Hannah Carpenter, 32
John, 32, 57, 151
Maria Chambless, 32
Mary, 30, 32, 151
Rachel, 151
Samuel, 151
Sarah, 72, 151
Thomas, 151
William, 151
ELLETT, Charles, 159
Elizabeth, 72
Hannah, 159
John, 73, 131
Rachel Carpenter, 143
ELLIOT, Hannah, 117
ELLIOTT, Charles, 117
Hannah, 117
William, 170
ELLIS, Isaac, 43, 103
ELLISON, Rachel, 139
Samuel, 58
ELLOTT, Charles, 139
ELLWELL, John, 250
Sarah, 250
ELMANN, Heinz, 180
ELMER, Mr., 235
ELMOR, Margaret, 251
ELWELL, Abraham, 248
Elizabeth, 248
Hannah, 248
James, 248

Joel, 248
John H., 248
Margaret, 248
Mary, 248
Nancy, 245
Phebe, 244
Samuel, 244
Susanna, 244
EMLIN, Elisabeth, 188
EMMEL, Anna Elisabeth, 186
David, 217
Elisabeth, 193, 203, 205
Hartman, 195
Margaretha, 195, 206
Martin, 195, 217
Peter, 193, 203, 205
Rosina, 195, 217
Rosina Margaretha, 195
Rosina-Carolina, 217
Sarah Margareta, 217
EMMELSON, Rosina, 208, 209
EMPSON, Cornelius, 83
ENDRESS, Christian, 224
Christn., 226, 227
ENGLE, Asa, 164, 170
Charles, 164
Hannah, 84
Joseph, 164
Joshua, 164
Josiah, 164
Levi, 164, 170
Martha, 164, 170
Mary, 164
ENOCH, Mary, 171
Thomas, 171
ETHRIDGE, John, 75
EVANS, Aaron, 67, 68, 109, 117, 123, 124, 128, 151, 155, 156
Amy, 117
Ann, 130, 155, 156
Aron, 32, 71

Benjamin, 137
Daniel, 66
David, 46, 69, 117, 137, 141, 157
Eleanor, 32, 151
Elizabeth, 157
Isaac, 137
Jacob, 117
Jael, 32
James, 32, 39, 93
Jane, 66, 154, 157
John, 67, 94, 115, 137, 150
Joseph, 137
Joshua, 168, 170
Levi, 117, 135
Mary, 39, 67, 72, 117, 120, 137
Milicent, 117
Milliscent, 70
Mr., 244
Nathan, 137
Nathaniel, 117
Prudence, 155
Rebeckah, 117
Ruth, 72, 129
Sarah, 32, 39, 137
Susanah, 117
Susanna, 50
EVENS, Elioner, 100
Mary, 125
Nathaniel, 100
EVINS, Jane, 113
EVIS, Elizabeth, 236
George, 236
Sarah, 236
EWIN, Susannah, 132
EWING, Susanna, 55

-F-

FAASEMEYER, Christina, 218
Georg, 218
Jacob, 218
FABER, Anna Maria, 183
Elisabeth, 181, 183, 188, 189
Friederich, 187
Heinrich, 186, 187, 189, 190
Henrich, 183, 188, 196, 201, 230,

231
Henry, 189
Hinrich, 181
Johann Hinrich, 186
Johannes, 189
Maria Elisabeth, 181, 186, 187
Maria Magdalena, 196, 201
Maria Margaretha, 181
FAIR, Hannah, 235
FAIRBANKS, Robert, 4
Sarah, 4, 74
FALCK, Elisabeth, 180, 184
Elisabetha, 178
Johann Peter, 184
Louisa, 178
Simon, 178, 180, 184
FALK, Anna Mar., 204
Louise, 196
FARTZEN, Eva, 199
FAUCET, Jonathan, 45
Lidya, 108
FENWICK, John, 74
FERREDGE, Samuel, 75
FERTH, John, 86
FETTERS, Ersamus, 100
FETTORS, Erasmus, 97
FIRTH, Edward, 82
Elizabeth, 24, 155
Ezra, 23, 67, 155
Hannah, 134
Henry, 25, 70
John, 15, 23, 24, 25, 55, 82, 89, 102, 132, 141, 154, 155
Judith, 23, 24, 25
Preston, 139
Preston Carpenter, 155
Samuel, 59, 135, 142, 143, 155
Sarah, 15, 23, 90, 127
Thomas, 60, 142, 155
FISCHER, Anna Margaretha, 195

Elisabeth, 214
Georg, 182, 185, 189, 192, 193, 195, 202, 215
George, 190
Johann, 214, 215, 219, 221
Johannes, 185
Juliana Margretha, 182
Magdalena, 215, 219, 221
Margretha, 182, 185, 189, 190, 192, 193
Maria, 196, 197, 199, 219
FISH, Amanda, 245, 248
Catherine, 248
Elizabeth, 248
Enos, 245, 248
Esther, 245, 248
Hannah, 248
John, 248
Joseph, 248
Sarah, 248
Tryphena, 248
FISHER, Catherine, 244
Elisabeth, 198
Georg, 198
Hannah, 170
Johann Matthey, 198
Margretha, 193
FISTAR, Adam, 190, 229
Christina, 190
Margareth, 190
FISTER, Adam, 186
Christina, 186
Johann Adam, 186
FITHIAN, Josiah, 251
FITZERAN, Maria, 206
Nicolaus, 206
FIX, Adam, 188, 191, 197, 198, 200, 201, 205, 231
Anna Barbara, 199
Barbara, 200
Charlotte, 204, 205
Christina, 191

Elisabeth, 188, 191, 197, 198, 201, 205
Elisbetha, 200
Maria, 209
Mariane, 210
FLACK, Elisabeth, 183
Johann Philip, 183
Simon, 183
Susanna, 183
FLANEGAN, Thomas, 252
FLEETWOOD, William, 82
FOERSTER, Elisabeth, 181
Hinrich, 181, 182
Magdalena, 184
Maria Elisabeth, 181
Miriam, 181, 182
FOG, Rebecca, 92
FOGG, Aaron, 33, 72, 146
Ann, 25, 26, 53, 68
Anna, 120
Charles, 24, 25, 28, 33, 39, 53, 62, 63, 107, 123, 124, 146, 155, 162
Daniel, 32, 161
David, 25
Ebenezer, 25, 33
Elijah, 157
Elisha, 33
Elizabeth, 25, 26, 63, 70, 120, 126, 140
Hannah, 24, 25, 28, 33, 39, 68, 128
Holm, 161
Holme, 25, 32, 33, 70
Holmes, 161
Isaac, 25
Job, 32, 33, 161
Joseph, 25, 26, 32, 97, 160, 161
Lidya, 161
Lydia, 32

INDEX 271

Mary, 24, 28, 32, 161
Prudence, 157
Rachel, 28, 70
Rebecca, 33, 119, 126, 127
Rebeckah, 25, 68, 127
Samuel, 69, 96, 97, 98, 104, 121, 157, 159
Samuuel, 104
Sarah, 24, 28, 33, 70, 109, 146, 155
Thomas, 33
William, 32
FOLLOWAY, Elizabeth, 123
John, 123
Nathan, 123
Samuel, 123
Thomas, 123
FOLWELL, Elizabeth, 47
Nathan, 57, 139
Samuel, 47
Thomas, 47, 56, 121, 141
William, 47, 121
FOOLETT, John, 91
FORCER, Eva, 198
FORD, Elizabeth, 250
FORESST, John, 75
FOREST, Francis, 76
FORREST, Ann, 236
Barbara, 236
Francis, 76, 77
John, 77, 78, 236, 243
FORRETT, Joseph, 75
FORT., Jam., 196
Mar Cath, 196
Maria Catharina, 196
FORTSCHER, Valentin, 199
FOSKER, Georg, 199
Johannes, 199
Salome, 199
FOSSIT, Lydia, 97
FOSTER, Abigail, 237
Amey, 239
Ann, 235, 240, 244
Hannah, 53

I., 248
Jeremiah, 237
Josiah, 53
Lydia, 53
Mary, 53, 237
Patient, 237
Rachel, 53, 132
Rebecca, 53
William, 235, 240
FREBEL, Anna Margareta, 207
Henrich, 207
Johann, 207
FREEDLAND, Elizabeth, 33, 54
Jonas, 33
Jonathan, 33
Lydia, 33
Sarah, 33
FREELAND, Jonas, 126, 133
FREETH, John, 108
FREISS, Dorcas, 208, 209
Jacob, 208, 209
Maria, 208, 209
Philipp, 208, 209
FRENCH, Kesiah, 52
Keziah, 129
Thomas, 251
FRETH, John, 82, 84
FREVEL, Anna Marg., 200
Catharina, 216
Elisabetha, 200
Joh., 200
Johann, 202, 216, 227
Johannes, 208, 209
Margareta, 202, 216
Margaretha, 227
Margarethe, 208, 209
Maria Margarethe, 208, 209
FREVLE, Johann, 215
Margare, 215
FREWEL, Heinerich, 231
Johannes, 231
FREYSEMEIER, Anna Maria, 192
Christian, 192

Helena, 192
FRIEAS, A.
Margretha, 191
Jacob, 191
Maria, 191
FRIEND, Ephraim, 252
FRIES, Anna, 176, 200, 232
Anna Margareta, 230
Anna Margaretha, 177
Anna Margreta, 180, 181
Anna Margretha, 186
Anna Maria, 181, 191, 229
Cath., 226
Catharina, 195, 200, 202, 205, 227
Catharine, 208, 209
Catherine, 197
Christina, 203
Dorcas, 202, 204, 207, 208, 209, 226
Eliesabeth, 191
Elis., 196, 198
Elisabeth, 188, 192, 202, 203, 233
Elisabetha, 230
Friderich, 208, 209
Friederich, 176, 177
Friedrich, 202, 205, 232
Georg, 202
Hanna, 205
Jacob, 176, 177, 179, 180, 181, 182, 183, 184, 185, 186, 188, 191, 192, 195, 196, 197, 198, 202, 203, 204, 207, 208, 209, 226, 229, 230, 231, 233
Joh. Fried., 200

Joh. Georg, 230
Joh. Henrich, 200
Johan, 195
Johan Georg, 195, 197
Johann, 202
Johann Georg, 230
Johann Heinrich, 179, 230
Johann Henrich, 202
Johann Peter, 184
Johann Philip, 183
Johanna, 198
John Friedr., 196
John Georg, 196
Marg., 196
Margaretha, 179, 183, 204
Margretha, 181, 182, 183, 184, 186, 188, 191
Maria, 229
Mary, 233
Peter, 230
Philip, 195, 197, 233
Philipp, 230
Phillipp, 231
Phoebe, 207, 231
Sara, 208, 209
FRIESS, Adam, 211
Anna, 207, 219
Anna Margretha, 178, 193
Catharina, 207, 210
Catharine, 213
Dorcas, 200, 213, 215, 216
Elisabeth, 206, 211, 212, 213, 216
Fridr., 207
Fridrich, 210
Friedrich, 213
Georg, 194
Jacob, 178, 179, 192, 193, 200, 206, 211, 212, 213, 215, 216
Johann, 215
Johann Georg, 178
Johann Peter, 206

Lydia, 210
Margareta, 209
Margaretha, 178, 179
Margretha, 191, 192
Maria, 200, 209, 215, 219
Maria German, 228
Mary, 213
Phil., 219
Philip, 213, 228
Philipp, 209, 215
Sarah, 216
FRITH, John, 86, 88, 107
Sarah, 87
FROLICKHEIMER, Elisabet, 195
FROLLINGER, Daniel, 193
Gabriel, 193
Margaretha, 193
FROMM, Conrad, 208, 209
Maria Margarethe, 208, 209
FRUN, Ann, 246
Uphain, 246
Wemen, 246
FRY, John, 250
FUCHS, Anna Marai, 224
Anna Margar., 204
Anna Maria, 190, 194, 199, 202, 218, 220, 225
Catharina, 225
Christina, 217
Christine, 225
Elisabeth, 220
Fridrich, 218, 220
Friederich, 188, 190, 199
Friedr., 224
Friedrich, 225
Isaac, 185
Jacob Wilhelm, 185
Joh. Friederich, 185
Joh. Georg, 202
Johann, 217, 224
Johann Frid., 202
Johann Friedr.,

194
Johann Jacob, 194
Johannes, 225
Juliana, 190
Magdalena, 206
Margareta, 217, 224
Rosina Maria, 199
Sophia Margretha, 185
FUCKS, A. Maria, 191
Friederich, 191
Johannes, 191
FULK, Louise, 197
FUREDGE, Will, 75

-G-
GAECK, David, 198
Georg, 198
Margaretha, 198
GAMSTER, John, 117
GARDENER, Mary, 68
GARDENOR, Hannah, 86
GARDINER, Joseph, 135
GARDNER, Ephraim, 48
James, 48
Joseph, 48
Mary, 48
GARISON, Seger, 252
GARNER, Ephraim, 132
Joseph, 136
GARRASON, Rachel, 250
GARRAT, George, 89
GARRAWN, Isaac, 250
GARRETT, Bartholomew, 236
GARRISON, Abigail, 236, 239, 242
Amey, 237
Arthur, 235
Benjamin, 238, 239, 240, 242
Catherine, 244
Daniel, 235
David, 234, 235, 240
Eleanor, 124
Elizabeth, 237
Gamaliel, 235
Hannah, 237, 238, 240, 243
Isaac, 238, 240,

INDEX 273

243
Jacob, 104
Jane, 235
Jeremiah, 234,
  235, 236, 237,
  239, 241, 243
Jeremy, 242
Joel, 237
John, 235, 237,
  242
Jonathan, 240
Joshua, 100, 234,
  237, 240
Mary, 234, 235,
  236, 238, 239,
  241, 242, 243
Miriam, 238
Phebe, 239, 241
Rachel, 238
Sarah, 234, 235,
  237, 240
Tamson, 238
Tamzon, 239
Tomson, 240, 242
GARTIN, David, 248
  Elishebe, 248
GARTON, Furman, 249
  John, 249
  Lydia, 248
  Rebeckah, 249
  Rhoda, 249
  Sherry, 248
GARWOOD, Thomas, 84
GASTON, David, 245
  Elizabeth, 245
  John, 245
  Lydia, 245
  Rhoda, 245
  Sherry, 245
GAUGER, Anna
  Barbara, 177
  Conrad, 177
  Georg, 188, 231
  Johannes, 177
  Maria, 188
  Susanna, 188
GAUKER, Georg, 196
  Maria, 196
GECK, David, 217
  Margareta, 217
GELBHOEFFER,
  Benjamin, 191
  Maria, 191
  Maria Barbara, 191

GELLHOEFER,
  Benjamin, 186
  Johannes, 186
  Maria, 186
GELLHOEFFER,
  Benjamin, 188
  Maria, 188
GELLOPER, Andreas,
  183
  Benjamin, 183
  Maria, 183
GERDRICK, Daniel,
  230
GERMAN, Catharina,
  191
  Elisabeth, 191,
    193, 226, 227
  Ezechiel, 226
  Johann Henrich,
    227
  Marx, 191, 193
  Ruben, 226, 227
  Sara, 193
GERVAS, Elizabeth,
  134
GIBBS, Boras, 51
  Burrough, 140
  Burroughs, 56, 134
  Edward, 56, 134,
    160
  Enoch, 51, 56, 134
  Hannah, 51
  Hepzebeth, 142
  Jonathan, 50, 71,
    139, 160, 162,
    163
  Lidya, 162
  Lucas, 51, 59, 73
  Lydia, 59, 140,
    160, 163
  Mary, 51, 141,
    159, 160
  Phebe, 51, 56, 134
  Phoebe, 73
  Richard, 51, 56,
    134, 159, 160
  Sarah, 51, 56,
    134, 140
  Solomon, 51, 56,
    134, 137
  Susannah, 73, 162
GIBONS, Joseph, 42
GIBSON, Daniel, 135
  Dorcas, 22

  Elizabeth, 22, 101
  Giddeon, 52, 127
  Gideon, 52, 71,
    135
  Hannah, 52, 128
  Jane, 150
  Joseph, 22, 46,
    97, 98, 101, 103,
    105, 107, 115,
    150
  Joshua, 52
  Jospeh, 97
  Rachel, 22
  Sarah, 22
GILBERT, Elizabeth,
  70
  John, 70
  Mary, 50, 70, 124
GILL, David, 59, 142
  John, 42, 59, 73,
    100, 142
  Joshua, 42, 98
  Prudence, 142
GILLESPIE, John, 244
GILLS, John, 171
  Prudence, 171
GILMAN, Elizabeth,
  235
  Hannah, 235
  Susanna, 235
GLAVES, Easter, 79
GLEAVES, Hester, 84
GODDIN, Edward, 84
GODING, Edward, 76
GODOWIN, Joseph, 66
GODWIN, Edward, 76,
  79, 80, 81, 84
  John, 87
  Joseph, 97
  Susanah, 97
GODWINN, Edward, 80
GONKLIN, Barbara,
  220
  Philipp, 220
GONRATH, Hinrich,
  181
GOODING, John, 86
GOODWIN, Abigail, 33
  Edward, 78, 82, 86
  Elizabeth, 33, 41,
    51, 55, 130
  Hester, 51
  John, 7, 12, 13,
    14, 16, 28, 54,

71, 86, 89, 90, 95, 99, 142
Joseph, 14, 21, 51, 97
Katharine, 7
Lewis, 28, 68, 126
Mary, 13, 28, 94, 123, 156
Mary Morris, 33
Phebey, 21
Rachel, 33, 41, 126
Richard, 13, 21
Sarah, 21, 33, 47, 103, 114, 129, 149
Susanah, 13, 14
Susanna, 16, 68
Susannah, 7, 12, 16, 119
Thomas, 16, 101, 102, 109, 117, 118, 149
William, 16, 28, 33, 41, 72, 102, 115, 121, 123, 125, 126, 128, 130, 156
GOSLIN, Isabel, 124
  Rebecca, 139
  Savery, 106
GOSLING, Isabel, 124
  Samuel, 124
  Sarah, 131
GRAEMEU, Anna Margreth, 177
  Cathrina, 177
  Mathias, 177
GRAFF, Anna Barbara, 185
  Anna Margretha, 186
  Elisabeth, 185
  Georg, 185, 186
  Jacob, 186
  Margretha, 186
  Peter, 186
GRAHAM, Judith, 242
  Richard, 242
  William, 242
GRANTLAND, Jane, 120
GRAOFF, William, 111
GRATINGER, Christian, 178

Maria Louisa, 178
Maria Margaretha, 178
GRAVES, Elizabeth, 108
  Joseph, 98, 105
  Margrett, 102
  Rebecca, 147
  Rebekah, 102
  Richard, 41, 91, 93, 94, 102
  Samuel, 43, 97, 100
  Thomas, 83, 84, 104, 118, 119, 147
GREEN, Ann, 251
  Athony, 170
  Enoch, 200
  Hannah, 128, 170
  Lewis, 170
  Martin, 170
  Mary, 170
  Nehemiah, 200
GREENMAN, N., 248
GREGG, Anne, 100
GREGORY, Elizabeth, 252
  Joseph, 250
  Samuel, 159
  Sarah, 50, 122, 159
  Walpole, 48, 50, 69, 122, 130, 159
GRIFFIN, Heziah, 172
  Jonathan, 172, 173
  Rebeccah, 250
  Robert, 1, 2, 73
GRIFFITH, Isaac, 59, 141
GRIGG, William, 43, 100
GRIMES, Archibald, 244
  Elizabeth, 238
  Judith, 234, 235, 240, 242
  Mary, 240
  Richard, 242
  William, 234, 235, 240, 242
  William G., 235
GRINNINGS, Rachel, 69

GRINSDALE, John, 67
GRINSLADE, Elizabeth, 55, 127, 152
  John, 46, 55, 73, 127, 152
GRINSLEY, Elizabeth, 118
  Hepzibah, 118
  Mary, 118
  Sarah, 118
GRISCOM, Andrew, 33, 70, 112, 152, 158, 176
  Benjamin, 58, 73, 158
  David, 163
  Deborah, 176
  Everat, 176
  Everatt, 54, 155, 159, 163
  John, 54, 140, 155, 163
  Jonathan, 59
  Leatitia, 158
  Mary, 154, 176
  Rachel, 33, 54, 130, 139, 141, 155, 163
  Samuel, 155, 163
  Sarah, 99, 176
  Susanna, 33
  Susannah, 176
  William, 33, 42, 47, 54, 60, 69, 73, 99, 112, 139, 155, 163, 176
GRISCUM, Andrew, 44, 106
GRISMEYERIN, Zusana, 178
GROAF, Elizabeth, 138
GROAFF, Abigail, 129
  Elizabeth, 64
GROFF, William, 71, 170
GROOM, William, 3
GRUBB, Henry, 76
GRUETH, Griffin, 173
  Heziah, 172, 173
GRUFF, Abigail, 72
GRUFFYTH, Isaac, 59
GUEST, Thomas, 60,

INDEX

143
GUY, Bridget, 82
  Richard, 74, 75, 76
GUYES, Richard, 74

-H-
HAAS, Abraham, 236
HACKET, Elizabeth, 96
HACKETT, Elizabeth, 126
HAEHNS, Margareta, 207
HAGLIN, Elizabeth, 244
  Mary, 241
HAHN, A. Margrta, 229
  Andreas, 188, 207, 211, 215, 219, 222, 226
  Anna Margretha, 186
  Apollonia, 195
  Catharina, 178, 179, 180, 200, 206, 207, 217, 219, 221, 227
  Catharine, 211
  Catherine, 225
  Cathrina, 177
  Charlotta, 228
  Chatarina, 178
  Christina, 177, 178, 181
  Daniel, 196, 211, 227
  David, 178
  Don, 226
  Elisabet, 196, 207
  Elisabeth, 179, 180, 181, 183, 186, 188, 191, 192, 193, 200, 204, 205, 206, 207, 211, 215, 217, 219, 221, 223, 225, 226, 227, 228
  Elisabetha, 225
  Georg, 178, 195
  George, 181
  Hanna, 221

Hesekiel, 222
J. Jacob, 192
Jacob, 200, 206, 211, 215, 221, 223, 226
Joh., 196, 211, 217, 219, 221
Joh. Jac, 219
Johan, 192
Johann, 180, 186, 188, 191, 206, 207, 212, 215, 217, 219, 221, 223, 226, 229
Johann Georg, 200
Johann Jacob, 181
Johannes, 181, 183, 200, 204, 205, 207, 211, 225, 227, 228
John, 193
Jonathan, 177, 193, 195, 217, 225, 226, 227
Jurg, 177
Ludwig, 177, 178, 179, 228
Lydia, 206
Margareta, 215
Margrete, 212
Maria, 177, 178, 181, 215, 221
Michael, 178, 179
Richard, 225
Sara, 211, 222
Sarah, 207, 215, 219, 226
HAHNN, Christina, 187
  Georg, 187
HAINES, Agnes, 175
  Ann, 71, 165
  Anthony, 110, 175
  Elizabeth, 56, 67, 164, 165, 176
  Ephraim, 72, 175, 176
  Grace, 57, 140
  Hannah, 134
  Hope, 165
  Hugh, 122, 134
  Jacob, 135, 164
  Jedidiah, 34
  Jemima, 133

Jeremiah, 48
Joel, 164
John, 34, 73
Joseph, 138, 175
Joshua, 170, 172, 173
Latitia, 72
Lydia, 34
Mark, 138
Martha, 34
Mary, 34, 69
Naomi, 134
Rachel, 129
Rebeckah, 175
Richard, 175, 176
Ruth, 169
Samuel, 164
Sarah, 133
Susannah, 165
William, 72, 165
HAINS, Ann, 51, 124, 126, 144, 175
  Anthony, 107, 112, 113, 175
  Beulah, 149
  Deborah, 149
  Elizabeth, 116, 149, 158
  Ephraim, 109, 124, 149
  Grace, 149
  Hugh, 45
  Jacob, 144
  Jemima, 175
  Jonathan, 123
  Joseph, 44, 175
  Leatitia, 130, 149
  Mary, 96, 144, 149
  Naomy, 175
  Nathan, 144
  Rebeckah, 175
  Reuben, 175
  Richard, 63, 107, 112, 120, 122, 149
  Sarah, 68, 144
  Susannah, 144, 149
  William, 144, 145
HALE, Henry, 16
  John, 16
  Mary, 16
  Thomas, 16
HALIDAY, James, 111
HALL, Abel, 67, 154

Ann, 9, 34, 35, 108, 134
Astill, 34
Charlotte, 34
Clemant, 102, 103
Clement, 13, 29, 34, 35, 94, 98, 125, 134, 149, 175
David, 35
Deborah, 34
Ebenezer, 154
Edward, 35, 118
Elizabeth, 9, 29, 33, 34, 102, 106, 107
Hannah, 9, 35, 89, 251
Hester, 118
Isaac Key, 34
James, 35
John, 34, 109
Joseph, 29, 33, 35, 72, 142, 149
Josiah, 34, 55
Lewis, 35
Lidia, 35
Lydia, 35
Margaret, 29, 34, 35, 112, 124, 134, 149, 175
Margaret Morris, 34
Mark, 154
Martha, 35
Mary, 33, 34, 57, 58, 114
Morris, 29, 34, 35, 72, 134, 149
Naome, 139
Naomi, 57, 138, 139
Nathaniel, 13, 33, 34
Nethaniel, 108
Prudence, 29, 34, 71
Rachel, 143
Rebecca, 34, 35
Rebeckah, 70, 125, 154
Rodra, 34
Samuel, 34, 35
Sarah, 9, 13, 29, 34, 35, 49, 57, 73, 81, 91, 122, 125
Stephen, 33, 73
Thomas, 35
William, 4, 9, 13, 29, 35, 79, 81, 82, 83, 84, 86, 90, 92, 94, 97, 98, 106, 114
HALLIDAY, James, 101, 102, 104
HALTER, Catharina, 195, 229
Hanns Martin, 228
Hans Martin, 229
Hs. Martin, 228
Joh. Martin, 230
HALTON, David, 217
HAMBY, Ann, 79
HAMILTON, Ann, 242
Archibald, 237, 242, 244
Elizabeth, 237
William, 242
HAMMEN, David, 179
Maria Magdalena, 179
HAMMER, Anna, 185, 232
Georg, 185
Sabina, 229
HAMMETT, Sarah, 140
HAMMITT, Sarah, 143
HAMMON, Richard, 244
HAMPTON, John, 251
HAMSCHER, Joh. Georg, 212
Johannes, 212
Maria Catherine, 212
HANBY, Ann, 41
William, 89
HANCE, Isaac, 34, 70, 133, 141, 159
John, 133
Joseph, 34, 159
Martha, 159
Mary, 34, 73, 159
William, 159
HANCOCK, Easter, 20, 145
Edward, 10
Elizabeth, 20, 141, 152, 160
Elizbeth, 79
Esther, 91, 149, 251
Grace, 13
Hannah, 12, 71, 92, 147, 152, 160, 161
Jane, 149, 151
John, 9, 10, 11, 12, 13, 80, 81, 82, 84, 86, 140, 152
Jonathan, 12
Joseph, 11, 147
Lidya, 71
Lydia, 137, 149
Marey, 86
Margaret, 84, 161
Margret, 62
Mary, 9, 10, 11, 12, 13, 123
Nathaniel, 10, 96, 98, 147
Nethaniel, 110, 156, 161
Prudence, 145
Rachel, 145, 149, 152
Rebeckah, 14, 17, 20, 65, 121, 122, 145
Richard, 17, 84, 87, 91, 92, 93, 94, 95, 99, 110, 145, 152
Ruth, 94
Samuel, 17, 20, 64, 94, 97, 98, 145, 149, 152, 156
Samuell, 92
Sarah, 10, 14, 20, 63, 67, 115
Susannah, 65
Thomas, 14, 97, 101, 104, 109, 123, 151
William, 14, 66, 68, 87, 89, 90, 92, 93, 94, 95, 97, 102, 107, 108, 147, 149, 151, 152, 156,

INDEX

160
HANDCOCK, John, 7
  Mary, 7
  Thomas, 96
  William, 7
HANDSCHUE, Rev., 183
HANDSHUCH, Johann
  Friederich, 181
HANES, Edward, 168
  Isaac, 49
  James, 141
HANNAH, Abigail,
  235, 240, 242
  James, 242
  Samuel, 235, 240,
  242, 243
HANS, George, 244
HANSCHUE, Rev., 182,
  185
HANSE, James, 53
  John, 51
  Joseph, 143
  Martha, 141
HANSON, John, 99
HANTSCHUE, Rev., 185
HARDING, Ann, 247
  Benjamin, 235, 247
  Catherine, 247
  Elizabeth, 235,
  247
  Henry, 247
  John, 247
  Lydia, 247
  Rachel, 247
  Thomas, 247
HARKER, Mary, 139
HARMAN, Joseph, 46
HARRIS, Abner, 33,
  147
  Aron, 33
  Chalkley, 33
  David, 147
  Enoch, 33
  Esther, 33
  Hannah, 33
  Hepzebeth, 142
  Hepzibah, 33
  Hester, 238
  Isaac, 147, 236,
  238
  Jacob, 33
  John, 33, 65, 70,
  147
  Jonathan, 33

Leatitia, 147
Mark, 33
Mary, 33, 236
Mercy, 236, 238
Nathan, 147
Ruth, 147, 154
Samuel, 33
William, 134, 147
HARRISON, Deborah,
  51, 126
  Esther, 82
  Hester, 8, 81, 82
  Isarel, 8
  Israell, 79
  Sarah, 8
HARST, Timothy, 82
HART, Ann, 15
  Dennis, 244
  Hannah, 60
  Jane, 15
  John, 15, 41, 44,
  63, 88, 89, 90,
  99, 110
HARTLEY, Catharine,
  149, 155
  Elizabeth, 72,
  133, 149
  Ester, 133
  Esther, 33
  Hester, 132, 133
  Mark, 156
  Mary, 37, 156
  Samuel, 156
  Sarah, 149
  Susannah, 73, 149,
  151
  Thomas, 66, 68,
  113, 149, 151,
  155, 156
HARTLY, Mark, 142
  Thomas, 138
HARTMAN, Anne Maria,
  212
  Daniel, 212
  Johannes, 212
HARTMANN, A. Maria,
  204
  Andreas, 208, 209
  Anna Maria, 200
  Anne Maria, 208,
  209
  Henrich, 204
  Johann, 200
  Johannes, 200,

208, 209
Maria Margretha,
  189
HARTSHORN, Robert,
  42, 100
HARTSHORNE, Hannah,
  100
HARVEY, Allice, 5
  Leonard, 5
HASELWOOD, Georg, 75
HASSELWOOD, George,
  76
HATCHESON, Robert,
  76
HAUCK, Martin, 198
HAUSSER, Christoph,
  179
  Johann David, 179
  Regina, 179
HAWES, Edward, 98
HAYER, Christine,
  197
  Conrad, 197
  Johan Georg, 197
HAYNES, Mark, 139
  Sarah, 104
  Thomas, 244
  William, 43, 103
HAYNS, Rebekah, 103
  Richard, 107
HAYRES, Joshua, 58
HAYSE, Andrew, 104
  Esther, 66
HAZE, Andrew, 100
HAZELWOOD, John, 88
HEA, Margaret, 244
HEADLY, Mary, 47
HEARLY, Henry, 8
  Mary, 8
  Sarah, 8
HEATH, Robert, 82
HEBNER, Joh., 206
HECKTOR, Anna Maria,
  212
  Caspar, 212
  Susanna, 212
HECTOR, Anna
  Catharina, 206
  Anna Elisabeth,
  202
  Anna Maria, 209,
  219
  Caspar, 199, 202,
  203, 206, 207,

209, 219
Christina, 219
Johann Catharina, 203
Johann Nicolaus, 199
Margareta, 207
Maria, 199, 202, 203, 207
HEFFT, Friedr., 223
Johann, 223
Susanna, 223
HEFT, Hanna, 212
Johannes, 205
John, 233
Margareta, 205
HEIER, Anna
Margareta, 203
Christian, 195
Christiana, 203
Christina, 201
Conrad, 195, 201, 203
Daniel, 195
HEINE, Johann Balthasar, 207
HEINS, Georg, 222, 226
Margaretha, 222
Patience, 222, 226
Wilhelm, 226
HEINTZ, Anna Margretha, 192
Liesabeth, 192
Peter, 192, 229
HEINZELMANN, Mathias, 180
HELMUTH, H., 223
Heinr., 206, 220
Heinrich, 208, 209, 213, 215, 216, 217
J. H. Ch., 202, 204, 220, 226
HENCKEL, Anna Maria, 210
Barbara, 212
Catharina, 210
Henrich, 210
Philip, 212
HENDRICKS, John, 95
HENDRICKSON,
Elizabeth, 250
John, 101

HENNE, Adam, 211, 224, 226
Anna Maria, 224
Christina, 226
Elisabeth, 211
Johannes, 211
Margareta, 224
Susanna, 224, 226
HENRY, Ann, 235, 244
Athey, 243
HENSHAW, Rachel, 42
HEOPFNER, Johannes, 203
HEPNER, A. Maria, 222
Anna Maria, 218, 223
Elisabeth, 222
Johann, 218, 222, 223
Juliana, 218
Magdalena, 223
Mathias, 218
HEPPEL, Johan Jacob, 177
Johann Adam, 178
Maria Barbara, 177, 178
Nicolaus, 177, 178
HEPPENER, Anna Maria, 201
Johannes, 201
HEPPNER, Anna Maria, 214
Johann, 214
HERB, Margretha, 180
Michael, 180
HERBSTLER, Barbara, 179
HERCHE, Johan, 195
HERDMAN, Johannes, 199
Maria, 199
Matthias, 199
HERGE, Barbara, 200
Johannes, 200
Salomon, 200
HERITAGE, Benjamin, 170
Joseph, 52, 129
Stephen, 171
HERMAN, Anna Catharina, 190
Barbara, 190

Friederich, 190
Joseph, 212
Maria, 212
HERMER, Joseph, 66, 151
Rebeckah, 67, 151
HERP, Charlotta, 206
Elisabeth, 206
Elisbeth, 206
Michael, 206
HERPE, Margarethe, 177
Maria Cathrina, 177
HERRIGE, Johannes, 197
HERRISON, Hester, 80, 81
HERRMANN, Anna Maria, 210
Friederich, 229
Joseph, 210
HESS, Christian, 221
David, 203
Johannes, 203
Margareta, 203
Maria, 221
Peter, 234
Tobias, 221
HEUER, Christina, 198, 224
Conrad, 198
Daniel, 224
Jacob, 198
Margareta, 224
HEUES, William, 86
HEWES, Benjamin, 34
Dewitt, 84
Edith, 34
Edward, 91
Elizabeth, 34
Ezekiah, 34
Hannah, 34, 61
Hezekiah, 72
Hiriam, 34
Isaac, 34
James, 20, 96, 98
Jane, 20
John, 34
Mary, 97
Rebecca, 34, 61
Sarah, 133
Thomas, 34, 94
HEWEY, Isaac, 54

INDEX 279

Robert, 54
HEWINGS, Susannah, 132
HEWIT, Ann, 244
HEWS, Aaron, 50, 127
  Edith, 59
  Edward, 94, 97
  Elizabeth, 145
  Ezekiah, 139
  Hannah, 108, 172, 173
  Hezekiah, 52
  James, 99, 118, 145
  Jane, 34
  Jemima, 113, 145
  John, 72, 113, 130
  Lidya, 127
  Rachel, 108
  Rebecca, 173
  Rebeccah, 172
  Sarah, 118, 127, 133
  Susannah, 66, 145
  Tabitha, 102
  Thomas, 107
HEYER, Christina, 206
  Conrad, 206
  Daniel, 228
  Johannes, 206
  Margarethe, 228
  Susanna, 228
HEYMUN, Elizabeth, 237
  John, 237
HIGBY, Rachel, 139
HIGHBY, Rachel, 140
HILDERBRAND, Mary, 128
  Mary Ann, 72, 128, 129
HILDERMAN, Ann, 126
HILGERT, Henr., 199
  Maria Magdal, 199
  Salome, 199
HILL, Aaron, 239
  Elizabeth, 19, 92, 95
  Hannah, 19, 100
  Krindaill, 79
  Krindall, 77
  Moses, 239
  Mullica, 170

Rebecah, 19
Rebeccah, 252
Sarah, 19, 100, 250
Thomas, 19, 98
HILLARD, Hannah, 34
  Reuben, 34
HILLIARD, Henrich, 207
  Salome, 207
HILMAN, Rachel, 112
HILTSHNER, Jacob, 193
HINDERLE, Sebastian, 195
HINKLE, Francis, 106
HINKLEY, Francis, 44
HINNE, Adam, 209, 221
  Elisab., 209
  Georg, 221
  Susanna, 209, 221
HINNEY, Adam, 217
  Elisabeth, 217
HINNIN, Johann, 189
  Maria Elisabeth, 189
HINRICH, Ann
  Elisabeth, 189
  Eva Maria, 189
  Johann Peter, 189
  Peter, 189
HINRICHS, Johannes, 188
  Maria, 188
  Peter, 188
HITCHNER, Elisabeth, 206, 208, 209, 230
  Georg, 201, 206
  Jacob, 206, 208, 209, 230
  Magdalena, 206
  Magdalene, 208, 209
  Mariana, 206
  Susanna, 206
HITSCHNER, Andr., 204, 218
  Andreas, 210, 211, 223
  Anna Barbara, 199
  Anna Maria, 205
  Barbara, 192, 193

Christina, 200, 210, 223
David, 221
Elisabeth, 200, 203, 204, 210, 211, 218, 221, 222, 223, 225
Elisbeth, 216, 226
Elizabeth, 212
Georg, 203, 207, 210, 216, 218, 220
Jacob, 198, 200, 203, 204, 206, 210, 211, 212, 216, 218, 220, 221, 222, 223, 225, 226
Joh. Fridrich, 218
Johann, 220
Johannes, 192
Magdalena, 198, 206, 207, 210, 218, 220
Margareta, 216, 218
Margarethe, 223
Maria, 207, 210, 225
Maria Anna, 216
Maria Magdalena, 204
Marian, 220
Mariana, 207, 218
Martin, 209, 210, 212, 216, 217
Matthias, 225
Peter, 192, 193
Sara, 210, 223
Sarah, 218
Susanna, 223
HITTSCHNER, Jacob, 193
  Joh. Martin, 193
  Magdalena, 193
HITTSHENER, Catharina, 192
HITZLER, Johann Melchior, 183
  Margretha, 183
  Peter, 183
HITZNER, Jacob, 202
  Magdalena, 202
HIZNER, Andr., 209

280 EARLY CHURCH RECORDS OF SALEM COUNTY

Elisabeth, 209
Sarah, 209
HOCH, Andreas, 196,
  199, 201, 205
  Christina, 199,
  201, 205
  Christine, 196
  Hanna, 201
  Jacob, 196
  Johannes, 205
  Susanna, 199
HOCHSCHEID, Joha.,
  191
  Johannes, 191
  Margretha, 191
HOCHSCHILD, Adam,
  178, 180
  Elisabetha, 178
  Loysa, 180
HOCHSHILD, Christ.,
  177
  Christina, 177
  Justus, 177
  Magdalena, 177
HODGE, Hannah, 125
HODGKINS, Thomas,
  41, 42, 96, 97
HODKINS, Thomas, 98
HOELTZEL, Anna
  Catharina, 185
  Elisabeth, 185,
  188, 189
  Elizabeth, 183
  Eva Elisabeth, 189
  Friederich, 188,
  189, 229
  Georg Fried., 185
  Georg Friederich,
  183
  Johannes, 183
  Maria Elisabeth,
  188
HOELZEL, Barbara,
  192
  Elisabeth, 191,
  192, 193
  Friederich, 191,
  192, 193
  George Friederich,
  193
  Louise, 196
  Maria Dorothea,
  191
HOELZER, Elisabet,
195
Friedr., 195
Margaretha, 195
HOEPNER, Anna Maria,
  210
  Jacob, 210
  Johannes, 210
HOEPPENER, Anna
  Barbara, 207
  Anna Maria, 207
  Johannes, 207
HOEYER, Conrad, 230
HOFF, Jurg, 229
HOFFAECKER,
  Heinrich, 191
  Margareth, 191
HOFFECKER, Heinrich,
  189
  Henrich, 187
  Joh. Adam, 189
  Margaretha, 187
  Margretha, 189
  Philip Henrich,
  187
HOFFMAN, Abigail,
  149
  Anna Margretha,
  183
  Anne Margrethe,
  211
  Elisabeth, 183,
  186
  Elizabeth, 146
  Eva, 193
  Friederich, 193
  Isaac, 72, 146
  Jacob, 137, 146
  Joh. Jacob, 211
  Johann, 184
  Johanna Margretha,
  184
  Johannes, 183,
  184, 211
  John, 146, 149,
  152, 160
  Jonathan, 152, 170
  Mary, 73, 149, 152
  Mary Ann, 67
  Mary Anne, 146
  Nancy, 203
  Naomy, 67
  Neomy, 146
  Samuel, 152
HOFFMANN, Eva, 203
Friedrich, 203
HOFMANN, Andreas,
  197
  Elisab., 207
  Elisabeth, 201,
  206
  Eva, 196
  Eva Maria, 197
  Friedr., 197
  Georg Friedrich,
  196
  Johannes, 202, 206
  Johannes Caspar,
  206
  Margaretha, 202
HOGBEEN, Lettisha,
  116
HOGBIN, Joseph, 6
HOHENSCHILD, Adam,
  229
  Anna Elisbeth, 229
  Johann Adam, 229
HOHENSHILD, Adam,
  178
  Louisa, 178
HOHENSHILDT, Adam,
  178
  Anna Elisabetha,
  178
  Maria Elisabetha,
  178
HOHENSHILT, Adam,
  178
  Anna Elisabetha,
  178
HOLBROOK, Robert,
  234, 235
HOLIDAY, James, 110
HOLINGSHEAD, Renier,
  115
HOLINGSWORTH, Ann,
  81
HOLLIDAY, James, 42
HOLLINDHEAD, Sarah,
  127
HOLLINSHEAD,
  Eleanor, 251
  Jacob, 45
  Sarah, 252
HOLLSHEID, Anna
  Rosina, 189
  Johan, 189
  Maria Margaretha,
  189

INDEX

HOLMES, Elizabeth, 97
  Mary, 135, 136
  William, 78
HOLSCHEIT, Anna Maria, 195
  Johannes, 195
  Margaretha, 195
HOLSCHIED, Johannes, 225
  Maria, 225
HOLSON, Rebecca, 169
HOLSTEN, Andrew, 251
HOLZSCHELD, Elisabeth, 221
  Johann, 221
  Maria, 221
HOLZSEITER, Johann, 217
  Maria, 217
HOOTON, Thomas, 5
HOPKINS, Charles, 251
HOPMAN, John, 106, 132
HORN, Anna Elisabeth, 186
  Anna Maria, 218
  Catharina, 218, 223, 224
  Christina, 186, 188, 190
  Joh., 215, 217, 218
  Johan, 190
  Johann, 188, 213, 217, 218, 224
  Johannes, 182, 186, 188, 203, 205, 208, 209, 223
  Johanns, 212
  Margar., 215
  Margareta, 203, 205, 213, 217
  Margarethe, 208, 209, 223
  Margrethe, 212
  Maria, 218
  Maria Elisbeth, 190
  Simon, 224
  William, 86
HOSER, Henry, 87

HOUSE, Mary, 128
HOUSEMAN, Mary, 128, 136
HOVEY, Isaac, 136
HOWARD, Hannah, 117
  Robert, 44, 120, 121
HOWART, Robert, 117
HOWEL, Elisabeth Johnson, 213
  Georg, 213
  George, 213
HOWELL, John, 6
  Lewis, 93
  Rebecca, 95
HOWES, James, 94
HOWEY, Abigail, 139, 165, 172, 173
  Ann, 165
  Benjamin, 139, 165
  Deborah, 58, 165
  Elizabeth, 165
  Isaac, 137, 139, 165
  John, 169
  Joshua, 58, 170
  Martha, 165
  Mary, 58, 139, 165, 170
  Naomi, 165
  Rebecca, 165
  Robert, 138, 165
  William, 53, 165, 172, 173
HOYER, Christina, 230
  Conrad, 231
HUCHINGS, Thomas, 110
HUCHINS, Roger, 94, 97
HUCKINGS, Achsah, 16
  Elizabeth, 16, 130
  Hannah, 16
  Hindrance, 16
  Huldah, 16
  John, 16
  Mary, 16
  Rebeckah, 124
  Roger, 16, 17, 252
  Samuel, 50
  Sarah, 16, 17
  Susanah, 16
  Susanna, 252

Thomas, 17
HUCKINS, Hannah, 96
  Mercy, 153
  Roger, 76
  Samuel, 153
  Thomas, 110, 153
HUDDY, Daniel, 21, 68, 96, 97, 98, 99, 102, 107, 145
  Elizabeth, 21, 145
  Joshua, 21
  Martha, 21, 64, 145
  Naomy, 155
HUDSON, Elizabeth, 65
  Isaac, 251
HUEST, Johann Fr., 225
  Johann Heinrich, 225
  Susanna, 225
HUETSCHNER, Andreas, 214, 215, 217
  Elisabeth, 200, 213, 214
  Georg, 214
  Hanna, 214
  Jacob, 200, 213, 214, 215
  Joh. Phil., 217
  Johann, 213
  Magdalena, 215
  Mariane, 214
  Martin, 213
  Mathias, 215
  Sarah, 214, 215, 217
HUGG, John, 80, 83
HUGGENS, Roger, 101
HUGGINGS, Elizabeth, 130
HUGGINS, Barbara, 113
  Elizabeth, 99
  Huldah, 98
  Mary, 113
  Patience, 118
  Roger, 75, 89, 90, 91, 92, 93, 98, 99
  Samuel, 71
  Thomas, 101
HUGHES, Benjaman, 18

Edward, 18, 92,
  95, 99, 101
Elihu, 18
Hannah, 18, 101
Joseph, 104
Ruth, 95
Tabitha, 18
HUGHS, Benjamin, 104
  Edward, 93
  James, 93
  Jane, 122
  John, 72
  Jonathan, 92, 94
  Joseph, 44, 104
  Thomas, 250
HUGINS, Roger, 99
HULING, Honor, 61
HUMBLES, Jane, 4
  Thomas, 4
HUMPHRES, Abraham,
  43, 103
  Hannah, 103
HUMPHREY, Ann, 236
  John, 236
  Rachel, 236
HUMPHREYS, Mary, 45
  Richard, 45, 47,
  113, 120, 121
HUMPHRIES, Mary, 45,
  47, 117, 118
  Richard, 45
HUMSCHIER, Maria
  Cath., 210
  Maria Catharina,
  210
HUNRT, William, 92
HUNT, Ann, 95
  Elizabeth, 101
  John, 101, 102
  Mary, 143
  Sarah, 16, 17, 41
  Thomas, 17
  William, 16, 17,
  41, 91, 92, 93,
  94, 96, 97, 98,
  99
HUNTER, Rebekah,
  102, 244
HURLEY, Henry, 79,
  80
  Mary, 80
  Sarah, 80
HUSE, Edward, 95
  William, 91

HUSES, Edward, 94
HUSINGER, Andreas,
  218
  Catharina, 218
  Joh. Georg, 218
HUTSCHNER, Anna
  Margar, 203
  Jacob, 197, 200
  Magdalena, 195,
  197, 200

-I-

IFFT, Anna
  Catharina, 185,
  209
  Catharina, 188
  Elisabeth, 188
  Joh., 209
  Johannes, 185, 188
  Margareta, 209
IFT, Anna Catherine,
  198
  Johannes, 198
ILGEN, A. Barbara,
  222
  Anna Barbara, 218
  Anna Margareta,
  218
  Anne Barbara, 212
  Barbara, 209
  Hanna, 209, 232
  Johann Christoph
    Wilhelm, 222
  L., 208, 209
  Lewis, 209
  Ludwig, 218, 220
  Ludwig A. W., 212
  Ludwig Albrecht
    Wilhelm, 222, 232
  Luois, 231
  Maria Magdalene,
  212
  Mr., 218
ILLGEN, Anna, 209,
  210
  Anna Barbara, 209,
  215
  Barbara, 223
  Catharina, 223
  Elisabeth, 215
  Ludw., 209, 210
  Ludwig, 209, 215,
  223
IMMEL, Martin, 205

Rosina, 205
IREDELL, Sybble, 165
  Thomas, 165
IRELAND, Prudence,
  124
IRESON, John, 77
IRVIN, Abigail, 171
ITSCHNER, Anna
  Maria, 223
  Jacob, 223
  Magdalena, 223
  Martin, 223
  Nancy, 223
IVEY, Elizabeth, 170
IVINS, Barzilla, 57
  Elizabeth, 57
  Hannah, 57
  Isaac, 57
  Margaret Ann, 57
  Mary, 57
  Thomas, 57

-J-

JACKSON, James, 238
  Joseph, 238
  Sara-Ann, 238
JACOB, Catharina,
  183
JAGGER, Aner, 235
  David, 237, 239,
  241, 242
  Deborah, 241
  Dorothy, 242
  Elizabeth, 235,
  236, 239, 240,
  242
  Eunice, 242
  Jemima, 239
  John, 239
  Jonathan, 235,
  236, 239, 240,
  242
  Joseph, 237
  Martha, 237, 241,
  242
  Mary, 237, 239
  Phebe, 235
  Rachel, 237
JAHNSON, Barbara,
  181
  Michael, 181
  Peter, 181
JAMES, Abigail, 47
  Edward, 43, 100

Hannah, 47, 48, 132
James, 47
John, 141, 142
Mary, 47, 139
Rebeckah, 100
Sarah, 47, 72
JANSEN, Catharina, 225
Daniel, 225
Johann Adam, 231
Johannes, 225
Juliana, 225
Margaretha, 225
Michael, 231
JANSON, Andreas, 201
Anna, 215
Anna Maria, 219
Barbara, 183, 185, 187, 188, 191, 197, 202, 207, 219
Catharina, 195, 219
Catharine, 211
Daniel, 191, 221, 223
Eliesabeth, 191
Elisabeth, 182, 185, 187
Gabr., 207
Jacob, 188, 215, 219, 220
Joh., 219
Juliana, 223
Margareta, 215, 219, 220
Margretha, 187
Maria Catharina, 182, 183
Michael, 185, 201, 211, 217, 221, 222, 223
Paul, 182, 185, 186, 187, 191
Peter, 183, 185, 187, 188, 191, 197, 200, 202, 219, 223
Philip, 185
Samuel, 197
Sarah, 223
Susanna, 201, 211, 217, 221, 222, 223
Wilhelm, 220
JANVIER, Geo. W., 247, 248
JAYNER, Jane, 242
Mary, 242
Peter, 242
JEANS, Ann, 90
JEFFERIES, Asa, 50
Barzillai, 49, 126
Berzillai, 49
Constantine, 49
Leatitia, 49
Lettitia, 49
Mercy, 50
Patience, 49
Richard, 35
Sarah, 35
JEFFERIS, John, 35
Joshua, 35
Massey, 35
Rebecca, 35
JEFFERS, Joshua, 51
JEFFERY, Gertrude, 11
Jane, 11
John, 11
JEFFREY, Jean, 90
JEFFRIES, Hannah, 58
Joshua, 58
Mary, 50
Rebecca, 58
Richard Ware, 58
Sarah, 58
JENINGS, Henry, 76, 77
Rachal, 117
Samuel, 83
JENNINGS, Ann, 47, 152
Anna, 128
Hannah, 47, 128, 152, 165
Henry, 3, 74, 77, 79
John, 72, 123, 126, 131, 161
Levi, 47, 128, 152, 165
Mary, 3
Mary Ann, 161
Rachel, 69, 165
Rebeccah, 138
Rebeckah, 161
Sam, 82
Sarah, 152
Thomas, 48, 128, 152, 165
William, 3
JERVIS, Elizabeth, 134
JESOP, Hannah, 120
JESS, David, 43, 104, 106, 107
James, 53, 130
Jonathan, 44, 109
Rachel, 124
Rebekah, 124
Ruth, 43
Sarah, 58
Zachariah, 69
Zacheriah, 124
Zachery, 124
JESSOP, Hannah, 47
JOHNSON, Amelia, 247
Anna Margretha, 228
Barbara, 180, 184, 205
Betsey, 247
Catharina, 184, 216, 222
Christina, 209
Elisabeth, 180, 190, 203, 232
Emme Ann, 247
Franklin, 247
Hanna, 216
Harriet, 247
Isaac, 247
Johann, 216, 222
Johann Henrich, 203
Johannes, 184
John, 239, 247
Maria Catharina, 180
Mary, 95, 235, 247, 251
Michael, 203, 208, 209
Paul, 180, 190, 232
Peter, 184, 205
Richard, 78, 80, 81, 82, 84, 86, 87, 89, 222
Samuel E., 247

Sarah, 247
Susanna, 203, 208, 209
William, 247
JONES, Hannah, 107
Jane, 63
John, 42, 94, 99, 118
Matthew, 235
Sarah, 125
Susannah, 104
JORDAN, A.
Margretha, 193
Adam, 217, 220
Catharina, 217, 220
Joh. Micha., 193
Samuel, 220
Zacharias, 217
JOSEPH, Edward, 96
JOST, Elizabeth, 218
Johann, 218
JUDITH, William, 238
JUNG, Adam, 213, 217, 218, 221, 223, 226
Anna Maria, 186
Catharina, 209
David, 213
Elisabeth, 217, 222
Hanna, 221
Henrich, 222
Louisa, 186, 197, 226
Louise, 195
Margareta, 209, 215
Margarethe, 222
Margrete, 212
Maria, 213, 217, 218, 221, 223, 226
Philip, 186, 195, 212, 222
Philipp, 197, 209, 215, 223
JUNGE, Johann
Philip, 183
Louisa, 183, 184
Louise, 184
Philip, 183, 184

-K-

KAEK, David, 200
Margareta, 200
KAENDEL, Anna Maria, 195, 197, 200
Elisabeth, 200
Henr., 195
Henrich, 197, 200
Margareta, 195
Susanna, 197
KAHK, David, 225
Margarethe, 225
KAKE, David, 207
Margareta, 207
KAMMER, Catharina, 198, 205
Elisabeth, 198
Georg, 198, 205, 222
Joh. Georg, 224
KAMMERER, Barbara, 194
Cath., 203
Catharina, 216
Catharina Barbara, 194
Catharine, 210
Christian, 200
Georg, 200, 210, 216
Joh. Georg, 194, 203
Johann, 216
Johann Georg, 203
Susanna, 210
KANDLER, Anna Maria, 219
Heinrich, 219
Jacob, 219
KANTZ, Johann, 184
KANUS, Anna Barbara, 177
Johan, 177
KARLL, Catharina, 188
Elisabeth, 188
Georg Martin, 188
KASBEY, Bradway, 18
Edward, 10, 11, 12, 17, 18
Elizabeth, 10, 11, 12, 17, 18
Mary, 10, 17
Mather, 12
KASBY, Susanah, 12

KASER, Jacob, 184
Maria Eva, 184
KAST, Andreas, 226
Anna Barbara, 226, 228
Elisabeth, 228
Jacob, 226, 228
KAUCHER, Anna
Barbara, 183
Anna Elisabeth, 183
Barbara, 179
Conradt, 179
Conrath, 183
Georg, 183
George, 182
Hans Juerg, 179
Jacob, 179
Margretha, 183
Maria, 182
Maria Appellona, 179
KAUFFMAN, Christina, 190
Gotlieb, 190
Hans George, 190
KAUFFMANN, Gottlieb, 187
KAUGER, Anna
Barbara, 181
Catharina, 181
Conrath, 181
KAUMANN, Eva, 188
Eva Maria, 185
Joh., 188
Johann, 185
KAUTZ, Adam, 211, 212, 214, 216, 219, 221, 223, 225
Anna, 191, 192, 201, 206, 210, 216, 218, 219, 221, 223, 225
Anna Barbara, 191
Anne, 211, 212
Barbara, 188, 211, 212, 214, 215, 216, 219, 221, 223, 225
Catharina, 200
Elisabeth, 225
Geo., 206
Georg, 191, 192,

200, 210, 211, 212, 216, 218, 219, 221, 223
George, 201, 232
Hanna, 206
Joh., 191
Joh. Adam, 215
Joh. Georg, 188, 216
Joh. George, 186
Johann, 216
Johann Adam, 188
Maria, 214
Sara, 211
KAUZ, Anna, 197, 201, 204
Anna Barbara, 207
Barbara, 207
Georg, 201, 204, 206, 207
Hanna, 206
Johann Georg, 197
KAY, Ann, 28, 149
Clement, 125
Isaac, 115, 149
John, 115
Joseph, 28, 44, 109, 115, 149
Josiah, 28, 51, 110, 129
Rebeckah, 28, 115, 125
KEAIS, Nathan, 33
KEASBEY, Bradway, 150
Ed, 81
Edward, 81, 82, 84, 86, 87
Elizabeth, 22, 87
Hannah, 132
Jane, 150
John, 22
Mary, 22
Matthew, 22
Sarah, 22, 150
KEASBY, Bradway, 28, 65
Edward, 28, 82, 86
Elizabeth, 28, 69
Matthew, 96
Prudence, 28
KEASEY, Sarah, 98
KEEN, Magdalen, 251
KEHK, David, 221,

224, 227
Margare, 221
Margareta, 221, 224
Margaretha, 227
KEHRMANN, Fridrich, 213, 219
Hanna, 219
Johann, 219
Margareta, 213
KELLER, David, 221
Elisabeth, 211, 214, 215, 219, 220, 221, 223
Georg, 214, 215, 219, 220, 221, 223
George, 232
Joh. Georg, 211
Sarah, 215
Susanna, 219
KELLEY, William, 76
KELLY, Elisabeth, 209
Georg, 209
Hephsiba, 126
Job, 50, 126
Johann, 209
William, 77
KENCK, Preacher, 207
S., 207
KENDEL, A. Maria, 222
Anna Maria, 204, 206, 225
Heinrich, 204, 206
Henrich, 212, 225
Susanna, 212
KENT, Elizabeth, 113
Margaret, 78
KENTIN, William, 79
KENTON, Mary, 79
William, 79
KERBY, Asa, 72
Hannah, 120
Jonathan, 72
KERMAN, Catharina, 222, 227
David, 227
Elisabeth, 196
Friedrich, 211, 222, 227
Henrich, 211
Marcus, 196

Margarethe, 222
Margrete, 211
KERMANN, Catharina, 225
Frierich, 225
Marcus, 232
KERRMANN, Bodo, 208, 209
Catharine, 220
Elisabeth, 203, 220
Fridrich, 208, 209, 220
Marcus, 203
Margar., 209
Margareta, 208, 209
KESBY, Edward, 80
KEY, Ann, 34
Joseph, 34
Josiah, 42
Rebecca, 34
KIDD, Isabel, 106
Martha, 98
KILLEY, William, 77, 78
KING, Susannah, 116
KINISH, John, 244
KINNY, Bartolome, 179
Maria, 179
Maria Catharina, 179
KINSEY, James, 59, 170
Jonathan, 48, 122, 123
KIRBY, Amos, 71, 120, 127
Ann, 168
Asa, 127, 162, 165
Benjamin, 35, 59
Ebenezer, 162
Elizabeth, 71
Hannah, 117, 162, 165
Jonathan, 69, 120, 158
Lydia, 59, 137
Marcy, 35
Mercy, 59, 158
Richard, 120, 121, 127
Samuel, 120, 127,

158
Sarah, 170
KIRMAN, Catharina
  Maria, 185
  Marcus, 185
  Maria Elisabeth, 185
KIRMANN, Elisabeth, 189
  Friederich Marcus, 186
  Marcus, 186, 189
  Maria Elisabeth, 186
KLEIN, Jacob, 189
  Jul., 194
  Maria, 189
  Matthaeus, 189
KLOBER, Jacob, 196
KNAPTON, Ann, 8
  Ben, 82
  Benamen, 81
  Benia, 86
  Beniaman, 77
  Beniamen, 87
  Beniamin, 79, 80
  Beniamm, 77
  Beniemen, 84
  Benimen, 80, 86, 87
  Benj, 86
  Benja, 89
  Benjamin, 8, 84
  Phebe, 8
  Phebey, 88
KNARRY, Anna Maria, 190
  Lorentz, 190
KNERI, Anna Maria, 197
  Lorenz, 197
KNERY, Anna Mar., 194
  Dewald, 194
  Lorenz, 194
KNIEST, Barbara, 178
  Johannes, 178
  Michael, 178
KNIGHT, John, 35, 137
  Sarah, 35
KNOPP, Theobald, 228
KOBEL, Anna Barbara, 195

Jac., 195
KOCH, Catharine, 198
  Christoph, 182
  Marcus, 196
  Margretha, 182
  Michael, 189
  Rudolph, 196
  Rudy, 198
  Sarah, 196, 198
KOECK, David, 230
KOEK, David, 205
  Elisabeth, 205
  Margareta, 205
KOELSCH, Johan
  Georg, 229
  Johann Juerg, 229
KOUS, Nathan, 60
KRADINGER,
  Christian, 179, 181
  Elisabeth, 181
  Georg Adam, 181
KRAEMER, Andreas, 182, 204
  Anna Margratha, 182
  Barbara, 189
  Cath., 194
  Charl., 194
  Charlotte, 196
  Jacob, 184
  Marg. Catharina, 199
  Margretha, 184, 186, 189
  Mathias, 182, 186
  Matthaeus, 189
  Matthias, 184, 199
KRAUSS, Christian
  Friederich, 182
KREEMER, Catharina, 192
  Johnnes, 192
  Matias, 192
KRONBERGER,
  Margarethe, 223
  Peter, 223
KRONEBERGER,
  Friedr., 199
  Johann, 215
  Margareta, 215
  Margrete, 212
  Peter, 212, 215
KRONENEBERGER,

Peter, 206
KRUMERIN, Barbara, 181
  Juerg, 181
KRUMREIM, Barbara, 178
  Georg Leonhard, 178
KRUMREIN, Barbara, 181, 185, 187, 228
  Catharina, 187
  Elisabeth, 181
  Georg, 179, 181, 183, 185, 187
  Georg Leonhardt, 228
  Henrich, 183
  Johann Christian, 181
KRUMREYN, Abraham, 179
  Barbara, 179
  Juerg, 179
KUEPER, Johannes, 177
KUHLEMAN, Christoph, 179
  Magdalena Juliana, 179
KUHLEMANN, Anna
  Maria, 198
  Christoph, 182, 190, 198
  J. C., 179
  Johann Martin, 198
  Magdalena Juliana, 182, 190
KUNTZ, Elisabeth, 179
  Isaac, 179
  Sophia Augusta, 179
KUNZE, J. C., 201
  Joh. Christ., 207
  Johann Christoph, 203, 204, 205

—L—
LACHS, Friedrich, 207
LADD, Elizabeth, 100
LAMBORN, Dinah, 60
  Richard, 60, 73

INDEX 287

LANG, Mary, 244
LANGENBACH,
　Elisabeth, 182,
　　188, 192
　Fomas, 192
　Michael, 182
　Paul, 182, 188,
　　192
LANNING, John, 118,
　1214
LANTENSCHLAEGER,
　Elisabeth, 195
　Johan Jacob, 195
　Michael, 195
LARAUNCE, George,
　101
LARRANCE, George, 97
LAUDENSLEGEL, Johan
　Georg, 193
LAUDESCHLEGEL, Anna
　Maria, 193
　Elisabeth, 193
　Joh. Michael, 193
LAUERER, Anna, 228
　Gottfried, 228
LAUTENSCHLAEGER,
　Elisabeth, 197
　Joh. Michael, 197
　Richard, 197
LAWRANCE, Hannah,
　113
LAWRENCE, Elizabeth,
　250
　George, 115
　John, 113, 114
　Josiah, 126, 159
LAWRICE, Abigail, 35
　Ann, 35
　Thomas, 35
LEAVER, Mary, 49
LECROY, John, 244
LEDES, Lavisey, 128
LEEDS, Louisa, 128
　Samuel, 52, 71
LEHMANN, Eva, 197
　Theobald, 197
LEIDENBERGER,
　Eberhard, 207
　Elisabet, 207
LEIDINGER, Maria
　Magdalena, 232
LEMAN, Dewald, 194
LEONARD, Hannah, 91
　Sarah, 4

Thomas, 4
LEUTENBERGER, Anna
　Margareta, 204
　Eberhard, 204
　Elisabeth, 204
LEWDEN, Rebeckah, 51
LEWIS, Ann, 53, 141,
　170
　Ellen, 75
　Hannah, 138, 141,
　170
　Jacob, 53
　John, 85, 86, 138,
　141, 170, 251
　Joseph, 53, 69,
　138, 140, 141,
　170
　Mary, 53, 123,
　138, 141, 170
　Sarah, 53
　Stephen, 91, 92,
　93, 94, 97, 99,
　100, 101
　Steven, 101
　William, 53, 138,
　141, 170
LICHT, Agnesa, 186
　Johannes, 186
LIGHTFOOT, Ann, 56
　Sarah, 55
LINCH, Sarah, 64
LINCK, Anna
　Margretha, 189
　Anna Maria, 194
　Joh. Georg, 194
　Johann Michael,
　204
　Johannes, 187,
　189, 194, 204
　Maria, 187, 189
　Mattaeus, 187
　Sophia, 204
LINK, George, 232
　Hans, 229
LINSEY, Sedons, 135
LINTER, Anna
　Catharina, 179
LIPINCOTT, Caleb,
　107
LIPPENCOTT, Abigail,
　170
　Julia Ann, 170
　Samuel, 73
　Thomas, 170

LIPPINCOAT, Jacob,
　104
LIPPINCOT, Jacob,
　101
LIPPINCOTT, Aaron,
　68, 145, 158
　Abigail, 35, 53,
　71, 144, 157
　Amey, 160
　Ann, 153, 156, 165
　Barzillai, 51, 129
　Barzillia, 72
　Benjamin, 42, 71,
　117, 122, 145,
　158
　Caleb, 165
　Charles, 54, 143
　Darius, 45, 113
　Deborah, 158, 165,
　167, 170
　Elizabeth, 52, 54,
　65, 129, 144,
　145, 158
　Freedom, 144
　Hannah, 103, 165
　Hope, 68, 145, 158
　Jacob, 42
　Jethro, 72
　John, 158, 168
　Joseph, 68, 113,
　123, 144, 153,
　156, 157, 160
　Joshua, 44, 71,
　115, 144, 168
　Leatitia, 135
　Lettitia, 165
　Lidya, 153
　Lydia, 73
　Mary, 69, 72, 102,
　113, 119, 132,
　145, 153, 165,
　169
　Mercy, 69, 144
　Mercy Kerby, 157
　Naomy, 118
　Rebecca, 137, 168
　Samuel, 35, 43,
　54, 106, 109,
　110, 111, 112,
　113, 143, 144,
　157, 165, 167
　Sarah, 103, 158
　Thomas, 35, 165
　William, 52, 127,

138, 165
LIPPONCOTT, Neomy, 119
LITHENS, Daniel, 246
  Enos, 246
  Margaret, 246
  Mary, 246
LITLE, Joseph, 228
  Nancy, 228
  William, 228
LIUS, Bartholomew, 87
  Jael, 88
  John, 86
LLOYD, Catherine, 251
  Hester, 236
  Obadiah, 236
  Obariah, 234
LOCK, Beata, 252
LODGE, Benjamin, 100
  Jane, 96
  Robart, 93
  Robert, 41, 89, 94, 95, 100
LONG, Mary, 244
LONGE, William, 77
LONGS, Sarah, 242
LONGSTAFF, Laban, 244
LOOY, Elizabeth, 172, 173
LOPER, Patience, 244
LORD, Azuba, 54
  David, 56
  Elizabeth, 244
  Hannah, 104
  Joshua, 43, 103
  Kesiah, 54
  Nathan, 54, 141
  Sarah, 54, 138
LOT, Mary, 244
LOTZ, Anna Maria, 187, 188
  Johann, 188
  Johann Friederich, 188
  Johannes, 181, 182, 186, 187, 195
  Maria, 186
LOUDEN, Reneir, 88, 89
  Renier, 93

LOW, Ann, 54
  Catharine, 54
  Hugh, 54, 135
  Lucy, 54
LOWDEN, Renier, 91
LOWDERBACK, Patience, 118
LOWE, Ann, 135
  Catharine, 135
  Lucy, 135
LOWNSBERRY, Rebeccah, 131
LOYD, Sarah, 209
LUETZ, Anna Maria, 191
  Joh., 191
LUKENS, Azor, 53
LUKIN, Azor, 131
LUMBY, Abigail, 244
LUMLEY, Edward, 241
  John, 241
  Rebekah, 241
  Sarah, 241
LUMMAS, Henry, 117
LUMMIS, Edward, 251
  Grace, 118
  Henry, 67
LUMMUS, Elisabeth, 226
  Jacob Fries, 226
  Wilhelm, 226
LUTZ, Anna Maria, 190
  Johan, 230
  Johann, 190
  Johannes, 190, 192
  Maria, 192
LUZ, Johannes, 178
LYDENIUS, Rev., 182
LYNCH, Joshua, 168, 170

-M-
MACCALL, Hannah, 73
MCCALL, Hannah, 138
MCCARTY, Elizabeth, 243
M'CASSON, Jacob Friederich, 182
  Maria Dorothea, 182
  William, 182
MCCATTS, Hannah, 138
MACCLANG, Ann, 235

  James, 235
  Mary, 235
MCCLEESE, Daniel, 244
MCFARLIN, Mary, 115
MCGEE, Abraham, 212
  Elisbeth, 212
  John, 212
MCGOOGAN, Margaret, 244
MACKASCEN, Maria Dorothea, 177
MACKASCHEN, Maria, 177
  Maria Dorothea, 177
  William, 177
MCKEE, Abraham, 215
  Anna, 215
  Elisabeth, 215
MCKEEN, Jane, 237
  John, 237
MCKINNE, Ann, 243
  Barnabas, 243, 244
  William, 243
MACKLERAY, Rachel, 129
MACKLIN, Anna Maria, 202
  Joh. Georg, 202
MCKNIGHT, Jane, 250
MCLANNING, Samuel, 251
MCNICHOL, Phebe, 130
MCNICHOLE, George, 22, 101
  Mary, 22
  Rebeckah, 22
MACNICHOLS, George, 43
MCNICHOLS, John, 156
  Mary, 115
  Rebecca, 137
  William, 137
MCNICKOLS, Andrew, 144
  Daniel, 144
  George, 144
  Hannah, 144
  Isaac, 144
  John, 144
  Margaret, 144
  Nethaniel, 144
  Phebe, 144

Rebeckah, 144
William, 144
MCPEAK, Rebeckah, 124
MADDOCK, John, 61, 75, 78, 82
MADDOCKES, Joseph, 76
MADDOCKS, Elizabeth, 5, 78
John, 5, 74, 79, 80
Joseph, 75
Ralfe, 5
MADERA, Christopher, 246
David, 246
Elizabeth, 246
John, 246
Nancy, 246
MADOCKS, John, 74
MAERTIN, Catharina, 190
Simon, 190
MAIER, Elisabeth, 179
Jacob, 179
MAISES, Maria, 212
MAISON, John, 87
Thomas, 87
MAKRE, Michael, 201
MALSON, Catharine, 251
MANARING, John, 250
MANCH, Adam, 215
Anna Maria, 215
Jacob, 215
Susanna, 215
MANN, Anna Barbara Kautz, 232
MANNE, Jacob, 219
Margareta, 219
Michael, 219
MANNY, Anna Maria, 221
Jacob, 221
Margareta, 221
Maria, 221
MARCHAL, Richard, 81
MARDERSTICK,
Catharina, 187, 189
Johann, 187
Johann Georg, 189

Johannes, 187, 189
MARIA, Gulielma, 132
MARINUS, David, 244
MARK, Friedrich, 207
MARLEY, Gregory, 2, 3
MARRIOTT, Joseph, 43, 102
Mary, 102
MARSHAL, John, 243
MARSHALL, Elizabeth, 240
Humphrey, 4
Issabell, 4
John, 240
Rebecca, 90
Richard, 78, 80, 81
Sarah, 88
Simon, 240
Thomas, 92
MARSHOH, Elizabeth, 237
Jane, 237
John, 237
MARSHOLDER,
Elisabeth, 208, 209
Jacob, 208, 209
MARTIN, Catharina, 186, 192
Georg Jacob, 186
Simon, 186, 192
MARTINI, Catharina, 184
Simon, 184
MARY, Anna Maria, 210
Edward, 6
Johannes, 210
Margrethe, 210
Susanna, 6
MASLEY, Gregory, 74
MASON, Aaron, 10, 25, 91, 152
Abigail, 25, 104
Ann, 10, 39, 72, 88, 132, 148, 152
Aron, 36, 93, 94
Barrott, 152
Elizabeth, 9, 10, 11, 12, 13, 19, 105, 119, 120, 143

Grace, 42, 103
Hannah, 19, 66, 72, 152
Isabel, 251
James, 13, 36, 94, 95, 119, 152
John, 8, 10, 11, 13, 19, 31, 36, 39, 48, 68, 79, 80, 81, 82, 83, 84, 86, 88, 89, 90, 91, 94, 97, 108, 109, 115, 135, 148, 152, 155, 159
Jonathan, 12
Joseph, 11
Leatitia, 152
Letitia, 36, 119
Martha, 11
Mary, 9, 31, 50, 65, 89, 152, 155
Melissa, 152
Millisant, 129
Rebecca, 36, 119, 152
Rebeckah, 13, 152
Reeve, 119
Ruth, 36, 152
Samuel, 11, 19, 25, 63, 96, 97, 98, 99, 108
Samuell, 94
Sarah, 8, 10, 11, 13, 19, 25, 49, 72, 94, 106, 115, 148, 152, 252
Susanna, 39, 72
Susannah, 31, 36, 119, 155
Thomas, 9, 10, 11, 12, 13, 19, 36, 84, 86, 87, 88, 89, 91, 92, 93, 94, 99
William, 10, 155, 159
MASSHOLDER,
Catharina, 219
Jacob, 219
MASSON, John, 84
MATERSTICH,
Catharina, 193
Jacob, 193

Johannes, 193
MATLACK, George, 49, 69
  Mary, 53
  Richard, 101
  Sarah, 122
  William, 53, 72
MATSON, Catharine, 251
  Elizabeth, 67, 152
  Hapzibah, 152
  Hephsiba, 126
  Mary, 118, 126, 152
  Mathias, 118, 152
  Sarah, 69, 152
MAUERER, Adam, 195
  Maria Catharina, 195
MAULE, Abigail, 242
  Benjamin, 237, 240, 242
  Eleanor, 236, 244
  Hannah, 237
  John, 237
  Lydia, 237
  Rebekah, 240
  Robrt, 236
  Sarah, 237
MAURER, A.
  Margretha, 191
  Adam, 183, 188, 191, 193, 196, 197, 204, 229, 230, 232
  Anna Margretha, 183, 188
  Cath., 193
  Catharina, 208, 209
  Christina, 191, 229
  Elisabeth, 181, 188
  Jacob, 181
  Joh. Georg, 208, 209
  Johann, 208, 209
  Maria Catharina, 197, 230
MAXFIELD, Elizabeth, 142
MAXWELL, Elizabeth, 36, 130, 142

John, 36
MAY, Anna Maria, 210
  Elisabeth, 220
  Jacob, 222
  Johann, 213, 215, 218, 220
  Johann Georg, 213
  Johannes, 210, 222, 225
  Margareta, 213, 215, 218, 220
  Margarethe, 222, 225
  Margrethe, 210
  Sarah, 225
MAYER, Christoph, 217
  Leonhard, 177
  Sarah, 217
  Wilhelm, 217
MAYHEW, Benjamin, 248
  Catherine, 248
  Elam, 248
  Eleazer, 247, 248
  Hannah, 240, 242
  Isaac, 248
  Israel, 242
  Jacob, 248
  John, 247
  Rebecca, 248
  Sarah, 247
  Stanford, 247
  Thomas, 240, 242, 244
  Uriah, 240
MEAD, Margaret, 46
  Richard, 46, 121
  Ruth, 46, 128
  Samuel, 46
  Sarah, 46
MEBOLD, Anna Christine, 196
  Christina, 189
  Georg, 189
  Johann Georg, 196
MECKLIN, A. Maria Barbara, 187, 189
  Georg, 218
  H. Georg, 187, 189
MEDAREY, Gertrude, 169
MEED, Sarah, 116
MEIER, Catharina,

182, 183, 185
  Elisabeth, 185
  Georg, 189
  I. Georg, 189
  Leonhard, 182, 183, 185
  Maria, 182
MEIR, Margaretha, 198
MEJER, Catharina, 180
  Johann Simon, 180
  Leonhard, 180
MELBOLD, Christina, 187
  Georg, 187
MENSCH, Adam, 181, 182, 184, 185, 187, 188, 189, 191, 197, 201, 202, 205, 213
  Andreas, 181, 196, 200, 210, 211, 213, 216, 217, 219, 221, 223, 224, 227
  Anna, 217, 224, 225
  Archebald, 224
  Barbara, 181, 182, 184, 185, 187, 188, 189, 197, 201, 202, 205, 210
  Beniamin, 209, 214, 217, 224
  Benjamin, 191, 210, 222, 227
  Cathar., 227
  Catharina, 213, 216, 217, 219, 221, 223, 224
  Christian, 216
  Christina, 209, 214, 219, 222, 225, 227
  Christine, 212, 216
  Daniel, 214
  David, 222
  Elizabeth, 214
  Hanna, 214, 222, 224, 227
  Joh. Adam, 181

Joseph, 227
Lydia, 219
M. Barbara, 191
Margaretha, 222
Maria, 217
Peter, 188, 203,
  205, 207, 209,
  212, 214, 216,
  219, 222, 225,
  227
Phebe, 227
Philippina, 227
Susanna, 184, 199,
  221
MENSH, Christine,
  208, 209
Peter, 208, 209
Susanna, 208, 209
MEOPALD, Anna, 231
Georg, 231
MEOPOLD, Christina,
  192
Georg, 192
MEPOLD, Georg, 230
MERCKEL, Georg, 209
Maria, 209
MERRION, Thomas, 84
MERTHENSBECK,
  Elisabeth, 191
Johan, 191
METZGER, Georg, 187
Johan Georg, 187
Ledi, 187
MEYER, A. Maria, 222
Anna Elisabeth,
  224
Anna Margaretha,
  178
Catharina, 179
Cathrina, 176, 177
Christoph, 224
Christopher, 219
Daniel, 222
Elisabeth, 192
Eva Cathrina, 178
Georg, 192
Joh. Leonhard, 178
Johan Jacob, 176,
  177
Johann Jacob, 229
Johann Juerg, 179
Johannes, 192
Leonhard, 176,
  177, 179, 229

Margareta, 219
Margarethe, 222
Maria, 229
Sarah, 219, 224
Simon, 229
MEYERER, Anna
  Margaretha, 178
Jacob, 178
Johann Jacob, 178
MEYERS, Christoph,
  211
Ester, 211
Sara, 211
MICHLER, Catharina,
  179
Eva, 179
Jost, 179
MICKEL, Elisabeth,
  223
Joseph, 226
Josua, 223, 226
Rosina, 223, 226
MIDDLETON, Hugh, 5,
  79
MIEHL, Elisabeth,
  213
Georg, 213
MILER, Georg, 192,
  193
Margaretha, 192
Michael, 192
Susanna, 192, 193
MILLAR, Catherine,
  241
Christiana, 241
Joost, 241
MILLER, Abraham, 36,
  71, 124, 140,
  161, 241
Adam, 199
Andreas, 202
Andrew, 23, 36,
  52, 57, 106, 112,
  130, 146, 175
Ann, 52, 73
Anna Margretha,
  188
Anna Maria, 192,
  205, 209
Benjamin, 30
Cathar., 200
Catharina, 190,
  197, 198, 199,
  201, 202, 204,

205, 206
Catharine, 236
Catrina, 192
Christiana, 236,
  238, 240, 243
Christina, 36,
  191, 234
Daniel, 36, 57
Ebenezer, 23, 35,
  40, 42, 45, 63,
  72, 97, 98, 100,
  108, 109, 111,
  112, 114, 125,
  134, 146, 156,
  175
Elisabeth, 205
Elizabeth, 30, 36,
  56, 161, 240, 243
Elizabeth Wyatt,
  35
Georg, 192, 193,
  201, 202, 204,
  224, 229
George, 190, 252
Hannah, 23, 35,
  40, 45, 52, 62,
  72, 175
Hannah White, 161
Hans. Michl., 190
Henry, 238
Isaac, 157
J. Philip, 192
Jacob, 188, 198,
  200, 201, 202,
  204, 206, 232
James, 35
Joh. Michael, 191,
  192
Johann, 214, 224
Johann Georg, 197
Johanna, 192
Johannes, 204,
  205, 206
John, 23, 46, 66,
  109, 147, 155,
  157, 234, 236,
  241, 243
Joost, 234, 236,
  238, 240, 243
Joseph, 36, 157
Josiah, 23, 35,
  36, 64, 112, 114,
  120, 123, 126,
  146, 155

Latitia, 72
Leatitia, 35, 36, 122, 146, 147, 155
Letitia, 119, 120
Lidia, 35, 52
Lidya, 52
Magdalena, 214
Margaret, 157, 236, 241, 243
Margareta, 214
Margaretha, 199
Margretha, 188, 191, 192
Maria, 190
Maria Appollonia, 201
Maria Catharina, 191, 192, 210
Mark, 23, 35, 40, 52, 114, 137, 141, 147
Mary, 36, 40, 52, 72, 146, 157, 236
Matthias, 231
Michael, 188, 191, 192, 197, 199, 201, 205, 206, 210, 229
Phebe, 35, 52, 140, 143
Pheobe, 52
Priscilla, 40, 71, 175
Pyle Smith, 36, 161
Rachel, 36, 146, 175, 243
Rebecca, 35, 36, 57
Rebeckah, 23, 66
Richard, 30, 35, 135, 146
Ruth, 35, 40, 73, 123, 128, 175
Samuel, 36
Sarah, 23, 36, 66, 160, 175, 224
Sarah Wyatt, 35, 36
Susanna, 188, 192, 193, 204, 206
Susannah, 190
Wilhelm, 210

William, 23, 36, 52, 59, 68, 73, 123, 130, 146, 157, 160, 161, 234
William Fister, 35
MILLS, Rebeckah, 115
Rebekah, 124
MINTZ, Anna Cathrina, 177
Philip, 177
MIRA, Catherine, 243
Jacob, 243
Margaret, 243
MIRE, Leonard, 244
MISHNER, Susanna, 170
MOFFETT, Andrew, 236
Mary, 236
Samuel, 236
MOHSHOLDER, Elisabeth, 203
Jacob, 203
MONIE, Michael, 202
MONROHE, Johanne, 231
MONY, Michael, 205
MOOR, Damaris, 238
Elizabeth, 238
Jedikiah, 239
Mary, 234, 235
Moses, 238
Nathaniel, 239
MOORE, Asa, 165
Atlantic, 165
Benjamin, 46, 157, 165
Chalkey, 157
Chalkley, 165, 167
Elizabeth, 165
Hanna, 234
Hannah, 46, 157, 165, 168
Hugh, 234
Jacob, 165
Joseph, 172, 173
Joshua, 165, 168
Josiah, 157
Kiturah, 165
Lewis, 98
Mary, 54, 135, 157, 165, 243
Priscilla, 165
Rachel, 165, 168

Rebecca, 73, 165
Rebeckah, 157
Richard, 243
Samuel, 165
Sybbl, 165
Thomas, 93, 165, 168
MORE, Thomas, 250
MORGAN, David, 169
Elizabeth, 169
Hannah, 169
Jonathan, 169
Mary, 252
Samuel, 252
MORIS, Lewis, 93
Rothrak, 81
Ruddea, 78
Rudera, 77
Rudrah, 80
MORRIS, Anthony, 77, 83
Daniel, 92
David, 8, 16, 17, 90, 92, 93, 94
Jael, 8, 9, 10, 104
Jane, 10, 16, 17
Jayel, 85
Jonathan, 6, 87, 89
Joseph, 6, 34, 89, 90, 91, 92, 93, 94, 97, 101
Joshua, 9, 16, 17
Lewis, 6, 90, 91, 92, 97, 99
Luis, 89
Prudence, 34, 101
Rothoray, 89
Rothrah, 82, 83
Rothrak, 8, 9
Rothrea, 78
Rudera, 79
Rudra, 6, 10
Ruthera, 82
Samuel, 91
Sarah, 6, 88
MORRISON, Ann, 162
Anna, 122, 130
Matthew, 162
MORRISS, Jael, 84
MORROW, Jane, 131
MOSES, Isaac, 49
MOSLET, Elisabeth,

INDEX 293

190
 Friederich, 190
 Heinrich, 190
MOSS, Abraham, 18,
 19, 22, 42, 43,
 64, 90, 92, 93,
 94, 96, 97, 98,
 99, 100, 101, 103
 Abram, 94
 Ann, 64
 Hannah, 18
 Hope, 64
 Isaac, 18, 112
 Rebeckah, 18, 19,
 22, 67
 Richard, 18, 22,
 101, 104
 Thomas, 19
MOUNCE, Ann, 168
 Peter, 168
MOUNT, Abigail, 134
MUCJLEROY, Rachel,
 129
MUEHL, Georg, 220
MUEHLENBERG, Henry,
 195
 Rev, 187, 188
MUELLER, Adam, 231
 Anna, 227
 Anna Catharina,
 180
 Barbara, 197
 Cath., 194, 198
 Catharina, 180,
 181, 182, 183,
 185, 186, 187,
 188, 194, 213
 Catharine, 198,
 211
 Catherine, 197
 Elisabeth, 222
 Elisabetha, 227
 Friederich, 227
 Georg, 186, 194,
 210, 230
 George, 198
 Hans Mich., 186
 Hans Michael, 184,
 185, 187
 Heinrich, 180, 206
 Jacob, 194, 197,
 198, 211
 Johann, 227
 Johann Michael,

182
 Johannes, 180,
 186, 210
 Magdalena, 210
 Margretha, 182,
 185
 Maria Catharina,
 184, 185
 Matthias, 222, 225
 Mich, 180
 Mich., 183
 Michael, 181, 182,
 185, 229, 231
 Sarah, 227
 Schena, 180
 Susanna, 186, 222,
 225
 Susanne, 198
MUENZ, Maria
 Catharina, 179
 Philipp, 179
MUHLENBERG, Henr.,
 230
 Magdalena, 230
MULFORD, Deborah,
 165
 Elizabeth, 165
 John, 236
 Martha B., 165
 Mary, 165
 Mary Ann, 165
 William, 165
MULLER, Cathar., 194
 Catharina, 197,
 201
 Georg, 194
 George, 194, 197
 Hans Michael, 184
 Jacob, 197
 Juliana, 187
 Margretha, 187
 Maria Catharina,
 184
 Mich., 194
 Michael, 177, 187,
 201
 Susanna, 194, 197
MULLFORD, Stephen,
 114
MURPHEY, John, 248
 Lettitia, 35
 Mahlon, 35
 Mary, 248
 Naomi, 35

Noah, 35
 Phebe, 248
 Rachel, 248
 Smith, 35
 William, 35
MURPHY, Elizabeth,
 246
 Mahlon, 59
 Naomi, 59
 Neah, 59
 Robert, 246
 Samuel, 246
 Smith, 59
 William, 59

-N-

NAEGLIN, Anna Maria,
 192
 Johan Georg, 192
NARTHEL, Christian,
 244
NASEL, Anna
 Catharina, 180
 Christian, 180
 Margreta, 180
NASSEL, Anna
 Margaretha, 179
 Christian, 179
NAZEL, Anna
 Margretha, 177
 Christian, 177,
 178
 Margretha, 178
NEALSON, Deborah,
 243
NEALY, Joseph, 244
NEFFT, Catharina,
 192
 Joh., 192
 Johanna, 192
NEGRO, Bethina, 235,
 239
NELSON, Anthony, 244
NESSIN, Anna, 177
NESTLER, Hanna, 201
 Joh. Gottfried,
 201
 Rahel, 201
NEVILLE, James, 74
NEWBOLD, Michael,
 57, 140
NEWBURN, John, 57
 Susanna, 57
 Susannah, 57

William, 57
NEWELL, James, 74, 75
NICHOLASON, Joseph, 79
　Martha, 170
NICHOLS, Abell, 84
　Christiana, 238
　David, 238
　John, 243
　Stephen, 5
　Thomas, 238
　William, 243
NICHOLSON, Abel, 2, 8, 9, 10, 12, 13, 14, 15, 24, 81, 82, 86, 87, 92, 93, 95, 97, 98, 99, 110, 129
　Abell, 79, 80, 81, 84, 86, 91, 92, 93, 94, 96, 99
　Able, 88, 89, 90
　Ann, 2, 12, 36, 62
　Beulah, 36
　Daniel, 36, 157
　Darkin, 36, 72
　Elisha, 36
　Elizabeth, 2, 36, 60, 110, 126
　Esther, 36
　Grace, 24, 46, 66
　Hannah, 36, 72, 112, 114
　Jael, 143
　James, 36
　John, 13, 15, 20, 36, 99, 106, 120
　Joseph, 2, 10, 80
　Mark, 52, 136
　Martha, 52, 129
　Mary, 8, 9, 10, 12, 13, 14, 15, 20, 52, 129
　Millicent, 36
　Milliscent, 156
　Noah, 36
　Rachel, 2, 9, 24, 36, 107, 127, 145, 156
　Ruth, 14, 36, 72, 94, 117, 145, 157
　Samuel, 2, 14, 24, 36, 52, 62, 65, 73, 74, 78, 96, 97, 98, 100, 107, 108, 109, 121, 129, 141, 142, 156
　Samuell, 79
　Sarah, 8, 20, 24, 36, 52, 115, 129, 156, 157
　William, 10, 36, 69, 94, 95, 142, 145, 156
NICKHOLSON, Rachel, 74
NICKOLSON, Abell, 86
NICKSON, Jane, 78
　John, 78
NIELSON, Deborah, 136
NIEU KIRK, Abraham, 234
　Cornelius, 234
　Rachel, 234
NIEUKIRK, Abraham, 234, 241, 243, 244
　Ann, 241, 243, 245, 247
　Barshaba, 245
　Bathsheba, 247
　Benjamin, 246
　Catherine, 246
　Christiana, 246
　Cornelius, 234, 237
　Elizabeth, 241, 245, 247
　Hannah, 246
　Janetie, 244
　Janitie, 234
　Mary, 245, 247
　Matthew, 245, 246, 247
　Nathaniel Reeve, 247
　Nieu, 234
　Rachel, 234, 237, 246
　Rebekah, 243
　Sarah, 237, 245, 247
NIXON, Isaac, 130, 138
　Joseph, 49
NOBLET, Anna, 122
　Margaret, 72
　Mary, 72
　William, 125
NOBLIT, Joseph, 104
　Leatitia, 121
　William, 125
NOLL, Anna
　Margretha, 193
　Anna Maria, 193, 203, 221
　Heinr., 208, 209, 221
　Hendrick, 231
　Henrich, 205, 211
　Joh., 193
　Johannes, 181, 205, 231
　Johannes Georg, 181
　Margareta, 208, 209
　Maria, 181
　Michael, 211
　Susanna, 205, 208, 209, 221
　Susanne, 211
NOLLE, Anna Maria, 183
　Johann Henrich, 183
　Johannes, 183
NORBERRY, Rebekah, 102
NORRIS, Isaac, 83
　Thomas, 133, 134

—O—

OACKEFOARD, Charles, 81
OACKFOARD, Wade, 81
OACKFORD, Charles, 81, 84
　Wad Sam, 87
　Wade, 84, 87, 88
　Wade Samuel, 87
OADS, Thomas, 5
OAKEFORD, Elizabeth, 89
　Isaac, 96
　William, 96
OAKFOARD, Charles, 82
　Samuel, 81

INDEX

OAKFORD, Aaron, 111
  Amos, 21, 152
  Ann, 108
  Benjamin Webber, 52
  Charles, 9, 10, 11, 12, 17, 20, 27, 80, 84, 90, 91, 92, 94, 96, 97, 98, 99
  Deborah, 65
  Easter, 20
  Elizabeth, 9, 17, 20, 21, 113, 161
  Esther, 17, 103, 104
  Grace, 67
  Hannah, 21, 101, 152, 161, 162
  Hester, 27
  Isaac, 101, 104, 109, 121
  Jacob, 64, 110
  James, 20
  John, 11, 21, 22, 43, 93, 97, 103, 152, 250
  Lettitia, 104
  Mable, 22
  Margaret, 27, 64
  Margret, 12, 87
  Mary, 9, 10, 11, 12, 48, 118, 120
  Rebeckah, 22
  Samuel, 22
  Sarah, 22, 133, 161, 162
  Susanna, 62, 98
  Susannah, 22
  Wade, 82, 90, 97
  Wade Samuel, 87
  Waid, 93
  William, 67, 104, 109, 116, 123, 160, 161, 162
OAKFROD, John, 62
OARKFORD, Waid, 92
OCHESBERGER,
  Henrich, 212
  Joh. Georg, 212
  Maria Christine, 212
OCHSENBECHER,
  Catharina, 201
  Henrich, 201
  Johann Jacob, 201
OCHSENBECKER,
  Christina, 219
OCHSENBERGER,
  Christine, 210
  Henrich, 210
OELBERS, Nicolaus, 230
OGDEN, Ann, 165, 166
  David, 166
  Esther, 154, 165, 168
  Hannah, 165, 236, 239
  Joel, 239
  John, 166, 236
  Jonathan, 239
  Joseph, 154, 165
  Marian, 135
  Martha, 165
  Mary, 154, 165, 167
  Mary Ann, 154, 165, 170, 172
  Richard, 236
  Samuel, 47, 67, 123, 129, 154, 165, 166, 169, 170, 171
OGDON, Hannah, 168
  Mary Ann, 168
  Palmira, 171
  Phebe, 171
  Rhoda, 171
  Samuel, 168
  Thomas, 171
OKEFORD, Charles, 80
OLBERS, Nicholaus, 190
  Nicolaus, 188
OLLINGER, Mary, 235
OSBORN, Josiah, 136
  Nathan, 136
  Phoebe, 136
  Rhoda, 136
  Thomas, 72
OSBORNE, Dunn, 170
  Nathan, 170
  Palmyra, 170
  Phebe, 170
  Rhoda, 170
  Thomas, 170
OTH, Elisabeth, 222

Henrich, 222
OTT, David, 198
  Elisabeth, 226
  Elisabetha, 227
  Georg, 211
  Heinrich, 227
  Henrich, 226
  Margareta, 204
  Margaretha, 226
  Margrethe, 211
  Martin, 204, 211, 226
OTTO, Bodo, 185, 186, 189, 191, 229
  Catharina, 191, 229
  Catharina Dorothea, 185, 186
  Dorothea Catharina, 189
OVEREND, Margret, 97
OWEN, Ann, 166, 169
  Benjamin, 169
  David, 169
  Elizabeth, 169, 170
  Griffith, 141
  Isaac, 141
  Jesse, 169
  Joseph, 169
  Joshua, 166, 169, 171, 172, 173
  Lewis, 43, 53, 104, 108, 126
  Prudence, 169
  Rachel, 168
  Rowland, 169
  Sarah, 169
  Sydney, 166
  William, 72
OXENBECHER,
  Christina, 204
  Henrich, 204
  Joh. Henrich, 204
OXLEY, Joseph, 48

-P-

PAGE, Abigail, 72
  Hannah, 72
  James, 145
  John, 34, 43, 51, 101, 122, 145,

146
  Mary, 116, 145, 146
  Rachel, 146
  Rebecca, 34, 121, 145
  Rebeckah, 70, 146
  Rebekah, 102
  Sarah, 118, 145
PAGET, Andrew, 250
PAINE, Mathew, 1
PAINTER, Adam, 209
  Georg, 209, 221
  Margareta, 209, 221
PALMER, Francis, 251
PANCOAST, Aaron, 166
  Amos, 166
  Anne, 166
  Caleb, 168, 170
  Hannah, 57, 166
PANCOCAST, Shadlock, 126
PANCOST, Isaiah, 47
  Jonathan, 47
  Shadlock, 47
PARIS, Daniel, 220
  Gabriel, 216
  Georg, 206
  Hanna, 225
  Johannes, 211
  Peter, 206, 211, 216, 220, 221, 224, 225
  Susanna, 206, 211, 216, 220, 221, 224, 225
PARKER, Elizabeth, 245
  Hannah, 245
  John, 245
  Julian, 245
  Richard, 245
  Samuel, 245
  Waity, 170
PARUIN, Jeremiah, 236
  Rebekah, 236
PARVIN, Ebenezer, 244
PATEN, Jany, 81
PATTERSON, Rachel, 115
PAUL, Elizabeth, 125
  Hannah, 125
  Richard, 125
  Samuel, 50, 71
PAULSON, Tonias, 244
PEARSON, Isaac, 84, 86
  Isaak, 84
PEDDRICK, Daniel, 136
PEDERICK, Elihu, 169
  Hannah, 50
  John, 170
  William, 58, 141
PEDNEY, Hannah, 81
PEDRICK, Ann, 166
  Anna, 116
  Charles, 27
  Daniel, 67, 129, 136, 158
  Elihu, 68, 137, 170
  Elizabeth, 26, 133, 150, 153
  Hannah, 32, 38, 64, 109, 150, 159, 166
  Hester, 26, 27, 133
  Hezekiah, 54
  Hugh, 66, 153
  Isaac, 32, 38, 123, 159, 166, 170
  James, 112, 150, 153
  Jesse, 133
  John, 54, 86, 158
  Kesiah, 129
  Keziah, 158
  Lydia, 166
  Martha, 32, 166, 168
  Mary, 38, 54, 89, 129, 158, 159, 166, 168, 250
  Michael, 108, 158
  Miles, 170
  Mirabe, 133
  Naomi, 54, 136, 158
  Neomy, 129
  Phebe, 159, 166
  Philip, 95, 150, 153
  Rebecca, 66
  Rebeck, 80
  Rebeckah, 69, 80, 150, 162
  Richard, 150
  Samuel, 26, 27, 102, 103, 104, 107, 110, 111
  Sarah, 27, 116, 133
  Susannah, 150
  Thomas, 54
  William, 101, 108, 112, 150, 166
PENTON, Sarah, 88
  William, 74
PERKINS, Ann, 166, 171
  Benjamin, 166, 171
  Elisabeth, 170
  Elizabeth, 166, 171
  Hannah, 166, 172
  Lettice Jane, 166
  Mary, 166, 171
  Rachel, 166, 171
  Sarah, 166, 171
  William, 166, 171
  Zebiah, 171
  Zibbiah, 166
PETER, Georg, 216
  Margareta, 216
  Susanna, 216
PETERSON, Andr., 209
  Anna Maria, 209
  Rachel, 115
  Samuel, 209
  Sarah, 131
PETTET, David, 171
  Jonathan, 171
  Joseph, 171
  Mary, 171
  Rachel, 171
  Sarah, 171
  Thomas, 171
  Woodnut, 171
PETTIT, David, 36, 60, 135, 161
  Jonathan, 36, 60
  Joseph, 36, 37, 51, 60, 71, 133, 135, 161
  Mary, 37, 60
  Rachel, 36, 60,

135, 161
Sarah, 36, 60, 135, 161
Thomas, 36, 60
Woodnut, 135
Woodnutt, 36, 60
PEW, Rebecca, 139
PFEIL, Catharina, 186
PFEILER, Christina, 224
David, 224
Georg, 227
Johann, 227
Margaretha, 227
Susanna, 224
PHILIPS, Elizabeth, 32
Margaret, 32
Samuel, 32
PHILPOTT, Mary, 120
PHOCER, Eva, 181
PHORCER, Sophia, 205
Valentin, 205
PHOZER, Adam, 183
Anna Eva, 183
Eva, 183
PIDGEON, Dorcas, 134
PIERPOINT, Sarah, 121
PIERSON, Ajabel, 241
Mary, 241
Zabulan, 241
PILGRAM, Anna, 193
Catharina, 200
Catharina Maria, 200
Francis, 200, 232
Johanna, 192, 193
PILGRAMM, Albrecht, 217
Algeby, 217
Bathsaba, 220
Bershabey, 213
Catharina, 220
Deamy, 213
Franz, 213, 217, 220
PILGRIM, Catharina, 206
Elisabeth, 206
Francys, 206
Franz, 209, 212
Moritz, 212

Pescheby, 212
PILLGRIM, Anna Maria, 190
Joh. Fried., 190
PIMM, Elizabeth, 127
Hannah, 127, 166
John, 72, 141, 168, 170
Joseph, 48, 127, 166
Levi, 127, 137
Lida, 127
Lidya, 71
Mary, 134, 141, 170
Terase, 168
Teresa, 127
Tharasa, 127
PINE, Lazarus, 239
Margaret, 239
Samuel, 170
PISTRAU, Adam, 188
Christina, 188
PITT, Edeth, 5
Joseph, 5
PITTMAN, Rebecca, 250
PLATS, Elizabeth, 19
Jane, 19
Jonathan, 19, 93
PLATTS, Jane, 20, 105
Jonah, 104
Jonathan, 20
Thomas, 19
PLATZ, Elizabeth, 226
Philip, 226
PLEDGER, Elizabeth, 1
Hannah, 106
John, 1, 79, 95, 96, 97, 98
Joseph, 1, 80, 113
PLENINGER, Catharina, 196
Math., 196
PLENNINGER, Catharina, 232
PLUMMER, John, 243
POLNELL, Charles, 203
John, 203
Nancy, 203

POPPLETON, Mary, 79
POSTHUMUS, Andreas, 200
POTTS, Elizabeth, 176
Jonathan, 35, 44, 63, 107, 136, 176
Lidia, 35
Lydia, 55, 72
Rachel, 58, 110, 139, 140
Sarah, 33, 35, 58, 59, 141, 176
Thomas, 63, 107
POUNDER, Asher, 127
POWEL, Elizabeth, 8, 9, 21
Jane, 21
Jeremiah, 8, 9, 21
Jerimiah, 82
Jerimy, 94
John, 20, 21
Mary, 8, 20, 21, 95, 243
Sarah, 20, 99
POWELL, Elizabeth, 8
Hannah, 80
Jeremiah, 8, 80, 91, 96
Jerimy, 94
Marry, 82
Samuel, 88
POWES, Joseph, 90
POWLSON, Catherine, 244
POWNER, Asher, 127
PRAWNER, George, 235
PRESTON, Abigail, 243
Elen, 74
Eliner, 61
Hester, 243
PREUS, Johann George, 232
PRINDESHOLTZ, Adam, 186, 188
Anna Maria, 186
Georg, 188
Johann Adam, 188
Johann Georg, 186
Maria, 188
PRINTESHOLZ, Adam, 192, 211
Elizabeth, 211

Jacob, 192
Maria, 192
PROBE, Catharina
  Hedewig, 179
  Johann Heinrich, 179
  Martha Juliana, 179
PROSS, Benjamin, 171
PROSSER, Ann, 53, 55, 130
  Benjamin, 53, 54, 130
  Elizabeth, 53, 54, 130, 170
  John, 54
  Martha, 53, 54, 130
  Mary, 53, 54, 130, 170
  Uriah, 53, 54, 130
  William, 53, 54, 170
  William Stephenson, 53, 55, 135
PURIANCE, Joanna, 236
  Mary, 238
  Samuel, 236, 238
PURUIANCE, Andrew, 243
  Margaret, 241
  Mary, 241, 243
  Samuel, 241, 243
PURVIANCE, Mary, 234, 240
  Samuel, 234, 240
  Susanna, 240
PYLE, Edith, 34
  Isaac, 34
  Jane, 34

-Q-
QUINTON, Marey, 86

-R-
RADYN, Margareta, 214
  Thomas, 214
RAEMEL, Catharina, 190
  Jacob, 190
  Magdalena, 190

RAEMMEL, Anna Cathr., 199
  Francisca Margaretha, 199
  Georg, 199
RAEMPSTER, Anna Margareta, 203
  Friedrich, 203
  Juliana, 203
RAISER, Anna Elisab., 202
  Christian, 202
RALPH, Sarah, 109
RAMEL, Anne, 210
  Catharina, 190
  Elisabeth, 210
  George, 190
  Jacob, 210
RAMELTON, Anna Catharina, 179
  Marius, 179
RAMMEL, Andreas, 220
  Anna, 215
  Catharina, 232
  Catharine, 208, 209, 211
  Christina, 208, 209, 210, 214, 218, 220, 222, 224, 226
  Christine, 208, 209
  Henrich, 222
  Jacob, 182, 184, 186, 187, 207, 215, 221
  Jean, 218
  Joh. Georg, 218, 221
  Johann Georg, 187
  Magdalen, 210
  Magdalena, 182, 184, 186, 187
  Maria Magdalena, 210
  Maria Margretha, 182
  Martin, 210
  Regina, 221
  Simon, 184, 208, 209, 210, 214, 218, 220, 222, 224, 226, 232
  Susanna, 215

RAMSTER, Adam, 182
  Joh. Georg, 182
  Margaretha, 182
RAY, Elizabeth, 37, 143
READ, Elizabeth, 252
  Samuel, 250
READKNAP, Joseph, 86
REAFORD, Lewis, 121
REAVE, Cynthey, 248
  Eliza Ann, 248
  Elizabeth, 248
  Esther, 248
  Mary V., 248
  Rachel, 248
  William, 248
REAVES, Joseph, 90
REDIKNAP, Joseph, 83
REDKNAP, Joseph, 85, 86, 87
  Rebeck, 84
REDMAN, John, 32, 37, 40, 48, 123, 124, 128, 142
  Mary, 32, 37, 48
  Mercy, 37, 48
  Rachel, 32, 37, 48
  Thomas, 43, 103
REDNAP, Joseph, 84
REDSTREAK, Elizabeth, 252
REEVE, Ann, 80, 81, 126, 146, 157
  Benjamin, 45, 46, 65, 67, 118, 122, 123, 150, 152, 174
  Beulah, 53
  David, 234
  Elenor, 174
  Eleonar, 175
  Elizabeth, 123, 175
  George, 146, 153, 157
  Hannah, 126, 141, 146, 157
  James, 152
  John, 53, 63, 112, 116, 118, 129, 174, 175
  Joseph, 37, 54, 72, 108, 112, 141, 145, 174,

INDEX 299

175
Joshua, 73, 140, 153
Josiah, 146
Leatitia, 135
Mark, 44, 107, 109, 111, 115, 126, 146, 157, 174
Martha, 37, 72, 175
Mary, 37, 106, 174
Milisent, 37
Milliscent, 109
Millisent, 175
Peter, 175
Rachel, 152
Richard, 60, 153
Ruth, 46, 150
Samuel, 37, 175
Thomas C., 37
William, 56, 72, 146
Zeruish, 234
REEVES, Benjamin, 123
Cynthey, 246
Elizabeth, 246
Ester, 246
Joseph, 62, 95, 104
Mary, 106
Milisant, 104
Rachel, 246
William, 246
REICHARD, Anna, 217
Joh. Georg, 217
Maria, 209, 217
REICHERT, Anna, 219
Balthasara, 219
Georg, 210, 212
Hanna, 219
Johann Georg, 219
REICHHARD, Anna, 215
Balthasar, 215
Hanna, 215
Joh., 215
Johann, 215
REIFFSCHNEDIER, Eqidius, 186
Johann Paul, 186
Margretha, 186
REIHLING, Vallentin, 230

REIL, Joh. Heinr., 194
Susanna, 194
REILING, Falentin B., 190
Margretha, 190
REILY, Mary, 72
REIMAR, Juerg, 180
REIS, Adam, 177, 181
Margretha, 179
REISS, Adam, 179, 180
Anna Margareth, 179
Margreta, 180
REMEL, Anna, 196
Anna Catharina, 196
Anna Elisabeth, 187
Catharina, 187
Georg, 187, 196
REMINGTON, John, 79, 80, 81, 82, 83, 84
William, 84
Witt, 84
REMMEL, Catharina, 189
Georg, 189
REMPEL, Anna Catharina, 191
Georg, 191
Joh. Martin, 191
REMPLE, Anna Catharina, 191
Georg, 191
Joh. Martin, 191
REMSTER, Andreas, 216
Barbara, 210
Beniamin, 224
Fridr., 207, 210, 216
Fridrich, 220
Friedr., 224
Friedrich, 222
John George, 214
Juliana, 207, 210, 216, 220, 222, 224
Philipp, 220
Susanna, 207
RENNOLS, Frances, 87

RENTON, Joseph, 7
Mary, 7
William, 7
RESER, Adam, 187, 188, 189
Anna Maria, 189
Catharina, 187, 189
Georg Adam, 189
Isaac, 187
Maria, 188
Maria Christina, 188
REUBEL, Rev., 180
REUER, Daniel, 220
Georg, 220
Johann, 220
Margareta, 220
REYNOLDS, Jane, 108
Samuel, 44, 63
RHEIEL, Heinrich, 192
Marcus, 192
Susanna, 192
RHEIL, Heinrich, 191
Maria Catharina, 191
Susanna, 191
RHEINHARD, Diedrich, 177
RHODER, Margareta, 204
Thomas, 204
William, 204
RICE, Griffith, 25
Philip, 22, 114
Sarah, 22, 25, 127
Thomas, 22, 25, 102, 103, 104, 107, 108
RICHARD, Gadfreed, 244
RICHARDSON, Edward, 239
Jane, 239
John, 239
Joseph, 239
RICHER, Annah, 249
Catherine, 249
David, 249
Elizabeth, 249
John, 249
Loas, 249
Mary, 249

Polly, 249
RICHINSON, Marey, 83
RICHMAN, Abijhai, 238
　Abraham, 242
　Ann, 244
　Harman, 234
　Isaac, 240
　John, 234, 238, 240, 242, 243
　Mary, 235, 244
　Rebekah, 238
　Sarah, 238, 240, 242
RICHMOND, Jacob, 251
RICK, Joh., 216
　Johannes, 203, 207
　Louisa Jung, 220
　Maria, 203
　Philipp, 220
　Sarah, 207, 209, 216
RIDGELEY, Nicholas, 251
RIDGEWAY, Daniel, 70
　Elizabeth, 163
　Hannah, 163
　Isaac, 49
　Jacob, 49
　Job, 49
　Martha, 49
　Rebeckah, 49
RIDGWAY, Ann, 37, 47, 166
　Beulah, 47
　Charlotte, 166
　Daniel, 37, 47, 127
　Elizabeth, 37, 47, 53, 135
　Eunice, 60
　Hannah, 37, 47, 53, 132, 134, 135
　Henrietta, 135
　Henry, 53, 131, 132
　Isaac, 166, 168
　Jacob, 137, 170, 172, 173
　Job, 37, 47, 154, 166, 168
　John, 37
　Joseph, 53, 132, 135

　Kezia, 137
　Lidia, 47
　Lidya, 70
　Mark, 172, 173
　Martha, 166, 168
　Mary, 47, 53, 132, 135, 172, 173
　Namoi, 166
　Phebe, 166
　Rachel, 37
　Rebecca, 132, 135
　Rebeccah, 53
　Rebeckah, 137
　Sarah, 72
　Teresa, 166
　Unis, 170
RIDLEY, James, 14, 82, 83
　Marey, 87
　Rebeccah, 82
　Rebeck, 86
　Rebeckah, 15
　Sarah, 14, 15, 87
　William, 14, 15, 87, 89, 91, 103, 104
RIDMANN, Anna Barbara, 177
　Anna Elizabeth, 177
　Johan Andreas, 177
RIDSCH, Adam, 214
　Catharina Mony, 214
RIDWAY, Ann, 122
　Mary, 122
RIEMSTER, Fridrich, 214
　Johann Georg, 214
　Juliana, 214
RIGHT, Thomas, 155
RILEY, Mary, 131
RISELY, Enoch, 136
RISLEY, Enoch, 53, 137
　Sarah, 136
RITTER, Johannes, 195
　Michael, 195
ROAN, Sarah, 122
ROBBINSON, Widow, 76
ROBERT, John, 108
　William, 108
ROBERTS, Esther, 139

　Hannah, 138
　Hester, 58
　John, 65, 123
　Ruth, 251
　Thomasin, 58
　Thomason, 139
　Waity, 170
ROBESON, Ann, 244
ROBINSON, Elizabeth, 244
　Euphan, 242
　John, 241, 242, 243
　Mary, 241, 242
　Mathew, 79, 80
　Matthew, 77
　Richard, 61, 75
　Richards, 74
　Thomas, 252
　William, 241
ROCKHILL, Clement, 151
　Hannah, 47, 132, 151, 156
　Joseph, 151, 156, 160
　Lida, 151
　Mary, 118, 151, 156
　Robert, 151
　Samuel, 151
RODER, Anna Catharina, 189
　Joh. Jacob, 189
RODGEB, Heinrich, 179
ROESER, Christian, 215
　Elisab., 215
　Elisabeth, 215
ROGEB, Joh Georg, 197
　Salome, 197
ROHKEP, Georg, 207
　Salome, 207
ROLSE, Josiah, 251
ROOKHILL, Joseph, 46
ROSE, Abigail, 237
　Abraham, 246
　Catherine, 246
　Eliza, 246
　Elizabeth, 235, 239, 246
　Ezekiel, 239

INDEX

Hannah, 234, 244
John, 234, 235, 237, 239, 246
Mary, 234, 235, 237
Phebe, 246
Rebekah, 246
Sarah, 246
William, 246
ROSS, Abraham, 184
Adam, 202
Anna, 179
Catharina, 179, 181
Eliesabeth, 191
Elisabeth, 185, 191
Georg, 189
Hanna, 189
Jacob, 179, 191
Johanna, 188, 191
Juerg, 179
Margretha, 184
Math., 196
Matias, 191, 229
Matthaeus, 188, 189
Matthias, 184
Michael, 185, 191
Phoebe, 202
Susanna, 196
Wilhelm, 202
ROTGEB, Barbara, 186
Georg, 186
Heinrich, 186
ROTH, Agnes, 195
Andr., 198
Andreas, 186, 188, 193, 195
Angnes, 193
Cath., 198
Catharina, 191
Elisabet, 195
Heinrich, 209
Margar, 209
Rosina, 198
Susanna, 193
Thomas, 209
ROTHER, Margarethe, 208, 209
Matthias, 208, 209
Thomas, 208, 209
ROTHGAB, Anna Barbara, 217

Jacob, 217
ROTHGAEP, Andreas, 211
Georg, 211
Salome, 211
ROTHGEB, Anna Maria, 183
Barbara, 180, 181, 183, 184
Catharina, 192
Georg, 192
George, 194
Heinrich, 180
Henrich, 181, 183, 184
Margretha, 191
Mary Magdalena, 194
Sallome, 192
Salome, 194
ROTHGEIBER, Cath., 209
ROTHGET, Barbara, 180
Heinrich, 180
ROTHKAEPP, Adam, 213
Georg, 213
Salome, 213
ROTHKAP, Anna Maria, 205
Barbara, 226
Eva, 205
Georg, 205, 211
Jacob, 226
Salome, 205, 211
Theodorus, 205
ROTHKEP, Anna Barbara, 202
Barbara, 202
Georg, 202
Salome, 202
ROTHKEPP, Georg, 224
Joh. Georg, 215
Salome, 215, 224
ROTHKERB, Joh. Georg, 221
Salome, 221
ROTHKOEP, Sara, 223
ROTHKOPF, Georg, 225, 226
Salome, 225, 226
ROTTER, Anna Elisabeth, 220
Catharina, 193

Dewald, 232
Elisabeth, 196, 205, 206, 207, 226
Jacob, 226
Johann, 196, 207
Johann Georg, 196
Johannes Michael, 200
Latitia, 226
Maria Elisabeth, 200, 207
Mariana, 226
Michael, 226
Simon, 205
Theobald, 196, 200, 205, 206
ROWLAND, Abigail, 41, 91
Samuel, 41, 91, 99
Sarah, 94
ROYALL, Elizabeth, 251
RUDOLF, Catharina, 203
Johannes, 203
Ludewich, 203
RUDOLPH, Catharina, 206, 213
Catharine, 208, 209, 212
Elisabeth, 212
Hans, 251
Joh. Adam, 206
Ludewig, 206
Ludwig, 208, 209, 212, 213
RUEBEL, Caspar, 180
RUH, Barbara, 180
Melchior, 180
RULAND, Moses, 73
Susanna, 140
RULON, Moses, 59
Susanna, 140
RUMSEY, Charles, 252
William, 76, 81, 82
RUMSY, Ruth, 251
Sarah, 252
RUNDEL, Warrnick, 94
RUNDLE, Warrick, 94
Warwick, 96
RUSEL, Phebe, 244
RUTTER, Catharina,

232
Theobald, 232

-S-
SAEJLER, A. Maria, 190
  Georg, 190
  Zacharias, 190
SAEUDER, Joh., 192
  Margretha, 192
SAGEL, Ann, 240
  Thomas, 240
SALGEYER, Elisabet, 196
  Jeremias, 196
  Joh Michael, 196
SANDERS, Abraham, 124
  Paul, 120
SANGHURST, Edward, 250
SARGE, Catharina, 224
  Peter, 224
  Susanna, 224
SATATHWYTE, Isaac, 95
SATTERTHWAITE, Isaac, 88
  Rebeckah, 100
SAUDER, Anna, 216
  Anna Maria, 217
  Carl, 176, 177
  Catharina, 226
  Cathrina, 178
  Christ., 194
  Christina, 187, 196, 202, 217
  Christine, 195
  Elisabeth, 191, 194, 202, 216, 229
  Georg, 226
  Jacob, 195, 198
  Joh., 202
  Johan, 195
  Johann, 202
  Johann Georg, 196
  Johannes, 194, 195, 198, 205
  Margaret, 195
  Margareta, 196, 202, 205
  Margaretha, 194, 198
  Maria, 202, 206
  Peter, 191, 202, 206, 229
  Phil., 202, 217
  Philip, 187, 192, 195, 196
  Philipp, 194, 202
  Simon, 196, 202, 216, 230
  Susanna, 202, 204
  Wilhelm, 178, 206
SAUGHER, Peter, 231
SAUL, A. Maria, 222
  Adam, 185, 190, 192, 193, 198, 200, 202, 206, 207, 210, 211, 213, 214, 219, 220, 224, 232
  Andreas, 219
  Anna Maria, 210, 213, 224
  Barbara, 211
  Elisabeth, 203, 205, 206, 207, 211
  Eva Margretha, 193
  Fridrich, 213
  Heinr., 206, 219
  Heinrich, 213, 224
  Henrich, 210, 211, 222
  Joh. Adam, 224
  Johann, 224
  Johann Adam, 205, 207, 208, 209, 210, 224
  Johann Philipp, 203
  Margareta, 200, 202, 205, 207, 208, 209, 213, 214, 219, 224
  Margaretha, 198, 206
  Margreth, 193
  Margretha, 185, 192
  Margrethe, 210
  Maria, 210, 211, 219, 220, 224
  Maria Eliesabeth, 190
  Philip, 206, 211
  Philipp, 205, 207
SAUNDERS, Abraham, 47
  Christopher, 76, 78
  Elizabeth, 47, 152
  James, 47, 152
  John, 47, 152
  Paul, 47, 152
  Rebecca, 47
  Rebeckah, 152
  Samuel, 47, 152
  Sarah, 55, 72
SAUTER, Catharina, 222
  Christina, 178
  Elisabeth, 204, 212, 222
  Georg, 222
  Johann, 204
  Johannes, 185, 186
  Juliana, 208, 209
  Margareta, 204, 208, 209
  Margretha, 185, 186
  Maria, 208, 209
  Peter, 185, 208, 209
  Philip, 183
  Philipp, 178
  Sara, 212
  Simon, 204, 212
SAUTHER, Anna Margaretha, 199
  Charles, 242
  Jacob, 242
  Johannes, 199
  Margaretha, 199
  Peter, 199
  William, 231, 244
SAVAGE, Mary, 114
SAVARY, Jacob, 217
  Samuel, 74
  Susanna, 217
SAVIG, Mary, 114
SAWYER, Elizabeth, 89
SAYRE, Prudence, 106
  Rachel, 128
  Ruth, 65
SCACK, Catharina, 190

INDEX

Wilhelm, 190
William, 190
SCATTERGOOD, Thomas, 57
SCHAEFER, Cath., 196
  Catharina, 194
  Catharine, 211
  Conard, 198
  Conrad, 201, 203, 211
  Elisabeth, 198, 201, 203, 211
  Jacob, 196
  Johannes, 194, 203
  Leonard, 198
  Margaret, 196
  Margreta, 194
  Thomas, 211
SCHAEFFER, Adam, 180, 187, 189, 191
  Christian, 221
  Conrad, 200, 204, 206
  Elisabeth, 204, 206
  Elisabetha, 200
  Margareta, 218
  Margaretha, 187
  Margreta, 180
  Margretha, 189, 191
  Maria, 221
SCHAFER, Conrad, 201
  Elisabeth, 201
SCHEIDNER, Andreas, 211
  Louisa, 218
  Louise, 211
  Phil., 218
  Philip, 211
  Philipp, 218
SCHEITNER, Hanna, 215
  Louise, 215
  Phil., 215
SCHENCK, William, 248
SCHENERMANN, Ge, 200
SCHEUERMANN,
  Barbara, 205, 207
  Jacob, 224
  Margareta, 224
  Mathias, 207, 224
  Matthias, 205
SCHIETS, David, 217
  Joseph, 217
  Louisa, 217
SCHIMP, A.
  Christina, 192
  Adam, 211
  Adreas, 192
  Andreas, 212, 224
  Anna, 224
  Anna Maria, 215, 216, 223
  Catharina, 223
  Charlotta, 223
  Charlotte, 211, 212, 216
  Daniel, 216
  Elisab., 217
  Elisabeth, 190, 191, 192, 202, 207, 215, 216
  Elizabeth, 211
  Georg, 215, 216, 223, 224
  Hanna, 216
  Joh., 192, 207, 223
  Johann, 202, 216, 223
  Johann Willhellm, 190
  Johannes, 190, 195, 211, 212
  Margareta, 223, 224
  Maria, 212, 224
  Maria Magdal., 223
  Phil., 215, 216, 217
  Philip, 191, 192, 212
  Sebastian, 223
  Wilhelm, 223
SCHIMPF, Andreas, 221, 225
  Anna Maria, 213, 214, 220
  Catharina, 221, 226
  Catherine, 225
  Charlotte, 225
  David, 198, 225
  Elis., 198, 199
  Elisab., 205, 209
  Elisabeth, 206, 213, 214, 220, 221, 223
  Elizab, 209
  Enoch, 225
  Georg, 213, 214, 220, 225
  Hanna, 221
  Johan, 198
  Johann, 213, 214, 225
  Johann Georg, 213
  Johannes, 225
  Margareta, 221
  Margarethe, 225
  Maria Magdalena, 222
  Peter, 199
  Phil, 221
  Phil., 199, 220
  Philip, 222, 223, 226
  Philipp, 206, 209, 221
  Philippp, 203
  Salome, 221
  Sarah, 220
  Sebastian, 221, 225
  Wilhelm, 222
SCHIMPH, Elisabeth, 182, 183, 187, 188, 189
  Elizabeth, 185, 187
  Joh., 187
  Johann George, 183
  Johannes, 182, 183, 185, 187, 188
  Margretha, 189
  Philip, 182, 187, 189
  Sara Elisabeth, 187
SCHIMPP, Andreas, 218
  Anna Maria, 217, 219, 220
  Catharina, 217, 224
  Elisab., 219
  Elisabeth, 217
  Georg, 217

Jacob, 217
Johann, 217, 219
Johann Wilhelm, 218
Lydia, 218
Margareta, 218, 224
Maria Magdal., 218
Phil., 217
Philipp, 220, 224
Susanna, 218
SCHITSHER, Anna Barbara, 190
Johannes, 190
Regina, 190
SCHLEICH, Jacob, 186
SCHLESMANN,
Catharina, 197
Christoph, 197
Johanna, 197
SCHMICH, Elisabeth Magdalena, 183
Philip, 183
SCHMICK, A. Maria, 222
Anna Maria, 203
Catharina Magdalena, 182
Elisabeth, 184, 222
Elisabeth Magdaelna, 186
Elisabeth Magdalena, 181
Friederich Reinhard, 184
Hanna, 222
Joh. Philipp, 178
Johann Heinrich, 186
Johann Wilhelm, 181
Johannes, 178
Johannes Philip, 182
Philip, 181, 182, 184, 186, 222
Sara, 222
Sovia Elisabetha, 178
Wilhelm, 203, 222
SCHMID, Anne Maria, 212
Balthasar, 199

Catharina, 199
Johannes, 196
Jonathan, 212
Wilhelm, 212
SCHMIDTHEINE,
Balthasar, 204
Catharina, 204
Elisabeth, 204
SCHMIDT, Abraham, 194
Anna Magdalena, 187
Appellona, 179
Appelona, 183
Appolonia, 195
Balth., 207
Balthasar, 198, 201, 204
Baltzer, 208, 209
Balzer, 212
Barbara, 182, 187
Catharina, 182, 201, 204, 207
Catharine, 198, 208, 209, 212
Christian, 179, 183, 185
Christina, 214
Elisabeth, 180, 212, 219, 225
Friedrich, 210, 211
Georg, 204
Hanna, 212
J. F., 228
Joh. Friederich, 208, 209
Joh. Henrich, 202
Johann, 180, 181, 187, 204, 209
Johann Balthasar, 198
Johann Balthasar Heine, 207
Johann Friedrich, 222
Johann Georg, 225
Johannes, 179, 182, 184, 199, 200, 201, 202
Margretha, 194
Maria, 209
Maria Barbara, 180, 181, 184

Nancy, 219
Philip, 212, 225
Philipp, 219
Pier, 210
Rosina, 199, 200, 201, 202, 204, 209
Rosina Maria, 201
Susanna Rosina, 194
SCHMIDTLEIN,
Balthasar, 197
Catharina, 197
Johannes, 197
SCHMITT, Barbara, 186
Johannes, 186
Magdalena, 186
SCHMUECK, Anna Maria, 213, 216, 217
Elisabeth, 203, 204
Joh Phil, 204
Joh. Henrich, 216
Margareta, 213
Phil, 203, 204
Wilhelm, 213, 216, 217
SCHMUENKER, Philipp, 228
Sovia Elisabetha, 228
SCHNEDIER, Joh. Georg, 183
Margretha, 183
SCHNEIDER, A. M., 193
Anna Margareta, 197
Anna Margaretha, 198
Daniel, 198
Elisabet, 198
Elisabeth, 182, 198, 217, 220, 226
Georg, 182, 185, 187, 193, 198, 201, 205, 217
George, 190
Hans Juerg, 180
Jacob, 226
Johan Georg, 197

Johann Michael, 197
Johannes, 185, 211
Margareta, 201, 205, 216, 217, 220
Margaretha, 185
Margrete, 211
Margretha, 182
Peter, 211, 216, 220, 226
Philip, 190
Samuel, 226
Wilhelm, 193, 216
SCHNID, Elisabet, 194
Johan Henrich, 194
Philip, 194
SCHNITZER, Anna Barbara, 183
Barbara, 187, 189
Georg, 207
Johann, 189
Johann Georg, 187
Johannes, 183, 187
SCHNIZER, Barbara, 192
Joh., 192
SCHOCH, Anna, 228
Anna Maria, 224, 225
Catharina, 193, 224
Catharina Jacobi, 185
Christina, 220, 221, 224, 227, 228
Christine, 220
Daniel, 224, 225
David, 224
Deobald, 185
Elisabeth, 224, 227
Jacob, 220, 221, 224, 227, 228
Joha, 193
Johann, 220
Wilhelm, 185, 221, 228
William, 193
SCHOG, Catharina, 194, 197
Daniel, 197

Wilhelm, 194, 197
SCHOLES, Edith, 8
John, 8, 79, 80
Rebeckah, 8
SCHOLL, Abijah, 227
Margaretha, 227
Wilhelm, 227
SCHOTT, Adam, 214
Fridr., 209
Fridrich, 199, 203, 214, 219, 220
Friedrich, 213, 232
Marg., 199
Margaretha, 199
Maria, 219
Maria Barbara, 203
Susanna, 199, 203, 209, 213, 214, 219, 220, 232
Wilhelm, 220
SCHRENCK, Rev., 184
SCHRODNER, Easter, 190
SCHROTNER, Ester, 179
Ester Margreta, 181
Esther, 179
Esther Margretha, 185, 186, 187
Michael, 179, 181, 185, 186, 187
SCHROTTNER, Michael, 178
SCHUCZ, Elisabeth, 203
Johannes, 203
Jost, 203
SCHUETZ, Elisabeth, 206, 207, 213, 215
Elisbeth, 206
Elizabeth, 213
Jacob, 210
Joh. Jos, 206
Joh. Jost, 215
Johann Adam, 215
Johann Georg, 207, 213
Johann Jost, 207, 213
Joseph, 198, 210,

213, 218
Louisa, 213
Louise, 198, 210
Susanne, 198
Wilhelm, 206
SCHUEZ, Elizabeth, 209
Isaak, 209
Joh. Georg, 209
SCHULTZ, Jacob, 193
SCHUMACHER, Dorothea, 201
SCHUMECK, Anna Margareta, 210
Anna Maria, 206
Elisabeth, 210
Elisabeth Margareta, 207
Johannes, 206
Phil., 210
Philipp, 207
Willh., 206
SCHUZ, Elisabeth, 203
Elizabeth, 201
Johannes, 203, 204
Joseph, 201, 204, 205
Jost, 203
Louisa, 201, 204, 205
SCHWAAB, Jacob, 209, 214
SCHWAB, Dorothea, 200
Jacob, 215
SCHWAEMLE, Elisabeth, 229
Johann, 229
Mrs., 229
SCHWAILLE, Catharina, 229
Michael, 229
Taylor, 180
SCHWAM, Johann, 180
Maria Elizabeth, 180
SCHWENK, Deobald, 183
SCOGGIN, Rebecca, 38
SCOLES, John, 82
SCOOLS, John, 81
SCULL, Abigail, 166
Abigail Lawrence,

166
  David, 167
  Gideon, 53, 72, 166
  Hannah, 167
  James, 166
  Offley, 166
  Paul, 166
  Ruth, 56, 138
  Sarah, 166, 167
SEAL, Ann, 208
  Anna Maria, 207
  Benjamin, 207
SEARS, Rachel, 128, 130
SEELEY, David, 241
  Deborah, 241
  Hannah, 239
  Henry, 238, 239
  Mary, 238, 239, 241
SEELY, David, 244
SEERS, Richard, 96
SEHLER, Anna Maria, 198, 203
  Hans Jacob, 198
  Salome, 203
  Zachar., 198
  Zacharias, 203
SEIGRE, Catharina, 226
  Jacob, 226
  Peter, 226
SEILER, Anna Maria, 188
  Catharina, 188
  Maria, 184, 185, 187, 188
  Maria Elisabeth, 187
  Wilhelm, 184
  Zacharias, 184, 185, 187, 188
SEISER, Ann Maria, 189
  Johannes, 189
SEITZ, Georg, 200
SELEY, Benjamin, 243
  David, 243
  Mary, 243
SENECKS, Bridgitta, 252
SERGER, Catharina, 202, 214

Catherine, 218
  Georg, 214
  Heinrich, 227
  Johan, 227
  Johann, 202
  Ludwig, 218
  Margaretha, 227
  Peter, 214, 218
  Philipp, 202
SERGIO, Catharina, 206
  Johann, 206
  Maria, 206
SERRIGE, William, 77
SHAEFFER, Adam, 183, 186
  Margretha, 183, 186
SHANES, Henrich, 194
SHARP, Ann, 171
  Anna, 56
  Anthony, 119, 122, 144
  Edward, 128
  Elizabeth, 127, 144
  Grace, 114, 126
  Hannah, 113, 144
  Isaac, 83, 84, 101, 128, 144
  Jacob, 56
  Jane, 56, 137, 169
  Margaret, 171
  Margret, 98
  Mary, 119, 144
  Rachel, 121, 144
  Rebecca, 56
  Samuel, 50, 121, 144
  Sarah, 138, 144
  Thomas, 83
  William, 86
SHARPLEY, Adam, 80
  Mary, 80
SHATERWITE, Isaac, 88
SHATTERWITE, Isaac, 88
SHAW, Anna, 235
  Annanias, 237
  Ephraim, 235
  Hezekiah, 244
  John, 235
  Mary, 235

Nathan, 235, 237
  Sarah, 235
  Zuhariah, 235
SHELDEN, Ester, 212
  Margrete, 212
  Odel, 212
  Richard, 212
SHEPARD, John, 106
  Nathan, 106
SHEPHARD, Mary, 50
SHEPHERD, John, 72
SHEPPARD, Ann, 175
  John, 63, 147
  Jonathan, 109
  Josiah, 159
  Mark, 63, 64, 104, 159, 175
  Mary, 68, 69, 134, 147, 175
  Moses, 147
  Nathan, 104
  Priscilla, 123, 147
  Rachel, 147
  Richard Wood, 147
  Sarah, 147, 159
  Thomas, 159
  William, 55, 141, 159
SHEPPERD, Priscilla, 117
SHERRY, Mary, 234, 235, 238, 240, 241
  Phebe, 241
  Priscilla, 238
  Ruampence, 235
  Samuel, 235, 238, 240, 241
  Sarah, 235
SHIELDS, William, 41, 96
SHIMP, Elisabeth, 216
  Phil., 216
SHIMPF, Elisabet, 195
  Johannes, 195
  Sebastian, 195
SHINTO, Ruth, 122
SHIP, James, 244
SHIPPEN, Edward, 83
SHIPPING, Edward, 82
SHIVERS, Mary, 103

SHNEIDER, Georg, 192
  Margretha, 192
  Wilhelm, 192
SHOOT, Margaret, 244
SHOURD, Christopher, 50
  Mary, 50
  Thomson, 50
SHOURDS, Benjamin, 37, 38, 49, 70
  Christopher, 124
  Elizabeth, 38
  Martha, 39
  Mary, 37, 38, 124
  Rachel, 37, 143
  Rhoda, 37
  Samuel, 37, 38
  Tamson, 124
  Thomason, 124
  William, 37, 39
SHREEVE, Abigail, 55, 140
  Abraham, 47, 155, 162
  Ann, 47, 162
  Edith, 47, 155, 162
  Elizabeth, 47, 135, 140, 162
  Hannah, 55
  Hope, 47, 155
  Job, 55, 131, 136, 140
  Marey, 47
  Mary, 131
  Mercy, 131
  Robert, 47, 155
  Thomas, 140
SHREVE, Elizabeth, 53
  Hannah, 53
  Job, 53
SHROUDS, Benjamin, 158
  Mary, 158
  Rachel, 158
  Rhoda, 158
  Samuel, 158
  Thomas, 158, 159
  William, 158
SHULTZ, Rev., 193
SHUTE, Hannah, 136
  Isaac, 136
  Lidia, 115
  Lydia, 116
  Rachel, 51, 136
  Samuel, 136
  William, 51
SICHERER, Magdalena, 204
  Theobald, 204
SICKEN, Beniamin, 209
  Charlott, 209
  Sarah, 209
SICKES, Mary, 96
SICKLER, Magdalena, 207
  Theobald, 207
SIDDEN, Hannah, 92
SIDDON, Ezekiel, 117
  Mary, 111
  Sarah, 89
  William, 95, 104
SIDDONS, Deborah, 20
  Edward, 24, 122
  Elizabeth, 23, 28
  Ezekiel, 22
  Hannah, 18
  Isaac, 24, 28
  Jane, 20
  Mary, 18, 19, 20, 21, 22, 23, 24, 28
  Sarah, 19, 29
  William, 18, 19, 20, 21, 22, 23, 24, 28
SIEGLIN, Georg, 202
  Jeany, 202
SILVER, Aaron, 104
  Abel, 64, 146, 153, 157, 160
  Able, 104
  Abraham, 139, 153, 166
  Abram, 56
  Adna, 166
  Amy, 66
  Anna, 161
  Archabel, 42
  Archabele, 34
  Archibald, 64, 89, 135, 151, 153, 157
  Elizabeth, 166, 167
  Elizabeth Bradway, 166
  Esther, 131
  Eunice, 69, 119
  Hannah, 112
  Hephzibah, 167
  Hester, 131
  Hope, 146, 153, 157, 160
  Horatio D., 167
  James, 153, 157
  Jane, 107
  Joseph E., 167
  Josiah, 166
  Martha Ann, 167
  Mary, 34, 58, 64, 101, 121, 151, 161, 166
  Mary Ann, 153, 158
  Phebe E., 167
  Rebecca, 72, 73, 135, 167
  Rebeckah, 153, 159
  Rhody, 118
  Ruth, 135
  Samuel, 66, 135, 167
  Sarah, 58, 166
  Sarah Knight, 166
  Seatitia, 161
  Seth, 72, 138, 161
  Silvia, 146
  Silviah, 146
  Susannah, 153
  Syliva, 72
  William, 70, 71, 112, 135, 159, 160, 167
  William B., 167
SILVERS, Aaron, 124
  Abraham, 167
  Mary, 70
  Rebecca, 60
  Rhoda, 69
  Sarah, 167
  Seth, 131
  Susannah, 72
SIMMONS, Stephen, 85
SIMPSON, Ann, 37
  Anna, 37
  Anne, 37
  Benjamin, 37, 136
  Hannah, 37, 136
  James, 37, 136
  Rebekah, 101

Thomas, 37
William, 37
SIMVELL, John, 240
  Margaret, 241
  Mary, 240, 241, 243
  William, 240, 241, 243
SKANK, Parson, 208, 209
SKENK, Minister, 204
SLEEPER, Abil, 46
  Sibil, 118
SLOAN, Joseph, 49, 133
SMART, Ann, 8, 25, 32, 38, 113, 160
  Anna, 38, 72, 160
  Catharine, 25, 38, 46, 71, 113
  Deborah, 14, 15, 16, 17, 25, 38, 160
  Edward, 16, 17
  Elizabeth, 2, 8, 9, 14, 81, 82
  Hannah, 2, 14, 38, 103, 160
  Isaac, 1, 2, 8, 9, 15, 25, 32, 38, 61, 73, 76, 77, 79, 80, 82, 104, 113, 136, 160
  Isabell, 9
  Jane, 38, 160
  John, 38
  Mary, 2, 14, 38, 60, 95, 142, 160
  Nathan, 2, 14, 15, 16, 17, 25, 38, 74, 87, 89, 90, 91, 92, 93, 94, 95, 97, 98, 99, 160
  Rebecca, 38
  Rebecka, 2
  Rebekah, 89
  Robert, 38, 160
  Roger, 1
  Sarah, 2
  Wilson, 38, 160
SMARTE, Isaac, 75
  Nathan, 75
  Sarah, 86

SMITH, Abigail, 147, 162
  Ann, 38, 123, 128, 132, 147
  Anna, 31
  Atilla, 38
  Beulah, 38
  Charity, 103
  Christopher, 31, 33, 38, 65, 108, 147, 153, 162
  Clark, 109
  Clement, 38
  Daniel, 1, 10, 12, 38, 78, 80, 81, 82, 85, 86, 134, 153, 172, 173
  Daniell, 79, 84
  David, 1, 7, 24, 38, 46, 50, 51, 61, 66, 110, 125, 134, 153, 158, 172, 173
  Deborah, 250
  Dorcas, 10, 12
  Dorothea, 129
  Dorothy, 38, 51
  Eleazer, 234, 235, 236, 239, 240, 242
  Elisha, 57
  Elizabeth, 10, 17, 33, 37, 38, 48, 61, 73, 90, 125, 133, 142, 147, 153, 172, 173, 240, 252
  Elonar, 104
  Esther, 38, 153
  Eve, 61
  Evi, 38, 134
  Grace, 37, 108, 140, 147
  Gulielma Maria, 54
  Hannah, 14, 15, 16, 17, 18, 38, 51, 100, 114, 119, 130, 131, 134, 153, 158, 172, 173, 240
  Henry Hill, 54
  Hill, 23, 38, 123, 131
  Jael, 143

James, 38
Jane, 2
Jeams, 90
Jeremiah, 1, 251
John, 1, 6, 7, 10, 14, 15, 23, 37, 54, 68, 74, 75, 76, 77, 78, 79, 80, 81, 82, 83, 84, 86, 87, 88, 89, 90, 91, 92, 93, 94, 97, 99, 100, 101, 114, 119, 126, 132, 143, 153, 155, 156, 171, 240
Jonathan, 1, 38, 61, 81, 86, 172, 173
Joseph, 87, 88, 89, 91, 92, 94, 96, 97, 114, 128, 132, 158
Joshua, 172, 173
Josiah, 38
Lucy, 37
Marmaduk, 129
Marmaduke, 51
Martha, 1, 10, 37, 75, 76, 235
Mary, 7, 16, 58, 73, 87, 102, 114, 133, 134, 140, 153, 234, 235, 236, 239, 240, 242
Mary Ann, 18
Meriman, 134
Milliscent, 155, 156
Oakford, 147
Pile, 106
Piles, 15, 104
Prudence, 37, 121, 148
Rachel, 37, 73, 95, 129, 147, 148
Rebecca, 31, 33, 38
Rebeckah, 51, 129, 153, 162
Rebekah, 235, 236
Richard, 23, 37, 42, 65, 92, 93,

94, 95, 97, 98, 99, 104, 107, 109, 119, 121, 138, 147
Robart, 90
Robert, 51, 91, 128
Roger, 77, 78
Samuel, 1, 15, 16, 17, 18, 72, 89, 127, 240
Sarah, 1, 7, 15, 23, 24, 37, 38, 63, 73, 80, 97, 113, 115, 126, 136, 140, 148, 242
Sarey, 80
Stephen, 57, 140
Susanna, 6
Susannah, 7, 10, 73, 153
Thomas, 2, 24, 38, 47, 62, 75, 82, 98, 111, 119, 130, 131
William, 6, 24, 38, 89, 92, 96, 97, 107, 114, 136
SMITHEY, Frances, 2
Francis, 74
SMYTH, Richard, 65
SNAG, Ann, 235
SOEFFNER, Elisabeth, 231
Johannes, 231
SOFRER, Johann, 205
Maria Elisabeth, 205
SOMERS, Ann, 166, 169
Chalkley, 166
Deborah, 166, 169
Elizabeth, 118, 129, 131
Elwood, 166
Guli Elma, 166
Hannah, 166
Isaac, 170
Jacob, 166
James, 166
John, 129, 131, 166, 167, 169, 170

Phebe, 166
Rebecca, 168
Richard, 166
Sarah, 166, 169
Tabitha, 166, 169
William, 166
SOMMERS, Anna, 51
David, 171
Elizabeth, 132
Hannah, 71
Jacob, 51
John, 132
Rachal, 119
Rebecca, 169
SORGE, Catharina, 216
Elisabeth, 216
Peter, 216
SORGER, Jacob, 219
Johann, 219
Nancy, 219
Susanna, 219
SPARK, Rachal, 119
SPARKS, Elizabeth, 234, 243
Jane, 234
Richard, 234
Simon, 234
Thomas, 234
SPICER, Jacob, 43, 102
SPOONER, John, 74
SPRINGER, Ann, 171
Mary, 138
SQUIBB, Caleb, 47, 117, 118
STACEY, Robert, 76
STAENGEL, David, 205
Queen, 205
Salomo, 205
STAENGER, Daniel, 196, 198
Queen, 198
Salomo, 198
STAM, Cathrina, 177
Charlotte, 200
Maria Catharina, 191
Maria Cathrina, 177
Sophia, 200
Wilhelm, 200
STAMM, Anna Margareta, 197

Catharina, 178, 206
Cathrina, 177
Charlotta, 182, 183, 184
Charlotte, 180
Elisabeth, 219
Georg Wilhelm, 192
Joh. Ludw., 197, 199
Johann Adam, 180
Johann Ludew., 201
Johannes, 177, 178, 180, 182, 183, 184, 197
Marg., 199
Margareta, 197, 200, 201
Margaretha, 199
Margretha, 178
Maria, 219
Maria Catharina, 201
Sophia, 199, 206, 210
Wilhelm, 199, 206, 210, 219
STAMME, Anna Margaretha, 179
Charlotte, 179
Johannes, 179
STANDLEY, Mary, 54, 130
STANLEY, Mary, 130, 134
STANLY, Mary, 61
STARKE, Elisabeth, 224
Johann, 224
Johann Georg, 224
STAUT, Joseph, 223, 226, 227
Rosina, 223, 226, 227
STEEL, Margate, 250
STEELE, Margate, 250
STEIN, Elisabeth Margareta, 218
STEINER, Rev., 184, 186, 187
STENGER, Adam, 194
Catharina, 194
Christian, 193
Christina, 209

Daniel, 196, 197, 199, 201, 209
Dorothea, 209
Eva, 201, 209
Franz, 209
Fridrich, 209
Guin, 200
Gwin, 200
Joh. Georg, 200
Louisa, 194
Philipp, 209
Queen, 194
Salome, 193, 194
Salomo, 197
Salomon, 194, 200
Sophia, 201
Susa Queen, 197
STEPHENS, John, 46, 120, 122
STEPHENSON, William, 130
STERGE, Catharina, 221
  Elisabeth, 221, 222
  Johann, 221, 222
STERTZ, Heinrich, 188
  Joh. Heinrich, 184
  Margretha, 188
STERZ, Heinrich, 209
  Joh., 209
  Nancy, 209
STETTET, David, 169
  Jonathan, 169
  Joseph, 169
  Mary, 169
  Rachel, 169
  Sarah, 169
  Thomas, 169
  Woodnut, 169
STEVENSON, Amelia, 38, 59
  Charles, 38
  Daniel, 38, 59
  Elizabeth, 6
  Emelia, 38
  James, 60
  John, 6, 38, 59
  Margaret, 60
  Mary, 6, 38, 59
  William, 59
  William Laurice, 38

STEWARD, John, 97
  Joseph, 98
STEWART, Amariah, 160
  Ann, 26, 37, 68, 73, 169
  Elizabeth, 26, 63, 108
  George, 37
  Hannah, 129, 130, 161
  James, 26, 68, 121, 153, 160, 161
  John, 26, 37, 67, 104, 107, 109, 112, 122, 160, 161
  Joseph, 26, 37, 160
  Lidya, 26
  Mark, 37
  Mary, 26, 37, 66, 153, 160
  Melisent, 26
  Mylasent, 161
  Rebekah, 37
  Samuel, 26, 37, 140, 142
  Sarah, 37, 160
  Thomas, 161
  William, 37, 160
STINGER, Daniel, 199
STOCKTON, Ann, 56, 137
STOM, Johann Ludew, 194
  Margretha, 194
STONEBANKS,
  Elizabeth, 239
  James, 238
  John, 238
  Joseph, 238
  Mary, 238, 239, 241
  Richard, 238
  Samuel, 241
  Thomas, 235, 238, 239, 241
  William, 238
STOY, Rev., 182
STRAEUB, Bastian, 193
  Georg, 193

  J. Georg, 192, 193
  Regina, 193
STRAND, Abraham, 61, 74
STRATTON, Aaron, 239
  Bethuel, 56
  Elias, 61, 171, 172, 173
  Elizabeth, 131, 170
  Gideon, 131, 139
  Hope, 52
  Isaiah, 69
  Josiah, 58
  Mary, 52, 73, 126, 131
  Phebe, 235, 239
  William, 170, 235, 239
STRAUB, Daniel, 230
  Georg, 232
  John, 232
STRAUCH, Joh., 195
  Margareta, 195
  Regina, 195
STRAUEB, Daniel, 191
STRAUP, Maria, 198
  Rahel, 198
  Sebastian, 198
STREET, Aaron, 38, 142, 157, 168
  Anna, 38, 157
  Aron, 38
  Elizabeth, 98
  Eunice, 38, 157
  John, 38, 157
  Lydia, 38, 157
  Mark, 138
  Mary, 38, 60, 171
  William, 38, 157
  Zadock, 38, 69, 122, 157
STRENGER, Daniel, 203
  Elisabeth, 203
  Eva, 203
  Guin, 195
  Jacob, 195
  Quinney, 203
  Salomon, 195, 203
  Sibylla, 203
STRETCH, Aaron, 26, 29, 114
  Bradwy, 10

Daniel, 90
David, 149
Deborah, 21, 26,
  29, 149
Elisha, 58, 148,
  163
Elizabeth, 26, 149
Elonar, 67
Eloner, 115
Esther, 110, 114
Hannah, 10, 11,
  46, 82, 83, 112,
  116, 126, 149,
  155
Jael, 147
Jail, 71
Job, 148
John, 251
Jonathan, 21, 63,
  70, 116, 123,
  124, 149, 155,
  158
Joseph, 10, 11,
  21, 26, 29, 63,
  65, 81, 82, 84,
  96, 97, 98, 109,
  147, 150, 250
Joshua, 65, 121,
  148, 154
Lidya, 148
Luke, 126
Mark, 149
Martha, 21, 147
Mary, 21, 70, 124
Millisent, 148
Nathan, 21, 26,
  29, 117
Peter, 97, 115
Rebeckah, 26, 29,
  117, 149
Samuel, 21, 107,
  126
Sarah, 58, 67, 82,
  98, 104, 113,
  147, 149
William, 58, 163
STRETSCH, Anna
  Maria, 216
Anne Maria, 212
Samuel, 212
Sarah, 216
Thomas, 212, 216
STRIBINGS,
  Elizabeth, 4

Henry, 4
STRING, David, 228
Louise, 228
Simon, 228
STROUD, Elizabeth,
  126, 157
Isaac, 49, 125,
  126, 157
Lidia, 49, 126
Lidya, 157
Mary, 126, 157
Thomas, 126, 157
STUART, James, 49
John, 62, 63
Joseph, 159
Lidia, 63
Mary, 49, 63
Samuel, 120
Sarah, 120
STUBBINES,
  Elizabeth, 13
Henry, 13
Samuel, 13
Sarah, 13
STUBBINS, Henry, 62,
  97, 98, 100, 146
STUBEN, Samuel, 86
STUBINS, Samuel, 86,
  87
Sarah, 88
STUMP, Christopher,
  244
STURZ, Barbara, 196
Elisabeth, 196
Georg, 196
STUTZ, Barbara, 208,
  209
Joh. Georg, 208,
  209
SUMMERS, David, 154
Elizabeth, 114,
  152, 154
Isaac, 45, 152,
  154, 159
Jacob, 124, 154
John, 44
Rachel, 72
Rebeckah, 154
Samuel, 45
SURKINS, Roger, 74
SURREY, Jonathan, 86
SURRIG, John, 87
SURRIGE, William, 82
SWAIN, Abraham, 140

Isaac, 113
Jacob, 54, 113
Mary, 118, 125
Samuel, 64, 109,
  113
SWINNY, Ann, 139

-T-
TAGGART, John, 48,
  154, 155
TAME, David, 240
Elizabeth, 239
Hannah, 239, 240,
  242
Joseph, 235, 239,
  240, 242, 243
Tossy, 242
TAMERUS, Anna Maria,
  188
Johann Adam, 185
Johann Peter, 188
Maria, 185
Peter, 185, 188
TANKERSLEY,
  Elizabeth, 88
TANZEBECHER,
  Cathar., 209
Catharina, 214,
  224
Georg, 224
Ludw., 209
Ludwig, 214
Maria, 224
TANZEBERGER,
  Catharina, 215
Ludwig, 215
TANZENBECHER,
  Catharina, 210
Christina, 210
Ludw., 224
Ludwig, 210
Mariagareta, 224
TARBEL, Abraham, 241
Elizabeth, 240,
  241, 242
Keturah, 242
Melicent, 240
Nathan, 234, 240,
  241, 242, 244
TATUM, Beulay, 167
TAYLOR, Anna Maria,
  214
Christopher, 94
Elizabeth, 94

Georg, 214
Isaac, 131
Margareta, 214
Martha, 73, 138
Peter, 214
TEAS, Charles, 56
  John, 56, 138
  Martha, 56
  Mary, 56
  Rachel, 56, 138
TEES, Charles, 138
  John, 138
  Martha, 138
  Mary, 138
  Rachel, 138
TEMERUS, Christian,
  198
TENDELSBECK, Anna
  Margaretha, 179
  Friederich, 179
  Friedrich, 176
  Margretha, 176,
    177
TENDELSPECK,
  Elisabet, 195
  Johannes, 195
TENDESLBECK,
  Friedrich, 177
TENNELSBERG,
  Susanna, 209
TENZENBECHER,
  Catharina, 213
  Johann Ludwig, 213
  Ludwig, 213
TEST, Abner, 27
  Benjamin, 27, 53,
    64, 112, 117,
    123, 126, 131,
    146, 153, 158,
    172, 173
  Clayton, 167
  David, 153
  Deborah, 53, 132,
    146
  Dorcas, 148
  Elenore Ann, 167
  Elizabeth, 27, 39,
    52, 53, 63, 64,
    108, 121, 130,
    132, 133, 138,
    148, 160, 167
  Frances, 62, 89,
    90, 92, 97, 102,
    109, 110, 112,
    114, 117
  Francis, 27, 64
  Hannah, 167
  Hope, 73, 148
  Isaac, 148, 153
  John, 27, 39, 65,
    73, 104, 109,
    130, 148, 160,
    167
  Joseph, 90, 92,
    93, 96, 97, 99,
    105, 106, 107,
    148, 167
  Leatitia, 27, 71
  Lettitia, 167
  Lidya, 148, 153
  Lydia, 148
  Martha, 148, 160
  Mary, 134, 148,
    167
  Rachel, 27, 39
  Rebecca, 53, 131
  Rebekah, 102
  Ruth, 27, 65
  Samuel, 39, 56,
    67, 106, 108,
    141, 148, 153,
    162
  Sarah, 39, 71,
    146, 148, 153,
    158, 167
  Thomas, 27, 167
  William, 103
  Zaccheus, 131
  Zacehues, 146
  Zachheus, 53
TEST'S, Abner, 121
TEYCKERT, Catharina,
  182
THACKERA, Thomas, 78
THACKERY, Elizabeth,
    154, 155
  Hannah, 128, 154
  Jacob, 135, 155
  Joseph, 155
  Stephen, 154, 172,
    173
  Thomas, 45, 154,
    155
  William, 154, 156
THANNEY, Elizabeth,
  171
  Hannah, 171
THOMAS, Abel, 45
  Ann, 19, 132
  Catharina, 216
  Elisabet, 212
  Elisabeth, 212,
    216, 222, 225
  Elisabth, 220
  Elizabeth, 91
  Hanna, 212
  Henrich, 222
  James, 19
  Johann Georg, 225
  John, 19, 41, 95,
    101, 112
  Mary, 91
  Rice, 98
  Valent., 199
  Valentin, 212,
    216, 220, 222,
    225
THOMASON, Anna
  Elisab., 224
  Valentin, 224
THOMPKINS, Mary, 125
THOMPSON, Aaron, 46,
    71, 115, 137, 148
  Abel, 46, 119
  Abraham, 15, 122,
    158
  Andrew, 2, 3, 4,
    8, 9, 11, 12, 13,
    14, 15, 17, 21,
    39, 40, 65, 66,
    74, 76, 77, 78,
    79, 80, 81, 84,
    86, 87, 88, 89,
    91, 92, 99, 123,
    125, 130, 151,
    155, 156, 159,
    160
  Ann, 10, 11, 12,
    13, 21, 39, 79,
    106, 109, 135,
    137, 158, 162
  Anne, 20
  Aron, 39
  Arron, 72
  Benjaman, 15
  Benjamin, 22, 23,
    29, 62, 104, 113,
    116, 154, 155
  Daniel, 20
  David, 39
  Deborah, 114, 148
  Doritha, 10, 11

Dorithy, 9
Edith, 20, 21, 30, 154, 155, 158
Elizabeth, 2, 3, 4, 13, 14, 15, 17, 18, 19, 22, 23, 29, 36, 39, 59, 61, 135, 139, 140, 147, 155, 156, 157, 169
Eupho, 239
Grace, 12, 13, 14, 15, 18, 21, 24, 39, 40, 56, 72, 108, 151, 159
Hannah, 9, 11, 12, 13, 14, 15, 19, 20, 23, 24, 39, 65, 139, 161
Isaac, 17, 108, 148, 157
Isabel, 9
Isabella, 4
Issabell, 2, 4
Jacob, 39, 158
James, 4, 10, 11, 12, 13, 17, 81, 84, 86, 87, 139, 161, 239
Jane, 4, 8, 9, 10, 15
Jemima, 113
John, 3, 4, 9, 12, 18, 20, 29, 38, 39, 70, 74, 77, 79, 80, 81, 84, 85, 86, 87, 113, 115, 142, 157, 158
Jonathan, 8
Joseph, 7, 14, 15, 16, 17, 18, 19, 24, 29, 39, 50, 63, 67, 76, 97, 98, 102, 109, 116, 118, 122, 145, 147, 156, 157, 162
Joshua, 13, 20, 21, 23, 29, 36, 39, 46, 48, 49, 50, 56, 57, 69, 72, 73, 96, 97, 98, 101, 107,
108, 109, 112, 115, 116, 118, 123, 128, 136, 151, 156, 160, 250
Judah, 119
Lidia, 10
Martha, 16, 17
Mary, 4, 11, 13, 20, 21, 22, 23, 24, 39, 70, 122, 130, 135, 143, 145, 147, 158, 161, 162
Mellicent, 29
Milissent, 22
Millicent, 162
Milliscent, 154, 158
Prudence, 73, 145
Rachal, 89
Rachel, 8, 24, 58, 67, 141
Rebecah, 7, 8, 11
Rebecca, 38, 39, 60, 73, 137, 143
Rebeccah, 39
Rebeckah, 8, 9, 14, 15, 23, 29, 66, 97, 145, 158
Rebekah, 30, 101
Ruth, 39, 73, 158
Samuel, 20, 24, 30, 97, 98, 148, 151, 154, 239
Samuell, 95
Sarah, 7, 12, 13, 14, 15, 16, 17, 18, 19, 21, 23, 29, 36, 39, 40, 55, 72, 87, 88, 93, 115, 133, 139, 147, 151, 157, 158, 160, 161
Siddon, 114
Susanna, 19, 135
Susannah, 11
Thomas, 3, 4, 7, 8, 9, 10, 11, 12, 14, 20, 21, 22, 23, 24, 65, 70, 78, 79, 80, 81, 82, 83, 84, 86,
87, 96, 97, 98, 102, 118, 122, 148, 158, 162
Will, 86, 87, 93
William, 4, 7, 8, 9, 11, 12, 13, 14, 15, 17, 18, 19, 24, 39, 72, 78, 79, 80, 81, 82, 84, 85, 87, 89, 91, 92, 97, 98, 101, 130, 131, 139, 158, 161
THOMSON, Andrew, 82
Ann, 235, 242
Elizabeth, 240, 251
Eupho, 240
Francis, 77, 235, 242, 244
James, 86, 240
John, 74, 82
Mary, 242, 243
Richard, 77
William, 86, 240
THORNE, Sarah, 136
THUERINGER, Anna, 184, 186
Catharina, 184, 191
Joh., 191
Johannes, 184
Johanns, 191
Michael, 184
TILAR, Mary, 79
William, 78, 79
TILER, Rachel, 130
TILLSHEFER, Jacob, 216
Joh. Georg, 216
Susanna, 216
TILLSHOEFER, Johannes, 194
Mariana, 194
Philipp, 194
TILSHEFER, Jacob, 210
Maria, 210
Susanna, 210
TILTON, Daniel, 109, 111
TILTONS, Daniel, 44, 109

TILZHEFER, Jac., 218
  Jacob, 218
  Sarah, 218
  Susanna, 218
TIMVELL, Mary, 239
  Sarah, 239
  William, 239
TINDAL, Benjamin,
    41, 43
  Esther, 41
  Mary, 41, 68
TINDALL, Benjamin,
    27, 103
  Esther, 151
  Hester, 27
  Joseph, 27, 119
  Mary, 27
  Rachel, 141
TINDELL, Elizabeth,
    88, 90
TODD, Mary, 119
TOFFEL, Anna
    Margaretha, 230,
    231
  Peter, 230
TOLE, Percifful, 76
TOMLINSON,
  Catherine, 59
  Joseph, 95
  Lydia, 42
  Mary, 64
  Othniel, 43, 101,
    105, 106
TOMSON, Andrew, 75
  John, 75
  Joseph, 88
  Thomas, 84
TONKINS, Mary, 125
  Samuel, 50, 70
TOOD, Elizabeth
    Green, 248
  Mary Cleveland,
    248
  Nathaniel, 248
TOOTTIT, John, 83
TOPY, Joseph, 234
TOSSY, Hannah, 243
  Jospeh, 243
  Sarah, 243
TOWE, Hannah, 238
  Joseph, 238
  Mary, 238
TOWNSEND, Abigail,
    39

Beulah, 39
Caleb, 39
Catharine, 114
Catherine, 46, 68
Daniel, 36
David, 45, 64
Hannah, 61, 171
Isaac, 60, 143,
  168
Jacob, 42, 65,
  151, 153, 162
Jesse, 60
John, 55, 151
Josiah, 60
Judah, 119
Judith, 60
Ketturah, 60
Keturah, 168
Mary, 123, 151,
  162
Peter, 49, 130
Rebecca, 55
Rebeckah, 151
Richard, 44, 151,
  162
Robert, 96
Sarah, 39, 69
TOX, Anna Maria, 190
  Frederich, 190
TRACEY, Jeremiah,
  129, 161
  Margaret, 161
TRACY, Jeremiah, 72,
  133, 162
  Margaret, 162
TROLLINGER, Anna
  Margretha, 179
  Elisabeth, 176,
  177
  Friederick, 179
  Gabriel, 176, 177,
  179
  Margaretha, 176,
  177
TUCKNISS, John, 58,
  140
TUFT, Jean, 94
TULLY, Anna, 242
  Azubah, 237
  Francis, 234, 235,
  237, 239, 241,
  242
  Gideon, 242
  Hannah, 234, 235,

  237, 239, 241,
  242
  Mary, 241
  Phebe, 242
  Priscilla, 234,
  235
  Robert, 234, 241,
  242, 244
  Samuel, 239
  Thebe, 235
TURNER, Ann, 244
  John, 251
TYLAR, Mary, 114
TYLER, Ann, 115
  Benjamin, 39, 59,
  62, 64, 102, 109,
  118, 175
  Catharine, 39
  Edith, 95
  Elizabeth, 68, 175
  Hannah, 175
  Hannah Gillasphey,
  39
  James, 118, 130,
  151
  Job, 39, 59, 143,
  175
  Johanna, 8
  John, 8, 71, 175
  Katrine, 8
  Leatitia, 70, 175
  Lydia, 72, 175
  Martha, 151
  Mary, 8, 39, 59,
  141, 175
  Naomy, 174, 175
  Neomy, 119
  Philip, 8, 103
  Phillip, 106
  Rachel, 59, 67,
  96, 175
  Rebeckah, 8, 65
  Richard, 39
  Ruth, 151
  Samuel, 104
  Temperance, 115
  William, 8, 39,
  80, 89, 92, 94,
  251
TYLEY, Edward, 102,
  103, 104
  Naomy, 118
TYLOR, John, 84
  Mary, 96

Philip, 89
William, 81, 82,
  84, 86, 87

-U-
UETZNER, Andreas,
  187
Anna Magdalena,
  186
Anna Maria, 186
Jacob, 181, 184,
  186, 187, 188,
  189
Johann Georg, 184
Magdalena, 181,
  184, 186, 187,
  188, 189
Margretha, 189
Maria Barbara, 181
UHSINGERS, Andreas,
  214
Catharina, 214
Simon, 214
UPMAN, Abertin, 191
Andreas, 191
Lorentz, 191
Margretha, 191
URICH, Barbara, 187
Henrich, 187
USINGER, Andreas,
  199, 200, 201,
  211
Johann, 201
Margareta, 201
UTZ, Jacob, 177
UTZEN, Jacob, 177
Maria Cathrina,
  177

-V-
VALENTIN, Adam, 183
VALENTINE, Robert,
  49
VAN CULAN, John, 114
VAN CULIN, John, 64
VAN LAHNEN, Georg,
  200
Jacob, 200, 230
Johanna Maria, 200
VAN METER, Hannah,
  234
Henry, 234, 241
Isaac, 234
Jacob, 241

Mary, 241
Samuel, 248
Sarah, 234
Susanna, 248
VANCULIN, John, 108
VANMETER, Adam, 245,
  248
Benjamin, 239
Catherine, 245,
  248
David, 235
Elizabeth, 247,
  242
Fetters, 236
Hannah, 235, 243,
  242
Henry, 234, 236,
  237, 239, 242,
  250
Isaac, 237, 243
James, 245, 248
John, 247
Joseph, 235, 243,
  244, 242
Joseph Neley, 247
Lydia, 245, 248
Mary, 234, 236,
  237, 239, 247
Mary Ann, 248
Nancy, 248
Rebeckah, 247
Rebekah, 234, 237
Richard, 245, 248
Samuel, 245
Sarah, 243, 242
Susannah, 245
Thomas, 247
William Alderman,
  247
VAUGHAN, Sarah, 113
VEAL, Hannah, 244
VERON, Ann, 55
VIAL, Nehemiah, 239
VICARY, Edward, 92
VICKARY, Edward, 16,
  17, 92, 93, 94,
  97, 100
Hannah, 16
Martha, 106
Mary, 100
Rebecca, 100
Rebeckah, 17
Richard, 104, 106
Sarah, 16, 17

VICKERY, edward, 103
Edward, 91, 97,
  98, 99, 103
Esther, 128
Mary, 62
Rachel, 115
Rebecca, 133
Richard, 97, 108
Samuel, 110
Sarah, 110, 113,
  116, 127, 128,
  129, 131, 132,
  133, 134
VICKRERY, Edward, 90
VINING, Mary, 251
VOZEN, Joh. Val.,
  209
Peter, 209
Sophia, 209

-W-
WACK, P., 203
WACKER, Christoph,
  197
Johannes, 192
Juliane, 197
Margretha, 192
WADDINGTON, Ann, 63
Elizabeth, 64, 108
Jane, 65
Jonathan, 124
Sarah, 125
WADE, Edward, 2, 73,
  74, 75, 76, 77,
  79
Esther, 98
Jane, 2
John, 2
Joseph, 11
Josiah, 92
Lydia, 95
Mary, 11, 62, 110
Prudence, 2, 73,
  83
Robert, 78
Samuel, 2, 11, 75,
  76, 77, 79, 80,
  81, 82, 84, 85,
  90
William, 74
WAETHER, Mary, 142
WAGNER, Maria
  Elisabeth, 183
Wilhelm, 184

WAGSTAFE, Sarah, 5
WAHL, Christina, 186
  Georg, 186
  Gottfried, 186
WAID, Hannah, 18
  Jayn, 81
  John, 94
  Joseph, 18, 92, 93
  Milisent, 18
  Samuel, 94
  Samuell, 93
WAIDE, Joseph, 91, 92, 94, 99
  Samuel, 91, 92, 94
WAINMAN, Hannah, 132
WAIR, Joseph, 84, 94
WAIRE, Joseph, 87
WAIT, Batholomew, 86
WAITHAM, William, 86
WAKER, Elizabeth, 86
WAKS, Joh. Nie., 228
WALCKER, Johannes, 186
  Maria, 186
WALDEN, Elizabeth, 12
  Hannah, 12
  Will, 86
  William, 12, 86
WALDREN, William, 87
WALKER, Hannah, 109
  Johannes, 190
  John, 79
  Joseph, 91
  Margareth, 190
WALL, John, 4
WALLACE, Mary, 116
WALTER, Carl, 180, 184
  Catharina, 180
  Eva, 179, 180, 229
  Johann Carl, 184
  Margaretha, 184
  Maria Margretha, 180
  Peter, 180
  Simon, 179, 180, 229
WALTHER, Johann, 186
  Margretha, 186
WAMSLEY, Ann, 13, 92
  Dynah, 9, 13
  George, 13
  Henry, 9, 13, 87, 88, 89
  Jonathan, 13
  Nathaniel, 9
WARD, Ann, 132
  Elizabeth, 55
  Gulimarah, 55
  Hannah, 133
  Isaac, 45, 55, 66, 72
  John, 51, 72, 133
  Joseph, 92, 94
  Mary, 55
  Rebecca, 113
  Rebeccah, 138
  Rebeckah, 55
  Samuel, 94
  Samuell, 81, 95
  Sarah, 55, 138
WARE, Bathsheba, 27
  Brown, 72
  David, 27, 40, 53, 129
  Elijah, 22, 41, 68, 137
  Elisha, 27, 150
  Elizabeth, 22, 27, 29, 38, 40, 41, 54, 62, 63, 128, 134, 141, 147, 158
  Grace, 136
  Hannah, 22, 27, 35, 63, 73, 133, 141, 147, 149, 158
  Isaac, 117
  Jacob, 29, 38, 40, 128, 132, 158
  Job, 27, 56, 72, 73, 147, 149
  John, 27, 29, 40, 63, 127, 133, 147, 154
  Joseph, 2, 7, 12, 22, 41, 53, 61, 62, 73, 77, 79, 80, 81, 82, 84, 86, 92, 96, 97, 98, 101, 102, 106, 128, 133
  Lydia, 41
  Martha, 7
  Mary, 12, 22, 27, 38, 40, 41, 69, 132
  Milicent, 40
  Miliscent, 132
  Milisent, 68
  Millicent, 27
  Naomi, 158
  Patience, 12
  Peter, 27
  Rebecca, 35, 134
  Rebeckah, 22, 117, 121, 122, 158
  Richard, 35, 125, 158
  Samuel Thompson, 40
  Sarah, 7, 22, 27, 28, 40, 53, 65, 69, 122, 125, 147, 149
  Solomon, 27, 28, 98, 149, 150
  Susanna, 140
WARNER, Abigail, 40, 56
  George, 40, 56, 129, 131, 161
  Phebe, 40, 129, 131, 161
  Pheobe, 56
  Phoebe, 136
  William, 56, 131, 161
WARRICK, Hannah, 11
  Mary, 11
  Thomas, 11
WATERS, Rebecca, 72, 133
WATSON, Jacob, 214
  Johann, 202
  John, 202, 214
  Maria, 202, 214
  Susanna, 202
  Temperance, 115
WAUK, Susanna, 203
WAYATT, Bartho, 88, 89
  Elizabeth, 90
WAYTT, Bartholomew, 89
WEATEN, Rachel, 251
WEATHERBY, Daniel, 244
  Sarah, 131
WEAVER, Ann, 139,

INDEX

140
Elizabeth, 52,
  139, 140
Josiah, 52, 139,
  140
Mary, 52, 139,
  140, 170
Susanna, 140
Susannah, 52, 139
Thomas, 61, 139,
  140, 172, 173
WEBB, Sarah, 138
WEBER, Henrich, 199
  Hers., 194
WECK, Anna Cath.,
  203
  Anna Maria, 203,
  225
  David, 221
  Jacob, 208, 209
  Joh. Nic., 203
  Joh. Nicol., 218,
  231
  Joh. Nicolaus,
  208, 209, 221,
  231
  Joh. Nicoluas, 210
  Johann Nicolaus,
  225
  Johannes, 210
  Margareta, 218,
  221
  Margarete, 208,
  209
  Margareth, 225
  Margrethe, 210
  Michael, 203
WECKLER, Catharina,
  217
WEEK, Marg., 199
  Margar, 199
  Mich., 199
WEEKS, Amos, 243
WEIBEL, Elisabeth,
  225
  Jesse, 225
  Martin, 225
WEIDENMEYER,
  Arbanus, 198
  Magdalene, 198
WEIL, Elisabeth, 214
  Johann Nicholaus,
  213
  Johann Nicolaus,
  214
  Margareta, 213,
  214
WEISER, Catharina,
  186
  Georg, 186
  Joh. Georg, 186
WEISS, Elisabeth,
  215
  Sarah, 215
  Sickel, 215
WELDE, Andreas, 178
WELES, Daniel, 84
WELLS, Danniel, 85
  Hannah, 55, 127
WENSCHEL, Carl, 218
  Catharina, 218
WENTZEL, Anna, 219
  Anna Margretha,
  183
  Anna Maria, 176,
  177, 178, 183
  Carl, 199, 210
  Catharina, 199
  Catharine, 210
  Daniel, 176, 177,
  210
  David, 210
  Ditorius, 210
  Eva, 210, 219
  Hanna, 199
  Hans Wilhelm, 178,
  185
  Joh. Wilhelm, 183
  Johan Wilhelm,
  176, 177
  Johann Wilhelm,
  183
  Johannes, 210
  Maria, 210
  Philip, 189
  Theodor, 192, 219
WENZEL, Adam, 198,
  227
  Anna Barbara, 205
  Anna Maria, 201,
  205
  Barbara, 227
  Carl, 203, 209,
  213, 216
  Catharina, 203,
  209, 213, 216
  Daniel, 212
  Elisabeth, 195,
  201, 205
  Enoch, 227
  Eva, 198, 201,
  205, 212, 215,
  221
  Margareta, 205
  Philipp, 195, 205
  Samuel, 195
  Sarah, 215
  Theodor, 212, 221
  Theodorus, 198,
  201, 205, 215
  Thoedorus, 192
  Wilhelm, 201, 205
WESCOTE, Abinidab,
  240
  David, 236, 239,
  240
  Davis, 236
  John, 239
  Rachel, 236, 239,
  240
WESEMEIER,
  Christoffer, 187
  Christoph, 189
  Georg, 189
  Helena, 187, 189
  Johann Heinrich,
  187
WEST, Bartholomew,
  79
WETHERLY, Edmond, 51
  Sarah, 53
WHARTON, Thomas, 120
WHEATEN, Rachel, 251
WHEELER, Dobson, 99
WHISTER, Casper, 103
WHITAKER, Abigail,
  245
  Enoch More, 245
  Hannah Lecok, 245
  Rachel, 245
  Recompence, 245
WHITALL, Abraham, 43
WHITCRAFT, Ann, 236
  Jane, 236
  John, 236
WHITE, Abigal, 13
  Christ., 75
  Christopher, 2, 3,
  9, 74, 76, 77, 79
  Easter, 79
  Elizabeth, 5, 7,
  21, 99

Esther, 2, 3, 82
Hannah, 9, 11, 12, 13, 21, 88
Hester, 12
John, 21, 78, 80, 83, 95, 97, 98, 99
Joseph, 3, 5, 7, 14, 76, 77, 78, 79, 80, 81, 82, 83, 87, 89, 92
Josiah, 9, 11, 12, 13, 80, 82, 84, 86, 87, 92, 93, 99
Josias, 3
Mary, 14, 112, 124
Rachel, 113
Rains, 112
Rayns, 81
Rebekah, 50
Reines, 5
Samuel, 5
Sarah, 118
Thomas, 2
William, 83
WHITEALL, James, 171
WHITEMORE, Martin, 66
WHITMORE, Martin, 110
WHITTAN, Ann, 12
James, 12, 13
Joseph, 13
Sarah, 12, 13
WHITTEN, James, 89
Jeams, 90
WHITTEUR, Elenor, 114
WHITTIN, James, 86
WHITTON,
Christopher, 77
Grace, 77
James, 82, 84, 86, 87, 91, 92, 93, 94, 95
Jeanes, 89
Sarah, 77, 78
WIAT, Bartha, 87
Bartho, 86
Bartholemew, 12, 80
Bartholomew, 8, 18, 19, 77, 78, 84, 87, 98
Batholemew, 82
Batholomew, 81
Bathomolew, 82
Elizabeth, 12, 18, 19, 110
Mary, 112
Sarah, 8, 12, 19
WIATT, Elizabeth, 154
John, 2
WICK, Joh. Nichol., 217
Joh. Nicol., 207
Margar., 217
Margareta, 207
WICKSELL, Parson, 190
Rev., 189
WID, Joh. Nicolaus, 199
Maria, 199
WIDDISH, Leuretia, 243
WIDMAYER, Hannah, 150
Martin, 66, 150
Mary, 150, 154
Virgin, 150
WIEAT, Bartholomew, 79
Batholomew, 79, 80
WIGGINS, David, 250
Hannah, 252
WIKSELL, Rev., 188
WILFORD, Kunigunda, 179
Leonhard, 179, 180
WILKINS, Sarah, 171
WILKINSON, Joseph, 44, 109
William, 75, 77
WILL, William, 94
WILLCOX, Mary, 3
Robert, 3
WILLETS, Amos, 40
Hannah, 40
Richard, 44, 109
WILLIAMS, John, 45
Marey, 84
WILLIS, Hannah, 51, 133, 161
Hester, 118
John, 97
Jourdan, 51, 161
Mary, 64
Prudence, 108
Sarah, 51, 124, 161, 169
Silas, 133, 161
Stephen, 116
Steven, 104
William, 88, 89, 92, 93, 94, 95, 96, 97, 98, 99, 110, 115, 116
WILLITS, Richard, 108
WILLS, Amos, 60
Hannah, 50, 140
James, 57, 171
William, 96
WILSON, Ann, 38
Betty, 118
Darkin, 40
Elizabeth, 41
Enoch, 243
Hannah, 40, 41, 140
Jane, 29, 40, 145
Jesse, 41, 61
John, 40
Mary, 118
Robert, 29, 38, 41, 44, 51
Robert Darkin, 40
Ruth, 40
Sarah, 52, 129
William, 29, 40, 72, 141
WINCKLER, Catharina, 184
Margretha, 184
WINTON, Hannah, 145
Jesse, 120
John, 96, 97, 106, 145
Samuel, 118
WISTAR, Bartholomew, 40
Casper, 40, 70
Catharine, 40
Catherine, 70
Charlotte, 39, 40
Cleayton, 40
Elizabeth, 40
Hannah, 40
John, 39, 40, 52,

128
Mary, 40, 124
Richard, 44, 70, 104, 105, 230
Sarah, 39
WISTER, Charlotte, 52
John, 52
WITHERS, Grace, 155
Mary, 59, 141, 142, 155
Samuel, 48, 69, 155, 156
WITSCHER, Charlotha Lowisa, 192
Herman, 192
Maria Chatarina, 192
WITTAKARS, Hannah, 103
WITTON, James, 84, 85
WOLBERT, Joh. Michael, 209
Maria Cath., 209
Philip, 209
WOLDEN, William, 89
WOLFF, Elisabeth, 192
Elizabeth, 193
Eva Margretha, 193
Heinrich, 192, 193, 229
J. Adam, 192
Joh. Martin, 191
M. Elisabetha, 191
Martin, 191, 229
WOLPERT, Carolina, 193, 194
Catharina, 191, 192, 193, 199
Catherine, 198
Elisabeth, 208, 209
Eva Rosina, 199
Georg, 196, 199, 202
George, 193
Hans Michael, 197, 205
Hans Peter, 197
Jacob, 212
Joh Michael, 196
Joh. Georg, 193, 194
Joh. Michael, 199, 212
Joh. Peter, 215
Johann Henrich, 207
Johann Matthias, 201
Johann Michael, 204, 207
Johannes, 196
Johnn Jacob, 193
Magdalena, 199, 201
Mar. Ma., 194
Margareta, 217
Maria, 202, 205, 207, 212
Maria Magdalena, 193, 196
Maria Margretha, 193
Mathias, 199
Matthias, 193, 201
Michael, 196, 201, 202, 208, 209
Peter, 196, 197, 199, 211
Rosina Carolina, 205
Rosina Catharina, 199
Rosina Marg., 196
Rosina Margaret, 196
Rosina Margareta, 196, 201, 204
Rosina Maria, 196
Samuel, 211
Sarah, 215
Sophia, 196, 197, 211, 215
WOLPORT, Catharina, 191, 193
Mathaias, 193
Matias, 191, 229
Michael, 191
Rosina Margreth, 191
Rosina Margretha, 191
WOOD, Ann, 52
Beulah, 140
Caleb, 40, 59
Charles, 245, 247
David, 40
Elizabeth, 77, 247
Hannah, 40, 175
Henry, 40
Isaac, 46
Isaiah, 245, 247
Jacob, 40, 59
James, 136, 140, 175, 244
Jane, 174
Jeremiah, 236, 245, 247, 251
John, 247
Josiah B., 247
Josiah Brick, 245
Juhaniah, 236
Laetitia, 64
Leatitia, 174
Lydia, 40
Mariah R., 247
Mariah Richman, 245
Priscilla, 63, 174
Rachel, 245, 247
Rebeckah, 247
Rebekah, 46
Richard, 28, 92, 93, 94, 95, 97, 106, 115, 123, 127, 140, 174, 175
Ruth, 40, 57, 63, 174
Sarah, 245, 247
Thomas B., 247
Thomas Brick, 245
WOODES, Rebeckah, 80
WOODHOUSE, Samuel, 84
WOODNIT, Richard, 83
WOODNUT, Ann, 25
Anne, 100
Betty, 118
Elizabeth, 72
Grace, 10
Hannah, 55, 118, 138
Henry, 25
James Mason, 25
Jonathan, 25, 106
Joseph, 16, 17, 19, 92, 94
Mary, 9, 10, 12,

19
  Rachel, 16, 17, 19
  Richard, 9, 10, 12, 25, 81, 82, 84, 86, 87, 91, 92, 99, 100, 107
  Sarah, 12, 25
  Thomas, 16, 17
WOODNUTT, Betty, 47
  Elizabeth, 33, 163
  Grace, 89
  Hannah, 73, 143, 163
  Henry, 110, 111, 114
  James, 41
  James Mason, 70, 163
  Jonathan, 41, 116, 163
  Joseph, 14, 90, 93
  Margaret, 41, 163
  Martha, 41
  Mary, 14, 41
  Preston, 41, 163
  Rachel, 41
  Richard, 14, 33, 88, 89, 90
  Sarah, 41, 163
  Thomas, 163
  William, 41
WOODROFE, Thomas, 75, 76, 77, 78
WOODROFFE, Thomas, 77
WOODROOFE, Edeth, 5
  Isaac, 5
  John, 5
  Mary, 5
  Thomas, 5, 76, 77, 78, 79
WOODSISE, Henrich, 217
  John, 217
  Maria, 217
WOODWARD, Isaac, 117
WOOLF, Elisabet, 195
  Henry, 195
  Susanna, 195
WOOLSEY, Barcheba, 236
  Benjamin, 237
  Bersheba, 237
  Israel Wharton, 236
  John, 236, 237
WOOLSTER, Magery, 135
WOOLSTON, Marjery, 55
WORE, Joseph, 85
WORGAN, James, 76
  Richard, 76
  Scisila, 76
  Scisly, 61
WORLDIN, Mary, 251
WORRICK, Thomas, 84
WORTHINGTON, Easter, 89
  Elizabeth, 252
  Ephraim, 90
  Robart, 41, 89, 90, 92
  Robert, 87
  Samuel, 90, 94
  Samuell, 41
  Sarah, 41
WRANGEL, C. M., 187
WRAY, Sarah, 133
WRIGHT, Amos, 40
  Benjamin, 34, 40, 47, 48, 154, 155
  Ebenezer, 40
  Elizabeth, 34, 40, 47, 72, 154, 162, 235
  Ezekiel, 45
  George, 40, 47, 142, 154
  Hannah, 40, 128, 158
  Isaac, 128, 158
  John, 47, 67, 94, 95, 96, 128, 158
  Joseph, 128, 158
  Lettitia, 40
  Mary, 40, 128, 158, 172, 173
  Nathan, 40, 47, 154
  Peter, 47, 55, 131, 154
  Priscilla, 40, 54, 131, 162
  Rebecca, 40, 54, 60, 131, 169
  Rebeckah, 137, 162
  Richard, 60
  Ruth, 34, 40, 47, 128, 139, 154
  Samuel, 46, 116
  Sarah, 40, 162
  Stephen, 40, 47, 54, 71, 131, 154, 162
  Thomas, 40, 91, 93, 154, 155
  William, 40, 73, 154
WRITE, John, 67
  Margret, 84
WUCHER, Christoph, 208, 209
  Judith, 208, 209
WUCKER, Barb, 198
  Christoph, 198
  Juliana, 198
  Wilhelm, 198
WUCKERT, Wilhelm, 195
WUERTZ, Anna Barbara, 232
WULBERT, Catharina, 218
  Heinrich, 218
  Maria, 218
  Mathias, 218
WULFORT, Margretha, 189
  Michael, 189
WULLFORT, Matteas, 187
WULPERT, Anna, 231
  Catharin, 196
  Catharina, 198
  Georg, 198
  Joh. Marth, 196
  Johannes, 196, 198
  Lydia, 220
  Peter, 198, 220, 231
  Susanna, 220
WULPERTH, Catharina Margaretha Rosi, 232
  Johann Michael, 232
WUPERT, Catharina, 198
  Matthey, 198
WUSTER, Anna, 182
  Catharina, 189

Catharina Barbara, 189
Charlotte, 182
Michael, 182, 189
WYAT, Bartholomew, 96, 97, 99
Barthomolew, 99
Elizabeth, 28
WYATE, Bartholomew, 91, 92, 93
Batholomew, 94
WYATT, Bartho, 91
Bartholomew, 43, 91, 92, 94, 99, 100, 101, 115, 125, 162
Batholomew, 92, 154
Elizabeth, 72, 154
Mary, 112, 154
Sarah, 94, 104
WYETT, Batholomew, 90
WYNKOOP, Rachel, 121

-Z-

ZAINES, Joseph, 252
ZANE, Jonathan, 104
Joseph, 108, 252
Nathan, 49, 69
Rebeckah, 68
Robert, 74, 75
ZANES, Joseph, 44
Nathan, 69
Rachel, 122
Robert, 78
ZIEGLER, Anna Maria, 216
Catherina, 204
Dewald, 211
Elisabeth, 199
Joh. Jacob, 206
Johann Adam, 211
Magdalena, 199, 204, 206, 213, 216, 218, 221
Magdalene, 211
Margaretha, 218
Martin, 213
Susanna, 221
Theobald, 195, 199, 204, 206, 213, 216, 218, 221

ZIGLER, Johannes, 197
Magdalena, 197
Theobald, 197
ZIMERMAN, Abraham, 191
Anna, 191
Magdalena, 192
Melchor, 192
ZIMMERMAN, Abraham, 179, 180, 183, 184, 185, 229
Adam, 201
Anna, 180, 183, 184, 185, 229
Catharina, 201
Johann Adam, 180
Johannes, 201
Magdalena, 188
Maria Catharina, 184
Matthaeus, 188
Melchior, 183, 184, 188
ZIMMERMANN, Adam, 205
Catharina, 205
Matthias, 205
ZOBEL, Adam, 181
Elisabetha, 178
Eva Ursula, 178, 181
Georg Adam, 178
Maria Barbara, 181

Other Heritage Books by Charlotte Meldrum:

Abstracts of Bucks County, Pennsylvania Land Records, 1684-1723

*Early Church Records of Burlington County, New Jersey
Volumes 1-3*

Early Church Records of Chester County, Pennsylvania, Volume 2
Charlotte Meldrum and Martha Reamy

Early Church Records of Gloucester County, New Jersey

Early Church Records of Salem County, New Jersey

Early Records of Cumberland County, New Jersey

Johnston County, North Carolina Marriages, 1764-1867

Marriages and Deaths of Montgomery County, Pennsylvania, 1685-1800

www.ingramcontent.com/pod-product-compliance
Lightning Source LLC
Chambersburg PA
CBHW070720160426
43192CB00009B/1256